DANIEL OGDEN

# Dragons, Serpents, and Slayers in the Classical and Early Christian Worlds

A SOURCEBOOK

# OXFORD
UNIVERSITY PRESS

Oxford University Press is a department of the University of Oxford.
It furthers the University's objective of excellence in research,
scholarship, and education by publishing worldwide.

Oxford   New York
Auckland   Cape Town   Dar es Salaam   Hong Kong   Karachi
Kuala Lumpur   Madrid   Melbourne   Mexico City   Nairobi
New Delhi   Shanghai   Taipei   Toronto

With offices in
Argentina   Austria   Brazil   Chile   Czech Republic   France   Greece
Guatemala   Hungary   Italy   Japan   Poland   Portugal   Singapore
South Korea   Switzerland   Thailand   Turkey   Ukraine   Vietnam

Oxford is a registered trademark of Oxford University Press
in the UK and certain other countries.

Published in the United States of America by
Oxford University Press
198 Madison Avenue, New York, NY 10016, United States of America

© Oxford University Press 2013

All rights reserved. No part of this publication may be reproduced,
stored in a retrieval system, or transmitted, in any form or by any means, without the
prior permission in writing of Oxford University Press, or as expressly permitted by law,
by license, or under terms agreed with the appropriate reproduction rights organization.
Inquiries concerning reproduction outside the scope of the above should be sent to the
Rights Department, Oxford University Press, at the address above.

You must not circulate this work in any other form and you must impose this
same condition on any acquirer.

Library of Congress Cataloging-in-Publication Data

Ogden, Daniel.
Dragons, serpents and slayers in the classical and early Christian worlds : a sourcebook /
Daniel Ogden.
pages. cm.
Includes bibliographical references and index.
ISBN 978-0-19-992511-7 — ISBN 978-0-19-992509-4
1. Dragons—Folklore.   2. Dragons—Religious aspects.   3. Dragons in the Bible.
4. Mythology, Classical.   I. Title.
BL795.D7O44 2013
398.24'540938—dc23         2012032468

1 3 5 7 9 8 6 4 2

Printed in the United States of America
on acid-free paper

わが最愛の妻
江里子に

# Contents

*List of Figures* xi

*Acknowledgments* xiii

*Abbreviations* xv

*Quick Key to Some Special Terms and Conventions Used in this Book* xvii

*Schema of Motifs* xix

*Introduction* 1

## PART ONE: THE CLASSICAL DRAGON

1. *The Genealogy of the Great Dragons* 13

2. *Typhon, Slain by Zeus* 19

3. *Python, Slain by Apollo* 39

4. *Heracles' Dragons (i): Baby Heracles and the Dragon Pair Sent by Hera* 45

5. *Heracles' Dragons (ii): the Hydra* 50

6. *Heracles' Dragons (iii): Ladon, the Dragon of the Hesperides* 57

7. *Heracles' Dragons (iv): Cerberus, the Hound of Hades* 63

8. *The Chimaera, Slain by Bellerophon* 75

9. *Medusa, Slain by Perseus* 82

10. *Lamia, Slain by Eurybatus and Others* 97

11. *The Dragon of Ares, Slain by Cadmus* 109

12. The Dragon of Nemea, Slain by the Seven against Thebes   119

13. The Dragon of Colchis, Slain or Sent to Sleep by Jason and Medea   125

14. The Dragon Pair Sent against Laocoon and his Sons   134

15. The Dragon of the River Bagrada, Slain by Regulus and his Army   141

16. Some Unique Dragon-Slaying and Dragon-Averting Narratives in Later Greek Sources   146

17. The Sea Monster of Troy, Slain by Heracles   153

18. The Sea Monster of Ethiopia, Slain by Perseus   162

19. Scylla, Slain by Heracles and Encountered by Odysseus   179

PART TWO: THE CHRISTIAN DRAGON

20. The Serpents of the Bible and its Apocrypha   187

21. The Dragons of the Early Hagiographical Tradition   196

22. St Philip, the Echidna and the Ophianoi   207

23. St Silvester and the Dragon of Rome   221

24. Saintly Tales Originating between the Fourth and Sixth Centuries AD   228

25. Saintly Tales of the Central Medieval Period   239

26. St Patrick and St George   247

APPENDICES

Appendix A: World-foundational Dragon-Slaying Tales from the Ancient Near East and India   257

Appendix B: Germanic Dragon Fights of the Eighth to Thirteenth Centuries AD   263

Appendix C: A Selection of Dragon- and Serpent-Slaying Tales of Folkloric Interest   271

*List of Editions Used*   281

*References*   289

*Index of Greek and Latin sources*   303

*General Index*   309

# List of Figures

1. The anguipede Echidna   13
2. The winged, anguipede Typhon   19
3. Python challenges Leto, with babies Apollo and Artemis   39
4. Baby Heracles throttles the serpent pair   45
5. Heracles and Iolaus battle the Lernaean Hydra   50
6. Ladon in his apple tree   57
7. Heracles brings Cerberus to Eurystheus   63
8. The Chimaera   75
9. Gorgon head   82
10. The anguipede Lamia with Apollo at Delphi   97
11. Cadmus slays the Dragon of Ares with a rock   109
12. The Dragon of Nemea devours baby Opheltes-Archemorus   119
13. Jason is regurgitated by the Colchis Dragon   125
14. The Vatican Laocoon   134
15. Regulus and his army slay the Bagrada Dragon   141
16. An anguipede Hecate's two dog-heads tear a soul apart between them   146
17. Heracles disguises himself as the sacrificial Hesione to enter the mouth of the Sea Monster of Troy   153
18. Sir Edward John Poynter, Perseus and Andromeda   162
19. Scylla   179
20. Eve and the Snake of Eden   187
21. The Ladder of St Perpetua   197
22. Filippino Lippi: St Philip and the Dragon of the Temple of Mars   207
23. Maso di Banco: St Silvester and the Dragon of Rome   221
24. Jean Fouquet: St Hilary of Poitiers confines the snakes of Gallinaria   228
25. Jost Amman: St Margaret of Antioch   239
26. Raphael: St George battles the dragon   247
A. Marduk battles Tiamat   257
B. Sigurd transfixes Fafnir   263
C. The Wonderful Legend of the Lambton Worm   271

# *Acknowledgments*

Thanks (once again) to my wife, Eriko, for drawing a number of the images that illustrate this book. Thanks also to Stefan Vranka, the editor at OUP, and to the typescript's most helpful anonymous readers.

Daniel Ogden
University of Exeter and UNISA

# *Abbreviations*

| | |
|---|---|
| *ANET³* | Pritchard 1969 |
| *ANRW* | *Aufstieg und Niedergang der römischen Welt* |
| *ATU* | Uther 2004 (i.e. 'Aarne—Thompson—Uther') |
| *CSEL* | *Corpus Scriptorum Ecclesiasticorum Latinorum* |
| *CTH* | Laroche 1971 |
| *DA* | Daremberg and Saglio 1877–1919 |
| *DK* | Diels and Krantz 1951–2 |
| *FGrH* | Jacoby et al. 1923– |
| *FHG* | Müller 1878–85 |
| *GGM* | Müller 1855–82 |
| *HRR* | Peter 1906–14 |
| *KA* | Kassel and Austin 1983– |
| *LCL* | Loeb Classical Library |
| *LIMC* | *Lexicon Iconographicum Mythologiae Classicae* |
| *MGH* | *Monumenta Germaniae Historica* |
| *ML* | Roscher 1884–1937a |
| *MWG* | Ogden 2009 |
| *NEB* | *New English Bible* |
| *PG* | Migne 1857–1904 |
| *PGM* | Preisendanz and Henrichs 1973–4 |
| *PL* | Migne 1884–1904 |
| *SH* | Parsons and Lloyd-Jones 1983 |
| *TrGF* | Snell et al. 1971–2004 |
| *RAC* | *Reallexikon für Antike und Christentum* |
| *RE* | Pauly, Wissowa and Kroll 1893– |
| *TUAT* | *Texte aus der Umwelt des Alten Testaments* |

# Quick Key to Some Special Terms and Conventions Used in this Book

Most Greek and Latin terms used in this book are supplied only in amplification of their English translations. It may nonetheless be helpful to supply initial glosses for the terms that recur most frequently, and so too for some less common English technical terms.

## GREEK TERMS

| | |
|---|---|
| *drakōn* | A large snake, often huge, often supernatural, marauding, man-eating and fiery: the Greek term most consistently used to signify 'dragon' |
| *drakontes* | The plural form of *drakōn* |
| *drakaina* | A female *drakōn* |
| *drakainai* | The plural form of *drakaina* |
| *kētos* | A sea monster, marine cousin to the *drakōn* |
| *kētē* | The plural form of *kētos* |

## LATIN TERMS

| | |
|---|---|
| *draco* | The Latin adoption of *drakōn* |
| *dracones* | The plural form of *draco* |

## ENGLISH TERMS

| | |
|---|---|
| anguiform | Creature wholly or partially of snake form or capable of manifesting itself in snake form |
| anguipede | Creature that combines a humanoid upper half with a serpentine lower half; the lower half can culminate either in a snake tail (or tails) or a snake head (or heads) |

## PARENTHESES IN TRANSLATIONS

| | |
|---|---|
| (…) | Text enclosed in round brackets translates material present in the ancient text, appropriately punctuated. |
| […] | Square brackets enclose editorial interventions in the translation of the ancient text: a quick explanation of an obscure term, or the supplying of the original Greek or Latin word translated. The latter is normally given in standard form (i.e. for nouns, the nominative singular or plural), but occasionally it is supplied in the actual grammatical form in which it appears in context when this is significant for the exegesis. |

## QUICK KEY TO SOME SPECIAL TERMS AND CONVENTIONS USED IN THIS BOOK

### NUMERICAL REFERENCES

**123**  Emboldened numbers, without prefix, refer to the basic series of Greek and Latin source passages from which the book is constructed.

**123** com.  Emboldened numbers followed by 'com.' refer to the commentary appended to the source passage denoted.

**A1, B2, C3**  Emboldened numbers prefixed by **A**, **B** or **C** refer to the series of texts and narrative summaries from non-Graeco-Roman cultures laid out respectively in Appendices A, B and C.

**M4.a.2**  Emboldened numbers prefixed by **M** and often of complex form refer to the schema of motifs that follows the introduction.

123  Unemboldened numbers, or numbers in other letter combinations, refer to the traditional divisions or lines of the text under discussion.

# Schema of Motifs

## M1. THE DRAGON'S FORM

**a. Dragons of fundamentally pure serpent form**: i. dragons of the form of a gigantic snake (13, 15, 17, 19–26, 28–32, 75–9, 81–95, 97–101, 124, 130–2, 134–52, 154–6, 160–2; cf. B1–10, C1–2, C4, C7–8, C12–15); ii. with a beard and/or a crest (21, 76, 78–9, 81, 83, 89, 92, 94–5, 98, 134, 158); *kētē* with crests (115); iii. with tongues that are 'three-forked' (4, 71, 78, 83, 98), or resemble swords (140, 158), or are significant in other ways (6, 8, 20, 55, 59, 89, 92, 95, 108 [with com.], 128, 134, B8); iv. with three rows of teeth (78, 83, 106, 119, 121); vi. with skin that is metallic (25, 78, 90, 133, 149), variegated (8, 15, 85, 149) or blue (20, 78, 133).

**b. Dragons of composite or complex forms**: i. dragons of the form of multi-headed, but otherwise pure, serpents (23–8, 119 [with com.], 162); ii. dragons consisting of a fundamentally humanoid or animalian body from which multiple smaller snake heads project (35, 37, 40, 43, 45, 55–6, 58–9, 66; cf. A8); iii. dragons otherwise compounded from multiple animal forms (5–8, 11–12, 48–53, 102, 119 [with com.], 120, 158); iv. dragons of anguipede form, male (5–8, 77) or female (1, 3, 5, 71–2, 74 [with com.], 76, 102); v. dragons with wings or the ability to fly (5, 11, 21, 55; cf. B11).

## M2. THE DRAGON'S FAMILY AND ITS GENERATION

**a. The dragon and its family**: i. dragons born or reared in a family of dragons (1–2, 13, 95, 121, 131); ii. dragons presiding over a brood or host of lesser snakes (1–2, 10–12, 14, 27, 72, 130, 134, 156; cf. 71, 153, 159); iii. dragons operating in pairs (10, 19–22, 75, 77, 92–6, 134, 145, 150).

**b. Generation and putrefaction**: i. dragons born of the earth itself (5, 11, 13, 15–17, 25, 53, 71, 76, 98; cf. 7); ii. dragons born from the body of a dead person (132 [with com.], 133, 151 [with com.], 161 [with com.]; cf. B2); iii. snakes (or other creatures) produced from the body of a dead dragon (58–9, 75, 79, 88); iv. immortal dragons (1, 23, 25, 28, 54, 67 119).

## M3. THE DRAGON'S HOME

**a. Inside the earth** (cf. M2.b.i): i. in the underworld (35–47); ii. in a cave (1, 5, 7–8, 72–3, 76, 78, 95, 98, 119, 131, 134, 136–7, 139–42, 145–8, 154, 157; cf. B1, C12), or specifically in a cave assimilated to the underworld (1, 98, 130, 136, 142); iii. in a tomb (132–3, 151; cf. 90, B2); iv. (re-)confinement of the dragon beneath the earth after defeat, under a mountain or in the abyss (5–9, 102, 126–7, 131, 134, 136–7, 142, 154; cf. 10, A8).

    b. **In woodlands**: i. in a sacred grove (**15, 28, 31–2, 34, 78, 81, 83–5, 87, 89–90, 98**), sometimes explicitly a walled one (**32, 90**); ii. in or under a tree (**24, 30**).

## M4. THE DRAGON AS GUARDIAN

   a. **Of a water source**: i. dragons as guardians of a water source (**15, 23–4, 75–6, 78–9, 81, 83, 88, 97–8, 101, 155, 160–2**; cf. A4, A5); ii. dragons reared in a water source (**24, 79, 98**); iii. dragons identified with or transformed into a water source (**9, 27, 73, 101**; cf. also A4); iv. dragon fights memorialised in a water source (**9, 73, 117, 134, 160–1**); v. sea monsters dwelling in the sea (**103–16**).
   b. **Of treasure**: i. dragons as guardians of treasure (**1, 28, 30–4, 85, 87, 89–91**; cf. B1–7); ii. the dragon's body incorporating treasure (**25, 75** [with com.]); iii. the dragon's metallic skin or crest (= M1.a.v; cf. M1.a.ii).
   c. **Otherwise**: i. dragons as guardians of the underworld (**35–47**); ii. dragons as guardians, in pairs, of a temple (**92–6**), a city (**134**) or a hermit cell (**145**).

## M5. THE MARAUDING DRAGON

   a. **The destruction of people**: i. locals or passers-by destroyed at random (**14, 16–17, 53, 68–74, 98–9, 119, 130–1, 143–6, 149, 154, 156, 160–1**); ii. the dragon's depredations contained by the sacrifice to it of young men (**73, 99, 142**), young women (**103–4, 106–16, 140**) or both (**160–1**), often selected by lot.
   b. **The destruction of cattle or crops**: i. cattle plundered (**23, 48, 71, 73, 121, 143–4, 146, 156**) or received in sacrifice (**161**); ii. crops plundered or poisoned (**45, 48, 52–3, 71**); iii. sea monsters brought to land in a crop-destroying tsunami (**104**) or belching brine over the crops (**103, 105**).

## M6. THE BATTLE OF FIRE

   a. **The dragon's fiery attributes and resources**: i. fiery venom, sometimes so described (**8, 83, 125**; cf., more generally, M8.a.i); ii. fiery breath, smoke or winds (**5–7, 48–53, 83, 98, 128, 134, 137, 154** [with com.], **162**; cf. B1–2, B8, B12, C2, C6) or a breath of fiery locusts (**134**); iii. fiery eyes (**5, 20, 42, 78, 82–3, 89, 92, 94, 98, 106, 121, 149**); iv. fiery crest (**89**); v. fiery belly (**134**), parodically represented as heartburn (**98**); vi. thunderbolts (**8**; cf. **126**); vii. fiery trees (**5**) or rocks (**5, 7**).
   b. **The slayer's fiery resources**: i. fiery saliva (**146** = M8.b.iii); ii. fiery breath or spirit (**83, 93, 98, 130, 149**; cf. C2), fiery fumigation with sulphur (**20, 130**; cf. **161** [com.], C12) or the use of horses with fiery breath (**98**); iii. fiery eyes (**134**); iv. thunderbolts (**5, 6, 8–9, 26, 134, 153**; cf. A1, A4–5); v. fiery arrows (**23, 27**); vi. fiery brands (**23, 27, 72**; cf. B6); vii. pyres (**20, 23, 125, 143–4**; cf. **26**, C1, C9–10); viii. fiery herbs (**100**); ix. fiery chains (**126**); x. the slayer's deployment of the dragon's own fire against it (**51, 124**; cf. C3–4, C7, C11–13). Cf., more generally, A1–2, A8.

## M7. THE BATTLE OF AIR

   a. **The dragon's production of bad air or bad winds**: i. deploying winds (**5–6, 8**; cf. A1); ii. breathing out pestilential breath (**59, 64, 72, 78, 83, 98, 106, 130,**

132, 134–7, 141–2, 144–5, 147–9, 155–6, 161; cf. C6, C12–13), even after death (6; cf. 30); iii. breathing out fiery or smoky breath (= M6.a.ii); iv. sucking victims into its maw (98, 143–4; cf. 139, C3, C6, 12–13); v. farting (150); vi. rotting in pestilential fashion after death, with special measures required for the disposal of the carcass (14, 30, 71, 97, 145–6, 153, 161–2; cf. B2).

    **b. The slayer's production of good air**: i. blowing upon the dragon and its snakes (127, 130); ii. blowing pipes to produce enchanting music (8; cf. C10); iii. making good winds (8; cf. A3); iv. fumigating (= M6.b.ii); v. making the sign of the cross in the air, by gesture or by sprinkling (134, 146, 150, 152, 156; cf. M11.b.v); vi. invoking the Holy Spirit, *Pneuma* (158).

## M8. THE BATTLE OF LIQUID

**a. The dragon's venom**: i. dragons deploying venom in the fight (4, 8, 20, 23–4, 26–7, 30, 41, 45, 59, 71–2, 78–9, 83, 92, 98, 106, 125, 130–2, 134, 137, 144–5, 148–9, 154, 156, 159; cf. A3, B2, B9, B12); ii. the dragon's venom produced by eating poisonous herbs (89) and in turn transforming harmless plants into poisonous ones (41, 47).

    **b. The slayer's corresponding liquids**: i. lethal poison-impregnated arrows (14) or poison-herb beds (100); ii. soporific decoctions (31, 43, 87, 89–90; cf. 134); iii. saliva (M6.b.i; cf. 134, C8); iv. dragon venom from his current opponent (131) or another one (30).

## M9. THE BATTLE OF SIGHT AND GAZE

**a. The dragon**: i. as unsleeping (29, 31, 40, 86–7, 89–90); ii. as casting sleep upon its victims (100); iii. as blinding or petrifying with its venom (79, 134); iv. with fiery eyes (= M6.a.iii); v. with piercing or petrifying eyes (6, 54, 59–62, 65, 81; cf. 64).

    **b. The slayer**: i. as casting sleep upon the dragon with drugs (= M8.b.ii); ii. as blinding the dragon with a thunderbolt (134); iii. as staring the dragon down (134, 150).

## M10. THE BATTLE OF SOUND

**a. The dragon**: i. as making a terrible sound, typically a hissing (5–6, 40, 55–6, 59, 71–2, 78–9, 83, 87, 89–90, 92, 94, 98, 132, 139, 145, 149, 158; cf. A1); ii. as singing or deploying an incantation against its victim (100: cf. C9–10); iii. as being deaf or deafening itself to its slayer's incantations (130 [with com.]).

    **b. The slayer deploys**: i. incantations or prayers against the dragon (87, 89, 100, 130, 134, 136, 141, 143–5, 147–8, 151, 153–4, 158, 160); ii. silent prayers against the dragon (150).

## M11. THE BATTLE OF CIRCLES

**a. The dragon's circularity**: as coiling and constricting (1, 4, 5, 8–9, 17, 20, 23, 40, 53, 71, 78–9, 81, 83, 86–7, 90, 92, 94, 97–8, 102, 106, 113–15, 123, 133–4, 144, 149, 151–2, 158, 162 and *passim*; cf. A9, B2, B9, B12, C10, C12–15); ii. as running around its opponent in a circle (158; cf. B2).

b. **The slayer deploys**: i. the curving *harpē* or sickle, which reflects the dragon's coils in its form and is well adapted for 'reaping' rampant snakes (**5, 54, 57, 59, 65, 113–16**); ii. circular purifications (**130**); iii. a circle of fiery herbs (**100**; cf. C8, C10); iv. a magical ring (**102**); v. by significant contrast, the sign of the cross (**134–5, 146, 150, 152, 156, 158, 160–1**; cf. M7.b.v).

## M12. THE SLAYER'S MEANS OF FORCE

a. **Bare hands**: i. with which he throttles the dragon (**19–22, 35, 37**); ii. or throws it over a precipice (**73**).

b. **Weapons**: i. stones or rocks (**5, 8, 39, 75–9, 83, 97, 106**; cf. A9); ii. club (**5, 23, 29, 33, 40, 72, 106**; cf. A5, A9); iii. arrows (**13–14, 17–18, 23, 27, 30, 39, 48, 71–2, 81, 83, 106**; cf. A3); iv. spear or javelin (**48** [com.]**, 51, 53, 65, 78–9, 81, 83, 98, 161**; cf. A2, A9, B12, C12, C14); v. sword or knife (**19, 35, 71, 79, 113, 123, 160–2**; cf. A2, A9, B1–2, B4–5, B11, C6, C12); vi. *harpē* or sickle (= M11.b.i); vii. ballista (**97–8**); viii. crosier (**151**).

c. **The slayer feeds himself to the dragon and kills it by hacking at it from within**: i. dying in the process (**99**); ii. surviving and emerging (**103, 105**; cf. **85** [com.], C6, C15).

## M13. DRAGON-SLAYING ASSISTANTS

a. **The human slayer**: i. with a human assistant, balancing the dragon's animal assistant (**23–4, 27**); ii. with a divine assistant, in classical narratives most commonly Athene (**1, 50, 54, 56, 59, 63, 75–6, 79, 85** [with com.]**, 88, 103**; cf. **5, 28, 53, 57–60, 66–7, 109**); in Christian narratives Jesus, an angel or a saint (**126, 128–9, 136, 148, 158**; cf. M10.b.i-ii); iii. with an animal assistant (**48, 50–1**).

b. **The divine slayer**: i. with a dragon assistant (**5** [com.]); ii. with a human assistant (**5, 8**: cf. A7).

## M14. COMPENSATION FOR THE SLAYING OF DRAGONS, AND THE MEMORIALISATION OF THEM

a. **Compensation**: i. an act or period of service by the slayer (**16, 71, 75**); ii. a human sacrifice (**71, 76**; cf. M5.a.ii); iii. the creation of replacement dragons or serpents (**75–9**).

b. **Acts of memorialisation**: i. the narrative itself of the slaying (*passim*); ii. a tune or song (**16, 56**); iii. a statue (**50, 92, 95**); iv. the preservation of part of the dragon's body as a trophy (**13, 53–4, 53, 58, 117**); v. the foundation of a city (**9, 71, 73, 75, 10**); vi. the foundation of a cult or festival (**16, 18, 71, 81–2, 84, 99, 101**); vii. the mourning of the dragon by nymphs or naiads (**83, 98, 106**; cf. **116**).

c. **The landscape remembers the battle**: i. in the shape or nature of mountains or hills (**5, 17, 117, 120, C12–15**; cf. M2b.i, M3.a); ii. in volcanoes (**5–7, 52**); iii. in its burnt appearance (**53**); iv. in the creation of a spring or river (= M4.a.iv).

## M15. SOME MOTIFS MORE SPECIFIC TO CHRISTIAN NARRATIVES

a. **The battle of belief and conversion**: i. the dragon and its sickening breath as embodying a community's commitment to pagan worship (**135, 136–7,**

147–8, 156, 160; cf. M7.a.ii); ii. the killing or mastery of the dragon as a demonstration of the power of faith (125–6, 128, 135–6, 145, 154, 160–1; cf. C8); iii. the killing or mastery of the dragon as bringing about (mass) conversion (134–7, 147, 160–1; cf. 130).

b. **The dragon is assimilated to**: i. the Devil (126, 131–2, 138, 140, 156, 158); ii. the Snake of Eden (132, 149–50); iii. a demon, and therefore subject to exorcistic expulsion to the wilderness (134–5, 147–8, 151, 154, 156; cf. also 162).

c. **Alternatives to the killing of the dragon**: i. the dragon's expulsion to the wilderness (= M15.b.iii); ii. the dragon's confinement to the underworld abyss (= M3.a.iv).

d. **Further themes**: i. the killing of the dragon associated with the reanimation of its most recent boy victim (127, 130–1, 132 [with com.], 135, 145, 149, 154, 161 [com.]); ii. the dragon trampled or trodden on (122, 125–6, 129, 145); iii. the dragon harnessed by the saint with an item of personal clothing and led like a dog on leash (126, 151, 154–6, 160–1); iv. the dragon burst open (131, 145, 149; cf. A3); v. the saint's appropriation of the dragon's vacated home for a monastery or hermitage (147, 150, 154, 156).

## M16. THE DRAGON RATIONALISED AND ALLEGORISED

a. **The dragon is rationalised as**: i. an ordinary snake (45, 101); ii. another animal (46, 64); iii. a man called Drakon, 'Dragon' (18, 34, 80; cf. 107, Keton); iv. humans of other names (52, 60–3, 65; cf. 69); v. a castle (27); vi. a rock (121); vii. a volcano (52); viii. a ship (118, 121 [com.]).

b. **The dragon is allegorised as**: i. desire (33); ii. the (flesh-eating) earth (47; cf. M2.b.i, M3.a); iii. terror (66); iv. seawater (67).

*Dragons, Serpents,
and Slayers in the Classical
and Early Christian Worlds*

# *Introduction*

If one asks a child of the modern West what he or she knows of dragons, the child is likely to offer a stereotype of the following sort: they are fundamentally serpentine; they come in a variety of colours, sometimes metallic, with green preferred; they have four legs, wings and lots of teeth; they breathe fire; they live in caves; they guard treasure; they eat people; and they are slain by knights or brave heroes. Of these details, the only one that does not really resonate for the dragons of classical antiquity is greenness, ancient dragons tending rather towards blueness or variegation. Examples of legged (including four-legged) dragons or winged (or wingless but nonetheless flying) dragons are rare in antiquity, but found they are. All of the other details suggested would have been equally recognisable as typical features of dragons by the children and indeed the adults of classical antiquity and the early Christian world that developed out of it.

But to speak of the typical features of ancient dragons is to disguise the wonderful variety that is to be found in their stories, which first emerge for us with the earliest surviving Greek literature, that of the seventh century BC, and never disappear from the Graeco-Latin tradition thereafter. This is a variety that this book seeks to showcase. Let us anticipate a few of these stories here.

Perhaps the best-known of all ancient dragon-slaying stories is Heracles' slaying of the marauding multi-headed Hydra of Lerna as one of his labours. She was seemingly undefeatable, for whenever Heracles lopped off one of her heads with his reaping sickle, two more would instantly grow in its place. Heracles eventually defeated her by having his companion Iolaus sear the stumps as soon as he lopped. Because of the help offered by Iolaus, Heracles' taskmaster Eurystheus refused to count the labour against his tally. It is less well-known that the Hydra too had had an ally in the battle, a sympathetic crab that pincered Heracles' toe.

Some dragons were unsleeping. Such a one was Ladon, the Dragon of the Hesperides, who hung in his apple tree to guard its golden apples. Such also was the Colchis Dragon, deployed by Aeetes to guard his golden fleece for him as it hung in a great oak. Only magic could overcome the Colchis dragon's wakefulness, and Aeetes' daughter, the young witch Medea, in love with Jason, helped the hero to steal the fleece by using her powerful drugs to plunge the creature, her erstwhile pet, into an unaccustomed slumber.

When Cadmus wished to found the city of Thebes at the site of the spring of Dirce, he had to contend with another guardian, the Dragon of Ares, which watched over the spring. Like other natural phenomena in the classical world, the spring could also be manifest as a virgin nymph or naiad, and it seems to have been the dragon's job to preserve her virginity for Ares. Cadmus killed the dragon with a great rock and then made a population for his new city by sowing its teeth in the ground, from which a crop of bronze-armed warriors sprung. This was one of the ways in which Cadmus was credited with being the first to discover metal. But Cadmus eventually had to pay compensation for killing Ares' servant, and both he and his wife Harmonia were themselves in due course transformed into dragons.

A number of recent movies have retold the tale of Perseus's delivery of the Ethiopian princess Andromeda from the serpentine sea monster for which she had been pinned out as a sacrifice. In the ancient narratives Perseus was able to hover over the creature on his winged boots and petrify it, in part at any rate, with the gaze of the head of the Gorgon Medusa that he was carrying with him. The tale initially resembles that of our friend Heracles' delivery of the Trojan princess Hesione from the sea monster for which she had similarly been set out as a sacrifice. But Heracles had had no magical instruments to rely upon, only his own mettle. Donning the princess's dress, he substituted himself for her and allowed the creature to swallow him as if he were a tastier morsel. Once inside, he hacked away at its liver until he killed it. When he emerged, he found that the monster's digestive juices had dissolved his hair.

Some ancient dragons combined other forms with their fundamentally serpentine nature. A good example of this is the Chimaera, who devastated Lycia with her fiery breath: she was a composite of serpent, lion and, surprisingly, goat. She was eventually destroyed by Bellerophon, who attacked her with his spear from the back of the winged horse Pegasus. A late version of this story tells how Bellerophon tipped his spear with lead and thrust it into the creature's fiery throat, whereupon the lead melted and suffocated her.

Composite in form too was Typhon, perhaps the greatest of all ancient dragons, amongst whose coils and proliferation of serpent heads there lurked a central, humanoid head as well as the noisy heads of many other animals. Typhon was created by Earth to supplant the Olympian gods, but after a battle of elemental and even cosmic proportions, in which the fire of his breath was countered by Zeus's thunderbolts, he was pinned down for eternity beneath Mt Etna in Sicily: it remains unclear whether the fire that continues to pour forth from the volcano is the dragon's own or that of the thunderbolts with which he was scorched.

Several monsters were termed *lamia* (or named Lamia). Most of them seem to have combined, in some form, the shapes of a serpent and a human female. Particularly intriguing is a group of *lamiai* said to have resided in Libya. They were massive, voracious serpents whose tails ended in the shape of a beautiful, naked young woman. They would conceal the bulk of their bodies behind sand dunes, exhibiting only their young-woman end to seduce and attract passing young men, their preferred diet. Once the young men came close enough, they would wheel round and gobble them down.

Most of the classical tales collected in this book, like all those mentioned here, are Greek in origin, though it must be conceded that the Romans often told them better. The Romans did have one home-grown dragon-slaying myth of their own, and a fine one it is too. When the Roman general Regulus and his army were confronted by the Dragon of the River Bagrada in Libya during the First Punic War, they turned to the high-tech super-weapons of the day, their ballistas (catapult engines), and eventually were able to overwhelm it with their missiles, though in doing so the army incurred a terrible curse from the naiads of the Bagrada river, whose pet the dragon had been, and this led to the force's eventual annihilation.

The Christian tradition of saintly dragon slayers grows directly out of the classical one, whilst incorporating, of course, an infusion of serpent symbolism from the Old and New Testaments. The most famous Christian dragon slayer of them all, St George, did not acquire his dragon until the twelfth century AD (so far as our evidence tells), but his dragon story is of a variety broadly established for other saints as early as the third century AD.

As a knight, St George is relatively hands-on in the method by which he disposes of his dragon, but other saints tend to rely on the power of prayer or the direct intervention of God to dispose of their dragons. St Philip discovers an entire city under the sway of a wicked tyrant and devoted to the cult of a great Viper. The city is fenced around by numerous other dragons and snakes, some of which he destroys some by calling down lightning upon them and others by staring them down with the light of the Holy Spirit in his eyes. Yet others he dispatches to the wilderness as if exorcising demons. He disposes of the great Viper herself by calling upon God to open up an abyss into which she is plunged, alongside her friend and ally, the tyrant.

Christian dragons, like their classical forerunners, often infect the air with their pestilential breath, and this can serve, in their stories, as a metaphor for the paganism the saint seeks to eradicate. A striking example is that offered by the Dragon of Rome, which lived at the bottom of a deep cave in the Forum, where it was fed by the Vestal Virgins. When its cult was terminated by the ascendant Christians, it breathed out a miasma that began to kill the people. St Silvester, the pope, descended to the dragon and drew a collar tight around its neck. The Dragon of Rome proved to be a popular creature, and the final victory over it was claimed for many several holy men, including one who discovered that it was a mechanical monster that had been in receipt of human sacrifices, impaling virgins upon its sword-like tongue as they fumbled towards it in the dark, unawares. Dragons had a number of ways of polluting the air and were notorious for doing so even after death with their rotting carcass. One of the dragons faced by St Callupan pollutes the air by the novel method of farting.

In classical times, women lacked the martial qualifications needed to destroy dragons, though Medea came close to doing so with her drugs. The more hands-off approach taken to dragon disposal typically adopted by Christian saints made space for female glory too, and St Victoria was the first to take the opportunity offered in banishing the Dragon of Tribulanum to the wilderness by the power of her prayer. When the jailed martyr St Marina encountered the Devil in her cell, manifest in the form of a great dragon, she too prayed. The dragon swallowed her nonetheless, but Jesus preceded her into its belly, bursting it open so that she could spring alive from it.

## WHAT IS A 'DRAGON' IN ANCIENT CONTEXT?

Let us think a little more precisely now about matters of definition. 'Dragons' can be challenging things to define, especially for those pursuing cross-cultural studies of them. But for those interested in 'dragons' in Greek and Roman antiquity, the relevant data set is actually quite easy to define. Our own word 'dragon' is ultimately derived from the Latin *draco*, which in turn is directly derived from the Greek *drakōn*. As even the most superficial perusal of the following sources will make clear, almost every creature featured this book is explicitly described in the ancient texts in whole or in part as a *drakōn* or a *draco*, and the remainder of them are described in terms that make it clear that they are creatures of the same type—terms, that is, relating to their physical nature, to their behaviour or to their story, and usually to all three of these together.

Continuity of terminology does not in itself entail continuity of meaning. However, as further perusal of the excerpts will make clear, a *drakōn* or *draco* was fundamentally a large serpent; it was often not merely large, but monstrously huge; it was often a marauding predator; it often had a supernatural nature or context of some sort; it was often fiery; and it was often slain by a hero figure. It will therefore be readily agreed that the modern English word 'dragon' remains, considerations of its derivational link apart, an appropriate word with which to translate the Greek and Latin terms in question, a point that will be reinforced when one considers the schema of the motifs most typically found in ancient dragon-slaying stories that precedes this introduction. In some later Greek and in some Latin texts other than those featured in this book, it is true, the terms *drakōn* and *draco* can be applied to what are ostensibly large but otherwise common or garden snakes, a consideration that may recommend the use rather of the English word 'serpent' as a default translation, a word embracing for us as it does both 'dragons' and 'snakes' in its semantic field. This is one of the reasons I have incorporated 'serpents' into the book's title; another is to honour the plagues of lesser snakes that are sometimes found to attend upon the *drakōn* or *draco*, or even to serve in its stead. However, given the importance I have placed upon highlighting the significance of the terms *drakōn* and *draco* in the texts we are considering, and the inconcinnity of tying the word 'serpent' to these terms whilst a number of the Latin texts under consideration also deploy the word the *serpens*, which is of course the source of our word 'serpent' and which also shares its semantic field, it has seemed best after all to retain 'dragon' to translate *drakōn* and *draco* and to serve as the prime umbrella term for the creatures of interest. The use of the term 'dragon' and its derivatives in the following translations always reflects, it should be noted, the use of the terms *drakōn* or *draco* or their derivatives in the original text; the relevant original term is usually supplied in addition in square brackets on its first appearance in each excerpt given, though only exceptionally thereafter.

Our adumbration of the ancient *drakōn* requires two glosses. First, Greek myth knew of a number of monstrous creatures, some of which we have already mentioned, that integrated the form of a *drakōn* with humanoid elements or elements of other animals, and these creatures too are featured in this book. This is because some of them at least can nonetheless be described in the ancient texts as a *drakōn* (or its female equivalent, *drakaina*) as a whole (e.g. Delphyne in **5**); because they are born into a *drakōn* family (e.g. **1–2**); or because, for all that the *drakōn* element may constitute a relatively small physical proportion of their body, it can even so be seen to dominate their natures. Medusa and the Gorgons have only hair that consists of *drakontes*, but the paralysing stare central to their nature and their story is derivative of ancient thinking about the *drakōn*; the Chimaera has only a *drakōn* tail, but the fire breathing central to her nature and her story is again derivative of ancient thinking about *drakontes*. Cerberus merely has a pelt covered in tiny *drakōn* heads, but when he slavers or vomits from his canine mouths, the distinctive, plant-mutating venom he produces can only come from his *drakōn* element. When one accepts creatures of this sort into the fold of the ancient 'dragon', one realises that rather few of the best-loved monsters of Greek myth remain outside it: the Minotaur and the Cyclops are perhaps the most distinguished exceptions.

Secondly, there is after all one category of creature featured in this collection that is not characteristically defined by the terms *drakōn* or *draco*. That is sea monsters, which are usually defined on the Greek side by the term *kētos* and on the Latin by the derived *cetus* or the native *belua*. The inclusion is justified because: they share with *drakontes* a fundamentally serpentine form; sea monsters appear in the canonical genealogies that link the great *drakontes* of myth (1–2); they also share certain minor physical features with *drakontes*, such as beards and crests, triple rows of teeth and fiery eyes; they participate in stories closely similar in type to those given to *drakontes* (the hero slays the creature to rescue a young victim set out for it to devour); and two myths merge *kētē* and *drakontes* with each other in different ways, a significant number when one considers that there are only two great *kētē* of pure nature in the mythical tradition anyway, that of Troy and that of Ethiopia. The creature Scylla seems to have started life as a *drakōn* but to morph into a *kētos* in the course of her tradition. And the *drakontes*, explicitly so described, of the Laocoon myth behave precisely as if they were *kētē* in breasting the sea to attack the coast of Troy.

If we ask why it is that snake-based monsters should have made such popular adversaries in ancient storytelling, I can do no better than refer to the words of Walter Burkert: 'Or take that favorite character of Near Eastern and Western mythology, the dragon. He is only the perfect crystallization of the role of the adversary in the combat tale. He is a snake, because this is the most dreaded and hated animal, having resorted to chemical warfare so long ago; he has a huge devouring mouth, because being swallowed and eaten is a most basic anxiety of every living being.' (Burkert 1979:20).

## THE SCOPE AND ORGANISATION OF THIS BOOK

This book's object is to provide an expansive series of translations of the many rich (but not always easily accessible) dragon and dragon-slaying narratives of the Greek and Latin tradition. It seeks to provide fairly detailed coverage of the pagan literature of classical antiquity and of Christian literature up until the end of the sixth century AD. With more selective coverage of the intervening period, it culminates with translations of the earliest and most influential accounts of the dragon and snake slayings of SS. George and Patrick, both first attested in the twelfth century AD but belonging squarely within the tradition of saintly dragon-slaying stories established many centuries before. Given the natures, quantities and distributions of the sources available, it has seemed more helpful to organise the classical material principally in accordance with theme, which in effect normally means the dragon or the slayer featured, but the Christian material principally in accordance with source date (with the notable exceptions of the material relating to SS. Philip and Silvester). The classical part of the book incorporates the vast bulk of the surviving literary texts that bear upon dragon-fighting traditions in any substantial way. Texts of substance normally are omitted only where they overlap strongly in their content with texts that have been included. The chapters typically open with the source, irrespective of date, that offers the most helpful balanced summary of the myth or tale in question in a broadly canonical form. Amongst other texts included in each case is the one that makes the earliest (literary) reference to the dragon in question and the one that provides the most expansive and richly detailed account of it. The evidence of the iconographic sources, which in fact consists almost entirely of vases, is introduced in commentaries, where it is capable of making a significant addition to that of the literary record.

In all, 162 excerpts or excerpt groups are provided (appendices apart). All the translations from Greek and Latin sources are my own, one virtue of which is that a measure of consistency has thus been achieved in the rendering of key terms and motifs. But I have also, with regret, found it necessary to introduce a small inconsistency between some of my translations: this is in the degree to which the dragons are represented as personalised. The Greek word *drakōn*, for example, is a masculine-gendered noun, and accordingly *drakontes* are inevitably referred to with masculine-gendered language, including masculine pronouns. In the want of other indicators, this can leave unclear the extent to which any given author personalised his dragon in his own mind—in other words, the extent to which he conceptualised his dragon, in our terms, as a 'he' or as an 'it'. My own choice between the adoption of 'he' and that of 'it' in referring to individual *drakontes* in the translations has sometimes been conditioned less by an estimate of the author's attitude towards his creature than by a desire to convey the narrative in hand with clarity and efficiency: it is often helpful, in a fast-paced text, to be able to distinguish a dragon 'it' from a slayer 'he'. Only rarely in ancient texts are dragons marked out as female by the use of the term *drakaina* and corresponding feminine pronouns. On these occasions, therefore, the dragon's femaleness certainly, if not necessarily its actual personalisation, is clearly of interest and importance to the ancient author, and in these cases I have been careful to use the pronoun 'she' in translation. The editions of the ancient texts upon which the translations are based are indicated at the rear of the book.

The presentation of the sources is basically on the model of that I adopted in my previous sourcebook, *Magic, Witchcraft and Ghosts in the Greek and Roman Worlds* (New York: Oxford University Press, 2002; 2nd ed. 2009). Each text (or group of texts) is headed by a brief title indicating its content and significance, its formal citation and specifications of its original language and date. Excerpts are followed by commentaries that seek to provide, to the extent that it is helpful or appropriate, further information about the nature of the source. But their principal purpose is to situate the source material in the broader context of ancient dragon-slaying literature, i.e. in that of the other passages contained within the sourcebook, and to this extent there is heavy use of cross-referencing, with parallel source texts indicated in bold figures. Although the narratives included here are refreshingly diverse, nonetheless many of them are underpinned by a tight set of productive motifs. These motifs have been organised into a systematic schema, which is presented directly before this introduction and which lists the principal occurrences of each motif. The schema has its own interest (a quick scan of it will be sufficient to convey to the reader all the principal features of the world of ancient dragons), but its sections and subsections are also often cited in the individual commentaries for efficiency's sake, and to avoid repeating lengthy lists of parallel passages whenever one of the more common productive motifs presents itself. The schema of motifs is also cited by means of a series of emboldened figures, these preceded by **M**. The commentaries further seek, where appropriate, to relate the material found in the classical and Christian texts to that of three other fields: world-foundational dragon-slaying tales found in texts of the ancient societies of the Near East and India, some of which may have had a direct impact on the shaping of the Greek material; the rich tradition of Germanic, especially Norse, dragon-slaying tales recorded up until the thirteenth century AD, which may or may not share an Indo-European inheritance with the Graeco-Roman material; and a (rather more arbitrarily selected) series of international folk tales of varying dates that exhibit story-type and motivic correspondences with the Graeco-Roman material. The texts of interest in each case, thirty-five in total, are summarised (occasionally quoted) in three corresponding appendices, and these are again cited by means bold figures preceded by **A** (Near Eastern), **B** (Germanic) or **C** (folk tale). Each of the sourcebook's principal chapters is concluded with a brief articulated bibliography of further reading in the author-date style.

## THE SYMMETRICAL BATTLE

Many of the recurring motifs of classical and early Christian dragon-fighting narratives speak for themselves or are most conveniently elucidated in the commentaries that follow, but an expansive set of interestingly symmetrical motifs call for special introduction here (**M6–M11** in the Schema of Motifs). The ancient dragon battles with a range of integral weapons, and these are often countered by their human or divine opponents on a like-for-like basis, though not always within the compass of an individual narrative. The dragon is above all a creature of fire, its fieriness being an imaginative extrapolation of the burning sensation caused by the natural viper's venom. But it is not only the dragon's venom that is fiery: so are its eyes and, as we have seen, its breath. The slayer counters the dragon's fire with his own saliva (the ancients considering human saliva to be scalding for snakes, and therefore the mirror image of snake venom), with thunderbolts, fiery arrows or brands, pyres, fumigations, parching herbs or a metaphorically fiery spirit. Sometimes the slayer is able to turn the dragon's own fire against it. The dragon also battles with air and wind, which it typically infects with its venomous, pestilential and smoky breath, again as we have already noted; after death its rotting corpse, so vast that it is difficult to dispose of, can similarly corrupt the atmosphere. Slayers counter with a magically destructive breath of their own, by fumigating (again), by making the sign of the cross in the air or by invoking the Holy Spirit. The poisonousness of the dragon's liquid venom is countered more directly, saliva aside, with poisonous or soporific herbal decoctions, with poison arrows or indeed with dragon venom, either that of dragon in question or that extracted from another dragon previously slain. The dragon can battle with its gaze or against its opponent's gaze in various ways. Most simply, it can be unsleeping, never closing its eyes, as we have seen; this notion too is an imaginative extrapolation from the behaviour of natural snakes, which cannot close their eyes. More actively, the dragon can emit fire from its eyes, petrify with them or blind its opponent by spitting venom. The slayer counters by casting sleep upon the unsleeping dragon with magical herbs, blinding the dragon with a thunderbolt or staring it down. In the field of sound, the dragon often makes a terrible hiss, but it can also bewitch its opponent by singing. The slayer counters by using his own incantations against the dragon. The dragon, however, has a further weapon up its sleeve: it can be deaf or can deafen itself to the slayer's incantation; we may note that all natural snakes are deaf. But the slayer can counter this too, with a silent incantation or prayer. Finally, dragons do battle with their coils: it is of coils that they almost wholly consist, and they are on occasion said to constrict. The slayer counters with circles of different kinds. Most strikingly, he fights dragons with a sickle that reflects the creatures' curving shape, as well as being well adapted to the reaping of a snaky neck. But he also does battle with circular purifications, circles of magical herbs or magic rings.

## THE LITERATURE

The texts presented in this volume are discussed, alongside many others, in my recent monograph, *Drakōn: Dragon Myth and Serpent Cult in the Greek and Roman Worlds* (Ogden 2013), to which readers are referred in the first instance for further analysis and references. That volume was written to address the surprising lack of general treatments of dragons in Graeco-Roman antiquity. Indeed, to the best of my knowledge, there has never been a monograph squarely devoted to the subject in any language. Much of interest may be found in two substantial and profound works of scholarship, Fontenrose's *Python* (Fontenrose 1959) and Watkins's *How to Kill a Dragon* (Watkins 1995), but these scholars are less interested in the culture of the Graeco-Roman dragon in itself than they are in the reconstruction of mythical or linguistic-poetic archetypes that may have underlain the dragon stories of a broad range of ancient cultures. Beyond these items relatively little of value is accessible to the English reader. For more focused discussions on Graeco-Roman dragons one must still turn to the relevant articles in the great classical dictionaries initiated in the nineteenth centuries (we stand on the shoulders of giants), the best being Pottier's article 'Draco' in the *Dictionnaire des antiquités grecques et romaines* (Pottier 1877–1919). Merkelbach's article 'Drache' in the more recent *Reallexikon für Antike und Christentum* (Merkelbach 1959) has the virtue of embracing the early Christian texts. There is material of interest in books devoted to snakes more generally in antiquity (Küster 1913, on snakes in Greek art and religion; Mitropoulou 1977, a samizdat treatment of gods and heroes in snake form; Sancassano 1997, on snakes in early Greek poetry; Grabow 1998, on snakes on black-figure vases; Jacques 2002, 2007, commentaries—of breathtaking learning—on the herpetological poems of Nicander). In shorter compass, Bodson's article 'Les grecs et leurs serpents' (Bodson 1981) also repays reading. If one wishes to investigate the mythological traditions introduced in this book in more detail, one should turn first to the great Sir James Frazer's two volumes devoted to Apollodorus in the Loeb Classical Library (Frazer 1921); his copious notes incorporate lists of parallel texts that are all but exhaustive. One turns in second place to Gantz's *Early Greek Myth* (Gantz 1993), the accessibility of which can disguise the vast scope of its accomplishment. And in the third place, for the ancient iconographical counterparts to these myths, which include much to surprise and delight, one turns to the relevant entries in the *Lexicon Iconographicum Mythologiae Classicae* (1981–99), soon, rumour has it, to be available online. Envy is the only explanation I can offer for recent attempts to disparage this superb work of reference. For the folk-loric context of some of the ancient dragon stories, one should turn to Hansen's authoritative *Ariadne's Thread* (Hansen 2002:119–30), and also to Röhrich's entry 'Drache, Drachenkampf, Drachentöter' in the *Enzyklopädie des Märchens* (Röhrich 1981). A well-informed and efficient summary of the dragon's role in the wider Western tradition is to be found in Evans' thirty-two-page article 'Semiotics and Traditional Lore: The Medieval Dragon Tradition' (Evans 1985).

## A NOTE ON THE OTHER DRAGONS OF CLASSICAL ANTIQUITY

The classical narratives collected in this book focus on the dragon fights of myth, which inevitably tend to cast the dragons in a negative and aggressive role. But the Greek and Roman worlds also knew dragons in a far more benign and positive aspect, in the context of cult. Unfortunately, this aspect lends itself to illustration in narrative only occasionally, and so it has not been made a focus of this sourcebook. Dead heroes sometimes morphed into snakes, or at any rate acquired serpentine affinities (**133**). Some of them developed helpful oracular powers, such as Trophonius (Bonnechere 2003) and Amphiaraus (Sineux 2007). Others, such as Cecrops and Ericthonius, could specialise in the protection of their erstwhile land (Gourmelen 2004). From the end of the fifth century BC onwards the uncomplicatedly benign gods of healing, wealth and good luck were often held to manifest themselves in the form of large dragons (as well as in humanoid form). An impressive series of relief stelae from fourth-century BC Attica shows Zeus Meilichios ('Zeus the Propitiated'), the god of wealth and good luck, appearing in friendly fashion before the gathered families of his grateful petitioners in the form of an enormous, rampant, vertically coiling serpent (Cook 1914–40:2.2,1091–1160, Mitropoulou 1977:112–55, Jameson et al. 1993:81–91, Lalonde 2006). Agathos Daimon ('Good Demon'), first attested in serpent form in early Ptolemaic Alexandria, ca. 300 BC, had a similar province. He is a curious character: in some ways he appears to have been a slain dragon like any other (**101**), but somehow he lived on beyond his slaying as a minor divine power, conferring his blessings on the city and its constituent households alike (Fraser 1972:1, 209–11, with associated notes, Quaegebeur 1975:170–6 and *passim*, Mitropoulou 1977: 155–68, Dunand 1969, 1981, Stoneman 2007:532–4, 2008:56–8). The great healing god Asclepius was often manifest in the form of a serpent, most splendidly so when travelling from one of his established sanctuaries to the place in which he wished to set up another one. One narrative that does deserve attention here is Ovid's wonderful first-century AD description of the god's transition from his original home at Epidaurus in the Argolid to his (additional) new home on the Tiber Island in Rome. He appears before the Roman ambassadors visiting his temple in Epidaurus in the form of a large and gracious dragon, and then of his own accord he slithers to the coast and onto their ship to signify his willingness to be taken to Rome and extend his cult there (Ovid *Metamorphoses* 15.622–744; for Asclepius more generally see Edelstein and Edelstein 1945, LiDonnici 1995, Riethmüller 2005, Melfi 2007–, Wickkiser 2008,

Petsalis-Diomidis 2010, *LIMC* Asklepios). When Asclepius manifested himself in humanoid form, he nonetheless famously carried a serpent avatar with him, as did his daughter Hygieia ('Health'). His wound around his staff; hers wound around her body and fed from the bowl she extended to it. In some of Asclepius's temples at any rate the great dragon god was manifest also in the form of the sacred snakes maintained there, snakes probably of the Four-lined rat snake variety (*Elaphe quatuorlineata*). As pilgrims slept ('incubated') in the temple complex overnight, these large but placid snakes would be brought to them and encouraged to give a lick or a gentle bite to their ailing body part (Aristophanes *Wealth* 633–747).

# Part One
## *The Classical Dragon*

# 1
# The Genealogy of the Great Dragons

We open with two genealogies that encompass several of the more famous great dragons (*drakontes*) and sea monsters (*kētē*) of Greek myth (1–2). A pivotal mother figure within these genealogies is Echidna (Viper), an anguipede who remains frustratingly obscured from view in ancient tradition. Perhaps, however, we can get some notion of her from a curious figure seemingly calqued upon her in a supposedly Scythian myth told by Herodotus (3). The genealogies tell us that the ancients did indeed think of their great dragons and sea monsters as belonging in a special category together, a point that also emerges from the canonical list of great dragons invoked by Seneca's Medea (4).

Figure 1 The anguipede Echidna. Pirro Ligorio (ca.1500–83 AD): 'Parco dei Mostri' (Monster Park), 1552 AD. Sacro Bosco di Bomarzo, Lazio, Italy. The Bridgeman Art Library.

13

## 1 Hesiod's influential genealogy of the great dragons

vii BC

Hesiod *Theogony* 270–336

Greek

Now Ceto bore to Phorcys the beautiful-cheeked old women, grey from birth, whom the immortal gods and earthbound humans know as the Graeae, Pemphredo of the fair dress and Enyo of the saffron dress, and the Gorgons, Sthenno, Euryale and the grievously suffering Medusa, who live beyond glorious Ocean at the end of the world, adjacent to Night, where the shrill-voiced Hesperides dwell. Medusa was mortal, but the other two were immortal and unaging. It was just with Medusa that he of the blue hair [Poseidon] lay in a soft meadow amid spring flowers. When Perseus chopped her head off, out jumped great Chrysaor and the horse Pegasus. Pegasus received his name from the fact that he was born beside the springs [*pēgai*] of Ocean, Chrysaor from the fact that he wielded a golden sword [*aor chryseion*] in his hands. Pegasus flew up, abandoning the earth, the mother of flocks, and came to the immortals. He lives in the house of Zeus, bearing thunder and lightning for Zeus the counsellor. Chrysaor made love with Callirhoe, the daughter of glorious Ocean, and sired the three-headed Geryon, whom mighty Heracles slew beside his rolling-footed oxen in sea-bound Erytheia, on the day on which he drove his oxen of the broad foreheads to sacred Tiryns, crossing the stream of Ocean and killing Orthus and the cowherd Eurytion in the misty stable beyond glorious Ocean.

**295.** And she* [probably Ceto; surely not Callirhoe] bore another irresistible monster, nothing like mortal men or the immortal gods, in a hollow cave, the divine, strong-minded Echidna ['Viper'], who in half of her body is a nymph with rolling eyes and fair cheeks, but in the other half is a monstrous snake, terrible and great, darting, eating raw flesh deep in hidden lairs in the sacred earth. There is her cave, down below, under a hollow rock, far from the immortal gods and mortal men. There the gods allocated to her a glorious home in which to dwell. And the baleful Echidna keeps watch under the earth in Arima, an immortal nymph, unaging all her days. They say that Typhon was joined with her in love, the terrible, violent and lawless creature with the nymph of rolling eyes. She conceived and bore strong-minded children. First she bore the dog Orthus, for Geryon. Then she gave birth again to the irresistible, unutterable, raw-flesh-eating Cerberus, the bronze-voiced dog of Hades with fifty heads, shameless and strong. And in the third place again she bore the Lernaean Hydra of baleful mind, whom the white-armed goddess Hera reared, implacably angry as she was with mighty Heracles. Heracles, the son of Zeus and also son of Amphitryon, slew her with pitiless bronze, alongside the war-loving Iolaus, at the devising of Athene, driver of the spoil.

**319.** And she* [probably the Echidna; possibly the Hydra] bore the Chimaera that breathed irresistible fire, terrible, large, swift of foot and strong. She had three heads. The first was of a fierce lion, the second of a goat, and the third of a snake, a strong dragon [*drakōn*].° In front she was a lion, in the rear she was a dragon, and in the middle a goat [*chimaira*], breathing forth the terrible might of burning fire. ° Pegasus and the good Bellerophon slew her.

**326.** And she* [probably the Echidna; possibly the Chimaera] was covered by Orthus and bore the deadly Sphinx, a doom to the Cadmeians, and the Nemean Lion. Hera, the chaste wife of Zeus, reared the lion and set him to dwell in the high ground of Nemea as a bane to men. There he destroyed the tribes of her own people, lording it over Nemean Tretus and Apesas. But the strength of mighty Heracles conquered him.

**333.** Ceto made love with Phorcys and bore her youngest child, a terrible snake [*ophis*] which guards all-gold apples within his great coils in his lair in the dark earth [i.e. Ladon]. This is the family of Ceto and Phorcys.

The Hesiodic hexameter poems *Theogony* and *Works and Days* are regarded as second only to the Homeric epics in antiquity amongst extant Greek literature. Much of the material they contain is of a traditional nature and may long antedate the (estimated) age of composition.

This richly detailed genealogy of the great dragons was to retain influence until the end of antiquity. In yoking together as it does most of the significant great anguiforms of Classical mythology—the Gorgons (**54–67**), Typhon (**5–12**), Echidna (**3**), Cerberus (**35–47**), the Hydra (**23–7**), the Chimaera (**48–53**) and Ladon (**28–34**)—it helps to establish the integrity of the concept of the dragon in antiquity (like is grouped with like), alongside two further criteria: the deployment term *drakōn*, which will be noted throughout this book, and the recurring set of motifs and story types associated with that term, as laid out in the Schema of Motifs. As we have noted in the introduction, the single greatest difficulty in dragon definition in an ancient context is presented by the *drakontes'* marine cousins, sea monsters, the creatures signified by the term *kētos*. In deriving most of the great *drakontes* from the archetypal *kētos* Ceto (*Kētō*), Hesiod helps unify the two groups conceptually. The two groups are further unified by the traditions relating to the dragon-pair sent against Laocoon (**92–6**) and to Scylla (**119–212**), which creatures, in different ways, seem to straddle the distinction between *drakōn* and *kētos*.

Creatures in this genealogy wholly devoid of *drakōn* affinities are few: Medusa's children Pegasus and Chrysaor (together with the latter's bride and son) and the Nemean Lion. It is worth noting, however, that Heracles brought a pet *drakōn* of his own along to help him in his fight against the lion (**25**). As to the less obviously *drakōn* members of the family, the Graeae, full sisters of the Gorgons (indeed fully identified with them in the rationalising tradition, **60**), were famous for sharing between them a single eye and a single tooth, the parts that might be considered characteristic of serpents (**54**). A unique source (schol. Euripides *Phoenissae* 1760) tells that the Sphinx's tail consisted of a dragoness (*drakaina*). Cerberus's less well distinguished elder brother Orthus (also known as Orthrus), the two-headed dog that died at Heracles' hands alongside his master Geryon, is given no dragon affinities in the extant literary tradition, but his tail sometimes takes the form of a serpent, à la Chimaera, in the iconography of the sixth and earlier fifth centuries BC (*LIMC* Orthros i 6, 14, 20, 21, 25). A great many of the creatures in this genealogy, it may be noted, are also multi-headed, or at least sometimes manifest as such.

The genealogy is articulated by a number of paratactic 'and she's, and upon three occasions, marked with asterisks, it remains uncertain to which previously mentioned female creature the 'she' refers. I have indicated in square brackets the antecedent I find the most probable upon each occasion, based upon the flow of the text and indeed the way in which it was usually interpreted by the later writers of antiquity, such as Hyginus (**2**; cf. Table 1). This need not of course reflect the intentions of the text's original composer(s), if indeed their intentions were strongly fixed. The repetition of the 'and she's at any rate serves to highlight the particular danger posed by female monsters, ever ready to produce a new brood (**M2.a.ii**). According to the understanding adopted here, the great focal mother of the dragons is the Echidna. As is commonly the case with dragonesses (*drakainai*), she is an anguipede in form (humanoid above the waist, serpentine below). Since her snake half is said to be raw-flesh-eating, her tail presumably ends in a snake's head; for the configuration, cf. the Giants (**5**) and the *lamiai* (**72**). Aristophanes gives his own Echidna a hundred heads (**37**), a property also ascribed to her consort Typhon (**5–6**). Presumably ninety-nine of these are snake's heads, though the comedian's description need not be canonical. The relationships of Hesiod's Echidna with Aristophanes', with Herodotus's Scythian Echidna (**3**) and with the Echidna encountered by St Philip at Ophiorhyme-Hierapolis (**134**) remain unclear, but two common themes should be noted. First, the Hesiodic, Aristophanic and Philippian Echidnas are all associated with holes in the ground: Hesiod's Echidna is here associated with the depths of the earth both in her birth and in her subsequent cave lair at Arima (for which cf. **7–9, 11**); Aristophanes casts his Echidna as a denizen of the underworld; and it is noteworthy too that Philip's Echidna ends up confined to an underworld abyss. Secondly, the Hesiodic, Herodotean and Philippian Echidnas are all presented first and foremost as progenitrixes.

Lines 323–4 (between '°...°'), describing the Chimaera, are identical with the Homer *Iliad* 6.181–2 (**49**), usually thought to be the prior location.

## 2    A later, flatter genealogy of the great dragons

ii AD

Hyginus *Fabulae* 151

Latin

From the Giant Typhon and Echidna there were born Gorgon, Cerberus the three-headed dog, the dragon [*draco*] that guarded the apples of the Hesperides across the Ocean [Ladon], the Hydra that Heracles killed at the Lernaean spring, the dragon [*draco*] that protected the ram's fleece in Colchis, Scylla, whose upper part was that of a woman but her lower part that of a dog [*canis*: recte *cetus*, 'sea monster'?], and she had six dogs [*canes*] sprouting from her, the Sphinx that was in Boeotia, the Chimaera in Lycia, whose front part was a lion and hind part a dragon [*draco*], whilst the *chimaera*-goat itself was in the middle. To Medusa the daughter of Gorgon and Neptune were born Chrysaor and Pegasus. From Chrysaor and Callirhoe was born three-bodied Geryon.

Hyginus's mythological handbook simplifies and expands the Hesiodic genealogy, concentrating the great dragons together as the immediate offspring of Typhon and Echidna. From Hesiod's genealogy the couple retain Cerberus and the Hydra and (probably) the Chimaera, and the Sphinx too. Then in addition Echidna's Hesiodic siblings Ladon and 'Gorgon' also become the couple's children, as do two further monsters not included in Hesiod's tree, the Dragon of Colchis and Scylla. There are several oddities amongst the details, as is often the case with Hyginus. Typhon is not normally regarded as a Giant, though he, like them, is produced by Earth as part of her sequence of attempts to overthrow the heavenly gods (**5**). Medusa and her two Gorgon sisters have mutated into a father and a daughter. The claim that Scylla's lower part was a dog probably originated in a scribal error: *canis*, 'dog' supplanting the less familiar *ceti*, 'sea monster', under the influence of the word *canes* that immediately follows in the sequence of the Latin. Much of this material is also to be found in the same text at *praefatio* 39.

## 3    The Scythian *echidna*, another great progenitrix

ca. 425 BC

Herodotus 4.8–10

Greek

**8.** From there Heracles arrived in the land now called Scythia, where he was overtaken by winter weather and frost. He pulled his lion skin over himself and went to sleep. In the meantime, his mares, which were pasturing whilst harnessed to his chariot, disappeared by some divine fortune.

**9.** When Heracles roused himself, he made a search for them combing the whole land over, eventually coming to a land called Wooded. There he found in a cave a creature who was half girl, an *echidna* [viper] of double form, whose parts above the buttocks were those of a woman, and those below of a snake. Upon seeing her he marvelled at her and asked her if she had seen his mares wandering anywhere. She replied that she herself had them and would not give them back to him until he had sex with her. Heracles had sex with her on this basis. She kept postponing the return of the horses, as she wished to be with Heracles for as long a time as possible, although Heracles just wanted to get them back and be off. Eventually she did restore them to him, and said, 'These mares came here and I saved them for you, and you have rewarded me for doing so, for I have three sons from you. Tell me what I am to do with them when they are grown. Am I to have them live here (for I myself rule over this land), or am I to send them off to you?' That is what she asked, and this is what they say Heracles replied: 'Whenever you see that the boys have become men, you will not go wrong if you do as follows: whichever of them you see stretching this bow as I do now and wearing this belt as I wear it now, have him make his home in this land. You must send out of the land the ones that fail in these tasks I impose. If you do this you yourself will be cheered and you will be following my commands.'

**10.** Heracles drew one of his bows (for up until that point he used to carry two) and he showed her the belt, and he handed over to her the bow and the belt that had a golden cup at the end of its clasp. After giving them over, he went off. When her sons had become men, the *echidna* named them. The first she called Agathyrsus, the second Gelonus and the youngest Scythes. She remembered Heracles' behest and followed his instructions. Two of her sons, Agathyrsus and Gelonus, did not pass the test and departed the land, exiled by their own mother, but the youngest of them, Scythes, did indeed pass it and remained in the land. And from Scythes the son of Heracles have been born all those that have ever been kings of the Scythians. And it is because of the cup that still up until now the Scythians wear cups on their belts. His mother ensured that Scythes remained. This is what those of the Greeks that live in Pontus say.

This delightful tale from the pioneering historian Herodotus, a Greek aetiology of the origin of the Scythian race, is included here for its portrait of the Scythian *echidna* or viper and her resemblance to the Hesiodic Echidna. They share an anguipede form, both being maiden above and serpent below, and both are featured in their texts primarily in the role of progenitrix. Like the Hesiodic Echidna's consort Typhon (**5, 8**), Herodotus's *echidna* is herself adept at stealing things and hiding them in caves. However, there is no particular reason to infer that Herodotus's creature, although she is an *echidna*, bears Echidna as a proper name, nor yet that she is supposed to be fully identifiable with the Hesiodic Echidna. Broadly similar stories, shorn of snake elements, were to attach, in the Persian realm adjacent to Scythia, to Alexander the Great and the Amazon queen Thalestris (Diodorus 17.77.1–3, Strabo C505, Justin 2.4.33, Curtius 6.5.24–32, all ultimately derivative of the late fourth-century BC Clitarchus) and to Rostam and Tamineh (Ferdowsi *Shahnameh* V.434–42, translated at Warner and Warner 1912:ii, 120–6 and Davis 1997:187–9, c. 1000 AD).

## 4 Medea culls the venom of the great dragons in preparing a fiery spell

mid-i AD

Seneca *Medea* 684–709

Latin

NURSE: ... Drawn by her magical incantations the scaly host abandon their holes and present themselves. Here a cruel snake [*serpens*] drags its monstrous body, sticks out its three-forked tongue and seeks out those to whom it is to bring death. It is astonished to hear her spell, winds its thick body in knot upon knot and forces them into coils. 'Small are the evils', she says, 'and worthless is the weapon which the depths of the earth produce. I shall seek my poisons [*venena*] in heaven. This, this is the time to start something more than ordinarily criminal. Let that snake [the constellation Draco] that lies like a huge torrent come down here, the knots of which touch against the two beasts, the greater and the lesser [Bears] (the greater one exploited by the Pelasgians, the lesser one by the Sidonians). Let Ophiuchus [Snake-Holder] finally release his tight grip on it, and let it pour forth its venom. Let Python respond to my incantations and present himself, he who dared attack the twin deities [Apollo and Artemis]. Let the Hydra come back, and every snake cut from it by Hercules' hand, renewing itself through its own butchery. And do you too, unsleeping snake first given rest by my incantations, abandon the Colchians and present yourself.' After she had called up the entire race of snakes, she heaped together her evil and ill-starred poisons...

This passage of typically Senecan gothic excess from his tragedy *Medea* is included here because, like the genealogies (1–2), it yokes together a series of great dragons from Graeco-Roman myth and speaks of an awareness of a canon of such creatures. Medea's nurse is describing her mistress's preparation of magical substances for the manufacture of a wedding dress for Glauce, who has stolen her husband Jason. The dress will explode into flames and burn the girl to ashes, together with her father (879–90). Accordingly, Medea makes use of the characteristically fiery venom of snakes. But the venom of common or garden snakes is not good enough for her purposes, and she summons to herself the great cosmic dragon, the constellation Draco, alongside a series of great dragons of myth, irrespective of whether at this point they are alive (the Dragon of Colchis) or dead (Python and Hydra). The motif of the manufacture of a fiery garment impregnated with the venom of a great dragon is taken over from the Heracles-Deianeira tradition (26). The Romans associated the magical summoning-together of snakes with the race of the Marsi, who lived beside Lake Fucinus (for whom see above all Augustine *De Genesi ad literam* 11.28.35); the practice is also found in 130.

### FURTHER READING

Hesiod's genealogy of *drakontes*: West 1966:243–59, Sancassano 1997:54–7, Hansen 2004:175.

The Scythian *echidna*: Ustinova 2005, Ogden 2011:149–50.

The dragons of Seneca's Medea: Hine 2000:178–81.

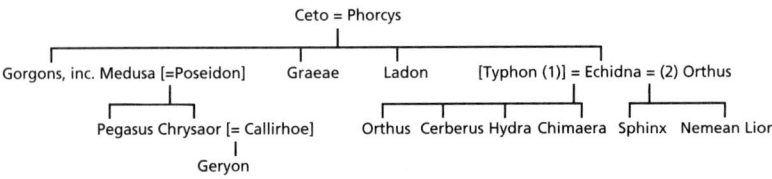

Table 1.1 Hesiod's genealogy of the great dragons.

# 2
# *Typhon, Slain by Zeus*

Typhon, who challenged Zeus for rulership of the world in a battle that reached cosmic proportions, is one of the most richly attested of the classical dragons. Already the subject of major section of Hesiod's *Theogony* (6), his assault on heaven is described in lavish detail by Nonnus in Late Antiquity (8). The later narratives, including Nonnus's (5, 8, 9), unexpectedly preserve seemingly very ancient motifs that link Typhon's backstory to the dragon narratives of Near Eastern culture. The model of Typhon's unsuccessful attack upon the heavenly gods was avidly taken up by Orphic thinkers, who produced no fewer than three calques for him in Ophion(eus), Chronos and Zeus-Sabazius (10–11). Typhon's physical form is represented in a number of

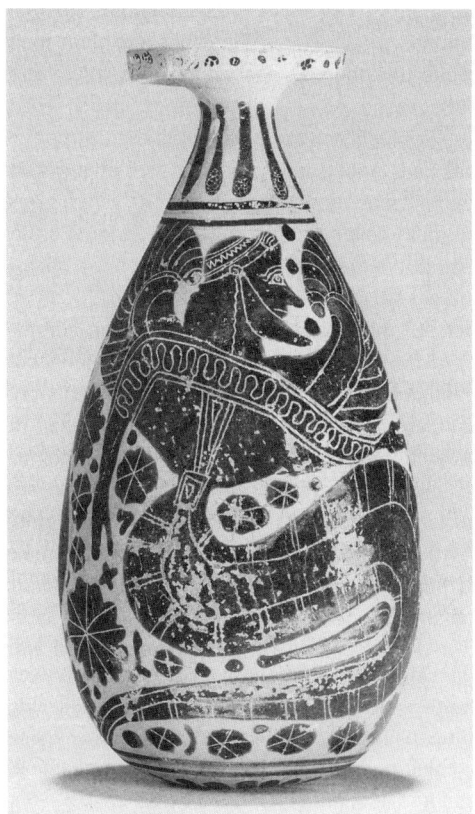

Figure 2 The winged, anguipede Typhon. Corinthian black-figure alabastron with a, ca. 620–590 BC. Private Collection. Photo © Christie's Images / The Bridgeman Art Library.

different ways in art and literature, but he is always fundamentally an anguipede. For Typhon's career as progenitor, with Echidna, of the other canonical great dragons, see also **1–2**.

## 5   Earth's attempts to overthrow the Olympian gods by producing the Giants and then Typhon: a summary account

ca. 100 AD

Apollodorus *Bibliotheca* 1.6.1–3

Greek

**1.** Earth, angry about the Titans, spawned the Giants, sired by Uranus. They were unsurpassable in the size of their bodies and mentally undefeatable. Their appearance was terrible, with long hair hanging from head and chin, and their feet consisted of scaly dragons [*drakontes*]. Some say they were born at Phlegra, others in Pallene. They hurled rocks and oak trees set ablaze at heaven. Porphyrion and Alcyoneus stood out amongst them all. The latter was actually immortal, provided he fought in the land in which he had been born. It was he that drove the cattle of the Sun out of Erytheia. The gods had an oracle that stipulated that none of the Giants could perish by their hands alone but would be killed if a mortal fought in alliance with them. When Earth learned this, she sought a herb that would prevent their being killed even by a mortal. But Zeus forbade Dawn, Moon and Sun to show their light, and he himself culled the herb first. He then called in Heracles as an ally, by means of Athene. Heracles shot Alcyoneus first, but when he fell upon the earth he began to recover somewhat. On Athene's advice, he dragged him out of Pallene.

**2.** In this way the Giant was killed. Porphyrion attacked Heracles and Hera in the battle. Zeus cast a desire for Hera into him. He tore her dress and made to rape her, and she called for help. Zeus struck him with his thunderbolt and Heracles shot him, killing him. As to the other Giants, Apollo shot an arrow into Ephialtes' left eye, and Heracles into his right one. Dionysus killed Eurytus with his thyrsus, Hecate Clytius with her torches and Hephaestus Mimas by belting him with anvils. Athene hurled the island of Sicily on top of Enceladus as he fled, and she flayed the skin from Pallas and used it to protect her own body. Polybotes was pursued through the sea by Poseidon and came to Cos. Poseidon broke off part of the island and threw it on top of him, the islet called Nisyrus. Hermes, wearing the cap of Hades, killed Hippolytus in the battle, Artemis killed Gration and the Moirai [Fates] killed Agrion and Thoon with clubs of bronze; Zeus destroyed the others by hurling thunderbolts at them. Heracles shot them all as they perished.

**3.** When the gods had conquered the Giants, Earth, angrier still, had sex with Tartarus and produced Typhon in Cilicia. He had the mixed form of man and beast. In size and power he surpassed all the creatures Earth produced. As far down as the thighs he consisted of a huge man-shaped bulk, so big that he stood proud of all the mountains, and his head often touched the stars. He had hands that extended on the one side towards the west and on the other towards the east, and from these projected the heads of a hundred dragons. Below his thighs he had massive coils of vipers [*echidnai*]. Their coils stretched up towards his head and emitted a loud hiss. His body was covered in wings. Rough hair blew in the wind from his head and his cheeks. Fire could be seen in his eyes. Such was Typhon in form and size when he attacked heaven by setting fire to rocks and throwing them at it, with much hissing and bellowing. He belched forth a great rainstorm of fire from his mouth. When the gods saw him rushing at heaven, they fled to Egypt, and, being pursued, changed their forms to those of animals. But Zeus struck Typhon from a distance with thunderbolts, and when he was close he dashed him down with an adamantine sickle [*harpē*]. He pursued him as he fled as far as Mt Kasios. This lies above Syria. Finding him wounded there he came to grips with him. Typhon wound about Zeus with his coils and held him fast. He took the sickle from him and cut through the sinews of his hands and feet. He lifted Zeus onto his shoulders and carried him through the sea to Cilicia. Arriving at the Corycian cave, he put him down. Similarly, he put away the sinews there, hiding them in the skin of a bear, and he set the she-dragon [*drakaina*] Delphyne as guard over them. The maiden was a half-beast [*hēmithēr*]. But Hermes and Aigipan stole the sinews and secretly fitted them back into Zeus. Recovering his strength, Zeus suddenly rode out of heaven on a chariot of winged horses. Striking him with thunderbolts, he drove Typhon to the mountain called Nysa. When he had been pursued there, the Moirai deceived him. For he tasted the ephemeral fruits, convinced that he would be strengthened. And so, as he was being pursued, he came again to Thrace. In fighting in the region of Haemus he threw entire mountains. But when these mountains were blasted back at him by a thunderbolt, a great deal of blood poured forth onto the massif. And they say that it is as a result of this that the massif is called Haemus ['Blood']. And as he was beginning to flee through the Sicilian sea, Zeus threw Mt Etna in Sicily upon him. This is a vast mountain. Still even now they say that there are blasts of fire from the thunderbolts that were thrown. Let so much and no more be said on this subject.

The most important mythological handbook to survive from antiquity is bequeathed to us under the name of Apollodorus. Earth produced three sets of progeny in her doomed attempt to overthrow the Olympian gods: the Titans, the Giants and then Typhon. The Titans are the murkiest of the three; as they are never explicitly attributed with any serpentine characteristics, we shall say no more of them. But the Giants and Typhon resemble each other closely both in their serpentine lower halves and in their ultimate fates, with Enceladus and Polybotes, like Typhon, ending their career pinned beneath islands—indeed, the very same one, Sicily, in the case of Enceladus. Since snakes were characteristically regarded as creatures of the earth (**M2.b.i, M3.a**), it is wholly appropriate that the Giants and Typhon alike should be given serpentine form: they are produced from the depths of the earth and returned to these depths in defeat.

The Giants are a novel form of anguipede: rather than having a single serpent tail beneath the waist, they have each of their two initially humanoid legs terminating in a serpent tail, or, in some instances, in a serpent head. References to their *drakōn* form are few and far between in the extant literary record (although see **59** and further Naevius F4 Strzelecki, Diodorus 1.26, Claudian *Gigantomachia* 8, 80–1, 111–13), but they are commonly, indeed definingly, depicted this way in classical art from the fourth century BC onwards, and this under the influence of the traditional representation of their half-brother Typhon. Intriguingly, in Giant-fight scenes from as early as the mid-sixth century BC, we find independent dragons fighting on the gods' side against the Giants.

Heracles, the mortal helper upon whom the gods depend to defeat the Giants, seems to play a similar role to that played by the otherwise anomalous Cadmus in Nonnus's account of the defeat of Typhon (**8**). The Giants were sired by Uranus in a striking fashion: Earth was impregnated by the drops of his blood that fell to land when Cronus castrated him in heaven (Hesiod *Theogony* 183–5); compare **59**, where the terrible serpents of Africa are sired by drops of blood falling onto the land from Medusa's severed head as Perseus flies over the country with it, and schol. Aristophanes *Clouds* 749a, where the poisonous herbs of Thessaly, so vigorously exploited by that land's famous witches, are created when Medea drops a box of her magical drugs from her *drakōn*-drawn flying chariot as she flies over the land. For the Giants and their snakes, see further **98**. With Athene's use of the flayed skin of the Giant Pallas to protect herself, compare the traditions relating to the Aegis, **53**.

Typhon is here the child of Earth by Tartarus. In the *Homeric Hymn to Apollo*, however, he is the parthenogenetic offspring of the goddess Hera (**14**). Apollodorus's physical description of Typhon, which leaves us in no doubt as to his *drakōn* nature, is an elaborated version of the inevitably simpler form in which he typically appears in art, which is as an anguipede, his human face bearded, with one, two or more snake's tails or snake's heads beneath the waist and a large pair of wings behind. Apollodorus makes it clear that at least some of Typhon's coils terminate in snake's heads (cf. **8**).

The battle between Zeus and Typhon as described here (and as already in Hesiod, **6**) is broadly reminiscent of the narrative in the late third-millennium BC Sumerian *Lugal-e* of the battle between the storm god Ninurta and the sea monster Azag-Labbu, who hisses like a serpent and attempts to seize the former's throne. In the course of their battle both set fire to the landscape (**A1**). But the specific topography of the Apollodoran story links Typhon even more strikingly to other Near Eastern dragon traditions. Apollodorus's account bases Typhon in the lands on either side of the gulf of Issus: Cilicia, including the Corycian cave, to the west, and Mt Kasios, the modern Jebel Aqra, to the south. Mt Kasios had been the location of the battle, attested in the fourteenth century BC, of the Canaanite storm god Baal-Sapon against the dragon Litan (or Lotan), the biblical Leviathan (**A5**; cf. **123**). It had also been the location of the battle of the Hurrian storm god Teshub against the dragon Hedammu (**A6**) and the related Hittite storm god Tarhunna's battle against the dragon Illuyanka (**A7**), both attested in Hittite texts of ca. 1250 BC. The latter myth offers an intriguing series of correspondences with the Apollodoran and Nonnian (**8**) versions of the Typhon myth, despite the lateness of their attestation:

1. Illuyanka removes Tarhunna's eyes and stores them in his house just as Typhon removes Zeus's sinews and hides them in a cave lair.
2. Tarhunna deploys others, both divine (Inara) and human (Hupasiya), to help him trick and defeat Illuyanka, just as Zeus deploys Hermes and Aigipan, according to Apollodorus here, and Pan, Eros and the human Cadmus, according to Nonnus (**8**). The Inara-Hupasiya episode, where Tarhunna brings in the mortal Hupasiya through the agency of the allied goddess Inara, also bears comparison with Apollodorus's description of the battle of the gods against the Giants here, in which Zeus has Athene bring in the mortal Heracles.
3. In both myths the defeated dragon is bound.

Both the Illuyanka tale and the Typhon tale can be seen to belong, more broadly, to folk-tale type ATU 1148B ('Thunder's Instruments'). The *Poetic Edda* (*Thrymskvida*) preserves a delightful Old Norse example of the type:

the giant king Thrym steals Thor's hammer, Mjöllnir, and buries it eight leagues under the earth, and the god must suffer considerable indignity to retrieve it.

Apollodorus's narrative illustrates well the persistent theme in Graeco-Roman dragon narratives of the symmetry of battle. Fire and fieriness are characteristic of *drakontes* (**M6.a**). Here Typhon flashes fire from his eyes, vomits it from his mouth, and hurls it up to heaven in the form of rocks he has set ablaze. In response, Zeus strikes Typhon with his fiery thunderbolts, thunderbolts that continue to give forth blasts from Typhon's burial place under Etna (but contrast **7** for Pindar's alternative interpretation of this fire). Zeus attacks Typhon with a sickle, *harpē*, ever the ancient dragon slayer's weapon of choice, since it reflects the dragon's own coils in its curving blade and its reaping function is well suited to a snaky physique (**M11.b.i**).

A recurring feature of terrible dragon fights is that they leave permanent memorials of themselves behind in the landscape (**M14.c**), several of which are mentioned here: the Corycian cave in Cilicia was Typhon's home; the islands of Nisyrus and Sicily are where they are because gods hurled them upon the Giants and Typhon; Etna's fire recalls Zeus's thunderbolts; Thracian Haemus is still reddened by Typhon's blood.

The she-dragon (*drakaina*) Delphyne was also, like the Giants and Typhon, and indeed like most of the she-dragons in Greek myth, an anguipede in form: her description as a 'half-beast' implies, of course, that she was also half-humanoid. The relationship between Delphyne and Typhon goes unspecified here. By default we might imagine that she was his consort, the role normally taken on by another anguipede she-dragon, that prolific progenitrix of dragons, Echidna (**1–2**); that Delphyne too might be a prolific progenitrix is implied by her name, seemingly built out of the word *delphys*, 'womb.' But in the *Homeric Hymn to Apollo* Delphyne is instead the foster-mother into whose care his parthenogenetic birth mother, Hera, gives him (**14**).

The detail of gods' flight to Egypt (cf. **8**) pays tribute to an old Greek aetiology of Egypt's many animal-shaped gods. According to this, Typhon, who had been identified with the Egyptian Seth since Hecataeus, in the early fifth century BC (*FGrH* 1 F300), chased the gods to Egypt, where they adopted various animal forms to hide from him (Nicander at Antoninus Liberalis 28).

## 6    The classic account of Typhon's attempt to overthrow Zeus

vii BC

Hesiod *Theogony* 820–80

Greek

But when Zeus had expelled the Titans from heaven, the massive Earth brought forth her youngest child, Typhon, after making love with Tartarus, through the agency of golden Aphrodite [goddess of love]. He accomplished his deeds by the might of his hands. The feet of the powerful god did not grow tired. From his shoulders grew the hundred heads of a snake, a terrible dragon [*drakōn*], and these flickered with dark tongues. Fire flashed forth from the eyes under the brows of his awesome heads. And from all his heads as he gazed [*derkomenoio*] fire burned. And there were voices in all his terrible heads that sent forth every kind of unspeakable sound. Sometimes they spoke in such a way that the gods could understand, and at other times they spoke with the voice of a loud-bellowing bull, unrestrainable in might, proud in voice, at other times again with the voice of a lion with shameless heart. At other times his voice resembled that of puppies, a wonder to hear; at other times again he would hiss, and the high mountains would reverberate. Indeed there would have been on that day an achievement no one could have done anything about, and he would have ruled over mortals and immortals, if the father of gods and men had not quickly realised what was happening. He thundered hard and loud and the earth resounded round about in terrible fashion, and so did the broad heaven above and the sea and the streams of Ocean and Tartarus beneath the earth. Great Olympus quaked beneath the immortal feet of the lord as he roused himself. And the earth groaned in response. The heat that they both generated took hold of the dark blue sea, the heat of the thunder and the lightning, and of the fire from the monster, and of the burning winds and the burning thunderbolt. The entire earth boiled, and so did the fire and the sea. The long waves beat about the shores at the violence of the immortals, and an unquenchable shaking arose. Hades trembled as he ruled over the dead below, and so did the Titans under Tartarus, those who live with Cronus, because of the unquenchable noise and the dread battle. When Zeus had raised high his might and taken up his weapons, thunder, lightning and the flashing thunderbolt, he struck him, leaping from Olympus. And he burned all the heads of the terrible monster on all sides. But when he had beaten him with blows and conquered him, Typhon crashed down lamed, and massive earth groaned. A flame flashed forth from that lord, smitten and struck with the thunderbolt in the obscure dells of the craggy mountain. The massive earth was burned over a wide expanse by an awesome vapour, and it melted like tin when smelted by strong craftsmen in well-drilled crucibles, or iron, which is the strongest substance. It is subdued in the dells of a mountain with burning fire, and it melts in the divine earth by the hands of Hephaestus. In this way then the earth melted in the gleam of flashing fire. Grieving in heart he cast him down into broad Tartarus. From Typhon is the wet might of the blowing winds, except for Notus [South Wind], Boreas [North Wind] and brightening Zephyr [West Wind]. For these are of the race of the gods, and they are a boon to mortals. But the others blow at random over the sea. Some fall upon the misty sea, a great bane to mortals, and rage in an evil storm. They blow from different directions at different times, scattering ships and destroying sailors. There is no defence against this evil for the men who encounter them on the sea. Other winds, blowing over the limitless, blooming earth, destroy the lovely works of the men that live upon it, filling them full of dust and harsh tumult.

The oldest and most influential account of the great battle between Zeus and Typhon. Hesiod does not give a complete description of Typhon's form, but the *drakontes* that project from his shoulders seem to correspond well enough with the arms that terminate in *drakontes* in Apollodorus's description (**5**). The fact that Typhon is able to emit the noises of a range of different creatures—human, bull, puppy and indeed snake—may suggest that, as in Nonnus's description of him (**8**), Hesiod's Typhon also boasted heads of many different animals, but there is nothing explicit to this effect. For his puppy voices, cf. those of Scylla (**119**).

Once again there is repeated emphasis on Typhon's fieriness. Fire flashes from under the brows of his *drakōn* heads, and he manipulates burning winds, as well as being the source of destructive winds more generally (cf. **M7.a**). Again Zeus replies with his burning thunderbolt. The fire Typhon finally emits in defeat seems to be connected more with the thunderbolt (cf. **5**) than with his own (cf. **7**).

In his use of the verb 'gazed', *derkomenoio*, Hesiod may be attempting to suggest an etymology of the term *drakōn* based upon the piercing stare characteristic of snakes: indeed the aorist participle of this verb takes precisely the form *drakōn*. Many (but not all) modern philologists hold that the two words are indeed related.

The description of Zeus rousing himself in response to Typhon's uproar may be more pointed than at first appears. Epimenides *FGrH* 457 F8 (= DK 3 B 8) subsequently tells us that Typhon was able to seize Zeus's palace whilst the god slept: Hesiod seems to be self-consciously contradicting an established account of this sort.

The allusion to Hephaestus may suggest that the poet already considers Etna to be the location of Typhon's final confinement: cf. 7.

## 7   Typhon's final confinement beneath Etna in Sicily

470 BC

Pindar *Pythians* 1.15–28

Greek

But all the things that Zeus does not love shudder when they hear the cry of the Muses, those that live on the land and in the resistless sea, and he who lies in dread Tartarus, the enemy of the gods, Typhon of the hundred heads. The well-known Cilician cave once reared him, but now the sea-penning banks above Cyme and Sicily weigh down upon his shaggy breast. A heavenly column confines him, snowy Etna, nurse of sharply cold snow the whole year through. From its remotest depths the most sacred springs of terrible fire are belched forth. By day its rivers pour forth a burning stream of smoke, but in the darkness a rolling red flame carries rocks into the flat of the sea with a crash. That reptile [*herpeton*] sends up the most terrible fountains of Hephaestus, a wonderful portent to look upon, and an amazing thing to hear of from those who are present. Such is the creature that is bound within the black-leaved peaks of Etna and in the plain, and a rough bed jabs into the whole of his back that lies upon it.

Pindar, the poet of victory odes, seems to arbitrate between the competing claims to Typhon of the Issus region and of Sicily and southern Italy (Cyme is more familiar under its Latin name of Cumae). Cilicia (Kilikia) is given as his birthplace, Sicily (Sikelia) as his final place of confinement. Both Greek toponyms bear a passing resemblance to the Hittite toponym Kiskilussa, the site of Tarhunna's battle against Illuyanka (A7). The two regions also competed over claims to a Greek toponym associated with Typhon and his consort Echidna, Arimoi or Arima, these being mentioned first in Homer, who speaks of Zeus lashing the earth with his thunderbolts around Typhon in the land of the 'Arimoi' (*Iliad* 2.781–3), and in Hesiod, who has Echidna keeping watch under the earth in Arima (1). Neither Homer nor Hesiod gives any indication as to where the place might be, but Callisthenes, in the fourth century BC (*FGrH* 124 F33), and Nonnus (8) locate it in Cilicia, and Strabo, in the early first century AD, identifies it with the island of Pithecussae, adjacent to Cyme, amongst other places (C626; cf. 9).

Pindar makes it fairly clear that the fires of Etna emanate not from the remains of the thunderbolts with which Zeus blasted Typhon (as in the Apollodoran version, 5), but from Typhon himself, a more satisfactory notion and perhaps the original one, as even in his confined state Typhon continues to hurl fire up from his mother, Earth, towards heaven. The original battle, and the continuing threat that Typhon constitutes, are rendered more immediate.

## 8 The most elaborate and expansive account of Zeus's battle against Typhon

V AD

Nonnus *Dionysiaca*
1.140–64, 184–202, 213–18, 234–53, 258–76, 294–309, 362–82, 387–403, 409–47, 463–71, 478–94, 507–20; 2.1–10, 20–52, 68–72, 237–58, 273–90, 314–17, 339–52, 364–90, 436–74, 508–39, 553–63, 606–24, 663–79

Greek

**1.140.** Cadmus came also to the bloody cave of Arima, when the mountain peaks, upheaved from their positions, were pounding at the gates of unbreakable Olympus, and when the gods flew off high over the Nile that knows not rainstorms and imitated the unreachable flight of birds, rowing an unfamiliar path through the airy winds, and the seven-zoned pole was lashed. For Zeus, son of Cronus, rushing to the bed of Pluto [daughter of Cronus] to sire Tantalus, the witless thief of heavenly cups, stored his ether-weapons in a recess of rock and hid his lightning. The covered thunderbolts belched forth smoke and the white crag was blackened. Springs were heated by the secret spark of the arrow barbed with fire. The Mygdonian cleft foamed and resounded with the steam of mountain torrents. Given the nod by his mother, Earth, Cilician Typhon extended his hands and stole Zeus's snowy weapons, his weapons of fire. Then, opening up his row of deep-sounding throats he let forth a cry of every sort of beast calling out in unison. The dragons [*drakontes*] that were fused with him hovered over the faces of his leopards, licked at the shaggy manes of his lions, turbaned their coiling and spiralling tails around the horns of his bulls and mingled the squirting venom of their long-tongued jaws with the foam of his pigs. He placed the weapons of Zeus, son of Cronus, in the cleft of a rock and stretched the forest of his hands up high into the ether. [164]

**184.** With dragging feet Typhon hoisted himself up into the realm of the clouds. Spreading out his great host of sprouting arms, he obscured the bright gleam of the cloudless ether as he shot forth his twisted army of snakes. One of them ran up over the edge of the polar circle and jumped along the spine of the heavenly Dragon [*Drakōn*, i.e. the constellation of Draco], hissing war. Another approached the daughter of Cepheus, matched the astral grip in which she was held with the circle of its own coil and constrained the bound Andromeda yet more tightly with a second bond, aslant beneath her ropes. A horned dragon [*drakōn…kerastēs*] wound around the tip of one of the Bull's horns, the constellation reflecting its own shape and, hanging in coils over its forehead, with open jaws goaded the Hyades, who mimicked the shape of the horned Moon opposite. Venom-casting straps of dragons, woven together, engirdled Bootes. Another dragon boldly darted upon seeing another snake on Olympus, leaping around Ophiuchus's viper-bedecked forearm, then wove itself into a second garland around Ariadne's crown, twisting its neck and coiling on its curving belly. [202]

**213.** Often he would brandish with threatening arm a bull recently released from its plough-tree and then hurl the similarly formed mimic of the [sc. horned] Moon at her, stopping her in her path and, halting her bulls' white yoke straps with their bridle, he hurtled himself against the goddess, pouring forth the deadly hiss of a venom-casting viper. [218]

**234.** Shining Ophiuchus, seeing the Giant's terrible snaky shape, shook the grey bodies of the fire-nurtured dragons from his evil-warding hands, launching his mottled, twisting dart. Whirlwinds roared around the fire. Raging viper arrows shot aslant through the air. Sagittarius, the bold archer, who runs alongside fish-shaped Capricorn, launched his arrow. The Dragon [*Drakōn*, Draco again], split between the two Bears, and manifest in the middle of the Wain circle, rolled the flashing coil of his celestial spine. [253]

**258.** Typhon seized the pinnacle of Corycius and brandished it. Crushing the stream of the Cilician river Cydnus, he scooped it up together with the city of Tarsus in a single hand. Then he moved on to the sea crags, launching rocky missiles into the serried waves of brine, lashing the sea after the ether. As the Giant advanced on the coil of his sea-washed foot, his loins could be seen still dry, standing proud from the water, and the resounding sea roared against only the middle of his thigh. His swimming dragons hissed war from their brine-resounding throats and attacked the sea, spitting venom. As Typhon stood in the weed-strewn seabed of the fishy ocean, his feet were planted in the depths, whilst his belly was of a level with the air, and was buffeted by clouds. Hearing the terrible roar of the high-maned lions of the Giant's head, the sea-lion kept itself hidden in the muddy gulf. And the whole host of sea monsters [*phalanx...kētōessa*] was pressed tight in the ocean, as the earth-born one filled up the whole sea, which was itself more expansive than the land, with flanks the water could not reach over. [276]

**294.** After he had passed out of the deep and onto the well-founded land, the counterfeit Zeus armed himself with a fire-hooked thunderbolt. The monster Typhon struggled to lift the weapons of Zeus the son of Cronus in his resistless hands, two hundred though they were, because of their weight, though the son of Cronus used to hoist them up with a single hand. No clouds formed over the Giant's dry hands, and the thunder sent forth only a dull noise, booming gently and without resonance. There was only the merest precipitation of a thirsty dew from the dropless rain in the dry air. The lightning flash was murky, and a weak fire shone with subdued gleam, like a flame in smoke. Feeling the hands of their inexperienced bearer, the thunderbolts, with their masculine fire, were feminised. Often they slipped from his unnumbered hands and jumped about of their own accord. The fires went astray for want of the accustomed hand of their heavenly bearer. [309]

**362.** Typhon was not destined to wield the weapons of Zeus any more. For Zeus the son of Cronus quitted the whirling pole with the bow-bearing Eros and encountered the itinerant Cadmus as he wandered in his search. He constructed a cunning plan together with him, twining together the threads of an evil-spindled Fate for Typhon. His companion, the goatherd Pan, gave Zeus, ruler of all, oxen, and flocks of sheep and lines of well-horned goats. He wove a hut from reeds, twisting and binding them together, and fixed it on the ground. He put the clothes of a shepherd around Cadmus's body, to disguise his form, and cloaked the counterfeit pasturer in mimicking dress. He brought deceptive pan pipes and gave them to intelligent Cadmus, to steer Typhon to his doom. Zeus called to the bogus herder and the winged charioteer of reproduction [Eros], and shared his plan with them: 'Good Cadmus, play your pipes, and heaven will be calm. If you are slow to do so, Olympus will be lashed. For Typhon is armed with our heavenly weapons. The aegis alone is left to me. But what will the aegis achieve in the battle against Typhon's thunderbolt?' [382]

**387.** [Zeus continues to address Cadmus.] 'Become a cowherd for one dawn-born day, and by playing your mind-robbing shepherd's pipes save the shepherd of the universe, lest I have to hear the sound of Typhon gathering clouds, or the thunder of a second, counterfeit Zeus, and so that I may stop him fighting with the lightning flash and launching the thunderbolt. If you are the recipient of the blood of Zeus and the stock of Inachian Io, charm the mind of Typhon with the evil-warding tune of your crafty pan pipes. I will give you a double gift in return for your labours. I will make you the protector of the harmony of the universe and the husband of Harmonia. And if you, Eros, initiator and spawner of fertile marriage, stretch your bow, the universe will no longer be awry. If everything derives from you, shepherd of love, then launch one further arrow, so as to save everything.

Since you are fiery, take up arms against Typhon, and let the fire-bearing thunderbolts return to my hand by your agency.' [403]

**409.** Cadmus played shrill deceitful music on his harmonious reeds, leaning his back against a nearby tree in a woodland pasture. Wearing the rustic clothes of a genuine pasturer, he sent the cunning tune to Typhon's ears, making soft breaths with inflated cheeks. Then, upon hearing the deceptive song, the music-loving Giant leaped up with his viper-coiled foot. He left Zeus's flaming weapons behind inside a cave with his mother, Earth, and sought out the nearby song of the mind-delighting pan pipes, following after the phrases. When Cadmus saw him near his copse, he took fear and concealed himself in a cleft in the rock. But the monster Typhon, with his head so high, noticed him as he tried to evade him and summoned him with a silent nod. He did not perceive the trick behind the vibrant music. He extended one of his right hands to the shepherd opposite, failing to see the toils of his destruction, and with his central, tawny, humanoid face he laughed and gave voice to hollow boasts: 'Goatherd, why are you frightened of me? Why do you put your hand over your eyes? A fine thing it would be if I were to chase a mere mortal man after the son of Cronus! A fine thing it would be for me to steal pan pipes together with the lightning! What do reeds and the fiery thunderbolt have in common? Keep the pipes for yourself, since Typhon has acquired another instrument [i.e. the thunderbolts], an Olympian one, which makes its own sound. Zeus, sitting cloudless, without his accustomed noise and with unresounding hands, has need of your pan pipes. Let him have the noise of your little bunch of reeds. I do not roll around worthless rows of reeds, but I join clouds to rolling clouds and make a bang that clatters through heaven. If you wish, I'll mount a friendly competition. You make a tune with your reeds, and I will crash with my thunder. Distend your cheeks with breath and blow with your lips, whilst my thunderbolts rumble when lashed with the breath of the great blower Boreas [North Wind]. Cowherd, you will be paid for your pipes. For when I control the throne of heaven, holding the sceptre in place of Zeus, I will bring you with me, quitting the earth for the ether, together with your pan pipes and, if you wish, your animals.' [447]

**463.** [Typhon continues to address Cadmus.] 'Blessed shepherd, come dine with Typhon in heaven. Make your song on earth today, and tomorrow you will do it on Olympus. As fit requital for your song I will establish your Olympian form in the circle of bright stars and fasten your sweet pan pipes to the heavenly Lyre. And, if you wish, I will grant you holy marriage with Athene. If the grey-eyed goddess does not please you, take instead Leto, Charis or Cytheria [Aphrodite], or marriage with Hebe. Only seek not the bed of my Hera.' [471]

**478.** [Typhon continues to address Cadmus.] 'But, cowherd, strike up the song of Typhon's victory. Sing of me as the new legitimate sceptre-bearer of Olympus, carrying Zeus's sceptre and wearing his tunic of lightning.' So he spoke, and Adrasteia [Nemesis] recorded all he said. But when Cadmus perceived that the son of Earth had at Fate's spinning run into his hunting net of his own accord, stricken by the sweet goad of the mind-delighting reeds, he gave voice to crafty speech, with sober mien: 'Since you were delighted to hear the slender sound of pan pipes, tell me, what would you do if I were to sing of your throne by plucking a hymn of victory on my seven-stringed lyre? I competed with the heavenly plectrum and surpassed Phoebus [Apollo] with my lyre. But the son of Cronus turned my fair-sounding strings to ashes with his thunderbolt to gratify his defeated son. But if ever I find again the vigorous sinews, I will make song with my plectrum and enchant all the trees and the mountains and the hearts of the beasts.' [494]

**507.** He had spoken. Typhon nodded with flashing brows and shook his hair. His locks vomited forth viper venom and the hills were soaked in it. He rushed swiftly back to his cave. Taking Zeus's sinews from there he presented them as gifts to tricky Cadmus, the sinews that had once fallen on the ground as he fought Typhon. The cunning shepherd expressed admiration for the immortal gift. He handled them gingerly, as if they were to be strings for his lyre, and hid them in a hollow rock, preserving them for Giant-slaying Zeus. Then sending forth a gentle breath with tightened lips, pressing the reeds and drawing a tune from them, he produced a yet pleasanter song. Typhon strained his many ears and listened to the tune, and did not know what was afoot. [520]

**2.1.** So Cadmus the son of Agenor, the counterfeit goatherd, remained there at the foot of the woodland pasture, drawing his lips back and forth across the open-ended pan pipes. Zeus, the son of Cronus, crept without a sound into the cave, without being noticed or challenged, and armed his hands again with his accustomed fire. A cloud covered Cadmus over and obscured his rock, lest Typhon discover the cheating trick and the secret thief of the thunderbolt and, wise after the event, kill the treacherous cowherd. But he, impelled by its sweet goad, just wanted to listen more to the heart-enchanting rhythm of the song. [10]

**2.20.** But the tuneful pasturer was enveloped in a shadowy twist of clouds, and the blown reeds fell silent. He put an end to his song. With battle frenzy Typhon soared through the air and rushed to the recess of his cave and looked frantically for the airborne thunder and the resistless lightning. With searching foot he sought out the fiery gleam of the thunderbolt he had stolen, but all he could find was an empty cave. Too late did he understand the tricky plots of the son of Cronus and the cunning counsels of Cadmus. Launching from crags, he leapt onto Olympus. Dragging out a twisting track with his snaky foot, he spat out and projected venom from his throat. Mountain streams surged as the monster rained down torrents from his viper hair on high. As he rushed to the assault, the steady, even plain of the Cilician land was shaken to its foundations beneath the weight of his dragon [*drakonteioisi*] feet. As the Taurus mountainside reverberated with a great crash, the nearby Pamphylian hills danced in fear. The water hollows of the land resounded, the projecting shores trembled, the recesses were shaken and beaches subsided as their sand was loosened by the stamp of his earthshaking feet. Neither pasture not beasts went unharmed at that time. The bears that ate raw flesh became a meal for the bear-jaws of Typhon's heads. The pale limbs of shaggy-breasted lions were devoured by the gaping mouths of his similarly formed lion heads. The cold lengths of earth-nurtured dragons were consumed by his vipers' maws. As birds of the air flew through the untrodden ether he dined on them with an adjacent maw. He preferred to eat the eagle that flew close, since it bore the name of Zeus's bird. He ate too the ox at the plough, and felt no pity upon noticing that its neck was chafed and bloody from the yoke band. [52]

**68.** The hollows of the earth were torn open and laid bare by the Giant's missiles. He set free the veins of water and, as the chasms were opened, the buried channels gushed fourth their springs, pouring water from the bosom of the land ripped open. [72]

**237.** Sleep whirred his shadowy wing and put to rest the whole of breathing nature. At that time the son of Cronus alone remained sleepless. Typhon relaxed his weary back and rested his heavy form on his ground bed, covering over his mother, Earth. She opened her folds, and her lairs gaped open to provide beds for his viper heads as they ducked into the ground. When the sun rose the many-armed Typhon went roaring into battle, all his throats crying out at once, calling upon great Zeus. The shout reached the firmly rooted, backwards-flowing bed of Ocean that surrounds the circuit of the world in its four divisions, yoking together the whole earth like a crown or a round turban. When the Giant spoke, he was answered not by a harmonious echo, but by a cacophony of all sorts of voices. As he armed himself with the many shapes of his nature, the howling of wolves rang out, as did the roaring of lions, the grunting of boars, the lowing of cows, the hissing of dragons, the cry of leopards with bold gaping mouths, the sound of bears gnashing their teeth and the mad yelping of dogs. Then the Giant shrieked threatening words at Zeus with his central humanoid head: 'My hands, crush the house of Zeus....' [258]

**273.** [Typhon continues to address Zeus.] 'I will enslave the four winds by force. I whip Boreas [North Wind], I drive Notus [South Wind] before me, I lash Eurus [East Wind], I will beat Zephyr [West Wind] and I will mix night with day with a single hand. My kinsman Ocean will carry water on high to Olympus with his throats of many springs. Lifting himself high above the five equivalent circles, he will flood the stars, and then the thirsty Bear can go wandering in the water whilst the Wain's plough tree is submerged! My bulls, shake the ethereal equator and bellow, shatter with your pointed horns the horns of the fiery Bull that resembles you. Let the cattle of the moon change their watery course, in fear of my bull-heads' resounding bellow. May the Typhonian bear spread wide the great gape of its shaggy jaws and harry the Olympian Bear. May my lion measure itself against the ethereal Lion and force it against its will from its Zodiac path.' [290]

**314.** [Typhon continues to address Zeus.] 'May Zeus, the son of Cronus, take on the role of Atlas and lift and bear the whirling heaven on his burdened shoulders, standing upright. Let him hear my wedding song and conceal his envy, when I become bridegroom to Hera.' [317]

**339.** [Typhon continues to address Zeus.] 'I shall loose those stout bonds and restore the Titans to the ether, and I will bring the earth-born Cyclopes [makers of Zeus's thunderbolts] to heaven to share the same roof. I shall manufacture further weapons of fire. For I need many thunderbolts, since I make war with two hundred hands, not merely two, as the son of Cronus does. I shall forge more lightning flashes, similar in form, but bigger, newer and with greater and brighter fire. Up high I will fashion another heaven, an eighth one, broader and higher, and decorate it with shinier stars. For the adjacent vault cannot cover Typhon in his entirety. To succeed the female children and male offspring of fecund Zeus, I will sire another prolific line of new blessed ones, all with many necks.' [352]

**364.** Zeus lashed the clouds, made a crashing bellow of thunder in the ether and trumpeted the song of war. He fitted clouds spirally over his breast to protect himself from the Giant's missiles. Typhon did not remain silent. In sending forth their bellow his ox heads served as automatic trumpets and made Olympus resound. The dragons mixed in together with them, the flutes of war, hissed. Typhon defended the ranks of his high-reaching limbs by fencing one great cliff off with another one until he had surrounded himself with a continuous row of closely packed broken crags, and he placed one wrenched-up rock upon another. The impression given was of an armed host. Crag leaned upon adjacent crag, hill upon hill, mountain upon mountain. Headlands, high in the clouds, pressed heavily upon many-valed headlands. Rocky hills formed helmets for Typhon, and his heads were protected by sheer-sided promontories. The fighting Giant had just a single body but many necks and hosts of hands, hosts of sharpened teeth in lion jaws and hosts of viper locks climbing over the stars. Typhon folded up trees with his hands and brandished them against the son of Cronus, and so too the other fair-leafed flora of the earth, which Zeus reluctantly turned to ashes with a single spark of the heavy thunderbolt he balanced in his hand. He threw many elms at Zeus, together with pines of similar age, and huge plane trees. He hurled white poplars at him like javelins. The earth's flanks were repeatedly torn open. [390]

**436.** The chief of the heavenly realm shook his fiery dart on high and made war, shifting from the left wing to the right, manifest up above. The many-armed Giant hastened to the water-carrying torrents. He interleaved his fingers, drew them tightly together and made a hollow with his capacious palms. With them he drew up mountain-coursing water from the midst of winter rivers, and with cupped hands he launched the streams he had detached and hurled them against the thunderbolt. But as it was struck by the torrent streams the ethereal fire gleamed through the water with a keener spark. The thirsty water boiled and turned to steam, and its liquid nature was turned dry by the red-hot metal. The bold but naive Giant was eager to extinguish the ethereal fire. But he did not realise that the fire-bright thunderbolts and lightning flashes are born of the rain-begetting clouds. Once again he seized the rocks of straight-cut caves from the riverbeds and was intent upon striking the breast of Zeus, unwoundable by iron. He launched a crag against him. Zeus blew gently, with just the tip of his lips, and the gentle breath turned the spinning rock aside, for all its great peaks. Typhon broke off a rounded island hill with his hand, whirled it around in the air in preparation for the throw, and launched it against Zeus's unshatterable face. He avoided the rocky missile aimed at him by leaning his head to one side. But Typhon caught a blow from the lightning, sent in response, on its hot, twisting course, and forthwith his rock was whitened at its point but otherwise blackened by telltale smoke. Typhon hurled a third rock. As it hurtled towards him the son of Cronus deflected it, redirecting it with the centre of the wrist of his boundless, extended hand, and sent it back against Typhon, like a bouncing ball. The rock returned, spinning high in the air on its backward journey, and the hill of its own accord shot the one that had shot it. He launched a fourth rock on a higher trajectory. It touched the tips of the tassels of Zeus's aegis and was rent in two. He threw another. It flew as swiftly as a storm, but Zeus shot it with a thunderbolt, and its half-burned remains were left to blaze. The crags could not tear open the rainclouds, but the hills were broken up when struck by the water-laden clouds. [474]

**508.** Father Zeus continued to make war. He launched and threw his familiar fire against his opponent, piercing his lions and striking the many-voiced ranks of his unnumbered throats with a heavenly hurricane. Zeus cast his missile. Part of its fire burned up Typhon's boundless hands, another turned his countless shoulders and their darting tribes of dragons to ashes. The ether's spear-points destroyed his countless heads. A spinning comet turned Typhon's hair to ashes, meeting him with sparks and itself projecting thick tresses of fire. Typhon's heads were on fire. As his hair caught light, the heavenly spark silenced and closed the mouths of his hissing locks. The venomous droplets were dried up in the jaws of the dragons as they withered. As the Giant battled, his eyes were reduced to ash by sooty smoke, whilst his cheeks were turned white as his faces were stuck by streams of snow. On four sides he felt the force of the four winds. For as he twisted his unstable eyes to the east, he was confronted with the fiery onslaught of neighbouring Eurus. If he looked to the stormy region of the Arcadian Bear, he was stricken by the heatless frost of the winter hurricane. If he tried to evade the blast of snow-casting Boreas, he was buffeted by darts both wet and burning. If he looked upon the sunset opposite the fearful east, he shuddered before stormy western Enyo [War] as he heard the sound of Zephyr's spring lash. At the southern foot of Capricorn, Notus whipped the aerial circle, blowing hot, bringing flaming heat and fiery vapours against Typhon. If again stormy Zeus poured down a shower of rain, Typhon washed all his skin in the painkilling streams, cooling the hot limbs battered by the thunderbolt. [539]

**553.** The son of Cronus inclined the balance of the equal fight in his favour. Typhon's mother, Earth, threw off her veil of trees to grieve, as she saw the smoke emanating from his heads. As his faces withered, the earth-born one's knees were slackened. Zeus prophesied his victory with crashes of thunder: this was his clarion. Made drunk by the fiery dart of heaven, and bearing a war wound inflicted by no mere iron, lofty Typhon keeled over and cast his back upon his mother, Earth. There he lay, sprawling his snaky limbs in the dust and belching forth fire. [563]

**606.** [Zeus addresses Typhon.] 'How was it that you were unable to evade the unwarlike fire of a little flash of lightning? Or why was it that with your countless ears you were scared to hear the slight noise of rain and thunder? Who made you so weak? Where are your spears? Where are your puppy heads? Where are the gaping maws of your lions and the earthly bellow of your sonorous throats? Where is the projectile venom of your dragon [*drakonteiēs*] hair? Do you no longer hiss with your circle of dragon hair? Where are the bellowings of the mouths of your bulls? Where are your hands that launch steep promontories? Are you no longer whipping the spiralling circles of stars? Do your boars' projecting tusks no longer whiten their chins, wet with drips of foam? Where are the terrible jaws of the raging bear, with their rictus grin? Nursling of the earth, yield before those of heaven. For with a single hand I conquered the ranks of your two hundred hands. Let three-pointed Sicily, ringed with steep-cragged hills, encompass Typhon, his hundred heads pitiably buried in the dust.' [624]

**663.** [Zeus addresses Cadmus.] 'Cadmus, you have garlanded the gates of Olympus with your pan pipes. I will memorialise your marriage with the heavenly Lyre. I will make you the son-in-law of Ares and Cytheria [Aphrodite]. You will receive gods as diners at your earthly wedding breakfast. I will come to your house. What other thing could be dearer to you to observe than the king of the blessed gods sitting at your table? If you wish to escape the waves of fortune, which wash this way and that, and to sail calmly across the strait of life, make sure you never anger Dircaean [Theban] Ares, the Ares that grows wroth when stripped of his progeny. By night reach your eyes up to the heavenly Dragon [*Drakōn*, Draco], make sacrifice at an altar holding a piece of fair-smelling snakestone, call upon Olympian Ophiuchus [Snake-Holder] and burn in the fire the many-hooked horn of the Illyrian deer so as to evade all the bitter things the compulsive spindle of the Fates spun and assigned to your lot—if the threads of the Fates comply.' [679]

Nonnus of Panopolis (Chemmis) in Egypt lived and wrote ca. 400 AD. He is a remarkable figure for producing deeply learned works of both pagan and Christian interest. Alongside this enormous hexameter pagan epic devoted to Dionysus, the *Dionysiaca* (a mere two of its forty-eight books are excerpted here), there also survives his *Metabole*, a hexameter paraphrase of the Gospel of John. Nonnus's overwrought and repetitive (as is quite apparent from these excerpts) account of Typhon's assault on Zeus and heaven was composed in an age when hagiographical dragon-slaying tales were already well established—the elaborate tales of the *Acts of Philip* (**134**) are probably older—but it includes among its motifs some that seem to reach far back into pagan tradition.

Much of the action takes place at the cosmic level, as Typhon battles against not merely heaven, but actually the constellations; even so, Cilicia, where Nonnus locates Arima (cf. **7**, with commentary), remains the focal point of the action on earth (1.140–64, 258–76, 2.20–52).

What is the form of Nonnus's Typhon? He is clearly an anguipede, with the serpentine nature of his feet repeatedly adverted. The description of them hissing in the brine as he wades into the sea entails that his serpent feet culminate in heads, as opposed to the more usual tails (1.258–76; cf. **5**). His two hundred hands are also said to take the form of snakes (1.184–202, 294–309). The description of Typhon scooping up water with his hands may imply that Typhon's individual arms are basically humanoid but terminate in snake fingers (2.436–74). Evidently his hands are fully usable as such: he can also use them to scoop up cities (1.258–76), fold up trees (2.364–90) and even offer a handshake to Cadmus (1.409–47). His central, speaking head is humanoid (1.409–47). His other animal heads, bringing the total to a hundred, are presumably arranged around this one atop his body, and these may include further snake heads (1,140–64, 2.606–24, etc.). The hair of his humanoid head is made up of a third or fourth set of snakes, à la Medusa, vipers that belch out venom and hang down over and engage with his animal heads, including those of leopards, lions, bulls, dogs and boars (1.140–64, 258–76, 2.20–52, 237–58, 606–24). Nonnus repeatedly casts Typhon as a Giant (1.234–53 etc.), which, strictly speaking, he was not, though he was closely related to them and closely aligned with them, as we have seen (**5**).

Nonnus's account of the ruse operated by Cadmus, Pan and Eros (1.362–2.10) builds on tales such as those found in Apollodorus (**5**) first of Zeus's exploitation of a mortal helper against the Giants, in that case Heracles, and secondly of Hermes's and Pan's stealing back of Zeus's sinews from Typhon. Looking rather further back, the role of Cadmus here, as a mortal helper to the storm god, seems to reflect that of Hupasiya in the ca. 1250 BC Hittite myth of Tarhunna's slaying of the dragon Illuyanka, as we have seen (commentary to **5**). Insofar as he seduces and distracts the dragon with music, and that too with the aid of Eros, god of sex, he also seems to reflect the role of Sauska, goddess of sex, in the similarly ca. 1250 BC Hurrian-Hittite myth of the storm god Teshub's defeat of the dragon Hedammu. Here the dragon is seduced by the goddess Sauska with music (again), alcohol and her nakedness (**A6**). Cadmus persuades Typhon by the charm of his pan pipes (it is a contrived inconcinnity that a monster of such terrible, cosmic proportions should be bewitched by such a slight instrument) to retrieve Zeus's stolen sinews from the cave in which he had stored them, on the supposition that he will construct a yet more charming instrument from them, a lyre (1.478–94). Cadmus then stores them in another cave in turn, from which Zeus can recover them and thereby proceed, as it seems, to recover his thunderbolts too from the cave in which Typhon had concealed them (1.507–20). This narrative, particularly when aligned with the Apollodoran one, conveys the impression of a deep identity between the sinews and the thunderbolts. Cadmus's better-established dragon affinities in the ancient tradition are incorporated into the narrative: he will encounter the great Dragon of Ares (2.663–79), and after his marriage to Harmonia the pair will themselves be transformed into dragons (1.387–403; cf. **77**). Zeus advises him—in vain, of course—to avoid the bad luck arising from his encounter with the Dragon of Ares by sacrificing to the constellation of Ophiuchus, the Snake Holder, whilst holding deer horn, the substance that ancient snake lore held to be more toxic to and aversive of snakes than any other (Pliny *Natural History* 8.118, Lucan 9.915–21, Aelian *On Animals* 2.9).

Typhon's relationship with the hollows of his mother, Earth, is intense: she directs him to the cave in which Zeus has concealed his thunderbolts; he in turn conceals them in another (1.140–64); it is not clear whether the cave in which he conceals Zeus's sinews is the same one or even a third (1.507–20). And when he sleeps his many serpent appendages slip into hollows Earth opens up for them in a fashion that seems almost incestuously sexual (2.237–258). Accordingly, his natural weapons and his natural armour are Earth's rocks (2.364–90, 436–74).

Nonnus is particularly taken with the theme of the symmetry of battle between Zeus and Typhon, and this works well with the recurring notion that Typhon, the 'counterfeit Zeus', seeks not merely to supplant Zeus but actually to become him, not least as wielder of his thunderbolts (1.140–64, 294–309, 478–94), as husband to Hera and as bestower of the other goddesses in marriage (1.463–71, 2.314–17). We hear much of the deployment of fire on both sides throughout (**M6**). Nonnus particularly likes to align Typhon's various animal heads with equivalent opponents: his dragon heads face dragons, his horned-dragon heads face horned bulls, his bear heads face bears, his lion heads face lions and even sea lions, and so on, whether actual animals, at the natural level (2.20–52), or animal-shaped constellations, at the cosmic level (1.184–202, 258–76, 2.273–90). Similarly, he casts horned bulls against the horned moon (1.213–18).

Three minor points may be made briefly. First, Typhon's role as all-too-fecund progenitor of further serpentine monsters is noticed (2.339–52; cf. **1–2**). Secondly, Typhon is initially said to attack whilst Zeus is distracted, seducing Pluto (1.140–64). Later on, all, Typhon included, sleep whilst Zeus alone remains awake (2.237–58). Both episodes may refract an ancient notion that Typhon had first attacked whilst Zeus slept (**5**, with commentary). Thirdly, as with the Orontes myth (**9**), Typhon releases underground water sources and makes rivers of them (2.68–72).

## 9  Typhon embodied in the Syrian river Orontes

ca. 24 AD–iv AD

Strabo C750–1 (ca. 24 AD)

Pausanias of Antioch *FHG* iv pp. 467–8, F3 (iv AD) = John Malalas *Chronographia* pp. 37–8 Dindorf

Greek

**Strabo:** The river Orontes flows past the city [of Antioch]. It originates in Coele-Syria, and thence it is taken underground, but it returns its stream to the surface, and, advancing through Apamea to Antioch, flows close to the city and then debouches into the sea near Seleuceia. The river was formerly called Typhon, but changed its name to that of the man who built a bridge across it, Orontes. They tell that somewhere here occurred the events concerning Typhon's being blasted with the thunderbolt and the Arimoi, about whom we have also spoken above. They say that Typhon was struck by the thunderbolts (he was a dragon [*drakōn*]) and he fled in search of a way underground. He cut into the earth with his coils, making the channel for the river, and by diving into the earth he broke open the spring. The name of the river derived from this.

**Pausanias of Antioch:** This same Perseus, after ruling the Persian land for many years, learning that Ionitans from Argos were living in the Syrian land, came to them in Syria at Mt Silpion, as to his own relatives. They received him with all honour and did obeisance before him. These same Argive Iopolitans recognised him because he too was descended from the race of the Argives. Rejoicing, [38] they hymned him. When there was a storm, the river adjacent to the city of the Ionitans [a precursor to Antioch] flooded badly. At that time it was called the Drakōn [i.e. Dragon], but now it is called the Orontes. Perseus asked the Ionitans to pray. In the course of their prayers and their mystic rites a ball of thunderbolt fire came down from heaven, which put a stop to the storm and checked the streams of the river. Perseus was amazed at the occurrence and at once lit a fire from that fire, and kept it by his side under guard. He carried this fire across the Persian lands to his own palace. He taught the Persians to honour that fire, which he said he had seen brought down from heaven for them. They have revered this fire as divine until this present time. Perseus himself founded a sanctuary for the Ionitans, which he called the sanctuary of the immortal fire. And similarly he founded a sanctuary of fire in Persia, and appointed trustworthy men to tend it there, whom he called magi. This Pausanias the most wise chronographer wrote.

The river Orontes flowed beneath Mt Kasios (cf. **5**). The river's distinctively serpentine course (cf. the Maeander) licensed this story of its creation, which could conceivably have been as old as the Canaanite, Hurrian and Hittite dragon-fight stories associated with Mt Kasios. But the interest in the great dragon river shown in these two texts derives principally from the attempts of the early Seleucid kings to aggrandise themselves and the two of their great capitals that the river linked, Antioch and Seleuceia in Pieria. The first Seleucus identified himself strongly with Zeus, not least in the act of founding the cities (Libanius *Orations* 11.85–8 [Förster i.2 pp. 464–5], John Malalas *Chronicle* 198–200 Dindorf), whereas Perseus offered the dynasty the virtue of being at once a good Greek hero with a pedigree from ancient Argos whilst also, supposedly, being the founder of the Persia named for him, the heartland of the vast territory of which Seleucus had made himself master (Hesiod *Catalogue of Women* FF125, 129 MW, Herodotus 7.150). The imagery of dragon and river is associated also with the foundation myth of another of the great Hellenistic royal capitals, Alexandria: **101**.

Zeus attacks the dragon with his fiery thunderbolts, as usual, and his son Perseus then replicates this by calling a ball of thunderbolt fire down from heaven against it, though fire no longer fights fire; rather, it dries up the watery river into which the creature of fire has, somewhat counter-intuitively, been transformed. In taking the fire back to Persia and causing it to be worshipped, Perseus founds the Zoroastrian religion. The Malalas passage surrounding his quotation of Pausanias of Antioch, which offers a curious version of the Medusa story, is given at **65**.

## 10 The Orphic doublets of Typhon (i): Ophion(eus)

vi BC–Hellenistic-Byzantine

Origen *Contra Celsum* 6.42 and 6.43 (248 BC), incorporating Pherecydes of Syros FF78 and 79 Schibli respectively (vi BC)

Apollonius *Argonautica* 1.494–5, 503–6 (ca. 270 BC)

**Origen:** 6.42. [Celsus says that] Pherecydes, a much older mythographer than Heraclitus, gives us one army drawn up opposite another one, Cronus the leader of the first and Ophion the leader of the second. He [Pherecydes] tells of their challenges and contests, and of the deal made between them, to the effect that whichever of them should first be cast into Ogenos [Ocean], the one that had thrust him out and prevailed should control heaven. And he [Origen] says that the mysteries that tell of the battle of the Titans and the Giants against the gods have a similar meaning, as do the Egyptian mysteries concerning Typhon [= Seth], Horus and Osiris.

| | |
|---|---|
| Schol. vet. on Lycophron *Alexandra* 1191 (Hellenistic-Byzantine) | 6.43. [Origen now speaks in his own voice.] For the snake [*ophis*], the origin of Pherecydes' Ophioneus, became responsible for man being cast out of the divine paradise.... |
| Schol. Homer *Iliad* 8.479 (Hellenistic-Byzantine) Greek | **Apollonius:** Orpheus picked up his lyre with his left hand and began to sing.... And he sang of how first Ophion and Eurynome the daughter of Ocean had control of snowy Olympus, and how the former was compelled by Cronus to yield his position of honour to him by the force of his hands, as the latter was by Rhea, and they were cast into the waves of Ocean. |
| | **Scholium to Lycophron:** Cronus threw Ophion down whilst Rhea wrestled Eurynome to the ground and then cast her into Tartarus, and they became king and queen of the gods. Zeus subsequently threw Cronus and Rhea too into Tartarus and seized power. |
| | **Scholium to Homer:** When Zeus had moved [lacuna]... after putting a mountain on top of him, wherefore it was called Ophionion. |

A series of rather similar myths attributed to Orpheus or Orphics plays with the traditional imagery of Typhon, his form and his battle for symbolic theological purposes all but inscrutable to us. The first Orphic equivalent of Typhon is *Ophiōn* or *Ophiōneus*. According to these texts, Zeus's father, Cronus, also had had to fight for his position on Olympus with a serpentine monster. The serpentine nature of Ophion is revealed by his names, derivative of *ophis*, 'snake', as well as by Origen's explicit if curious testimony. If Ophion's consort Eurynome resembled in form the daughter of Ocean of the same name spoken of by Pausanias (Periegetes) at Phigalia (8.41), then she was a humanoid female above the waist and a fish below. Nonnus's confusion of Eurynome with Harmonia (*Dionysiaca* 8.158–61), who was transformed into a dragoness (**75, 77**), may imply a tradition that she was a dragoness, perhaps an anguipede one like Typhon's own consort, Echidna (**1**). Philo of Byblos's reference to the Ophionidae, 'children of Ophion', suggests that, like Typhon, Ophion was a great progenitor of other troublesome creatures (*apud* Eusebius *Praeparatio Evangelica* 1.10.50).

The lacunary scholium to Homer seemingly relates to a slightly different (or differentiated) Ophion, a Giant, no doubt an anguipede one, who suffered a similar fate to his fellow Giants Enceladus and Polybotes in the gigantomachy (**5**), and indeed to Typhon again in his battle with Zeus. The syntax of such text as survives here may suggest that it was not Zeus himself that placed the mountain on top of this Ophion, but rather another male god.

## 11 The Orphic doublets of Typhon (ii): Chronos

| | |
|---|---|
| ii BC–Byzantine Athenagoras *Legatio* 18 (176–7 AD) Damascius *De principiis* 123.2, i p.318 Ruelle = DK 1.B.12 (515–29 AD), incorporating Hieronymus of Rhodes (iii BC) and Hellanicus of Tarsus (ii BC) Schol. Homer *Iliad* 2.793 (Hellenistic-Byzantine) Greek | **Athenagoras:** According to Orpheus water was the origin of everything. From water was produced mud, and from both of these was engendered an animal, a dragon [*drakōn*] with the head of a lion attached to it, and between them was the face of a god, Heracles and Chronos by name. This Heracles produced an overweening egg. This was filled with the power of its sire, and the pressure broke it in two. Its pointed upper part came to be heaven and its lower part the earth. There came forth from it a two-bodied [i.e. hermaphrodite?] god. |
| | **Damascius:** The Orphic theogony relayed by Hieronymus and also by Hellanicus, if in fact they are not indentical, is as follows. There was water in the beginning, it tells, and matter, and from these the earth was formed. This is the initial pair of principles it proposes, water and earth. The latter is friable by nature, but the former glues it and holds it together. It passes over the single principle that |

preceded these two principles, because it cannot be spoken of. This quality is demonstrated precisely by its failure to speak of it.The third principle after this pair, that is, water and land, was produced from them. It is a dragon [*drakōn*] with the heads of a bull and a lion attached to it, and it has the face of a god in the middle. It has wings on its shoulders, and is called 'unaging Chronos [Time]' and also 'Heracles'. Ananke ['Necessity'] is combined with Chronos and is of the same nature as bodiless Adrasteia [Nemesis], stretching her arms out across the entire universe to touch its limits. I think this is said to be the third principle of substance, except that the theogony conceptualised it as male and female together, to make the point that it was the generating cause of all things. And I think that the theogony in the *Rhapsodies* passed over the first pair of principles together with the single principle that preceded the two and is passed on by the act of silence, to make its first principle the third one that comes after the pair, on the basis that this is the first to be in some way expressible and susceptible to the understanding of men. In this theogony Chronos holds the highest position of honour. He is unaging and the father of Ether and Chaos. Anyway, according to this theogony, this Chronos dragon produces children that are each threefold: Ether, which it says is liquid, and boundless Chaos, and in the third place after these misty Erebus [Underworld]. It conveys that Chaos comprises a triad analogous to that comprised by Ether, though it is a triad defined by power rather than by generation. So the theogony's third child is misty Erebus, whereas Ether is generative and at the top, not a uniform substance, but liquid, and boundless Chaos is in the middle of them. Amongst these, it says, Chronos produced an egg, this tradition making Chronos's offspring an egg and born amongst these entities, because it is from them that the third perceptible triad proceeds. What is this triad? It is the egg. The dyad is made up of the natures in it, the male and the female, and the multitude is made up of all the different sorts of seed in the middle of it. Third after these is a bodiless god with golden wings on his shoulders, who has the heads of bulls growing out of his flanks, and has on his head a monstrous dragon resembling all kinds of shapes of animals. This god should be construed as the mind of the triad, the multitude the middle part and the dyad the power. The egg itself is the generative principle of the third triad. The third god is part of this third triad. And this theogony hymns Protogonos and calls Zeus the organiser of all things and of the whole universe. For that reason he is also called 'Pan'. This is what this genealogy supplies about the perceptible principles.

**Homeric scholium:** *In Arima, where they say the beds of Typhon are.* They say that Earth was angry at the killing of the Giants and slandered Zeus to Hera. She went off to Cronus and told him. He gave her two eggs, smearing them with his own semen, and he bade her bury them in the earth. He told her that they would produce a power [*daimōn*] that would remove Zeus from his rule. Since she was angry, she placed them under Arimon in Cilicia. When Typhon had been produced, Hera became reconciled with Zeus and told him everything.

The second Orphic equivalent of Typhon is Chronos. The theogonies relayed by Athenagoras and Damascius kaleidoscope the imagery of the Ophion myth. The physical descriptions of the Chronos *drakōn*, and the claim that he was born of the earth (or 'mud') clearly mark him out as a Typhon-like figure, whilst his name, Chronos, evidently plays on that of Cronus, Ophion's opponent. As in the Typhon narratives of Apollodorus and Nonnus (**5, 8**), roles are found for Zeus, Heracles and Pan, though their identities here are radically different. Like Typhon and Ophion too, Chronos is signally a progenitor. He can be construed as generating children either with Ananke-Adrasteia as a female consort in the Echidna role (1–2) or, to the extent that he is himself identified hermaphroditically with Ananke-Adrasteia, by parthenogenesis (cf. the traditions of Typhon's own parthenogenesis, 6). The Hieronymus cited by Damascius is probably the mid-third-century BC Peripatetic Hieronymus of Rhodes. Hellanicus remains obscure; he is unlikely to have been the famous classical historian of that name (24, 75, 103). The Orphic *Rhapsodies* were hexameter verses: the many fragments of them that survive (Kern 1922 FF59–235) indicate them to have been post-Hellenistic for the most part.

The Homeric scholium seems to fold elements of a similar Orphic theogony, with the involvement of Cronus (rather than Chronos) and the eggs, into a more conventional version of the Typhon myth, Typhon retaining his name and his associations with Hera, Arima and Cilicia.

## 12  The Orphic doublets of Typhon (iii): Zeus-Sabazius

ca. 200 AD

Clement of Alexandria
*Protrepticus* 2.16 p. 14 P

Greek

What if I were to add what remains? Demeter becomes pregnant, and Kore is reared, and her father Zeus has sex again in turn with Pherephatte [Persephone, Kore], his own daughter, after her mother, Deo [Demeter], forgetting his former abomination, Zeus, the father and corrupter of his daughter, and he has sex with her after becoming a dragon [*drakōn*], in which form, however, he was detected. The token for those being initiated into the Sabazian mysteries is 'the god across the bosom'. This is a dragon, crawling across the bosom of those being initiated. This is proof of Zeus's lack of self-control. And Pherephatta conceives a bull-shaped child. Anyway, an idolatrous poet says:

> the bull the father of the dragon and the dragon the father of the bull, on the mountain the hidden thing, the herdsman, the goad...

He refers, I think, by 'the herdsman's goad' to the narthex [a staff topped with a pine cone], which the Bacchi decorate with garlands.

The third, and more etiolated, Orphic equivalent of Typhon is Sabazius. This theogony shares with the Typhon myth and the other Orphic theogonies laid out above (11–12) a focus on a pair of progenitor dragons, the key male dragon now, with yet more kaleidoscoping, being identified with Zeus himself. The date of his theogony's original concoction is unclear, but it was already known to Athenagoras when he wrote his *Legatio* (20) between 176 and 180 AD.

### FURTHER READING

Giants and the gigantomachy: Vian 1951, 1952a, 1952b, Dörig and Gigon 1961, Hardie 1986:85–156, Vian and Moore 1998, Gantz 1993:445–54.

Typhon and his oriental analogues: Schmidt 1884–1937, Holland 1900, Teipel 1922, Porzig 1930, Vian 1960, Worms 1953, Fontenrose 1959:70–93, Walcot 1966:9–26, West 1966:379–97 (on 820–80), 1997:300–4, Detienne and Vernant 1978:107–30, Burkert 1979:5–10, 1992:94–95, Beckman 1982, Ballabriga 1990, Höckmann 1991, Blaise 1992, Gantz 1993:48–51, Penglase 1994:191–6, Watkins 1995:448–63, Touchefeu-Meynier and Krauskopf 1997, Sancassano 1997:77–96, Hansen 2002:305–14, Lane Fox 2008:255–73.

Seleucid foundation mythology: Ogden 2011:89–102.

The Orphic reflexes of Typhon: Fontenrose 1959:230–9, Kirk et al. 1983:7–74, West 1983:176–226, Schibli 1990:78–103, Ahbel-Rappe 2010:498–9.

# 3
# *Python, Slain by Apollo*

For all its modern fame, antiquity has bequeathed us no expansive literary account of Apollo's slaying of the Delphic dragon, which was known in both male and female variants. The Delphic dragon is also referred to in **4, 71** and **83**.

### 13   Apollo's slaying of Python at the Delphic Oracle: a summary account

ii AD

Hyginus *Fabulae* 140

Latin

Python was a huge dragon [*draco*], the son of Earth. He had been accustomed to give responses from an oracle on Mt Parnassus before Apollo. He knew that he was fated to be killed by the offspring of Leto. At that time Zeus lay with Leto the daughter of Polus. When Hera discovered this she brought it about that Leto should give birth in a place that the sun could not reach. When Python perceived that Leto was pregnant by Zeus, he began to pursue her in order to kill her. But by the command of Zeus the North Wind picked Leto up and took her to Poseidon. He protected her, but so as not to undo what Hera had already done, he took her to the island of Ortygia, which he covered over with waves. Since Python could not find her, he returned to Parnassus. But Poseidon brought Ortygia back up to a higher level, and the island was subsequently called Delos. There Leto, holding onto an olive tree, gave birth to Apollo and Artemis, to whom Hephaestus gave

Figure 3 Python challenges Leto, with babies Apollo and Artemis. Lost Apulian red-figure neck amphora, earlier iv BC. Drawing by J.H.W. Tischbein, at Hamilton and Tischbein 1791–5:iii fig. 4.

arrows as a gift. Four days after they were born, Apollo exacted vengeance for his mother. For he came to Parnassus and killed Python with his arrows (for that reason he was called Pythian), and he threw his bones into a tripod cauldron [*cortina*] and deposited them in his temple. He made funeral games for him, which are called the Pythian games.

Hyginus offers a summary of the canonical version of the myth of Apollo's slaying of the Delphic dragon, here the male Python. The tradition assigns a range of different motivations to Apollo: it was, as here, to avenge the (male) dragon's attack upon his mother Leto (so too **15**); or it proceeded from Apollo's selfish desire to seize the oracle for himself (Callimachus *Hymns* 4.84–93); or Apollo was more altruistically concerned to clean up a marauding menace that was no good to anyone (so too **14, 16–17**). Whilst Apollo's statuary often gives him a curiously modestly sized and still-living Python as attribute, the iconographic record for the actual slaying of Python is surprisingly meagre. But in such illustrations of it as do survive Apollo is typically shown as a babe in his mother's arms and stretching a bow as tall as he is himself against the dragon, images that reflect the vengeance motivation. Narratives deploying the other motivations imply that the Apollo that slew Python was an adult, or at any rate an adolescent. For the memorialisation of Python at Delphi see **16**. For another example of a dragon-slaying baby, cf. Heracles and the dragon pair sent by Hera, **19–22**.

## 14 The dragoness Delphyne, her slaying and her rotting

ca. 590 BC

*Homeric Hymn* (3) *to Apollo* 300–9, 349–73

Greek

**300.** Nearby was the sweetly flowing spring, where Lord Apollo, the son of Zeus, killed the dragoness [*drakaina*], shooting from his stout bow. She was fat and huge, a wild monster, who did much harm to people on the earth, much harm to people themselves and much to slender-footed sheep, for she was a blood-reeking bane. And once she received from Hera of the golden throne the terrible, harsh Typhon, and reared him, a bane to mortals. Hera bore him when she was angry with father Zeus, when the son of Cronus produced glorious Athene from the top of his head. [309]

**349.** When Hera's months and days were completed with the cycle of the year, and the seasons followed each other, she bore a creature that resembled neither gods nor mortals, the terrible, harsh Typhon, and reared him, a bane to the gods. At once cow-eyed lady Hera took him up, carried him and gave him over, an evil thing to another evil thing, and she received him. Typhon did much harm to the glorious tribes of people. Whoever encountered the dragoness would be carried off by his day of doom, until Lord Apollo, who does his work from afar, sent powerful poison against her. And she, rent by harsh agonies, lay gasping badly and rolling over the place. There was a loud and terrible cry. She writhed back and forth, again and again, through the wood, and she gave up her life, breathing it forth in the form of blood. And Phoebus Apollo gloried over her: 'Now rot [*pytheu*] here on the man-feeding earth. Nor will you, living still, be an evil cause of destruction to mortals who, eating the fruit of the earth that gives much nourishment, bring perfect hecatombs to this place. Neither will Typhon ward cruel death from you nor the Chimaera of the evil name, but in this place the black earth and beaming Hyperion [Sun] will cause you to rot.' So he spoke, boasting. And darkness covered her eyes. And the sacred might of the Sun caused her to rot there, as a result of which the place is now called Pytho. And they call the lord Pythian in epithet, because in just that place the might of penetrating Helius [Sun] caused the monster to rot. [373]

This sub-Homeric text offers the earliest narrative of Apollo's great Delphic dragon slaying of any substance, and the only narrative of substance to give us a dragoness, a *drakaina* (though cf. **16**). Later sources supply a name for the female variant: Delphyne (e.g. Callimachus F643 Pfeiffer). The elaborate play with *pyth-* terms towards the end of this passage strongly suggests that the more familiar variant with the male dragon named Python was already well-known. The name Python offers a supposed etymology for the toponym Pytho, the byname of Delphi, but is also linked to a key motif in the dragon narrative, indeed in many international dragon narratives: the pestilential rotting of the creature's corpse (**M7.a.vi**). The name Delphyne similarly offers a supposed etymology for the toponym Delphi itself and may also have a speaking significance for the tale. *Delphys* means 'womb': the prospect, if it is implied, that the dragoness may be mother to a brood of similar creatures is a terrible one; at any rate, she is foster-mother to the terrible Typhon. (Here it is Hera, rather than Earth—as in **5, 6, 8**—who is birth mother to Typhon, but Earth is still involved in his production, as, in the section omitted, Hera makes appeal to her in order to conceive him.)

Beyond the assertion that Delphyne was a dragoness, we are told nothing of her form here. Apollodorus, however, makes it clear that she was an anguipede, a female humanoid above the waist and a serpent below (**5**).

In Apollo's crowing words over the dying Delphyne we once again get the sense of a fellowship of mythical dragons (cf. **4**): if Typhon has a strong personal connection to Delphyne, the same can hardly be said of the Chimaera.

## 15 The earliest substantial narrative of the battle with Python

ca. 412 BC

Euripides *Iphigenia in Tauris* 1234–57

Greek

Lovely is the offspring of Leto [Apollo], whom once she bore in the fruit-bearing hollows of Delos, the golden-haired one, skilled in the lyre, and who delights in the good aim of the bow. She, his mother, brought him from the sea ridge and the glorious place of birth to the peak of Parnassus that revels with Dionysus, Parnassus of flooding waters. There the mottled-backed, dark-eyed dragon [*drakōn*] occupied a grove, well shaded with leafy laurel, a huge monster of the earth, and tended the chthonic oracle. Phoebus [Apollo], though still a baby, though still playing in your mother's arms, you killed it, and succeeded to its place, in charge of the divine oracle. You sit on the golden tripod, on an unlying throne, disbursing prophecies to men from your divine inner sanctum, neighbour of the streams of Castalia, occupying a hall at the centre of the world.

Euripides' choral ode comprises the earliest substantial narrative of Apollo's killing of Python. Again he is held to have done it as a babe in Leto's arms and therefore, presumably, in revenge. As often, the *drakōn* is portrayed as living in a grove (**M3.b**); the link to the water source, the spring of Castalia, remains indirect (**M4.a**).

## 16 Aspects of the memorialisation of the killing of Python

ca. 100 AD

Plutarch *Failure of Oracles, Moralia* 414b and 417f–18c

Greek

**414b.** [Ammonius speaks.] 'They tell that our oracle here [Delphi], which is the oldest and most distinguished in repute, was deserted and left inaccessible for a long time because of a dangerous beast, a dragoness [*drakaina*]. However, they misunderstand the nature of the oracle's period of inactivity, and put the cart before the horse. For it was the oracle's abandonment that attracted the beast, and not the beast that caused the abandonment.'

**417f.** [Cleombrotus speaks.] 'But those that fall furthest short of the truth are the Delphic theologians that think that the god once had a fight against a snake for the oracle. They allow poets and prose writers to state this in their theatrical competitions, as if deliberately contradicting the holiest rites they enact.' Philip (for the historian was in attendance) was surprised at this and asked him what holy rites he thought the competitors contradicted. 'These ones,' he said, 'to do with the oracle, into which the city recently initiated all the Greeks from Thermopyle to Tempe. For the hut built here in the region of the threshing floor on an eight-year cycle is not the lair or hole of the dragon [*drakōn*], but a representation of the home of a tyrant or king. The silent assault made upon it is made along the so-called Dolonian road. The Labyadae [a Delphic clan] escort the boy of two living parents along this road with lighted torches before throwing the fire into the hut, overturning the table and fleeing through the gates of the sanctuary without turning round. The rites are rounded off with the boy's wanderings, his period of service and the purifications at Tempe. All of these rites lead one to suspect that there was an act of great boldness that gave rise to pollution. For it is completely risible, my friend, to think that Apollo killed the beast and fled to the borders of Greece in need of purification, and then made libations there and did what men do when they are placating and calming the wrath of demons [*daimones*], whom they call "avenging spirits" [*alastores, palamnaioi*], as if they pursue the memories of some unforgettable [*alēsta*] and ancient [*palaia*] pollutions.' [418c]

**421c.** [Cleombrotus speaks, supposedly relating the words of a Persian sage.] 'He said that no eight-year exile in Tempe was imposed upon the slayer of Python, but that after he had been cast out he went to another universe. He subsequently returned after a cycle of nine huge years, purified and truly "shining" [*Phoibos*], and took over control of the oracle that had been guarded by Themis in the meantime.'

Plutarch was a priest of the Delphic oracle. These are excerpts from one of his recherché discussions of it, cast in dialogue format. The learned Ammonius, consonantly with the dialogue's general subject matter, ostentatiously contradicts a traditional understanding of the oracle's history, namely that the dragon from which Apollo took the oracle had been of a marauding variety. His presentation of the dragon in question as female (cf. **14**) reflects what can only have been a minor tradition by Plutarch's day, and so is also a token of his learning. Cleombrotus, with similar ostentation, contradicts what was evidently the usual interpretation, right or wrong, of rites performed at the oracle on an eight-year basis. The usual interpretation was that they re-enacted and memorialised Apollo's killing of (the male dragon) Python. The notion that Apollo should have gone into exile and into service for an eight-year period as part of his expiation of the killing of the dragon corresponds with traditions attaching to Cadmus and the killing of the Dragon of Ares (**75**). Cleombrotus's assertion that the hut belonged to a tyrant or king reflects the rationalising tradition found in **18**. We can be more certain that it was indeed the dragon fight that was remembered and celebrated in a musical competition incorporated into the quadrennial Pythian games: the competition was for tunes played on the *aulos* (double oboe) in the so-called Pythian measure; the different phases of the measure corresponded to the different phases of the dragon fight (Strabo C421–2, Pollux *Onomasticon* 4.78–9, 4.84, hypothesis A to Pindar *Pythians*).

## 17 Python: the dragon in and of the landscape

late iii AD

Menander Rhetor *Peri epideiktikon* 3.17 pp. 441–2 Spengel

Greek

Apollo killed Python, who had occupied Delphi, with his own darts. I shall expand a little in order to explain who Python was. The earth brought forth a variety of dragon [*drakōn*] neither expressible in words nor easy to believe in when hearing of. This laid waste to all the land in the region of Delphi and Phocis and then occupied Parnassus, the greatest mountain of all those under heaven, falling short neither of Olympus nor the Ida near us. It covered this over with its coils and loops, and no part of the mountain was left exposed. It held its head over the peak, raising it aloft up to the ether. When it needed to drink, it took in rivers whole, and when it needed to eat, it devoured complete herds. It rendered Delphi inaccessible to all. No one lived in the place. The oracle of Themis was deserted. The god realised that the people were suffering outrageous things about which they could do nothing, and he wanted by all means to give them useful prophecies by which their lives were destined to be fortunate, and so he killed this Python too in a single shooting and with the same barbs and darts [sc. as Tityus].

Again, a marauding Python and an altruistic Apollo. Of particular interest here is the author's expression of the *drakōn*'s vast size, which contrives to identify it with the landscape in which it lived and to present it as a sort of elemental force: a common theme in ancient and indeed more recent dragon narratives (**M3.a, M14.c**), and one wholly appropriate to a son of Earth.

## 18 Python rationalised

ca. 330 BC

Ephorus *FGrH* 70 F31b

Greek

[Ephorus says that] when he set out from Athens to Delphi, Apollo went by this road along which the Athenians send the Pythian embassy. When he came to the Panopaeans he destroyed Tityus, who controlled the place, a violent man beyond the law. The Parnassians encountered him and indicated that there was another difficult man, Python by name, also known as Drakōn ['Dragon']. When Apollo shot him they shouted out 'Hie Paian' in encouragement. It was from this that the custom of singing the paean began for those on the point of joining battle. The hut of Python was burned at that time by the Delphians, just as they still do now, to make remembrance of what happened at that time. What could be more mythical than Apollo shooting and punishing Tityuses and Pythons and making the journey from Athens to Delphi and traversing the whole earth? If Ephorus did not assume that these things were myths, why did he have to call the Themis of myth a woman, and the Drakōn of myth a person, unless he wanted to blend together the type of history and the type of myth?

As in other cases too (**M16.a.iii**), the supernatural dragon of the original myth is rationalised into 'a man called Dragon'. Note again the memorialisation of the killing of the dragon in ritual and cult (cf. **M14.b.vi**).

## FURTHER READING

Apollo and Python: Turk 1884–1937, Fontenrose 1959, Geisau 1963, Bömer 1969–86:1, 138–45 (on 1, 438–51), Sourvinou-Inwood 1987, Gantz 1993:38, 88–9, Watkins 1995:461–2, Gourmelen 2004:377–80.

Python's iconography: Kahil 1966, 1994, Lambrinudakis and Palagia 1984:301–3.

# 4
# Heracles' Dragons (i): Baby Heracles and the Dragon Pair Sent by Hera

In this chapter and the three that follow, we look at the four sets of dragons slain or overcome by Heracles, in biographical order: the first belongs to his childhood, the latter three to his labours. Given that Heracles faces dragons so many times, one might be tempted to think of him as a specialist in dragon slaying. However, on the one hand the tradition gives Heracles an inordinate number of monsters to contend with—and by no means just

Figure 4 Baby Heracles throttles the serpent pair. Fresco, Casa dei Vettii, ca. 50–79 AD, Pompeii, Italy. Alinari / The Bridgeman Art Library.

in the context of his canonical labours—and on the other, as we have noted in the introduction, the dragon element was the most common one across the board in Greek monsters. A further pair of *drakontes* attacks a further pair of human children, probably twins, in the tale of Laocoon (**92–6**); a single *drakōn* attacks a single baby in the tale of the Dragon of Nemea (**81–4**).

## 19   The earliest account of baby Heracles' battle against the dragon pair sent by Hera

soon after 476 BC

Pindar *Nemeans* 1.33–59

Greek

I gladly cling to Heracles on the great peaks of virtues, stirring up an ancient tale. This tells how, as soon as the son of Zeus came down from his mother's womb into the amazing light, fleeing her birth pangs, together with his twin brother, Hera of the golden throne caught sight of him as he was put into his saffron swaddling clothes. But the queen of the gods, angry in heart, dispatched dragons [*drakontes*] at once. When the gates were opened, they entered the broad recess of the chamber, eager to fold their swift jaws round the children. But he held his head up straight and ventured into battle for the first time. He grabbed the two snakes by the neck with his two hands, and they could not escape. As they were choked, time blew away the souls from their huge frames. Unendurable fear struck the women who happened to be attending Alcmene's childbed, and indeed she herself, without her dress though she was, rose from her bed and attempted to defend against the brutes' violent attack. Quickly, the leaders of the Cadmeians all together came running with their bronze weapons, and Amphitryon, stricken with sharp agonies, arrived brandishing in his hand his sword, denuded of its scabbard. For troubles of one's own press upon every man the same, but in no time at all does the heart recover from another's grief. There he stood, suffused with an amazement that was both pleasant and difficult to bear. For he saw his son's extraordinary spirit and power. The immortal gods had reversed the speech of the messengers.

Zeus had disguised himself as the mortal Amphitryon in order to sleep with the man's wife, Alcmene. She has now given birth to twins, Heracles and Iphicles. Whilst Amphitryon is generally spoken of as Heracles' father, he is in fact the scion of Zeus, whilst Iphicles is genuinely Amphitryon's. Zeus's wife, Hera, resentful of the affair and the child, sends the dragons to kill Heracles.

In claiming that he recounts an 'ancient tale' the lyric poet Pindar may, perhaps, protest too much. There is no trace of this story prior to his ode, and it is conceivable, as some scholars believe, that he has in fact invented it, perhaps on the model of the tale of Laocoon (**92–6**), as a suitable anticipation of the great dragon battles that were already established for Heracles in his later life (**23–47**).

Pindar's vignette of the baby Heracles choking a dragon in each of his hands corresponds well with the subsequent representation of the episode in the further three accounts of it given here (**20–2**) and also in art, where Heracles is typically shown on splayed knees forcing one dragon's head down to the ground, whilst lifting the other up above him (e.g. *LIMC* Herakles 1598, 1600, 1602, 1606–8, 1613, 1619, 1621, 1624–8, 1638, 1650, 1651, 1663).

## 20  The most elaborate account of the battle against the dragon pair, and its aftermath

270s BC

Theocritus 24.10–33, 56–9, 82–100

Greek

**10.** When the Bear was turning towards her midnight setting opposite Orion, who displays his great shoulder, then Hera of many wiles dispatched two dreadful monsters, dragons [*drakontes*] bristling with dark blue coils, over the flat threshold, empty space between the doorposts. Her hostile intent was that they should eat baby Heracles. And they, the pair of them, uncoiled themselves and rolled their blood-sucking bellies over the ground. Evil fire shone forth from their eyes as they went, and they spat out a heavy venom. But when, their tongues a-flicker, they approached the babies, then the dear children of Alcmene woke up, since Zeus knows everything, and light was created throughout the house. Iphicles shouted out at once when he noticed the evil beasts and saw their shameless teeth over the edge of the hollow shield [serving as their cradle], and kicked away the woollen bedspread with his feet in his rush to flee. But Heracles flew at them with his hands and bound them both in a heavy grip, grasping them by the throat, where deadly snakes keep their baleful venom, which even the gods abominate. In response the pair entwined themselves round the child with their coils, the late-born child, suckling at the nurse, ever without tears. But before long, their spines in agony, they let him go again and tried to find release from the compelling grip.... [33]

**56.** And he kept showing the creeping creatures to his father, Amphitryon, leaping about on high, delighting in his boyhood, and, laughing, he set down before his father's feet the terrible monsters, quietened by death. [59]

**82.** [Tiresias prophesies.] It is fated that after completing twelve labours he will live in Zeus's house, but a pyre in Trachis shall have all of him that is mortal. He will be called the son-in-law of the immortals who incited these hole-dwelling brutes to destroy the baby. But, my lady, let there be a fire ready beneath the ashes, and prepare dry wood from the camel's thorn, the Christ's thorn or the bramble, or dry wood from the wild pear, that swirls in the wind. Burn the dragon pair [*drakonte*] on wild firewood in the middle of the night, at the point at which they themselves wished to kill your child. And in the morning one of the serving women should gather up the dust from the fire, take it to a precipitous rock over a river and be sure to cast it all beyond the borders, and she should come back without turning behind her. Fumigate your house with purifying sulphur first, then sprinkle the house with harmless water mixed with salt, in accordance with custom, using a garlanded branch. Sacrifice to Zeus above a male pig, so that you may always be above your enemies.' [100]

Once again we have a vignette in which Heracles grasps one of the two attacking dragons in each hand. The Hellenistic poet Theocritus does much here with the motifs of fire that belong with *drakontes* (**M6**). The pair flash fire from their eyes. Once killed, their bodies must be burned on a pyre for purposes of purification (the casting out of ashes beyond the land's border is particularly associated with purification of monstrous births: Diodorus 32.10, Phlegon of Tralles *Mirabilia* 2, Phrynichus Arabicus *Praeparatio Sophistica* 15.23 de Borries) and perhaps even simple safety. This action, at the beginning of Heracles' life, as the prophet Tiresias makes explicit, anticipates the end of it, for Heracles is destined eventually to kill himself by throwing himself onto a pyre in Trachis, and that too to escape from the burning venom of another dragon, the Hydra (**26**). After this the house must be subjected to further purification rituals that again exploit fire: sulphur will be burned to fumigate the house; for fumigation against a (live) dragon and other snakes, see **130**.

## 21 The dragon pair flies: a dramatic dialogue

ca. 200 BC

Plautus *Amphitruo* 1091–1124

Latin

BROMIA: After your wife began to give birth today, when the pains arose in her womb, as happens when women give birth, she called upon the immortal gods to bring her help, her hands washed and her head covered. Then at once there was a huge crash of thunder. At first we thought your house was falling down. Your whole house shone as if it were gold.

AMPHITRUO: Please spare me from this sort of stuff, once you've had enough of your joking. What happened then?

BROMIA: In the meantime none of us heard your wife moaning or wailing, and there she was: she'd given birth instantly and without any pain.

AMPHITRUO: I'm happy about that, however she has been treating me.

BROMIA: Forget all that and listen to what I have to say. After she had given birth, she told us to wash the boys, and we got on with it. But the boy that I washed, how large he was! How strong he was! No one was able to bind him into his swaddling clothes.

AMPHITRUO: What you tell is incredible. If it's true, then I do not fear to suggest that my wife was secretly aided by the divine.

BROMIA: You'll be even more amazed by what I'm going to tell you. After he was laid in the cradle, two huge crested snakes flew down into the house's central pool. At once they both reared their heads.

AMPHITRUO: Goodness me!

BROMIA: Don't worry! But the snakes looked around at all of us with their eyes. After they had caught sight of the boys, they made for the cradle at high speed. I tried to drag the cradle and pull it backward, this way and that, fearing for the boys and trembling for myself. The snakes chased me all the more keenly. But when the boy I mentioned caught sight of the snakes, he quickly jumped out of his cradle and made a direct charge at them. He grabbed them swiftly, one in each of his hands.

AMPHITRUO: What you're saying is amazing. The story you're telling is all too terrifying. For, poor me, my limbs are seized with shivering at your words. What happened next? Speak on!

BROMIA: The boy slaughtered both snakes. Whilst this was going on, he called upon your wife in clear voice...

AMPHITRUO: Who did?

BROMIA: The highest ruler of gods and men, Zeus. He said that he had secretly slept with Alcmene, and that the boy who had overcome those snakes was his son. He said that the other boy was yours.

Plautus composed his comedy *Amphitruo* in ca. 200 BC but, in accordance with his usual practice, will have based the play upon a Greek original of the fourth or third century BC, which, in this case, we are unable to identify. For this climactic scene of revelation, delivered by the maid Bromia, the humour is largely left aside.

The dragons are described here as crested, and in ancient art *drakontes* were indeed frequently portrayed as both bearded and crested (**M1.a.ii**). Bromia's assertion that the dragons flew down into the house's pool may imply that they were also winged. However, *drakontes* did not need to be winged to fly: those that draw Medea's flying Chariot of the Sun are sometimes depicted in art as winged (*LIMC* Medeia 39, 46, 51, 53, 55, 57, 58, 62, 63, 66), but sometimes as wingless too (*LIMC* Iason 70–3, Medeia 29, 36, 38).

## 22 Amphitryon uses the dragon pair to identify which of the twins is his own son

ca. 454 BC–ca. 100 AD

Apollodorus *Bibliotheca* 2.4.8 (ca. 100 AD), incorporating Pherecydes F69a Fowler (ca. 454 BC)

Greek

When the child was eight months old, Hera sent two massive dragons [*drakontes*] against his bed, wishing to destroy the baby. Alcmene called to Amphitryon for help, but Heracles, standing alone, choked and destroyed them with his two hands. Pherecydes says that Amphitryon put the dragons into the bed, as he wanted to discover which of the two children [*sc.* Heracles and Iphicles] belonged to him, and that when Iphicles fled whilst Heracles stood firm he discovered that it was Iphicles that had been sired by him.

It is unusual for Pherecydes to be credited with a mythical variant that did not become canonical. Later tradition was also to attribute a paternity test involving venomous snakes to the partly magical snake-wrangling race of the Psylli, based in the Libyan Syrtes. They would put the snakes into their children's cradles, and the snakes would wilt away before those of true Psyllus blood (Agatharchides of Cnidus *FGrH* 86 F21a-b, ii BC).

**FURTHER READING**

Robert 1920–6:2, 619–21, Brendel 1932, Woodford 1983, 1988.

# 5
# *Heracles' Dragons (ii): the Hydra*

The remaining three of Heracles' dragons the hero encounters in the course of his labours. In the second of these he destroys the multi-headed Hydra, arguably the most famous of all the dragons of classical antiquity. It is a great pity that no elaborate expansive literary account of her slaying, of which there must once have been many, has survived for us. By contrast, the Hydra thrives in the iconographic record, and that too from an early stage: a pair of

Figure 5 Heracles and Iolaus battle the Lernaean Hydra; the crab can be seen between Heracles' legs. White-ground lekythos, ca. 500–490 BC. Musée du Louvre. The Bridgeman Art Library.

50

bronze fibulae are able to tell us that the canonical version of the tale, crab and all, had already become established by ca. 700 BC (*LIMC* Herakles 2019–20). The Hydra is mentioned also in **1–2, 4, 28, 30–1, 46, 59, 83**; cf. also **119** com.

## 23  Heracles' slaying of the Hydra: a summary account

ca. 100 AD

Apollodorus *Bibliotheca* 2.5.2

Greek

The second labour he [Eurystheus] assigned to him was to kill the Lernaean Hydra. This was reared in the swamp of Lerna and used to venture forth onto the plain and plunder the cattle and the land. The Hydra had a huge body and nine heads, eight of them mortal, but the middle one was immortal. Heracles mounted his chariot, with Iolaus as his driver, arrived at Lerna and brought his horses to a halt. He caught sight of the Hydra on a hill beside the springs of Amymone, where she had her lair. He pelted her with lighted arrows and compelled her to come out. As she came out he overpowered her and kept tight hold of her. The Hydra attached herself to one of his feet and wound herself around it. He beat her heads with his club, but he was not able to achieve anything. When he had beaten one head, two new ones grew up. A huge crab came to help the Hydra, biting his foot. Therefore, when he had killed it, he himself too called in Iolaus, who, setting light to part of the nearby wood, seared off the stumps of the heads with brands and prevented them from rising up. Having overcome the re-growing heads in this way, he cut off the immortal one, buried it and placed a heavy rock on top, beside the road through Lerna that leads to Elaeus. He sliced up the body of the Hydra and dipped his arrows in the venom. But Eurystheus claimed that this labour should not be counted amongst the ten, for Heracles had not overcome the Hydra alone but with the help of Iolaus.

Apollodorus's summary is actually the most substantial narrative of the Hydra episode we possess. The Hydra is given vastly differing tallies of heads in the tradition. Most commonly they are numbered nine, or at any rate in multiples of three. But Simonides and Palaephatus, amongst others, gave her fifty (F569 *PMG*; **27**) and Euripides, amongst others, a hundred (*Heracles* 1188). For the notion that the Hydra's middle head was in some way special, see also **25**. For its immortality, cf. Ophion's central head (of three), which was said to be that of a 'god' (**11**). The notion that a monster's serpentine head should in some way live on after the death of the monster proper and continue to be effective is also found in the traditions of the petrifying head of Medusa (**54, 59–62, 64–5**).

In her seizing of cattle and plundering of the local area, the Hydra's behaviour is that of a typical marauding dragon (**M5**). Like many *drakontes*, the Hydra is also tightly associated with a water source, in this case the multiple streams of the spring of Amymone and the Lernaean marsh that proceeds from them (cf. **24; M4.a**). Compatibly, her name consists simply of the Greek word for 'water snake'.

As often, fire, reflective of the dragon's own fiery venom, proves to be the most effective tool against her, in the cases both of Heracles' arrows and of Iolaus's brands; it may also be implied that the Hydra was driven into the blazing wood. For more of the battle of fire between Heracles and the Hydra see **26**.

## 24 Some early literary references to the Hydra

vii BC–ca. 400 BC

Pausanias 2.37 (ii AD), incorporating Pisander of Camirus *Heraclea* F2 West/F3 Davies (vii–vi BC)

Panyassis *Heraclea* F8 West/F3 Davies (early v BC)

Euripides *Heracles* 1274–5 (ca. 414 BC)

Schol. Plato *Phaedo* 89c (Hellenistic-Byzantine), incorporating Hellanicus F103 Fowler (later v BC) and Herodorus of Heraclea F23 Fowler (ca. 400 BC)

Greek

**Pausanias (Pisander):** A plane tree grows at the source of Amymone. They say that the Hydra was reared under this plane tree. I am persuaded that this beast surpassed other *hydras* [water snakes] in her actual size, and that her venom had an incurable property, with the result that Heracles poisoned the tips of his arrows from it. In my opinion she had a single head, and not several. But Pisander of Camirus gave the Hydra many heads instead of just the one, so that the beast might seem more fearful and his poetry might receive more attention.

**Panyassis:** The Crab. This is thought to have been placed amongst the stars by Hera, because when Heracles was killing the Hydra with the help of others, it alone jumped out of the lake and bit his foot, as Panyassis says in his *Heraclea*. Heracles, angered, crushed it with his foot. As a result of this it has received great honour, being counted amongst the twelve signs of the zodiac.

**Euripides:** [Heracles speaks.] I killed the Hydra, the double-headed growing-back dog...

**Schol. Plato (Hellanicus, Herodorus):** 'Not even Heracles...': The proverb is 'Against two not even Heracles.'... Herodorus and Hellanicus say that when Heracles was killing the Hydra, Hera sent a crab against him. Since Heracles could not fight against two, he called in Iolaus as an ally. This was the origin of the proverb.

As is apparent from Pausanias's wording, the Hydra is named for the common water snake, a creature she hardly resembles save for her devotion to water. He finds, as perhaps Pisander had already found before him, a strong association between the Hydra and the streams of the Amymone spring, and possibly with its plane tree too. The canonical multi-headed Hydra and the spring alike, let it be noted, boast a dendritic structure. Pausanias was not the only second-century AD rationaliser to suppose that the Hydra had only a single head: cf. also Heraclitus *De incredibilibus* 18 (Hydra), where it is explained that the impression of many heads was afforded by the brood that surrounded her; for further rationalising of the Hydra, see **27**.

The significance of Euripides' poetically allusive description of the Hydra is disputed. For this translator it represents the earliest extant assertion of the well-known conceit that the Hydra grew two heads back for every one lost; cf. **23–7**.

Panyassis, Hellanicus and Herodorus find a balance of some sort between the aides deployed on both sides of the battle, though they dispute which one was called in first; the debate remains implicit in Palaephatus too (**27**). The question of Heracles' integrity is at stake, a question cynically exploited by Eurystheus in denying Heracles credit for the labour (**23**).

## 25 The Hydra's golden head, and Heracles' pet dragon

early i AD (?)–ix AD

Photius *Bibliotheca* cod. 190, 147b22–8 (ix AD), resume of Ptolemy son of Hephaestion (i–ii AD?), incorporating Aristonicus of Tarentum *FHG* iv p. 337

He [Ptolemy son of Hephaestion] says that Aristonicus of Tarentum says that the middle head of the Hydra was golden. He says that Alexander of Myndus says that an earth-born dragon [*drakōn*] fought alongside Heracles against the Nemean Lion. This dragon had been reared by Heracles, accompanied him to Thebes and remained in Aulis, and it was the one that ate the sparrow's nestlings and was then turned to stone.

F2 (i AD?) and Alexander of Myndus *FGrH* 25 F5 (early i AD?)

Greek

Ptolemy, son of Hephaestion, also known as Ptolemy Chennos, was evidently a mine of recycled obscure information on the dragons of Greek myth.

The claim that the Hydra's middle head was golden should be compared with Apollodorus's that it was immortal (23), and also with the tradition that the many-streamed spring of Amymone, with which the many-necked Hydra was so closely identified, was created when the girl Amymone dropped a golden water vessel on the ground and waters gushed forth through it (Propertius 2.26.45–50, Philostratus *Imagines* 1.8). Was it held that the Hydra's golden head had somehow been formed from the water vessel?

The unique information that Heracles, serial battler against *drakontes*, should have reared a *drakōn* of his own to help him fight other monsters intrigues; he also has an ultimately positive relationship with the Scythian *echidna* (3). His pet's fate was to become the *drakōn* at the heart of a celebrated omen described in the *Iliad* (2.303–32): as the Greeks were sacrificing at a spring beneath a plane tree (cf. 24) in Aulis prior to embarking upon their campaign against Troy, a *drakōn* appeared (from the spring?) and devoured the nine sparrows that were nesting in the tree before being turned to stone. The seer Calchas expounded the omen as meaning that the Greeks were destined to take Troy in the tenth year.

## 26   The Hydra's slow revenge

468–ca. 30 BC

Diodorus 4.36 and 38 (ca. 30 BC); Sophocles *Trachinae* 831–8 (468–406 BC)

Greek

**Diodorus:** 4.36. Whilst he was making his way Heracles arrived at the river Evenus and came across the centaur Nessus ferrying people across the river for a fee. He ferried [Heracles' wife] Deianeira across the river first, fell in love with her because of her beauty and so tried to rape her. But she shouted out to her husband and Heracles shot the centaur. Nessus, in the midst of congress and dying almost instantaneously because of the severity of the blow, told Deianeira that he would give her a love charm to prevent Heracles from desiring sex with any other women. He urged her to take the semen that he had dropped on the ground, blend it into olive oil and the blood that dripped from the arrow, and smear it over Heracles' tunic. Nessus expired immediately after giving this advice to Deianeira. She followed his instructions, collected up his semen and put it in a jar, dipped the arrow into it, and kept the jar secret from Heracles. He crossed the river....

4.38. Heracles planned to make a sacrifice at Cenaeum. He sent his servant Lichas to his wife, Deinaeira, in Trachis. He had been entrusted with the order to fetch the tunic and cloak he usually wore for sacrifices. Deianeira learned from Lichas of Heracles' love for Iole. She wished to have more love herself, so she smeared the tunic with the love charm given her by the centaur, to his destruction. In ignorance of this, Lichas took the clothing to the sacrifice. Heracles put on the smeared tunic. The effect of the corrupting drug was gradual, but he met with great disaster, for the arrow had been armed with the viper's venom. And so as the tunic destroyed his body's flesh with its heat, Heracles, in the utmost pain, killed his servant Lichas, disbanded his army and returned to Trachis. Ever more oppressed by the sickness, Heracles sent Licymnius and Iolaus to Delphi to ask Apollo what he should do about it. But Deianeira was overwhelmed by the magnitude of Heracles' disaster and, feeling guilty about it, ended her life with a noose. The god's response was that Heracles should be taken to Mount Oeta, together with his military equipment, and that they should build a huge pyre beside him. Zeus would take care of the rest. When Iolaus and his men had done what was asked and were watching from a distance to see what would come about, Heracles despaired of his prospects, mounted the pyre and asked anyone who approached to ignite it. No one else had the courage to heed him, and Philoctetes alone was persuaded to do it. He lit the pyre and was given Heracles' bow and arrows in thanks for his service. Thunderbolts fell at once from the sky and the entire pyre was consumed. When Iolaus and his men subsequently came to collect the bones, and could find no trace of them, they supposed that Heracles had passed from the realm of mortals to that of the gods, in accordance with the oracles.

**Sophocles:** [The chorus of women of Trachis speak.] If the centaur's resistless trickery coats his flanks in a cloud of death once the venom has melted into him, the venom born of death, the venom born of the variegated dragon [*drakōn*], how could he see another sun, or even this very day, as he is bonded to the dread form of the Hydra?

Though long disposed of by this time, the Hydra still contrives to be the eventual cause of Heracles' own death in turn. Her venom passes into Nessus's blood and perhaps too into his semen (which Deianeira may well have assumed to be the active ingredient in her erotic charm), and so eventually comes to be smeared over Heracles' skin, to inflict a burning that can only be quenched by fire in turn. Once again we have the theme of a symmetrical battle of fire (**M6**).

The events summarised by Diodorus are expounded at length in Sophocles' tragedy *Trachiniae*, from which a brief but important passage is supplied here—important because it makes it explicit that the burning agent in Deianeira's lotion derives from the Hydra's venom and because it specifies, though we could hardly have doubted it, that the Hydra, usually referred to only by her proper name, is indeed a *drakōn*. The final phrase in the Sophocles passage is a little obscure (and subject to textual dispute), but it appears that 'the dread form of the Hydra' should be taken to refer again to the Hydra's venom, by synecdoche.

In the Diodoran material the deployment of Zeus's thunderbolts explains why no trace of Heracles' bones should have been found, but, after the god's iconic battle with Typhon, his thunderbolts can be seen as an ultimate weapon to use against a dragon and its works (**5, 6, 8–9**).

Despite my title, the long-dead Hydra does not achieve her revenge over Heracles by any design of her own. The story as told initially seems to be one rather of a revenge contrived by Nessus. It is just possible, however, that Nessus, contrite in death, genuinely means to help Deianeira with a charm he believes will warm Heracles up again with love for her. Thus an ancient love spell seeks to cast its victim symbolically into a bathhouse furnace and proclaims: 'Bring me (insert her name)...today, from this hour, burning in her soul and her heart, quickly, quickly, now, now' (*PGM* VII.467–77 = *MWG* no. 208; iii–iv AD). Heracles' insufferable torments will then have been the result of Deianeira's using an excessive dose of the charm, just as the concubine of Philoneos contrived to poison her master to death by giving him an excessive dose of a love potion (Antiphon 1.14–20 = *MWG* no. 77; 430–11 BC).

Theocritus, as we have seen, finds a symbolic link between the pyre that ultimately burns Heracles at death and the pyre used to burn the dragon pair that had attacked him at birth (**20**).

# Chapter 5: Heracles' Dragons (ii): the Hydra

## 27 The Hydra rationalised

ca. 300 BC–iv AD

Palaephatus 38 (Greek; ca. 300 BC)

Heraclitus *De incredibilibus* 18 (Greek; ii AD)

Servius on Virgil *Aeneid* 6.287 (Latin; iv AD)

Greek, Latin

**Palaephatus:** It is said of the Lernaean Hydra that it was a snake with fifty heads but a single body, and that whenever Heracles removed one of her heads, two grew back. And the crab came to aid the Hydra. And then Iolaus came to help Heracles, because the crab was helping the Hydra. If anyone believes that any of this happened, he's a fool. The snake is ridiculous. How is it that, whenever Heracles removed one head, he was not devoured by the remaining ones, and made to suffer for it? The case was rather something like this. Lernus was king of the village, and the village took its name from him. All men lived in villages at that time, and it is the Argives that now occupy that particular village. At that time there were the states of Argos, Mycenae, Tyrene and Lerna, and a king was appointed to rule each of them. The other kings were subject to Eurystheus, son of Sthenelus, son of Perseus, for he had control of the greatest and most populous state, Mycenae. But Lernus refused to be subject to him. So they made war upon him for this reason. At the defile that led into the region of Lerna there was a strong castle, and fifty brave archers guarded it, manning its tower continuously, day and night. The castle was called 'Hydra'. Eurystheus sent Heracles to take the castle. Heracles and his men shot fire against the archers on the castle's tower. Whenever one of them was struck and fell, two more archers stepped up in place of that single one, since the one that had been slain before them was brave. When Lernus was constrained in war by Heracles, he hired some Carian mercenaries. The man that brought the army for him was called Carcinus [Crab], and he was stout and warlike. With his help Lernus held out against Heracles. Then Iolaus, son of Iphicles and Heracles' nephew, came to help him with an army from Thebes. He drew near to the tower attached to the Hydra castle and fired it. With this force Heracles took the archers, destroying the Hydra castle and its army alike. After this happened people wrote that the Hydra was a snake and made the myth up to fit.

**Heraclitus:** It is said that the beast [the Hydra] had many heads, this not being true. Probably she had many young, which, accompanying her and helping their mother, aided her in destroying her attackers.

**Servius:** The 'beast of Lerna' refers to the Hydra, a snake of huge size, which lived in Lerna, a marsh in Argive territory. In Latin it is called the Excetra, because three heads used to grow when one had been cut off. When its heads kept growing back threefold, for all that Heracles was hacking them off at a vigorous rate, he brought fire and burned it up, as the story goes. He is said to have dipped his arrows in its venom. But it is established that the Hydra was in fact a place that belched forth waters that laid waste to a neighbouring town. Here many streams burst forth from a single confined one. When Heracles saw this he burned the place up and so confined the streams of water. Now the Hydra was named from water [*hydōr*].

Palaephatus's rationalising of the Hydra myth is typical of his art and indeed that of other rationalising writers before and after him (**M16**). Palaephatus adhered to the principle that the mythical past was in reality just like the present, and so nothing could be permitted to have happened in a myth that could not happen in the world of his own day. All the monsters, then, had to go, somehow or other (preface). Palaephatus's most notorious rationalising technique is fully on display here: difficult terms—the Hydra, the martial crab—

are arbitrarily displaced into proper names. Palaephatus's slightly contrived description of the castle and its tower (which has provoked some editors to question the text as transmitted) derives from a desire to visualise the castle on the model of the traditional image of the Hydra: the relatively low-lying castle proper corresponds to the Hydra's main body and trailing tail, the tower attached to (*sc.* the side of) it corresponds to its rampant lower neck and the fifty archers atop the tower correspond to its divided upper necks and their heads.

Heraclitus's rationalisation of the Hydra as a mother snake surrounded by her young should be compared with his remarkably similar rationalisation of Cerberus, as he himself acknowledges (**46;** cf. also **52**).

Servius's rationalisation is a clever one: it neatly respects the meaning of the Hydra's Greek name ('water snake') and the creature's shape, with necks branching forth from a single body, as well as the manner of its containment, fire. The novel claim that the creature was able to grow back three heads, as opposed to two, for every one lost is striking. It is founded—if one does not press the implications of the actual arithmetic too hard—in the common notion that its (static) number of heads was a multiple of three, most often nine (cf. **23**, with commentary). The name Excetra may have originated in a garbled borrowing of the Greek term or name Echidna, 'Viper', via Etruscan.

## FURTHER READING

Robert 1920–6:2, 444–7, Amandry 1952, Fontenrose 1959:356–8, Amandry and Amyx 1982, Venit 1989, Boardman 1990a, Kokkorou-Alewras 1990a, Gantz 1993:384–6.

# 6
# *Heracles' Dragons (iii): Ladon, the Dragon of the Hesperides*

The fetching of the golden apples of the Hesperides was the eleventh labour imposed on Heracles. The earliest mention of Ladon, the Dragon of the Hesperides that canonically guarded the apples by hanging in their tree with them, comes in Hesiod's great genealogy of dragons (**1**), where, uniquely and intriguingly, it is said that he 'guards all-gold apples within his great coils in his lair in the dark earth.' This is a rather different image of Ladon from anything found later and suggests something rather Fafnir-like (cf. **B2–7**). For ancient dragons' caves see **M3.a.ii**; for their guardianship of treasure see **M4.b**; and for their guarding of things inside caves see specifically **8** and **78**. It seems to be implied that for Hesiod, Ladon still lives and continues his guardianship. Ladon is also mentioned, **1** aside, in **2** and **98**.

Figure 6 Ladon in his apple tree, fed from a phiale by the Hesperides. Campanian red-figure hydria, ca. 350–40 BC. Private Collection. Redrawn by Eriko Ogden.

## 28 A summary of variant accounts of Heracles, Ladon and the golden apples of the Hesperides

ca. 100 AD

Apollodorus
*Bibliotheca* 2.5.11

Greek

When Heracles had completed his labours in eight years and a month, Eurystheus refused to accept the labour of the stables of Augeas and that of the Hydra and imposed an eleventh labour, namely to fetch golden apples from the Hesperides. Some have told that these apples were in Libya, but they were not. They were on Mt Atlas in the land of the Hyperboreans. Earth made a gift of them to Zeus upon his marriage to Hera. An immortal dragon [*drakōn*] guarded them, the child of Typhon and Echidna, with a hundred heads, and its cries were of every variety. Alongside it the Hesperides too guarded the apples, Aigle, Erytheia, Hesperia and Arethusa.... [An extended narrative of Heracles' long trek to the Hyperboreans intervenes.] Prometheus told Heracles not to go for the apples himself, but to take the sky over from Atlas and send him instead. Persuaded by the advice, this is what he did when he came to the Hyperboreans. Atlas reaped three apples with the help of the Hesperides and came to Heracles. But he now refused to hold the sky [there is a lacuna in the text here in which Heracles apparently began to fool the recalcitrant Atlas into taking back the sky, supposedly temporarily] and that he wished to make a cushion for his head. Upon hearing this Atlas put the apples on the ground and took the sky over from him. And so Heracles picked them up and went off. Some say Heracles did not get the apples from Atlas, but that he reaped them himself after killing the guardian snake. He brought the apples and gave them to Eurystheus. And he in turn made a gift of them to Heracles. Athene took them from him and carried them back. For it was not holy that they should be laid down anywhere.

The general function and significance of the golden apples of the Hesperides elude explanation. Apollodorus's account finds their origin in the earth, where, as we have seen, Hesiod had said that Ladon guarded them (1). As for the location of the Hesperides, the canonical view was indeed that they were located in the extreme west of 'Libya', that is, North Africa. Apollodorus uniquely gives Ladon a hundred heads. He is almost always portrayed as a single-headed serpent, though he can have two or three heads in some of his earliest surviving iconography, ca. 550–400 BC (two heads: *LIMC* Herakles 2692, 2714, Ladon i 12, 15; three heads: *LIMC* Herakles 1702/2680, Ladon i 13, 16). His varied range of cries recalls those attributed to his father Typhon (6).

Apollodorus provides two broad variant versions of how Heracles was able to get the apples, the first involving an immortal Ladon, the second a mortal one. In the first of these the role of the guardian Ladon is ultimately ignored when it comes to the seizing of the apples, which is managed by the proxy Atlas (for Heracles' confidence trick upon Atlas here, cf. the folk-tale type ATU 1530, 'Holding Up the Rock'). In the second variant Heracles duly kills the mortal Ladon to get the apples he guards, in a more predictable fashion. But there was at least a third variant too, as we shall see (31). Eurystheus's return of the apples to Heracles, telegraphically recounted here, should not be understood as a late gesture of kindness from the tyrant. Rather, like the head of Medusa that Polydectes demands of Perseus, they are something of a liability to their possessor, since to lay them on the ground evidently incurs some kind of divine punishment (perhaps the eternal return of the sky to Atlas's shoulders was his punishment for putting them down).

CHAPTER 6: HERACLES' DRAGONS (III): LADON, THE DRAGON OF THE HESPERIDES

## 29 The image of Heracles' battle against Ladon translated to the stars

early v BC–ii AD

Hyginus *Astronomia* 2.6.1 (ii AD), citing [Eratosthenes] *Catasterismi* 1.4 (i BC?) and incorporating Panyassis *Heraclea* F10 Davies/ F15 West (earlier v BC)

Latin

'The man on his knees': Eratosthenes says that this figure is Heracles, positioned above the dragon [*draco*], about which we spoke above, and that he is prepared for battle, holding his lion skin in his left hand and his club in his right. He is trying to kill the dragon that is the guardian of the Hesperides, which is thought never to have closed its eyes under the compulsion of sleep, by virtue of which it is proven all the more to have been suitable as a guardian. Panyassis also speaks about this in his *Heraclea*. Jupiter admired their battle, and so placed it in the stars. Now the dragon holds its head rampant, while Heracles, leaning on his right knee, strives to force down the right side of its head with his left foot. He raises his right hand in a strike, whilst his left is thrust forward with the lion skin. He seems to be fighting with all his strength.

Hyginus speaks no longer of an immortal dragon but of an unsleeping one, a quality Ladon shares with another dragon famous for guarding a golden treasure, the Dragon of Colchis, which guards the golden fleece (86–7, 89–90). Both dragons are characteristically depicted in ancient art as coiling in a tree alongside their treasure. The unsleeping dragon was an easy thing to imagine for the Greeks: after all, snakes cannot close their eyes.

## 30 A vision of Ladon in death

ca. 270–45 AD

Apollonius *Argonautica* 4.1396–1407

Greek

They [the Argonauts] came to the sacred plane on which Ladon, the snake of the earth, had until the day before been guarding the golden apples in the garden of Atlas. Round about the Hesperides nymphs used to busy themselves, singing delightful songs. But at that time, slain by Heracles, he lay cast down at the stump of the apple tree. The tip of his tail alone was still quivering. He lay breathless from his head all the way down his black spine. Flies were drying up over the putrid wounds made by the arrows that left behind them the bitter venom of the Lernaean Hydra in the blood. And close by the Hesperides with their silver arms on their blond heads lamented shrilly.

For the Hellenistic epicist Apollonius, Heracles had evidently cut down the apple tree to get the apples (was it of a vast height?). In killing Ladon with his arrows tipped with the Hydra's venom, Heracles has employed one dragon for the killing of another (**M8.b.iv**): this is one way of getting on terms with the dragon's terrible weaponry. The theme of the dragon's breath is tacitly raised. The dead Ladon can no longer emit the poisonous breath so often associated with serpents (**M7.ii**), but his putrefying body gives rise to a terrible stench of its own, in this case with the aid of the remnants of the Hydra's venom, which was itself famous for its stink: the river Anigrus acquired its permanent bad smell when Pylenor washed off in it the wound that he had received from Heracles' Hydral-venom–impregnated arrow (Pausanias 5.5.10). The word translated here as 'putrid' (*pythomenoisi*) belongs to the same verb exploited to give a folk-etymological derivation of the name Pytho from the rotting corpse of the Delphic dragon (**14**). The flies that are killed by the rising stench resemble in small compass the overflying birds that the living Bagrada Dragon could drop from the air and into its mouth with its pestilential breath (**98**).

Apollonius is actually only one of two sources, the other being Probus (on Virgil *Georgics* 1.205 and 244) to give the Dragon of the Hesperides the name Ladon. In its structure, SYLLABLE + -*ōn*, it resembles several other *drakōn* names, Typhōn, Pythōn, Glycōn (Lucian *Alexander* 18, etc.), and indeed the word *drakōn* itself, which could also function as a proper name.

## 31  How trustworthy were the Hesperides?

ca. 454 BC–ca. 65 AD

Pherecydes F16c Fowler (Greek; ca. 454 AD)

Virgil *Aeneid* 4.480–6 (Latin; ca. 19 BC)

Seneca *Hercules Furens* 524–32 (Latin; ca. 65 AD)

Greek, Latin

**Pherecydes:** Pherecydes says that when Hera was being married by Zeus and the gods brought her gifts, Earth came with the golden apples, branches and all. Hera was amazed by them and gave the command that they should be grown in the garden of the gods, which was beside Atlas. But since the apples were forever being stolen by his daughters, she set a snake, which was of enormous size, to guard them.

**Virgil:** [Dido speaks of a witchlike priestess located in northwest Africa.] Near the boundary of Ocean and the setting sun is the most remote land of the Ethiopians, where greatest Atlas twists on his shoulder the sphere that is set with blazing stars. From this region a priestess of Massylian race has been pointed out to me, the guardian of the temple of the Hesperides. She used to give the dragon [*draco*] its meals, and she looked after the sacred boughs on the tree, sprinkling moist honey and sleepy poppy.

**Seneca:** CHORUS: O Fortune, how you hate brave men! How unfair are the spoils you distribute to the good! Let Eurystheus rule in ease and leisure! Let the one born of Alcmene deploy in war after war the hand that bore up the sky. Let him cut back the fertile necks of the snake [*serpens*, i.e. the Hydra], let him deceive the sisters [i.e. the Hesperides] and bring back the apples, after the dragon [*draco*] set to watch over the valuable apples has given his vigilant eyes over to sleep.

Apollonius and Apollodorus (**28, 30**) suggest that the Hesperides girls and Ladon cooperated fully in the guarding of the golden apples, but this frustratingly allusive series of texts hints that things may have been more complicated. It is likely that the daughters of Atlas who according to Pherecydes kept stealing the apples initially, occasioning the need for Ladon, were none other than the Hesperides themselves, who were indeed sometimes considered to be daughters of Atlas (e.g. Diodorus 4.27.2). Virgil's witchlike priestess seems to be closely identified with the Hesperides, whose temple is her concern: like the Hesperides themselves in classical Greek art, she feeds Ladon. It is no surprise that she should feed him honey, for this was the normal offering given to sacred snakes maintained in sanctuaries in the ancient Greek world (for all that snakes cannot, of course, eat it). But why is she feeding the dragon sleepy poppy? This looks like a reminiscence of the idea that the Hesperides themselves had drugged the congenitally unsleeping Ladon in order to steal the apples from under his nose. Again classical Greek art (*LIMC* Hesperides 2–4, 7, 28, 41, 36, 63, Ladon i 6, 9) appears to support this notion, sometimes showing one Hesperid feeding Ladon from a dish on one side of his apple tree whilst another Hesperid filches apples from the other side. In light of this, the Seneca passage seems to suggest that Heracles deceived the Hesperides into drugging Ladon and taking apples to give to him. Once again classical Greek art supports the notion, showing a Hesperid handing over apples to Heracles, with Eros (Love) sometimes in attendance: Heracles' deception must have

CHAPTER 6: HERACLES' DRAGONS (III): LADON, THE DRAGON OF THE HESPERIDES      61

taken the form of a seduction (*LIMC* Herakles 2703, 2707a, 2717, 2719, 2726, Hesperides 36; cf. Hesperides 38, 62). The notion that the Hesperides should have drugged the unsleeping Ladon to sleep may be derivative of the witch Medea's treatment of the similarly unsleeping Colchis dragon, which similarly hung in a tree to guard its golden treasure (**87, 89**).

## 32   Ladon, Atlas and Perseus

8 AD

Ovid *Metamorphoses* 4.633–62

Latin

Here was Atlas, son of Iapetus, who outstripped all men with his huge body. Under this man as king were the end point of the earth and that part of the sea that puts its waters beneath the Sun's panting horses and welcomes his tired axles. A thousand flocks used to wander through his grassy fields, and so did a similar number of cattle. No neighbours attempted to encroach upon his land. The foliage of his trees shone with gold and covered branches of gold and fruit of gold. 'Guest-friend', Perseus said to him, 'if the distinction of high birth impresses you, Jupiter is my father. But if you are rather an admirer of deeds, you will be amazed at mine. I am looking for shelter and rest.' But Atlas remembered the ancient oracle (Parnassian Themis had given it): 'Atlas, there will come a time when your tree is stripped of its gold and a son of Zeus will have title to this booty.' Fearing this, Atlas had enclosed his orchard with solid walls and had entrusted it to a huge dragon [*draco*] to guard. He kept away all strangers from his territory. To Perseus too he said, 'Go far away, lest the glory of actions about which you lie forsakes you, and so too Jupiter. He added force to his threats and tried to drive him off with his hands as he tarried and as he blended strong words with calm ones. Perseus was lesser in strength (for who could equal Atlas's strength?), but he said, 'Since you hold my good will in contempt, accept this gift.' He turned back and from his left side brought forth the squalid face of Medusa. Being the size he was, Atlas became a mountain. His beard and hair disappeared into woods, his shoulders and hands into ridges. What had previously been his head became the pinnacle on the top of the mountain. His bones became stone. Then, aloft, he grew vastly in all directions (thus, gods, you decreed it), and the whole sky, together with all its stars, rested upon him.

The poet Ovid explains how Atlas was transformed from huge humanoid into a mountain by means of Medusa's head (cf. **59**). Perseus was Heracles' great-grandfather, and both alike were sons of Zeus. Given that this encounter precedes Heracles' theft of the apples, it is incompatible with variants in which Heracles interacts with a still humanoid Atlas (**28**). Here the apples are said to belong to Atlas himself in his humanoid form, and it is for him—and no doubt too his daughters—that Ladon guards them.

## 33   Heracles' battle against Ladon and his seizure of the golden apples allegorised

ca. 400 BC (?)

Herodorus of Heraclea F14 Fowler

Greek

Heracles is written of as wearing the skin of a lion in place of a tunic, carrying a club and acquiring three apples. They told the story that he seized the three apples after killing the dragon [*drakōn*] with his club. That is to say, he overcame the multifarious thoughts of bitter Desire by means of the club of Philosophy, wraping himself in Noble Thought, like a lion skin. And in this way he acquired the apples, which is to say the three Virtues, Not-getting-angry, Not-being-devoted-to-money and Not-being-devoted-to-pleasure. For by means of the club of a Stalwart Soul and the protective skin of the bravest, prudent Reason, he prevailed in the earthly contest against base Desire, persisting in the philosophical life until his death, as the most wise Herodorus wrote.

This summary of Herodorus's allegory is somewhat inconsistent. For instance, does Heracles' club stand for Philosophy or Soul?

## 34  Heracles' battle against Ladon and his seizure of the golden apples rationalised

ca. 30 BC

Diodorus 4.26.2–4

Greek

As his final labour Heracles undertook the fetching of the golden apples [*mēla*] and sailed back to Libya. The mythographers have expressed different views about these apples. Some say that there were golden apples in some gardens or other of the Hesperides in Libya, and that they were continuously watched by a most fearsome dragon [*drakōn*]. Others say that the Hesperides kept herds of sheep that stood out for their beauty, and that they were called 'golden sheep' [*mēla*] in a poetic style because of their beauty, just as Aphrodite is called 'golden' because of her beauty. Others again say that the sheep were of a particular colour that resembled gold and acquired their description for this reason, and that Drakōn was appointed overseer of the flocks, a man who excelled in the strength of his body and in courage, and that he watched the flocks and killed those that made bold enough to attempt to rustle them. Each man will be able to decide about such things however he persuades himself. But Heracles killed the guardian of the apples and brought them back to Eurystheus. Having completed his labours, he waited to receive the gift of immortality, in accordance with Apollo's prophecy.

The historian Diodorus's writings reflect the work of the ii BC rationalising mythographer Dionysius Scytobrachion at this point. The notion that the golden apples were really golden sheep, the term *mēlon* signifying both equally in ancient Greek, was a popular one in ancient writers: cf. also Agroetas *FGrH* 762 F3 (iii BC) and First Vatican Mythographer 1.38 (ix–xi AD). More popular still was the notion that stories about the terrible *drakontes* of myth originated in the mundane activities of men called Drakōn (**M16.a.iii**), for good reasons or none at all. Such stories are told also of Python (**18**), the Dragon of Ares (**80**) and even the dragon sire of Alexander the Great (Ptolemy son of Haephaestion *apud* Photius *Biblotheca* cod. 190, p.148a). Ladon in particular is reduced to a man called Drakōn also by Agroetas and the First Vatican Mythographer as cited, as well as the ii AD Heraclitus (*De incredibilibus* 20), the iv AD Servius (on Virgil *Aeneid* 4.484) and the xii AD Tzetzes (*Chiliades* 2.36.378–80).

### FURTHER READING

Robert 1920–6:2, 488–98, Scherling 1924, Brommer 1942, Matthews 1974:66–71, Brazda 1977:89–132, Boardman 1990a, 1990b, Kokkorou-Alewras 1990b, McPhee 1990, 1992, Gantz 1993:25, 412, Sancassano 1997:63–6, Hansen 2002:197–201.

# 7
# *Heracles' Dragons (iv): Cerberus, the Hound of Hades*

As the twelfth (or eleventh) of his labours, Eurystheus imposed upon Heracles the task of fetching Cerberus, the terrible hound of Hades, from the underworld and bringing him back to him in the Argolid. Those familiar with more modern representations of the hound Cerberus will know of his three dog heads, but may be unaware of his strongly serpentine origins. In his earliest iconography, that of the archaic and earlier classical periods, from ca. 590 BC onwards, he is characteristically represented with a serpent tail, a serpent rising from each of his heads or serpents sprouting out all over his body (*LIMC* Herakles 2553–4, 2560, 2571, 2579, 2581, 2586, 2588, 2595, 2600, 2603–6, 2610–11, 2614, 2616, 2621, 2628). This anguiform nature only occasionally becomes explicit in the literary tradition, though much is made of it by Euphorion, Apollodorus and Seneca (**35, 40, 42**), and it fundamentally underpins Hecataeus's rationalising account (**45**). For Cerberus see also **1–2, 59, 98, 102, 120**. For Cerberus's brother dog Orthus, also occasionally anguiform, see **1** (with commentary).

Figure 7 Heracles brings Cerberus to Eurystheus, who hides in a *pithos*-jar. Archaic Ionian Hydria from Cerveteri, ca. 530 BC. Musée du Louvre. The Bridgeman Art Library.

## 35   A summary account of Heracles' mission to fetch Cerberus

ca. 100 AD

Apollodorus *Bibliotheca* 2.5.12

Greek

A twelfth labour was imposed on Heracles to bring Cerberus from Hades. He had three dog heads, a tail consisting of a dragon [*drakōn*] and on his back he had heads of snakes of all kinds. When he was preparing to go off for Cerberus, he went to Eumolpus in Eleusis, as he wished to be initiated. But he was not able to see the mysteries until he had been purified of the murder of the centaurs, and so he was purified by Eumolpus and then he was initiated. He came to Taenarum in Laconia, where there is the mouth of a descent to Hades, and he went down through this. When the souls saw him, they fled, except for those of Meleager and the Gorgon Medusa. He drew his sword against the Gorgon as if she were alive, but Hermes told him that she was an empty ghost. Arriving near the gates of Hades, he found Theseus and Pirithous, who had made a suit to marry Persephone and was bound. When they saw Heracles they stretched out their hands to him in the hope that they would rise again through his strength. He took Theseus by the hand and roused him up, but although he wanted to make Pirithous rise again the earth moved and he had to let him go. He rolled the rock off Ascalaphos. Because he wanted to provide blood for the ghosts, he slaughtered one of the cattle of Hades. But Menoetes the son of Ceuthonymus, who looked after the cattle, challenged Heracles to a wrestling match. Heracles caught him round the middle and broke his ribs, but he let him go at Persephone's request. He asked Pluton for Cerberus, and Pluton [Hades] told him to take the dog if he could gain control of him without the weapons he had. He found Cerberus at the gates of the Acheron. Protected with a breastplate and draped in the lion's skin, he threw his hands round the dog's neck and refused to let go, mastering and choking the beast until he subjected him to his will, although he kept being bitten by the snake that constituted his tail. So he took him and went on his way, making his ascent through Troezen. Demeter turned Ascalaphus into an owl. Heracles showed Cerberus to Eurystheus and took him back to Hades.

Apollodorus asserts that Heracles descended to Hades through the underworld entrance at Taenarum (cf. **40, 45**), but returned with him through another one at Troezen (cf. Pausanias 2.31.2); whether the change in underworld passage was deliberate or not on Heracles' part remains unclear. The differing places of descent and ascent may be due in part to the competing claims of different Greek cities on behalf of their local underworld entrances. As we shall see, other cities too laid claim to a role in Heracles' famous labour (**41–2**).

Heracles undergoes initiation (cf. **38**) before descending, both to fortify himself against the terrors of the underworld and perhaps also to gain some knowledge of its topography, which would aid his journeys there and back. Those initiated, as Heracles was, at Eleusis were given an anticipatory show of the terrors of the underworld in the course of their initiation (Origen *Contra Celsum* 4.10), whilst other Orphic-Dionysiac initiates were buried with inscribed gold leaves that included route directions to help them find their way through the underworld to a blessed destination (for the best edition and translation of the tablets, see Bernabé and Jiménez San Cristóbal 2008). Lucan (**59**) suggests that Heracles was able to soothe the hissing of Cerberus's snakes with Orphic song.

Heracles' encounter with the ghost of the Gorgon, whose status as either living or dead Heracles might well have been concerned about, given the continuing effectiveness of her decapitated head, perhaps pays tribute to

CHAPTER 7: HERACLES' DRAGONS (IV): CERBERUS, THE HOUND OF HADES

the *Odyssey* episode in which Odysseus consults the ghosts he has called up at the Acheron. Odysseus finally abandons his consultation when he becomes overwhelmed by the fear that Persephone might send a Gorgon head up from Hades for him (11.633–5).

Heracles' wrestling match with Menoetes looks like a displacement of the variant motif found in art whereby Heracles had to fight not Cerberus himself in order to take him, but his owner, Hades, in order to win the right to do so (e.g. *LIMC* Herakles 2553).

For the notion that Heracles had to subdue Cerberus without arms, or at any rate without conventional arms, see **39–40**.

### 36   An early mention of Cerberus, and his function explained

vii BC

Hesiod *Theogony* 767–74

Greek

And there, before this, stand the resounding halls of the strong god of the underworld, Hades, and dread Persephone. A terrible and pitiless dog guards them in front, and he has an evil craft. He fawns and wags his tail and waggles both ears at those who are coming in, but he does not allow them to come out again. Rather, he keeps watch and eats whomever he catches going outside the gates of strong Hades and dread Persephone.

The *Iliad* (8.367–8) and the *Odyssey* (11.623–6) already refer to Heracles' labour to fetch Cerberus up from the underworld as a commonplace, though neither actually names the dog. He is given his name in the *Theogony*'s genealogy of dragons (**1**), and in this passage from the same text his function is explained. Contrary to many modern—illogical—assumptions, perhaps influenced unduly by Virgil (**43**), Cerberus does not guard the underworld against intrusion from without but rather keeps the ghosts penned up within. To this extent, for all his fearsomeness, he may be regarded as a friend and ally of the living. And as it happens, in his canonical form Cerberus is never credited with the direct killing of a living person, although he is the inadvertent creator of the poison aconite (**41**); a much-altered Cerberus is, however, said to have killed Pirithous (**45**). It is difficult to imagine what final sanction Cerberus does in effect exercise against the ghosts, devour them though he may: they cannot die twice, as Eustathius notes (**41**).

### 37   Cerberus's keeper Aeacus, the circling dogs of the underworld and the Echidna

405 BC

Aristophanes *Frogs* 465–77

Greek

[Aeacus addresses Heracles.] O you are disgusting, shameless, brazen and accursed, accursed, accursed in every possible way! You are the one who drove off our dog Cerberus. You grabbed him in a stranglehold and shot off, and then escaped with him at a run, the dog that I used to watch over. But now you are caught round the middle. So are you confined by the black-hearted rock of the Styx and the crag of the Acheron, dripping in blood, and also by the circling dogs of the Cocytus and hundred-headed Echidna, who will tear apart your guts. The moray eel of Tartessus will latch onto your lungs and the Teithrasian Gorgons will draw out your bloodied testicles, together with your guts. I will run hot-foot to fetch them.

Cerberus's wrangler Aeacus is understandably angry to see, in this comic play, the return to the underworld of the man who stole his dog. The implication that Cerberus is merely one of many dogs that police the underworld, with others running a protective circuit around it, is intriguing, as is his association with the Echidna. The Echidna is associated with the depths of the earth elsewhere (**1, 134**), but here alone is she given the hundred heads that make her such a good match for her consort Typhon (for Typhon's hundred snake heads see **5–6**). Given that Hesiod's description of her (**1**) implies that her single snake tail ends in a devouring snake head, perhaps the hundred heads are to be construed similarly as attached to a hundred snake tails. Elsewhere in this same play Heracles notes that upon descending to the underworld one encounters 'tens of thousands of snakes and strange-looking beasts' (*Frogs* 143). The moray eel of Tartessus (in south-western Spain) is a bizarre comedic take on the sorts of monsters and horrors that traditionally inhabit the underworld's Tartarus. A Gorgon in itself would constitute a much more traditional underworld horror (cf. Homer *Odyssey* 11.633–5; **35**), but in this case the opportunity is seized to take a satirical swipe at some (female?) inhabitants of the Attic deme of Teithras.

## 38   Persephone freely gives Cerberus to Heracles

ca. 30 BC

Diodorus 4.25.1, 4.26.1

Greek

**4.25.1.** Having completed his tenth labour, he received the command from Eurystheus to bring Cerberus from Hades into the light. Assuming that it would help him in this labour, he went to Athens and participated in the Eleusinian mysteries. At that time Musaeus son of Orpheus presided over the rite.

**4.26.1.** According to the myths that have been handed down to us, this Heracles descended into the regions of Hades. He was welcomed by Persephone as a brother would have been. By the grace of Persephone he brought up Theseus together with Pirithous, liberating them from their bonds. He was given the dog bound up and brought it away against all expectation and exhibited it to people.

For Heracles' preparation for descent to the underworld by being initiated into the Eleusinian mysteries, cf. **35, 42**. For Persephone's free gift of the dog to Heracles, see further **42** again.

## 39   Heracles commanded to master Cerberus without iron or shield

Hellenistic-Byzantine

Schol. Homer *Iliad* 5.395–7

Greek

They say that Heracles was commanded by Pluton [Hades] to master Cerberus without shield or iron, and that he used his lion skin instead of his shield, and that he made stone points for his arrows, and that after his victory when the god opposed him again Heracles became angry and shot him.

For the tradition that Heracles was commanded by Hades to master Cerberus without iron or conventional shield, cf. **38, 40**.

## 40   The most elaborate account of Heracles' dragging of Cerberus out of the underworld

ca. 65 AD

Seneca *Hercules Furens* 782–829

Latin

[Theseus speaks.] After this the palace of greedy Dis [Hades] hoves into view. This is where the savage Stygian dog terrorises the shades, shaking his three heads and baying loudly as he guards the kingdom. Snakes lick his head, filthy with gore. His neck bristles with vipers, and to form his twisting tail a long dragon [*draco*] hisses. His spirit matches his appearance. As he senses the movement of feet, he lifts his shaggy locks with their quivering snakes and with pricked ears catches the sound made. He is, after all, accustomed to detect the shades. When Heracles, son of Zeus, stood close, the suspicious dog sat in his cave and was a little afraid. Then, all at once, he struck terror into the silent world with a heavy barking. The threatening snakes hissed all across his shoulders. The roar of the terrible voice issuing forth from his three mouths terrified even the shades in the realm of the blessed. Then Heracles took from his left arm the wild, grinning Cleonaean head [the pelt of the Nemean Lion] to defend himself with it, and shielded himself with the generous cover it offered. In his conquering right hand he brandished his great club. He wheeled the club around to strike blow upon blow in an unrelenting assault, first on one side, then the other. The dog was tamed and gave up his threats. Tired, he hung all his heads and came fully away from his cave. His two masters watched in fear from their thrones and commanded that the dog should be taken. Heracles asked for me too, and they gave me to him.

**807.** Then, stroking the monster's heavy necks with his hand, he fitted a lead of adamant upon him. Forgetting himself, the dog, the unsleeping guard of the dark kingdom, submissively dropped his ears, allowed himself to be led, acknowledged his new master, obedient with lowered head, and beat both his sides with his snake-bearing tail. But when they came to the shores of Taenarum, and the strange radiance of the light he had never known struck his eyes, he recovered his spirit, tamed though he had been, and shook his great chains in rage. He almost carried his victor off, as he pulled back, forcing him to bend forwards and shift his stance. Then Heracles looked to my hands too. With our twin might we both dragged the dog, raging with anger and battling in vain against us, and brought him out onto the world's surface. When he saw the bright daylight and caught sight of the unclouded expanses of the shining sky, he shut his eyes tight and drove out the hated day. He turned his gaze back and sought the ground with all of his necks. He buried his head in the shadow cast by Heracles. Then a packed crowd arrived, shouting for joy, their foreheads wreathed with laurel, to sing the deserved praises of the great Heracles.

Theseus's monologue in Seneca's tragedy offers by far the most elaborate description of Heracles' dragging of Cerberus out of the underworld to survive from antiquity. Theseus's own direct involvement in the extraction is anomalous.

Seneca pays much attention to Cerberus's snakes, making it clear that he not only has a snake tail, but also that snake heads grow from his neck and shoulders, a configuration that honours the image type of Cerberus often found on archaic and classical Greek vases. Despite all this, Seneca sympathetically and successfully represents Cerberus's personality as very much that of a dog, in both his aggressive and submissive phases. It is not clear where Cerberus is to be imagined to have found the gore that befouls him. The Land of the Blessed, to which the sound of Cerberus's barking reaches, is normally conceived of as a separate division of the underworld, at some remove from the principal home of the unhappy shades.

Seneca subscribes to the tradition that Heracles was permitted by Hades and Persephone to take Cerberus on condition that he could master him himself, and probably too to the tradition that Hades also made the proviso that he should do this without recourse to metal weapons, given that Heracles is only said here to have used his club and his lion's skin (cf. **35, 39**).

For the nature of the underworld entrance at Taenarum, see **45**. Seneca adopts the theme of Cerberus's terror at the unaccustomed daylight upon his first emergence from the underworld normally associated with the tradition of his emergence at Heraclea Pontica, but can say nothing of the aconite, which was associated only with that particular underworld entrance.

The joyful crowd that greets Heracles and Theseus as they emerge with Cerberus marks the start of Heracles' triumphant parade of the dog back to Eurystheus in the Argolid; cf. 42.

## 41  Cerberus is dragged up at Heraclea Pontica and creates the poisonous aconite with his slaver or his vomit

earlier iv BC–Byzantine

Xenophon *Anabasis* 6.2.2 (Greek; earlier iv BC)

Ovid *Metamorphoses* 7.406–19 (Latin; 8 AD)

Pomponius Mela 1.92 (Latin; ca. 43 AD)

Schol. Apollonius *Argonautica* 2.353 (Greek; Hellenistic-Byzantine), incorporating Herodorus of Heraclea F31 Fowler (ca. 400 BC) and Euphorion F41 Lightfoot (later iii BC)

Schol. Nicander *Alexipharmaca* 13b (Greek; Hellenistic-Byzantine)

Dionysius Periegetes 788–92 (Greek; ii AD)

Eustathius *Commentary on Dionysius Periegetes* ad loc. (Greek; xii AD)

Greek, Latin

**Xenophon:** ... the Acherusian Chersonese [adjacent to Heraclea Pontica], where Heracles is said to have gone down for the dog Cerberus, where now they show the indications of his descent at a depth of more than two stades...

**Ovid:** In order to kill Theseus, Medea made up some aconite, which she had once brought with her from Scythian shores [i.e. Heraclea Pontica]. They say that it grew up from the teeth of the echidnaean dog. For there is a blind cave with a dark gape. The way slopes downwards, and it was along this that the Tirynthian hero dragged up Cerberus, struggling and averting his eyes from the daylight and the shining rays, with chains twisted from adamant. He was roused to a frenzied anger and filled the breezes with three sets of barking all at once and besprinkled the green fields with white foam. Men hold that this foam developed and took nourishment from the fertile and fecund soil and acquired the power to harm. Because these plants thrive on the hard crag, the country folk call them 'aconite'.

**Schol. Apollonius:** 'Projecting promontory': This is a headland near Heraclea, which local people call Acherousion. Herodorus and Euphorion in his *Xenios* say that Cerberus was brought up there by Heracles and vomited up bile, out of which the drug called aconite grew.

**Scholiast to Nicander:** They say that aconite grew up from Cerberus's vomit. For it is told that when Cerberus was brought up from the underworld he could not endure the rays of the sun and vomited, and this plant was born from his vomit.

**Pomponius Mela:** First on the Black Sea the Maryandyni inhabit a city given them, as they say, by the Argive Heracles. It is called Heraclea, which supports the claim. Nearby is an Acherusian cave that goes down all the way to the ghosts, it is said, and it was out of here that they think Cerberus was dragged up.

**Dionysius Periegetes:** ... and the sacred plain of the Maryandyni. There they say that the great bronze-voiced dog of infernal Cronides [Hades], dragged up by the hands of great-minded Heracles, cast forth from its mouths a running slaver, which the earth took up, and there it produced a bane...

**Eustathius on Dionysius Periegetes:** In the land of the Mariandyni there grows a deleterious plant, the aconite, about which myth says that the bronze-voiced Cerberus, the hound of Hades, when he was being dragged up from Hades by the great-minded Heracles, went terribly mad and threw out of his mouth a slavering juice or liquid. The earth there took it up and produced the bane of the aconite. This is the name of the poison, against which it is impossible to struggle.... Arrian [*FGrH* 156 F76a] writes as follows about such things: 'On the far side of the river Sangarius the Mariandyni are neighbours of the Paphlagonians. There the city of Heraclea is founded, where the Cimmerians, eating aconite-grass, suffered misfortune. For it was their ancestral custom to eat grass.' Of old the aconite, they say, was harmless but later it became an evil drug because of its poison, which dripped from the vipers [*echidnai*] that grew out of Cerberus's head, and damaged the grass. And no doubt someone being smart with this myth and putting down this labour of Heracles will say that Heracles did nothing good here. For a Cerberus staying below is not as great a bane for mankind as a Cerberus brought up. For formerly he sat over the dead, who cannot die twice, but when he appeared in the world above and created the aconite he became a great evil for the living.

Taenarum and Troezen (**35, 40**) were not the only places to lay claim to Heracles' Cerberus labour. Heraclea Pontica also laid claim to his return at any rate and, since it was named for him, may conceivably have done so since its foundation, ca. 560 BC. Heraclea identified the hole through which Heracles had returned as a cave in the valley of its local Acheron river (not to be confused with the famous Acheron of Thesprotia), a cave that also served the city as an oracle of the dead and was the place where the Spartan regent Pausanias, victor over the invading Persians at the battle of Plataea, called up the ghost of the woman he had killed, Cleonice, in the early 470s (Plutarch *Cimon* 6, *Moralia* 555c, Pausanias 3.17, Aristodemus *FGrH* 104 F8). Perhaps the previous dislodging of Cerberus had made it easier for the ghosts to leave, or at any rate present themselves at the edge of, the underworld at that point.

The tradition is undecided as to whether the Cerberan substance that gave birth to the aconite was the dog's slayer or, more touchingly, vomit induced by terror at the daylight the dog had never seen before. Either way, although (Eustathius aside) we assume the substance came from his dog mouths, its poisonous nature can only have been generated by Cerberus's serpentine element. See further **41**.

When Ovid gives the epithet 'echidnaean' to Cerberus, he may be alluding to the vipers (in Greek *echidnai*) that grow upon him (cf. **40**) or to Cerberus's mother, Echidna (**1–2**): perhaps both.

## 42  Heracles parades Cerberus through Greece as he takes him back to Eurystheus

ca. 416 BC–ca. 500 AD

Seneca *Hercules Furens* 49, 55–63 (Latin; ca. 65 AD)

Euphorion F71 Lightfoot (Greek; later iii BC)

Euripides *Heracles* 610–19 (Greek; ca. 416 BC)

Critias *Pirithous* TrGF 43 F1 lines 10–14 (Greek; before 403 BC)

Hesychius s.v. *eleutheron hydōr* (Greek; ca. 500 AD)

Greek, Latin

**Seneca:** [Juno speaks.] It is not enough for him just to be able to return from the underworld. The limitation placed upon the shades is undone.... A way back has been laid open from the deepest realm of the ghosts, and the sacred rites of dreadful death lie exposed. But he exults over me, exhilarated by his breaking open of the shades' prison, and with arrogant hand he leads the black dog through the cities of Greece. I saw the daylight shrink back upon sight of Cerberus, and the sun grow pale. I too was shaken with terror, and I took fear at the order I had given as I looked upon the threefold necks of the defeated monster.

**Euphorion:** ...yellow...profuse...foaming...falling down underneath his shaggy belly from behind, the dragons [*drakontes*] that constituted his tail licked around his sides. His dark blue eyes flashed like lightning. Whenever iron is broken, such flashings leap up through the air, from furnaces or from Meligounis [the island of Lipara near Hephaestian Sicily], whilst the anvil resounds to the hammer, or they leap up through sooty Etna, dwelling-place of Asteropos. Heracles came to spiteful Eurystheus's Tiryns alive, up from out of Hades after completing twelve labours, and the fearful women marvelled at him together with their children at the crossroads of Midea, abounding in barley.

**Euripides:**
AMPHITRYON: Did you actually go down to the house of Hades, my child?
HERACLES:     Yes, and I brought the beast of three heads into the light.

AMPHITRYON: Did you get control of him with a fight or by gift of the goddess?
HERACLES: With a fight. I was fortunate to have seen the rites of the initiates.
AMPHITRYON: So is the beast in the house of Eurystheus?
HERACLES: A grove of Chthonia [Demeter 'of the earth'] and the city of Hermion [Hermione] are minding him.
AMPHITRYON: And Eurystheus doesn't know that you have come up from the earth?
HERACLES: No, he doesn't. I came here first to see what was going on.
AMPHITRYON: How is it that you spent so much time under the earth?
HERACLES: I took time because I was escorting Theseus out of Hades, father.

**Critias:** [Heracles addresses Aeacus, warder of Hades and wrangler of Cerberus.] I come here under compulsion, subject to the commands of Eurystheus, who has sent me to bring the dog of Hades back alive to the gates of Mycenae. He has no wish to see the dog, but he thought he had discovered in this labour something I would be unable to accomplish.

**Hesychius:** In Argos slaves that are being freed drink from the spring of Cynadra, because it was by this route that Cerberus escaped and got his freedom.

These passages shed a few points of light on Heracles' parading of Cerberus through Greece en route back to Eurystheus. It is noteworthy that neither Midea nor, especially, Hermione, at the end of its peninsula, is on any direct route to Mycenae, Argos or Tiryns (the various homes given to Eurystheus) from either Taenarum or Heraclea Pontica.

Euphorion's description of Cerberus (cf. **41**) gives him a tail consisting of multiple *drakontes* and eyes that flash forth fire, like many ancient dragons (**M6.a.iii**).

In the Senecan prologue Juno regrets her harrassment of Heracles (cf. **19–20, 22**) and scorns Heracles' triumphant parading of Cerberus through Greece. The notion that the daylight should shrink back upon sight of Cerberus is a witty inversion of the established notion that Cerberus rather shrank back in terror at the unaccustomed daylight as Heracles dragged him out of the underworld (**40–1**).

In the Euripidean conversation, Amphitryon's question as to whether Heracles had to fight for Cerberus alludes to two variant traditions, that according to which Heracles had to fight Hades for Cerberus and that according to which Persephone freely gave Cerberus to Heracles (**38**). A grove of Demeter in her underworld aspect would be a comforting place for a traumatised Cerberus to rest (cf. **41**). Hermione also had the added benefit of famously being so close to the underworld itself, via its own local entrance to it, that those buried there were absolved of the duty to pay the ferryman (Strabo C373). Hermione was in fact one of the several places that claimed to have been the site of Heracles' emergence from the underworld (Pausanias 2.35.10), and Euripides' use of it as a staging post in Cerberus's journey here seemingly pays tribute to that tradition.

For Aeacus's role as Cerberus's wrangler in the underworld, see **37**. Eurystheus's dismay at being unexpectedly confronted with Cerberus is well illustrated on a Caeretan hydria of ca. 530–20 BC, on which Heracles restrains an excited, snake-covered dog whilst a desperate Eurystheus comically tries to hide from him inside a large earthenware storage jar or *pithos* (*LIMC* Herakles 2616).

In asserting that Cerberus escaped in returning to the underworld, Hesychius implies a more interesting conclusion to his surface sojourn than Apollodorus, who notes merely that Heracles took him back to the underworld after showing him to Eurystheus (35). Hesychius seems to state that Cerberus got back into the underworld through the spring itself, the name of which was perhaps folk-etymologised as 'Dog Water.'

## 43   The Sibyl drugs Cerberus in his lair to allow Aeneas to enter the underworld

ca. 19 BC

Virgil *Aeneid* 6.417–25

Latin

Cerberus makes these realms resound with three-throated barking as, a monstrous form, he lies in the cave opposite. The seer [the Cumaean Sibyl], seeing his neck bristle with snakes, throws a pellet, made drowsy with honey and drugged meal. He, opening his three throats in ravening hunger, snatches it up as it is thrown, relaxes his massive back, sprawls on the ground and extends his vast bulk over the whole cave. Aeneas gets past the entrance, and, with the guardian buried in sleep, swiftly moves on from the bank of the wave of no return.

So, in Virgil's epic, the Cumaean Sibyl smuggles Aeneas past Cerberus on his way down into the underworld, where he will learn of Rome's future glory. The passage is unique and remarkable for its implicit but inevitable contradiction of Hesiod (36) in suggesting that Cerberus idly guards the underworld from intrusion from without. In drugging Cerberus to sleep, and that too specifically in light of his serpent element, the Sibyl takes on the role of Medea as she drugs the Colchis dragon for Jason (87, 89) and the Hesperides as they drug Ladon for Heracles (31), and in so doing offers further confirmation that Cerberus belongs, in his nature and in his story world, with the other great dragons.

## 44   Cerberus speaks!

ca. 160–80 AD

Lucian *Dialogues of the Dead* 4

Greek

MENIPPUS: Cerberus, since I'm related to you as being a 'dog' myself, tell me, by the Styx, what sort of condition was Socrates in when he came down to you? Since you're a god, you're probably able not just to bark but also to speak in human fashion, when you wish to do so.

CERBERUS: Seen from afar, Menippus, he seemed to approach with composed face and have no fear of death, and this was the impression he wanted to give to those who stood outside the entrance to the underworld. But when he had taken a look down into the abyss and seen the dark, and when I had bitten him and dragged him on by the foot as he tarried because of the hemlock, he wailed like babies do, wept for his children and became desperate to find some escape.

MENIPPUS: So the man was just a charlatan philosopher, and did not really hold death in contempt?

CERBERUS: No, but when he began to see that his lot was unavoidable, he emboldened himself and made as if he was content to suffer what he was by all means bound to, so that the watching bystanders would admire him. In general I could say of all such men that they are bold and brave as far as the entrance to the underworld, but it's what they find inside that constitutes the unfailing test of them.

| | |
|---|---|
| **Menippus:** | How did I seem to you as I made my descent? |
| **Cerberus:** | You alone, Menippus, made your descent in a fashion worthy of your sort, along with Diogenes before you, because you came in without compulsion or force, but willingly, laughing, and pouring scorn on all around. |

A satirical dialogue pointing up the irrational fear of death that can be expected even in the most strong-willed and principled of philosophers. Socrates' composure in the face of death had been documented in Plato's *Phaedo* (*passim*), as indeed had the effects upon him of the hemlock poison with which he was executed, and which numbed his body from the feet up. (Some think the *explicit* reference to hemlock here is intrusive, holding that Cerberus's point is made more effectively if Socrates is slowed solely by his own hypocritical fear of death rather than by the poison.)

The third-century BC Menippus of Gadara, a frequent anti-hero of Lucian's, ever cheerful in the face of death, like Diogenes before him, was a Cynic philosopher. The name of the Cynics (*kynikoi*) was actually derived from word for 'dog' (*kyn-*), possibly because they had initially congregated at Athens's Cynosarges (White Dog) gymnasium, and the philosophers themselves were accordingly commonly referred to as 'dogs.'

It need hardly be said that Cerberus, god or otherwise, was not normally attributed with a human voice; nor were any of the great *drakontes* of Greek myth, with the significant exception of Typhon, who had a humanoid head and who, with his premature boasts, might be thought to have spoken rather too much (8). Nor was it a normal duty of Cerberus's to speed the entry of the newly dead into the underworld. He is given the job here only to highlight Socrates' hypocrisy. Cerberus is not strongly characterised in the speech given to him: he delivers the wise lessons of the levelling underworld with the same urbane assurance as its other denizens do throughout the *Dialogues of the Dead* and Lucian's other Menippean works. But in his case the contrast between manner and exterior is more striking, and particularly pleasing.

## 45 Cerberus rationalised (i) as a pure serpent

early v BC–later ii AD

Pausanias 3.25.4–6 (Greek; later ii AD), incorporating Hecataeus *FGrH* 1 F27 (early v BC)

Hyginus *Astronomia* 2.14 (Latin; ii AD)

Greek, Latin

**Pausanias:** On the promontory [at Taenarum] there is a temple made like a cave and before it an effigy of Poseidon. Some of the Greeks composed poems in accordance with which Heracles brought up the hound of Hades at this point, although there is no way bearing under the earth through the cave, nor is one readily persuaded that there is some underground house of the gods into which souls are gathered. But Hecataeus of Miletus found a plausible explanation. He said that a terrible snake was reared at Taenarum, and that it was called 'the hound of Hades' because anyone it had bitten was bound to die at once because of the venom, and he said that Heracles brought this snake to Eurystheus. Homer (for he first called what Heracles brought 'the hound of Hades') neither gave it any name nor fashioned it from multiple forms as in the case of the Chimaera. Later poets gave it the name Cerberus and made it resemble a dog in general, but said that it had three heads. But no more did Homer say that it was a dog, man's best friend, than if he called a dog of Hades when it was a dragon [*drakōn*].

**Hyginus:** But others maintain that the constellation of Ophiuchus is Heracles killing the snake at the river Sagaris in Lydia, which was killing people in large numbers and stripping the riverbank of crops.

Hecataeus's very early rationalisation of Cerberus serves to demonstrate how dominant the notion of his dragon element was in the archaic and early classical periods. It is also the earliest attested rationalisation of any of the great *drakontes*. The equally rational Pausanias objects that the cave at Taenarum, at the tip of the Peloponnese's Mani peninsula—which functioned, like Heraclea Pontica (**41**) as an oracle of the dead (Plutarch *Moralia* 560e–f and *Numa* 4; *Suda* s.v. *Archilochos*)—was finite and permitted no passage down to or up from the world of the ghosts below. For the Chimaera see **48–53**.

Hyginus's brief statement of a myth potentially projected into the stars (the technical term is 'catasterised') in the constellation of Ophiuchus is puzzling: on the one hand there is no river Sagaris in Lydia; on the other a carnivorous snake does not devour crops (though the fire-breathing Chimaera destroyed crops with her breath: **48–9**). The Sagaris is probably a garbled version of the river Sangarius, which is not in Lydia but in adjacent northern Phrygia, the river Eustathius tightly associates with Heraclea Pontica, Cerberus and the creation of the aconite (**41**). And this provides the clue that the Sagaris snake may have originated in another rationalisation of Cerberus. Does the destruction of the crops refract Cerberus's corruption of the local grasses into the poisonous aconite?

## 46  Cerberus rationalised (ii) as a dog or dogs

earlier iii BC–ii AD

Philochorus *FGrH* 328 F18b (earlier iii BC)

Heraclitus *De incredibilibus* 33 (ii AD)

Greek

**Philochorus:** The snatching of the girl Persephone by Aidoneus, the king of the Molossians, who had an exceptionally large dog called Cerberus, with whom he subsequently destroyed Pirithous, who had come to him to snatch his wife together with Theseus. Heracles happened by and saved Theseus as he was about to be destroyed in the same way as Pirithous had been.

**Heraclitus:** The truth of Cerberus could be the same as about the Hydra. For he had two puppies. Since they always walked alongside their father he seemed to have three heads.

Philochorus rationalises the underworld by bringing its apparatus to the surface and making it the realm of a mortal king. Hades becomes Aidoneus; no doubt he is made king of the Molossians because they lived adjacent to the Thesprotians, in whose realm was the most famous of the underworld entrances and oracles of the dead, that of the river Acheron (Pausanias 9.30.6). In all this, Cerberus is reduced to a mere mortal dog, however large, and paradoxically given the opportunity for the first time actually to kill to someone.

Heraclitus's telegraphic note on Cerberus also implies similarly that his origin lay in a mortal dog, or rather the lazy misperception of a trio of them; cf. his rationalisations of the Hydra, to which he refers (cf. *De incredibilibus* 18 Hydra; cf. **24**, commentary), and also of the Chimaera (**52**).

## 47  Cerberus allegorised as the flesh-devouring earth

ix–xi AD

First Vatican Mythographer 1.57

Latin

Tale of Hercules and Tricerberus. Hercules, descending to the underworld to rescue Theseus, feared lest Tricerberus might attack him and tear him apart. So he attacked Cerberus himself and dragged him out of the underworld. When he saw the unaccustomed light of the world above, he cast forth foam from his mouth. It is said that from this foam was born the poisonous herb by the name of aconite. For Cerberus is the earth, which is the devourer of all bodies, whence he is called Cerberus, as if *creo-boros*, that is 'flesh-devouring'.

The name Tricerberus celebrates the dog's three heads. *Creoboros* is a genuine Greek word and does indeed mean 'flesh-devouring', but it has no part to play in the genuine etymology of Cerberus's name, which remains obscure. For the aconite, cf. **41**.

## FURTHER READING

Cerberus: Hartwig 1893, Robert 1920–6:ii, 483–88, Eitrem 1921, Robertson 1980, Smallwood 1990, Gantz 1993:22–3, Sancassano 1997:67–9.

Entrances to the underworld and their associations with oracles of the dead: Ogden 2001, 2010.

# 8
# The Chimaera, Slain by Bellerophon

The tale of Bellerophon's slaying of the Lycian composite dragon, the Chimaera, as one of a brief series of three labours is already told in the *Iliad*. The Chimaera was enormously popular in art from the time of this seventh-century poem onwards, as was Bellerophon's winged horse, Pegasus. But whilst the Chimaera endured in the literary tradition, she received little further elaboration there. The Chimaera's claim to be regarded as a 'composite *drakōn*' may initially seem rather slight, given that her *drakōn* element makes up only a small proportion of her body, that is, her tail. But her signature fiery breath is characteristic of *drakontes* (**M6.a.ii**; cf. **M7**), and her fundamental nature, clearly, is that of *drakōn*: evidently the tail wags the dog. For the Chimaera see also **1–2, 14, 45**.

Figure 8 The Chimaera. Etruscan amphora, ca. 500 BC. Archaeological Museum, Milan. © Mondadori Electa / The Bridgeman Art Library.

## 48 Bellerophon's battle against the Chimaera: a summary account

ca. 100 AD

Apollodorus *Bibliotheca* 2.3.2

Greek

Iobates read the letter and ordered Bellerophon to kill the Chimaera in the belief that he would be destroyed by the beast. It was not easy for many men, let alone just one, to catch her. Her forepart consisted of a lion, her tail of a dragon [*drakōn*] and she had a third head in the middle, that of a goat, through which she sent forth fire. She laid waste to the land and plundered the cattle. For although she was a single creature, she had the power of three beasts. It is said too that this Chimaera was reared by Amisodarus, as Homer too has said, and she was spawned by Typhon and Echidna, as Hesiod relates. Bellerophon mounted himself on Pegasus, the winged horse he had that was born of Medusa and Poseidon. He flew high into the air and shot the Chimaera from the back of him.

Of all ancient dragons, it is the Chimaera that is most frequently and consistently associated with the breathing of fire (**M6.a.ii**), and the fire breathing is usually associated, as here, with the middle, goat's head. Perhaps this is to bestow a degree of formidability on the one of the creature's heads that threatens to be risible rather than terrible. As a destroyer of land and plunderer of cattle, the Chimaera is characterised as a typical marauding dragon calling for heroic intervention.

In the most typical iconography of the battle, Bellerophon forces his spear down into the Chimaera below from the back of Pegasus (e.g. *LIMC* Pegasos 152). This vignette was ultimately to mutate into the canonical medieval and Renaissance image of St George killing his dragon (cf. **160–1**). In other scenes the tale's two fantastical creatures are displayed, with or without the less interesting Bellerophon himself, facing each other in an elegant mirrored composition (e.g. *LIMC* Pegasos 209).

For the Chimaera's place in dragon genealogy, referred to here, see **1–2**.

## 49 The earliest account of the Chimaera, and its context amid the labours of Bellerophon

vii BC

Homer *Iliad* 6.152–95, 16.328–9

Greek

**6.152.** In a nook of horse-rearing Argos is the city of Ephyre [Corinth]. This is where Sisyphus was, who was the trickiest of men, Sisyphus the son of Aeolus. He had a son, Glaucus, and Glaucus in turn had a son of his own, the blameless Bellerophon. The gods gave him beauty and desirable manliness. But Proetus contrived wicked things against him in his heart. He drove him from his people of the Argives, since he was better by far. For Zeus wielded his sceptre over him. Proetus's wife, the lady Anteia, developed a mad lust for Bellerophon and wanted to sleep with him in secret. But in no way could she persuade the sensible and high-minded Bellerophon. So she made up lies and spoke to King Proetus as follows: 'May you die if you do not kill Bellerophon, who wanted to sleep with me against my will.' So she spoke, and the king was gripped by anger at the sort of thing he heard. He fell short of killing him, however, for he could not bring himself to do that in his heart, but he sent him to Lycia, giving him baleful symbols, drawing them, many and fatal, in a folded tablet. He bade him show them to his father-in-law, to his doom. But he came to Lycia with the blameless escort of the gods. When he came to Lycia and the river Xanthus, the king of broad Lycia honoured him generously. He entertained him for nine days and sacrificed nine oxen. When the tenth rosy-fingered dawn manifested itself, he questioned him and asked to see whatever message he brought from his son-in-law Proetus. But when he had digested his son-in-law's wicked message, he first bade him slay the irresistible Chimaera. She was of divine descent and did not belong to mankind. In front she was a lion, in the rear she was a dragon [*drakōn*] and in the middle a goat [*chimaira*] breathing forth the terrible might of burning fire. He slew her trusting in the portents of the gods. In the second place he fought the glorious Solymi. He said that the battle against them was the most difficult one he entered of all his battles against men. And in the third place he slew the Amazons, the equivalents of men. As he was returning the king contrived another cunning plot against him. He selected the best men from the whole of broad Lycia and set an ambush for Bellerophon with them. But they did not come home, not at all. For the blameless Bellerophon slew them all. When he recognised that Bellerophon was the mighty scion of a god, he kept him with him, and gave him his daughter in marriage, giving half of the whole of his kingdom. And the Lycians cut out for him a plot of land far superior to all the others, beautiful for growing and for ploughing, for him to maintain himself with. [195]

**16.328.** . . . Amisodarus [sc. of Lycia], who reared the irresistible Chimaera, an evil to many people. [329]

Blink and you will miss it. This narrative contains the foundational account of the Chimaera, so far as the later ancient tradition is concerned. Neither the Chimaera's backstory nor the great battle itself was ever really elaborated beyond Homer's few words, with the exception of the details first that Bellerophon fought her from the back of Pegasus (**48, 50**), and secondly that he killed her with molten lead (**51**).

One could wish to know more of the mysterious Amisodarus. But as to the Chimaera herself, Homer hints that she is a typical marauding dragon ('an evil to many people'; cf. **48**). As to fire breathing, the Homeric syntax leaves it unclear (an ambiguity the translation has attempted to replicate) whether the Chimaera is said to breathe fire *tout court* or specifically through her goat head, as Apollodorus (**48**) and many other subsequent writers were to understand it, and as did a vase of ca. 600–575 BC (*LIMC* Chimaira 21). If the fire breathing is to be dissociated from the goat head specifically, then one might imagine the Chimaera rather to breathe fire from all three mouths (as stipulated by Hyginus *Fabulae* 57: 'it was said to breathe fire from its threefold mouth'), or from her front head, that of the lion (as in the scholium to Homer, **52**). Whatever the case, the Chimaera's fire-breathing capacity is inevitably dependent ultimately upon the one head that ironically is never singled out as the fire breather: the serpent one.

Bellerophon is self-evidently another Heracles figure, sailing as he does through a series of labours designed to destroy him. But unlike Heracles' labours, Bellerophon's are unified by an underlying theme: the female. The Chimaera is female; the Amazons were a race of warrior women, as is well-known; and later tradition tells us that the Solymi lived in a bizarre society that was possibly matriarchal but certainly matrilineal, for they named themselves for their mothers (Herodotus 1.173). Bellerophon's battle against the female is anticipated in his initial difficulties with Anteia (subsequently Sthenoboea) and ultimately resolved in his marriage to the daughter (subsequently Philonoe) of the Lycian king (subsequently Iobates; cf. **48**). His role as a warrior against the female in abstract becomes even more explicit in a tale preserved by Plutarch (*Moralia* 248). According to this, after the Amazon battle Bellerophon waded into the sea and asked Poseidon to avenge him on Iobates by rendering his land sterile. As he returned onto the land, a huge tsunami followed behind. The men could do nothing to stop Bellerophon, but the women confronted him, pulling up their dresses and exhibiting their genitals, and Bellerophon retreated before them, taking the wave back with him. For this reason the Xanthians, like the Solymi, named themselves for their mothers. The ultimate symbol of sterility is driven back by the ultimate symbol of fertility. All this serves to highlight the Chimaera's femaleness. As we have noted before (1), female dragons carry the additional threat of producing a vast new brood of their own kind. From the sixth century onwards artists sometimes attempted to represent the Chimaera's femaleness by making her lion head emphatically that of a lioness (e.g. *LIMC* Chimaira 4).

In an indirect way, the Homeric tale constitutes, in Bellerophon's final marriage to the daughter of Iobates, the first example in Western tradition of the hero winning the girl through the slaying of the dragon; the link between the slaying of the Chimaera and the marriage becomes more direct in the Hesiodic *Ehoiai* (F43a lines 81–8 MW). The most striking example of this motif in the classical world is found in the tale of Perseus and Andromeda (**108–11, 113–16**).

We note in passing that this tale contains the only awareness of writing—or so it is understood by Apollodorus at any rate (**48**)—in the Homeric poems. Is it an indistinct and appropriately portentous recollection of the long-lost Linear B system of the Myceneans? Or an innovative first reference to the newly arrived Phoenician-derived alphabetic system?

## 50   Athene helps Bellerophon master the winged horse Pegasus

464 BC

Pindar *Olympians* 13.60–6 and 84–90

Greek

**60.** The Danaans shuddered before Glaucus, who came to them from Lycia. He boasted to them that his father's [Bellerophon's] rule, rich plot and hall were in the city of Pirene. Once he suffered much in his ambition to put a yoke on Pegasus, the son of the snake-visaged Gorgon, at the springs, until the maiden Pallas Athene brought for him the gold-banded bridle. [66]

**84.** Indeed strong Bellerophon eagerly captured the winged horse, stretching the gentle device around his jaw. Mounting the horse at once, and armed with bronze, he turned to the game. In due course, with Pegasus, he slew the female army of Amazon archers, striking them from the cold bosom of the open air, and the fire-breathing Chimaera and the Solymi. [90]

Once again the Chimaera is described as fire-breathing. As so often too, the hero is aided in the task of defeating the dragon by the goddess Athene, who helps him tame Pegasus, the winged horse, that he will need to do it (cf. **M13.a.ii**). For the birth of Pegasus from the severed neck of Medusa, see **58, 66–7**.

## 51   Bellerophon kills the Chimaera with molten lead

xii AD

Tzetzes *Commentary on Lycophron* Alexandra 17

Greek

…Riding on Pegasus, Bellerophon slew the Chimaera by coating his spear with lead and throwing it into her fire-breathing mouth. The lead was melted by this fire and killed her. A person who exercised foresight was said to be guarding against the fire of the Chimaera, in accordance with the myth, as Lysias [F439 Carey] says.…

Tzetzes, for all his lateness, can usually be relied upon for accurate knowledge of classical literature, and the fascinating detail he uniquely preserves about the manner in which Bellerophon killed the Chimaera presumably has an ancient pedigree ('uniquely preserves' because Theopompus *FGrH* 115 F412 [reproduced out of sequence at Dritter Teil B Texte p. 742] must, alas, be considered spurious, a figment of the fertile imagination of the Renaissance humanist Natale Conti). This sort of dragon-killing technique, in which the dragon is either fed something fiery or something glutinous that seals up its own fire inside it and causes it to overheat and explode, is widely attested in international dragon-slaying tales (**C3–4, C7, C11–13**), though only here in a classical context, the Septuagint apart (**124**).

## 52 The Chimaera rationalised

ca. 24 AD–Byzantine

Strabo C665
(Greek; ca. 24 AD)

Pliny *Natural History* 2.236
(Latin; ca. 79 AD)

Schol. Homer *Iliad* 6.181
(Greek; Hellenistic-Byzantine)

Heraclitus *De Incredibilibus* 15 (Greek; ii AD)

Greek, Latin

**Strabo:** Next is Anticragus, a steep mountain. The town of Carmylessus is situated on this, in a gorge. After this is Cragus, a mountain with eight spurs and a city of the same name. Myth locates the tale of the Chimaera around these mountains. In fact not far from here is the Chimaera, a gorge which stretches up from the shore.

**Pliny:** Nor with Mt Etna alone does nature rage and threaten to burn up lands. Mt Chimaera burns in the territory of Phaselis, and that too with a flame that dies neither by day nor by night.

**Schol. Homer:** If her greater and fore part was that of a lion, she would have been called a 'Lion'. She was therefore basically a goat [*chimaira*], and that is how she got her name, but she had the head of a lion and the tail of a snake. So she is introduced as breathing fire though her lion mouth.... Some say that there is a mountain in Lycia which is called Chimaera. This blows up fire in its middle part, and its peaks are infested with many wild beasts.

**Heraclitus:** In drawing the picture of this creature Homer says that she was a lion in front, a dragon [*drakōn*] behind and a goat in the middle. The truth could have been as follows. A woman ruling the region had in service two brothers by the name of Leon [Lion] and Drakon. Since she violated her oath and killed guest-friends, she was slain by Bellerophon.

Dragons were often strongly rooted in their landscapes, either being born of the earth itself or living in caves and holes within it. It is unsurprising, then, that the Chimaera should be rationalised as a landscape feature and most persuasively as a volcano, as by Pliny and the Homer scholiast. The latter's assertion that the volcano in question blows fire up in its middle part of course honours the tradition that it was the Chimaera's middle, goat, head that breathed fire (cf. **49**, with commentary), contradicting the scholiast's own (frankly obscure) reasoning that the mythical creature breathed fire through her lion mouth. Heraclitus's pattern of rationalisation matches that which he deploys in the cases of the Hydra (**27**) and Cerberus (**46**), in accordance with which the origin of multiple-headed creatures is found in the correspondingly named individual's entourage.

## 53 Athene slays the Aegis-Gorgon

before 412 BC–ca. 30 BC

Diodorus 3.70.3–6
(ca. 30 BC), incorporating
Dionysius Scytobrachion
*FGrH* 32 F8 (ii BC)

Euripides *Ion* 987–97
(before 412 BC)

Greek

**Diodorus:** They tell that this goddess [Athene] chose virginity for all time, excelled in self-control and discovered most of the crafts, being exceptionally shrewd. She was also competitive in war. She excelled in courage and might and achieved a great deal worthy of recollection, not the least of which was the slaying of the so-called Aegis, an awe-inspiring creature in all ways difficult to defeat. It was born of Earth and by nature cast forth a terrible flame from its mouth. It first appeared in the region of Phrygia, and burned up the land, which to this day is called 'Burnt Phrygia' [Phrygia Catacaumene]. Then, without respite, it attacked the mountains in the Taurus region and burned up the woods all the way to India. After that it returned to the sea in the region of Phoenicia and burned up the woods on Mt. Lebanon. Journeying through Egypt and across Libya, it arrived in the western lands and finally made its attack on the woods in the region of Ceraunia. As the land was being put to the flame in all directions and some of the people were being killed whilst others were abandoning their fatherlands and displacing themselves over long distances, they say that Athene overcame the beast, in part with cleverness, and in part with courage and strength, and killed it. She fastened its hide around herself and wore it on her breast. This was, on the one hand, to cover and to protect her body against subsequent dangers and, on the other, as a memento of her martial valour and deserved reputation. But Earth, the mother of the beast, grew angry and sent up the so-called Giants to challenge the gods. But they were subsequently killed by Zeus, who was aided in battle by Athene, Dionysus and the other gods.

**Euripides:**
CREUSA: Listen now. Do you know the Earth-born battle?
OLD MAN: I know it, the battle the Giants raised against the gods at Phlegra.
CREUSA: That was the time Earth bore the Gorgon, a terrible monster.
OLD MAN: As an ally for her children and a burden for the gods?
CREUSA: Yes. And the goddess Pallas [Athene], daughter of Zeus, killed her.
OLD MAN: Is this the story that I have heard from of old?
CREUSA: ...that Athene keeps her skin over her breast.
OLD MAN: ...which they call the *aegis*, the dress of Athene?
CREUSA: She acquired this name when she 'attacked' the spear of the gods.
OLD MAN: What wild form did the *aegis* have?
CREUSA: A breastplate armed with the coils of a viper [*echidna*].

Although there is no explicit mention of the serpentine in Diodorus's unique account of the Aegis, we can be sure that her form incorporated a serpentine element, both from the fact that snakes were an integral part of the *aegis* apron her hide was to provide, and from the fact that she was fire breathing, a key characteristic of *drakontes* (**M6.a.ii**). The Aegis boasts a number of affinities with other *drakontes*. As a creature with a name derived from 'goat' (*aig-*), as (again) a breather of fire and as a marauder and burner of Asia Minor, she most strongly resembles the Lycian Chimaera (**48, 52**). As a monster defeated by Athene herself in battle, rather than by one of the many dragon-slaying heroes sponsored by her (**M13.a.ii**), she resembles the Giants (**5**). As a fiery child of Earth created in parallel to the Giants, she also resembles Typhon (**5–8**). As the source of the *aegis* apron famously worn by Athene, she resembles Medusa, slain by Perseus (**54, 58**). The tale prompts one to look again at the bizarre Chimaera and ask whether she too may have originated in an attempt to account for the *aegis* apron's constituent elements of goatskin, Gorgon head (the iconographic origin of which is usually thought to have originated in frontal lion faces) and serpents, which fringe both the goatskin and the Gorgon head inset within it. A unique image of the Aegis monster may survive on a pot of ca. 410 BC (*LIMC* Pegasos 232). This shows Athene, resting on her spear, standing over a dead beast fully resembling the Chimaera, but with the Chimaera's slayer Bellerophon nowhere to be seen. The implication is surely that Athene has just killed the beast herself with her spear. Furthermore, the painter draws particular attention to Athene's *aegis* apron by giving it a distinctively enlarged Gorgon head: he means, surely, to give us its aetiology in a compressed narrative.

The Euripidean exchange would be all but unintelligible were it not for Diodorus's words on the Aegis, to which this which this particular Gorgon, as a monstrous child of Earth slain directly by Athene, was evidently equivalent. The Greek verb 'attacked' vaguely resembles, in some of its parts (*aïx-*), the root for 'goat' upon which the term *aegis* is based (*aig-*). (Note that Diggle's text rearranges the traditional order of lines in this passage.)

## FURTHER READING

Robert 1920–6:i, 179–85, Roes 1934, 1953, Amandry 1948, Dunbabin 1951–3, Schmitt 1966, Burkert 1983:52–3, Jacquemin 1986, Krauskopf 1986, Gantz 1993:23, 312–16, Lochin 1994, Collard et al. 1995:79–83.

# 9
## *Medusa, Slain by Perseus*

The tale of the three Gorgon sisters, who could turn men to stone with their gaze, and of Perseus's decapitation of the single mortal sister, Medusa, is well-known. As with the Chimaera, serpents make up a proportionately small part of the bodies of Medusa and the other Gorgons, for all that they often occupy prominent positions within their physical make-up, most commonly serving as their hair. But as with the Chimaera, the Gorgons' signature activity, that of a destructive stare, is one characteristically associated with serpents and dragons (**M9.a**). Their nature too, then, is fundamentally that of the *drakōn*. The Homeric *Iliad* mentions *gorgoneia* or Gorgon-faced images serving as shield

Figure 9 Gorgon head. Stone antefix from the Portonaccio Temple, Veii, ca.500. Museo Nazionale di Villa Giulia, Rome. Alinari / The Bridgeman Art Library.

devices (11.36–7) and seems to consider the Gorgon face on the *aegis* worn by Athene similarly to be an image rather than an object (5.741–2; cf. **53–4**). The *Odyssey* speaks of an actual detached Gorgon head housed in the underworld: Odysseus flees from his consultation of the ghosts for fear that Persephone might confront him with it (11.633–5). But it is in Hesiod's *Theogony* that we first learn, in brief outline, of Perseus's mission to fetch the head of the Gorgon Medusa (**1**). For Medusa and Gorgons see further **2, 32, 35, 37, 48, 50, 53, 79, 102, 108, 110–16, 118**.

## 54   An early summary of Perseus's mission to take the head of Medusa

ca. 454 BC

Pherecydes F11 Fowler

Greek

Perseus and his mother [Danae] lived in Seriphos with Dictys. When Perseus had become a youth, Polydectes, the maternal brother of Dictys, who happened to be king of Seriphos, saw Danae and fell in love with her, but was at a loss as to how to sleep with her. So he prepared a feast and invited many to it, including Perseus. Perseus asked what the price of attendance was. Polydectes said, 'A horse.' Perseus said, 'The head of the Gorgon.' On the sixth day after the feast, when the other banqueters brought their horses, so did Perseus. But Polydectes would not accept it, and demanded instead the head of the Gorgon in accordance with Perseus's promise. He said that if Perseus did not bring it, he would take his mother. Perseus was vexed and went off, lamenting his fate, to the remotest corner of the island. Hermes appeared before him, interrogated him and learned the reason for his lamentation. He told him to cheer up and led the way for him. First he took him to the Graeae, the daughters of Phorcys, named Pemphredo, Enyo and Deino. Athena told him the way. He stole from them their eye and tooth as they were handing it between themselves. When they realised this, they shouted out and besought him to give them back to them. For the three of them had been using one [sc. tooth and eye] by turns. Perseus said that he had them and would give them back if they directed him to the Nymphs that had the cap of Hades, the winged sandals and the pouch [*kibisis*]. So they showed him, and Perseus gave them their things back. He went off to the Nymphs with Hermes and asked them for the equipment. He put on the winged sandals, slung the pouch around himself and put the cap of Hades on his head. Then he travelled in flight to the region of Ocean and the Gorgons, with Hermes and Athena accompanying him. He found the Gorgons asleep. These gods instructed him to cut off the head whilst turning away, and in a mirror they showed him Medusa, who alone of the Gorgons was mortal. He approached, cut off her head with his sickle [*harpē*] and, putting it in his pouch, fled. The other Gorgons, realising what had happened, pursued him. However, they could not see him, because of his cap of Hades. When Perseus arrived at Seriphos he came before Polydectes and bade him gather the people so that he might show them the Gorgon's head, in the knowledge that when they saw it they would be turned to stone. Polydectes assembled the people and bade him show the head. Perseus turned away, took it out of his pouch, and showed it. The people saw it and were turned to stone. Athena took the head from Perseus and mounted it upon her goatskin [*aigis*]. He gave the pouch back to Hermes and his sandals and cap to the Nymphs.

Pherecydes has already told the tale of Perseus's birth: Danae's father, Acrisius, king of Argos, told by Apollo that his daughter Danae was destined to bear a son that would kill him, imprisons her in an underground chamber lined with bronze. Even so Zeus is able to impregnate her, falling in the form of golden rain through the chamber's skylight and into her lap. In due course the child she bears is discovered, and Acrisius seals mother and son together inside a chest and casts it into the sea. It washes ashore on the island of Seriphos, where it is discovered by the kindly fisherman Dictys, who takes Danae and Perseus on as his own family (Pherecydes F10 Fowler; cf. **56–7**). Apollodorus offers a summary that closely resembles the two Pherecydean fragments (*Bibliotheca* 2.4.1–2).

The monster-slaying mission on which Polydectes sends Perseus resembles those upon which Eurystheus sends Heracles (**23–47**) and on which Iobates, king of Lycia, sends Bellerophon (**48–52**): in each case it is trusted that the hero will not return alive. The significance of Perseus's initial declaration to Polydectes, 'The head of the Gorgon', remains obscure in this compression of Pherecydes' original words by the scholia to Apollonius. If the Seriphians already knew that the decapitation of Medusa would result in the birth of the magnificent flying horse Pegasus (**1, 58**), then it is possible that the wicked and cunning Polydectes manipulated the proud youth Perseus into contracting to bring him the best of all horses.

Perseus is helped in his mission by the gods Hermes and Athene, to the latter of whom he will eventually give the prize of the Gorgon's head for her *aegis*. These gods regularly attend Perseus in the iconography of his quest.

Perseus's mission comprises encounters with three groups of females in all, the Graeae (or Phorcides) and the Nymphs, before the Gorgons themselves. The Hesiodic *Theogony* had told in its genealogy of the great dragons that the Graeae (there just two, Pemphredo and Enyo) were full sisters of the Gorgons (**1**). As such, one might have expected the Graeae also to exhibit some *drakōn* qualities. There is no explicit mention of any such in the tradition, and the meagre iconographic record for them seems to depict them merely as harmless blind women (*LIMC* Graiai). But their two focal body parts, their mysteriously transferable eye and tooth, could be held to be the two body parts symbolic of the staring, biting serpent. It may be noted that in some versions of her story the serpentine Lamia had detachable eyes (**68–9**). The Nymphs, of whom we know little, appear to have been benign. According to other traditions, Perseus was armed by Hermes himself, the winged sandals being the god's own (**57, 59**).

As to Perseus's other special equipment, the shield and cap of Hades suggest different understandings of the mechanism by which Medusa petrified her victims. The use of the mirrored shield (cf. **58**) presupposes that the Gorgon's opponent is normally petrified when he looks at her, as does Perseus's turning away as he strikes. But the use of the invisibility-conferring cap of Hades presupposes rather that the opponent is petrified when she looks at him, as does Perseus's approach to Medusa in her sleep. The need for the *kibisis*, a specially proofed toxic container for the Gorgon's head, suggests the same: if a normal bag would have been petrified by the head, this cannot have been due to any gaze on the bag's part. The *harpē*, often represented in art as a weapon with an awkward combination of sword and curving sickle blades, was the Greek hero's appropriate weapon of choice against serpentine monsters: **M11.b.i.**

## 55  A marvellously animated relief image of Stheno and Euryale's pursuit of Perseus

vi BC

[Hesiod] *Shield* 216–37

Greek

And on it there was the child of Danae, Perseus the knight. Neither did he touch the shield with his feet, nor was he far from it, a great marvel to tell, since he was not at all supported by it. For this was how the glorious lame god [Hephaestus] made him with his hands, from gold. Around his feet he had winged sandals. Round his shoulders was placed a sword, bound in black, hanging from a baldric of bronze. He flew like thought. The whole of his back was occupied by the head of a terrible creature, the Gorgon. Around it ran the silver pouch [*kibisis*], a marvel to see. A gleaming fringe of gold hung from it. Around the lord's temples lay the cap of Hades, which brought with it the dread darkness of night. Perseus, son of Danae, strained to speed along. After him rushed the Gorgons, unapproachable and unutterable, desperate to seize him. As they crossed over the pale adamant the shield resounded with a great ringing, sharp and shrill. At their girdles a pair of dragons [*drakonte*] hung and hovered, bending their heads forwards. They flicked their tongues about. They gnashed their teeth whilst casting out wild stares. And over their terrible Gorgon heads shook great Fear.

This is the second text of any substance (after **1**) to speak of Perseus's mission against the Gorgons. The vignette describes Stheno and Euryale's pursuit of Perseus after he has taken their sister Medusa's head. It offers the first literary acknowledgement that the Gorgons comprised a serpentine element of some sort; they are seen to sport similar serpent belts in sixth-century BC art (e.g. *LIMC* Gorgo 113, and 289, the latter being the Corfu pediment). The Gorgons are ostensibly metallic here, in the first instance because they constitute decorations on a metal shield, but Apollodorus was subsequently to describe them as partly metallic in themselves: 'The Gorgons had heads about which scaly dragon snakes coiled, and great tusks as of pigs, hands of bronze and golden wings, with which they could fly' (*Bibliotheca* 2.4.2). For the attention drawn to the sound they make as they fly, cf. **56**. Perseus's wearing of the cap of Hades and the reference to the Gorgons' wild stares suggest that Stheno and Euryale, like Medusa, also had the power to petrify. Perseus already has much of his special equipment here: the cap of Hades aside, he also has his flying sandals and his pouch (*kibisis*).

## 56  The lamentation of the fair-cheeked Medusa's sisters Stheno and Euryale as they pursue Perseus

490 BC

Pindar *Pythians* 12.6–26

Greek

He [Midas of Acragas] conquered Greece in the craft which Pallas Athene once invented, interweaving the destructive lamentation of the bold Gorgons. She heard it pouring from their virginal, unapproachable heads of snakes as they toiled hard when Perseus shouted out, bringing a third part of the sisters as doom to sea-girt Seriphos and its peoples. Indeed he blinded the divine family of Phorcus [the Graeae or Phorcides], and he made his contribution feast bitter for Polydectes, and so too the forceful slavery he had inflicted on his mother and the compulsion of the bed, after stealing away the head of the fair-cheeked Medusa. He was the son of Danae, and the son of a spontaneous flow of gold. But when the virgin goddess had saved the dear man from these labours, she made a tune for double oboes [*auloi*] that consisted of all sounds, so that she might imitate with her tools the noisy grief emanating from the swift jaws of Euryale. The goddess was the inventor, but she invented it for the possession of mortal men, and she called it the measure of many heads, a glorious reminder of competitions that draw the people, and travelling frequently through thin bronze and the reeds that dwell beside the city of the Graces [Orchomenos] with its fair dancing lawns...

Pindar's allusive narrative refers to a number of episodes in Perseus's quest, but out of sequence. The focal point is that Athene made a tune for the double oboe to reflect the lamentation of Stheno and Euryale upon finding their sister decapitated and during the pursuit of Perseus. For the notion that the sounds the Gorgons emitted (cf. **55**) might have been deleterious, a sonic equivalent to their gaze, cf. Nonnus *Dionysiaca* 30.264–7: 'Did you see the stone-transforming eye of Stheno or [*sc.* hear] the invincible bellowing throat of Euryale herself?' For the memorialisation of a dragon fight in a tune for the double oboe, cf. **16**. Pindar refers to Medusa as 'fair-cheeked': this is an early indication of the notion that Medusa did not sport the terrible face of the *gorgoneia* (Gorgon faces) of archaic art, but rather the face of a beautiful girl, for all her serpentine hair. In due course stories would be developed to explain this configuration (**58**).

## 57   Perseus's ambush of the Graeae, and his catasterisation

earlier v

Aeschylus *Phorcides* F262 i *TrGF* = [Eratosthenes] *Catasterismi* 22

Greek

Star of Perseus. It is told of Perseus that he was set in the stars because of his glory. For when Zeus had sex with Danae in the form of gold, he sired him. He was sent against the Gorgons by Polydectes, and he received from Hermes the cap and the sandals, in which he made his journey through the air. It is thought that he also received from Hephaestus an adamantine sickle [*harpē*]. As Aeschylus the tragic poet says in his *Phorcides*, the Gorgons had the Graeae as advance guards. These had one eye and they used to hand it from one to another to keep guard. Perseus watched for the hand-over, seized it and threw it into the Tritonian lake. In this way he was able to approach the Gorgons as they slept. He took off the head of Medusa, which Athene put around her own breast, while for Perseus she made a place amongst the stars, from which he can be observed holding the Gorgon's head.

Aeschylus's tragedy *Phorcides* seems to have been influential in the development of the myth of the Graeae and the Gorgons. This summary of the play indicates that the Phorcides (Graeae) and the Gorgons were located, with Lake Tritonis, in Africa (cf. **1, 58–9**), and it has the virtue of explaining how Perseus was able to ensure that the Gorgons were sleeping as he approached them.

## 58   The transformation of Medusa and the creation of the snakes of Libya

8 AD

Ovid *Metamorphoses* 4.617–20, 772–803

Latin

**4.617.** While he [Perseus] hovered victorious over Libyan sands, drops from the bloody head of the Gorgon fell down. The ground took them up and animated them into snakes of different forms, and as a result of this that land is packed with and infested by snakes. [620]

**4.772.** Perseus, descended from Agenor, explained that there was a place lying beneath icy Atlas, securely protected by its solid mass. At the entrance to this place lived twin sisters, the Phorcides, who shared the use of a single eye. With stealth and cunning trickery he grabbed hold of the eye by inserting his hand as it was being passed between them. Travelling over remote and untrodden routes, and rocks bristling with broken woods, he alighted upon the Gorgons' house and saw, throughout the roads and ways, statues of men and wild beasts transformed from their former selves into stone by Medusa's gaze. But he himself had only looked at dreadful Medusa's image reflected in the bronze of the shield which he carried in his left hand, and whilst she herself and her snakes were in the grip of heavy sleep. He snatched the head from her neck, and Pegasus, fleeing swiftly on his wings, and his brother [Chrysaor] were born from the blood of their mother. He also told of the genuine dangers of his long journey, and the straits and lands he had seen beneath him from on high, and the stars he had touched with his beating wings. Nonetheless, he fell silent before they hoped. One of the several princes took up the conversation and asked why Medusa alone amongst the sisters had had snakes mixed in with her hair. The guest said, 'Since you seek to know something worth telling, hear the explanation of the thing you look for. She was very beautiful in form and the jealous hope of many suitors. Nor in her whole form was any part more lovely than her hair. I met someone who told me he had seen it. The director of the sea [Poseidon] is said to have violated her in the temple of Athene. Athene, daughter of Zeus, turned away and covered her chaste face with the *aegis*. And so that this should not go without punishment, she turned the Gorgon's hair into foul water snakes. Now too, in order to strike her enemies with fear and terrify them, she displays the snakes she created on her breast.' [803]

Ovid narrates the episodes of Perseus's Gorgon mission partly out of sequence, so that the vignette of Perseus hovering over Africa with the decapitated head precedes the tale of the decapitation itself. Lucan similarly derived the poisonous snakes of Africa from the drops of Medusa's blood, **59**; cf. the notion that the poisonous herbs of Thessaly, land of witches, were sown when Medea overflew it in her flying chariot and cast a chest of herbs from her stores to the ground (Scholiast Aristophanes *Clouds* 749a).

Ovid's evocative description of the Gorgons' house indicates that they turned their victims into perfect stone simulacra of their former selves, 'statues'. Classical Greek art suggests that they had originally been held to transform their victims rather into unshaped stones (*LIMC* Polydektes nos. 7–8; cf. **60**).

The tale of Athene's (it might be thought undeserved) transformation of Medusa serves an aetiology of the beautiful-*gorgoneion* type that came to prevail from classical Greece onwards. Ovid elsewhere implies that Poseidon took the form of a bird to effect the violation (*Metamorphoses* 6.119–20). For another serpentine punishment for sacrilegious sex in a temple, cf. **93**. Ovid is all too aware that his origin tale for Medusa excludes the possibility that her sisters shared her snaky form, as they traditionally did. His suggestion that the *aegis* existed prior to the addition of Medusa's head to it is curious.

## 59   A witty expansive description of the killing of Medusa, and once again the snakes of Libya

65 AD

Lucan *Pharsalia* 9.619–99

Latin

Why the Libyan air is inundated with such great pests [venomous snakes] and is fecund with death, or what it is that secretive nature has mingled into her soil, our careful researches have not been sufficiently powerful to discover. But a tale propagated throughout the world in place of the true reason has deceived the centuries. On the remotest borders of Libya, where the heated earth receives the hot Ocean as the sun goes down, are the broad and unkempt fields of Medusa, daughter of Phorcys. They are not sheltered by the foliage of groves or made soft by the plough, but are rough with the rocks that had been seen by the face of their owner. It was in her body first that harmful nature reared the cruel pests. From her throat snakes poured forth their high-pitched hisses with flickering tongues. They would lash Medusa's neck, and she was delighted by this. In the fashion of female coiffure, the snakes hung loose over her back but rose up straight over her forehead. Viperous venom flowed when she combed her hair. This was the part of unfortunate Medusa that all could look upon scot-free. For whoever had the chance to fear the grin and mouth of the monster? Who, of those who looked at her directly, did Medusa allow to die? She snatched forth the hesitating fates and acted before fear. Limbs perished whilst they still held their breath, and the shades, not yet sent forth, grew rigid beneath the bones. The hair of the Eumenides only inflicted madness. Cerberus softened his hissing before Orphean song, and the son of Amphitryon looked at the Hydra when he conquered it. But her father, Phorcys, the second power in the sea, feared this monster, as did her mother, Ceto, and her very sister Gorgons. She was able to threaten sky and sea with an unfamiliar solidification and draw earth over the whole world. Birds suddenly fell from the sky, together with their additional weight. Wild beasts stuck to their rocks. Whole races that lived in the neighbouring areas of Ethiopia grew rigid in marble. No animal endured her vision, and her very snakes, pouring themselves backwards, used to avoid her face. She turned Atlas into crags, the Titan who stands beneath the pillars of the west. When heaven feared the Giants who stood on snakes once at Phlegra she erected mountains, and the Gorgon put an end to the massive war of the gods from the middle of Pallas's breast. To this place Parrhasian wings carried Perseus, born of Danae and a divine cloud. The wings belonged to the Arcadian inventor of the cithara and the oil of the wrestling ground [Hermes]. And suddenly, flying headlong, he raised his Cyllenian sickle, the sickle already red with the slaughter of another monster, for it had been used [by Hermes] to kill Argus, guardian of the cow that Zeus loved. Virgin Pallas brought help for her winged brother. She made a deal for the head of the monster and instructed Perseus to turn around to face the east at the border of the Libyan land and to traverse the Gorgon's kingdom with backward flight. She gave him in his left hand a shield shining with yellow bronze, in which she instructed him to look at rock-making Medusa. She was overwhelmed with sleep that was destined to draw upon her the eternal peace of death, but not completely. Most of her hair kept watch, and the water snakes defended her head by straining forth from her hair. But the remainder of the snakes lay across the middle of her face and shaded her eyes. Pallas herself directed Perseus as he trembled and directed the Cyllenian sickle that quivered in his right hand as he turned away, rupturing the broad boundary of the snake-bearing neck. What an expression the Gorgon had on her face, slain with a wound inflicted by curved iron! With what great venom am I to think that her mouth breathed, and what great venom of death am I to think that her eyes poured forth? Not even Pallas could look, and the face of Perseus, even turned away, would have been frozen, if the Tritonian [Athene] had not spread the thick hair and covered her face with snakes. Thus he seized the Gorgon and flew into the sky on his wings. He gave thought to his journey and was minded to take a shortcut through the air, if he could cut through the middle of the cities of Europe. But Pallas ordered him not to harm the fruit-bearing lands and to spare the populations. For who would not look up into the ether with such a great thing flying over?

He turned his wings to the Zephyr and travelled over Libya, which was sown with no cultivation and lay open to stars and sun. The orbit of the sun presses the earth close and burns it up. Nor in any other land does the shadow fall so high into the sky and interfere with the path of the moon, if the moon, forgetting her curving path, runs straight along the signs of the zodiac and does not avoid the shadow either to the north or to the south. Although that earth was sterile and its fields fecund for no good creature, they took up the venoms of Medusa as she dripped with decay, and so too the dreadful dews from that wild blood. The heat helped these dews and cooked them into the crumbly sand. Here the putrefaction which first moved its head from the dust raised up the sleep-bringing asp with its swollen neck....

The epicist Lucan's description of the killing of Medusa, the most detailed to survive from antiquity, is an excursus from his narrative of the depredations made by the terrible snakes of Libya (cf. **58, 97–8**) upon Cato's army. As often in ancient texts, 'Libya' is here used to define Africa more or less as a whole and extends to its western coast, the traditional home of the Hesperides, the Graeae and the Gorgons. Poisonous snakes inundate the air because of the noxious fumes they, like many of the great dragons, are held to project (**M7.a.ii**).

As often with Lucan, there is humour: Medusa's snakes form themselves into the elaborate back-combed coiffure found in the mid-first-century AD busts of Roman matrons. The further conceit that her frontal snakes back-comb themselves because even they live in terror of her eyes is a sweet one. The role of a matron's hair oil is taken over by the snakes' dripping venom. Lucan's intriguing image of Medusa's snakes remaining alert and on guard while she sleeps implicitly contradicts Ovid's vignette of her snakes sympathetically sleeping as she does (**58**) and nicely invokes the notion that snakes in any case never sleep.

For Lucan, Medusa's petrification process is so instantaneous that the soul does not even have a chance to leave the body but is frozen within it. For her dropping of birds from the sky cf. the Bagrada dragon's dropping of birds from the sky with its noxious breath, here so that they may be eaten (**98**). As Lucan competitively magnifies the motifs of the poetic repertoire, Perseus can no longer merely turn away from Medusa as he kills her—he must fly backwards across Africa before even meeting her.

## 60  Rationalisation (i): the Graeae and the Gorgons identified

ca. 300 BC

Palaephatus 31

Greek

*On the daughters of Phorcys.* Concerning these too a rather ridiculous story is noised about, to the effect that Phorcys had three daughters who had just one eye and used it by turns. The one who was using it inserted it into her head and in this way she was able to see. And so, with one of them passing on the eye to the next, they could all see. Then Perseus sneaked up on them from behind and seized their eye and refused to give it back unless they told him where the Gorgon was. At any rate this is how they tell the story. He cut off her head, went to Seriphos, showed it to Polydectes and made him stone. This too is somewhat ridiculous, that a living man should be turned to stone after looking at the head of a corpse. For what power does a corpse have? Anyway, something along the following lines is what actually happened. Phorcys was a man of Cerne. The Cernaeans are Ethiopians by race and inhabit the island of Cerne outside the Pillars of Hercules, but they cultivate Libya along the Annon river as far as Carthage. They have a lot of gold. This Phorcys ruled over the islands outside the Pillars of Hercules, and there are three. He made a four-cubit gold statue of Athene. The Cernaeans called Athene Gorgon, just as the Thracians call Artemis Bendis, the Cretans Dictyna and the Spartans Oupis. Anyway, Phorcys died before dedicating his image in the sanctuary. He left three daughters, Stheno, Euryale and Medusa. These did not want to marry anyone, and, dividing up the property, they each took over the rule of an island. They decided not to dedicate the statue of Gorgon at that point, nor yet to divide it up, but by turns they stored it for themselves in a treasury. Phorcys had had a companion, a fine and respectable fellow, and they used him in every matter just like an eye [*ophthalmos*]. Perseus was an exile from Argos, and he lived as a pirate, plundering sea vessels, making use of his boats and his personal strength. Upon learning that here was a kingdom run by women, with much gold and few men, he arrived on the scene. To begin with, he moored his boat in the strait between Cerne and Sarpedonia, and he captured Eye [Ophthalmos] as he was sailing across from one to the other. He told Perseus that there was nothing to take from them worth mentioning apart from the Gorgon, and he indicated the amount of gold it contained. When Eye failed to arrive in his turn, in accordance with what he had said, the girls came together and accused each other. But when they had denied that they had him, they wondered what could have happened. At this point, whilst they were together, Perseus sailed to them and told them that he himself had Eye, but that he would not give him back to them unless they told him where the Gorgon was. He made the additional threat that he would kill them too if they didn't tell him. Medusa refused to show him, but Stheno and Euryale showed him. So he killed Medusa and gave Eye back to the others. Taking the Gorgon he cut it up. Making ready his trireme, he put the head of the Gorgon on it and gave the name of Gorgon to his ship. He sailed around in this, exacting money from the islanders, and he killed those that refused to give. In the same way he sailed to Seriphos and asked for money from the Seriphians. They asked him for a few days to collect the money. So they gathered together stones of human length, put them in the marketplace and abandoned Seriphos. Perseus sailed in again to demand the money and, coming to the marketplace, found no people, but the stones of human length. So Perseus told the remaining islanders, if they refused to provide money, 'Make sure that you do not suffer the same fate as the Seriphians, who were turned to stone when they saw the head of the Gorgon.'

The traditional homeland of the Gorgons, in the extreme west of Africa, is respected. The rationalisation follows to its end a tendency latent in the canonical tradition, namely the identification between the Gorgons and the Graeae. There is plenty of Palaephatus's characteristic arbitrariness and under-motivation, with key terms deferred into the names of individuals or things. Whilst the story about the Seriphian stones may appear peculiarly arbitrary, it does at least allude to the earlier tradition, observable in the iconography (cf. **58**, commentary), according to which the gaze of the Gorgon turned victims into rough stones rather than neat statues of their former selves.

## 61 Rationalisation (ii): the Gorgons as a race of warrior women equivalent to the Amazons

ii BC–ca. 30 BC

Diodorus 3.52, 54, 55 (ca. 30 BC), recycling Dionysius Scytobrachion *FGrH* 32 F7 (ii BC)

Greek

**52.** There have been several races of women in Libya that were warlike and much admired for their bravery. For we learn from tradition that the race of Gorgons, against which Perseus is said to have marched, was outstanding in its valour. That the son of Zeus, the best of the Greeks of his day, should have accomplished a great labour in his campaign against these women may be taken as proof of their superiority and power.....

**54.** Myrina, queen of the Amazons, is said to have assembled an army of 30,000 infantry and 3,000 cavalry. They were very keen on using cavalry in their wars. They used the skins of large snakes for shielding armour and for arms of attack, swords and spears.... They say that Myrina was asked by the Atlantians to attack the land of the Gorgons mentioned above. The Gorgons drew up their army against the Amazons. A violent battle ensued, and the Amazons, gaining the advantage, destroyed a great many of their opponents and took no fewer than 3,000 of them alive....

**55.** ... The Gorgons in later times increased their power again. Perseus the son of Zeus made war on them in the age when Medusa was ruling them. Finally both these and the Amazon race were destroyed root and branch by Heracles when he travelled towards the west and set up his Pillars in Libya....

The Gorgons are remodelled as a race of warrior women after the fashion of the famous Amazons, whose society, though bizarre, is at least theoretically conceivable. Once again the traditional homeland of the mythical Gorgons is respected, but the Amazons are dragged to join them in Libya from their traditional homeland of Themiscyra in Asia. The Amazons are in turn assimilated to the Gorgons by being given arms made of products derived from Libya's notorious snakes (cf. 58–9).

## 62 Rationalisation (iii): Medusa as a courtesan whose beauty stops men in their tracks

ii AD

Heraclitus *De incredibilibus* 1, 9, 13

Greek

**1. On Medusa.** They say that this woman turned to stone those that saw her, and that when Perseus chopped her head off, a winged horse came out. This is the truth of the matter. She was a beautiful courtesan, with the result that those who saw her were stopped in their tracks as if turned to stone. We too say, 'I saw her and was turned to stone.' When Perseus arrived she fell in love, devoured her property and destroyed her youthful beauty. After losing her youthful looks and her property she aged like a horse. The 'head' is the flower of her youthful beauty, which Perseus took from her.

**9. On Perseus.** It is told that Hermes gave winged sandals to him. For Hermes was an expert in training for the running track, in which Perseus was distinguished. For spectators, marvelling at his speed, said that wings had been attached to his feet, just as we are in the habit of saying of swift runners that they 'fly'.

**13. On the Phorcides.** People suppose that these used a single eye and were forever taking it from the one who had it to use. It is likely that three blind women used a single guide for walking.

Heraclitus prefers to find the origins of his fantastic stories in the misinterpretation of originally metaphorical exclamations. The detail of Medusa aging like a horse purports to offer an explanation for the myth of the birth of Pegasus.

## 63  Rationalisation (iv): Medusa as a wild woman of Libya

ii AD

Pausanias 2.21.5–7, incorporating Procles of Carthage *FHG* iv pp. 483–4 F1

Greek

Not far from the building in the marketplace of the Argives is a heap of earth. They say that the head of the Gorgon Medusa lies inside this. Leaving aside the fantastic, this is what is said of her besides. She was the daughter of Phorcus and after her father's death she ruled over those who lived around Lake Triton. She went out to hunt and she led the Libyans into battle. At the time in question she encamped her army opposite Perseus's force (for Perseus was accompanied by picked men from the Peloponnese), and she was killed by a ruse during the night. Perseus was amazed at her beauty even though she was dead, so he cut off her head to show the Greeks. But this other account seemed to be more plausible to the Carthaginian man Procles, son of Eucrates. The desert parts of Libya produce various beasts, the reports of which are incredible. Amongst them are wild men and wild women. Procles said that he had seen one of these men brought to Rome. So he conjectured that one of these women had strayed from her people and, arriving at Lake Tritonis, destroyed the locals, until Perseus killed her. It was held that Athene helped Perseus in the deed, because the people around Lake Tritonis are sacred to her.

The supposedly Argive tale of Medusa casts her as a Libyan queen and a warrior woman after the fashion of **60–1**, and as a mesmerising beauty after the fashion of **62**. The wild-woman rationalisation attributed to the Carthaginian Procles anticipates rather the rationalisations offered by **64–5**. As can be seen, the rationalised versions of Greek myths form a semi-independent tradition of their own. The date of Procles is unknown, but the context suggests that he could not have written prior to the second century BC.

## 64  Rationalisation (v): Gorgons as terrible wild animals

early i AD (?)–early iii AD

Athenaeus 221b–e (early iii AD) = Alexander of Myndus F i.6 Wellmann (not in *FGrH*; early i AD?)

Greek

As to the Gorgons and the fact that certain animals really exist that have the ability to turn men to stone, Alexander of Myndus explains as follows in the second book of his *History of Flocks*: 'The Numidians in Libya, where the animal is found, call the *gorgon* the "downward-looker". As most say, on the basis of its skin, it resembles a wild sheep, but as some say, a calf. And they say that is has a breath of such a kind that it destroys anyone that encounters the animal. It has hair hanging down from its forehead over its eyes. Whenever it manages to shake this aside (this is difficult because it is heavy) and cast its gaze, it kills the person it sees, not with its breath, but with the natural beam from its eyes, and renders him a corpse. It was discovered in the following fashion. Some of those who marched with Marius against Jugurtha saw the *gorgon*. They thought that it was a wild sheep on account of the fact that it held its head down and moved slowly. They started towards it as if to kill it with their swords. But the animal was startled, shook aside the hair that lay over its eyes and immediately made corpses out of those that attacked it. As others did the same thing again on different occasions and were killed, with those approaching it always perishing, some men looked into the nature of the animals by asking the locals. Some Numidian knights ambushed the animal from a great distance at Marius's behest, killed it with a javelin and brought it to the general.'

Here the Gorgon is rationalised, in natural-historical mode, into a wild animal, though the fantastical nature of the animal so created can hardly be said to belong to the world of reason. As a terrible variety of animal resident in Libya, this *gorgon* resembles the partly rationalised Lamia, 72.

## 65 Rationalisation (vi): Medusa's head as a tool of late antique magic

v–vi AD

John Malalas
*Chronographia*
pp. 35–9 Dindorf

Greek

Perseus's father, Picus-Zeus, taught him to do and perform the sorcery of the abominable skull cup, teaching him all its mysteries and impious errors. He told him, 'You will conquer all your public enemies by means of it, and so too your personal enemies and every hostile man. All who look into the face itself will be blinded and stilled as if dead and slaughtered by you.' In due course Perseus followed the instructions of his own father, Picus-Zeus, and later, after his father's death, and when he had come to the fullness of manhood, he conceived a desire for the kingship of Assyria, in envy of the children of Ninus, his uncle, the brother of his father. After consulting an oracle he went off to the land of Libya. On the road a maiden, a local girl, met this same Perseus. She had wild hair and eyes. Stopping her, he asked, 'What is your name?' And she freely told him, 'Medusa'. He got hold of her by her hair and cut off her head with the sickle-headed spear he carried. Perseus took this same head and at once consecrated it with mystic rites, just as he had been instructed by his father Picus when he taught him the error of accursed sorcery. [36] He brandished this head to aid himself against all enemies, personal and public, and used it to subjugate them and to slay them. He called the head Gorgon because of the 'efficiency' of its service and its 'effectiveness' against his opponents [cf. *gorgos*]. From there he passed into the Ethiopian land, which was ruled by Cepheus. He found there a sanctuary of Poseidon. He entered it and found a girl staying there. She had been dedicated to the sanctuary by order of her own father Cepheus. She was called Andromeda. He dragged her out of the sanctuary and raped her because she was beautiful, and then took her to wife. He sailed away from that land. Coming to Assyria, he arrived in Lycaonia. They recognised him and at once rose up in revolt and made war on him. Making use of the power of the Gorgon's head, he conquered the Lycaonians....[37]...After giving thanks he set out from there across the Argaean mountain to Assyria. Having defeated the Assyrians and slain Sardanapallus, their king, a man of his own family, he subjugated them. He ruled them for fifty-three years and called them Persians after his own name, removing their kingdom and their name from the Assyrians. He planted trees and called them *perseae*. He did not just do it there, but he also planted *perseae* in Egypt as monuments to himself. And he taught the Persians the rite of the accursed and godless skull cup of Medusa. Because of this instruction he called their land that of the Medes. ...[38]...After some time King Cepheus, the father of Andromeda, came against him from Ethiopia and made war upon him. Cepheus was unable to see because of old age. Perseus, hearing that he was making war on him, became very angry and went out against him brandishing [39] the head, and he showed it to him. Because he was unable to see, Cepheus rode against him on his horse. Perseus did not realise that he could not see, and reasoned that the head of the Gorgon he held was no longer working. So he turned it towards himself and looked at it. He was blinded and frozen like a corpse and killed. After that the son of Perseus and Andromeda ruled the Persians, established by his own grandfather Cepheus, the king of Ethiopia. Cepheus gave an order, and the accursed head of the Gorgon was burned. He returned to his own country, and thereafter the family of Perseus remained as rulers of the Babylonian land.

It might be thought, again, that the rationalisation of the Medusa myth into a tale of magic of this sort is no rationalisation at all, but Palaephatus (cf. **27** for his project) might nonetheless have approved: snaky-haired Gorgons were not observable phenomena of the ancient world, but the practice of magic certainly was an observable phenomenon, and so, in particular, was that of skull-based magic. In one of the Greek Magical Papyri, a fourth-century AD text reflecting a second-century AD original, we learn, for example, of a series of magical spells ascribed to one Pitys involving the manipulation of a skull that has been consecrated in accordance with the due rites; rites are also offered for the deactivation of such skulls (*PGM* IV.2006–2139).

The wild-girl Medusa seems partly reminiscent of **63**. As is quite typical of ancient rationalisation narratives, the sequence of events narrated seems arbitrary and under-motivated, building to an impression of random cruelty on Perseus's part. It is difficult to judge the tone of the tale of Perseus's death. A Christian denigration of a pagan hero, chiming with the impression of cruelty? Slapstick-comic? A witty aetiology of the statue type, already famous in antiquity, of Perseus holding the Gorgon's head aloft (e.g. *LIMC* Perseus 64)? The relationship between the terms 'Medusa' (*Mědousa*) and 'Medes' (*Mēdoi*) is hard to sell.

The passage omitted here between §§37–8 is printed in full at **9**. This gives Perseus a further *drakōn* to slay in the form of the river Orontes, also known as Drakōn, and he does so by calling down balls of fire upon it from the sky.

## 66   Rationalisation (vii); allegorisation (i): Perseus as Virtue overcomes the Gorgons as Terrors

late v AD

Fulgentius *Mitologiae* 1.21

Latin

They say that Perseus was the slayer of the Gorgon Medusa. They had it that there were three Gorgons, of whom the first was Stheno, the second Euryale and the third Medusa. I believe it unnecessary to tell their story, because it has been told by Lucan and Ovid, poets familiar even to those of just an elementary education. Theocnidus, the historian of antiquities, says that Phorcus was a king who left behind him three rich daughters. Of these Medusa, who was the eldest, increased her wealth by cultivation and farming, which is why she was called 'Gorgo', as from 'Georgigo'. For in Greek farmers are called *georgi*. She was said to have a snake-like head because she was rather clever. Perseus envied her rich kingdom and so killed her. He was said to be winged because he came with a fleet of ships. By taking away her head—that is, her capital—he made himself richer and took possession of no small kingdom. Then he invaded the kingdom of Atlas too, as it were, with the Gorgon's head—that is, with her capital—and compelled him to flee onto a mountain, wherefore it is said that he was turned into a mountain. However, let us explain what the Greek imagination wanted to express with such subtle imagery. They had it that the Gorgons were three to symbolise the three types of Terror. The first is that Terror that weakens the mind, the second is that Terror which sprinkles the mind with a deep terror, the third is that Terror that not only clouds the mind but also the vision. This is how the three Gorgons got their names. For in Greek Stheno means 'weakness'; hence we apply the term *asthenia* too to feebleness. The second name, Euryale, means 'broad depth'; hence Homer calls Troy *euryaguia*, that is 'Troy with wide streets'. And they named Medusa from *mē idousa*, on the basis that she 'cannot see'. Perseus killed these Terrors with the help of Athene, which is to say that Virtue killed them with the help of Wisdom. He flies whilst turning back, because Virtue never looks upon

Terror. Perseus is said to carry a mirror because these Terrors are not confined to the heart, but also create images. Pegasus is said to be born from Medusa's blood to be an allegory of Fame. For when Virtue has cut down Terror it generates Fame. And that is why Pegasus is said to fly, because Fame is winged. Hence Tiberianus speaks of 'Pegasus about to fly across the whinnying ether.' And this is why Pegasus is said to have broken forth a spring for the Muses with his hoof, because the Muses properly devote themselves to describing the fame of heroes or proclaim that of men of old.

This discussion awkwardly blends rationalisation with allegorisation: one ought not to be able to apply both processes successfully to the same text. The project of rationalisation assumes that an original true narrative has become distorted in the surviving version. The project of allegorisation assumes rather that the surviving version accurately preserves an original coded message. The latter normally seeks to expose a hidden narrative with a moral force; the former often, willy-nilly, exposes a distinctly amoral one. The earlier part of the discussion here rationalises the myth of Medusa in traditional style (again the rationalisation of myth has its own, partly parallel tradition to that of the canonical narrative), and indeed is strongly reminiscent of **60**; again the narrative thread is arbitrary and amoral. The subsequent allegorising discussion justifies its claims by appeal to supposed Greek etymologies in a series of contrived ways and with different levels of success. The first element of *Eury-alē* does indeed mean 'broad', but the second means 'leap', and seemingly describes the distinctive kneeling-running leg configuration characteristically given to the pursuing Gorgons in archaic art, as on the Corfu pediment (*LIMC* Gorgo 289). *Stheno*, derived from the noun *sthenos*, does not mean 'weakness' but rather its opposite, 'strength'; the related term *asthenia* does indeed mean 'feebleness' or 'weakness' by virtue of being the opposite of *sthenos* (it is marked by the initial alpha-privative). *Mĕdousa* signifies 'queen' and is a long way from its supposed etymological phrase *mē idousa*, 'not having seen'; it is furthermore curious that Medusa should have been one that did not see rather than one that did indeed see. A broadly similar discussion is to be found in the work of the ix–xi AD First Vatican Mythographer (2.20 Zorzetti).

## 67 Allegorisation (ii): Perseus as the sun slays Medusa as evaporated seawater

xii AD

Tzetzes, commentary on Lycophron *Alexandra* 17

Greek

Perseus is the Sun and the fast motion of the heaven. Athene is the air and the exhalation that moves the heaven. For it is moved by exhalations. Perseus is said to dart and rush to emphasise the point. This exhalation of air sends him to the Gorgons, that is, the sea and the body of waters called Gorgon, to strike it. For *gorgos* means 'striking'. Athene sends him to slay Medusa, the part of the sea that consists of the finest particles, because it resembles her. For in fact the entire sea is like air, and its finest element is transformed into air. So Perseus or rather the Sun, set moving by the motion of heaven, does not slay Stheno and Euryale, that is, the powerful, outstretched sea, for he cannot transform it or draw it up because it is immortal and cannot be transformed. Medusa alone he slays because she is mortal, striking her with his sword, or rather he transforms the topmost, fine water with his swift motion and draws it up. At Medusa's beheading Chrysaor and Pegasus leap from her neck. For as the sun and the air draw up, as I said, the topmost, finer and vaporous water, the heavier water is carried back down and streams [*pēgazein*] and pours forth, and they call this 'Pegasus' because it gushes down (for dull matter is carried downwards). But the finest-particled and the most ethereal water is transformed into a fire-like substance, wherefore they call it Chrysaor ['Golden Sword']. The day is carried up riding on this Pegasus of water, which is carried upwards by the motion of the heaven and the drawing of the sun. For the heaven is sphere-shaped and it moves from east to west, carrying the sun around with it. When the sun wheels round to the hemisphere below the earth, night comes on. As the sun runs up again from beneath the sea and the earth to the upper hemisphere, from where it draws up the so-called Pegasus vapours, it creates the day.

Tzetzes, no doubt drawing on older Greek tradition, offers a meteorological allegoresis of the Medusa story which, contrived though it is, is largely self-explanatory.

**FURTHER READING**

Glotz 1877–1919a, 1877–1919b, Roscher 1884–1937c, Furtwängler 1886–90, Kuhnert 1897–1909, Ziegler 1912, Robert 1920–6:i, 222–45, Blinkenberg 1924, Marinatos 1927/8, Krappe 1933, Hampe 1935–6, Besig 1937, Caterall 1937, Woodward 1937, Will 1947, Langlotz 1951, 1960, Howe 1952, 1953, 1954, Yalouris 1953, Croon 1955, Riccioni 1960, Schauenberg 1960, Goldman 1961, Feldman 1965, Sparkes 1968, von Steuben 1968:13–17, Zinserling-Paul 1979, Karagiorga 1970, Phinney 1971, Floren 1977, Belson 1980, Hughes and Fernandez Bernades 1981, Halm-Tisserant 1986, Napier 1986, Krauskopf 1988, Krauskopf and Dahlinger 1988, Paoletti 1988, Schefold and Jung 1988, Vernant and Ducroux 1988, Dillon 1990, Jameson 1990, Roccos 1994, Wilk 2000, Ogden 2008.

# 10
## Lamia, Slain by Eurybatus and Others

Lamia's name is usually held to have originated in that of the Mesopotamian child-attacking demoness Lamashtu, who is also believed to have had an impact on the iconography of the Gorgons. Lamashtu is often portrayed as lion headed, clutching a snake in each hand, with a rampant animal on either

Figure 10 The anguipede Lamia with Apollo at Delphi. Attic white-ground lekythos, ca. 475–50 BC. Musée du Louvre. Redrawn by Eriko Ogden.

side, in the so-called Mistress of Animals configuration; she rides on an ass, whose function is to carry her away to where she can do no harm. The Graeco-Roman evidence for Lamia holds much of interest, but also offers many frustrations: it is seemingly divided between an archetypal woman or creature named Lamia and a series of individual creatures termed *lamia*. It is uncertain whether *lamias* are to be imagined as flesh or ghost. Of the three most compelling narratives seemingly of relevance, two (Statius and Dio) withhold the designation *lamia* from the monster described, whilst a third (Antoninus Liberalis) applies the term *lamia* but declines to describe the monster so designated.

## 68   The myth of the archetypal Lamia

280 BC–Byzantine

Duris of Samos *FGrH* 76 F17 (ca. 280 BC)

Schol. Aristophanes *Peace* 758, selections (Hellenistic-Byzantine)

Greek

**Duris:** Duris in the second book of his *Libyca* says that Lamia was a beautiful woman in Libya. Zeus had sex with her. Because of Hera's envy towards her she lost [*or:* destroyed] the children she bore. Consequently she became misshapen through grief, snatched other people's children and killed them.

**Schol. Aristophanes *Peace*:** Lamos, the city of the Laestrygonians, is named after Lamia.... Lamia is said to have been the daughter of Belus and Libye. They say that Zeus fell in love with her and took her from Libya to Italy, and it is from her that the city of Lamia in Italy is named. Thereafter, Zeus had sex with her but did not evade the notice of Hera. She, in envy towards Lamia, ever killed the children that were born of her. And she, because she was so upset about her own children dying, secretly stole and killed the children of others, through envy. This is the reason that they say that nurses invoke Lamia against little children when they want to frighten them. It is said that by the will of Hera Lamia was constantly sleepless, so that she spent her days and nights in grief, until Zeus took pity on her and made her eyes removable, so that she could take out her own eyes and put them back again. It is said that she received from Zeus the gift of being able to transform herself into whatever she wanted. This is what I found in a note.

These sources preserve what appear to have been the myth of the archetypal Lamia and the aetiology of her function as a bogey for children. This is not to say that the notion of an archetypal Lamia preceded the notion of *lamiai* as a category of monster. Nothing here explicitly declares that this archetypal Lamia had a serpentine element, as the creatures that were subsequently to bear her name did, but her detachable eyes give one pause. They are strongly reminiscent of the Graeae, who were also female denizens of Libya, and who, we have argued, may have evinced a serpentine element of their own (**54**). They were at any rate full sisters to the serpentine Gorgons (**1**). Indeed, the motif of Hera's destruction of Lamia's beauty after her seduction by Zeus should be compared with that of Athene's destruction of Medusa's beauty after her seduction by Poseidon (**58**). The notion that the city of Homer's Laestrygonians should have been named after Lamia (schol. Theocritus 15.40 makes Lamia their erstwhile queen) is lent plausibility by the fact that she and they alike devour human beings.

## 69 The archetypal Lamia rationalised

later v BC–ii AD

Diodorus 20.41.2–6 (ca. 30 BC), incorporating Euripides F472m *TrGF* (later v BC)

Heraclitus *De incredibilibus* 34 (ii AD)

Greek

**Diodorus:** They [Ophellas and his army, in 308 BC] encamped at Automala. As they marched on from there they encountered a mountain that was steep on both sides. In the middle of it was a deep ravine, and from this rose up straight and sheer a pinnacle of rock. At the base of the rock was a very large cave, covered over with ivy and yew. They say that this is where queen Lamia was born, who was outstanding in her beauty. The passage of time thereafter rendered her appearance bestial, because of the wildness of her nature. For all the children that were born to her died. She was crushed by her suffering and came to envy the fertility of other women. So she commanded her men to snatch the babies from their mothers' embraces and kill them at once. And so it is that still now in our own age the story about this woman is kept alive with children and her mere name is absolutely terrifying for them. Whenever she got drunk, she gave liberty to all to do whatever they wanted without being observed. Since she did not interfere with what was going on at time, the people of her land supposed that she could not see. And so some people invented the myth that she put her eyes in a vessel, using this motif as an image for the negligence caused by drinking wine, on the basis that the wine took away her sight. One could also invoke Euripides as witness to the fact that she was born in Libya. For he says: 'Who does not know the name, most reproachful for mortals, of Lamia, Libyan by birth?' [F472m *TrGF* = 922 Nauck].

**Heraclitus:** They tell that when Zeus had sex with her, Hera turned her into a wild beast, and that whenever she becomes mad she takes out her eyes and puts them in a cup, and that she eats flesh and human beings. This could be the truth. Since she was beautiful, Zeus, the king, approached her, but Hera snatched her away, dug out her eyes and threw them into the mountains. After that she lived an oppressive life without support. Because she went to live in the wilderness, unwashed and untended, she seemed to become a beast.

Here we have two rationalisations of the myth of the archetypal Lamia. Heraclitus's is somewhat half-hearted. As to Diodorus, Automala was at the southernmost point of the Syrtes, which corresponds well with the homeland of Dio's (unnamed) *lamia* creatures, **72**. Nothing here, again, speaks directly of a serpentine nature, though Diodorus's evocative description of Lamia's cave home (which makes a better lair for a monster than it does a birthplace for a queen) seems particularly appropriate to a dragon and should be compared in particular with the mountain-cave home of Antoninus Liberalis's Lamia-Sybaris (**73**).

## 70 Lamia: from individual to category

ca. 500–630 AD

Hesychius s.vv. *Lamia, lamiai* (Greek, ca. 500 AD)

Isidore of Seville *Etymologies* 8.11.102 (Latin, ca. 630 AD)

Greek, Latin

**Hesychius:**

*Lamia.* A beast. And an ancient Libyan woman of this name.
*lamiai.* Apparitions [*phasmata*]. Or gluttonous people. And a fish.

**Isidore:**

*lamiae.* Stories tell that they are accustomed to snatch up babies and 'tear them apart' [*laniare*]. They are so called specifically from their 'tearing apart'.

These two lexicons from the end of antiquity illustrate the simultaneous deployment of the term *lamia* as a proper name for the archetypal individual (i.e. Lamia) and as a term for the category of monster related to the archetype. The description of the monster category as 'apparitions' may bear upon their ability to shape-shift (cf. **68**, **74**), or it may be that the term carries its more particular common meaning of 'ghost'. That the category of *lamias*, as baby-devourers, might be construed as a variety of ghost accords with the notion that the restless ghosts of girls who had died before becoming mothers might be particularly resentful and dangerous. Indeed it is possible that the category of *lamias* could at one level be conceived of as each a manifestation of the vengeful ghost of the archetypal Lamia. The applications of the term to gluttons and to a variety of doubtless greedy fish are metaphorical. Needless to say, Isidore's Latin-based derivation of the Greek term is false. The following passages focus on examples of the *lamia* category. The serpentine nature of these is readily apparent.

## 71   Coroebus slays a baby-devouring *lamia* sent by Apollo against Argos

ca. 92 AD

Statius *Thebaid*
1.562–669

Latin

[Adrastus speaks.] The god [Apollo] had struck down the bluish monster of the winding coils, the earth-born Python who encompassed Delphi with seven black circles, abraded the ancient oaks with his scales and, lolling at the spring of Castalia, gaped with mouth of three-forked tongue in thirst for food for his black venom. His arrows were spent on countless wounds. He left Python's body covering a hundred acres of the land of Cirrha [Delphi], not fully unwound even so, and then, looking for new purifications for the killing, alighted upon the home, far from rich, of our own Crotopus. His house was kept by his daughter, admirable for her grace and piety, a girl just verging upon womanhood and pure of the bed. She would have been fortunate, had the Delian Phoebus [Apollo] not had sex with her in secret. For she was taken by the god beside the wave of the Nemean river. When Cynthia [the moon] was recovering the full disk of her face for the tenth time thereafter, the pregnant girl gave birth to Leto's starry grandson. She feared punishment, for her father would not have pardoned her for being raped. She made for the pathless countryside and secretly amongst the sheepfolds entrusted her son to the mountain-roaming warden of a flock to rear. The grassy couch offered you no bed worthy of your birth so great, child, nor did the steading woven from oak twigs. Your limbs kept warm, wrapped in the bark of the wild strawberry, and the hollow pipe urged you to gentle sleep, as did the sharing of ground with the flock. But the fates denied even that home. For as he lay without care on the turf of the green earth and gazed at the sky with mouth agape, the dreadful hunger of dogs devoured him with bloody bite and tore him apart. When a messenger brought news to the shocked ears of his mother, the sire, the shame and the fear were driven from her mind. Without checking herself, and in a state of madness, she filled the house with cruel lamentations. With breasts bared, she met her father and told him all. He was unmoved and commanded that she fall in black death, for all that she wanted it for herself—an unutterable thing! All too late, Phoebus, did you recall your love and contrive a consolation for her sad death: a monster conceived in the deepest part of the Acheron, in the Furies' unspeakable halls. The monster had the face and breast of a girl but from her head there rose a snake [*anguis*], hissing continuously, parting her ruddy forehead. Then this dread blight slid into rooms by night with scaly gait, snatched newborn souls from the bosoms of their nurses, devoured them with bloody bite and grew fat on the grief of the land. But Coroebus, outstanding in arms and spirit, could not tolerate this and chose to confront the monster with a band of picked youths, the foremost in strength and keen to enhance their repute, even at the expense of their lives. She was on her way after raiding another set of homes and at the gateway between two roads. The bodies of two small children hung by her side, and already her hooked hand was fast in their guts and her iron-shod talons were growing warm in their soft hearts. He confronted her, with his ring of men pressing close on every side, and buried his huge iron sword deep in her hard breast. He searched out the deepest hiding places of her soul with his flashing blade and at last returned his monster to the Jupiter of the depths [Hades] to keep. It is a joy to go and examine closely her eyes, black in death, the unspeakable spillage of her womb and her breast filthy with congealed gore. This was the monster that had taken the lives of our people. The young men of Argos stared in amazement. After the tears, the rejoicing was great but remained muted. By way of empty consolation for their grief, they pounded her lifeless limbs with hard staves and knocked the rough teeth from her jaws. But, do what they might, they could not satisfy their anger. The birds circled her corpse by night with clamour, but they abandoned it uneaten, and they say that the ever-active dogs left it hungry, whilst the wolves gaped in terror at the body with mouths dry. The death of his lost avenger caused the Delian [Apollo] to attack the wretched people with even greater savagery. Sitting in the shade atop double-peaked Parnassus, he cruelly launched arrows of pestilence from his pitiless bow, and he burned up the fields and lofty dwellings of the Argives, casting a pall of cloud over them. Sweet lives slip away. Death cuts the threads of the sisters [the Parcae] with his sword and carries the city he has taken in his grasp to the shades. The king asks the cause: What is this pernicious fire from the sky? Why does the Dog Star rule over them the whole year long? The same authority, Paean [Apollo], commands in reply that the youths responsible for the killing of the bloody monster should be put to death for her sake. Blessed was Coroebus for his courage, and destined to win long-lasting glory across the centuries! He did not ignobly deny the arms he had taken up for the sake of his land or hesitate to meet certain death. He presented himself and stood on the threshold of the Cirrhaean temple and angrily gave voice to his righteous anger:

**642.** 'Thymbraean [Apollo], I approach your home neither sent by another nor as a suppliant. My piety, my courage and my pride have brought me here. I am the one that slew your deadly abomination, cruel Phoebus, the one you are trying to flush out with black clouds, darkened daylight and the black corruption that emanates from the hostile sky. But even if rabid monsters are so dear to the gods above, if the death of men is a smaller loss to the world and savage heaven is so merciless, what have the Argives done to deserve this? Best of the gods, it was preferable that you cast me and me alone before the Fates. Or is that a sweeter thing for your heart, that you should see homes desolate, and that the whole countryside should be ablaze with farmers' pyres? But why do I delay your weapons and your hands by speaking? Our mothers are waiting, and the final prayers are being made for me. This is enough. I have done nothing to make you wish to spare me. So ply your quiver and stretch your sounding bow and send me down to death, a distinguished soul, but already as I die dispel the grey pall that that hangs over Inachian Argos.'

**661.** Fairness favours the deserving. Leto's blazing son shied away from killing him. Humbled, he gave the man the sad reward of life. The evil clouds scattered from our sky. Coroebus departed from Apollo's threshold in amazement after prevailing in his prayer. From this time our solemn feasts have been repeating these due rites every year, and offerings renewed each year placate Apollo in his temple. [669]

This frequently engaging narrative from Statius's Theban epic contrives neither to name nor to give explicit categorisation to its delightful monster. The monster formally earns her place in this section because the ix–xi AD First Vatican Mythographer, in his brief account of the same episode, defines her as a *lamia* (2.66 Zorzetti). The claim is unique and late, but thoroughly plausible: she specialises, as do other *lamias*, in the devouring of babies (**68–70**), and as a Delphi-associated monster she corresponds well with Nicander and Antonius Liberalis's Lamia-Sybaris (**73**). Other sources for the episode apply different terms to the monster: at *Palatine Anthology* 7.154 she is a *kēr* ('death demon'); at Pausanias 1.43.7–8 she is a *poinē* ('punishment').

The monster in question is well described: she is an anguipede of 'scaly gait', with the upper body and head of a girl. The hissing snake that grows up from the top of her head seemingly corresponds to her snake 'foot' to make a complete serpent interrupted by a human upper body. Her arms end in hooked claws with which babies are skewered prior to being devoured. In all regards the description corresponds with the monster depicted on a ca. 470–60 BC white-ground Attic *lekythos*, an image the standard iconographical lexicon misattributes to Python (*LIMC* Apollon 998 = Python 2). The monster stands unthreateningly before Apollo, who sits on the *omphalos* and beside a tripod to signify his Delphic aspect. The tripod also alludes to the founding of the city of Tripodisci, 'Little Tripods', that other sources (e.g. Pausanias 1.43.7–8) tell us Coroebus was instructed by Apollo to found in expiation for his slaying of the monster. He was to find the site by carrying a tripod from the Delphic temple as far as he could until he dropped it.

It is significant that Coroebus should address Apollo in the context of the sending of such a monster by his rare epithet 'Thymbraean'. The temple of Thymbraean Apollo proper, on the Trojan plain, was inhabited by *drakontes*, and it was he who dispatched a pair of them to kill and eat the children (NB the devouring of children again) of Laocoon (**93, 96**). Statius seems conscious of the paradox, in Delphic context, that Apollo should have struck down one dragon there only to dispatch another from the same place to do his work for him. Indeed, by some accounts the dragon he himself killed at Delphi was a female anguipede like this *lamia* (**5, 14**).

'The unspeakable spillage of her womb' may simply be Statius's way of describing the disembowelling of a female monster. It is just conceivable that he means to tell us that the monster was pregnant (a demonic version of the dead girl?) and that a yet more terrible threat, a serpent brood, lay in store for Argos, had not Coroebus intervened. *Lamias*, it seems, are destined to be ever childless.

The detail of the Apolline pestilence following immediately upon the killing of the dragon reminds us of stench created by the killing of the Delphic dragon by Apollo himself (**14**), for all that, here, the pestilence is not directly associated with the *lamia*'s corpse. For the association, direct or indirect, of a fertility-destroying pestilence with a god's sending of an avenging serpentine monster, cf. the tales of Hesione and Andromeda in which a god-sent sea monster's attack upon the land goes hand in hand with a fertility-destroying tsunami (**104, 108, 114**).

In other accounts of this episode the daughter of Crotopus is named as Psamathe, and her child as Linus.

## 72  The *lamiai* creatures of Libya and their devouring of young men

ca. 100 AD

Dio Chrysostom
*Orations* 5.1, 5–16, 18–21, 24–7

Greek

**1.** To elaborate upon a Libyan myth ...

**5.** It is said that long ago there was a species of creature that was dangerous and wild and it occurred chiefly in the uninhabited regions of Libya. For this land even today seems to produce all sorts of animals, and not least reptiles. Amongst these was the species that forms the subject of this disquisition. Its body was a composite of the most unrelated parts, and it was wholly strange. It used to range as far as the Syrtes on our sea [i.e. the gulf of Sirte on the Mediterranean] for its food. It used to hunt other wild beasts, lions and leopards, just as they in turn hunt deer and wild asses and sheep. But it delighted most in making men its prey. And this is why it used to approach places of habitation, all the way up to the Syrtes. The Syrtes is a gulf of the sea that projects far into the land to the distance of three days' uninterrupted voyage. But once one has sailed into the gulf it is impossible to sail out of it again. For shallows, conflicting currents and extensive sandbanks render the waters by all means unnavigable and intractable. The seabed in that region is not clearly defined. Rather, it is hollow and sandy and lets the water in; it has no fixity. This is the cause, I suppose, of the sandbars and the great mounds of sand that are created in it. The same phenomenon occurs on land, too, where it is caused by winds, but in the sea it is caused by waves. The land that surrounds the gulf is more or less the same, desert and sand dunes. But at any rate, should people be shipwrecked and come inland from the sea, or should any native Libyans pass through the region out of necessity or be wandering in it lost, the beasts would appear and snatch them.

**12.** This was the nature and appearance of their bodies: they had the female face of a beautiful woman, and exceptionally beautiful breasts, chest and neck. No mortal girl or bride at the peak of her loveliness could possess such beautiful attributes, nor could a sculptor or a painter represent them. Their skin shone brightly, and the souls of all who looked into their eyes were gripped with love and desire. But the remainder of their body was hard and armoured with scales, and the lower part was all snake [*ophis*]. At the very end was the snake's shameless head. These beasts are not said to have been winged, like sphinxes, nor, like them, are they said to have conversed, but they just made a high-pitched hiss, like dragons [*drakontes*]. They were the fastest of all land animals, so that no one could ever escape them. They relied on their strength to catch other animals, but deceit to catch people. They would reveal their chests and breasts and enchant men just by looking at them, inflicting upon them a terrible longing for sex. Men would approach them as if they were women. They would remain still and repeatedly cast their eyes down in imitation of a decent woman. But when the man had come close they would snatch him up. For they also had beast-like hands, which they would keep concealed up until this point. Anyway, the snake would bite them at once and kill them with its venom. And then the snake and the remainder of the beast would both alike devour the corpse.

**16.** This myth, not fashioned for a child …

**18.** They add that a certain king of the Libyans attempted to annihilate this race of creatures in anger at their destruction of his people. It happened that many of them were living there after taking over a dense, wild wood beyond the Syrtes. He assembled a large army and tracked down their lairs. For they were easy to spot because of the snake trails and the terrible smell they emitted. He surrounded them from all sides and threw fire in. The creatures were trapped and perished together with their broods. The Libyans fled with all haste from the place, pausing for rest neither by night nor by day until they made camp by a certain river in the belief that they had achieved a significant head start. But as soon as all the creatures that had been away on the hunt realised that their lairs had been destroyed, they chased the army down at the river and destroyed it to the last man, finding some of them asleep, and others in a state of exhaustion. So at that time the king's project of eliminating the species remained unfulfilled. Later on, when Heracles was cleansing the whole world of beasts and tyrants, he came to the wood too. He set the place ablaze. Of the creatures that escaped out of the fire, those that joined battle with him he struck and killed with his club. Those that tried to run off he killed with his arrows. [21]

**24.** Would you like me to give the younger ones a further titbit of the myth? So fervently do they believe in the myth and hold it to be true that they say that at a later point a creature of this species once appeared to some Greek sacred ambassadors who were travelling to the oracle of Ammon with a large escort of cavalry and archers. They thought they saw a woman lying on a sand dune. She wore a hide over her head, as the women of Libya do, but she was exposing her chest and breasts and extending her neck backwards. They assumed that she was a prostitute who had come from a village to profit from their number. Two young men, struck by her looks, approached her, one ahead of the other. The creature seized the first one, dragged him down into a hole in the sand and devoured him. The second young man, running past and seeing what happened, shouted out and called for help to the rest of the host. But the creature launched itself at him, projecting its snake end, killed him and went off with a hiss. The body was found in a rotten and putrid condition. The Libyan guides would not allow anyone to touch it, on the ground that all who did so would die. [27]

Like Statius, Dio's show oration does not use the word *lamia* here. That he nonetheless has *lamia*s in mind is clear from his emphasis on the Libyan, and specifically Syrtian, setting of his material, and his comparison of it, more than once, to a myth for children: cf. **68–9**. The *lamia*s he describes strongly resemble Statius's in so far as they are anguipedes with the head and torso of girls and have beast-like hands, and in so doing they further guarantee the identity of Statius's monster as a *lamia*. But they differ from his monster in the one respect that their snake heads are sited not atop their humanoid heads, but at the end of their snake tails, the better to support the marvellous hunting technique Dio describes for them.

The archetypal Lamia and Statius's *lamia* had a taste for babies. These *lamiai*, like Philostratus's (**74**), seem to have a taste rather for vigorous and sexually active young men.

In their Libyan setting these creatures should be compared to the terrible snakes of Libya that Lucan describes at length (**59**, with commentary). And when we hear of Heracles' war of annihilation against these *lamias*, we are reminded of Diodorus's account of Libya's female warrior races of yore, the Amazons and the Gorgons, both of whom Heracles is said to have extirpated (**61**). The lengthy preliminary account of the Syrtes serves to create an appropriate atmosphere of inevitable doom prior to the introduction of the monsters themselves.

## 73   Eurybatus throws Lamia-Sybaris off Mt Cirphis

ii BC–ii AD

Antoninus Liberalis
*Metamorphoses* 8
*Lamia or Sybaris*
(ii AD), paraphrasing
Nicander (ii BC)

Greek

Nicander tells the story in the fourth book of his *Metamorphoses* (*Heteroioumena*). Beside the foothills of Mt Parnassus, on the south side, there is a mountain which is called Cirphis, near Crisa. On it there is still now a gigantic cave in which a huge and overweening beast used to live, and some called it Lamia, others Sybaris. This beast would venture abroad on a daily basis and snatch up flocks and people from the fields. The Delphians had been deliberating about moving their city and consulted the oracle as to what land they should turn to. The god indicated that they would be delivered from their misfortune if they had the heart to stay where they were and expose beside the cave a citizen lad. They did just as the god said. Lots were drawn, and it fell to Alcyoneus, the son of Diomus and Meganira. He was his father's only child, and fair both to look at and in the nature of his personality. The priests garlanded Alcyoneus and took him off to the cave of Sybaris. As a god would have it, Eurybatus, the son of Euphemius and descended from the river Axius, a young but noble-minded man, on his return from Curetis, happened upon the boy as he was being led off. He was smitten with love and asked the purpose of their journey. He thought it terrible that they should not resist the beast by force, but should stand by and watch the boy be slain in pitiful fashion. He took the garlands from Alcyoneus's head, put them on his own and bade them take him off in the boy's place. When the priests had taken him off, he ran up and snatched Sybaris from her lair. He brought her forth to where all could see and hurled her from the rocks. As she was carried down she struck her head against the foothills of Crisa. The creature herself, thus wounded, disappeared from view, but a spring emerged from that rock, and the locals call it Sybaris. And it was in the name of this spring that the Locrians too founded the city of Sybaris in Italy.

What is the form of Lamia-Sybaris? Nothing is said of it, though her *modus operandi*, not least her devouring of people, suggests she is a dragon. And this is suggested too by the strong general correspondences between this narrative and that of the *drakōn* of Thespiae (**99**): there again a youth is selected by lot for exposure to a monster; and again too his lover substitutes himself for the lad to confront the creature (in this case going to his death). We may even go so far as to suggest that she was an anguipede—not merely on the basis of comparison with Statius and Dio (**71–2**), but because the anguipede is the characteristic default form taken by supernatural dragons strongly characterised as female (**M1.b.iv**). As commonly, the dragon is tightly associated—indeed fully identified—with a water source; cf. above all **9** and more generally **M4.a**. As with the tradition of Coroebus's *lamia* (**71**, with commentary), an indirect link is established between the killing of the monster and the foundation of a city.

## 74 Apollonius of Tyana exposes a *lamia* in Corinth before she devours one of his pupils

ca. 220 AD

Philostratus *Life of Apollonius* 4.25 (= *MWG* 60)

Greek

It happened that at that time one Demetrius was studying philosophy in Corinth. He had taken up into his system all the strength of the Cynic doctrine. Later on Favorinus was to make repeated generous mentions of him in his own writings. His relationship towards Apollonius was comparable to that which they say Antisthenes adopted towards the wisdom of Socrates, for he followed him about in his eagerness to learn and applied himself to his writings, and he directed towards Apollonius the most respected of his associates. Among these was the Lycian Menippus, twenty-five years of age, quite sensible enough, and with a body so finely toned that he gave the appearance of being a beautiful gentleman athlete. Many thought that a foreign woman was in love with him, a woman who in turn seemed beautiful and quite gentle. She also claimed to be rich. But all this was wholly false, a complete deception. When he had been walking unaccompanied down the road to Cenchreae, an apparition [*phasma*] met him, materialised in the form of a woman, clung to his hand and claimed that she had been in love with him for a long time, that she was Phoenician and that she lived in one of the Corinthian suburbs, using the name of one or other of them. 'When you arrive there during the evening', she said, 'I will be singing a song for you, and I'll give you wine, the like of which you have never drunk before. There will be no competitor for my love to give you any trouble, but I shall live with you, a beautiful woman with a beautiful man.' The young man was enticed by these words. He was strong in all other aspects of the philosophical life, but could not resist sex. So he went to see her in the evening and thenceforth paid constant visits to her, as if to a catamite, not yet perceiving that she was an apparition. Apollonius eyed up Menippus as a sculptor would do, drew a sketch of him, watched him, and came to a conclusion about him. 'You are a beautiful man, and you are pursued by beautiful women, but you are warming a snake [*ophis*] on your bosom, and it is a snake that warms you.' Menippus was taken aback. 'Because your woman', Apollonius continued, 'is not marriageable. And why? Do you believe that she loves you?' 'Yes, by Zeus', he said, 'since she behaves towards me like a woman in love.' 'Would you marry her?' 'Yes, for it is a delightful thing to marry a woman who loves you.' So Apollonius asked, 'When's the wedding?' 'I'm burning to do it', he said—'perhaps tomorrow.' So Apollonius waited for the drinking party, and then stood over the guests once they had come, saying, 'Where is the gentle lady for whose sake you have come?' 'Here', said Menippus, and began to rise from his couch with a blush. 'To which of the two of you does the silver and the gold all the other finery with which the drinking room has been decorated belong?' 'To the woman', said Menippus, 'for this is all I own,' and he pointed to his rough philosopher's garment. 'Do you know about the gardens of Tantalus', said Apollonius, 'which exist and do not exist at the same time?' 'Yes, we know about them from Homer [*Odyssey* 11.582–92],' they replied, 'for we have yet to go down to Hades.' 'You must believe these decorations too to be such, for they are not substantial, but merely appear to be. So that you may accept what I say, the good bride is one of the *empousa*s, which many consider to be *lamia*s and bogies. These female creatures fall in love, and they crave for sex, but most of all for human flesh, and they use sex to ensnare the men upon whom they wish to feed.' 'Shut up,' she said, 'and get out.' She pretended to be repulsed by what she heard, and I supposed she jeered at the philosophers, to the effect that they were always talking rubbish. But then the golden cups and the pretended silver were shown to be made of air, everything flew from sight, and the wine pourers and the cooks and all the servants disappeared after their unmasking by Apollonius. The apparition pretended to cry and asked him not to subject her to torture or to compel her to admit what she was. However, Apollonius was insistent and would not release her. She admitted that she was an *empousa* and that she was feeding Menippus fat with pleasures as a prelude to eating his body. For it was her practice to feed upon beautiful young bodies, since their blood was pure. I have had to tell this story at length because it happens to be the best-known of all the Apollonius stories, for a great many people are familiar with it, in as much as it occurred in the middle of the Greek mainland. However, they have only had access to a summary version, to the effect that he once captured a *lamia* in Corinth, but they do not yet know what her purpose was and that he acted to protect Menippus. My version of the story comes from Damis and his writings.

Familiarity with the modern English-language metaphor of clasping a snake to one's bosom must not blind us to the fact that Apollonius here is telling poor Menippus that his fiancée is literally a snake.

This *lamia*, explicitly described as such, like those of Statius and Dio (and perhaps too that of Antoninus, **71–3**), combines in her form the elements of beautiful woman and snake. However, it seems that this one does not combine the two forms in a composite body, but rather displays the two forms at different times, as a shape-shifter. The sources for the archetypal Lamia, we recall, draw attention to her change of form, albeit in a rather different way, from beautiful woman to monster (**68**). Philostratus's *lamia* is described also as an apparition, *phasma*, a term that, as we have noted (**70**), may allude specifically to her shape-shifting ability, but may also subscribe to the simpler notion that she is indeed fundamentally a ghost (either of a dead girl or even of the archetypal Lamia). It is noteworthy that ancient ghosts generally possessed the ability to shift between animal forms (cf. Lucian *Philopseudes* 29–31).

Like the *lamia*s of Dio (**72**), this *lamia* has a taste for vigorous and sexually active young men rather than little babies, as in the case of the archetypal Lamia and the *lamia* of Statius (**68–71**). The notion, suggested by Apollonius here, that *lamia*s should feel genuine erotic desire or even love for the young men that they must eat casts them as tragic creatures. Is their desire for sex part of some eternally doomed drive to (re)acquire babies?

This *lamia* is also defined as an *empousa*. The precise nature of these creatures too remains obscure, but when ancient scholars implausibly explain the term on the basis that they went on one foot (as if reflecting the words *hen* + *pous*), they seem to envisage them as anguipedes: schol. Aristophanes *Frogs* 293; *Suda* and *Etymologicum Magnum* s.v. *empousa*. Indeed the Aristophanic joke under elucidation by his scholiast may itself also imply that *empousai* were anguipedes, though the case is not a straightforward one. Beyond that, *empousai* seem to have been denizens of the underworld (Aristophanes *Frogs* 288–95; cf. **71**) and either to have served as demonic apparitions visited upon people by Hecate or actually to have constituted manifestations of Hecate herself (cf. again the ancient scholarship cited above), who was also at times an anguipede (**102**). Plutarch further identifies the term *empousa* with *poinē* (*Moralia* 1101c), which brings us back once again to Statius's *lamia* (**71**, with commentary).

## FURTHER READING

Lamia and *lamia*s in general: Rohde 1925:590–3, Fontenrose 1959:44–5, 100–4, 119–20, 1968:81–3 Vermeule 1977, Scobie 1983:21–30, Boardman 1992, Johnston 1999:161–202 (with care), Hansen 2002:128–30, Resnick and Kitchell 2007.

Lamashtu and her relationship to Lamia: Farber 1983, Burkert 1992:82–7, 197 n.3, West 1995 esp. 292–303.

# 11
# *The Dragon of Ares, Slain by Cadmus*

The tale of Cadmus's slaying of the Dragon of Ares at the spring of Dirce, the site of the city of Thebes which he will go on to found, is perhaps the purest and simplest of ancient dragon-slaying tales in its essentials. Particular interest attaches to the brood of Spartoi, the 'Sown Men' produced from the dragon's teeth; to the possibility that metal was first discovered by mankind either in its carcass or in the arms of the Spartoi; and to the figure of Cadmus, who has form as a dragon slayer, having helped Zeus slay Typhon (8), yet is destined to be transformed into a dragon himself together with his wife Harmonia (77, 79). For the Dragon of Ares see also **8, 88, 135**.

Figure 11 Cadmus slays the Dragon of Ares with a rock. Red-figure Paestan crater, ca. 330 BC. Musée du Louvre, Collection Durand. Alinari / The Bridgeman Art Library.

## 75 Cadmus slays the Dragon of Ares: a summary derived in part from Hellanicus and Pherecydes

ca. 454 BC–ca. 100 AD

Apollodorus *Bibliotheca* 3.4.1 (cf. Hellanicus F51 Fowler, later v BC, and Pherecydes F22a Fowler, ca. 454 BC) and 3.5.4 (ca. 100 AD)

Greek

**3.4.1–2.** Apollo told Cadmus not to concern himself with Europa [his lost sister], but to follow a cow that would show him the way, and to found a city wherever it fell down tired. Having received the oracle, he made his way through the land of the Phocians and then encountered a cow amongst the herds of Pelagon. He followed behind it. Passing through Boeotia, it lay down at the point where the city of Thebes is now. Wishing to sacrifice the cow to Athene, he sent some of his men to get water from the spring of Ares. A dragon [*drakōn*] guarding the spring, which some said was born of Ares, killed the majority of those sent. Cadmus became angry and slew the dragon and, on Athene's advice, sowed its teeth. When the teeth had been sown men rose up from the ground under arms, whom they called the Spartoi [Sown Men]. These men killed each other, some in the course of arguments, knowing what they were doing, and others without realising it. Pherecydes says that Cadmus, seeing the armed men growing up out of the earth, threw stones at them, and they, thinking that they were being attacked by each other, fell to fighting. But five remained over, Echion, Oudaios, Chthonios, Hyperenor and Peloros. In return for his killing [of the dragon], Cadmus was indentured to Ares for a long year. For a year at that time was equal to eight modern ones. After his period of service Athene bestowed a kingdom upon him, and Zeus gave him Harmonia to wife, the daughter of Aphrodite and Ares.

**3.5.4.** Cadmus left Thebes with Harmonia and went to the Encheleans [Eel People]. The Illyrians were making war on them, but the god prophesied that they would beat them if they had Cadmus and Harmonia as their leaders. The Encheleans were persuaded and so made them their leaders against the Illyrians, and conquered them. Cadmus became king of the Illyrians. After this Cadmus turned into a serpent [*drakōn*], together with Harmonia, and was sent by Zeus to the Elycian fields.

Apollodorus credits Pherecydes at least for his narrative of the Spartoi episode (cf. Pherecydes F22a Fowler). But, confusingly, a scholium to Homer (schol. Homer *Iliad* 2.494), which offers a summary of the myth that runs closely parallel to Apollodorus's, credits rather Hellanicus's *Boeotiaca* (F51 Fowler) as its source. Hellanicus stipulated that Zeus arranged Cadmus's marriage to Harmonia in order to prevent the angry Ares killing him.

In many ways this is a classic old Greek dragon-slaying narrative. Firstly, the dragon in question is tightly associated with a water source, which it guards (**M4.a.i**). Other sources name the spring as Dirce (**76, 79**). Second, the slaying of the dragon is associated with the founding of a city (**M14.b.v**). Third, restitution must be made for the killing of the dragon, in this case by Cadmus's period of service (cf. **16**; **M14.a**); the curious equation of one ancient year to eight modern ones looks like an attempt to resolve conflicting traditions as to the length of Cadmus's service. The sowing of the dragon's teeth to produce a crop of indirect children may also be seen as a form of restitution. The names of the Earth-born Spartoi speak: Echion means 'viper', Oudaios and Chthonios both mean 'of the earth' and Peloros means 'monstrous'. And a third variety of restitution is made when both Cadmus and his bride, Harmonia, are themselves transformed into dragons.

Hyginus, in the second century AD, gives brief summary accounts of Cadmus's killing of the Serpent of Ares (*Fabulae* 178) and of Cadmus and

Harmonia's transformation into serpents in turn (6) in terms similar to those of Apollodorus here. But he also notes, telegraphically, that 'Cadmus, the son of Agenor, was the first to discover and make bronze, at Thebes' (274.4). The combination of the claims that Cadmus killed the Serpent of Ares with a stone, disposed of the ensuing Spartoi similarly with stones and then discovered bronze at Thebes is suggestive. Fuller accounts may have said either that bronze was first brought forth from the earth in the armour worn by the Earth-born men, or that Cadmus discovered the precious substance inside the body, perhaps specifically the head, of the Dragon of Ares once he had killed it: cf. the Hydra's golden head (**25**) and the precious stones that Philostratus says can be found inside the heads of the marvellous serpents of India (*Apollonius* 3.8). Beyond the ancient world, we may compare also the body-hardening properties of the blood of the slain Fafnir (**B3, B6**).

## 76   Further early light on the Dragon of Ares

410–9 BC

Euripides *Phoenissae* 638–48, 657–75, 818–21, 931–41, 1006–12, 1060–6.

Greek

CHORUS: [638] Tyrian Cadmus came to this land, for whom a four-legged heifer fulfilled an oracle by throwing herself down in untamed fashion, in the place where it was divinely foretold that he should dwell in the wheat-bearing plains of his home, where the waters of Dirce, fair of stream, spread across the verdant and deep-sown lands. [648]...[657] There was the guardian, the bloody, savage-minded dragon [*drakōn*] of Ares, watching over the flowing, fertile waters, its glancing pupils darting in all directions. Cadmus killed it with a marble rock when he came to wash his hands. He threw it against its bloody head with a lob from his beast-destroying arm. He cast the teeth that fell to the ground into the deep-sown land, at the advice of the motherless goddess [i.e. Athene]. Therefrom the earth sent up beyond its topmost surface a fully armed display. Iron-hearted killing rejoined them to the dear earth and wet with their blood the earth that had exhibited them to the sun-warmed breezes of the ether. [675]

CHORUS: [818] You bore, o Earth, you bore once, according to the barbarian [i.e. Phoenician] rumour I learned, I learned once in my home, the teeth-sired race from the beast-eating purple-crested dragon. This race is the most beautiful occasion of reproach for Thebes. [821]

TIRESIAS: [931] This man must be slaughtered in the chambers where the earth-born dragon was overseer to the spring of Dirce, and give his red blood to the earth of Cadmus as an offering, because of the ancient anger of Ares, who avenges the murder of the earth-born dragon. If you do this you will acquire Ares as an ally, and if the Earth receives fruit in place of fruit, and mortal blood in place of blood, you will have the Earth well disposed towards you, the Earth which once sent up for us the golden-helmeted crop of the Spartoi. A person from this family must die, one who is descended from the jaws of the dragon. [941]

MENOECEUS: [1006] By Zeus with the stars and by murderous Ares, who established the Spartoi that once rose from the earth as lords of this land, I will go and stand on the top of the battlements, sacrificing myself into the deep, dark precinct of the dragon, where the prophet indicated, and I will liberate the land. [1012]

CHORUS: [1060] May we become mothers so, may we become mothers to fine children, dear Pallas Athene, who spilled the blood of the dragon with a cast of a stone, urging Cadmus's mind to the deed, from which a frenzy of greedy powers sped over this land. [1065]

The setting is the attack of the Seven against Thebes upon that city. Tiresias prophesies that Ares, god of war, remains angry with the city over the killing of his serpent, as does its mother, Earth (still more compensation is evidently needed), and that Thebes can accordingly hope to survive the current war only if she appeases both parents by sacrificing a Theban of pure descent from the Spartoi. Only the young Menoeceus, son of Creon, fits the bill, and the lad nobly kills himself.

As often happens, it is Athene who inspires or supports heroes in their battles against the great dragons (**M13.a.ii**). Euripides' reference to the Dragon of Ares' purple crest is one of the earliest mentions in the literary record of a dragon's crest or beard, though both are prolific in earlier art (**M1.a.ii**); the ruddiness attributed to the crest here is realised in an illustration of Cadmus's slaying of the dragon on a fine red-figure Paestan vase of ca. 330 BC, with red paint used to highlight and pick out the monster's beard and crest (*LIMC* Kadmos i 25).

It appears from a series of passing references here that the former lair of the serpent, from which—or within which—it guarded the spring of Dirce, was some sort of chasm adjacent to the current city wall, from which Menoeceus was able to hurl himself into it. Elsewhere in the play Creon refers to 'the serpent's [*drakonteios*] crags' as a local landmark, possibly the same site (1315).

## 77  The transformation of Cadmus and Harmonia into snakes

ca. 450–406 BC

Euripides *Bacchae* 1330–9, 1355–60 (410–9 BC).

Euripides F930 *TrGF* (ca. 450–406 BC)

Philostratus *Imagines* 1.18

Greek

**Euripides *Bacchae*:**

DIONYSUS: [1330] You [Cadmus] will change and become a dragon [*drakōn*], and your wife, whom you received from Ares even though you are mortal, will be transformed into a beast, and take on the shape of a snake. This is what the oracle of Zeus says. Together with your wife you will drive a chariot drawn by calves, leading barbarians. You will sack many cities with your unnumbered army. But when you raid the oracle of Loxias [Apollo], you will make for yourself a wretched return home. Ares will save you and Harmonia and establish a life for you in the Land of the Blessed. [1309]

CADMUS: [1335]...And furthermore for me it is fated to lead a mixed barbarian army against Greece, and as a dragon [*drakōn*] I shall take the daughter of Ares, Harmonia, my wife, with the wild nature of a dragoness [*drakaina*], against the altars and tombs of the Greeks, in charge of armed divisions. [1360]

**Euripides F930 *TrGF*:** Alas, half of me is becoming a dragon [*drakōn*]! My child, embrace what is left of your father!

**Philostratus:** [An imaginary painting is described.] And there [sc. on Cithaeron] are Harmonia and Cadmus, but they are not as they were. For they are becoming dragons [*drakontes*] up to their thighs, and they are already covered in scales. Gone are their feet, gone are their buttocks, and the transformation of their form

CHAPTER 11: THE DRAGON OF ARES, SLAIN BY CADMUS

is creeping up their bodies. They are astonished and embrace each other, as if trying to hold on to what remains of their bodies so as not to be deprived of them.

For the context of Cadmus's and Harmonia's transformation into dragons and their martial role as such, see **75, 79**. The F930 *TrGF* fragment is preserved without context; it may well describe Cadmus's transformation into a serpent, perhaps specifically, in this case, into an anguipede ('half of me'), as in the transformation subsequently imagined by Philostratus, whose vignettes can elsewhere be seen to refract the world of Euripides (**111**).

## 78 An elaborate account of Cadmus's battle with the dragon

8 AD

Ovid *Metamorphoses* 3.28–98

Latin

An old wood stood violated by no axe. In its midst was a cave covered over thickly with twigs and withies, making a low arch with its structure of stones. It was fertile in rich waters. Buried in this cave was a snake of Mars [Ares], remarkable for its golden crest. Its eyes flickered with fire, its whole body swelled with venom. Three tongues flickered, its teeth were arranged in three rows. The Tyrians [i.e. Cadmus and his Phoenician companions], with luckless step, stopped at this grove on their journey. The jar, lowered down to the waters, made a noise, and the dark blue serpent [*serpens*] lifted its head out of the length of its cave and gave out a terrible hiss. The jars fell from their hands, the blood left their bodies, and a sudden trembling seized their stricken limbs. The snake rolled its scaly coils in rounded gatherings and threw them up into huge arcs. With more than half of its body lifted high into the gentle breezes, it looked down over the entire grove. Its body was as great as the one you would see if you gazed upon the full length of the snake that separates the twin Bear constellations. Without delay it snatched up the Phoenicians, whether they were pulling out their weapons, whether they were making to escape, or whether terror was preventing them from doing either. Some it killed with its bite, others with the embrace of its extensive coils, others again with the blast of its venom, deadly with corruption. Now the sun, at its highest point in the sky, reduced the shadows to their minimum. Cadmus, born of Agenor, wondered what was delaying his comrades and followed their tracks. His shield was a hide torn from a lion, his weapons a spear of shining iron and a javelin and a spirit superior to every weapon. On entering the grove he saw the slaughtered bodies and the victorious enemy, with its massive body, hanging over them, licking their wretched limbs with a bloody tongue. 'Bodies most loyal to me, I shall be either the avenger of your death, or your companion in it,' said Cadmus. So he spoke and with his right hand he picked up a huge rock, the size of a millstone, and hurled it, with great exertion. Lofty walls and their high towers would have been damaged by its impact, but the serpent remained unwounded. It was protected by its scales as if by a breastplate, and it repelled the violent blow from its skin by the hardness of its black hide. But this hardness did not overcome the javelin as well. This lodged, fixed in the middle of the curve of its twisting back, and the entirety of its iron point penetrated into its guts. The wild creature twisted back its head towards its back, saw the wound and bit onto the shaft that was fixed there. When, with much force, it had loosened the shaft on all sides, it eventually managed to rip it out of its back. But even so the iron point remained stuck in its bones. That was the point at which, this new cause being added to its normal rage, its throat swelled with full veins, and white foam splashed over its deadly snarl. The earth resounded as it scraped over it with its scales, and it infected the corrupted air with a black breath of the sort that issues from a Stygian mouth. Now it would coil round and fashion a monstrous circle from its coils; now it would stand up rampant, straighter than a tall beam; now it would surge forward with huge force like a river made violent by rains and crush the woods that lay in its way down with its breast. The son of Agenor conceded a little ground, deflected its attack with his lion-prize shield and frustrated the mouth that pressed upon him by defending himself with his spear. The snake raged and vainly attempted to deal wounds to the hard iron. It fixed its teeth around the point. Now it was that the blood began to flow forth from its venomous palate and bespatter the green grass. But the wound was just a superficial one, because the snake dragged itself back from the blow and drew its damaged neck backwards. By giving ground it tried to prevent Cadmus's blow from striking home or penetrating more deeply. But at the same time the son of Agenor, relentlessly following the snake, drove on the iron he had lodged in its throat until an oak tree blocked its way as it went backwards and its neck became pinned to the wood. The tree bowed under the serpent's weight and bewailed the fact that its trunk was being lashed by the tip of its tail. As the victor contemplated the bulk of the enemy he had overcome, a voice was suddenly heard (it was difficult to tell whence it emanated, but nonetheless, heard it was): 'Why, son of Agenor, do you gaze at the serpent you have killed? You too will be gazed at in the form of a serpent.'

Ovid offers an extensive account of Cadmus and the founding of Thebes, including the episodes of the search for Europa and of the battle with the Earth-born or Spartoi, at 3.1–137. Only the richly detailed narrative of the central battle with the serpent is offered here.

Ovid makes much of the traditional themes of a dragon's sacred grove (**M3.b.i**), its cave lair (**M3.a.ii**) and its guardianship of waters (**M4.a.I**), wrapping them together seemingly by placing the serpent's cave lair in the grove and the spring of Dirce seemingly within a well-like structure at the mouth of the serpent's cave lair.

As it so often is, the dragon is fiery, flashing fire from its eyes (**M6.a.iii**). As so often too, the serpent is said to belch forth a noxious breath (**M7.a.ii**). Ovid compares the fumes that the serpent emits with the mephitic vapours traditionally associated with the ancient world's underworld entrances, in a nexus of thought that Silius Italicus will develop still further in the case of the Bagrada Dragon (**98**).

The configuration in which the serpent first presents itself as it leaves its cave is the artificial one that is so popular in the iconography of the great supernatural serpents, and mentioned above (*LIMC* Kadmos i 25): the serpent is evidently conceptualised here as rampant in its forepart, whilst its hind part spirals vertically like a Catherine wheel.

The mysterious prophetic voice at the end of the quoted passage makes it clear that Cadmus's own future transformation into a serpent (**75**, **77**) will constitute some sort of punishment or compensation for the killing of Ares' serpent.

Since Cadmus and his men bear arms of metal, indeed actually of iron, it seems that Ovid does not subscribe to the notion that Cadmus first discovered bronze only in the body of the serpent or in the weapons of the dead Earth-born or Spartoi (75, with com.). It is intriguing, nonetheless, that he should compare the dragon's skin to a breastplate (M1.a.v; cf. M4.b).

## 79  An expansive account of Cadmus's battle with the dragon, from the end of antiquity

v AD

Nonnus *Dionysiaca* 4.348–463

Greek

**348.** The cow's prophetic hoof gave way and she sank to the ground, revealing the site of the city to be. But when the Pythian oracle from the resounding crypt was fulfilled, Cadmus set the sacred cow beside an incense-laden altar and looked for streaming spring water, so that he could purify his divining hands and pour a libation of holy water over the sacrifice. For the soft fruit of the burgeoning crop had not yet made its appearance in wine-growing vineyards [i.e., it was not yet the custom to use wine in sacrifice].

**356.** He brought his feet to a standstill at dragon-rearing [*drakontobotos*] Dirce. He stood in amazement to see the dapple-backed snake of Ares present itself there, slithering sideways, and coil around the spring with snaky bond. It frightened off the army, as great as it was, that was accompanying Cadmus. It bit one man beneath the chest with its flashing jaws. It attacked and rent another with its bloody tooth. It tore out the life-preserving liver of a third man who fought against it, and laid him out dead. A dusty and disordered crest ran over its neck, slipping down from its stout head. It panicked another man by leaping over the side of his temple. It ran unchecked over the chin of another again, and cast venomous dew into his eye, drawing a mist over the brightly shining eyeball as the lid closed. It snatched up the foot of another. Tearing at it with its jaw, it held it in its bite. From its teeth it spat out green foam onto the youth's body, and his body was frozen by the green venom and turned the colour of livid iron. Another gasped under the blows from the jaws, as his cerebral membrane gushed violently out of his head at the venomous bite. Gore from his liquidised brain ran out of his dripping nose.

**365.** The swift dragon [*drakōn*] crawled up Cadmus's shins and bound him threateningly. Then, with an upwards lurch it elongated its body and leaped at the round boss of his oxhide shield. With his feet entwined by its twisted spirals, the man toiled under the weight of its viperish, trailing tail. The burden was dreadful. As he tried, weighed down, to stand upright and bear it up, the snake dragged on him and pulled him down to the ground. It unlocked its bitter mouth and the bloody gateway of its cruel, gaping, raw-eating gullet stretched wide. It inclined its head and shook it, and arched and coiled the central part of its neck.

**389.** When Cadmus was failing, Athene approached. She shook her *aegis* with its viperish Gorgon-head of hair, omen of victory to be. The people-delivering deity cried out at the bewildered man:

**393.** 'Cadmus, ally of Giant-slaying Zeus in the din of battle, are you frightened to see a single snake? Placing his trust in you for battle the son of Cronus cast down Typhon, bedecked with all those dragon [*drakonteios*] heads. Stop trembling before the hiss emanating from the creature's teeth. Pallas Athene gives you encouragement. Bronze-clad Ares will not deliver his guardian snake beside bloody Dirce. Rather, when you have killed it, take the beast's dreadful teeth, sow the earth all around with the viperish fruit and reap the snaky harvest of Giant war. Unite the ranks of the Earth-born ones in a single doom, leaving just five alive. Let the splendid crop of the Spartoi spring up for the Thebes that is to be.'

**406.** So speaking, Athene encouraged the dismayed Cadmus before brushing the depths of the air with her swift foot and entering the house of Zeus. He braced himself against the rich earth and brandished the well-rounded marble boundary marker of an extensive farm, a weapon of rock. He threw the stone straight and with it dashed the top of the dragon's head. He drew his sharp knife from his thigh and cut at the beast's neck. He hacked the head from the body and laid it to one side, but its tail jerked in the dust and unravelled its familiar coils. Then the dragon lay dead, outstretched on the ground. Violent Ares cried out over the corpse, overburdened by his anger. It was due to this anger that Cadmus would change his form, his limbs mutating into coils, and take on the alien shape of a serpent's visage in the furthest reaches of the Illyrian land.

**421.** But that was destined for a later time. At this point he collected the fruit of the serpent's doom in his bronze helmet, the dismal crop of the beast's jaws. He brought a plough from Athene's local precinct and drove it into the land, cutting a war-begetting furrow in the dark earth, and sowed a long row of the venomous teeth. A self-fertilizing crop of Giants sprang up. One of them shot up, lifting his head, and shook the upper part of his chest in its breastplate. Another jutted his head out and reached his dreadful shoulder over the opened earth. Another bent his upper body forwards from the navel. Another grew up from the ground half-made, brandishing an earth-nurtured weapon. Another shook the bending plume with which he jutted forth, whilst not yet showing his chest. Though still crawling forth from his mother's womb, he was already beginning to fight with vigour against the unfrightened Cadmus, wearing the armour that had grown with him. What an amazing sight! Eileithyia [goddess of childbirth] armed the one of whom his mother had not yet been delivered. And one of them launched the spear that had been born with him, groping about and still only half emerged. Another drew the entirety of his body swiftly up into the light, but left the tips of his feet unmade and fixed still in the soil.

**441.** Cadmus did not forget Athene's command. He reaped the stalks of the re-growing Giants. He hit one above the breast with a spear as swift as the wind. Another Cadmus struck on the collarbone and the side of his stout neck and tore through the bones of his hairy throat. He shattered another by launching a rock at him whilst he had emerged only as far as the belly. Blood flowed in rivers from the awful Giants. Ares slipped in the gore and bloodied his limbs, and Victory's tunic was reddened with purple splatters of blood as she stood beside the battle. Another Cadmus struck with his sword in the hip as he fought and cut through his waist and at the same time the surface of the oxhide shield that had been born with him. The killing was limitless. As the Giants were cut down and slain by the sword a stream of death-blood gushed forth.

**455.** Following the sensible advice of Pallas Athene, Cadmus lifted a rock over the heads of the Earth-born. Drunk with bloody craving for war, they held a revel-rout in Ares' honour. They destroyed each other with the iron that was born with them and themselves were entombed in the dust. One struggled against another. As an Earth-born one was killed, the surface of his oxhide shield darkened as it was spotted and wetted with reddening gore. The crop of the field was cut down by the earth-sword's kin-killing point. [463]

Nonnus had given Cadmus an important role in his expansive account of Zeus's great fight against Typhon (8), alluded to in passing here (394–6); now he returns as the star in an elaborate account of the dragon fight that is traditionally his own. Dragon fights were clearly close to Nonnus's heart.

The notion that the dragon should have been reared in or by the spring of Dirce matches the notions that the Hydra was reared in the spring of Amymone (24) and that the Bagrada serpent was similarly reared in the river of that name (98; **M4.a.ii**). Nonnus further makes it clear that the serpent is also the special guardian of the spring (**M4.a.i**), though once again the reason for the guarding of the spring is left obscure. Nonnus gives us no clear idea of the dragon's size: the general impression is of a large monster, but the fact that it can knot itself round Cadmus's feet or run over one of his soldier's chins suggests something rather slender, however long.

Athene is ever the supporter of heroes in their dragon fights (**M13.a.ii**). In brandishing her viperish *aegis* she seems to bring one dragon to fight another (cf. **M8.b.iv**).

As always, one can see in Cadmus's sowing of the dragon's teeth a way of making good for the destruction of the dragon (alongside his period of service). But Nonnus also makes it more explicit here (417–20) than any earlier extant source that Cadmus's own eventual transformation into a serpent is also in some way a compensation and restitution for the killing of the Serpent of Ares (Nonnus refers to the eventual serpentine transformation of Cadmus also at *Dionysiaca* 5.121–5, 44.107–18 and 46.364–7). The characterisation of the Earth-born Spartoi as 'Giants' is curious in the context of mythological tradition but makes sense in so far as the true Giants were indeed similarly Earth-born and could in other contexts boast serpentine qualities of their own. (cf. **1**).

Some inconcinnities may be remarked upon. If Ares' dragon has hitherto successfully guarded the spring, then it ought to lie in uncultivated, virgin land, nor indeed would one have expected there to have been any signs of occupation or civilisation at the site of the city of Thebes to be. Yet in fighting the dragon at the spring itself, Cadmus is able to stave its head in with the boundary stone of an extensive farm, whilst a local shrine of Athene can offer him the convenient loan of a plough. (The motif of the boundary stone is likely to be much older than Nonnus: it appears to have been borrowed from the Dragon of Ares tradition into the Dragon of Nemea tradition by Statius as early as the end of the first century AD [**83**].) There is some primitivism here: wine has not yet been discovered, and so water alone can be used for sacrificial libation. But the notion that the battle against the dragon should have taken place in an age before the discovery of metal has clearly been lost. It matters not that the Earth-born 'Giants' should grow from the ground complete with metal arms, for they are sown from the teeth of the dragon, the body of which, as we have seen, may in other accounts have been the source of Cadmus's initial discovery of metal. But Cadmus already has a knife with which to hack off the dragon's head and a bronze helmet in which to collect its teeth.

The brief narratives of the dragon's predations upon Cadmus's army as it chases the men off are reminiscent of Lucan's celebrated account of the depredations of the dreadful snakes of Libya upon Cato's army (Lucan 9.700–838; cf. **59**).

## 80 The Dragon of Ares and the Spartoi rationalised

ca. 300 BC–ii AD

Palaephatus 3 (ca. 300 BC)

Greek

A certain ancient story tells that Cadmus killed a snake, took out its teeth and sowed them in his own land. Then men sprung up with weapons. If this were true, no one would ever have sown anything other than snake's teeth. And even if they could not grow in other lands, nonetheless they would be sown in the land in which they formerly grew. This is the truth. Cadmus, a man of Phoenician race, came to Thebes to compete for the kingship [sc. of Phoenicia] with his brother

Phoenix. At that time the king of Thebes was Drakon, the son of Ares. He had all the usual wealth of kings, and in particular he had some elephants' tusks. Cadmus killed him and ruled in his place. The sons of Drakon made war on him, but Cadmus's sons stood by him. The friends of Drakon, since they were worsted in battle, snatched Cadmus's money and the elephants' tusks, which lay in the temple, and fled off home. They were scattered in different directions, some to Attica, some to the Peloponnese, Phocis and Locris. Starting out from those places they made war on the Thebans, and they were tough warriors, since they spoke the same tongue and they knew the land. When they had fled after snatching the tusks, the citizens would say this: 'Such are the ills that Cadmus did us in killing Drakon. For as a result of those teeth many good men have become scattered [*spartoi*] and fight against us.' The myth was elaborated on this basis.

Elements of this Palaephatus chapter are confusing, either because of its originally eliptical nature or because of corruption in the manuscript tradition. It remains unclear how Cadmus expected to compete for the throne of Phoenicia with his brother and its eponymous current king Phoenix by coming to Thebes. The dragon of the myth is rationalised in the most typical and unimaginative way, by transmutation into 'a man called Drakon'; the resolution of the dragon's teeth is, by contrast, delightfully whimsical and surreal.

## FURTHER READING

Robert 1920–6:1, 100–14, Fontenrose 1959:306–20, Vian 1963:76–176, Vermeule 1971, Servais-Soyez 1981, Paribeni 1988, Tiverios 1990, Gantz 1993:469–70, Gourmelen 2004:381–400.

# 12
# *The Dragon of Nemea, Slain by the Seven against Thebes*

As the Seven passed through Nemea on their way to attack Thebes, they sought water. The slave nurse Hypsipyle put her charge, the baby Opheltes, down in the grass as she went to fetch it for them from a spring. There the baby was killed by a dragon, either by accident or by design. The Seven killed the dragon in revenge and established the Nemean games in memory of the child. For other baby and child victims of dragons, see **19–22, 68–71, 92–5**.

### 81  Euripides' account the Dragon of Nemea recovered

412 BC–ii AD

Euripides *Hypsipyle* FF754a, 757 *TrGF* (412–406 BC; Greek)

Hyginus *Fabulae* 74 (ii AD; Latin)

Greek and Latin

**Hyginus:** The seven leaders, who were en route to attack Thebes [i.e. the Seven against Thebes], stopped off in Nemea, where Hypsipyle, the daughter of Thoas, enslaved as she was, was serving as nurse to Archemorus or Opheltes, the son of King Lycus. She had been given an oracle that she should not lay the child down on the ground before he could walk. So the seven leaders, who were going to Thebes, came to Hypsipyle in their search for water and asked her to show them water. She fearfully put the boy down on the ground...there was some very tall parsley beside the spring, in which she laid the boy down. Whilst she was

Figure 12 The Dragon of Nemea devours baby Opheltes-Archemorus as he makes appeal to his nurse Hypsipyle. Red-figure Paestan crater, fragment, ca. 360 BC. Bari Museum. Redrawn by Eriko Ogden.

119

handing the water to them, the dragon [*draco*] that was guardian to the spring devoured the boy. But Adrastus and the others killed the dragon and pleaded Hypsipyle's case before Lycus. They established funeral games for the boy, which take place every four years, and in which the victors are rewarded with wreaths of parsley.

**Euripides:** F754a *TrGF*....a spring is shaded...a dragon [*drakōn*], living nearby to it...with fierce gaze...shaking its crest, fear of which...shepherds when quietly in...to do...to a woman everything happens...has come...not...a guard.

F757 *TrGF.* Amphiaraus:...child...and we...dragon...threw a javelin...and him run...coiled around...and we, seeing...and I shot...for it was a beginning for us...Archemorus...[then later in the fragment]...grant us to bury...for he will be famous...a competition for him...crowns....will be envied...in this....will be remembered...was named...in the grove of Nemea...she is not responsible...with good...she will make you and your son...

Hyginus's mythical summaries often reflect the plots of particular tragedies, and his summary of the myth of Opheltes-Archemorus and the Dragon of Nemea broadly reflects the plot of Euripides' lost *Hypsipyle*, as is demonstrated by surviving fragments of the play (including fragments beyond those reproduced here); cf. also, in this regard, schol. Pindar *Nemeans*, Hypothesis 2.

The first of the Euripidean fragments given appears to derive from an establishing scene in which the dragon and its role of guardianship are introduced. We note that the creature bears a distinctive badge of a supernatural *drakōn*, a crest (**M1.a.ii**). In the second of the fragments Amphiaraus narrates how he and others killed the dragon with javelin and arrow. He notes that the death of the boy symbolises the 'beginning of doom' for the Seven (cf. **82**) and so gives him an additional name, Archemorus, that signifies this. He then asks the boy's mother, Eurydice, for permission to bury him and to establish the Nemean Games to celebrate his memory, and speaks in defence of Hypsipyle.

Once again a dragon lives in a grove (**M2.b.i**) and protects a water source (**M4.a.i**). The killing of the dragon is followed by an act of memorialisation in the establishment of the cyclical Nemean Games (**M14.b.vi**); however, this was conceptualized as a memorial for the boy killed by the dragon, Opheltes-Archemorus, rather than for the dragon itself.

The iconography of the boy Opheltes-Archemorus was curiously calqued on the iconography of baby Heracles in his battle with the dragon pair sent against him by Hera. Both are shown in a splayed kneeling position and raising a single arm aloft. Baby Heracles does this to throttle one of the dragons (*LIMC* Alkmene 8, 11) but for Opheltes-Archemorus the gesture becomes a vain appeal for help (*LIMC* Archemoros 2, 7).

## 82 The earliest extant reference to the Dragon of Nemea

earlier v BC

Bacchylides *Epinicians* 9.10–14

Greek

In that place [Nemea] the red-shielded half-gods, the picked men of the Argives, first competed in honour of Archemorus, whom an enormous yellow-glancing dragon [*drakōn*] slew as he slept, a portent of the coming death.

CHAPTER 12: THE DRAGON OF NEMEA, SLAIN BY THE SEVEN AGAINST THEBES   121

This is the earliest extant reference to Dragon of Nemea. The lyric poet Bacchylides already knows the tale, it seems, of the renaming of the dead boy in the light of the doom that his death represented for the Seven. 'Yellow-glancing' may refer to the commonplace notion that a dragon had fiery eyes (M6.a.iii).

## 83 The Dragon of Nemea is slain by Hippomedon and Capaneus, in the most expansive account of the episode

91–2 AD

Statius *Thebaid* 4.716–22, 739–45, 775–96, 5.505–87

Latin

**4.716.** Only Langia sustains her waters, silently, albeit by the command of a god, she too in a remote and shaded place. Archemorus had not yet bestowed upon her a tearful name by being snatched away, and the goddess was not spoken of. Even so, she preserves her grove and her stream in her out-of-the-way place. Huge glory awaits the nymph, when the games, sweated over by Achaean leaders, and the black third-year festival will renew honour for sad Hypsipyle and sacred Opheltes. [722]

**4.739.** Wandering through the woods, in accordance with Dionysus's plan, they suddenly see Hypsipyle, beautiful as she grieved. From her breast hangs Opheltes, although he is not her own, but the unfortunate offspring of Inachian Lycurgus. Her hair is in disarray, nor are her clothes those of a rich person, but there are marks of royalty in her face, and her station is not buried in her bitter circumstances, but shines forth. [745]

[Adrastus proceeds to ask Hypsipyle for water.]

**4.775.** [Hypsipyle replies.] 'Come with me now, to see if Langia keeps her waters streaming continuously....'... At once, so as not to be too slow a leader to the Pelasgians, she lays down the wretched nursling (alas!), clinging to her as he was, in the adjacent grass—this is how the Fates twisted their threads—and she consoles his sweet tears as he objects to being put down with a heap of flowers and a gentle murmur.... But the child, in the bosom of the green earth and the deep grass, now crushes flat the tender grass by crawling forwards, struggling along, face down, and now he calls upon his dear nurse, crying out in need of milk. Smiling again, and intending words that struggle against gentle lips, he is awestruck by the sounds of the groves, or plucks what he finds before him, or drinks in the daylight with broad face. He wanders around in the grove, unaware of troubles and without concern for his own life. [796]

**5.505.** In the meantime a serpent [*serpens*], born of the earth, the sacred terror of the Achaean grove, rose up in the fields, and with a loose drawing motion now drove its monstrous self forwards, now left its back behind it. There was a bluish fire in its eyes. The green foam of its swollen venom was poised in its mouth. Three tongues flickered. There were three ranks of barbed teeth. A splendid but cruel crest projected from its gilded forehead. The peasants said that it was sacred to Jupiter the Thunderer, who presided over the place and received the meagre offerings made on forest altars. Now the serpent twined around the the temples of the gods, gliding with wandering coil, now it wore away the oaks of the wretched forest and smashed enormous ash trees in its coils. Often it stretched itself out across rivers, lying on both raised banks at once, and the river, bisected by its scales, seethed up. But at other times, when all the land was gasping at the behest of Ogygian Dionysus, and the trembling nymphs [i.e. the naiad springs] lay hidden in the dust, it twisted its winding frame backward on the ground more savagely and curved its sides around, and raged dangerously with the fire of its parched venom. It rolled over ponds, dry lakes and failing springs, and wandered in empty riverbeds. Tentatively, it now lifted back its mouth and licked at the liquid air, and now, facing downwards as it grated over the groaning fields, it cleaved to the earth, in case the green plants should exude any moisture. But, wherever it applied its mouth, the grasses, stricken by the hot blasts of its breath, collapsed, and the field died before its hissing. It was as large as the Snake that separates the ether from the Artic Plough and extends to the South and the foreign sky. It was as big as that snake too [i.e. Python] that twisted round the twin peaks of sacred Parnassus with its coils, until, transfixed by you, Delian Apollo, it carried with it a forest of arrows, with a hundred wounds. Little boy, what god allotted to you so weighty a fate? Did you already lie dead before this foe, when scarcely at the very threshold of life? Was it all so that you might die in a fashion worthy of such a great tomb, and become sacred for the peoples of Greece throughout the centuries? You died, boy, when grazed by the lashing tip of the serpent's tail (it knew it not), and at once sleep fled from your limbs, and your eyes opened only into death. But when your shocked, dying cry was released into the breezes, and then fell silent in your mouth, your complaints broken short, just as utterances go unfinished when people dream, Hypsipyle heard, and, lifeless herself, snatched along her sickened knees which baulked at the easy course. She was already sure of disaster, foreboding it in her mind, and she scanned everything with hasty gaze, searching over the ground and repeating in vain the words known to the small child. He was nowhere to be seen, and the meadows had already lost his fresh tracks. The sluggish enemy slumbered in the greensward, gathered into a spiral, and occupied broad acres, its neck laid out upon its slanting belly. The unfortunate woman shuddered at the sight and fired the deep grove with her long cry. The serpent was not disturbed; it merely continued to lie there. The tearful howls reached the ears of the Argives. As soon as they were alerted, on the leader's nod the Arcadian knight Parthenopaeus, fired up, sped to find the cause and brought back the explanation. Then, finally, the fierce creature stirred its scaly neck in response to the glinting of the arms and the cries of the men. With a huge exertion Hippomedon snatched up a rock, with which a field had been marked off, and, raising himself aloft, drove it through the empty air. It whirled with the motion of the stones hurled against gates barred in war. The leader's valour was fruitless: the snake had already swung its pliable neck backwards and defused the blow as it made contact. The earth reverberated and the densely entwined foliage was torn apart throughout the pathless groves. Capaneus came up to challenge the snake with an ash-wood spear, and cried out, 'But you will never escape the wounds I deal you, whether you are the wild inhabitant of a trembling grove, or a source of pleasure granted to the gods (and would that you were). You would not do so even if you were to carry on this back of yours a Giant to join battle with me.' The trembling spear flew and entered the monster's gaping mouth. It cut the wild bonds of the three-furrowed tongue. Then it shot out through the standing crests that decorated its flashing head. Coated with the gore of the black brain, it lodged itself deeply in the ground. The agony had hardly coursed through the entirety of its frame, but, rolling itself up swiftly, it encompassed the weapon, tore it out and fled back with it into the hidden shrine of the god. There it stretched out its great bulk over the ground and hissed out its life in supplication at its master's altars. You mourned for him, indignant marsh of akin Lerna [home of the Hydra], Nymphs accustomed to sprinkle the snake with spring flowers, the fields of Nemea it crawled over, and the wood-dwelling fauns of every grove, with your pan pipes. Zeus himself had called for his weapons from the height of the ether, and clouds and storms were gathering. But his anger was too small, and Capaneus was held not to deserve the greater weapon. The draft alone of the launched thunderbolt caught the top of his helmet crest. [587]

Statius's narrative of the tale of Opheltes and the Dragon of Nemea is too discursive to merit quotation in full. The key portions are given here and can be contextualized against the Hyginus summary (**81**).

The action is overseen by Dionysus, who has dried up all the water sources in the region except for the Nemean spring in order to bring Opheltes and the Seven to their fates. The Nemean spring is now given a name, Langia, and seemingly identified with a nymph or naiad thereby (cf. **76, 79**), but with what pedigree it remains unclear. The spring waters a grove sacred to Zeus and houses a shrine to him. The Dragon of Nemea, which lives in the grove and guards the spring, is, consequently, also sacred to Zeus and is to some extent watched over by him. In the final lines of the quoted material Zeus is on the point of coming to the defence of his dragon by hurling a thunderbolt at Capaneus. At the last minute he thinks better of it and deflects it. The relationship between Zeus and his dragon is reminiscent of that between the Dirce-guarding Dragon of Ares and its god (**75–80**).

Several commonplaces may be noted: the great dragon is twice said to sport a golden crest (**M1.a.ii**). It is also said to possess fiery venom (**M6.a.i**), to have a fiery and parching breath (**M6.a.ii**) and to flash fire from its eyes (**M6.a.iii**). These last themes are carried across, metaphorically at any rate, to its human opponents: Hypsipyle 'fires' the grove with her cry of grief; Parthenopaeus is 'fired up' as he rushes to investigate (**M6.b.ii**).

Statius rings some changes in comparison to the Euripidean tradition. The dragon kills the boy not purposefully or to eat, but unwittingly with a brush of its tail: the conceit serves to convey not only its vast size, but its sluggish insensitivity in the parching heat Dionysus has created. The dragon is no longer killed by Adrastus, but by Hippomedon and Capaneus. Hippomedon's hurling of a boundary stone against the dragon recalls the method by which Cadmus famously dispatched the Dragon of Ares (specifically the tradition reflected at **79**).

The local nymphs and spirits mourn the dead dragon, with which they evidently feel a kinship; cf. the naiads that mourn the death of Silius's Bagrada serpent (**98**).

The Dragon of Nemea is compared, bombastically, to the constellation of Draco (cf. **4, 8**), and also, more understandably, to its fellow supernatural *drakontes*, the Delphic Python (**13–18**) and the Lernean Hydra (**23–7**). Once again, one senses that the ancients possessed a notional canon of great *drakontes* (cf. **4**).

## 84 The myth of the Dragon of Nemea in relation to the cults observed there

later ii AD

Pausanias 2.15.2–3

Greek

At Nemea there is a temple of Nemean Zeus which is worth seeing, except that, when I saw it, its roof had fallen in, and there was no effigy left there. There is a grove of cypresses around the temple, and they say that Opheltes was put into the grass there by his nurse and destroyed by the dragon [*drakōn*]. The Argives make sacrifice to Zeus in Nemea as well, and they elect a priest to Nemean Zeus. And they give a running prize for men in full armour at the wintertime Nemean festival. The grave of Opheltes is there. Around it is a stone wall, and there are altars within its circuit. There is an earthen barrow, the tomb of Lycurgus, father of Opheltes. They call the spring 'Adrasteian' either because it was discovered by Adrastus or for some other reason.

Pausanias's brief description of the sacred area of Nemea in his own day makes it easy to see how the myth of the Dragon of Nemea and the mortals involved with the creature was inscribed in the topography and cult practices that had, no doubt, given rise to it in the first place, and of which it was the aetiology (**M14.b.vi**).

## FURTHER READING

Robert 1920–6:3, 933–6, Bond 1963, Simon 1979, Pülhorn 1984, Cockle 1987, Miller 1990, Gantz 1993:345–6, 511, Krauskopf 1994, Boulotis 1997, Collard et al. 2004:169–258, Pache 2004:95–134.

# 13
## The Dragon of Colchis, Slain or Sent to Sleep by Jason and Medea

For all its fame, Jason's encounter with the Dragon of Colchis, as he steals the golden fleece it guards, is the subject of only a few extant extended narratives, as the relatively modest length of this section illustrates. According to Apollonius's canonical summary of the wider Argonaut legend, Pelias, the wicked king of Iolcus, received a prophecy that Jason would kill him, so he sent the young man on a mission to fetch the golden fleece from Colchis, where it was kept by Aeetes, a mission from which Jason was not expected to return: cf. Eurystheus's imposition of labours upon Heracles, in particular those of the Hydra (**23–7**) and Cerberus (**35–42**); the Lycian king's imposition of labours upon Bellero-

Figure 13 Jason is regurgitated by the Colchis Dragon. The Duris Cup, Attica, ca. 470 BC. Vatican Museums and Galleries. The Bridgeman Art Library.

125

phon, in particular that of the Chimaera (**48–51**); and Polydectes' imposition of the Medusa labour upon Perseus (**54–9**). Jason assembled a group of companions to travel to Colchis with him, and they took the name Argonauts from their ship, the Argo. After many adventures along the way, Jason arrived in Colchis, and Aeetes offered to give Jason the fleece if he completed the task—as, again, he was not expected to—of yoking his massive bronze-footed bulls and then using them to sow a field with the teeth of the Dragon of Ares (cf. **88**). Aeetes' daughter, the young witch Medea, fell in love with Jason and anointed him with drugs of invincibility so that he might after all complete the task against expectation. The frustrated Aeetes refused to surrender the fleece and plotted to kill Jason and the Argonauts by other means, but before he could do so Jason stole the fleece from the grove where it was kept and watched over by the Dragon of Colchis, which Medea drugged to sleep for him. After many further adventures Jason, the Argonauts and Medea, now his wife, found their way back to Iolcus, where, with a combination of genuine magic and simple deceit, Medea tricked Pelias's daughters into killing him (Apollodorus *Bibliotheca* 1.9.16–27). The Dragon of Colchis is also mentioned at **2, 4**.

## 85  The earliest literary account of Jason's encounter with the Colchis Dragon.

462 BC

Pindar *Pythians* 4.242–50

Greek

Immediately Aeetes, the amazing son of Helios, told him [Jason] of the shining skin and the place in which the sacrificial knives of Phrixus had stretched it out. But that was a labour that he did not expect him to complete. For it lay in a copse, adjacent to the aggressive jaws of a dragon [*drakōn*], which surpassed in breadth and length a fifty-oared ship, fashioned by the blows of iron tools... with devices he slew the grey-eyed dappled-backed snake, Arcesilaus, and he stole away Medea with her co-operation, Medea the slayer of Pelias.

As is often the case, the great dragon lives in a grove, possibly, as in other cases, and as in **87** and **90**, a sacred one. Pindar presents us with a vignette that corresponds in part with the most traditional iconography of the Dragon of Colchis, which shows the golden fleece hanging, sometimes stretched, in the branches of a great tree, with the dragon also hanging in the branches, or winding around the trunk, to guard it. It is difficult, however, to imagine how a dragon the breadth and length of a ship could contrive to live in any tree.

Was Medea already involved in the dragon episode, so far as Pindar was concerned? His account is a glancing one, and it may not, therefore, be significant that he makes no explicit mention of Medea in direct connection with the dragon. However, the 'devices' with which Jason slew the snake may well allude to the deployment of some variety of magic or deceit on Medea's part. This may have been the drugging of the dragon to sleep, an event that was to become canonical.

But there is another possibility. The marvellous Duris cup (*LIMC* Iason 32), painted shortly before Pindar wrote, ca. 470 BC, shows the fleece hanging in its tree in the background, whilst in the foreground a dragon so massive that there is room only to show its (elaborately and beautifully crafted) head, disgorges a bedraggled Jason. The female figure in attendance is not Medea but Athene, as ever the champion of dragon slayers. (Some much cruder scenes from the seventh century BC of men emerging from the mouths of dragons, without tree or fleece, may, however, depict the same subject.) This scene reports an intriguing episode completely unattested in the extant literary tradition. Why does the dragon, having swallowed Jason, disgorge him? If it has found him indigestible, this may well have been due to the continuing effects of the invincibility lotion with which Medea had coated Jason prior to the trial of the bulls and the (Colchian) Spartoi.

## 86 Medea takes credit for the killing of the Colchis Dragon

431 BC

Euripides *Medea* 480–2

Greek

MEDEA: And I killed the dragon [*drakōn*] that kept safe the all-golden fleece, embracing it in the many folds of its coils, unsleeping ever, and I held up for you the light of deliverance.

Speculations about the significance of Pindar's words (**85**) aside, Euripides' tragedy makes the earliest explicit and direct association of Medea with the killing of the Dragon of Colchis, an association that would thenceforth be canonical, although in the context of the play it is conceivable that the claim is tendentious.

The dragon is described as 'unsleeping', as guardian dragons often are (of course, the common or garden snakes upon which they are modelled cannot close their eyes). To the extent that Medea's claim is to be taken seriously, the word's use here suggests that Medea had used her magical drugs to send the dragon to sleep, as she does in later sources, so that it could be slaughtered with ease either by Jason or indeed by herself.

## 87 The most influential account of Medea's drugging of the Dragon of Colchis

ca. 270–45

Apollonius *Argonautica* 4.123–66

Greek

Jason and Medea came down the path to the sacred grove in search of the giant oak, over which the fleece had been cast, like a cloud that glows red under the fiery rays of the rising sun. But the snake, watching out with its sleepless eyes, stretched out its long neck to meet them as they came and gave out a monstrous hiss. The long riverbanks and the vast grove reverberated around them. This was heard by the inhabitants of the Colchian land who lived a long way from Titanian Aea [i.e. Colchis itself], by the debouch of the Lycus, which splits off from the roaring river Araxes and mixes its sacred stream with the Phasis. They combine their streams into one and debouch into the Caucasian sea. New mothers woke in fear and, distressed, threw their hands round their babies, who were sleeping in the crooks of their arms, and who shook at the hiss. As above smoldering wood unnumbered circles of sooty smoke coil upwards and one ever rises quickly after another, ascending from below in spirals, so then did that huge creature gather its unnumbered coils, covered over with dry scales. The girl came before its eyes as it coiled. In a sweet voice she invoked Sleep, highest of the gods, to help her in bewitching the monster. She cried out to the night-wandering queen, the underworld goddess [Hecate, patron of witches], to look kindly upon her project. The son of Aeson [Jason] followed her, scared, but the snake was already bewitched by her song and was unfolding its long, spiralling spine and straightening its countless circles, just as a black wave, silent and without noise, rolls over a calm sea. Even so, it raised its terrible head aloft and was eager to enfold the pair of them in its ruinous jaws. But she sprinkled its eyes with a fresh-cut sprig of juniper, dipping this pure herb into her potion to the accompaniment of her incantations. The intense smell of the drug cast sleep round about. The snake lay down and rested its jaw just where it was. Its endless coils were unfurled a long way behind through the wood of many trees. Then, as the girl instructed him, he seized the golden fleece from the oak. But she stood her ground and smeared the head of the creature with her drug, until Jason himself bade her return to his ship, and she left the shady grove of Ares.

Apollonius's account of the Dragon of Colchis episode (and indeed of the Argonaut saga as a whole) was the most influential in antiquity. It also represents the earliest explicit entry into the literary tradition of the motif of Medea drugging the dragon to sleep with her herbs and incantations, though vases from ca. 380 BC onwards show her, often in oriental dress, approaching the snake to drug it either with a sprig with which to sprinkle its eyes, a dish from which it is to drink or a witch's box of herbs (*LIMC* Iason 38–43, 46, 47b). The iconography closely resembles that of the Hesperides feeding Ladon, possibly for the similarly deceitful purpose of stealing, or allowing Heracles to steal, his golden apples (**31**). It is implicit that Medea herself has nothing to fear from the dragon and that it trusts her. Persumably she had hitherto been its keeper, it her pet. Perhaps that is why the dragon is merely drugged and left alive. Jason, alas, is left with little opportunity to display valour here.

Why do new mothers in particular fear for their babies upon hearing the great dragon's hiss? Do they perhaps imagine that a *lamia* is coming to take them (cf. **68–70**)?

## 88  Athene divides the Dragon of Ares' teeth between Cadmus and Aeetes, who deploys his half in the trial he imposes upon Jason

ca. 270–45 AD

Apollonius *Argonautica* 3.1176–90

Greek

They [the Argonauts Telamon and Aethalides] came and their journey was not in vain. When they had come King Aeetes gave them as a trial the intractable teeth of the Aonian dragon [*drakōn*], which Cadmus slew in Ogygian Thebes, when he encountered it during his search for Europa. It was the guardian of Ares' spring. There he settled after being escorted by a cow, which Apollo, by way of prophecy, gave him to lead his way. The Tritonian goddess [Athene] dashed the teeth from its jaws and gave them as gift to Aeetes and to the slayer himself. Cadmus the son of Agenor sowed them on the Aonian plains and created an Earth-born people from all those that were left behind by the spear when Ares had reaped them down. Aeetes readily gave the teeth to be taken to the ship, for he did not think that Jason would make an end to this trial, even if he cast the yoke upon the oxen.

A rare explicit explanation of how it was that both Cadmus himself and Aeetes came to have handfuls of the teeth of the Dragon of Ares to sow to produce Earth-born warriors. Aeetes, as we have seen, uses his as part of the elaborate trial he sets Jason (**75–6, 79–8**). Apollonius's narrative of Jason's actual battle with the Earth-born follows at 3.1340–1407. So, like Cadmus, Jason encounters both a guardian dragon and a host of warriors sown from a dragon's teeth, albeit in reverse order. One has to wonder whether parallel versions of the Argonaut saga existed in which the Earth-born warriors faced by Jason were derived not from the teeth of Cadmus's dragon, but from those of his own dragon, the Dragon of Colchis, which he would accordingly have killed first. (Such a notion was adopted by Ray Harryhausen in his marvellous 1963 movie *Jason and the Argonauts*: here Aeetes hacks the teeth from the Hydra-shaped Dragon of Colchis that Jason has already killed to create a final, climactic trial for him. In a bravura scene of stop-motion animation, the Earth-born warriors are conceptualized as slightly larger than life-size skeletons.) Once again, Athene's presence looms where great dragons are slain.

## 89  An expansive and engaging account of the Colchis Dragon episode

ca. 80 AD

Valerius Flaccus *Argonautica* 8.54–121

Latin

So Medea said and with rapid step made her way along the pathless course. Jason stuck close by her side and was feeling sorry for her in her journey, when suddenly he saw a huge flame in the midst of the clouds, and the darkness shimmering with a cruel light. 'What is that redness in the sky? Which star shines so dismally?' he said. The maiden answered, as he trembled, 'See, you are looking at the eyes and the wild stare of the dragon [*draco*] himself. He shakes those thunderbolts from his crest. I am the only one that he looks upon with fear. He has the habit of calling me by choice, and he asks me for food with a fawning tongue. Come, tell me now, would you prefer to carry off the spoils from him whilst he is awake and sees you, his enemy, or do I rather plunge his eyes in sleep and give you a tamed snake?' He remained silent, so forcibly was he gripped by awe for the maiden.

**69.** And now the Colchian stretched up her hands and wand to the stars, pouring out spells with a barbarian metre, and she began to rouse you up, father Sleep: 'All-powerful Sleep, I, the Colchian, bid you now come from all over the world and enter this dragon alone. Relying on your horn, I have often overcome the waves, the clouds, the thunderbolts and whatever flashes throughout the heaven. But now, now, come to me in greater force, most like your brother Death. For you too [Dragon of Colchis], most faithful guardian of the Phrixean sheep, it is at last time to turn away your eyes from your object of concern. What trick do you fear whilst I am standing by you? I myself will look after the grove for a brief while. In the meantime lay aside your long toil.' He could not abide, though tired, to abandon the Aeolian gold, nor to give his eyes over to the rest he had been permitted, much as he would have liked to. Struck by a cloud of first drowsiness, he shivered and shook the sweet sleep from his body. But on the other side the Colchian maiden continued to foam with Tartarean spells and shake about all the silences of her bough of Lethe [forgetfulness]. She overwhelmed his struggling eyes with an incantation against them, and with tongue and hand she tried all her Stygian power, until sleep was in control of his blazing anger. Now his lofty crests sank down. His head, under compulsion, and his huge neck nodded down from the fleece, like the Po in backward flow or the Nile dispersed into seven rivers or the Alpheos as it arrives in the Hesperian world. Medea herself, when she saw the head of her dear dragon on the ground, threw herself upon him and put her arms around him, and wept for herself and for her nursling, to whom she was being so cruel. 'This was not how you looked when late at night I brought you offerings and feasts, nor was I like this when I put honey cakes in your gaping mouth and faithfully nourished you with my herbs [*or*: poisons, *venena*]. How heavy your bulk as you lie! How slowly you breathe as you lie there motionless! At least, unfortunate one, I have not killed you! Alas, you are destined to experience a cruel daylight! Soon you will see no fleece, no shining offering under your shade. So withdraw, and pass your old age in other groves, and forget me, I beg you. Nor let your hostile hissing drive me forth over all the sea. But you, son of Aeson [Jason], dispel all delays, seize the fleece and flee! With my drugs I extinguished my father's bulls and I gave the Earth-born warriors over to death. See, you have the body of the dragon sprawling before you, and now at last, I trust, I have finished my crimes.' Then the hero asked her by what route he should carry himself up to the top of the gold-bearing tree. 'There,' she said, 'come, climb over the snake himself and press your steps into his back before you.' There was no delay. The descendent of Cretheus [Jason] put his trust in her words, scaled his way up to the top of the ash tree, high as it was, the branches of which were still keeping safe the ruddy skin, the like of illuminated clouds or Iris [the rainbow] when she undoes her dress and glides to meet blazing Apollo. Jason snatched up the prize he had longed for, his final labour. Only reluctantly did the tree surrender the memento of Phrixus's flight, which it had borne through long years. It groaned, and dismal darkness surrounded it. They left …

Valerius's *Argonautica* was in general closely modelled on Apollonius's (87). In this passage it is easy to see at once both the impact of the model and the extent to which Valerius has elaborated winningly upon it, not least in the sympathetic description of the dragon's battle to stay awake before the onslaught of Medea's sleep-casting magic, and in Jason's use of the sleeping dragon as a ladder by which to reach the fleece.

The fiery eyes traditionally associated with the great dragons are well realised here (**M6.a.iii**). The dragon crest, common in art (**M1.a.ii**) is also presented as fiery in itself (cf. **M6.a**).

The notion, implicit in Apollonius, that hitherto Medea has been the dragon's keeper and it her beloved pet is here made explicit, and is deployed to poignant effect. In her apologetic speech to the dragon, Medea alludes to her former regular feeding of it with *venena*. The term could denote (like its Greek equivalent, *pharmaka*) either magical herbs or more simply poisons, and the latter will, paradoxically, have been the primary meaning here, for it was a commonplace in the ancient world that snakes stoked up their venom by devouring poisonous plants, to which they were themselves of course immune (Homer *Iliad* 22.93–4, Aelian *Nature of Animals* 6.4). But the close association between herbs of magical and those of more simply poisonous effect shows how easily the ancients could have imagined Medea substituting one kind for the other as she fed the snake. Honey cakes were the offerings traditionally given to the sacred snakes (some real, some imaginary) kept in the shrines of the Graeco-Roman world. Little use they would have been to the real snakes, however, for they are of course purely carnivorous.

## 90 Orpheus masterminds the seizure of the fleece from the Colchis Dragon

iv AD or later

*Orphic Argonautica*
887–1021 (=*MWG* No. 71)

Greek

**887.** [Orpheus speaks] When Medea had secretly quit the house of Aeetes and arrived at our ship, we then tried to work out the easiest way to go to take the golden fleece from its sacred oak. We turned it over in our minds, none of us holding that the task was hopeless. For great deeds are required of heroes, though it was becoming apparent that we had reached the nadir of our troubles. For before the house of Aeetes and the fast river a terribly high enclosure, some fifty-four feet high, confronted us. It was defended by towers and well-polished blocks of iron and crowned by seven parapets in a circle. In it there were three gigantic gates fitted with bronze. A wall ran atop them, decorated with golden battlements. At one of the gateposts was a statue of the far-seeing lady, brandishing flashing fire [i.e. Hecate]. The Colchians worship her as Artemis of the Gates, the one who runs in din, terrible for men to see and terrible for them to hear, unless one has come to rites of initiation and purificatory sacrifices. All these purifications were kept hidden by the initiating priestess, Medea of the terrible bed, together with the girls of Cyta. No mortal entered within by that route, stepping over the threshold, whether a man of the city or a stranger, for the terrible goddess prevented them by all means, the queen that breathes madness into her fiery-eyed dogs. In the furthest recess of the enclosure was a sacred grove, shaded by flourishing trees. In it there were many laurels and cornels and tall plane trees. Within this the grass was carpeted with low-growing plants with powerful roots. Famous asphodel, pretty maidenhair, rushes, galingale, delicate verbena, sage, hedge mustard, purple honeysuckle, healing cassidony, flourishing field basil, mandrake, hulwort, in addition fluffy dittany, fragrant saffron, nose-smart, there too lion's-foot, green briar, camomile, black poppy, *alcua*, allheal, white hellebore, aconite and many other noxious plants grew from the earth. In the middle a stout oak tree with heaven-high trunk spread its branches out over much of the grove. On it hung, spread out over a long branch, the golden fleece, over which watched a terrible snake, a monster deadly to mortals, which cannot be described. For it was decked with golden scales and it wound up around the trunk in its huge coils. It tended the tomb of chthonic Zeus as it guarded the fleece. Untiring but without sleep, it scrutinized its surroundings with grey eyes, rolling its shameless gaze this way and that.

**934.** But when we learned the true situation regarding Mounychian Hecate and the dragon's [*drakōn*] guardianship—for Medea explained everything to us clearly—we sought an unexpected way to accomplish the woeful task, namely to propitiate and sway Artemis the Huntress and approach the monstrous beast, so that we could steal the fleece and return to our homeland. Then Mopsus, who knew about these things because of his prophetic abilities, urged the other heroes to beseech me and to give me the job of propitiating Artemis and of bewitching the overweening beast. So they stood around me and begged me. But I commanded the son of Aeson [Jason], and these two strong fellows, Castor the horse tamer and Pollux the good boxer, to accomplish the task together with Mopsus, the son of Ampyx. Alone of the others, Medea accompanied me.

**950.** When I arrived at the enclosure and the divine abode I dug a triangular pit in some flat ground. I quickly fetched some logs of juniper, dry cedar, prickly boxthorn and much-lamenting black poplars, and I made a pyre of them in the pit. Knowledgeable Medea brought many drugs, taking them from the coffers of an incense-laden crypt. At once I fashioned figures from barley meal [the text is briefly corrupt]. I threw them onto the pyre and slaughtered three all-black puppies as a sacrifice to the dead. With their blood I mixed copper sulphate, soapwort, a sprig of safflower, and in addition odourless fleawort, red alkanet and bronzeplant. Then I filled the bellies of the puppies with this and placed them on the logs. I mixed the bowels with water and poured it round the pit. Dressed as I was in a dark mantle I sounded bronze cymbals and made my prayer. The Furies readily gave heed, breaking forth from the caverns of the cheerless abyss, Tisiphone, Allecto and divine Megaira, brandishing the flame of death in their dry pine torches. At once the pit was kindled, and the deadly fire crackled. The dirty flame sent its smoke high. At once, on the far side of the fire, the cruel Fearful Ones assembled themselves. One could not bear to look upon them. One of them had a body of iron. Mortals call her Pandora. With her came a shape-shifter, who could be seen to have three heads, a deadly monster that could not be described, Hecate, child of Tartarus. A horse with a long mane leaped from her left shoulder. On her right shoulder one could see a dog with a maddened face. In the middle was a snake of wild form. With both hands she held well-hilted swords. They wheeled around the pit in circles, this way and that, Pandora and Hecate. The Poinai [Punishments] leaped with them. Suddenly the wooden guardian statue of Artemis dropped its pine torches to the ground and raised its eyes to heaven. Her attendant dogs fawned. The bolts of the silver bars were loosed and the beautiful doors of the thick, strong wall flew open, and the mighty grove within was revealed.

**988.** I crossed the threshold. Then Medea, the daughter of Aeetes, the glorious son of Aeson and the Tyndarids hurried across too, and Mopsus followed along. But when we could see the lovely oak nearby and the plinth of the Zeus of Visitors and the altar base, at that point the dragon spun round and raised his head and fearful jaws from underneath the broad coils in which he had wound them. He emitted a deadly hiss. The boundless ether resounded. The trees cracked, shaken from the bottom of their roots. The shaded grove cried out. My companions and I were seized by trembling. Alone amongst us Medea kept an unflinching heart in her breast. For she had picked with her hands cuttings of baneful roots. Then I matched my divine voice, resounding deeply, to my lyre, plucking its lowest-pitched string, and sent an unuttered word from silent lips. I invoked Sleep, lord of the gods and of all men, to come and bewitch the might of the strong dragon. He heeded me at once and came to the land of Cyta. Sending to sleep tribes of ephemeral men, powerful blasts of winds, waves of the sea, springs of ever-flowing waters, streams of rivers, beasts and birds, and bringing stillness to everything that lived and moved, he travelled by the power of his golden wings. He came to the land of the hard Colchians. A deep sleep suddenly descended upon the eyes of the monstrous dragon, like death. He laid out his long neck, his head drowsy under the weight of its scales. Medea of the dreadful destiny marvelled to see it. She encouraged the glorious son of Aeson [Jason] and sent him to seize the golden fleece quickly from the trunk. Jason heard her and did not disobey. He took up the vast fleece and came to the ship. The Minyan heroes were overjoyed and lifted their hands to the immortal gods, who inhabit wide heaven.

The fourth-century AD or later *Orphic Argonautica* presents itself as an autobiographical retelling of the Argonaut myth by Orpheus himself. The pattern of events resembles that of Apollonius's poem, but the narrator pads his part. Here he virtually usurps Medea, taking over her role as caster of sleep upon the dragon; and this he does by the means proper to himself, his enchanting lyre as opposed to Medea's drugs. But even so, Medea fares better than poor Jason, who is now reduced to the role of third-in-command, little more than a passive dogsbody.

The text offers us the most elaborate description of the sacred grove in which the dragon lives and does its work of guarding the fleece (cf. **M3.b.i**). Within this, the dragon is described, curiously, as tending the tomb of chthonic Zeus. We may compare the wider ancient notion of a tomb-dwelling serpent born out of the body of a dead hero (cf. **132–3, 151, B2**). The rite Orpheus directs for the opening of the doors of the sacred enclosure corresponds to that with which Apollonius's Jason activates his invincibility lotion by calling up Hecate (3.1026–1224). Like that rite too, it has strongly chthonic or even necromantic overtones, with its pit, its sacrifice of black puppies and its voodoo dolls. For the dragon aspect of the goddess Hecate herself, see **102**.

Like Valerius Flaccus, the *Orphic Argonautica* draws attention to the terrible effects of the Colchis Dragon's hiss.

## 91 The subsequent career of the Dragon of Colchis

later iv BC–xii AD

Lycus *FGrH* 570 F3 (later iv BC) = Timaeus *FGrH* 566 F53 (ca. 260 BC), at Tzetzes *Commentary on Lycophron* Alexandra 615 (xii AD)

Greek

After the capture of Troy, Diomede threw some stones from the walls of Troy into his ship for ballast. Coming to Argos, he narrowly escaped being murdered by his wife and moved on to Italy. At that point he found the Colchian dragon [*drakōn*] laying waste to Phaeacis and killed it. He had the golden shield of Glaucus, and the dragon had mistaken it for the golden ram's fleece. He was greatly honoured for this, and so he made statues of himself out of the stones from Troy that he had thrown into the ship, and set them up all over the plain there. Later on Daunus killed him and cast the statues into the sea. These were carried out to sea by the waves but then returned to their bases. Timaeus tells us this, and so does Lycus in his third book.

This fragment, attributed to both the historians Timaeus and Lycus by Tzetzes in his commentary on Lycophron's *Alexandra*, is the unique source for this curious coda to the myth of the Dragon of Colchis. It presumes, of course, that the dragon had been left alive rather than killed by Jason and Medea, as in **87**, **89–90**. That the dragon should still be attempting to track down the lost golden fleece is touching. By what means it had made its way from Colchis to southern Italy one can hardly imagine.

### FURTHER READING

Heydemann 1886, Jessen 1914, Robert 1920–6:3, 794–6, Séchan 1927, Lesky 1931, Simon 1954, Zinserling-Paul 1979, Vojatzi 1982:87–94, Braswell 1988:6–23, Neils 1990, Schmidt 1992, Gantz 1993:358–60, Clauss and Johnston 1997, Isler-Kerényi 2000.

# 14
# The Dragon Pair Sent against Laocoon and his Sons

The story of Laocoon, somewhat anomalous in our collection for featuring a dragon fight from which the dragons emerge victorious and yet receive no comeuppance, was already known to Arctinus in the seventh century BC (*Iliou Persis*, as summarised in Proclus's *Chrestomathia*). The tale is well-known, constituting as it does one of the most celebrated and mysterious episodes of Virgil's *Aeneid*. As the Trojan priest Laocoon is making sacrifice in the final

Figure 14 The Vatican Laocoon, Hellenistic. Vatican Museums and Galleries. Alinari / The Bridgeman Art Library.

134

hours of the Trojan War, a pair of dragons cross the sea to devour him and his young sons for a reason that, in context, remains unclear.

**92** Laocoon and his twin sons are devoured by a pair of serpents at Poseidon's altars on the Trojan coast in the last hours before the fall of Troy

19 BC

Virgil *Aeneid* 2.199–231

Latin

[Aeneas speaks.] At this point another greater thing is cast before us, something to shudder at far more, and it disturbs our hearts, which do know not what is in store. Laocoon, selected by lot to be priest of Neptune [Poseidon], was slaying a huge bull at the traditional altars. When—lo!—from Tenedos twin snakes [*angues*] breast the sea, crossing the calm depths with their immense coils (I shiver to tell the tale) and make for the shore side by side. Their breasts are upright and their bloody crests are higher than the waves. The remainder of them skirts over the sea behind and coils their immense bodies in circles. The foaming main resounds. And by now they were occupying the fields. Their blazing eyes were suffused with blood and fire, and they were licking their hissing lips with flickering tongues. Bloodless at the vision, we scatter. They make a beeline for Laocoon. And first each of the two serpents embraces the tiny bodies of his two sons, winds around them and feeds upon their unfortunate limbs by biting. Then they snatch up Laocoon himself as he runs to help them and brings weapons, and bind him in their huge coils. And now, after embracing him twice around the middle and looping their scaly bodies twice around his neck, they tower over him with their heads and high necks. Meanwhile, he strives to tear apart their knots with his hands, his fillets soaked in gore and black venom. At the same time his dreadful screams reach the stars, screams that resemble the bellowings when a wounded bull flees from the altar and shakes the loose axe from its neck. But the twin dragons [*dracones*] escape to the highest shrines with a glide and make for the acropolis of cruel Tritonis [Athena], and they hide themselves under the feet of the goddess and the circle of her shield. And then, indeed, a new terror crawls into the trembling hearts of all, and they say that Laocoon has deservedly paid the price for his crime, since he damaged the sacred oak [sc. of the Trojan horse] and hurled his wicked spear into its back.

Virgil's narrative is the most famous and influential account of the Laocoon episode, with a central vignette that corresponds well with that of the equally famous Laocoon statue group found on the Palatine, where Pliny had known it to be housed in Titus's palace (*Natural History* 36.37). This triumph of the Hellenistic baroque is now on display in the Vatican.

Virgil's description of the dragons as they breast the sea seems to evoke the traditional iconography of *drakontes* travelling over land, in which they are shown rampant and coiling vertically, like a Catherine wheel, as in the image of the Dragon of Ares on the Paestan crater of ca. 330 BC, where the dragon's beard and crest are also picked out in bright red paint (*LIMC* Kadmos i 25; cf. **76**).

Virgil's narrative derives much of its power from its disinclination to explain which god lies behind Laocoon's killing and why. The opening lines suggest that his death may serve as a portent, and therefore they implicate Apollo. The simile comparing Laocoon's screams to those of a bull wounded at the altar suggests that Poseidon may have chosen to substitute the bull Laocoon has been offering him with the man himself. And selection by lot is, we may note, a motif often associated with the offering of human sacrifices to dragons or sea monsters (see **73** for Lamia-Sybaris; **99** for the Dragon of Thespiae; **106** for the Sea Monster of Troy). The refuge taken by the dragons, their task done, with Athene's cult statue suggests that it is she who has sent them, though why she should have done so remains unclear. In speaking of one of the dragons hiding itself under the circle of Athene's shield, Virgil visualises her cult image in the form of Phidias's well-known Athene Parthenos statue of the Athenian Parthenon. In this, too, a massive serpent coiled under the circle of the statue's shield, though its identity remains uncertain: Ericthonius (Pausanias 1.24.7; cf. 1.18.2)? The temple-guarding snake maintained on the Acropolis by the priestess of Athene Polias (Herodotus 8.41)? Or the serpent that fights alongside Athene in the Gigantomachy (**3**)?

**93**  An ancient commentary upon Virgil's narrative

iv AD

Servius on Virgil *Aeneid* 2.201, incorporating Bacchylides F9 Maehler (early v BC) and Euphorion F95 Lightfoot (later iii BC)

Latin

As Euphorion says, after the arrival of the Greeks the priest of Neptune [Poseidon] was killed with stones because he had not prevented their arrival with sacrifices. Afterwards, when the Greeks were departing and wished to sacrifice to Neptune, Laocoon, the priest of Thymbraean Apollo, was chosen by lot, as is customary when an appointed priest is wanting. He had committed sacrilege by having sex with his wife, Antiope, before the image of the god, and because of this he was killed together with his sons by dragons [*dracones*] sent against him. So this is how the story goes, but the poet [Virgil] excuses the Trojans on the ground that they were deceived in their ignorance. Others say that Neptune had once been insulted by Laomedon, and so he did not have an appointed priest at Troy. Whence it is thought that Neptune was actually hostile to the Trojans and that he used the priest to show them what they deserved. Neptune himself shows this elsewhere in saying, 'Although I wanted to overturn the walls of foresworn Troy, built by my own hands...' [*Aeneid* 5.810–11]. As to the fact, however, that the dragons went to the citadel, that is, the temple of Minerva [Athena], either she herself was hostile to the Trojans, or it was a sign that the state would perish. Bacchylides speaks about Laocoon and his wife and about the dragons coming from the islands of Calydnae and being transformed into people.

Servius's commentary on Virgil (**93**) offers valuable background to Laocoon's story and directly confronts the problem of the identity and purpose of the aggressor god:

- Apollo, specifically in his Thymbraeus aspect, acting in revenge for Laocoon's sacrilege, as Euphorion contended? This notion is found in the earliest extant iconography of the Laocoon episode, a pair of southern Italian vase images of the late fifth and early fourth centuries BC (*LIMC* Laokoon 1–2). These show the aftermath of the attack, with the serpents coiling around the cult statue of Apollo Thymbraeus (as opposed to that of Virgil's Athene) whilst continuing to munch on the children's severed limbs. This entails that they were devoured actually in the god's temple, where the statue would have been situated, and Tzetzes eventually asserts that this was so (on Lycophron *Alexandra* 344–7). This notion also accords well with the fact that the punishment was carried out by a pair of *drakontes*, for such a pair is associated with the temple of Apollo Thymbraeus on the Trojan plain in traditions relating to a second pair of human twins, Helenus and Cassandra (**96**).

- Poseidon, acting in revenge for the neglect of his cult, either after Laomedon, the erstwhile king of Troy, had cheated him of his payment for building the city walls, or after the murder of his former priest (a cause of sufficient outrage in itself, of course)? This notion accords well with the circumstances of the attack: Poseidon-sent serpentine monsters breast the sea to make an attack on the Trojan coast, just as in the myth of Hesione and the Sea Monster of Troy (**103–6**). In that case the victim was the daughter of *Lao-med-ōn*; here the victims are the sons of *Lao-co-ōn*.

- Athene, as the fact that Virgil's serpents make for her statue once their work is done suggests? Despite what Servius says, Athene's motivation remains obscure, but her action can be partly contextualised. First, it recalls the scene on a ca. 500 BC Attic *lekythos* illustrating the violation of Athene's temple and cult image by Ajax the Less as he rapes the captive Cassandra before it. As he goes about the attack he is himself attacked by a large serpent identical in configuration with the one that forms the blazon on the cult image's shield (*LIMC* Erechtheus 47 = Aias II 42 = Grabow 1998 K92). It is intriguing, in the light of Virgil, that this serpent too should be so closely identified with the shield of Athene's cult statue. In this case the creature would seem to be one of Athene's serpent aides, one of the sort that fights alongside her in the Gigantomachy (cf. **5**). Secondly, it recalls another Trojan War myth in which Philoctetes is attacked by a snake on an island off the Trojan coast. According to some accounts, the island in question was Tenedos, the island from which Virgil brings the serpents to attack Laocoon (Proclus *Cypria* arg. 9, Apollodorus *Epitome* 3.27). According to others, he was bitten on the islet of Chryse, off Lemnos, by a snake that guarded the shrine of the goddess Chryse-Athena (Sophocles *Philoctetes* 263–70, 1326–8 with schol., Tzetzes on Lycophron *Alexandra* 911–12).

The humans into which Bacchylides says that the serpents were transformed after their work are named as Porcis (or Porces or Porceus) and Chariboea by other sources (Lycophon *Alexandra* 347, with Tzetzes *ad loc.*), and perhaps were already so named by Bacchylides. The *drakontes* were thus a male-female pair, which in fact is true of all *drakontes* pairs in ancient myth and cult where their sexes are identifiable (see **77** for Cadmus and Harmonia; cf. also, on the cultic side, Asclepius and Hygieia, Agathos Daimon and Agathe Tyche).

## 94 A doggerel account of the Laocoon episode

ca. 60 AD

Petronius *Satyricon* 89

Latin

The priest of Neptune [Poseidon], Laocoon, his hair loose, reaches across the whole crowd with his shout. Then, drawing his spear back for the throw, he damages the horse's belly, but destiny slows his hands. The weapon bounces back from the blow and gives us trust in the trick. A second time, however, Laocoon steels his weak hand and tries to break through the lofty flanks with a double axe. The captive youths within mutter, and as they do so the oaken mass breathes with the foreigners' fear. The captive young men proceed towards the capture of Troy, and bring complete war upon it with a novel deceit. But see, other portents! Lofty Tenedos pushes its back out into the sea. There the swollen straits rise up, and the waves, torn, wash back, smaller and more calmly. Their sound carries a long way, like that of oars in the silent night, when fleets press the sea and the surface, driven back by oars, groans at the fir-wood ship sitting upon it. We look back. The waves carry snakes [*angues*] with doubled coils to the rocks. Their breasts, swelling up, drive back the foam like high-sided ships. Their tails give forth noise. Their crests, standing proud of the sea, shine like their eyes. A lightning ray burns the water, and the waves tremble at their hissings. Our minds are stupefied. Laocoon's twin sons are standing dressed in sacred fillets and Phrygian clothing. The flashing snakes suddenly bind them with their bodies. They grab the snakes' mouths with their little hands, neither to help himself, but each helping his brother. Their pious gestures are mirrored, and death itself destroys the boys, pitiful in their fear for each other. See, the boy's father, a weak ally, adds to the tally of death. The snakes attack the man and, gorged upon death, drag his limbs to the ground. The priest, now a sacrificial victim, lies among the altars and beats the earth. And so Troy, destined to perish, its sacred rites profaned, has first destroyed its gods.

Petronius's parodic piece of doggerel, its language contrived and its conceits awkwardly repetitive, depends heavily upon the *Aeneid* (**92**) for its conception of the Laocoon episode, as a hack poet might well have done. Particularly striking is the saccharine pathos of the vignette in which each boy attempts to fight off the dragon that devours his brother as he is himself devoured by the other one. The heavy emphasis laid upon the fiery and flashing nature of the serpents serves to indicate what commonplaces these had become in the representation of such creatures (**M6.a**).

## 95   The lair of the *drakontes*; Laocoon is spared but blinded

iii AD

Quintus Smyrnaeus
*Posthomerica* 12.444–97

Greek

Laocoon continued to urge his comrades to destroy the horse with raging fire. But they would not listen to him, because they dreaded the anger of the gods. Then great-hearted Athene contrived on top of that another more shameful thing, against the unfortunate sons of Laocoon. There was a cave high on a rough rock, unreachable by men, in which terrible beasts of the accursed race of Typhon still dwelled, in the recesses of the island, facing Troy from its position in the sea, that people call Calydna. From there she roused up the violence of dragons [*drakontes*] and summoned them to Troy. And they, started by the goddess, immediately shook the whole island. The sea resounded as they made their way, and the waves parted. They surged forwards, tongues flickering. The sea monsters [*kētē*] shuddered. The nymphs, the daughters of Xanthus and Simois, wailed loudly around about. The Cyprian [Aphrodite] was grieved from her vantage point on Olympus. And they quickly came to where the goddess [Athene] directed them, against the unfortunate boys, sharpening their destructive teeth with their shaggy jaws. The Trojans turned to cowardly flight, when they saw the dreadful monsters in their city. No stout man dared to stay put, even if he was otherwise fearless in his strength. An implacable terror and woe seized hold of all as they fled before the beasts. The women raised a cry of lamentation. Indeed one of them forgot her own children as she tried to avoid a hateful fate. Troy groaned as people rushed about, for many crushed together and scraped their limbs. They cowered in the streets. Laocoon was left apart with his sons. For the accused Ker [Death-Demon] and the goddess bound them to the spot. The dragons snatched up in their baneful jaws both the sons as they trembled before their doom and stretched out their hands to their dear father. But he did not have the strength to help them. From around, and from a distance, the Trojans watched and wept, dumbfounded in their hearts. The two dragons, having accomplished against the Trojans the hateful command of Athene's design, disappeared beneath the ground. And a monument to them can still be seen, at the point at which they entered the temple of Apollo on the sacred acropolis. But before the temple the Trojan sons, assembling together, built a cenotaph for the children of Laocoon, who were destroyed in implacable fashion. Over it their father poured tears from his blind eyes. Their mother wailed over the empty tomb, lamenting much and expecting something even worse. She wept for the disaster brought about by her husband's folly and was in fear of the anger of the blessed gods. And as when a nightingale, grieving greatly, laments over her bereft nest, concealed in a thicket, a nightingale whose offspring, voiceless and too young yet to sing aloud, conquered by the powerful jaws of a shaggy serpent have bequeathed her grief, and, immensely distressed, she bemoans her empty house with a great cry, so did Laocoon's wife mourn the grievous death of her children, lamenting over the empty tomb. And together with this she had further grief over her husband being struck blind.

The epicist Quintus is peculiarly emphatic that the dragons were sent by Athene, but even so pays tribute to the Apolline tradition by sending the dragons, their work done, into the ground in Apollo's shrine on the Trojan acropolis (however, this ought not to have been the shrine of Apollo in the aspect of Thymbraeus, because that was out on the Trojan plain at the confluence of the rivers Thymbrius and Scamander: Strabo C598). In describing the dragons as 'of the accursed race of Typhon', he knowingly associates them with the other great marauding *drakontes* of Greek myth (cf. **1–2, 4**).

Calydna or Calydnae is an island group adjacent to Tenedos, off the Trojan coast. This may have been the original home of the dragons in the tradition, with Virgil (**92**) transferring it to Tenedos in order to foreshadow the fall of Troy more directly, since that was where the Greek fleet was lurking, ready to return. The description of the dragons' lair as a cave high on a rock overlooking the sea recalls the Homeric description of Scylla's lair, a creature similarly caught between the identities of *drakōn*, 'dragon', and *kētos*, 'sea monster' (**119**; cf. **93**). Quintus, however, differentiates his *drakontes* from the ocean's run-of-the-mill *kētē*, for he has the latter shudder at the former, rendering them all the more terrible. The dragon's jaws are shaggy because they are bearded (**M1.a.ii**).

## 96 *Drakontes* lick out the ears of the baby twins Helenus and Cassandra in the temple of Apollo Thymbraeus, conferring the gift of prophecy

Hellenistic-Byzantine

Schol. Homer *Iliad* 6.76

Greek

It is said that Helenus was the twin brother of Cassandra, and that when they had been born they were left alone in the temple of Apollo Thymbraeus. Dragons [*drakontes*] cleaned out their hearing, and from that point on they had the gift of prophecy.

The learned twelfth-century AD Tzetzes (on Lycophron *Alexandra* 347) relates the same tale at greater length, but in a partly rationalised form, in which Apollo is reduced to the status of priest of his own temple, which is instead now dedicated to the sun. He specifies, interestingly, that it was a *pair* of *drakontes* that licked out the babies' ears. He speculates as to whether the babies were left behind accidentally or by design, so as to benefit from a known and customary blessing.

How did the serpents' aural cleansing work? We should compare the ancient traditions relating to the prophet Melampus. He was given the gift of prophecy by some grateful orphan snakes that similarly cleansed his ears, allowing him to understand the predictive language of birds (Hesiod F261 MW, Apollodorus *Bibliotheca* 1.9.11). And here we may compare in turn the striking episode of Norse mythology in which Sigurd/Siegfried learns to understand the predictive language of birds by tasting the blood of the heart of the dragon Fafnir (**B4–7**).

Another Trojan War episode that took place at the temple of the Thymbraean Apollo was Achilles' murder of Troilus. The scene, which receives little attention in the extant literary tradition, was repeatedly illustrated on archaic Spartan vases, and a series of three of them dating to ca. 560 BC shows a pair of snakes crawling over or out of the temple (*LIMC* Achilleus 257, 261, 264). It would be good to know whether we are dealing with the same serpent pair in each of these three episodes, which all take place within a single short generation, or whether Apollo Thymbraeus's unnumbered serpents ever liked to operate in pairs.

For Cassandra's broader affinity with serpents, see the commentary to **93**.

## FURTHER READING

Kleinknecht 1944, Knox 1950, Simon 1984, 1992, Himmelmann 1991, Gantz 1993:646–9.

# 15
# The Dragon of the River Bagrada, Slain by Regulus and his Army

The story of Regulus's killing of the Dragon of the Bagrada is remarkable for being a dragon-slaying tale fashioned for a strongly historical, as opposed to mythical, context, a rare quality it shares with **101**. But it is thoroughly unique for being the only significant home-grown classical Roman dragon-slaying story, which is surprising given the extent to which the Romans loved to appropriate and elaborate the dragon-slaying stories of the Greeks.

### 97  The Livian account of Regulus's battle against the Dragon of the Bagrada

ca. 14–37 AD

Valerius Maximus 1.8 ext 19, summarizing Livy

Latin

Since we are touching upon these things that fall beyond the bounds of familiar reason, mention should also be made of the serpent [*serpens*], the story of which is intriguingly and elegantly told by Titus Livy. He says that this snake at the Bagrada river in Africa was of such a great size that it prevented the army of

Figure 15  Regulus and his army slay the Bagrada Dragon. Hand-coloured engraving by Jan Collaert (1566–1628 AD), after Jan van der Straet (Joannes Stradanus, 1523–1605 AD): 'Venationes Ferarum, Avium, Piscium' (Hunts of Beasts, Birds and Fish), plate 42. The Stapleton Collection. The Bridgeman Art Library.

141

Regulus from using the river. It snatched up many soldiers in its huge mouth and crushed many with the coils of its tail. The snake could not be penetrated by the throwing of javelins. In the end they attacked it from all sides with stone missiles hurled from ballistas, and it collapsed under the rain of heavy blows. The snake seemed more terrible to all the cohorts and the legions than Carthage itself. Because the waters were contaminated by its blood and the region was polluted by the pestilent gases of the recumbent corpse, Regulus removed the Roman camp from that point. He adds that the skin of the creature, a hundred and twenty feet in length, was sent to Rome.

The action is set in 256/5 BC during the First Punic War between Rome and Carthage. The Bagrada is the modern Medjerda in Libya, the land home to Gorgons, *lamias* and many terrible snakes (**58–61, 63–5, 68–70, 72**). The first mention of the serpent tale we know of was made by Q. Aelius Tubero, who wrote in the mid-first century BC and whose account, summarised by Gellius, seems to have been broadly similar to Livy's, for which it may, indeed, have served as a source (*HRR* F8 at Aulus Gellius 7.3). The Tiberian-era Valerius Maximus's summary of Livy's early Augustan-era account, which is also lost in its original form, is rather fuller than that offered by *Periocha* 18. The Latin sources consistently apply the term *serpens* to the monster, the term that in Latin is deployed to correspond to the Greek *drakōn* about as much as the more tailored *draco*. For what it is worth, the one Greek source to discuss the episode, Cassius Dio (F42.23 = Zonaras ii p. 209 Dindorf), does indeed deploy the term *drakōn*.

Though a uniquely Roman story in some ways, it makes appeals to some themes well established in the Greek tradition: the serpent's protection of and special bond with a water source (**M4.a**); the resistless polluting stench of its corpse (**M7.a.vi**). The use of ballistas, the exciting and relatively new super-weapons of the day, to overcome the terrible monster somewhat anticipates the modern B-movie in which the United States overcomes the space alien with its nuclear missiles. Given that the serpent is said eventually to collapse under the blows of the ballista darts, we should perhaps imagine that it had been attacking in the rampant configuration familiarly adopted by *drakontes* in ancient art. If an item 120 feet in length was indeed sent back to Rome from the army in Libya, it is hard to imagine what it in fact was.

## 98 A highly elaborated account of Regulus's battle against the Dragon of the Bagrada

ca. 83–103 AD

Silius Italicus *Punica* 6.140–293.

Latin

**140.** [Marus speaks.] The murky Bagrada cuts though dry sands with slow pace. No other river in the Libyan land extends its muddy waves farther or envelops the wide plains with its still depths. Here, desperate for water, which the land does not supply in plenty, we happily established our camp in those wild regions. Nearby was a motionless grove that kept itself in colourless shade, Styx-like and unpenetrated by the sun. From it there burst forth into the air a thick exhalation that gave off a foul smell. Within lay a dreadful home, a huge cave twisting beneath the earth and dismal darkness without light. I shudder again as I remember it. A deadly monster, produced by the earth's anger, the like of which hardly any age of men will have seen, a serpent [*serpens*] extending over a hundred ells, dwelled on that lethal riverbank and in those Avernian groves. Lions caught at the spring used to sate the voraciousness of its huge stomach and venom-pregnant belly, or herds driven to the river by the heat of the searing sun, or birds drawn to it down through the air by the foul heaviness and corruption of its breath. Half-eaten bones lay on the ground, bones which it had vomited up in its black cave after laying waste to flocks and sating itself to the point of dyspepsia on its horrible feast. When it wanted to assuage the burning produced by its fervid eating in the river's fast-flowing swell and the foaming waves, it was already laying its head on the edge of the opposite bank before it had plunged the entirety of its body into the stream. I made my way, unaware of such a great threat, accompanied by Aquinus from the Appenines and Avens from Umbria. We wanted to investigate the grove and enjoy its peaceful atmosphere. But a silent dread entered our limbs as soon as we approached it, and our limbs stiffened with a strange chill. Even so, we entered, praying to the Nymphs and the power that presided over the unfamiliar river. We dared to commit our trembling and much-quivering steps to the secret grove. See! From the vestibule and the very mouth of the cave there burst forth a Tartarean whirlwind and a blast harsher than that of the cruel East wind. A tempest rose and poured out of the huge hole, twisting forth a storm mixed with the cry of Cerberus. Terrified at the prospect of disaster, we exchanged glances. The ground resounded, the earth moved, the cave began to fall in, and the shades seemed to be coming out. The serpent was bigger than those with which the Giants were armed when they attacked heaven. It was bigger than the one that made Heracles weary in the waters of Lerna. It resembled the snake of Juno [i.e. Ladon] that guarded the branches clothed in gold. That was the size of the snake that burst forth from the earth, raising its head aloft. It scattered its first slaver into the clouds and befouled heaven with its gape. We fled in different directions and, breathless with fear, tried to raise a cry of alarm in vain. For the hissing filled the entire grove. Avens, blinded by sudden fear, and reprehensible for doing it (but he was compelled by fate), hid himself in the huge trunk of an ancient oak in the hope that he could evade the unspeakable monster. I myself can hardly believe it. It dragged up the bulk of the lofty tree with its huge coils, tore it up from its base and roots and overturned it. Then it snatched him up as he trembled and called upon his comrades with his final words and, sucking him down with its black throat (I saw it as I looked back), it put him away in its hideous belly. The hapless Aquinus had entrusted himself to the river and the tumbling waves and was swimming in speedy flight. It attacked him in the middle of the stream and fed upon his limbs, after bringing them back to the bank (what an unspeakable variety of death!).

**204.** So it was granted to me to escape the dreadful monster, such cause for tears. As much as my sickened mind allowed me to, I hastened my step and revealed the details to my leader. He groaned in pity for the bitter lots of the young men. And as he was fiery for fights, war, battles and the enemy, and he burned with a great love of daring, he gave the command that arms be snatched up quickly and that the cavalry, which had experienced all forms of war, should mobilise itself. He himself rushed forward, spurring on his horse with his foot. A band armed with shields hurriedly followed at his command, bringing up heavy ballistas, torsion catapults for use against walls and the huge-pointed spear used to shatter lofty towers. And now when the horses' hooves, leaping over the grassy plain, surrounded its deadly habitat with a resounding noise, the serpent, aroused by the whinnying, slid out of its cave and hissed forth Stygian heats from its smoking mouth. A terrible fire flashed forth from its twin eyes. The height of its raised crest exceeded that of the grove and the high treetops of the wood. Its tongue flickered and flashed through the air with a three-forked movement and leaped up and licked the ether. But when the trumpets blasted, it was alarmed, reared up its huge body, then, settling back, grouped together the rest of its bulk under its breast in twisting coils. From that stance it darted into dread war and, quickly unravelling its spirals, extended its full bulk with straightened body and at once reached to the faces of those far distant from it. All the horses snorted in dismay at the serpent. They did not respond to the light rein and breathed out frequent fires from their noses. Rearing up, the snake nodded its high head from side to side on its swollen neck. Then, goaded by anger, it now snatched some men up aloft, now delighted in crushing them down beneath its great weight. Then it would suck down the black gore, breaking their bones, and, with blood flowing from its mouth, agape, it would change its victim and abandon half-eaten limbs. The ranks of soldiers were giving way before it, and the victorious snake was overwhelming squadrons that had ridden far back with its pestilential breath. Then the leader quickly called the host back into battle and encouraged them with the following words: 'Do we, the youth of Italy, turn tail before a snake and confess that Italy is not equal to Libyan snakes? If its breath has fought you down in your feebleness, and your courage has weakly drained away at the sight of its gape, I will proceed with vigour and alone will be sufficient to do battle with the monster.' This he shouted, and without fear he hurled his swift spear through the air with lightning arm. The hurl was successful, and the point lodged directly in its forehead, aided in the force of its impact by the fact that the creature was rushing against it with ardour, and it settled in its head, quivering. The men raised a shout to the stars and their voices, suddenly poured forth, reached to the ethereal halls. Immediately the earth-born monster raged with anger. It scorned flight and the experience of pain was new to it. Then for the first time in its long life did it experience iron. The swift attack the creature made, goaded by pain, would not have been in vain, had not Regulus, with his skill in riding, turned away his horse and evaded it as it darted forwards. When it continued the pursuit of the wheeling horse by twisting its flexible back, Regulus swiftly evaded it by yanking the rein with his left hand.

**261.** But Marus was no mere spectator amid such events, and his right hand was not inactive. My spear was the second in the monster's massive body. At any point now it would have been licking the hindquarters of the horse, tired from the struggle, with its three-forked tongue. I hurled my weapon and at once directed the cruel snake's war lust towards myself. Hence the soldiers followed my lead and competitively threw their spears with their right hands and diverted the wild creature to other focuses for its anger, until a ballista stopped it short with a blow designed for walls. From that point finally its strength was broken. It could no longer raise its damaged spine in the rigid fashion it used to for making its attack, nor could it raise its head into the clouds as it was used to doing. We pressed upon it more vigorously, and now a *falarica* bolt was plunged deep into its belly and lodged there, and swift arrows stole away the sight from both its eyes. The black cave of its deep wound, with its gaping jaws, breathed forth a noxious slaver. Now the end of its tail was pinned to the ground because of the javelins heaped onto it and the weight of the poles. Now at last it threatened with only a tired gape. Finally a beam, driven from a torsion catapult with a screech, broke its head apart with a great crack. The snake unravelled itself along the rampart of the riverbank and finally breathed out into the breezes the dark cloud of venom that escaped from its mouth. A bellow burst forth from the sad river, and mutterings poured forth from the lowest depths. Suddenly the grove and the cave and the riverbanks, sounding in response to the trees, gave forth a tearful howl. Alas, with what future penalties were we destined to atone for our battle! How great were the punishments, how intense were the angers we had to experience! Our pious prophets explained the matter. They advised us that we had destroyed with our hands the servant of the Naiad sisters whom the river Bagrada nurtured in its warm water, and that we would face perils subsequently as a result. Then this spear was given to me by your father, Serranus, as a reward and as a prize for dealing the second wound, this spear that was the first to drink the blood of the sacred serpent. [293]

Marus recounts the Bagrada Dragon episode from the First Punic War in an epic devoted to the Second. Many established themes from the Greek tradition are found: the dragon is born of the earth (**M2.b.i**); it is the protector of a water source (**M4.a.i**); it is associated with a grove (**M3.b.i**) and a cave (**M3.a.ii**), which are indeed identified with each other; it sports a crest (**M1.a.ii**) and a three-forked tongue (**M1.a.iii**); it flashes fire from its eyes (**M6.a.iii**) and emits a fiery breath (**M6.a.ii**; and it is noteworthy that Silius lays emphasis upon the fieriness of Regulus as he matches himself against the snake, and upon the metaphorically fiery breath of his horses—cf. **M6.b.ii**); and its breath is a venomous and pestilential stench (**M7.a.ii**).

The dragon's association with its water source is in fact highly developed. It is lamented by the river's Naiads, whose nursling it had been. Just as the anger of Ares pursues Cadmus for the killing of his serpent at Thebes (**75, 78–9**), and that of Zeus pursues Capaneus, if only briefly, for the killing of his serpent at Nemea (**83**), so the anger of the Naiads will pursue Regulus and his army. It will come to fruition in the destruction of the army at the imminent Battle of Tunis (Polybius 1.26–34) and the subsequent torture and execution of Regulus himself at the hands of the Carthaginians (Aulus Gellius 7.4, Augustine *City of God* 1.15, [Aurelius Victor] *De viris illustribus* 40 etc.: different tortures are offered).

The imagery of the underworld is heavily exploited here (Styx, Avernus, Tartarus, Cerberus, shades). The motif of the dragon's stench is combined with that of its cave lair to produce the conceit that the serpent's home is an underworld entrance. Underworld entrances, caves or lakes, were traditionally associated with the emission of noxious vapours: Lake Avernus in the Italian region of Campania was the most notorious in this regard. The serpent is creatively said to exploit its noxious breath to feed on birds, by using it to drop them out of the sky as they flew over; this pays tribute to ancient traditions of Avernus, which reputedly killed the birds that flew over it with its mephitic emissions (Virgil *Aeneid* 6.236–42). There is allusion too, no doubt, to **59**, where Medusa drops birds out of the sky with her petrifying gaze. Furthermore, the wound the soldiers open up in the dragon with their *falarica* bolt is in turn compared to an underworld entrance, as a black cave of noxious breath.

There is some further engaging creativity here. The killing of Aquinus in his tree trunk is novel. The notion that a dragon might give itself heartburn by eating too eagerly charms.

Once again we are given the notion of an implicit canon of great dragons (cf. **4**) into which Silius is eager to inscribe his Bagrada Dragon: it is compared with the serpents of the Giants (cf. **5**), the Lernaean Hydra (**23–7**), Ladon (**28–34**) and, perhaps, indirectly, Cerberus (**35–47**).

## FURTHER READING

Basset 1955, Spaltenstein 1986 (on Silius Italicus 6.140–293), Stothers 2004.

# 16
# Some Unique Dragon-Slaying and Dragon-Averting Narratives in Later Greek Sources

This section collects a number of significant dragon-fight narratives that are each uniquely attested in a later Greek source. Each one individually is of some interest.

Figure 16 An anguipede Hecate's two dog-heads tear a soul apart between them. Attic black-figure lekythos, ca. 470 BC. Athens, National Museum. Redrawn by Eriko Ogden.

CHAPTER 16: SOME UNIQUE DRAGON-SLAYING AND DRAGON-AVERTING NARRATIVES

## 99  Menestratus sacrifices himself to kill the Dragon of Thespiae in Boeotia

Later ii AD

Pausanias 9.26.7–8

Greek

In the city at Thespiae there is a bronze statue of Zeus the Saviour. They explain that a dragon [*drakōn*] was once devastating the city, and the god gave the command that the ephebe [young adult, around 18–20 years of age] chosen by lot each year should be given to the beast. They say that they do not remember the names of those that were killed. But they tell that when the lot fell upon Cleostratus, his lover Menestratus devised a plan. He had a bronze breastplate made with a fish hook pointing upwards on each of its little segments. He put this breastplate on and handed himself over willingly to the dragon. His purpose was, in handing himself over and being killed, in turn to kill the beast. In return for this Zeus has acquired the epithet 'Saviour'.

As often, a dragon-slaying story was remembered in connection with a cult (**M14.b.vi**), and, as often in his *Tour of Greece*, Pausanias links a good story to an artefact to be seen. This story is strongly reminiscent of that of Lamia-Sybaris (**73**): in that story too a handsome youth (Alcyoneus) is chosen by lot for sacrifice to the dragon, whereupon a warrior in love with him (Eurybatus) substitutes himself for the boy, takes on the dragon and destroys it. The major point of difference is that Menestratus is himself killed in the process, whereas Eurybatus survives.

The episode may bear comparison with the early tradition, if we have reconstructed it aright, in which Jason, rendered impregnable my Medea's drugs, was devoured by—and possibly even allowed himself to be devoured by—the Dragon of Colchis (**85**, with com.). At any rate, it certainly bears comparison with the tradition of the sea monster of Troy, which was destroyed by Heracles when he substituted himself for the sacrificial victim laid out for it, Hesione, allowed himself to be swallowed by it and hacked away at the monster's liver from within (**103–5**). The motif is also found, vestigially, in connection with Perseus's destruction of the sea monster of Ethiopia (**112**).

In its motif of the spiked armour, the tale bears comparison with a number of international dragon-slaying traditions, not least British ones: see the marvellous tales at **C14** and above all **C15**. The motif of a special armour devised for battle with serpents is found also in **B12**.

## 100  A Thessalian witch destroys a sacred snake with her magical herbs

iii BC–ii AD

[Aristotle] *Mirabilium auscultationes* 845b

Greek

In Thessaly they say that the sacred snake [*hieros ophis*] kills all living beings, not just if it bites them, but even if it just touches them. Therefore, whenever it appears and they hear its voice (and it appears only rarely), the snakes and the vipers and all the other beasts flee. In size it is not great but moderate. They say that once in Tenos, the city in Thessaly, a sacred snake was killed by a woman. The killing took place in the following fashion. The woman drew a circle, laid down herbs [*pharmaka*] and entered the circle, together with her son. Then she imitated the voice of the creature. The creature sang in response and approached. As it sang, the woman fell asleep, and then it came closer still, with the result that she was not able to resist sleep. But her son lying beside her roused her by pummelling her at her own bidding, for she had explained to him that if she fell asleep, both she herself and he would perish. But, she explained, if she compelled the beast and drew it on, they would be delivered from it. And when the beast came into the circle, it was immediately drained of moisture.

The *Mirabilium auscultationes* (*Marvellous Things Heard*) pseudonymously ascribed to Aristotle and transmitted with his corpus is difficult to date. It may have a post-Aristotelian, early Hellenistic core, but this appears to have been elaborated over the centuries, up until the second century AD, if indeed not beyond even this point.

There does not appear to have ever been a Tenos in Thessaly. Almost certainly the tale, in its ungarbled form, related rather to the well-known island of that name. This island's traditional difficulties with snakes are indicated by its by-name of Ophioussa, 'Snake-Land.' The action will have been attracted to Thessaly by the role of the Thessalian witch (Thessaly was famous for its witches) in the tale. The term *hieros ophis* would normally apply to a benign temple-dwelling snake (actual or imaginary), but here it seems to serve rather as the type name for a terrible variety of snake. To understand the tale fully, one has to supply a suppressed premise, namely that the woman must keep singing in order to compel the snake into the deadly herb-barrier; otherwise, it will be able to leap over the barrier and kill her.

The tale deploys a number of the recurring themes of ancient dragon-slaying narratives. Most striking is that of the magic circle (**M11.b**). There is much parallelism in the battle. The tale gives us the reciprocal human use of fire against the serpent's fieriness (**M6**). Although no flame burns, the magical herbs have the effect of parching the serpent to death (cf. the modern custom of sprinkling salt on slugs). And parching herbs are in a sense very much the equivalent of the serpent's venom, when we bear in mind the conceit that serpents create their venom by devouring poisonous herbs in the first place (89, with com.). We also have the deployment of an incantation against the serpent (**M10.b.i**), and this too is clearly marked as a weapon that mirrors and reciprocates the mysterious singing of the serpent itself. Of particular interest is the serpent's casting of sleep upon the witch (**M9.a**). Sleep casting might be thought to be an activity that generally belonged rather with ancient witches and magicians (e.g. Apuleius *Metamorphoses* 2.25: a witch in the form of a weasel casts sleep upon Thelyphron), and indeed it is precisely by sleep casting that Medea traditionally overcomes the normally unsleeping Serpent of Colchis (87, 89–90; cf. 31, 43, **M9.b.i**). So either the serpent has appropriated the witch's technique or, again, it shares it with her as reciprocal weapon. Since the sleep casting is associated with the serpent's song, we may conjecture that the witch's equal and opposite song had indeed aimed—inter alia—to cast sleep or drowsiness upon the snake.

This tale should be compared with the Tyrolean folk tale from Friedlach reproduced at **C10**. Here we find a sorcerer, Fridelo, charming a plague of snakes towards himself as he sits in the centre of a ring of (this time actual) fire, into which they plunge. But as the sorcerer directs the charming music of the flute towards the snakes, so the terrible queen of the snakes directs a ringing sound of her own against him. The threat advertised in the Thessalian tale is here realised: the queen is able to leap across the ring of fire and kill the sorcerer, albeit dying herself too in the process.

CHAPTER 16: SOME UNIQUE DRAGON-SLAYING AND DRAGON-AVERTING NARRATIVES

## 101  Alexander the Great has the Agathos Daimon dragon killed at the foundation of Alexandria

ca. 300 AD

*Alexander Romance*
1.32.5–13 A ~ Armenian
§§ 86–8

Greek (and Armenian)

They began to build Alexandria from the Middle Plain and so the place took on the additional name of 'Beginning', on account of the fact that the building of the city had begun from that point. A dragon [*drakōn*] which was in the habit of presenting itself to people in the area kept frightening the workmen, and they would break off their work upon the creature's arrival. News of this was given to Alexander. He gave the order that on the following day the dragon should be killed wherever it was caught. On receipt of this permission, they got the better of the beast when it presented itself at the place now called the Stoa and killed it. Alexander gave the order that it should have a precinct there and buried the dragon. And he gave the command that the neighbourhood should be garlanded in memory of the sighting of Agathos Daimon. He commanded that the soil from the digging of the foundations should all be deposited in one particular place, and even up until this day a large hill is there to be seen, called the 'Dung Heap'. When he had laid the foundations for most of the city and measured it out, he inscribed five letters, alpha, beta, gamma, delta and epsilon: alpha for 'Alexander', beta for 'king', gamma for 'scion', delta for 'of Zeus' and epsilon for 'founded this unforgettable city'. Beasts of burden and mules were at work. When the foundations of the heroon [hero shrine] had been laid down <he set it [i.e. the stele on which he had inscribed the letters] in on a pillar>. There leaped out from it a large host <of snakes>, and, crawling off, they ran into the four [?] houses that were already there. Alexander, who was still present, founded the city and the heroon itself on the 25th Tybi. From that point the doorkeepers admitted these snakes to the houses as Agathoi Daimones. These snakes are not venomous, but they do ward off those snakes that do seem to be venomous, and sacrifices are given to the hero himself <, as snake born>. They garland their beasts of burden and give them a holiday since they helped in the foundation of the city by carrying loads. Alexander ordered that the guardians of the houses be given wheat. They took it and milled it and made porridge [?] and gave it to the snakes in the houses. The Alexandrians preserve this custom until today. On the 25th of Tybi they garland their beasts of burden, make sacrifice to the Agathoi Daimones that look after their houses and make them gifts of porridge.

The passage quoted is drawn from the earliest preserved version of the Alexander Romance, the so-called alpha recension recoverable from a single poor Greek manuscript copy, 'A', and the Armenian translation of what was evidently a rather better manuscript. The alpha recension would have been composed ca. 300 AD, but it contains material of differing vintages, some of which, including the basics of the material quoted here, seems to date back to the early Ptolemaic period. The angle brackets in this translation mark passages lost from the A manuscript that have been supplied from the Armenian translation.

The *Romance* has told us just prior to this section (31.7) that Alexander's architects and surveyors had laid the city of Alexandria out between two branches of the Nile called the Drakon ('Dragon') and the Agathodaimon (i.e. Agathos Daimon). It is clear, therefore, that the troublemaking dragon is an embodiment and protector of these waterways, and that, in heroic form, it will continue as the protector of the city built between them. For the killing of a dragon at its water source in association with the foundation of a great new city, compare Cadmus's foundation of Thebes in association with his killing of the Dragon of Ares at its spring (**75–6, 78–9**). We have noted too that the Seleucids seem to have invoked the imagery of the mastery of a dragon river (the Orontes) in association with the foundation of their capitals at Seleuceia-in-Pieria and Antioch (**9**).

After the narrative of the killing of the Agathos Daimon dragon, the passage goes on to describe the restitutive cults that ensued from it (**M14.b.vi**): a public one based in the hero shrine or heroon built for it, and a set of private ones based in the individual houses of Alexandria in which offerings are made to snakes that are evidently considered to be, at some level, the original Agathos Daimon redivivus.

The narrative is not always clear. A substantial description of the building of the hero shrine for Agathos Daimon is confusingly followed by the assertion that the Alexandrians (of what era?) gave sacrifices 'to the hero himself <, as snake born>.' It makes little logical sense to describe a snake as 'snake born', and so the hero mentioned here is not Agathos Daimon but Alexander himself, who was indeed famously sired by a gigantic *drakōn* that slept with his mother, Olympias (Plutarch *Alexander* 2–3). Alexander's dragon siring is alluded to in this context because it explains his ability to achieve mastery over the Agathos Daimon dragon, indirect as this was. The Greeks knew of several races of 'snake-born' men (Ophiogeneis) who were immune to snakebite and so had a special ability to control the creatures (Strabo C588, Pliny *Natural History* 28.30–1, Aelian *Nature of Animals* 12.39).

As a dragon-slaying story fit for one of Alexander's stature, this does not, admittedly, cut the mustard: Alexander does not even encounter the dragon directly, but merely superciliously orders its destruction from afar at the hands of nameless workmen. Although the *Alexander Romance* is hardly a rationalising document in general—rather, seeking the fantastical out—this narrative does have the look of a rationalised version of a more traditional heroic dragon fight. Was there an earlier version of the *Romance* in which Alexander rather faced the Agathos Daimon dragon in person, one on one?

Later recensions of the *Romance* at any rate (and just possibly looking back to earlier ones) felt the need for Alexander to fight a dragon in more traditional fashion. So it is with the seventh-century AD Greek derived Syriac version of the *Romance*, the fight narrative of which is summarised at **C3** (cf. also **C4**). Although on the face of it this is a very different tale from the alpha recension's Agathos Daimon story, an etiolated link between the two may be indicated first by the Syriac tale's emphasis upon the dragon's association with a river, not least in view of the fact that nothing is really done with this motif, as well as the fact that this dragon too has a shrine in which it is worshipped.

## 102 Eucrates encounters a terrifying manifestation of a serpentine Hecate and sends her back to the underworld

ca. 170s AD

Lucian *Lover of Lies* 22–4

Greek

**22.** 'Listen to this then,' said Eucrates, '—and I have witnesses to it—something I saw five years ago. It happened to be around harvest time in the year. I was on the farm at midday. I left the workers to their grape picking and went off on my own into the wood. I had something on my mind I wanted to mull over. Once I was under the tree canopy, there came, first of all, a barking of dogs, and I guessed that my son Mnason was at sport and running to hounds, as so often, and that he had come into the forest with his comrades. But that was not it. Soon there was an earthquake and, simultaneously, a shout like thunder. I saw a fearsome woman approaching me, almost half a stadium's length high. In her left hand she held a torch and in her right a sword twenty cubits long. Below the waist she had a snake foot [*ophiopous*]; above it she resembled a Gorgon, so far as concerned the look in her eyes and her terrible appearance, I mean. Instead of hair, writhing dragons [*drakontes*] fell down in curls around her neck, and some of them coiled over her shoulders. See, my friends,' he said, 'how my hair stands on end at my mere telling of the story.'

**23.** As he spoke Eucrates showed off the hairs on his forearm, supposedly bristling from fear. Ion, Dinomachus and Cleodemus and their fellows gaped at him in rapt attention, old men being led along by the nose, virtually doing obeisance before such an implausible colossus, a woman the height of half a stadium's length, a giant bogey. In the meantime I reflected that men of this sort associated with the young to teach them wisdom, and were admired by many, but that it was only their white hair and their beards that distinguished them from babies. In fact, babies were less gullible than they were.

**24.** And so Dinomachus asked, 'Tell me, Eucrates, how big were the goddess's dogs?'

'They were taller than Indian elephants,' came the reply, 'similarly black and shaggy, with dirty, matted hair. Anyway, when I saw her, I came to a halt and at the same time turned back the seal-ring that the Arab had given me to the inside of my finger. Hecate stamped on the ground with her dragon foot [*drakonteiōi podi*] and created a huge chasm, as deep as Tartarus. Presently she jumped into it and was gone. I steeled myself and bent over it, after taking hold of a tree that was growing near the hole, to stop myself falling into it headlong from vertigo. Then I saw everything in Hades, Pyriphlegethon, the lake, Cerberus and the dead, whom I could see so clearly that I even recognized some of them. I got a good view of my father, still dressed in the clothes in which we had buried him.'

'What were the souls up to, Eucrates?' said Ion.

'Just as you would expect,' said he, 'they were lounging in the asphodel meadow, passing the time of day with their friends and relatives.'

'Now let the disciples of Epicurus argue against holy Plato and his book on souls,' said Ion. 'But didn't you see Socrates himself and Plato among the dead?'

'It was just Socrates I saw', said he, 'but I didn't get a very good view even of him. I guessed his identity because he was bald and pot-bellied. I didn't identify Plato. For one must, I believe, be honest with friends. But anyway, as soon as I had had a good look at everything, the chasm closed up. Some of the servants, Pyrrhias here among them, were looking for me and they arrived on the scene before the chasm had fully shut itself. Tell them whether I'm telling the truth, Pyrrhias.'

'Yes you are, by Zeus,' said Pyrrhias, 'and I heard a bark through the chasm, and I could see the gleam of fire through it, I suppose from her torch.'

I laughed when he tacked on the details of the barking and the fire for good measure.

Lucian's dialogue *Lover of Lies* or *Philopseudes* ostensibly satirises the credulous and their love of fantastical stories of magic and the supernatural, some nine examples of which are recounted in course. Eucrates' tale of his encounter with Hecate is one of them. Amongst the others are Ion's tale of the Chaldaean snake blaster (**130**) and Eucrates' tale of *The Sorcerer's Apprentice* (*Lover of Lies* 33–6), the earliest known version of that famous story.

Hecate is described as an anguipede. As such she takes the form most commonly associated with female *drakontes* (**M1.b.iv**). The affinities with the sometimes ghostly Lamia or *lamias* seem particularly relevant in view of Hecate's own ghostly associations. In addition to her snake foot, she also boasts Gorgon-like dragon hair. A dragon part is integrated into the *Orphic Argonautica*'s Hecate in a different way: there a dragon head is the central one of her three (**90**). An innocent reading might suggest that Hecate's elephantine dogs are separate and accompanying creatures, but her iconography suggests that that are integrated into her form. A striking image of ca. 470 BC (*LIMC* Hekate 95), actually the earliest positively identifiable image of the goddess to survive, represents her as an anguipede, her serpent tail making one large coil behind her clothed humanoid form, and with a pair of dogs emerging as far as their forelegs from the lower part of her humanoid frontage. The dog heads tear apart a soul, one of its arms in each mouth. The overall configuration is therefore remarkably similar to the canonical configuration given to Scylla in her iconography (**119**, with com.). Sword and fiery torch are amongst the goddess's familiar attributes, the latter perhaps saluting, inter alia, the fieriness of the *drakōn*.

The combination of the motifs of the approach of Hecate and the opening up of the underworld seems to have had a pedigree: in a fashion that remains obscure, Virgil's Sibyl performs rites for Aeneas which bring the approach of Hecate, as is again indicated by the sound of her dogs barking, and immediately upon this approach—and presumably *propter* as much as *post*—the earth opens up in Avernus to allow the pair to enter the underworld (*Aeneid* 6.255–62). The motif of the earth opening up specifically to swallow a terrible dragon down into the underworld is already found in **9** (Typhon), but it features more strikingly in some of the early hagiographic dragon fights, notably that of Thomas (**131**) and above all that of Philip (**134**), in which again the terrible female dragon, the Echidna, is swallowed up into the underworld when the earth opens up in response to Philip's prayer. Given the probability that Lucian's tale of the Chaldaean snake blaster (**130**) is in part a parody of early Christian storytelling, it is quite possible that this, his Hecate tale, is likewise. In both cases exotic oriental sorcerers and their accoutrements will have been substituted for Christian saints and their prayers.

The use of the ring against the serpentine Hecate should be compared with other uses of appropriately circular weapons against dragons (**M11.b**). For the activation of a magical ring by turning the bevel round to the inside of the hand, cf. Plato *Republic* 359d-60b (the ring of Gyges). In the ancient world and more recent ones alike, midday has often been imbued with a sinister significance and held to be a time at which demons might manifest themselves.

## FURTHER READING

Agathos Daimon: Harrison 1912:277–316, Cook 1914–40:ii.2, 1125–9, Ganschinietz/Ganszyniec 1918 and 1919, Jakobsson 1925 esp. 151–75, Rohde 1925:207–8 n. 133, Tarn 1928, Taylor 1930, Visser 1938:5–8, 65–6, Nilsson 1967–74:ii, 213–18, Bernand 1970:i, 82–99, Fraser 1972:1, 209–11, with associated notes, Quaegebeur 1975:170–6 and *passim*, Mitropoulou 1977:155–68, Dunand 1969, 1981, Pietrzykowski 1978, Sfameni Gasparro 1997, Hillard 1998, 2010, Jouanno 2002:75–6, 105–8, Stoneman 2007:532–4, 2008:56–8.

Lucian *Lover of Lies*: Schwartz 1951, Ebner et al. 2001, Ogden 2007.

# 17
# *The Sea Monster of Troy, Slain by Heracles*

We pass now to the category of the ancient *drakontes*' marine cousins, *kētē* (singular *kētos*) or sea monsters. The extent to which these serpentine creatures overlap with *drakontes* in their physiology and story worlds is discussed in the introduction. The two most distinctive *kētos* traditions of Greek myth resemble each other strongly: in both cases a hero comes across a young virgin who has been pinned out by the shore as a sacrifice for the marauding sea monster to eat; he kills it and delivers her. The earlier attested of these is the tale of Heracles and Hesione, and we turn to it first. It should be noted that neither Heracles' killing of the Sea Monster of Troy nor his killing of Scylla (**121**), for all that they add to his not inconsiderable tally of (quasi-)dragons felled, constituted 'labours' undertaken at the behest of Eurystheus: both killings were voluntary acts by a hero driven to rid the world of its monsters. For

Figure 17 Heracles disguises himself as the sacrificial Hesione to enter the mouth of the Sea-monster of Troy and kill it from within. Red-figure column-crater, ca. 350–25 BC. Perugia, Museo Nazionale. Redrawn by Eriko Ogden.

the possible influence of the sea-monster-of-Troy myth on St George's dragon-slaying tale, see **160** com.

## 103 A Homeric allusion to the Sea Monster of Troy and an ancient commentary upon it

later vii BC–
Hellenistic-Byzantine

Homer *Iliad*
20.144–8 (vii BC)

Schol. Homer *Iliad* 20.147
(Hellenistic-Byzantine),
incorporating Hellanicus
F26b Fowler (later v BC)

Greek

**Homer:** After saying this, Poseidon of the dark hair led them to the high, heaped-around wall of the divine Heracles, which the Trojans and Pallas Athene had built for him when he was fleeing before the sea monster [*kētos*] and avoiding it, when it chased him from the shore to the plain.

**Schol. ad loc., quoting Hellanicus:** Poseidon and Apollo built the [sc. Trojan] wall for an appointed price, when Zeus had ordered them to serve Laomedon. Laomedon broke his oaths and his agreements by withholding the pay and driving them off. In anger Poseidon sent a sea monster [*kētos*] against the country, which destroyed the people that encountered it and the fruits that had been produced. Laomedon consulted an oracle and was given the response that he should put his daughter Hesione out as food for the sea monster and rid himself of the trouble in that way. So he put his daughter out but proclaimed that he would give his immortal horses to anyone who slew the sea monster. Zeus had given these to Tros [the grandfather of Laomedon] in return for Ganymede [Tros's son, of whom Zeus was enamoured]. Heracles arrived and promised to succeed in the contest. Athene made a bulwark for him, the so-called heaped-around wall. Heracles entered the belly of the sea monster through its mouth and destroyed its flanks. Laomedon secretly exchanged the immortal horses for mortal ones and gave them to Heracles, and so Heracles drove these horses off. The story is in Hellanicus.

The earlier part of the narrative reflected by Hellanicus, in which Poseidon and Apollo built the walls of Troy for Laomedon, only to be cheated by him of their pay for doing so, is referred to several times elsewhere in the *Iliad* (5.638–51, 7.452–3, 21.441–57), but the quoted passage is the poem's unique reference to the sea monster sent in punishment by Poseidon.

As is immediately clear from Hellanicus's narrative, we have here an early manifestation of the story type familiar from the St George narrative (**160–1**) in which an itinerant hero fights a serpent in order to deliver a girl who has been pinned out for it. In classical antiquity the story type is also to be found in the tale of Perseus, Andromeda and the Sea Monster of Ethiopia (**108–116**)—which resembles this one strongly in so many respects—and, with a boy victim and a homosexually motivated hero, in the tale of Eurybatus, Alcyoneus and Lamia-Sybaris (**73**) and that of Menestratus, Cleostratus and the Dragon of Thespiae (**99**). And like St George, but unlike Perseus, Heracles refrains from taking the girl he delivers as his sexual partner afterwards.

More specifically, the motif of the hero getting himself inside a dragon or a sea monster so as to be able to destroy if from within—which, though known to Hellanicus, may not have been known to Homer—is also found in the traditions of the Sea Monster of Ethiopia (**112**) and of the Dragon of Thespiae (**99**). It is perhaps refracted also in the Christian tale of Marina of Antioch and her dragon (**149**). It is in any case found in widely international dragon-slaying tales: see the Persian tale from ca. 1000 AD in the *Shahnameh* of Ferdowsi, in which Esfandyar rides a chariot covered in projecting swords into his dragon's mouth (v 1591-4; translated at Warner and Warner 1912:v.125-8); the Scottish tale of the blacksmith of Kirkcudbright, who defeats the White Snake of Mote Hill by feeding himself to it wearing a suit of armour with retractable spikes (**C15**); or the Orkney tale, in which Assipattle destroys the Stoor Worm by sailing a boat into its mouth, then disembarking to attack its liver (**C11**).

Two minor points on the sea monster. Carnivorous sea monsters would not normally have been expected to devour the fruits of the land, so perhaps it destroyed them by belching brine over them, as in Lycophron's allusions to the myth (**105**). We must assume that the bulwark Hellanicus tells us Athene—ever the patroness of heroes fighting serpentine monsters (**M13.a.ii**)—built for Heracles had an entrance just big enough for the sea monster to stick its head through, so that Heracles could get inside its mouth as it did so and gaped and groped around in an attempt to devour him.

In its full expanse, the tale of the building of Troy's walls (up to and including the Hesione episode) exhibits a striking range of structural and motivic correspondences with Snorri Sturluson's Old Norse account—monsterless, alas—of the building of the walls of Asgard by a mountain giant with the help of his marvellous horse Svadilfari, sire of Odin's eight-legged horse Sleipnir. The Aesir gods cheat the giant of his promised reward, the sun, the moon and the goddess Freyja (*Prose Edda*, *Gylfaginning* 42). It is unclear whether Snorri's tale is an ancient folkloric cousin of the Trojan tale or represents a more recent direct adaptation of it (Trojan mythology was surprisingly well-known in medieval Iceland).

## 104  Heracles slays the Sea Monster of Troy to rescue Hesione: a later summary account

ca. 100 AD

Apollodorus *Bibliotheca* 2.5.9

Greek

It had happened that at that time the city [of Troy] was in a bad way because of the anger of Apollo and Poseidon. For Apollo and Poseidon wanted to test the arrogance of Laomedon, and so, turning themselves into the form of men, they promised to fortify Pergamum for wages. They did the job, but he refused to give them their wages. And so Apollo sent a pestilence [*loimos*] and Poseidon a sea monster [*kētos*], which was carried up to Troy by a flood, and which snatched up men on the plain. Oracles stated that there would be deliverance from the disasters if Laomedon put out his daughter Hesione as food for the sea monster, so he put her out, fastening her to the rocks near the sea. Heracles, seeing her put out, promised to save her if he could have from Laomedon the mares which Zeus had given him to make good the rape of Ganymede. Laomedon said he would give them, and Heracles killed the sea monster and saved Hesione. But Laomedon refused to pay the wages, and Heracles sailed off after threatening to make war on Troy.

Heracles' eventual return to Troy, his sacking of it and his killing of Laomedon are narrated at 2.6.4. At this point Heracles takes Hesione as a war captive and gives her as a prize to Telamon, to whom she was to bear Teucer as an illegitimate half-brother to the famous Ajax. Heracles also allows her to redeem one of the other captives for the price of her fine veil (or mirror, according to other accounts). She chooses Priam, who was to live to become king of Troy in the age of the Trojan War and the assault of the *drakōn* pair upon Laocoon (**92-5**).

Apollodorus supplies some further narrative details, which may or may not have been known to Homer or Hellanicus. Given their established spheres of activity, it makes good sense that Apollo should have punished Troy with a pestilence whilst Poseidon did so with a flood and sea monster. But since a pestilence, a *loimos*, was conceived of primarily in terms of a sterility, it could well have been one and the same with the briny flood. Here the sea monster is carried onto the plain by the flood. In Lycophron's allusions to the myth (**105**; and cf. again **103**), the sea monster more strikingly carries itself onto the plain and belches forth the flood from its mouth. The earliest extant image of the Sea Monster of Troy, much misinterpreted in recent times, shows it being carried into shore in a surging wave from which its head projects: *LIMC* Hesione 3 (ca. 575–50 BC).

In the summary of the tale preserved at Diodorus 4.42 (ca. 30 BC), we are told, in a common sacrificial motif (**M5.c.ii**), that the sea monster's victim was selected by lot from amongst all the children of the Trojans, but nonetheless the lot fell upon Hesione.

## 105 Obscure but intriguing references to the Sea-monster-of-Troy tale in an artful Hellenistic poem

early ii BC

Lycophron *Alexandra* 31–6 and 470–8, 951–5

Greek

**31–6.** [Cassandra speaks.] Alas, my poor nurse [i.e. Troy], burned before too by the army-bearing pines [i.e. ships] of the lion of the three evenings [i.e. Heracles], who once disappeared into the jaws of the jag-toothed dog [*kuōn*] of Triton [a sea god]. The still-breathing carver of livers, seething in the steam of a cauldron on flameless hearths, dropped the hair of his head on the floor...

**470–8.** The chatterer [Phoenodamas], who had sired threefold daughters, standing in the assembly of the people, once urged that she [Hesione] should be dispatched as a dismal dinner to the grey dog, which was reducing all the land to mud with brine whenever it belched up waves from its jaws, flooding all the ground with a turbulent triple wave. But instead of the anticipated woodpecker [i.e. Hesione], it drew into its throat a scorpion [i.e. Heracles] and bewailed the weight of its evil suffering to Phorcus [the sea god], desiring to find counsel to assuage the pain.

**951–5.** Others will inhabit the land of the Sicanians, coming in their wandering to the place where Laomedon, galled by the disaster of the intended meal of the sea monster [*kētos*], had sailors expose as food for flesh-eating wild beasts the daughters of Phoenodamas whom he gave them.

The *Alexandra* traditionally ascribed to Lycophron is a poem in the form of a extended prophecy delivered by Cassandra (cf. **96**), for whom Alexandra is a by-name. It is a work of such compression and studied obscurantism—the latter at least befits prophecy—that it is all but unintelligible without the surviving ancient and Byzantine commentaries upon it by Tzetzes and others, which are exploited in the following exegesis (these are directly quoted elsewhere in this volume: **51, 67, 91**).

The *Alexandra* subscribes to the view, which may already have been Hellanicus's (**103**), that the sea monster belched forth the briny flood over the plain of Troy rather than itself being carried onto the plain in a briny flood. The triple wave it created perhaps proceeded from its triple rows of teeth (**106**; cf. **M**). The poem implies that Heracles got himself inside the monster not by use of a bulwark, as in Hellanicus, but more directly by substituting himself for its intended sacrificial victim, Hesione—metaphorically, a scorpion for a woodpecker. This variant is illustrated on a fine fourth-century BC Etruscan red-figure vase on which a beardless but muscle-bound Heracles strides into the gaping mouth of the sea monster, draped in Hesione's cloak and drawing his sword as he goes (*LIMC* Hesione no. 6). Heracles then spent three days inside the monster, hence the 'three evenings', and destroyed it by hacking into its liver (as opposed to its flanks more generally, as Hellanicus says). The Phorcus to whom the sea monster cried out in pain is the progenitor, alongside Ceto (*Kētō*), the archetypal *kētos*, of most of the great dragons of Greek myth (1). By the time Heracles emerged, the vapour of the monster's digestive juices had dissolved his hair. Curiously, the *Alexandra* twice refers to the sea monster as 'dog', possibly because there can sometimes be something doglike about the heads of sea monsters in their traditional Greek iconography, or possibly under the influence of the Scylla tradition, a sea monster who incoporated dogs in her form (119–21).

The commentaries also shed light on the obscurely referenced Phoenodamas episode. They explain that Laomedon tried to compel this Trojan noble to sacrifice one of his three daughters to the sea monster, but to protect them he called an assembly and shamed Laomedon into sacrificing his own daughter Hesione to the sea monster instead, since the fault was his. In revenge, Laomedon had Phoenodamas's three daughters transported to Sicily, where they were to be abandoned to wild animals. However, the river Crimisus took the form of a dog (significantly, in view of the *Alexandra*'s characterisation of the sea monster as a dog?) and had sex with one of them, siring Aigestes, who went on to found Egesta and other cities on the island.

## 106  The most elaborate account of the Sea-monster-of-Troy episode to survive

ca. 80 AD

Valerius Flaccus *Argonautica* 2.451–578

Latin

**451.** As Alcides [Heracles] and his companion Telamon were skirting the pleasantly curving shore a cry reached their ears, repeatedly carrying its mournful sound to them as the noise of each broken wave receded. In amazement they pressed ahead and followed the voice's empty path. Now it could be heard distinctly. What man or god was the virgin abandoned to a harsh death not calling upon? At this the men hastened with greater alacrity, determined to help. It was just like when a bull has filled the pathless place with a sharp bellowing, as he carries on his high back a lion that is attempting to break him with its bite, and a band of farmers and countrymen, assembling from a scattering of shacks, come together with blind shouting. Heracles came to a halt. Straining to see from a high crag he espied the murderous manacles, the girl's exhausted face and her eyes swelling with tears, just as when ivory, for all that it is lifeless, nonetheless weeps under the compulsion of great art, or when Parian marble takes on features and names or fluid colours tell amazing stories. The leader said, 'Girl, what is your name, your family? Tell us about your fate here. Why do chains restrain your hands?' She trembled and lowered her eyes in sad shame. 'I do not deserve these sufferings,' she said. 'You can see my parents' final gifts to me, crags decorated with purple and gold. We are the once-happy stock of Ilus—happy until envious Fortune abandoned the household gods of Laomedon. First there were diseases, the temperate atmosphere was driven from the clear sky, and the fields burned with funeral pyres, outdoing each other, when all at once there was a terrible noise and waves disturbed Ida's groves and the homes of the animals in them. See, suddenly there rose out of the sea a beast [*belua*], a huge monster. You could not measure it in terms of any chunks of land or in terms of our sea. A group of young people is given to this raging monster amid the embraces and wailings of their parents. This the lots instruct, this is what horn-bearing Ammon [the oracular god based at Siwah in Egypt] instructs, the condemnation of a virgin's life and the body that had drawn the lot of Lethe [the underworld spring]. The cruel urn consigns me to the crags. But if now the Phrygians' protective deities are returning and you are come in fulfilment of the promise made by the auguries and the lot of the gods, the one for whom, after his vow, my father now rears hoof-footed white horses in his grasslands, the established reward of my deliverance, please say so, and, I pray, deliver me and exhausted Pergamum from the monster. You have the ability to do so, for I did not see such a broad chest even when Neptune was joining the city walls to the stars, nor was Apollo graced by such shoulders and such a quiver.' Her plea was enhanced by its location, and the most dismal appearance of the shore that was held captive, the tombs and the sky that pressed upon the city. Just such was the path to Nemea he had seen, with pity, in its sufferings, and the path to Erymanthus, and the rivers of poisoned Lerna.

**497.** In the meantime Neptune gave the signal from afar, and at once the monster-bearing gulf bellowed and the Sigean bane pushed high the waters of the strait. Its flickering eyes flashed in a grey cloud, and a thunderous uproar shook its mouth, curving with a triple row of teeth. Its tail returns over the sea over which it has already measured its course, and its neck, aloft, snatches forwards the spreading coils. The sea laps up against its flank as it weighs upon it with its thousand coils. Its own storm drives it forwards as it rushes, with the shores in terror. Smaller than this are the billows with which the wave of the cloud-bringing South Wind comes. Not so strongly does the African wind triumph over the deep. Not so strongly does Orion, holding onto his father's reins, lift up the sea with the snorting breaths of his two-hooved horses. See, Telamon was amazed to see the leader grow fierce for the battle he had chosen to take on. His muscles bulged, and he was huge in his armour. The heavy quiver beat against his back. Heracles prayed to his own father, the sea gods and his own arms. He leaped onto a crag and shook with horror to see the sea upheaved from its depths and the expansive coils of the lofty monster. The monster resembled the North Wind when it rises from the vales of cold Hebrus [a Thracian river] and drives the swift clouds over the Riphaean mountains but has still to embrace the entire world with a pitch sky. The beast at once advanced its terrible bulk and craggy back and approached with its huge shade. You would think Ida was quaking and being dashed apart and that towers cast down were rising again. Heracles grabbed his bow and burdened the monster with the whole cloud of arrows from his quiver. It did not stir any more than the great Mt Eryx stirs from its foundations whenever rains try to carry it down into the valleys. Now the space between them was short and no longer suitable for a flying weapon. Then he groaned as he realised the madness of the hopeless enterprise. The girl was silent in her shame and again grew pale. He threw his weapons from his hands and scanned the crags and nearby rocks. All the rocks that time and with it the winds or the crashing of the sea had made loose, he tore up, shaking them free from the bottom of the deep sea. And now the sea creature [*pistris*] was upon them with all its length and gaped for its pitiful booty from close quarters. Heracles stood high in the midst of the waters and received it as it attacked him. He got in first by slamming its rising neck with a rock. Then he heaped upon it the stout blows of his knotted club. The beast sank down to the bottom of the sea, unfurling itself to the entire length of the shallows.

The Idaean mother [Cybele] and her chorus and the rivers raised the cry of lamentation from the tops of the hills. At once the shepherds rose up from the crags and the shaded vale and made their way to the city with great cries. From here Telamon, carrying the message, called his comrades, and at once they were horrified to see the ship in the sudden wash of blood. Heracles shot up the crags to the pinnacle of the harsh rock and removed the girl's hands from the cliff and the chains that were holding them, and he fitted the armour on his proud shoulders. From that point he sought out the king, crossing the shore he had rendered safe in triumph. In this way a victorious bull stalks through meadows, swollen in neck and lofty in shoulders, when he comes back to the high-built fold of his familiar flock and his ancestral grove, and to the loves he has avenged in war.

**550.** A band of Phrygians emerging from their long period of darkness came out to meet him. Laomedon came dragging along his little son, together with his wife. He lamented sadly that his horses were demanded as due reward. Some of the people surrounded the battlements of the lofty wall and wondered at the young man in the strange arms. The king looked at him gloomily and was slippery with sharp cunning. He came up to him and spoke with a father's love, but without true joy: 'Greatest of the Greek-born, whom chance itself drove to this place, although you were not seeking the Sigean shore or feeling pity for the deaths in our Troy, if the story is true that Zeus is your father and you are of the stock of the Thunderer on high, you are one of us, and you come to your kin. We share the same sire and glory of descent, although we are separated and live on shores remote from each other. You come too late after all my tears, after all the sacrifices made by fathers. How small now is the glory that attaches to your achievements! But come now, bring your comrades within your brother's walls. Let tomorrow's light show you the chariot pair in the opened stables.' This is what he said, but he was turning over silent treachery and a dreadful crime in his heart, namely how he could slay him when he was shut in his chamber and heavy with sleep, and cheat the oracular response by seizing his quiver. For he had heard that Pergamum was fated to fall twice to the weapons of Heracles. But who now could avert fate from the kingdom of Priam? In the unmoving ages the night assault of the Greeks, the race of the Aeneadae [the descendants of Aeneas] and the glories of a better Troy [Rome] remain fixed. 'Our journey', said Tirynthian Heracles, 'rushes us to the mouth of the Scythian sea. We shall soon return here to your shores, and I will take away the stipulated reward.' Then Laomedon called upon the gods and promised to give him more gifts. Now the Phrygians wept at their tyrant's faithless promises and the dangers he was bringing on pitiful Troy. [578]

This is the only elaborated literary account of the Sea Monster of Troy to survive from antiquity. Valerius has chosen not to pursue the most distinctive motif of the Hesione tradition, Heracles' entry into the sea monster's belly, but instead he has the hero kill the creature, less intriguingly, with blows from his familiar attribute, his club. Here Apollo's pestilence and Poseidon's flood and sea monster are represented as two quite distinct attacks.

There is much in this narrative, above and beyond the tale's general shape, to align the sea monster with the great *drakontes*. First, it is indirectly compared with the Lernaean Hydra (cf. **4**). There can be no doubt that the physical description of the sea monster coming to shore over the water at 497–505 is calqued upon the movement of a snake over land. And, like the great *drakontes*, this sea monster seemingly has fiery ('flickering') eyes (**M5.a.iii**). The grey cloud that surrounds them may be one of sea spray or even smoke

(**M6.a.ii**). The sea monster's triple rows of teeth match those attributed to *drakontes* (**M1.a.iv**). The mourning for the sea monster by Cybele and her chorus and the rivers should be compared with the mourning of the nymphs for Statius's Dragon of Nemea (**83**) and that of the water nymphs for Silius's Bagrada Dragon (**98**; cf. **M14.b.vii**).

Unsurprisingly, given the tight similarities the tradition of the Sea Monster of Troy exhibits with that of the Sea Monster of Ethiopia (**108–118**), appeal is made to that parallel tradition. The oracle of deliverance issued by the Egyptian Ammon looks as though it has been lifted directly out of the Ethiopian story, where it seems much more appropriate (**108**). Hesione's repeated cry is reminiscent of Andromeda's echoing cry as she faced her monster (**110**). The indirect comparison of Hesione in her peril to a white marble statue is a commonplace of the Andromeda tradition (**110, 113, 115**). In describing the sea monster as of 'craggy' (*scopulosa*) back, Valerius assimilates it to the crags (*scopulos*) on which Hesione has been pinned out. We cannot help but think here too of the Sea Monster of Ethiopia, which was actually transformed by Perseus, using Medusa's head, into a seashore crag like the one upon which Andromeda was pinned out for it (**111, 115**).

*Belua* is the native-Latin term most commonly called upon to translate the Greek term *kētos*, although its own meanings are much wider. *Pistris* (or *pristis*) can denote any large sea creature.

## 107   The Sea Monster of Troy rationalised

ca. 300 BC

Palaephatus 37

Greek

This is said of the sea monster [*kētōs*], that it kept attacking the Trojans from the sea and that if they gave it girls for food [*borán*], it would go away, but if not, it would destroy their land. Who does not realise that it is vain for men to make contracts with fish? This is how it was. A great and powerful king had a large fleet. He subdued the entire seaboard of Asia Minor. People had to pay him a 'subvention' [*phóron*], which people also call 'tribute'. Men of those days did not use money, but goods. Some of the cities had been required to give horses, others oxen and still others girls. This king was called Kētōn, but the barbarians called him Kētos. So he would sail round the coast at the appointed time, demanding his tribute and ravaging the lands of all those who refused to give. As he arrived at Troy, so too did Heracles with an army of Greeks. King Laomedon hired him to help the Trojans. Kētōn disembarked his army and began to march. Heracles and Laomedon intercepted him, each with his own army, and killed him. This is the event from which the myth grew.

Once again, a serpentine creature is rationalised in the most unimaginative way, by transformation into a person with the monster's designation as their proper name (**M16.a.iii–iv**). Why does Palaephatus need to invoke a barbarian misinterpretation of the king's name? Why could he not simply have been called Kētos in the first place? Perhaps because the Greek noun *kētos* is a neuter form and so was felt to be inappropriate as a personal name for a man (we should not be deceived by its *-os* ending). Kētōn, by contrast, had a distinctively masculine ending, which also, interestingly, recalls that of *drakōn* and indeed the proper names of several *drakontes*, Typhon, Python and Ladon.

It is hard to believe that the terms *borán* and *phóron* resembled each other closely in their pronunciation in ca. 300 BC, but nonetheless Palaephatus seems to depend upon such a notion to explain how the subvention supposedly given to Kētōn metamorphosed into the 'food' given to the sea monster in myth. Perhaps Palaephatus had originally, before manuscript corruption, used rather the term *phorbán*, the very term that Euripides uses in describing Andromeda being exposed 'as food' for the Sea Monster of Ethiopia (**109**).

## FURTHER READING

Drexler 1886–90, Schmidt 1907:3–12, Robert 1920–6:ii, 549–58, Weicker 1912, Brommer 1955, Milne 1956, Fontenrose 1959:347–50, 1983, Lesky 1967, Burck 1976, Gantz 1993:400–2, 442–4, Oakley 1997.

# 18
## The Sea Monster of Ethiopia, Slain by Perseus

Perseus's delivery of Andromeda from the sea monster for which she had been pinned out as a sacrifice is another of the better-known classical myths. (One should not be misled by recent movies into thinking that the sea monster in question was the Kraken of the Norse sagas as opposed to the *kētos* of Greek tradition.) Within Perseus's biography, the episode takes place as he flies across Africa on his winged sandals with the head of Medusa after decapitating her (**54–9**). Indeed, according to some versions of the Andromeda tale, Perseus uses the freshly decapitated head to petrify the *kētos*. After this epsiode, and with Andromeda as his wife, he returns to Greece, in the first instance using the Gorgon head to petrify Polydectes and the wicked Seriphians (**54, 60**). It is often held that the tale of Perseus and his *kētos* eventually inspired the famous tale of St George and his dragon (**160–1**), but in fact the early versions of the St George story have far more in common rather with the Hesione tradition (**103–6**). For Andromeda (without specific mention of the sea monster) see also **65**.

### 108  Perseus slays the Sea Monster of Ethiopia to rescue Andromeda: a summary account

ca. 100 AD

Apollodorus
*Bibliotheca* 2.4.3

Greek

Anyway, Perseus put the head of Medusa in his pouch and went back. The Gorgons, roused from sleep, pursued Perseus, but they were not able to detect him because of his cap, since he was hidden by it. When Perseus had arrived in Ethiopia, over which Cepheus was king, he found his daughter Andromeda laid out as food for a sea monster [*kētos*] of the deep. For Cassiepeia the wife of Cepheus had competed with the Nereids in beauty and had boasted that she was better

Figure 18  Sir Edward John Poynter, *Perseus and Andromeda* (1836–1919 AD). Private Collection. Photo © The Fine Art Society, London / The Bridgeman Art Library.

than all of them. As a result of this the Nereids became angry, and Poseidon, becoming angry alongside them, sent a flood-tide against their land and the sea monster too. Ammon gave a prophecy of deliverance from the misfortune if Andromeda, the daughter of Cassiepeia, was given to the monster to eat. Cepheus did this under compulsion from the Ethiopians and bound his daughter to a rock. Perseus, seeing her and falling in love with her, promised to kill the monster for Cepheus if he would give him the girl to wife once he had saved her. Oaths were sworn to this effect, and Perseus faced the monster, killed it and released Andromeda. But Phineus plotted against him. He was Cepheus's brother and formerly had had Andromeda betrothed to him. Perseus discovered the plot, showed him and his fellow conspirators the head of the Gorgon and turned him to stone in an instant.

Apollodorus's summary probably derives from Pherecydes, ca. 454 BC. The parallels between this tale and that of Hesione and the Sea Monster of Troy (103–6) (which, in Valerius Flaccus's version, 106, is in any case actively assimilated to this one) are self-evident, as are its broader affinities with the tales of the slayings of land-based *drakontes* such as those of Lamia-Sybaris (73) and the Dragon of Thespiae (99). Note also that the brief phrase to the effect that Cepheus had to sacrifice Andromeda under the compulsion of the Ethiopians suggests that he was faced, like Hesione's father Laomedon, with a Phoenodamas-like figure.

What was the nature of Phineus's plot? The Andromeda tale falls neatly into the international folk-tale type ATU 300 ('The Dragon-Slayer'), and a coda to this story may hold the key. According to the coda, after defeating the dragon or other terrible beast, the hero cuts out its tongue as a trophy. After he has collapsed in sleep, exhausted, or has left the scene, his wicked rival for the hand of the king's daughter, who has been offered as bride to whoever is able to slay the creature, finds the carcass and cuts off its head, taking it back to the king, declaring himself the slayer and demanding the girl. Upon his subsequent arrival at court, the hero is able to prove his own achievement and claim by producing the tongue. A striking example of this full story type is to be found in Gottfried von Strassburg's *Tristan und Isolde* (B8).

### 109  The reconstruction of Euripides' lost *Andromeda* (i); some key testimonia and fragments

412 BC

Euripides *Andromeda* Testimonium iii.a (a) (= [Eratosthenes] *Catasterismi* 15 and 17) and FF115a, 120, 129, 129a, 136, 145, 146 *TrGF*.

Greek

**Testimonium iii.a (a): [Eratosthenes] *Catasterismi* 15 and 17**

15. Star of Cepheus. This star is fourth in the row...Cepheus was, as Euripides says, king of the Ethiopians, and father to Andromeda. It seems that he put out his daughter as food for the sea monster, and that Perseus the son of Zeus saved her. For this reason he himself too was set among the stars by Athena's decision.

17. Star of Andromeda. She is placed in the stars on account of Athene, as a reminder of Perseus's labours. Her arms are outstretched, in the position in which she was set forth for the sea monster [*kētos*]. In response to this, after being saved by Perseus, she elected not to remain with her father and mother, but voluntarily went off to Argos with him, with noble thoughts in mind. Euripides tells the story clearly in the drama he wrote about her...

**F115a**

ANDROMEDA: ...to expose as food [*phorbán*] for the sea monster [*kētos*].

**F120**

CHORUS [to Andromeda]: Your father is without pity, who abandoned you to Hades to die on behalf of your land, and you are the most overburdened of mortals.

**F129**

PERSEUS [to Andromeda]: O maiden, if I were to free you, will you be grateful?

**F129a**

ANDROMEDA [to Perseus]: Take me for yourself, stranger, whether you want me to be a servant or a wife or a slave.

**F136**

PERSEUS: Eros, you are the king of gods and people. You should either stop telling people that beautiful things are beautiful, or you should work alongside lovers as they struggle through the toils you have created for them, so that they can be successful. If you do this you will be honoured by the gods. But if you do not do this you will be deprived of the thanks with which men honour you by the teaching of love.

**F141**

[Speaker unidentified, probably Cepheus.] I do not allow the taking up of illegitimate children. Although they are in no way inferior to legitimate ones, they ail by law. This is something one must guard against.

**F145**

MESSENGER [?]: I see the sea monster [*kētos*] speeding from the Atlantic sea to its maiden feast.

**F146**

MESSENGER [?]: The whole community of shepherds rushed in, one carrying an ivy cup of milk, to revive him from his labours, another the brightness of vines.

Little survives of Sophocles' *Andromeda*: the evidence of its representation on pots suggests that it was mounted ca. 450 BC, that Andromeda was 'hung out' (F128a *TrGF*) for the sea monster between two poles and that the scene of the action was Ethiopia.

Euripides' Andromeda of 412 BC is also lost, but it evidently was hugely influential in antiquity, and so we devote this and the following two sections to its reconstruction—a reconstruction which its lasting influence, indeed, renders possible. The extant fragments selected for reproduction here are those that focus on the sea monster–slaying episode and its immediate context; further fragments of value for this are supplied with the following section. Their context within the drama can be readily understood from Apollodorus's summary of the myth, **108,** and from the testimonia for the play from the Eratosthenic *Catasterismi* (of perhaps the first century BC).

The coincidences between FF136, 145 and 147 on the one hand and the Perseus vignette of Philostratus's *Imagines* (**111**) are striking. F136 may at first appear to have little to tell us in itself of the play's focal action, but it becomes more meaningful in the light of a wonderful illustration of Euripides' play on a fine Apulian *loutrophoros* vase of c. 350–40 BC, *LIMC* Perseus 189. Here Perseus challenges the sea monster from the front, whilst Eros does indeed help him struggle through his toil by riding on the monster's back. Moderns may initially be baffled by F145, in which the sea monster is said to be speeding to, inevitably, the Ethiopian coast from the Atlantic. But for the ancients Ethiopia stretched the entire breadth of Africa, beneath Egypt and Libya, and had an Atlantic coast (this proves, incidentally, that Euripides' tragedy was indeed set in Ethiopia as opposed to Joppa, which some have doubted despite the explicit assertion of the testimonia, of F147, 'Ethiopians' and the strong indication of Philostratus, **111**). F141, in debating the ethics of illegitimacy, may derive from an attempt by Cepheus to justify his exposure of Andromeda to the monster; see further the commentary to **111**. F115a is of interest not least for helping us to understand Palaephatus's rationalisation of the parallel myth of the Sea Monster of Troy: see **107**.

The testimonia focus upon the ending of the play, in which it will have been foretold that Athene would translate the principal characters involved in the sea-monster episode to the stars after their deaths.

## 110 The reconstruction of Euripides' lost *Andromeda* (ii): Aristophanes' parody of it in his *Thesmophoriazusae*

411 BC

Aristophanes
*Thesmophoriazusae*
1009–1135, incorporating
Euripides *Andromeda*
FF114–15, 117–18, 122,
124–5, 127

Greek

MNESILOCHUS: Ah, gods, Zeus Soter, there is hope! It seems that the man will not betray me. He has just given me a secret sign by running out as Perseus, to the effect that I must become Andromeda. I already have the chains, at any rate. It's clear that he will come to save me, for otherwise he would not have flown past. **Dear maidens, my dear ones [F117 *TrGF*], how could I get away and escape the Scythian's watch? Do you hear there? I'm speaking to you, the woman in the cave [F118 *TrGF*]!** Say yes, and let me go to my wife. The man that tied me up was without pity, and I am the most wretched of mortals. Despite having escaped, just about, from a putrid old woman, I am done for even so. For the Scythian guard, set to keep an eye on me some time ago, has hung me out, done-for and friendless, as a meal for crows. **Can you see?** It is not with choral dances nor with peer girls that I stand here *with a voting funnel*. But, *bound in tight chains, I have been set forth as food for the sea monster* [*kētos*] Glaucetes. *Mourn for me, o women, not with a wedding paean, but with a song of binding. A wretched woman, I have suffered wretched things, alas for me, alas for me,* and I have experienced other *lawless sufferings from my own relatives. I beseech the fellow as I kindle up my many-teared lament of Hades, oh! oh!* [F122 *TrGF*]—that first shaved me, who dressed me in saffron, and in addition to these things sent me to this sanctuary, where the women are. Oh for my fate, which a god brought forth! Oh I am accursed! Who will not see my unenviable suffering in the company of evils? Would that the fiery star of the sky might destroy the barbarian! For it is no longer dear to me to see the immortal flame, since I have been hung out: throat-cutting agonies, a dark journey to the dead!

ECHO: Hello, dear girl, may the gods destroy your father, Cepheus, who exposed you.

MNESILOCHUS: Who are you, you who pity my suffering?

ECHO: I am Echo, the joking reflector of words, who last year in this same place assisted Euripides in his competition [*sc.* to win the prize for the year's best tragedy]. But, o child, you must do your part and lament in pitiful fashion.

MNESILOCHUS: And you must then lament in reply after me.

ECHO: I'll look after that. Just begin speaking.

MNESILOCHUS: **O holy night, how long is the chariot journey you pursue as you ride across the starry back of the sacred ether, through most holy Olympus!**

ECHO: ...through Olympus.

MNESILOCHUS: **Why ever have I, Andromeda, been allotted an excess of troubles, wretched as I am and about to meet my death [FF114–15 *TrGF*]?**

| | |
|---|---|
| Echo: | ... allotted. |
| Mnesilochus: | Wretched for my death... |
| Echo: | Wretched for my death... |
| Mnesilochus: | You will destroy me, old woman, with your wittering. |
| Echo: | ... with your wittering. |
| Mnesilochus: | Yes, by Zeus, your interference is too burdensome. |
| Echo: | ... too burdensome. |
| Mnesilochus: | My good man, allow me to sing my monody, and I'll be grateful. Stop! |
| Echo: | Stop! |
| Mnesilochus: | Go to the crows! |
| Echo: | Go to the crows! |
| Mnesilochus: | What's wrong? |
| Echo: | What's wrong? |
| Mnesilochus: | You're talking rubbish! |
| Echo: | You're talking rubbish! |
| Mnesilochus: | You'll be sorry! |
| Echo: | You'll be sorry! |
| Mnesilochus: | You'll wail! |
| Echo: | You'll wail! |
| Scythian: | You here, what are you chattering about? |
| Echo: | You here, what are you chattering about? |
| Scythian: | I'll call the presidents. |
| Echo: | I'll call the presidents. |
| Scythian: | What's the trouble? |
| Echo: | What's the trouble? |
| Scythian: | Where's that voice coming from? |
| Echo: | Where's that voice coming from? |
| Scythian: | Is it you that's chattering? |
| Echo: | Is it you that's chattering? |
| Scythian: | You'll be sorry! |
| Echo: | You'll be sorry! |
| Scythian: | Are you laughing at me? |
| Echo: | Are you laughing at me? |
| Mnesilochus: | No, by Zeus, but this woman beside us here is. |
| Echo: | ... Beside us here. |
| Scythian: | Where is the damned woman? |
| Mnesilochus: | Look, she's escaping. |
| Scythian: | Where, where are you running to? You won't get away with it! |
| Echo: | You won't catch me! |
| Scythian: | Are you still making noises? |
| Echo: | Are you still making noises? |
| Scythian: | Seize the damned woman! |
| Echo: | Seize the damned woman! |
| Scythian: | Chattering and accursed woman! |
| Euripides: | **O gods, to what land of foreigners have I come with swift sandal? Cutting a path through the midst of the ether, I work my winged foot. I, Perseus, am voyaging to Argos over the swell of the sea and the Pleiad, with the head of the Gorgon [F124 *TrGF*].** |
| Scythian: | What are you saying? You have the head of Gorgos the secretary? |
| Euripides: | I said 'the Gorgon's head.' |
| Scythian: | I'm saying 'Gorgos' too. |

| | |
|---|---|
| EURIPIDES: | Well now. What is this mound I see *and a goddess-like virgin moored to it as if a ship* [F125 *TrGF*]? |
| MNESILOCHUS: | **Stranger, pity me in my great wretchedness. Free me from my bonds** [F128 *TrGF*]! |
| SCYTHIAN: | Will you not shut up, accursed thing! You dare to talk when you are about to be killed? |
| EURIPIDES: | **O maiden, I pity you as I see you hanging here** [F127 *TrGF*]. |
| SCYTHIAN: | She's not a maiden, but a sinful old man, a thief and a criminal. |
| EURIPIDES: | You're talking rubbish, Scythian. For she is Andromeda the daughter of Cepheus. |
| SCYTHIAN: | Look at her fig. It doesn't seem very small, does it? |
| EURIPIDES: | Pass her hand to me, so that I may touch the girl, pass it, Scythian. All men have diseases, and I myself have been seized by desire for this girl. |
| SCYTHIAN: | I don't envy you. But if his arsehole was twisted round here, I would not have any problem with you taking him and buggering him. |
| EURIPIDES: | Why do you not allow me to release her, Scythian, and fall onto the bed and the bridal couch? |
| SCYTHIAN: | If you're so desperate to bugger the old man, then drill a hole through the plank and bugger him from behind it. |
| EURIPIDES: | No, by Zeus, but I'll undo her bonds. |
| SCYTHIAN: | In that case I'll whip you. |
| EURIPIDES: | I'll go ahead and do it. |
| SCYTHIAN: | In that case I'll cut off your head with this sabre. |
| EURIPIDES: | Alas! What shall I do? To what words am I to turn? But this man's barbarian nature would not understand them. For to apply new wisdom to dull people is to waste one's time. I must deploy some other device suitable to this man. |
| SCYTHIAN: | The accursed fox, how he tried to make a monkey out of me! |
| MNESILOCHUS: | Remember, Perseus, in what misery you leave me! |
| SCYTHIAN: | So do you still want to taste the whip? |

Euripides' relative, the gruff Mnesilochus, has been detected infiltrating the women-only Thesmophoria festival in drag in order to spy upon the women's plans to have Euripides killed for defaming their sex in his tragedies. Chained against a plank, it seems, he is kept under guard by an obtuse Scythian archer, one of classical Athens's so-called policemen, all of whose utterances are expressed in an appropriately barbarous and pidgin variety of Greek (no attempt is made to represent the effect of this in the translation). Meanwhile, Mnesilochus and Euripides attempt to engineer the former's escape by re-enacting famous scenes from the latter's *oeuvre*. Here Euripides attempts the rescue in the guise of his Perseus, casting Mnesilochus in the guise of his Andromeda.

The dialogue, much of which is in tragic (or paratragic) diction, includes a number of quotations from Euripides' play, some direct, some modified for their new context or for comic effect, identifiable with the help of the ancient commentaries. Directly quoted material is in boldface type here; modified material is in bold italics.

Whereas in Sophocles' *Andromeda* the girl had been tied, arms outstretched, between two poles to await the monster (à la Fay Wray in *King Kong*), in Euripides' play she was tied into the mouth of a cave. One of the play's striking effects, and one ripe with the comic potential exploited by Aristophanes, was the repetition of the final words of Andromeda's utterances by the echo in the cave behind—or, rather, by the nymph Echo, denizen of the cave.

In the modified fragment F122 Aristophanes takes the opportunity for a satirical swipe at Glaucetes by comparing him to the sea monster. Other comedies indicate that he was a glutton for seafood (Aristophanes *Peace* 1008, Plato Comicus F114 K-A); his name is in any case suggestive of Glaucus, a fish-tailed, Triton-like sea deity (for whom see **120**). The Gorgon's head gives Aristophanes the opportunity to joke at the expense of another public figure, one Gorgos, who is otherwise unknown to us. The reference to the voting funnel is not certainly understood, but it looks, at some level, like a characteristic Aristophanic swipe at the paraphernalia of Athens's radical democracy.

The ancient commentaries tell us that the original lines behind F125 had Perseus compare the pinned-out Andromeda to a beautiful stone statue, a conceit that Ovid and Achilles Tatius were to borrow (**113**, **115**), and that Valerius Flaccus was to transfer to Hesione (**106**). For Euripides the principal purpose of the comparison was likely to have been to make the point that Andromeda stood as starkly white amongst the otherwise black population of Ethiopia: see **111**.

Mnesilochus's 'fig' is his penis, which would have been manifest on the comic stage in the form of a giant leather phallus. The remnants of Mnesilochus's disguise as a woman do not fool the Scythian, slow though he may be, and he is understandably surprised by Euripides' apparent confusion.

## 111 The reconstruction of Euripides' lost *Andromeda* (iii): a vignette reflecting the play's focal action

mid-iii AD

Philostratus *Imagines* 1.29

Greek

But this is not the Red Sea [i.e., the Indian Ocean], and this is not the land of the Indians. The people are Ethiopians, and a Greek man in Ethiopia. I think, my boy, you must have heard of the contest the man is undertaking, and that too of his own accord, because of love. They say that he killed an Atlantic sea monster [*kētos*] that was attacking the herds and the people on the land. The painter admires the story and shows pity for Andromeda, because she was put out for the sea monster. The contest is already over, and the sea monster is cast down before the shore, weltering in gushing blood. That is why the sea is red. Eros is releasing Andromeda from her bonds. Eros is painted with wings, in the traditional fashion, but, in less traditional fashion, he is represented as a young man, breathing hard and not yet recovered from his struggle. For, before the task, Perseus had struck up a prayer to Eros to present himself and fly down upon the beast, and come he did and heeded the Greek man. The girl is sweet, because fair in Ethiopia, and her form itself is also sweet. She would outstrip a Lydian girl in grace, an Attic girl in dignity and a Spartan girl in healthy physique. Her beauty is enhanced by the occasion. For she seems to be in a state of disbelief, joy and shock. She looks at Perseus and sends him something of a smile. He lies, not far from the girl, on the sweet and frankincense-like grass, dripping sweat to the ground and keeping the Gorgon hidden from view, lest folk should happen upon it and become stone. Many are the cowherds offering him milk and drinks of wine, Ethiopians sweet in the unusualness of their colour and their grim smiles. Most of them are obviously rejoicing alike. Perseus welcomes these gifts and, leaning on his left elbow, lifts his chest, swollen by his hard breathing, and gazes at the girl. He lets the wind take his purple cloak, which is speckled with drops of blood and the gore the beast breathed upon it in the fight. The descendants of Pelops [who was famous for his ivory shoulder] are nowhere by comparison with Perseus's shoulder.

For the exertion has added bloom to his ruddy beauty, and his veins stand proud, which is what happens to them when hard breathing takes over. He wins much admiration from the girl.

The *Imagines* is a collection of so-called ecphrases, virtuoso literary recreations in words of (usually imaginary) works of material art, painting or statuary. This one describes a Perseus-and-Andromeda scene, as do the further ecphrases at **115–16**. Often in ecphrasis scenes are described that it would in fact be impossible to represent in a single image. In this case we may wonder whether any artist could fully represent at once all the emotions attributed to Andromeda. Imaginary though the supposed original image might be in this case, it should be noted that Andromeda frescos were popular in the houses of 79 AD Pompeii (*LIMC* Andromeda i 67–71, 73–4, 78, 83–9, 102–4, 109–10, 118, 120, 209–11, 222, Perseus 66–73, 229–30), and no doubt throughout the rest of the Graeco-Roman world in that era.

In speaking of Eros heeding Perseus's prayer and coming to help him in the fight (cf. Euripides *Andromeda* F136 *TrGF*), of the Atlantic origin of the sea monster (cf. F145 *TrGF*) and of the herdsmen coming to comfort Perseus with milk and wine after the fight (cf. F146 *TrGF*), Philostratus shows that he has Euripides' tragedy very much in mind as he composes his vignette (**109**). As such, it may give us a good impression of the play's action, particularly that described in its messenger speech. The notion that Eros should have flown down upon the beast perfectly matches the fashion in which he is shown riding it on the Apulian *loutrophoros* vase that illustrates Euripides' play, *LIMC* Perseus 189 (cf. **109**, with commentary).

It is just possible, given that Perseus is fretting about whether an innocent local might catch sight of the Gorgon's head, that he has had it recently unsheathed, and therefore that he has deployed it against the sea monster (cf. **115**). This too could have been a Euripidean motif.

Philostratus makes it clear that the Ethiopians, presumably including Andromeda's parents, were black, whilst Andromeda herself was white. Again, this motif is presumably taken over from Euripides, who would himself have taken it over from Sophocles. It is tempting to link this paradox with Euripides *Andromeda* F141 (**119**), which indicates that illegitimacy was at issue in the play. Perhaps Cepheus believed, in view of her colour, that Andromeda was an adulterine bastard foisted upon him by his wife and was for this reason all too ready to give her over to the monster. This may explain why Andromeda complained of the 'lawless sufferings' she experienced at the hands of her own relatives, which seems to hint that she had greater cause for complaint against them than their accession to the will of an oracle (**110**: F122). It may also explain why she chose to go off with Perseus when her ordeal was over (**109**: testimonia, *Catasterismi* 17). No doubt Andromeda's whiteness was in fact due to some other mysterious cause.

## 112 Perseus enters the sea monster's mouth to attack its liver

early ii BC

Lycophron *Alexandra* 834–46

Greek

And he [sc. Menelaus] will see bastions of Cepheus, and the kick traces of Hermes Laphrius, and the twin rocks at which the *kepphos*-bird [storm petrel?] leapt, in desire for its meal. But he came and snatched up in his jaws instead of the female [i.e. Andromeda] a male, the golden-fathered 'eagle' [i.e. Perseus], the winged-shoed liver wrecker. The hateful whale [or: monster—*phalaina*] will be slain by the blade of the reaper; it will be stripped out. This reaper will have relieved the equine birth pangs of the neck-delivering stone-eyed weasel [i.e. Medusa; weasels were held to give birth through their necks] and will make statues of men from their toes upwards, enveloping them with stone, the stealer of light from the triple-wandering guiding [i.e. the Graeae/Phorcides].

Another allusive and obscurantist passage from Lycophron. He speaks of Perseus's killing of the Sea Monster of Ethiopia in terms very similar to those in which he (and others) speak of Heracles killing the Sea Monster of Troy (105, with commentary). Here, alluding to the protagonists with the imagery of birds, Cassandra prophesies that Perseus, he of the winged sandals, after stealing the eye of the Graeae and decapitating Medusa (54–9), will substitute himself for Andromeda, the female sacrifice the sea monster expects to devour, and so get inside its mouth. He will then kill it by wrecking its liver. This is a unique claim in the context of the Sea Monster of Ethiopia tradition, and one must ask whether Lycophron is reporting an established but to us otherwise unattested variant, or is transferring the motif from the Sea Monster of Troy tradition in anomalous and maverick fashion. The latter seems more likely.

## 113   An elaborate account of the Sea Monster of Ethiopia

8 AD

Ovid *Metamorphoses* 4.663–739

Latin

**663.** The son of Hippotes [Aeolus] had closed the winds in their eternal cell and Lucifer, brightest star in the high sky, who tells men to go to work, had risen. Perseus took up his wings again and bound them to his feet on both sides. He girded on his hooked weapon and cut through the clear air by plying his sandals. He had flown over and adjacent to countless races when he caught sight of the peoples of the Ethiopians and the territory of Cepheus. Their unjust Ammon had given the order that Andromeda should undeservedly pay the penalty for what her mother had said. As soon as the descendant of Abas [Perseus] saw her arms tied to the harsh rocks (he would have thought she was a marble statue, were it not that a gentle breeze had stirred her hair and her eyes flowed with warm tears), he was set aflame despite himself. He was dumbstruck. Preoccupied by the impression of the beauty he had seen, he almost forgot to shake his wings in the air. As he stopped, 'Oh,' he said, 'you do not deserve those bonds but rather the ones by which amorous lovers are joined to each other. I ask you: tell me the name of the land and your own name, and tell me why you wear these chains.' At first she kept silent and, as a maiden, did not dare to speak to a man. She would have covered her face in modesty with her hands if she had not been tied back. But she filled her eyes with welling tears, which was something she was still able to do. As he pressed her again and again, she feared that she might seem to be refusing to confess crimes, and so she told him the name of the land and her own, and the size of her mother's confidence in her own beauty. She had yet to tell him the whole story when the wave crashed, and the beast [*belua*] came forth from the vast sea to the attack. It engulfed the wide waters beneath its breast.

**691.** The maiden screamed. Her mourning father and, together with him, her mother stood by, both desolate, but she with greater reason. They had no aid to offer, but they produced tears suited to the occasion and wailing, and cleaved to the bound body. The visitor addressed them as follows: 'You will have plenty of time to grieve in the future, but there is only a brief time in which to bring succour.

I am Perseus, born of Jupiter and her whom, imprisoned, Jupiter filled with fertilising gold [Danae], Perseus, vanquisher of the snake-tressed Gorgon, the man who dared to travel through the winds of the air upon beating wings. If I were to seek this girl's hand in marriage, I would surely be preferred as son-in-law to all comers. But to such great gifts of wooing I essay to add a deserving deed, if only the gods look kindly upon me. I contract to marry her: so may she be delivered by my valour!' They accepted the pact. Who would hesitate to do so? Her parents begged him to save her, and in addition promised the kingdom as a dowry. And lo, just as a swift ship cuts a furrow through the waters, prow first, impelled forwards by the sweating arms of youths, so did the wild creature, driving the waves apart with the force of its breast. Its distance from the crags was equivalent to the amount of air across which a Balearic sling can cast the leaden bullet it hurls. At once, the young man soared aloft into the clouds, his feet driving him up from the earth. As a shadow of the man appeared on the surface of the sea, the wild creature attacked the shadow it saw. And as Jupiter's bird [the eagle], when it sees a serpent [*draco*] offering its dark back to Phoebus [the sun] in an open field, attacks it from the rear and fixes its greedy talons in the scaly neck to prevent it from twisting back its savage mouth, so, hurtling headlong in swift flight through the open air, Inachides [Perseus] attacked the wild creature's back and buried his sword in its right shoulder, up as far as the curving hilt, as it bellowed. Damaged by the deep wound, it repeatedly raised itself aloft into the air, buried itself in the waters, and twisted around in the fashion of a wild boar that a pack of barking hounds has at bay. Perseus avoided its greedy bites with his swift wings. Where the beast was exposed, he repeatedly struck it with his sickle-shaped sword—first the back, covered over with hollow shells, then its ribs, on its flanks, then at the point at which its tail tapered off narrowly into a fish. The beast belched forth from its mouth waves mixed with ruddy blood. His wings grew heavy with moisture from the spray. He no longer dared trust his soaked ankle wings. Espying a rock, the topmost part of which jutted from the waters when they were calm but was covered over with water when it was upheaved, he got a firm foothold on it. Holding on to the highest part of the ridge of the rock with his left hand, he drove his sword repeatedly, three times and four times, through the animal's flank. Applause and acclaim filled the shores and the home of the gods above. Cassiope [= Cassiepeia] and Andromeda's father, Cepheus, rejoiced and hailed Perseus as their son-in-law, proclaiming him succour and salvation of their house. The girl, prize and occasion alike of the labour, stepped forward, liberated now from her chains. [739]

It is the Latin poets Ovid and Manilius (**114**) that preserve for us the most elaborate and enjoyable accounts of Perseus's killing of the Sea Monster of Ethiopia. Ovid's action is well grounded in Ethiopia, with the participation in the story of the relatively local Egyptian god Ammon (cf. **108**). Perseus attacks the monster with his *harpē*, the sickle sword so well adapted to the slaying of anguiform monsters, and perhaps with an additional regular sword too (cf. **114**; **M11.b.i, M12.b.v**). Ovid pays much attention to the erotics of the scene and to the psychology of Andromeda, who is again projected as a white statue (cf. **110, 115**).

As a (temporarily) winged son of Jupiter, the comparison, in simile, of Perseus to an eagle seems particularly apposite; we may take comfort, therefore, in the parallel comparison of the sea monster to a dragon (*draco*). That aside, Ovid's allusions to the sea monster's physical form—particularly its shoulders and tapering fish tail—make it clear that he envisages a sea monster of a sort typical in ancient art, with a relatively wide upper body and forearms.

## 114 An elaborate and astronomically flavoured account of the Sea Monster of Ethiopia

earlier i AD

Manilius *Astronomica* 5.538–618

Latin

The constellation of Andromeda is next. She appears in the right of the sky when Pisces has risen by twelve degrees. The fault of her dread parents once led her to be put out as a sacrifice, when the hostile sea threw itself upon all its shores, the land was submerged and shipwrecked, and what had been Cepheus's kingdom became the open sea. There could only be one expiation for these crimes, the surrender of Andromeda to the maddened sea, so that the creature [*belua*] could devour her gentle limbs. This was her wedding. Relieving the suffering of the people with her own, the weeping victim was decked out for her sacrifice. She put on the dress that had not been intended for this kind of vow, and the funeral without funeral of the living virgin was hastened on. As soon as they had come to the shore of the hostile sea, her soft arms were stretched over the hard rocks. They fastened her feet to the crags and chained her up. The virgin girl, doomed to die, was suspended in the shape of a cross. But even as she was offered in sacrifice she preserved the modesty of her demeanour. The tortures themselves enhanced her beauty. Gently throwing back her snowy neck, she seemed retain control over her figure. The folds of her dress slipped down her arms, and her loose, flowing hair clung to her shoulders. Andromeda, halcyons made lament as they flew around you and they mourned your lot with piteous song! They shielded you by overlapping their wings! The sea halted its waves at the sight of you, and for your sake it held back from drenching the rocks in its usual way! A Nereid lifted her face from the flowing waters, and, in pity for your lot, wetted even the waves with her tears. The breeze itself, refreshing your hanging limbs with its gentle breath, made a tearful sound across the tops of the cliffs.

**567.** At long last that happy day brought Perseus, victorious over the monstrous Gorgon, to the shore. When he saw the girl hanging from the rock, Perseus, the one whom his Gorgon-enemy had not been able to stop short with her face, froze, and he could scarcely keep hold of the spoils in his hand. The vanquisher of Medusa was vanquished by Andromeda. He envied the very rocks and called the chains lucky to hold such limbs. After learning from the girl herself the reason she had been put out as a sacrifice, he resolved to go to war with the sea so that he could marry her. He was not to be deterred even if a second Gorgon should confront him. Speeding through the air, he brought relief to her weeping parents by promising to save her life. Making the deal to marry her, he returned to the shore. By now the heavy sea had begun to swell, and its waves fled in a long rank before the bulk of the monster that drove them forwards. It cut through the waves and lifted its head from them. It belched forth sea. The waters resounded around its teeth, and the ocean surged even within its mouth. Behind rose its huge coils with their massive loops. Its body occupied the sea, and the ocean resounded on every side. Even the mountains and the rocks dreaded its attack. Unhappy virgin, what was your expression at that time, even though such a great champion was at hand! How you lost your breath to the breezes! How your limbs were drained of all their blood when you yourself saw your doom from your hollow in the rocks, the creature swimming for its sacrifice and carrying the sea with it, and how tiny a prize you made for the sea!

**592.** Then Perseus flew up with a shake of his winged sandals and launched himself from the sky against the enemy, fixing the iron stained with the Gorgon's blood into it. The beast came up against him, raising its head out of the flood. Powering itself aloft on its twisting coils, it sprang forth from the water and lifted its whole body high. But, however high it lifted itself, launching itself from the deep, Perseus ever flew back and upwards by the same amount, mocking it with his aerial agility, and he struck the head of the sea monster [*cetus*] as it came up. It would not yield to the man, but chomped at the air in its rage. Its teeth crashed together in vain without inflicting any wound. It blew a spout of seawater skywards and drenched Perseus as he flew through the bloodied liquid. It sprayed the ocean over the stars. The girl, the cause of the fighting, watched the fight, and now, forgetting herself, sighed as she feared rather for her impressive champion. Her mind was in a greater state of suspense than her body. Eventually the beast sank down, its body perforated and filled with seawater, and returned again to the surface of the waves. It covered a vast expanse of sea with its huge carcass. Even in that state it was terrible and a thing a virgin should never have had to look upon. Perseus, the victor, washed his body off in the flowing water and flew from the waves to the high crags. He released the girl from the rock and from the chains that bound her to it, the girl betrothed in battle and now about to marry with the dowry of her life, saved by her husband. Perseus's feat gave Andromeda her destiny in the sky and led to her sacred representation in the stars as the prize of such a great battle. The monster that fell in that battle was no less dreadful than the Gorgon herself, and the sea was liberated of it. [618]

The constellation of Andromeda is the starting point for Manilius's excursus on the mythical episode. The most striking feature of his account is its highly eroticised presentation of the suspended Andromeda. The vignette of Perseus's freeing Andromeda from the rock after defeating the sea monster was a particularly popular one in Roman art (*LIMC* Andromeda i 67–71, 73–4, 78, 83–9, 209–11, 222).

The monster is conceptualised as strongly serpentine, with its massive looping coils, upon which it powers itself up into the air. The conceit of Perseus nimbly flying ever just out of its reach as it surges upwards is a winning one. When the sea monster sprays the ocean over the stars, Manilius reminds us of the principal theme of his astronomical work and also magnifies the battle to the cosmic scale, as Nonnus was later to do for Typhon (8).

Once again, the weapon used is the *harpē* (cf. 113; M11.b.i). It is difficult to imagine, nonetheless, how such a small weapon could have made any impact on a creature of the size the sea monster is implied to be, let alone penetrate to its inner organs, as is implied when the monster belches forth blood. Was the Gorgon's blood, which remained on the *harpē*, venomous, and did this play a contributory role in the creature's demise?

## 115  Another vignette of Perseus's slaying of the Sea Monster of Ethiopia

later ii AD

Achilles Tatius *Leucippe and Clitophon* 3.6.3–3.7.9

Greek

Euanthes was the painter [sc. of a temple fresco]. The picture showed Andromeda and Prometheus. Both were bound. This is the reason, I believe, that the artist brought them together. The paintings constituted twins in other ways too. The place of binding for both was rocks. The executioners for both were wild beasts: for Prometheus a creature from the air; for Andromeda a creature from the sea. Their deliverers were two related Argives: for Prometheus, Heracles; for Andromeda, Perseus. Heracles shot the bird that came from Zeus, whereas Perseus fought against the sea monster [*kētos*] that came from Poseidon. The former took his stance on the ground as he shot; the latter hung in the air with his wings. The rock was recessed in such a way as to fit the girl. The recess suggested that it had not been made by hand, but that it was natural. For the painter had made the cavern of stone rough, as if the earth had produced it. Andromeda was sitting within her shelter. If you were to consider her beauty, you would find that the vision resembled a new kind of statue, but if you were to consider her chains and the sea monster, a rough and ready grave. Beauty and fear were mixed in her face. Fear sat on her cheeks, but beauty flowered from her eyes. Her cheeks were not completely pale, but they had a pink blush, and had been lightly shaded red. Care had been taken with the flower of her eyes. They resembled violets just as they begin to wither. This was how the painter decorated her with a comely fear. She spread her arms out across the rock. The chains bound each of her hands to the rock with a manacle above. Her hands hung down like grape clusters from a vine. The girl's arms were pure white but changing their colour to livid, and her fingers seemed to be dying. This was how she was bound, ready to receive death. She stood there dressed in bridal garb, just like a bride adorned for Hades. Her tunic was full-length and white. The weave was fine, like spiders' webs, not like that made from sheep's fleeces, but like that winged wool the threads of which are drawn from trees and woven by Indian women. The sea monster, coming up from below directly before the girl, opened the sea up before itself. Most of its body was surrounded by waves, with only its head breaking the surface of the water. But the shadow of its body had been painted beneath the salty water: the ridges of its scales, the curves of its neck, its crest of spines, the coils of its tail. Its jaw was massive and long. It gaped open all the way down to the join of the shoulders, and then immediately came its belly. Between the sea monster and the girl Perseus had been painted coming down from the air. He was coming down against the creature completely nude. He wore just a cloak round his shoulders and sandals on his feet to which wings were connected. On his head he wore a felt cap. This was meant to suggest the cap of Hades. In his left hand he brandished the Gorgon's head and held it before him like a shield. It was frightening even in paint. Its eyes stared out, the hair on its temples stood on end, and the serpents (*drakontes*) were roused. So threatening was it even in a picture. This was the weapon Perseus held in his left hand. He was armed in his right hand with a double-shaped piece of iron, formed into both a sickle and a sword. Both blades began from a common handle, and for half its length the iron formed a sword, but from that point it was split in two, and one part ran straight, the other was curved. The straight part continued as a sword, just as it had begun, whilst the curved part became a sickle, so that with a single blow the first part drove in a deep wound, whilst the second part achieved a slashing cut. This was the drama of Andromeda.

As with Philostratus's account (**111**) we have here another Second-Sophistic ecphrasis, a literary exposition of a work of art (in this case, imaginary).

Once again, it is made clear that the monster had a strongly serpentine nature (cf. **114**). The notion finally emerges in later texts such as this one (cf. also **116**) that Perseus should actually have deployed against the sea monster the obvious super-weapon he had at his disposal—the Gorgon's head—though the notion may already have been Euripides' (**111**, with com.), and it may be implicit too in Conon's rationalisation of the Andromeda story, composed at the turn of the eras (**118**). The notion first emerges in the iconographic on a fourth-century BC Etruscan cup (*LIMC* Perseus

192). Achilles Tatius's conceptualisation of the fight as a battle between two serpentine forms is palpable. But Perseus also retains his signature weapon, his *harpē* or sickle sword, here described in some detail. If the description seems to suggest a weapon too cumbersome to be usable, it nonetheless reflects well some images of the *harpē* in classical art (e.g. *LIMC* Perseus 68).

As in the Manilian account (114), all the attention is on the figure of Andromeda, her beauty, her eroticism and her psychology in her desperate hour. The notion that Andromeda resembled a statue in her beauty is derived ultimately from Euripides (110) and is shared also with Ovid (113). Achilles Tatius shares with Manilius the conceit that Andromeda's offering to the sea monster is a sort of perverted wedding for her.

## 116 Perseus's slaying of the Sea Monster of Ethiopia from the perspective of the Nereids that sent it

ca. 160–80 AD

Lucian *Dialogues in the Sea* 14 and *The Hall* 22

Greek

**Dialogues in the Sea:**

TRITON: Your sea monster [*kētos*], o Nereids, which you sent against Andromeda, daughter of Cepheus, did not harm the girl, as you were expecting, but is itself now dead.

NEREIDS: By whom was it killed, o Triton? Did Cepheus set the girl forth as if a piece of bait, and then attack it and kill it, lying in ambush with a great force?

TRITON: No. But I think, o Iphianassa, that you know Perseus, the child of Danae, who was cast into the sea together with his mother by his maternal grandfather, and whom you took pity on and saved.

IPHIANASSA: I know of whom you speak. He is likely to be a young man, very noble and beautiful to see.

TRITON: This is the man that killed the sea monster.

IPHIANASSA: Why, o Triton? This is not the way in which he should have repaid us for saving him.

TRITON: I will tell you the whole story. He was sent against the Gorgons, to complete some labour for his king, but when he arrived in Libya...

IPHIANASSA: How, o Triton? Alone? Or did he bring allies besides? The journey is a difficult one otherwise.

TRITON: Through the air. For Athena put wings under him. Anyway, when he came to where they lived, they were sleeping, I believe, so he chopped off Medusa's head and flew off.

IPHIANASSA: How did he look upon them? For they cannot be looked at. Or rather, if ever someone does look upon them, he never sees anything else after them.

TRITON: Athena held her shield in front. I heard him relating this story to Andromeda and Cepheus afterwards. Athena let him see the reflection of Medusa in her shiny shield, as in a mirror. He took her by the hair with his left hand and, concentrating on the reflection and holding his sickle in his right hand, he cut off her head, flying aloft before her sisters awoke. When he came to the coast of Ethiopia here, now skimming the ground close, he espied Andromeda exposed on some prominent rock, pegged to it, exceptionally beautiful, by the gods, with her hair loose, and half naked, mainly below the breasts. At first he felt pity for her fate and sought the reason for her condemnation. But gradually he was overcome by love and decided to help her—for it was fated that the girl should be saved. And when the sea monster approached—a very fearsome thing—with a view to eating Andromeda, the young man launched himself into the air with his sickle unsheathed, struck the beast with one hand and displayed the Gorgon with the other, turning the sea monster to stone. It died and at the same time most of it, all of it that had seen Medusa, was frozen. He undid the virgin's chains and supported her with his arm as she gingerly made her way down from the slippery rock. He is now marrying her in Cepheus's palace and will take her back to Argos. So, instead of death, she has found for herself a marriage of no ordinary sort.

IPHIANASSA: For my part, I am not very upset about what has happened. For in what way did the girl wrong us, just because her mother used to boast and claimed to be more beautiful?

DORIS: The reasoning was that, as her mother, she would in this way have had to grieve over her daughter.

IPHIANASSA: Let's not bear a grudge over those things, o Doris, if a barbarian woman has made some claim greater than she should. She has compensated us enough in her fear for her child. So let us rejoice in the marriage.

**The Hall:** As you enter you see on the right a romance set in Ethiopia blended with Argive myth. Perseus slaughters the sea monster [*kētos*] and takes Andromeda. Shortly he will marry her and take her off. This is a supplementary scene in the depiction of his flight to the Gorgons. The painter has represented a great deal with efficiency, the girl's shyness and her fear—for she looks down on the battle from the cliff above—and the young man's daring, driven by desire, and the invincible appearance of the creature. It attacks with its spines bristling and terrifying with its gaping maw. Perseus shows it the Gorgon with his left hand and with the right he hits it with his sword. That part of the sea monster that has seen Medusa is already stone, but that part that remains alive is being hacked at with the sickle [*harpē*].

In *Dialogues in the Sea* Lucian, ever the engaging satirist, gives us a left-field take on the tale of Andromeda and the sea monster, showing us the perspective of the Nereids who sent the sea monster in the first place. One might have expected them to express a little more regret than they do over the fate of their creature. In *The Hall* Lucian gives us the ecphrasis of an Andromeda fresco with which his imaginary hall is decorated (cf. **111, 115**). In both texts here Lucian has Perseus deploy the Gorgon head against the sea monster (cf. **115**).

The exchange of the *Dialogues in the Sea* begins by referring to an episode in Perseus's childhood. Acrisius, king of Argos, received a prophecy that he would die at the hand of a grandson by his daughter Danae. So he locked her up in an underground chamber to prevent her impregnation. Zeus, however, poured himself through the chamber's skylight in the form of golden rain to impregnate her with Perseus. She reared her son in secrecy in her cell, but when the child was detected, Acrisius enclosed them both in a chest and cast them into the sea. The chest washed ashore on the island of Seriphos, which was to be the starting point for the adult Perseus's mission against the Gorgon. Perseus was subsequently reconciled with his grandfather, but of course the prophecy had by all means to be fulfilled, and the hero killed the old man accidentally with a stray cast of a discus (see Pherecydes FF10 and 12 Fowler).

## 117 Phoenician Joppa appropriates the tale of Andromeda and the sea monster

iv BC–later ii AD

[Scylax] *Periplus* 104 = GGM p.79 (Greek; iv–iii BC)

Strabo C43 (Greek; ca. 24 AD)

Pomponius Mela 1.11 (Latin; ca. 43 AD)

Pliny *Natural History* 5.69, 5.128, 6.182, 9.11 (Latin; ca. 79 AD)

Josephus *Jewish War* 3.420 (Greek; ca. 75 AD)

Pausanias 4.35.9 (Greek; later ii AD)

Greek and Latin

**Ps.-Scylax:** *Joppa*. A city. They say that this was where Andromeda was put out for the sea monster [*kētos*].

**Strabo:** And there are some who transfer Ethiopia to the Phoenicia near us, and they say that the Andromeda story took place in Joppa. But people do not tell this story out of geographical ignorance; rather, they present it in the form of a myth.

**Pomponius Mela:** In Palaestine... there is Joppa, founded before the flood, as they say, where the inhabitants claim that Cepheus ruled with this as their evidence. Certain ancient altars retain the title of him and his brother Phineus, together with a great deal of reverence. Indeed, they exhibit the monstrous bones of the sea's creature [*belua*] as a clear token of the event celebrated in songs and stories and of Andromeda saved by Perseus.

**Pliny:** 5.69. Phoenician Joppa, more ancient than the [sc. Deucalian] flood, as they say, sits upon a hill before which lies a rock on which they exhibit the traces of Andromeda's chains. The Ceto of myth is the object of a cult there.

5.128. Next in the Phoenician sea, in front of Joppa, is Paria, which is all built up, where they say Andromeda was cast out for the creature [*belua*].

6.182. It is clear that Ethiopia dominated Syria and our coast in the age of Cepheus because of the myths of Andromeda.

9.11. In his aedileship [58 BC] Marcus Scaurus exhibited amongst the rest of his marvels the bones of the creature [*belua*] to which Andromeda was said to have been exposed, after bringing them to Rome from the Judaean city of Joppa. The skeleton was forty feet long. The length of its ribs exceeded those of an Indian elephant, and the thickness of its spine was one and a half feet.

**Josephus:** And at Joppa there are steep crags and rocks projecting into the sea, where the marks made by Andromeda's chains are still shown, and give credence to the ancient myth....

**Pausanias:** The land of the Hebrews gives forth ruddy water, nothing short of the colour of blood, near the city of Joppa. The water is hard by the sea, and the people there tell this story about the spring. After Perseus killed the sea monster [*kētos*], for which the daughter of Cepheus had been set forth, he washed his hands of the blood there.

These largely geographical and topographical writers report, from the fourth or third century BC onwards, an initially surprising counter-tradition that Andromeda was exposed for the sea monster at Joppa, the modern Jaffa, port of Tel Aviv (cf. also **118**). The Joppans touted evidence for their claim. In the first century BC they were exhibiting the sea monster's bones (whale bones?), which Scaurus then brought to Rome, as Pliny tells us. Perhaps the Joppans were able to claim them back so as to be exhibiting them again in the first century AD, as Mela tells us, or perhaps, resourcefully, they had found themselves another set. They could also point to the marks made by Andromeda's chains on their seaboard rocks, as Pliny and Josephus tell us, and to the permanently bloodied spring in which Perseus washed himself off after the battle, according to Pausanias (Manilius too draws attention to Perseus's act of ablution after the kill (**114**).

Pliny confusingly identifies the sea monster (*kētos*, *cetus*) with *Kētō* or Ceto, which looks like an appeal, at some level, to Hesiod's great progenetrix of *drakontes* of the same name (1), and he tells us that the Joppans gave her a cult. The local goddess in question was probably Astarte or Atargatis, who was represented as fish tailed, and whom the Greeks knew as *Der-kētō* (Diodorus 2.4; Lucian *Syrian Goddess* 14).

## 118  Andromeda's sea monster rationalised

Turn of the eras

Conon *FGrH* 26 F1 *apud* Photius *Bibliotheca* cod. 186

Greek

Book 40. He tells the story of Andromeda differently to the Greek myth. For he says that there were two brothers, Cepheus and Phineus. The kingdom of Cepheus was later renamed Phoenicia, but at that time it was called Joppa, taking its name from the seaboard city of Joppa. Its original borders stretched from our sea as far as the Arabs that live beside the Red Sea. Cepheus had a very beautiful daughter, Andromeda, and she was wooed by Phoenix and Phineus the brother of Cepheus. After thinking long and hard about both options, Cepheus decided to give her to Phoenix, but to conceal his will by arranging for the girl to be snatched by her suitor. She was snatched from a deserted islet to which she was in the habit of going in order to sacrifice to Aphrodite. When Phoenix had snatched her in a ship (this was called *Sea Monster* [*Kētos*], either because it resembled the creature or by chance), Andromeda, thinking that she was being snatched without her father's knowledge, with plaintive cry raised a wail and called upon people to help her. Perseus, the son of Danae, happened to be sailing past and was seized with pity and desire at his first sight of the girl. He sank the boat, the *Sea Monster*, and he slew its crew, who were all but turned to stone with amazement. This is the origin of the sea monster [*kētos*] of Greek myth, and of the men frozen into stone by the Gorgon's head. Anyway, he took Andromeda to wife, and she went off and sailed to Greece by Perseus's side and made her home in Argos, where he was king.

Conon's rationalised narrative (cf **M16,a**), as summarised here by Photius, may imply awareness of an unrationalised variant of the myth in which Perseus deployed the Gorgon's head against the sea monster (cf. **111, 115–16**). It is noteworthy too that he subscribes to the Joppa line (**117**), whilst attempting to stretch considerably the territory the term 'Joppa' might denote. The suggestion that Phoenix's ship was called *Sea Monster* because it resembled one is somewhat self-defeating for a rationalising narrative.

### FURTHER READING

Roscher 1884–1937b, Glotz 1877–1919b, Wernicke 1894, Kuhnert 1897–1909, Robert 1920–6:2, 222–45, Caterall 1937, Woodward 1937, Rathmann 1938, Langlotz 1951, Brommer 1955, Schauenberg 1960, 1981, Hetzner 1963, Phillips 1968, Burck 1976, Alexiades 1982, Boardman 1987, 1997, Schefold and Jung 1988, Dillon 1990, Klimek-Winter 1993, Roccos 1994, Balty 1997, Ogden 2008:67–99.

# 19
# *Scylla, Slain by Heracles and Encountered by Odysseus*

Scylla, who famously devours crewmen from Odysseus's ship as it passes her crag in the *Odyssey*, is a somewhat curious and *sui generis* monster. In art her primary affiliation would appear to be with sea monsters, but the literary record seems to indicate that she had once had affinities with *drakontes* too. Scylla is also mentioned in **2**.

**119** The Homeric account of Scylla

vii BC

Homer *Odyssey* 12.73–126, 234–9

Greek

**73.** [Circe gives Odysseus directions for his voyage home.] '...Of the two crags the one reaches to wide heaven with its sharp peak and is shrouded in a lowering cloud. The cloud never dissipates, nor is the sky around the peak ever clear from the beginning to the end of summer. No mortal man could climb it or reach its top, not even if he had twenty hands and feet. For the rock is smooth, as if it had been polished. In the middle of the crag is a murky cave, facing west, towards Erebus. You and your men must direct your ship past this, glorious Odysseus. Nor could even a man of great vigour shoot an arrow from the ship and reach the hollow cave with it. That is where Scylla lives, with her dread bark. Indeed, her voice is

Figure 19 Scylla. Etruscan terracotta ledge / Museo Nazionale Etrusco, Chiusi. Alinari / The Bridgeman Art Library.

only as loud as that of a newborn puppy [*skylax*], but she herself is a wicked monster. No one could take joy in seeing her, not even if it were a god that were meeting her. She has twelve feet, all *aōroi*, and six very long necks. On each neck there is a terrible head, and in each of them three rows of close-packed teeth, full of black death. Half of her body's length remains in the hollow cave, but she projects her heads forth from the dread hole and fishes from it. She scans around the crag in hopes of catching dolphins, sea dogs or even a substantial sea monster [*or:* whale—*kētos*], the creatures that the resounding sea rears in vast numbers. There are no sailors yet that can claim to have fled past her with their ship and emerged unharmed. For with each of her heads she carries away a man, snatching him up from his dark-prowed ship.

'You will see that the other crag lies lower, Odysseus. They are close to each other: you could even shoot an arrow from one to the other. On it there is a great fig tree, full of leaves. But beneath it divine Charybdis repeatedly sucks down the black water. She shoots it forth three times each day, and three times each day she sucks it down again in dread fashion. I pray that you not be there when she sucks the water down, for not even Poseidon, the shaker of the earth, could save you from that disaster. Rather, hug Scylla's crag and row your ship swiftly past it, for it is a far better thing to lament the loss of six of your ship's crew than that of all of them together.'

So she spoke, and I said to her in reply, 'Come now goddess, tell me truthfully, if there is any way to escape destructive Charybdis whilst defending against the other monster, when she attacks my crew?'

So I spoke, and she, goodly among goddesses, replied immediately: 'Reckless man, once again you look to warfare and the toil of battle! Will you not concede before the immortal gods? I tell you she is not mortal, but an immortal blight, dread, grievous and wild, and you could not overcome her in battle. There is no defence against her. The best thing is just to flee from her. For if you tarry by the rock to arm yourself, I fear that she might shoot out as many heads down to you, and seize the same number of men a second time. But row vigorously and invoke Crataeis, the mother of Scylla, who bore her as a bane to mortals. She will stop her shooting at you again.' [126]

**234.** [Odysseus now narrates the corresponding portion of the voyage.] We sailed up the narrows, lamenting. On the one side was Scylla, whilst on the other divine Charybdis repeatedly sucked down the briny water of the sea. Whenever she vomited it forth she would seethe and swirl in her entirety like a cauldron on a great fire, and her spray would fall upon the tops of both crags high above. Whenever she drained down the briny water of the sea, her inner tumult was exposed in its entirety, and the surrounding rocks resounded terribly. The darkened sand of the land was exposed beneath her. Whitening fear seized my men. We turned our gaze upon her in fear of doom. That was when Scylla seized six of my crew from my hollow ship, the six that were best with their hands and in their might. Looking back to my swift ship and to my crew, I just saw their feet and hands as they were they were hoisted aloft. They cried out and called upon me by name—the final time they were to do so—grieved in their hearts. As when a fisherman on a projecting rock casts down titbits with his long rod as bait for the small fish, sends forth into the sea the horn of the ox of the field, catches the grasping fish and jerks them out of the water, just so were the men hoisted up to the rock, gasping as they went. There in the entrance to her cave she devoured them as they cried out and stretched out their hands to me in their dread dying struggles. That was the most pitiable of all the things I saw with my own eyes, amongst all the toils I experienced as I traversed the paths of the sea. [259]

On their way back home from Troy, Odysseus and his men have rested on the divine witch Circe's island. Circe instructs them in how to continue their journey. They must pass through a narrow strait, subsequently identified with the Strait of Messina, where they will encounter the twin perils of Scylla and Charybdis. The first passage contains Circe's words of advice, the second Odysseus's narrative of experiences in the strait.

In art from the mid-fifth century BC (*LIMC* Skylla i 2–3, 8–9, 12–13, 19, 69, 75) and later in literature, Scylla has a canonical form: the upper body of a maiden and a serpentine lower body ending in a fish or *kētos* tail, sometimes two. From the region of the join project a series of dog heads, sometimes accompanied by corresponding forelegs. There are occasionally six of these, but the constraints of artistic representation usually reduce the number.

But the Homeric Scylla evidently differs markedly in her configuration. There is no indication that she has any humanoid part. The only indication of an affinity with sea monsters is the fact that she feeds herself from the sea, but then sea monsters are actually said to be part of her regular diet in this way. (Her triple rows of teeth are characteristic both of sea monsters (106) and of *drakontes* (78, 83) alike (cf. M1.a.iv).) There is only a weak indication that any part of her resembles a dog. This comes in the comparison of her call to that of a puppy, which might imply that she has dog heads, though her call is presented as paradoxical in the context of her form, and the comparison seems to be motivated primarily by a desire to provide an etymology for her name.

The Homeric Scylla is certainly serpentine, however. She has long necks that she can drop down the side of her cloud-high cliff to snatch sea creatures and humans from the waters below, and these are said to constitute only half her length. She would seem broadly to resemble the Hydra (a point well made by schol. Homer *Odyssey* 12.89). We can say nothing more of her feet or legs. The meaning in context of the adjective used to describe them, *aōroi*, is unknown, and so it has been left untranslated. The notion that Scylla's mother Crataeis (Strong One) should have borne her as a bane to mortals suggests that for the Homeric tradition Scylla never had any form other than the one he describes for her. Later sources identify Crataeis with Hecate, but there is no reason to think that the Homeric tradition made this equation.

Odysseus's narrative of his actual encounter with Scylla is admirably cinematic. Our gaze, like his, is drawn to the horrors of Charybdis, and too late we wheel round with him only to catch sight of the flailing limbs of his companions as they are hoisted aloft by Scylla.

## 120 Scylla transformed from beautiful Nereid to monster by Circe's drugs

8 AD

Ovid *Metamorphoses* 14.8–74

Latin

From there Glaucus swam through the Tyrrhenian sea with stout hand and came to the drug-bearing hills of Circe, daughter of the Sun, and to her palace, which was full of bogus animals. As soon as he saw her and they had exchanged greetings, he said, 'As a goddess, I beg you, have pity on a god, for you alone are able to alleviate my love. May you only find me worthy of it! Lady Titan, no one knows better than I do the great power of drugs, for it was by them that I was myself transformed. Let me tell you the cause of my frenzy. On the coast of Italy, opposite the walls of Messina, I caught sight of Scylla. It shames me to tell you of the promises, prayers and fond words I used—all scorned. If there is any power in incantation, then please start an incantation with your sacred mouth. Or, if a drug is stronger, then please deploy the tried and tested strength of an effective one. I do not ask you to cure me or heal these wounds. There is no need to cool my love; rather, let her share my burning passion.' No one had a nature more subject to the flames of love than Circe, whether the cause of this lay in herself or Venus had made it so in anger at her father's revelation. This was her reply: 'It is better to pursue a woman who is willing, who prays for you and who is a victim of that same desire. You were yourself deserving of pursuit, and you certainly could have been pursued. If you give cause for hope, trust me, you will be pursued yourself. Lest you doubt it, and so that you may have confidence in your beauty, see, despite being a goddess, despite being daughter of the radiant Sun, despite being so powerful with incantation and herb alike, even I pray that I may be yours. Scorn the one that scorns you, reciprocate love to the one that pursues you, and so give what is due to both women with a single act.' Such was her suit, but Glaucus replied, 'Leaves will grow in the sea and seaweed on the tops of mountains before my love will change, so long as Scylla remains alive.' The goddess was outraged. She could not harm Glaucus himself (nor would she wish too, loving him as she did), and so she directed her anger at the woman that was preferred to her. Upset by the rejection of her love, she immediately compounded her notorious herbs with dreadful juices. As she blended them, she mixed in Hecate's incantations. She put on a blue cloak and left her court, making her way through the ranks of the wild beasts that fawned upon her. She sought out Rhegium, opposite rocky Zancle. She proceeded over the surging waters, upon which she placed her steps as if on dry land, and ran across the surface of the sea with dry feet. There was a small bow-shaped pool. This was Scylla's favourite place to relax. She used to withdraw there to escape the heat of the sea and the air, when the sun's disk was in mid-sky and at its fullest, and from its zenith contracted the shadows to their smallest. Circe polluted and corrupted the pool in advance with her monster-making drugs. She poured these in and sprinkled the waters with a harmful root. Thrice nine times she mumbled with magical lips an incantation obscure with strange and impenetrable words. Scylla arrived and descended into the water as far as her midriff, when she saw that her loins were disfigured with barking monsters. At first she had no notion that they were part of herself. She fled in fear and tried to drive away the excitable dog heads, but as she fled she drew them along with her. As she felt over her body for her thighs, legs and feet, she found maws like Cerberus's in place of those parts. She was standing on hungry dogs and surrounding her foreshortened loins and jutting belly below with the bodies of the wild beasts. Glaucus, who loved her, wept and shunned marriage with Circe, who had deployed the powers of her drugs too viciously. Scylla remained where she was and, as soon as the opportunity presented itself, stripped Odysseus of his crew for hatred of Circe. She would subsequently have sunk the ships of the Trojans, had she not first been transformed into the rocky crag, prominent there to this day. The sailor avoids the crag too. [74]

Ovid has previously told us how the fish-tailed sea god Glaucus has fallen in love with Nereid Scylla and been rebuffed by her (*Metamorphoses* 13.898–968). For the reasons given above, it seems unlikely that the Homeric poets knew anything of this tale of scorned love and the transformation of Scylla from humanoid form. So far as we can tell, it originated in the third century BC with the poetess Hedyle of Samos (Athenaeus 297b; cf. *SH* no. 456).

Ovid's description of Scylla's transformation focuses entirely on her dogs and omits all reference to her sea-monster or fish tail, presumably because this could not in itself have been repulsive to the fish-tailed Glaucus. Circe had been well-known from the *Odyssey* itself for using her drugs to transform people into animals (10.229–43, etc.), and she had been associated with the production of hybrid, compounded forms at least from the time of Apollonius (*Argonautica* 4.672–82). Aphrodite's (Venus's) cause for resentment against Circe's father, the Sun, was that he had revealed her affair with Ares to her husband Hephaestus (*Odyssey* 8.302). Since Ovid has Circe deploy 'Hecataean incantations' against Scylla (Circe is herself variously projected as a close relative of Hecate's), he presumably does not think, as some others did (121), that Hecate was Scylla's mother.

Whereas Homer makes it clear that Scylla plundered all passing ships alike, Ovid makes her attack upon Odysseus's ship a specific act of revenge against Circe, presumed to be still fond of Odysseus after his sojourns with her. The 'Trojans' referred to are Aeneas and the Trojan refugees, en route to their new lives in Italy, where they will become the ancestors of the Romans.

We remain under-informed about the circumstances of Scylla's further transformation into a crag. One suspects the indirect influence of the Andromeda tradition, in which Perseus transformed at least part of the sea monster into rock with the Gorgon head (116), and also the influence of the rationalising tradition that found the origin of the myth of the monster in the treacherous and creature-infested rocks of the Strait of Messina (121).

## 121  Heracles kills Scylla; and a rationalisation of her myth

Hellenistic-Byzantine

Dionysius of Samos *FGrH* 15 F2 (Hellenistic). Schol. Lycophron *Alexandra* 45 (selections; Hellenistic-Byzantine)

Greek

**Dionysius:** Scylla was the daughter of Phorcys and Hecate, and was of an amazing size. She had twelve feet and six heads, three rows of teeth in each of her mouths and fiery eyes. The remainder of her body was hidden from sight, thrust deep within a cave, and adhered to the rock. She had six long heads that enabled her to reach down from the rock to a ship before the crew knew what was happening. Heracles is said to have killed her when he was driving the cattle of Geryon and saw her plundering some of them. Her father compelled her back to life with fire. The story is in Dionysius.

**Scholia to Lycophron:** Heracles was driving the cattle of Geryon from Erytheia. When he arrived at the strait between Italy and Sicily, Scylla, as she was called, snatched some of the bulls and killed them and so she too was killed by Heracles in turn. Later her father Phorcys heated her up and boiled her using torches and made her live again. Scylla was a beautiful woman who went with Poseidon. Amphitrite became envious and cast drugs into the spring at which Scylla used to wash herself, and so she was turned into a wild creature.... Scylla is a promontory that projects into the sea near Rhegion in Sicily. Beneath it there are many large rocks full of hollows and caves in which creatures of the sea dwell. When boats are cast against the rocks and shattered by the water from Charybdis, the creatures eat their crews.... Heracles was the wisest of men and of great leadership. When he was sailing past these parts with the cattle of Geryon he lost some of them there. So he improved the area with certain works. Whence they invented the myth that he killed Scylla. Phorcys, that is the sea, her father, made her treacherous. He brought her back to life with 'torches', which is to say that with the motion of the sun, marking the passing of time, the sea wore down Heracles' improvements and works and returned her to her former treacherousness.

Dionysius's affiliation of Scylla to Hecate makes sense if one compares her canonical configuration in art (**119** com.), which differs from the physical description he actually supplies, with the earliest extant image of Hecate and Lucian's physical description of her (**102**).

Dionysius's claim that Scylla adhered to the rock of her cave fascinates: was it somehow congenital with her, like a snail's shell, or had she grown inside her cave so as to be trapped in it? The exact nature of her Scylla's revivification by her father remains frustratingly obscure. But revived she had to be if it was desired that she should be killed by the great dragon slayer and cleanser of beasts, Heracles, and yet still be alive to attack Odysseus, as Homer had told, in a later generation.

The scholiasts' claim that Scylla was transformed not by Circe but by the sea goddess Amphitrite, envious wife of Poseidon, may antedate the Circe tradition. This variant recalls the Medusa myth variant in which she too began life as a beautiful woman who slept with Poseidon and was subsequently transformed into a serpentine monster by a resentful goddess, in her case Athene, because she had violated her temple (**58**).

The scholiasts' rationalisation of the myth of Heracles and Scylla is largely self-explanatory: the myth of Scylla arose out of the treacherous rocks of the strait themselves and the sea creatures that frequented them. Heracles improved the safety of the strait with some marine engineering, but with the passage of time his works were undone, the strait became treacherous again and so Scylla, as it were, returned to life. Palaephatus (20), who describes Scylla's serpentine tail as that of a snake (*ophis*), offers a different rationalisation of her myth: 'Scylla' was the name of a pirate boat that raided the strait (cf. **118**). Another again is offered by Heraclitus (*De incredibilibus* 2), who tells that she was in origin 'a beautiful island-dwelling courtesan, and she had gluttonous, shameless dining companions.' The word for 'shameless' here (*kunōdeis*) literally means 'doglike' (cf. **46**, **52**).

## FURTHER READING

Waser 1894, Schmidt 1913, Shepard 1940:43–8, 75–8, Boosen 1986:5–63, Andreae and Conticello 1987, Buitron-Oliver 1992:136–53, Gantz 1993:258, 731–3, Jentel 1997, Andreae 1999.

# Part Two
## The Christian Dragon

# 20
# The Serpents of the Bible and its Apocrypha

The Greek translation of the Hebrew Bible (Old Testament), the Septuagint ('LXX'), was initiated by Ptolemy II Philadelphus (r. 282–46 BC), and the bulk of the work was completed within a century or so of his death (however, note introduction to **124**). From this point on the Hebrew Bible's snakes and dragons might legitimately be considered as contributing to the Greek (and later Roman) imaginary of the dragon. But the chief interest of the Septuagint's snake and dragon material lies in the influence it was eventually to have, in the context of hagiography, upon the Graeco-Roman tradition of dragon-slaying narratives.

**122  The Septuagint's snake of Eden**

iii–ii BC

Septuagint, Genesis 3.1–20

Greek

The snake [*ophis*] was the cleverest of all the beasts on the earth that the Lord God had made. The snake said to the woman, 'Why is it that God told you, "You must not eat from any tree in the garden?"' The woman said to the snake, 'We eat of the fruit from the trees in the garden, but as for the fruit of the tree that is in the middle of the garden, God said, "Do not eat from it, and do not even touch it, so that you may not die."' The snake said to the woman, 'You will not die. But God knew that

Figure 20 Eve and the Snake of Eden. Fresco, Church of San Michele al Pozzo Bianco, Bergamo, xiv AD. Alinari / The Bridgeman Art Library.

your eyes would be opened upon whatever day you ate from it, and you would resemble gods in your knowledge of good and evil. The woman saw that the tree was good for eating and pleasing for the eyes to look upon and attractive to think about. She took of its fruit and ate. She gave some of it to her husband, and they ate it together. The pair's eyes were opened, and they perceived that they were naked. They stitched together the leaves of the fig and made loincloths for themselves. In the evening they heard the voice of the Lord God as he strolled in the garden, and Adam and his wife hid from the face of the Lord God amidst the trees of the garden. The Lord God called to Adam and said, 'Adam, where are you?' Adam said to him, 'I heard your voice as you strolled in the garden and I took fear, because I am naked, and I hid.' God said to him, 'Who told you that you were naked? Surely you did not eat from the one tree I forbade you to eat from?' Adam said, 'The woman, whom you gave me for company, gave me some fruit from the tree, and I ate it.' The Lord God said to the woman, 'Why did you do this?' The woman said, 'The snake deceived me, and I ate.' The Lord God said to the snake, 'Because you have done this, you shall be accursed beyond all the other cattle and wild beasts of the earth. You will travel on your breast and your belly and eat earth all the days of your life. And I shall establish a hatred between you and the woman and between your seed and hers. Man will be wary of your head, and you will be wary of his heel.' He said to the woman, 'I will increase your sufferings and your wailing. In suffering shall you give birth. You will be dependent upon your husband, and he will be your lord.' To Adam he said, 'Because you listened to the words of your wife and you ate from the one tree I forbade you to eat from, the earth will be accursed in your working of it. In suffering will you eat from it all the days of your life. It will produce thorns and prickles for you, and you will have to eat the food of the field. By the sweat of your face shall you eat your bread, until you return to the earth from which you were taken, because you are earth and you will go back to the earth.' Adam called his wife 'Life' [Zoe, i.e. Eve], because she was the mother of all living people.

The book of Genesis in its original Hebrew form is considered a product principally of the sixth and fifth centuries BC. Some of the dragons encountered by saints in the following passages are compared or identified, including by themselves, explicitly or implicitly, with the snake of Eden (e.g. **129, 131, 134**).

## 123 The Septuagint's reflexes of Leviathan and Rahab

iii–ii BC

Septuagint, Psalms 73.13–14, 103.25–6 (originally x–vi BC), Isaiah 27.1 (originally late viii BC), Job 3.8, 9.13, 26.12–13, 40.25 (originally iv BC)

Greek

**Psalms 73.13–14 [= Hebrew Bible 74.13–14]:** By your power you exercised control over the sea, and you dashed together the heads of the dragons [*drakontes*] on the sea. You crushed the heads of the dragon [*drakōn*, i.e. Leviathan] and gave it as food to the Ethiopian peoples.

**Psalms 103.25–6 [= Hebrew Bible 104.25–6]:** This is the great, expansive sea. In it are creatures of which there is no number, small ones together with large. Ships fare across it. This is the dragon [*drakōn*, i.e. Leviathan], which you moulded for playing with.

**Isaiah 27.1:** On that day God will bring his holy, great and strong sword against the dragon [*drakōn*, i.e. Leviathan] as it flees, against the twisting dragon-snake [*drakōn ophis*], and he will slay the dragon [*drakōn*].

**Job 3.8:** May the one that will subdue the great sea monster [*kētos*, i.e. Leviathan] curse it [sc. the day of my birth].

**Job 7.12:** Am I the sea or a dragon [*drakōn*], in view of the fact that you established a guard over me?

**Job 9.13:** God does not reverse his anger. The sea monsters [*kētē*, i.e. the partisans of Rahab] were made to bow down by him.

**Job 26.12-13:** With his strength God stopped the sea, with his skill he dealt a wound to the sea monster [*kētos*, i.e. Rahab]. The gates of heaven fear him, and by his command he killed the rebel dragon [*drakōn*].

**Job 40.25-6:** Will you catch a dragon [*drakōn*] on a hook or put a muzzle on his nose? If you fix a ring into his nostril, will you pierce his lip with a circlet?

**Job 41.6:** Who will open the gates of his face? There is terror in the circle of his teeth.

**Job 41.10-13:** Light gleams in his sneezing. His eyes look like the morning star. Burning torches issue from his mouth and hearths of fire are cast forth this way and that. Smoke issues from his nostrils, as from an oven burning with a charcoal fire. His breath is charcoal embers, and a flame issues from his mouth.

**Job 41.23-6:** He makes the abyss boil like a bronze cauldron. He controls the sea as if it were a little bottle of oil, and Tartarus as if it were his captive. He regards the abyss as a place for pleasant strolls. There is nothing like him on earth, made as he is for the mockery of my angels. He sees every height, and he himself is king of everything in the waters.

The above passages should all be considered in the light of the corresponding passages of the Hebrew Bible of which they are translations or adaptations (cf. **A9**). Whereas the Hebrew Bible gives its sea monsters the names Leviathan and Rahab, almost certainly to be identified with each other, the Septuagint eliminates the names entirely. For the most part it accommodates both under the generic terms *drakōn* (dragon), *kētos* (sea monster) and *ophis* (snake), but some of the Hebrew Bible's references to them are eliminated entirely (thus Septuagint Psalms 88.10–11 [= Hebrew Bible 89.9–10] and Septuagint Isaiah 51.9–10). For the direct influence of Leviathan and Rahab and their Greek reflexes on the hagiographical tradition, see **160**.

## 124 Daniel, Cyrus and the Dragon of Babylon

ii BC

Septuagint, Bel and the Dragon (Theodotion version) 23–7

Greek

And there was a great dragon [*drakōn*] and the Babylonians worshipped it. And the king [Cyrus the Great] said to Daniel: 'You will not be able to say that this is not a living god [sc. in contrast to the idol of Bel]. Do obeisance before it!' And Daniel said to Cyrus, 'I will do obeisance before my God, because he is the living God. But king, give me the authorisation, and I will kill the dragon without knife or staff.' And the king said, 'I give it you.' And Daniel took pitch and fat and hair and boiled them until they congealed. He then made cakes [*mazai*] and gave them into the mouth of the dragon. Upon eating them the dragon burst open. And Daniel said, 'Behold the object of your worship!'

The Septuagint's later, apocryphal book Bel and the Dragon survives in two Greek translations from a lost Aramaic original composed in the late second century BC. It tells a pair of tales in which Daniel deflates false gods worshipped by the Babylonians under the Persian king Cyrus the Great (the historical Cyrus ruled ca. 559–50 BC). Despite its Aramaic origins, the feeding of cakes termed *mazai*, as here in this Greek translation, to serpent gods was a

Graeco-Roman cultural practice and widely attested as such (e.g. Pausanias 6.20.2–6, 9.39.1, Aelian *Nature of Animals* 11.16). And so we may wonder whether the tale was developed in a culturally mixed Judaeo-Greek context. The idea with the pitch is evidently to deploy the dragon's own fire against it: as the dragon kindles the pitch with its fieriness, it overheats from within and explodes. This motif probably existed in the Greek tradition of dragon-slaying stories: a version of it is attested for Bellerophon's killing of the Chimaera, albeit in a very late source (**51**), and it is found in the Syriac *Alexander Romance*, a seventh-century translation of a lost Greek original, **C3** (cf. also **C4**). The book of Bel and the Dragon was incorporated into the book of Daniel in the Latin Vulgate (as chapter 14 thereof), and this was presumably the route by which the motif found its way into an extended and delightful range of more recent European dragon-slaying folk tales, including British ones (**C7, C11–13**). So far as the following hagiographical texts are concerned, we may broadly compare the tale of Marina of Antioch, whose holiness causes her dragon to burst open when it swallows her (**149**).

## 125  Snake imagery in the works of Luke: Jesus's words and Paul's Maltese viper

ca. 60 AD

Luke 10.19 and (Luke) Acts 28.3–6

Greek

**Luke:** [Jesus addresses his converts.] See, I have given you the power to trample on snakes [*opheis*] and scorpions, and upon all the enemy's strength, and he will be able to harm you in no way.

**Acts:** Paul gathered together a mass of dry sticks and put them on a pyre. A viper [*echidna*], escaping from the heat, latched on to his hand. When the Maltese saw the creature hanging from his hand, they said to each other, 'By all means this man is a murderer. Although he has been saved from the sea, justice has not allowed him to live.' But he shook the creature off into the fire and suffered no harm. They expected that he was about to become inflamed [*pimprasthai*] or suddenly fall down dead. But as they anticipated this and watched him for a long time, and nothing untoward happened, they changed their opinion and said he was a god.

Jesus's proclamation with its motif of trampling on snakes (for which cf. also Mark 16.18) refers back to God's words at the conclusion of Genesis's Eden story (**122**); note also, more remotely, **A3**. It is acknowledged in turn in some of the hagiographical narratives that follow (**M15.d.ii**).

As in the classical tradition (**M6**), Paul fights his fiery snake, or at any rate the would-be fiery snake, which was expected to 'inflame' his hand by its bite, with fire. The motif of committing a snake to a pyre (cf. **20, 23**) is picked up most strikingly in the tale of Hilarion and the Dragon of Epidaurus (**143**). For Paul's viper see also **161** (com.).

## 126  The Revelation Dragon and his re-emergence as Beliar

ca. 95 AD–iv AD

Revelation 12–13, 20.1–3 (ca. 95 AD)

**Revelation:** 12. A great sign was seen in the sky, a woman dressed in the sun, the moon beneath her feet, on her head a crown of twelve stars. She was with child in her belly, and she cried out at the birth pangs and laboured to give birth. Another sign was seen in heaven: lo! it was a great red dragon [*drakōn*], with seven heads and ten horns and on his heads he had seven crowns, and his tail swept a

*Questions of Bartholomew* 4.7–17, 18–28, 46, 60 (iv AD or earlier)

Greek

third of the stars from heaven and cast them onto the ground. The dragon stood opposite the woman who was about to give birth so that he could devour her child whenever she did so. She bore a male child who was destined to shepherd all peoples with an iron rod. Her child was snatched up to God and to his throne. And the woman fled into the desert where a place had been made ready for her by God, so that they could maintain her there for twelve hundred and sixty days. There was a war in heaven, and Michael and his angels made war upon the dragon. The dragon made war with the aid of his angels, but he was not strong. No place was found for them in heaven any more. The great dragon was cast down, the ancient snake [*ophis*], the so-called Devil and Satan, the one that causes the entire inhabited world to stray. He was cast down to earth, and his angels were cast down with him. Then I heard a great voice in heaven saying: 'Now has come the deliverance and power and kingship of our God and the power of Christ himself, because the accuser of our brothers has been cast down, the one who day and night accused them before God. They have conquered him through the blood of the Lamb and through the word of their witnessing, and they did not love their own lives to the point of death. So rejoice, heavens, and those that live in you! But woe betide the earth and the sea, because the Devil came down to you with a great anger, knowing that he has little time.' When the dragon saw that he had been cast down to the land, he pursued the woman that had borne the boy, and the two wings of the great eagle were given to the woman, so that she could fly to her place in the desert, where she was maintained for a year, two more years and a further half year safely remote from the face of the snake. The snake cast forth from its mouth water like a river after the woman, so that she would be carried away by it. The earth came to the aid of the woman and opened its mouth and swallowed down the river that the dragon cast from his mouth. The dragon grew angry at the woman and went off to make war upon the rest of her progeny, those who keep the commandments of God and bear witness to Jesus, and he took up his position on the shore of the sea.

13. I saw a beast coming up out of the sea, with ten horns and seven heads, and ten crowns on its heads and a blasphemous name upon each of its heads. The beast I saw was like a leopard, and its feet were as those of a bear, and its mouth was as the mouth of a lion. The dragon gave it his might and his throne and great power. One of its heads had been mortally severed, but its death blow had been healed. The whole of the earth were in wonder behind the beast, and people worshipped the dragon because he had given power to the beast, and they worshipped the beast too, saying, 'Who resembles the beast, and who is able to fight against it?' The beast was given a mouth with which to make great claims and blasphemies, and it was given the power to do this for forty-two months. It opened its mouth to blaspheme against God, and blasphemed against his name and his home and those who lived in his home. The power was given to it to make war against the holy and to conquer them, and so too power over every tribe and people and language. All the people that live on the earth will worship it, if their name has not been written in the book of life of the slaughtered lamb from the time of the creation of the universe. If anyone has an ear, let him hear! If anyone is for imprisonment, he goes off to imprisonment! If anyone is to die by the sword, let him die by the sword! Such is the steadfastness and faith of the holy. I saw another beast coming up out of the earth. It had two horns like a lamb, and it spoke like a dragon. It exercised all the power of the first beast in front of it. It made the earth and those that lived on it worship the first beast, the one with the mortal blow that had been healed. It brought

about great signs, including the making of fire come down from heaven to earth in front of men. It led those that dwelled on the earth astray by means of the signs it was granted to it to bring about in front of the beast, and told them to erect an idol to the beast that had the blow of the sword and lived on. It was granted to it to give life to the idol of the beast, so that the idol could speak and bring it about that all those that did not worship the idol of the beast should be killed. It brought it about that all men, small and great, rich and poor, free and slave should be given a brand on their right hand or their forehead, and that no one should be able to buy or sell unless he had the brand, which was the name of the beast or the number of its name. This is the understanding. Let the intelligent person reckon out the number of the beast, for it is the number of a man. Its number is 666.

20. And I saw an angel coming down from heaven, with the key of the abyss and a large chain in his hand. He conquered the dragon, the ancient snake, that is the Devil or Satan, and bound him for a thousand years. He cast him into the abyss, and locked him in, making a seal over him, so that he should no longer lead the races of men astray before the completion of the thousand years. After this he must be released for a short time.

**Questions of Bartholomew:** 7. Jesus manifested himself again and Bartholomew said to him, 'Lord, show us the antagonist of mankind, so that we may observe his nature, what it is that he does, whence he starts from and what sort of power he possesses that equipped him to spare not even you yourself, but rather have you suspended on the wooden cross.'

Jesus looked at him and said, 'Braveheart! You are asking for something you are unable to look at.'

Bartholomew became upset and fell at Jesus's feet. He began to say the following: 'Inextinguishable, eternal light, Lord Jesus Christ, you who have bestowed the grace that adorns the world upon all to those that love you, you who have bestowed the everlasting light by virtue of your presence in the world, you who [lacuna] the substance above in speech, you who accomplished your father's work, you who changed Adam's grimace to cheerfulness, you who put an end to Eve's grief with a joyful face, by virtue of your virgin birth, do not begrudge it me, but grant me what I ask for.'

This is what he said. Jesus raised him and said to him, 'Bartholomew, you want to see the antagonist of mankind? I declare that upon sight of him, you will fall down on your face and become as dead, and so will the apostles and Mary alongside you.'

But they all said to him, 'Lord, let us see him.'

[lacuna] to the angels that keep guard over Tartarus. He nodded to Michael to blow his trumpet in the height of heaven. There was an earthquake, and out came Beliar under the control of 660 angels, and he was bound in chains of fire. He was 1,600 cubits in length and 40 in breadth. His face resembled a lightning bolt of fire. His eyes were dark. A malodorous smoke emanated from his nostrils. His mouth was like a chill cavern, and just one of his wings extended for 80 cubits. As soon as they saw him the apostles fell down on the earth on their faces and became as dead.

Jesus approached the apostles, raised them up and gave them a breath [*or*: spirit—*pneuma*] of power. He said to Bartholomew, 'Draw near to him, Bartholomew, trample on his neck with your feet, and he will tell you the nature of his work and how he deceives mankind.'

Jesus stood at some distance from the apostles. [Verse 17 is out of place in the text and omitted from the translation here.]. Frightened, Bartholomew said, 'Lord Jesus, give me the border of your cloak, so that I may be bold as I approach him.'

Jesus said to him, 'You cannot take the border of my cloak, for this cloak of mine is not the one I wore before my crucifixion.'

Bartholomew said, 'I am frightened, Lord, lest he gobble me down just as he spared not your angels.'

Jesus said to him, 'Is it not at my word that everything happens? Was it not by the will of my father that [lacuna] was made subject to the spirit? So follow my command, and go in my name and ask him what you want.'

Bartholomew trampled on his neck and forced his face to the ground, all the way down to his ears. Bartholomew said to him, 'Tell me who you are and what your name is!'

He replied to him, 'Relieve the pressure on me a little and I will tell you who I am, how I came here, what my work is and what is the nature of my power.'

Bartholomew relieved the pressure upon him and said to him, 'Tell me what you have done and everything you are doing now.'

Beliar said in reply, 'If you wish to know my name, I was at first called Satanael, which means "God's messenger".' But when I disowned the stamp of God, I was given the name Satanas, which means "Tartarus-keeping messenger".'

Bartholomew addressed him again: 'Reveal everything to me and conceal nothing from me!'

He replied to him, 'I swear to you by the power of the glory of God that I am unable to conceal things from you even if I want to do so, for my confuter stands beside us. For if I had my power, I would have destroyed you like the one before you. Now, I was made to be the first angel. For when God was making heaven he took a handful [*drax*] of fire and made me first, and then Michael second.' ... [28]

46. Bartholomew said, 'Shut up, dragon [*drakōn*] of the abyss!'

60. Then Bartholomew ordered him to return to Hades.

Chapter 20 of the Revelation passage was to become one of particular importance for the hagiographical tradition. It offers a clear model for Christian heroes to battle the Devil himself manifest in the form of a dragon (**131–2, 134, 138, 140, 149, 150, 156**). For the casting of the dragon into the abyss, one could imagine that Typhon offered a classical precedent, in his confinement beneath the earth (**5, 7–9**). We will encounter a number of saints similarly casting their own dragons into underground abysses (**M3.a.iv**). Many more will bind their dragons, as Michael does (**M15.d.iii**). In particular, Silvester will chain up the Dragon of Rome in a hole in the ground (**136–7**). On a more general level, the Revelation Dragon seems to exercise a strong impact upon the *Shepherd of Hermas's* revelatory vision of a *kētos* (**128**). For Michael and the Revelation dragon see also **161** (com.).

The (non-biblical) *Questions of Bartholomew* (probably broadly identifiable with the *Gospel of Thomas* referred to by Jerome) supplies an entertaining sequel to Michael's defeat of the Satan-dragon, now going under the name of Beliar. The narrative leaves us in no doubt as to his serpentine form: his dimensions indicate him to be a creature of some elongation. He also sports wings. The vignette of his being brought forth from Hell in chains under a guard of 660 angels for display is a striking one. He is very much a creature of fire: his face consists of a bolt of lightning, he oozes stinking smoke and he has been manufactured by God from a handful of fire—the word for 'handful,' *drax*, evidently being proffered as a folk etymology for *drakōn*. And, as usual, fire must be fought with fire: he is bound in fiery chains. In treading on Beliar's neck, Bartholomew follows the Lukan exhortation to trample on snakes (**125**). Bartholomew's exchange with Jesus about the border of his cloak is curious, not least since the request is confused. But the motif was to have a successful career in the hagiographical tradition, where we repeatedly find saints fitting their dragons with leads manufactured from an item of their personal clothing (**151, 154, 156, 160-1**). The dragon is made to confess his identity like any demon under the compulsion of exorcism. As we will see, dragons are often assimilated to demons in the hagiographical tradition and accordingly dealt with appropriately by exorcistic means (**M15.b.iii**). For the adventures of Bartholomew, see also **134**.

## 127  The infant Jesus destroys a viper that has bitten Jacob and revives his brother

ii–vi AD

*Gospel of Thomas* 16.1–2 (A), p. 147 Tischendorf

Greek

Joseph sent his son Jacob to bundle up logs and bring them to his house. The child Jesus accompanied him too. As Jacob was gathering the firewood, a viper [*echidna*] bit his hand. He was laid low and on the point of death. Jesus came near and blew upon [*katephusēse*] the bite. Immediately the pain ceased and the creature was burst, and Jacob was immediately restored to health.

The *Gospel of Thomas*, one of the apocryphal infancy gospels, has Gnostic and Manichaean affinities. It contains some wonderful tales of the childhood of Christ. In the most celebrated of these the boy Jesus is accidentally jostled by another boy as he runs past. Jesus strikes him dead; when the boy's parents complain to Joseph about it, he strikes them blind (2). It is hard to date the text as we have it. Quasten (1949–60: 1, 123–5) holds the text in its surviving form to be an expurgated version deriving from the sixth century AD at the earliest. But its antecedent (or antecedents) were already known in the early third century AD, when it (or they) were referred to by Hippolytus (*Refutations* 5.7) and Origen (*First Homily on Luke*), and possibly ca. 180 AD, when a tale in the text was referred to by Irenaeus (1.13.1). Hippolytus considers his *Gospel of Thomas* a product of the Naassenes; it is hard to believe, however, that the quoted story pitting Jesus against a snake would have appealed to that snake-loving sect (see **134** [with com.]). Cyril of Jerusalem regarded his *Gospel of Thomas* rather as a Manichaean product (*Catecheses* 4.36, 6.31; 347–8 AD).

We note the strong motival correspondence with Luke's tale of Paul in Malta, **125**, in which again a viper (*echidna*) strikes as firewood is collected. But the particular interest of this tale lies in the kaleidoscopic correspondence of several of its motifs with those of the *Acts of Thomas* tale (**131**; cf. also **130, 132** [with com.], **145, 149, 154** [with com.]) and above all those of Lucian's tale of the Chaldaean snake blaster (**130**, ca. 160–80 AD). In the latter the farm slave Midas is bitten by a viper (*echidna*) as he ties up the vines. He is miraculously healed by the Chaldaean, who then proceeds to destroy all the snakes of the farm, including a *drakōn*, by blowing upon them. Whatever the date of the snake tale in the *Gospel of Thomas*, it probably preserves an arrangement of motifs subsequent to and derivative of the arrangement found in Lucian.

On the one hand the *Gospel of Thomas* seems to simplify and syncopate the Lucianic motifs; on the other the association of human breath with snake destruction (as opposed to snakebite healing) was long established in the classical tradition. But the syncopation is admittedly effective: it is a nice idea that the snake should be destroyed automatically as its evil works are undone.

## FURTHER READING

The Septuagint: Gooding 1963, Collins 2000, Fernández Marcos 2000, Pietersma and Wright 2007, Rajak 2011.

Genesis: Cassuto 1961:138–77, Morris and Sawyer 1992, Stordalen 2000.

Leviathan and Rahab: Day 1977, Batto 1992, Beaude 2000.

Old Testament Apocrypha: Goodman et al.2012.

Use of the terms *drakōn* and *ophis* in the New Testament: Foerster 1935 and Foerster et al. 1957.

Luke: Marshall 1978:427–30, Green 1997:417–20, Bovon 2008:56–8.

Acts: Johnson 1992:460–7, Pesch 2003:295–300, Pervo 2009:665–78.

The Revelation Dragon: Batto 1992:174–8, Koch 2004.

Questions of Bartholomew: Kroll 1932:71–82, Kaestli 1988.

Gospel of Thomas: Quispel 1957, Wilson 1960, Fallon and Cameron 1988, Valantasis 1997, Uro 2003, Gathercole 2012.

# 21
# *The Dragons of the Early Hagiographical Tradition*

We turn now to the earliest dragons of the hagiographical tradition. A number of important texts are gathered here, though only one of them incorporates a hagiographical dragon fight proper, the early third-century AD tale of St Thomas (**131**). However, Lucian's parodic, pagan tale (**130**) indirectly but securely attests that dragon fights of this sort were already well established in hagiography half a century before. Also given here are two early hagiographical texts that deploy dragon imagery in interesting ways whilst falling just short of offering a full-blown battle (**128–9**). The intriguing tale of St John (**132**) seems to kaleidoscope the motifs of a tale similar to the Thomas one to produce a dragon that curiously fights on the side of the angels, whilst at the same time making an appeal to some pagan thinking about snakes (**133**).

## 128 Hermas's faith is tested by the vision of a terrible dragon

130–50 AD

*Shepherd of Hermas* vision 4 (4.1–3)

Greek

My brothers, the vision I saw twenty days after the last one occurred offered an example of the suffering to come. I was travelling into the country on the Campanian Road. It is about ten stades from the main road, and the region is easy to travel through. As I walked on my own I asked the Lord to bring to pass the revelations and visions he had shown me through his holy church, so that he might make me strong and bestow repentance upon those of his servants who had stumbled, so that his great and glorious name might be glorified, because he had considered me a worthy person to reveal his miracles to. As I glorified him and thanked him, I was answered by what sounded like a voice. 'Do not doubt, Hermas.' I began to question myself, and said, 'How can I doubt when I have been so well grounded by the Lord, and when I have seen such glories?' I advanced a little further, my brothers, and lo! I saw a cloud of dust rising to heaven, and I started to say to myself, 'Is this a herd of cattle coming and stirring up the dust?' The cloud was about a stade distant from me. As the cloud of dust became greater and greater I supposed that it was something divine. The sun illumined it a little, and lo! I saw that it was very large beast like a sea monster [*kētos*], and fiery locusts were pouring forth from its mouth. The beast was around a hundred feet in length, and its head resembled a vase. I started to cry and to ask the Lord to deliver me from it, and I remembered the saying I had heard: 'Do not doubt, Hermas.' So, my brothers, I clothed myself in my faith in the Lord and remembered the great things he had taught me. Taking courage, I gave myself to the beast. The beast started at me with such a surge that it could have destroyed a city. As I came close to it, the sea monster, enormous as it was, stretched itself out

# Chapter 21: The Dragons of the Early Hagiographical Tradition

Figure 21 The Ladder of Saint Perpetua. Illuminated Manuscript of Conrad of Hirsau's *Speculum Virginum*. Walters Art Museum, Baltimore. Redrawn by Eriko Ogden.

on the ground and did nothing except stick its tongue out. It made no movement at all until I had passed it. The beast had four colours on its head, black, fiery-and-bloody, gold and white. After I had passed the beast and gone about thirty feet further, lo! a virgin met me adorned as if she had stepped out of her bridal chamber, dressed from head to toe in white and with white shoes, and wearing a veil over her forehead. Her veil was in the form of a turban. She had white hair. I knew from former visions that she was the church, and I became happier. She greeted me with the words 'Hail, fellow.' I greeted her in turn, 'Hail, Lady.' In answer she said, 'Has nothing met you?' I said to her, 'Lady, a beast of such a size that it could destroy peoples. But I was delivered from it by the power of the Lord and his great mercy.' 'You were delivered from it successfully,' she said, 'because you threw your anxieties off upon God and you opened your heart to the Lord, trusting that you could be saved by nothing except his great and glorious name. For this reason the Lord dispatched the angel in charge of wild beasts, whose name is Thegri, and he fastened its mouth so that it could not harm you. You have escaped great suffering because of your faith, and because you did not have doubt upon seeing such a huge beast. Take yourself off, therefore, and report his great deeds to the Lord's elect, and tell them that this beast is an example of the great suffering that is to come. So, if you prepare yourselves, repent with all your heart and come to the Lord, you will be able to escape it, if your heart is pure and beyond reproach, and you serve the Lord blamelessly for all the remaining days of your life. Throw your anxieties off upon the Lord, and he himself will sort them out. Trust the Lord, doubters, because he is all-powerful. He diverts his anger from you, and he sends his scourges upon you when you doubt. Woe betide those who have heard these words and ignore them. It would have been better for them not to have been born in the first place.' I asked her about the four colours the beast had on its head. She replied to me, 'Once again you are curious about such matters.' 'Yes,' I said, 'Lady, tell me what they are.' 'Listen,' she said, 'the black represents the world in which you live. The fiery-and-bloody colour represents the fact that this world must perish in blood and fire. The golden part represents you, the ones who have escaped this world. For just as gold is refined in fire and so rendered useful, so too you who dwell in the world are being refined in your souls. You who stand your ground in the fire will be purified by it. For just as gold loses its dross, so too you will lose all your grief and difficulties, you will be purified and you will be rendered useful for the building of the tower. The white part represents the age to come, that of the elect of God. Because those chosen out by God for eternal life will be the stainless and pure. So do not stop speaking into the ears of the saints. For you have the example of the great suffering that is to come. But you have only to wish it, and it will be nothing. Bear in mind what was written before.' After saying this she went off, and I did not see where. For there was a cloud, and I turned back in fear, thinking that the beast was coming.

The creature fought by Hermas in his vision is curiously described not as a *drakōn* but as something resembling a sea monster, a *kētos*. However, it clearly resembles a *drakōn* in many regards: it is a landlubber, is elongated, has a lolling tongue and shoots a fiery substance from its mouth. Given its visionary context and the symbolism written into its own body, the creature is reminiscent of the Revelation dragon (**126**) and indeed its beast. The description of Hermas's encounter with the creature has something in common with the description of Philip's encounter with his desert *drakōn* (**134**); inter alia, both creatures initially present themselves in a cloud. To this extent the passage is useful for further indicating the conceptual closeness between *drakontes* and *kētē*.

## 129  St Perpetua steps on a cowed dragon under her stairway to heaven

203 AD

*Passion of SS. Perpetua and Felicitas* 4.3–9

Latin

I saw a bronze ladder of marvellous height. Its height reached to heaven. It was narrow, so that no one could climb up it except in single file. Into the sides of the ladder was fixed every kind of iron blade: swords, spears, hooks, knives and darts. So if anyone were to climb up it in careless fashion or without fixing his gaze upwards, he would be gored and his flesh would cleave to the blades. Under the ladder itself lay a dragon [*draco*] of miraculous size, which came out and attacked people as they tried to climb up and deterred them from attempting to do it. Now Saturus went up first, the one who subsequently gave himself up for us (for we were in the house that he himself had built). But he had not been present at the time we were arrested. When he reached the top of the ladder he turned and said, 'Perpetua, I will help you up. But make sure that dragon doesn't bite you.' I said, 'It will not harm me, in the name of Jesus Christ.' Hesitantly, as if afraid of me, the creature stuck its head out from underneath the ladder. I trod upon its head as if it were the first step, and mounted up. I saw an enormous garden, and in the middle of it a tall, grey-haired man in the dress of a shepherd, and he was milking his sheep. Many thousands of people in white stood around him. He lifted his head, looked at me and said, 'You did well to come, child.'

St Perpetua's prison autobiography survives in both Latin and Greek, with the Latin version now believed to have been the original; it may well have been edited by Tertullian. Once again, as in **128**, the *drakōn* appears in a vision rather than in the waking world, perhaps saluting Revelation. Perpetua's treading on the dragon's head is a clear tribute to God's curse against the snake of Eden (**122**) and to the Lukan exhortation to trample upon serpents (**125**). The imagery of the ladder reflects Jacob's ladder to heaven (Genesis 28.10–12).

## 130  Lucian's Chaldaean snake blaster: a parody of an early Christian dragon-slaying narrative type

150s–80s AD

Lucian *Lover of Lies* 11–13= *MWG* no. 49 (Greek; ca. 170s AD); Apuleius *Metamorphoses* 8.19–21 (Latin; 150s–80s AD)

Greek and Latin

**Lucian:** Said Ion, 'I'll tell you an amazing story. It took place when I was a lad, just about fourteen years old. Someone came with news for my father that Midas the vine-dresser, a generally strong and hard-working slave, had been bitten by a viper [*echidna*] at around noon, and was lying there with his leg already going rotten. For as he had been tying up the vine tendrils and winding them around the props, the creature had crept up on him and bitten him on his big toe. Then it had slipped off again and shot down its hole, whilst he was left to wail, dying from the pain. This was the news, and then we saw Midas himself being carried in on a stretcher by his fellow slaves, his whole body swollen and livid. He looked clammy, and he was only just still breathing. My father was upset, but a friend who happened to be present said, 'Don't worry. For I'll go after a Babylonian fellow, one of the Chaldaeans, as they say, right away, and he will cure your man.' To make a long story short, the Babylonian came and set Midas back on his feet by driving the venom out of his body with an incantation. Also, he tied a rock he had chipped off a virgin's tombstone to his foot. You may think this a rather ordinary achievement. Even so,

Midas himself picked up the stretcher on which he had been brought and went off straight back to the farm. That was the power of the incantation and the piece of tombstone. And the Babylonian did other things too that were truly marvellous.

He went out to the farm at dawn, recited seven sacred names from an old book and purified the place with a torch, encircling it three times. He called out all the reptiles within its boundaries. There came as if drawn to the incantation many snakes, asps, vipers, horned snakes, darting snakes, common toads and puff adders [*or possibly*: 'puff toads'—*phusaloi*]. Only one old dragon [*drakōn*] was left behind, unable to crawl out or too deaf to hear the command. The mage said there was one missing, and chose out the youngest snake and sent it with a message, and shortly that snake too arrived. When they were all assembled, the Babylonian blew upon [*enephusēse*] them all. At once they were all burned up by the blast [*phusēmati*], and we looked on in amazement.'

'Tell me, Ion,' I said, 'did the young snake that took the message lead the snake of, as you say, advanced age back by the hand, or did the old snake have a stick with which to support himself?'

**Apuleius:** [Lucius tells of an experience he had in Thessaly whilst transformed into an ass. At the time he and other animals were in the possession of a band of runaway slaves. The slaves had just been attacked by locals in the mistaken belief that they were bandits, and they were recovering from their ordeal, relaxing on a hillside.] In the meantime an old man caught sight of us from the top of the hill. The nanny goats grazing around him declared him to be a shepherd. One of our party asked him whether he had any milk he could sell us, either liquid still or on the point of congealing into cheese. He shook his head for some time before asking us, 'Are you thinking of food or drink or indeed any other form of refreshment in these circumstances? Do none of you know the nature of this place in which you have settled down?' With this he rounded up his little animals, turned and made off to some far point. What he had said and his action in fleeing struck our herdsmen with no small fear. In their terror they were desperate to ask about the nature of the place, though there was no one to tell them about it. But then another old man drew near on the road. He was huge but bowed by the years, leaning over his stick and dragging his tired feet, and he was in floods of tears. When he saw us, with great lamentation he reached out to the knees of each of the young men [*sc.* in a gesture of supplication] and begged them:

'In the name of your good fortune and protective deities, so may you come hale and hearty to an age as advanced as mine! Help a decrepit old man: retrieve my little boy from the underworld and restore him to me in my greyness. My grandson, my delightful companion on this journey, was trying to grab hold of a swallow that was singing in a little hedge, but he fell into a hole that opened adjacent to the base of the bushes. He is now in danger of losing his life. I know that he is alive because I can hear his crying and his repeated calls to his grandfather, but I cannot help him because the strength of my body has failed, as you see. But it is easy for you with the boons of youth and strength to help a most unfortunate old man and to save that boy, the youngest of my family and my sole heir.'

We all felt compassion for him as he begged us in this way and tore his grey hair. But one, braver in heart, younger in age and stronger in body than the others, and the only one of the party to have come away unharmed from the previous battle, jumped up at once and asked where the boy had fallen down. The old man indicated some thorny bushes in the distance, and the young man followed after him keenly. When we had been refreshed by our fodder and the men had tended to themselves, they each picked up their packs and took to the road. To begin with they raised their voices and repeatedly called that young man's name. They were concerned by the long delay and dispatched one of their own to go and get him, one who could find him, remind him that it was time to be off, and bring him back. After a little while he brought himself back, all atremble and of the pallor of box-wood. He reported an amazing tale of his fellow slave. He has seen a massive dragon [*draco*] pinning him down on his back and eating him, and it had already devoured most of him. But he had had seen no sign anywhere of any wretched old man. Upon learning this, and putting it together with the words of the shepherd, who had been warning them precisely about this savage denizen of the district and no other, they forsook that accursed place and gave themselves to a swifter flight even than their prior one, and they drove us on, beating us with frequent blows of their clubs.

Ion's tale is the first to be related in the *Philopseudes*, for the nature of which text see **102**. Though it has been doubted in the past, it is clear that this narrative is, inter alia, a knowing parody of the dragon-slaying story type in early hagiographical tradition, and therefore constitutes the earliest testimony to the entry of the dragon fight into the hagiographical tradition. A clue to its Christian background is to be found in the distinctive New Testament motif of Midas leaping up after his instantaneous cure to carry home the stretcher on which he had been brought (cf. Matthew 9.6–7, Mark 2.9 and 11–12, Luke 5.24–5, John 5.8–9). But decisive are its strong thematic connections with both the Jesus-and-Jacob episode in the *Gospel of Thomas* (**127**) and Thomas's own dragon-slaying episode in the *Acts of Thomas* (**131**), both of which coordinate the revivification of the dragon's last victim, a youth, with the dragon's own destruction: a constellation of motifs with no known precedent in pagan literature, though one that was to go on to have a *grande fortune* in the Christian tradition (**M15.d.i**). Furthermore, each of these two texts employs, in different ways, the motif of blowing to dispatch its dragon. In the former case Jesus does so by blowing upon the bite it has delivered; in the second Thomas does so by compelling the dragon to inflate itself to the point of bursting by re-ingesting its own venom.

In the Jesus and Thomas tales the snake that is destroyed is simply the snake that has bitten and (almost) killed. The vengeance of Lucian's practitioner is much greater: he destroys all the snakes on the farm, including its vipers, which group, we must assume, includes the original miscreant. The focal role given to the *drakōn* itself amongst the snakes destroyed seems to resemble subsequent Christian sources rather better than it does anything from the pagan repertoire, in particular Philip's desert dragon and dragon of the rocks (**134**) and Clement of Metz's dragon (**157**), all three of which preside over hosts of smaller snakes.

But there is also an overlay of pagan apparatus too: the recasting of the Christian saint as a Chaldaean (cf. Iamblicus *Babyloniaca*, as summarised at Photius *Bibliotheca* 74b); the application of the binding action of a restless ghost, that of a girl dead before marriage, by means of a chip from her tombstone (though cf. Philip's use of the saliva of the living virgin Mariamne to heal harm inflicted by serpents in **134**); and the use of a magic circle against the serpents (cf. **100**; cf. **M11.b**). The healing incantation could equally well be read as a motif from the pagan tradition (it is the sort of thing attributed to the magical race of the snakebite-healing Psylli: e.g. Plutarch *Cato Minor* 56) or as a saintly prayer.

The symmetrical battle of fire and air is well displayed here. As to the former, viper bites were conceived of as fiery (e.g. Lucian *Dipsads* 4) and as such lay at the heart of the fundamental notion that dragons were creatures of fire (**M6.a**). To this fire on the snakes' part the Chaldaean replies not only with the sulphur, which he burns in fumigation, but also with the fire of his own marvellous breath. As to the latter, the *phusaloi* can be assumed to be producers of noxious breaths that pollute of the local atmosphere. The Chaldaean replies to this again with his sulphur fumigation and again with his act of blowing upon the reptiles. (Later on, at any rate, blowing could be used against a wider range of opponents in hagiography: in the mid fourth-century AD *Lives of SS. Cyprian and Justina*, the holy virgin Justina dispatches the demon sent by the mage Cyprian to seduce her by blowing upon it, §5.)

Lucian makes mock of the deafness of the old *drakōn* and projects it as almost pathetic in this regard, but, as Lucian's narrative in any case makes clear, deafness can render a snake immune to incantation and therefore particularly dangerous, a notion discussed (in admittedly a somewhat confusing way) by Avitus of Vienne (*De spiritalis historiae gestis* 2.303–13). In reality all snakes are deaf.

The tale from Apuleius's novel *Metamophoses* is supplied in further elucidation of final sentences of the Lucian passage. The second old man is of course none other than the dragon manifesting himself in human form to deceive the slaves. Even when transformed, the dragon cannot disguise his hugeness, which, for a dragon, goes hand in hand with advanced age. The humanoid disguise hints at the underlying dragon too in the stooping and the dragging gait. Presumably, then, the ancient dragon could only disguise himself as a correspondingly ancient human, but even so the disguise works particularly well in context, when the party has just encountered a similarly elderly man. For a dragon capable of disguising itself as a man, cf. **162** and, more generally, **72, 74**.

When one realises that terrible dragons can manifest themselves as old men with walking sticks, the scoffing rhetorical question with which Tychiades closes the Lucian passage can be seen to carry a sinister undertone. Given the dragon-escorting role of the youngest snake in the Lucian passage, it is intriguing too that Apuleius's dragon should, in his disguise, speak of himself being accompanied by the youngest memory of his family, for all that he belongs in his inevitably lying tale. (The existence of the hole too is confined to the realm of the dragon's lying tale, but even so it is evocative of a dragon's home, not least in its comparison to the underworld: see **M3.a.ii**.)

It is just possible that Apuleius's tale originated with Lucian himself, if, as some believe, the 'Lucius of Patras' that Photius tells us was the author of the Greek novel upon which Apuleius's was based is to be identified with our own Lucian of Samosata (Photius *Bibliotheca* cod. 128). We can infer little from the fact that the précis of the Greek original transmitted with Lucian's *oeuvre*, the *Onos*, does not include the tale. (I thank D. Felton for drawing the Apuleius passage to my attention.)

## 131  St Thomas slays a dragon in India

ca. 220–40 AD

*Acts of Thomas* 30–3 (edited)

Greek

**30.** And the apostle went out to go off to where the Lord had commanded. When he was near the second milestone and had veered off the road a little, he saw the fallen body of an attractive young man lying on the ground. . . . He turned to his followers and said, 'This deed did not come about of its own accord, but the enemy did it, and his purpose in doing so was to be able to attack us through it. And see that he did not make use of any other form, or achieve it through any other creature other than the one that is subject to him [sc. the snake].'

**31.** When he had said this, a great dragon [*drakōn*] came out of its hole, beating its head and shaking its tail against the ground. In a booming voice it said to the apostle, 'I will tell you directly why I killed him, since you have come for this purpose, to investigate my work.' The apostle said, 'Yes, speak.' The dragon said, 'There is a beautiful woman in this village opposite. As she passed by me I saw her and fell in love with her. I followed her and kept watch over her. I found this young man kissing her. He also had sex with her and did other shameful things with her. It has been easy for me to reveal this to you, for I know that you are the twin brother of Christ and are always trying to abolish our race. Because I did not wish to upset this woman, I did not kill him there and then, but waited for him to pass by in the evening, and I struck him and killed him then, not least because he had the effrontery to do this on the day of the Lord.' The apostle asked it, 'Tell me from what kind of seed and from what kind of race you are sprung.'

**32.** And it said to him, 'I am a reptile of reptile race, a harmful creature born of a harmful creature.... I am the son of the one who forms a girdle around the sphere. I am kin with the one who is beyond the Ocean, whose tail lies in his own mouth. I am the one who entered Paradise through the fence and said to Eve everything my father commanded me to say to her. I am the one that kindled Cain and fired him up to kill his own brother,... I am the one that dwells in and occupies the abyss of Tartarus....'

**33.** When that dragon had said this as the whole crowd listened, the apostle raised his voice to its full volume and said, 'Stop henceforth, most shameless creature, and in your shame perish utterly. For the end of death has overtaken you. Do not dare to declare what you did through the agency of those that have become subject to you. I command you in the name of the Jesus that hitherto has been doing battle with you by means of his own men, that you suck out the venom you cast into this man, draw it out and take it from him.' And the dragon said, 'The hour of my end is not yet upon me in the way that you declared it. Why do you compel me to take back what I cast into this man and die before my time? For indeed that is the time of my father's end, whenever he draws up and sucks out what he cast into creation.' The apostle said to him, 'Reveal now the nature of your father.' The dragon approached, placed its mouth over the young man's wound and sucked the bile out of him. And gradually the young man's skin, which was livid, grew white again, and the dragon was inflated [*ephusato*]. And when the dragon had drawn up all the bile into itself, the young man leaped up, stood on his feet and then ran and fell at the feet of the apostle. The dragon, having become inflated [*phusētheis*], burst open and died. Its venom and bile spilled out. And in the place in which its venom was spilled there opened a great chasm, and the dragon was swallowed down. The apostle said to the king and his brother, 'Direct workmen and fill that place up, lay foundations and build houses over it, so that it may be a house for visitors.'

The apocryphal *Acts of Thomas* exhibit both Gnostic and Encratite affinities. The action takes place during St Thomas's mission to India. The fundamental correspondence with the Gospel of Thomas tale (**127**) and in particular with Lucian's *Philopseudes* tale (**130**) is striking. Again the destruction of a snake is coordinated with the instantaneous revivification of its final, youthful victim

(**M15.d.i**). And again the act of blowing is central to the remedy. Whilst Thomas makes his *drakōn* suck its venom out, the narrative is careful to specify that this resulted in a blowing up, an inflation, of the *drakōn*, to the point at which it burst. The motif of the opening up of the earth to swallow the body of the *drakōn* and take it back down to the abyss corresponds with the denouement of the *Martyrion of Philip*, in which the earth opens up to swallow the wicked Echidna (alive, in this case, **134**). But this motif too is found in another of the *Philopseudes'* tales, that in which Eucrates uses a magical ring to open up a chasm down to the underworld, which swallows down a massive serpentine Hecate (**102**). Almost certainly Lucian is parodying the Christian story type in this episode too. It is worth noting that the Acts of Thomas as we know them are thought to have been composed in Edessa, some twenty-five miles from Lucian's hometown of Samosata. It is tempting to think that this story type had already been thriving in the region for half a century at least, and that it was this that inspired Lucian's parodic account. (It must be stressed, however, that we do not know where amongst his many and prolonged travels around the Roman Empire Lucian actually composed the *Philopseudes*.)

As often in Christian texts, the *drakōn* identifies itself with the snake of Eden (**M15.b.ii**) and with Satan, also declaring itself to be a son of Satan (**M15.b.i**). The notion that a serpent might fall in love with a human being, bizarre and mendacious as it seems in its context here, is nonetheless a classical one (Aelian *Nature of Animals* 6.17, 8.11).

## 132 A dragon mysteriously manifests itself to prevent the violation of a Christian woman's corpse

ca. 150–80 AD

*Acts of John* 71–86

Greek

[John and his brethren come to Ephesus and lodge in the house of Andronicus and his beautiful wife, Drusiana, who has given up sex for the sake of godliness. Here a certain Callimachus develops an obsession with her and sends her billets-doux, in response to which she develops a fever, takes to her bed and prays to God to die, since she has become an obstacle to virtue in another. And die she does. But this is not the end of Callimachus's passion, and he bribes Andronicus's steward, Fortunatus, who has the keys to Drusiana's tomb, to open it so that he can have sex with her corpse. He begins to strip the body in preparation. (62–71)]

**71.** As they were saying this, and only the usual shift was left on her body, a strange vision was seen, one that all that do these things ought to see. A snake [*ophis*] appeared from somewhere and struck at the steward with a single bite and killed him. But it did not strike at the young man, but wound itself around his feet, blowing out [*apophusōn*] a terrible hiss. When he had fallen down, the snake got on top of him and sat there.

[A beautiful young man manifests himself, whom Callimachus recognises to be an angel. The angel covers Drusiana's body again with his cloak and flashes sparks of light from his eyes into Drusiana's. He turns to Callimachus and tells him to die so that he may live. When John, Andronicus and the brethren arrive at the tomb, this is the scene that confronts them. The angel explains that he has come to rescue Drusiana's body from its impending shame and then ascends into Heaven. (72–3)]

**73.** John, turning to the other part of the tomb, saw the young man, the first of the Ephesians, Callimachus (for this is what he was called), and the enormous snake sleeping on top of him, and Andronicus's steward, who was called Fortunatus, dead. [...]

**75.** John looked at the collapsed Callimachus and told the venomous reptile, 'Depart from the one that is destined to serve Jesus Christ.' [...]

[Callimachus begs to be admitted to the Christian fold. John proceeds to raise Drusiana from death (she may return to life now that she no longer constitutes a temptation to Callimachus), and she in turn raises Fortunatus from death, despite his dubious entitlement to such a privilege. But the raised Fortunatus remains unconverted (75–85).]

**86.** After praying and glorifying God, John came out of the tomb, having shared the Lord's Eucharist with the brothers. When he had arrived at Andronicus's house, he said to the brothers, 'Brothers, a spirit in me has prophesied that Fortunatus is about to die of blackness from the bite of the snake. Let someone go quickly and find out whether this is true.' One of the young men ran and found him dead for good and that the blackness, spreading over him, had reached his heart. He came back and reported to John that Fortunatus had been dead for three hours. And John said, 'Keep your child for yourself, Devil.'

The *Acts of John* also exhibits Gnostic affinities. The narrative excerpted here is too long to supply in full, and only the key details relating to the marvellous snake are supplied. Once again we have the snake's last victim, Fortunatus, restored to life (indirectly) by a saint, and this time from a categorical state of death (cf. **M15.d.i**). But since the person is wicked and remains unconverted by his experience, the serpent's venom is permitted once again to do its work, and continues where it left off. Again too we have a snake 'blowing out' its venom (**M7.a.ii**). For the critical change in the colour of the victim's body, compare Lucian's Midas (**130**).

We hear nothing of the snake after John has ordered it off Callimachus. It is significant that we are not told of its destruction: it is, after all, on the side of the angels, paradoxical though this may be. Its mysterious emergence 'from somewhere' as the corpse is stripped leads one to think of the classical notion of the snake produced from the corpse of a dead hero, as exemplified in **133**. The same conceit may lurk behind the tale of Marcellus of Paris's dragon (**152**).

## 133 In the background to the St John tale: the classical notion that heroes could be transformed into snakes after their death

iii BC–earlier iii AD

Diogenes Laertius 5.89–90 (Greek; earlier iii AD; = Heraclides of Pontus F16 Wehrli), incorporating fragments of Demetrius of Magnesia (i BC) and Hippobotus (ca. 200 BC)

Virgil *Aeneid* 5.86–96 (Latin; 19 BC)

Greek, Latin

**Diogenes Laertius:** Demetrius of Magnesia also tells the following story about Heraclides [sc. in his *Namesakes*]: 'He kept a dragon [*drakōn*] from when he was a child and continued to do so after he was grown. When he was about to die, he ordered one of his trusted men to conceal his body, but to put the dragon on the bier, so that he might appear to have migrated to the gods. Everything was done. As the citizens were following Heraclides' body and singing his praises, the dragon, hearing the shouting, ducked out from the shroud and threw most of the people into disarray. Afterwards everything was revealed, and Heraclides was seen for what he truly was, not what he had appeared to be.' I have a poem on him which goes like this:

> Heraclides, you wished to bequeath to all men the rumour
> That after dying you continued to live as a dragon
> But you were deceived, my clever fellow. For the dragon was just a beast

And you too were caught out as just a beast, not a wise man.
Hippobotus tells this story too.

**Virgil:** [Aeneas is making offerings at the tomb of his father Anchises.] From the depths of the shrine a slippery snake [*anguis*], so huge that it could make seven coils, drew forth its loops seven times over. It calmly enfolded the tumulus and slid amongst the altars. On its back were blue markings, and spots of brightly burning gold illumined its scales. Its resembled the rainbow in the clouds that casts a thousand different colours against the sun. Aeneas stopped short at the sight. Eventually the serpent [*serpens*] insinuated its long body amongst the sacrificial bowl and shining cups and tasted the food. Then it withdrew again into the depths of the tumulus, without harming anyone, quitting the altars it had tasted. All the more keenly did Aeneas resume the offerings he had begun to make to his father, uncertain whether he was to consider the creature to be the spirit of the place [*genius loci*] or the servant of his father.

These two classical texts illustrate the notion that the body of a distinguished hero could produce a serpent, either as an embodiment of his partly divine nature, or as a guardian of his tomb. We might also point to Pliny's claim (*Natural History* 16.234) that Scipio Africanus's estate at Liternum boasted a cave in which there lived a dragon (*draco*) that guarded his ghost, and to Plutarch's tale of the death of Cleomenes III of Sparta (*Agis and Cleomenes* 60). According to this, as Cleomenes' body hung on display in Alexandria, a large dragon (*drakōn*) manifested itself and coiled around his head, warding the birds off, and so the women of Alexandria made offerings to him, declaring him a hero and a son of gods. As noted, similar notions may lurk behind some Christian *drakōn* narratives, **132** and **152**.

## FURTHER READING

*Shepherd of Hermas*: Quasten 1949–60:i, 92–105, Peterson 1954, Wilson 1995, Ehrman 2003, Lipsett 2011.

*Passion of SS. Perpetua and Felicitas*: Quasten 1949–60:i, 163–4, Rossi 1984, Amat 1996, Godding 2000, Bremmer 2012, Heffernan 2012.

Lucian's Chaldaean snake blaster: Radermacher 1905, Müller 1932:38–47, Schwartz 1951:41–3, Ebner et al. 2001:50–2, 118–20, Ogden 2007:65–104.

*Acts of Thomas*: Bornkamm 1933, Klijn 1962, Bremmer 2001.

*Acts of John*: June and Kastler 1988, Bremmer 1996, Lalleman 1998.

# 22
## St Philip, the Echidna and the Ophianoi

It is to St Philip that the richest of all early hagiographical dragon-slaying narratives attach. Two closely related fourth-century AD Greek texts, the *Acts of Philip* and the *Martyrion* of Philip, bestow upon him three major dragon fights—doublets in origin, no doubt, but each now strongly differentiated and of considerable interest in its own right. These tales are important not only for their complex engagement with the classical dragon-slaying tradition, but also for the light they shed upon the religious battles of their own day. For Philip see also **161** (com.).

Figure 22 Filippino Lippi (ca. 1457–1504 AD): St. Philip and the Dragon of the Temple of Mars. Fresco, south wall, Strozzi Chapel, Santa Maria Novella, Florence, ca. 1497–1502 AD. The Bridgeman Art Library.

207

## 134   St Philip goes to war against the Echidna, her attendant dragons and her snakes in Ophiorhyme-Hierapolis

mid- to late iv AD

*Acts of Philip* 8.4 (G), 8.7 (G), 8.15 (G), 8.16–17 (V), 9 (V), 11.2–8 (A), 13.1–4 (A), 14.1–3 (A), 14.7–9 (A), 15.1 (A), *Martyrion of Philip* 2 (A), 7 (V), 12–17 (V), 19–20 (V), 24 (V), 26–8 (V), 32 (V), 39 (V), 42 (V)

Greek

**Acts of Philip 8.4 (G).** [Jesus explains the mission upon which he dispatches Philip, Bartholomew and Mariamne.] 'And you yourself, Mariamne, change your dress and your look. Put off all appearance of being a woman, including the summer dress you are wearing. Do not let its fringe trail on the ground. Do not fold it up, but cut it off, and go with your brother Philip to the city called Opheorhymos, which signifies "Road of the Snakes". For the people of that city worship the mother of the snakes, the Echidna [Viper]. Whenever you enter that city, if there is nothing female about your form, the snakes will see that you have nothing to do with the form of Eve. For the form of Eve is a woman, and Eve is of this same form. But the form of Adam is a man, and you know that a hatred of Eve arose for Adam from the beginning. This was the beginning of the snake's war with man. The snake formed a friendship with the woman, and Adam was deceived by his wife, Eve. And it was because of Eve that Adam put on the snake's slough [i.e. clothing], that is, its venom. And because of this slough the old enemy found a place to lodge in Cain, the son of Eve, whence he made him kill his brother Abel. So, Mariamne, shun the poverty of Eve and thereby enrich yourself.'

**8.7 (G).** [Jesus continues.] 'Now, my brothers, fear not the bites of the snakes, nor their venom. For their mouths will be sealed before you and their threat nullified. If they raise their heads, apply to them the sign of the monad. If the vipers come out, wear the sign of the cross, and this will make them bow their heads.'

**8.15 (G).** Philip and his companions rejoiced at the Lord's instructions and promises. Philip left, accompanied by Bartholomew and Mariamne. After kissing the Saviour's right hand, they began their journey to the land of the Ophianoi.

**8.16–17 (V).** When they had come up into the wilderness of she-dragons [*drakainai*], as they walked there, lo! a great leopard came out of the woods on the mountain. Upon seeing the apostles of the Lord it ran and threw itself at their feet and said to them in a human voice, 'I abase myself before you, servants of God's greatness and apostles of the only-born son of God: command me to speak perfectly.'

17. Philip said, 'In the name of Jesus Christ, speak!' The leopard acquired a perfect human voice and began to say, 'Hear me, Philip, you who escort people to the word of God. It happened that early last night I came across a herd of goats on the opposite side of the mountain of the she-dragon [*drakaina*], the mother of snakes, and I snatched a kid....' [In due course the leopard and the kid itself, similarly endowed with human voice and consciousness, add themselves to Philip's team.]

**9 (V).** The apostles, Philip, Bartholomew and Mariamne, together with the leopard and the goat, travelled together for five days. Then, when they were on the road in the early morning, after the midnight prayers, lo! a great and dark [*gnophōdēs*] wind suddenly blew up, and a very great and dark dragon [*gnophōdēs drakōn*] attacked the servants of God from out of the darkness [*gnophos*] itself. It had a blackened back, and its belly consisted of brazen embers and sparks of fire. Its body extended beyond a hundred cubits. There attended upon it a host of snakes and a host of the offspring of snakes. The whole desert place, extensive as it was, shook. Seeing this, Philip said to Bartholomew and Mariamne, 'Now we need help from the Saviour. Let us remember the words of Christ, who sent us on our mission and said, "Fear nothing, neither persecution, nor the snakes of that place, nor the misty dragon [*zopheros drakōn*]." So let us stand like firmly fixed pillars before God, and our enemy's entire power will be nullified, and its threat will fail. So let us pray, and let us purify the air by sprinkling from cups, and this misty creature will be rendered still, and its smoke will be halted.' So they took their cups and prayed as follows: 'You bedew every pyre and you bridle darkness; you cast the bit onto the mouth of the dragon. You nullified its anger. You diverted the wickedness of the enemy, and you submerged it in its own fire; you shut up its lair and blocked its exits and slapped down its pride. Come with us in this desert, for it is by your will that we make our course, and at your command.' Turning, Philip said to Bartholomew and Mariamne, 'Now, stand up and lift up your hands with the cups you possess, sprinkle the sign of the cross into the air, and behold the glory of the Lord.' And immediately there was a flame of lightning and it blinded the dragon and the creatures that depended upon it. At once the dragon and the snakes were withered up, and the rays of light penetrated the openings of the lairs and pulverised the eggs of the snakes. The apostles covered their eyes, since they were unable to look directly at the manifest miracle of the lightning. And in this way they continued to make their way unharmed, praising our Lord Jesus Christ. Amen.

**11.2–8 (A).** [The apostles continue their journey towards Ophiorhyme.] As Philip, Bartholomew and Mariamne rejoiced, there was an earthquake in the region, and tumult and disruption could be heard from a nearby place in which there was a great pile of broken stones. From it there came a confusion of voices and they said, 'Take yourself off once and for all from here to where you belong, servants of unnameable God, just as we are going to stay where we belong. How long will you oppose us in your desire to eradicate the demon race? We have never killed any passer-by. But uniquely at your arrival we have become enfeebled. We are fifty demons of a single nature, and we have been given this little place in which to live. But you, the servants of Christ, have crossed over all the earth under heaven to bring destruction upon us, and alongside you Jesus, the son of God, has alone destroyed countless races of demons. And see, we now forsake this cave, since we are forcibly expelled from it. We admit that henceforth we have been reduced to nothing. For the one who was crucified for us made our former nature wither away.'

3. The apostle said, 'I tell you in the name of the crucified one to show us what your former nature was.' And the dragon [*drakōn*] that was amongst them replied, 'The trick in Paradise, that is the source of my nature, and that was where he who now wants to destroy me through you cursed me. For then, after withdrawing from the garden that grew everything, I found a place to lurk in Cain, on account of Abel. I put female beauty before the angels and cast them down from on high. They sired enormous sons...[text corrupt]. These, when they were grown, began to devour men like locusts. The flood wiped men out, and they begat the race of demons and snakes, when the staff of Moses proved the nature of the wise men and the mages of Egypt. For we are the fifty snakes that the dragon of Moses devoured at that time. Henceforth, Philip, you have victory over us.'

4. The apostle, the servant of God, looked to heaven and said, 'Holy Jesus, continuance of the shadowless light, glory of your Father, strength of the weak, word of your Father since before time, the one who appeared on earth in the form of a man, come now and fortify me, because the host of demons in this desert mars your world. Tarry not, master, but speed your help to me.' Praying in this way, he cried out and said, 'I adjure you in the glorious name of the Father, in the name of his only-born son, in the name of the highest God, show yourselves, demons, show your number, and show what form you are.' At once a great cry came forth,

amidst uproar: 'Go forth now, children of Blackness [*Melania*] and Bitterness, swiftly, for our inevitable doom is at hand.'

5. The demons came forth from the tumble of stones in the form of reptiles, fifty snakes raising their heads to ten cubits in height (for each one had a length of over sixty cubits), and they said in a single voice, 'You come forth too, the one that told us to come out. For we are children of your race.' Then there was an earthquake so great that Bartholomew and Mariamne would have fainted had not Philip fortified them by saying, 'Whoever you are that are summoned by the snakes, which are wicked demons, come out, you on account of whom the earth shook, for you have already been defeated and all your strain has withered away.' At once there stood amongst the snakes a huge dragon of around a hundred cubits, all soot, and it belched forth fire and a great deal of venom in a bursting torrent. It had a beard of twenty cubits and a head like a hilltop that balanced a crest of iron [a conjectural interpretation of the obscure and possibly corrupt text at this point], and its whole body was like fire.

6. It raised itself up to a great height and said to Philip, 'Philip, son of thunder, what is this power so great that you are able to cross through our region? Why have you been so keen to slay me too, like the dragon in the desert? But I adjure you in the name of the one that gave you this power, do not slay us and do not annihilate us in the thunder of your anger. Send us to the mountains of Labyrinth, so that we may make our den there and change our forms and serve you with our demon power. Just as we served our just lord Solomon in Jerusalem (and it was by virtue of our service that he built God's temple), so let us complete a dwelling in this place for you in six days, and it will be called the Church of the Living God. And I will make seven eternal springs flow forth in the name of the crucified one. Only do not annihilate us.'

7. The apostle said, 'How will you be able to build, as of reptile nature and as snakes, given that all building is the work of human craft? In the name of the power of Jesus I now command you and these fifty snakes to change your birth form and display a human shape.' The dragon said, 'Listen, Philip, our nature is misty and dark [*gnophōdēs*]. Our father is called Darkness [*Skotos*], and our mother Blackness [*Melania*], and they begat us dark, black, light-footed, hook-haired, kneeless, wind-legged, misty, spark-eyed, sharp-chinned, bristle-haired, unpleasant, women-mad and hermaphrodite.' Then the dragon uttered the deepest of groans before continuing: 'Philip, since you are so strong, see our form!' And at once the dragon and the fifty snakes revealed their true form and flew off right away, like winds, and cried out, 'Let us bring the building at once!' Before three hours had passed they had brought fifty tall columns through the air, and they said, 'Arrange these columns as you wish, Philip, and on the sixth day you will see the building, the seven springs and the consecration of the church.'

8. After six days the building had been completed, and rivers gushed forth. In a few days more three thousand men, together with many women and small children, were attracted to the spot, and they glorified Christ. The dragon revealed itself in the form of a rather black Ethiopian and said, 'We are off, Philip, to a place we will no longer be seen by you, so that you may not order us to build there too. We have had enough. We have been defeated.'

**13.1–4 (A).** The apostles were travelling to the city and with them were the two animals that thought themselves human. Philip was signalling to the leopard to guide them along the road to the city. Coming to the summit of a mountain, they looked down and saw lying on the mountainside the city to which the Lord had sent them. Looking down, they saw men before the city, and they said to each other, 'Let us go to these men and ask them the name of the city.' As they went, the men saw them and came to meet them. Every man of that land had a snake upon his shoulder from which he read signs. They enquired of their snakes as to who these people were that were coming towards them. This was their sign. They would unleash their snakes against visitors. If they were not bitten by the snakes, then the snakes were showing them that the visitors were of the same abomination. But if the visitors were bitten by the snakes, then the snakes were showing them that they were enemies, and the men would not allow them into the city.

2. When the apostles drew near to talk to those men (they were seven in number), each of them put his own snake down, and the snakes rested their heads on the ground before the apostles and remained there, biting their own tongues. The men inferred that they too worshipped the Echidna. Philip proceeded on his way with the others. The people of the country observed the unreasoning animals accompanying them and talking like men, and they were amazed.

3. When they arrived at the city itself, lo! there were two great dragons [*drakontes*] before the city gate, one on the right and one on the left, mounting guard against all visitors trying to enter this city. They would breathe into their eyes and blind them. As the apostles approached, the dragons reared their heads, saw them at the gate and roared to each other. When Philip looked at them they saw the ray of light of the monad shining in his eyes and at that very time they turned their heads away and died.

4. Entering the city, the apostles found near the gate an empty clinic, in which no healer was based. Philip said to Mariamne, 'See, our Lord has anticipated us and prepared this clinic of the soul for us. Let us occupy it, and we will take some rest, because we have worn ourselves out and become tired on the road.' To Bartholomew he said, 'Where is the medicine chest the Saviour gave us when we were in Galilee? Let us base ourselves in this clinic and look after people, until we see the plan the Saviour has for us.'

**14.1–3 (A).** Near that place was the house of a rich man called Stachys, who had been blind for forty years. When he heard Philip saying these things as he was sitting at his window, he wept before his children and said, 'Help me and take me to the people based at the gate. For they can cure my eyes and restore the light to me.' His sons said to him, 'Who are those healers?' Stachys said to them, 'They are the people based at the gate, whom I heard saying, "Let us base ourselves in this clinic and heal all suffering and all disease."'

2. His sons got up, and with them his slaves, and, taking him by the hand, they led him to the apostles. He fell on the ground, prostrated himself before them and said, 'I beg you, the visitors who have come to this city, surely for the sake of me and my disability, to heal me too. For, let me tell you, for three days I have been seeing strange dreams, and for forty years I have not seen the light of the sun. Before I was blinded, I was a persecutor of visitors and Christians. For I was at the head of all those who worshipped the Echidna and the snakes that were near my house, in the street [*rhymē*] called Ophiorhyme. For all in the city worship snakes.

3. 'This is what happened. I was lying on my bed—I had my eyes open—and I was looking at my bedroom ceiling. I saw some snake eggs, and some baby snakes emerged from them. I thought about this and said, "Are these gods? I will take a little of the liquid from the snake eggs and put it in my eyes, to see if they have any curative power." But when I put the liquid from the eggs into my eyes, they were damaged and inflamed [*en phlegmonēi*] for a full ten years. At that time my wife was still alive, and she used to go to the mountain and bring back dew

from the plants and put it into my eyes every day, and that afforded me some relief. One day she rose at dawn and went to the mountain to bring me dew, and an enormous beast attacked and wounded her. She died from the wound, because there was no healer to heal her. From that time until now I haven't seen the light, not have I seen my sons' faces.'

**14.7–9 (A).** Philip drew Stachys to himself, extended his hand, dipped his finger in Mariamne's mouth and smeared the saliva around his eyes...[lacuna]...and he laid on for them a grand reception, roasted some cattle from the field and strained out a fine wine for them.

8. The report of this spread through the entire city and people said, 'Come and see the god-fearing men. One of them opened Stachys's eyes after he had not seen the light for forty years. No doubt the power of God is with them, since the craft of human healers cannot achieve such a great act of healing.' A great crowd gathered at his house because of Philip and his companions, and all ran to see the sick and the possessed being cured, and those with jaundice or dropsy being healed.

9. Philip baptized the men, Mariamne the women. All the crowds marvelled greatly that a leopard and a kid goat were pronouncing the 'Amens'. In those days there was uproar everywhere, amongst the common people, the great the small, the rich, the poor. To our God [lacuna].

**15.1 (A).** The ruler in that city was called Tyrannognophus [Tyrant of Darkness], and he had a wife named Nicanora, who was Syrian by birth. She had been thrown overboard from her ship during a storm and had made her way inland to that city. Because she was rich, Tyrannognophus took her as his wife. The snakes of the city bit her because she was a stranger. Her body was damaged by the venom, and she was in a state of continual torment. When she heard that Stachys had recovered his sight, she asked her slaves to take her to his house. They took her off without her husband's knowledge. The apostles were within, being attended by Stachys.

**Martyrion 2 (A).** When Philip had arrived in the city of Ophiorhyme, which is called Asian Hierapolis, he was received by one of the faithful named Stachys. He was accompanied by Bartholomew, one of the seventy disciples of the Lord, and his sister Mariamne, and by the disciples that followed him. Philip set about baptizing the men, Mariamne the women. This city had the following custom. They used to take all the children that were born to the sanctuary and cast them before the Echidna. She would lick them with her tongue, and it was by this sign that they became partners of the snakes. But during Philip's stay in the city the people were baptized in the name of the Father, the Son and the Holy Ghost. They stopped associating with the Echidna and all turned to the apostles. The snakes would not bite those who were baptized because of the sign of the cross. Philip and Bartholomew remained in the city and went about it destroying the snakes, tending to the sick and taking care of the widows, orphans and poor, providing them with food, wine and oil from their three jars [the creation of these three miraculously inexhaustible jars is described at *Acts of Philip* 15.5]. All the men of the city left their work and ran to Stachys's house when they heard about Philip's deeds.

**7 (V).** Philip was saying this to the assembled crowds on account of their ancient worship of snakes and the Echidna. They used to set up images of them and abase themselves before them, and for that reason Hierapolis was also called Ophiorhyme.

**12–17 (V).** When all had just pronounced the 'Amen' with the apostle Philip, lo! the tyrant came, Nicanora's husband, like a wild and crazy horse. He seized his wife by her cloak and shouted, 'Nicanora, did I not leave you on your couch? Where did you get the strength to come to these mages? How were you relieved of the inflammation of your eyes? Unless you tell me who the healer is I will punish you in a variety of ways and without pity.'

13. She said in reply, 'Throw off your tyranny, forget your wickedness, abandon your temporal way of life, put off your base mind's bestial nature, flee the bitter dragon [*drakōn*] and its desires, cast away the tools and weapons of the man-slaying snake, renounce the unclean and accursed wickedness of idols, which are the enemy's territory and a dark prison. Clothe yourself in a clean and respectable life, so that you may become holy and be able to know my healer and have his name. If you want me to remain by your side, make ready to abide in chastity, in abstinence and in fear of the true God. In that case I will live with you always. Purify yourself of idols and all their uncleanness.'

14. When the tyrant, her husband, heard these words, he seized her by the hair of her head, dragged her, kicked her and said, 'Better that you be put to the sword than that I should see you prostituting yourself with these mages. I see that you have become embroiled in the magic of these deceivers. I will kill you first in a dreadful way, and then I shall humiliate and kill these people too in the most dreadful fashion. They will not be spared.' Turning, he said to his men, 'Bring out those mages and schemers!' The executioners ran to the house of Stachys, seized hold of Philip, Bartholomew and Mariamne and dragged them to where the proconsul was. The most faithful Stachys and all the faithful followed them.

15. On sight of them the proconsul [i.e. the tyrant] gnashed his teeth and said, 'Torture these mages who have deceived so many women and men, youths, girls and those who claim to be god-fearing. They are abominations.' He commanded that rawhide straps be brought, and that Philip, Bartholomew and Mariamne be beaten. After the whipping he commanded that they should be bound by the feet with the straps and dragged through the city's squares to the gate of the city's sanctuary. A great crowd gathered, so great that hardly anyone can have remained at home. All were amazed at their endurance and perseverance, as they were dragged in a violent and inhumane fashion.

16. After torturing the apostle Philip and the saints with him, the proconsul commanded that they be brought to the sanctuary of the idol of the Echidna and confined there. The saints drew strength from their faith in Christ and were fortified by the endurance of saints. All together they glorified God in pronouncing 'Amen' in loud voice.

17. When Philip the apostle and Bartholomew and Mariamne had been shut into the sanctuary of the Echidna, the priests of the Echidna gathered at the same place, and so too did a crowd of some seven hundred men. They ran to the proconsul and shouted, 'Punish these mages, strangers, corrupters and deceivers of men for us! Since they arrived in our city, it has been filled with evil deeds. They even killed the snakes, the sons of our goddess. They have closed down the sanctuary and its altar is abandoned. We have found no offerings of wine for the Echidna to drink and so go to sleep. If you wish to know that they are indeed mages, look, see how they wish to bewitch us by saying, "Live a life of chastity and dignity, believing in God"; see how they got into the city; how they did this without the dragons blinding them; how the dragons did not drink their blood; and how the dragons themselves that guard our city against all strangers where cast down by these men.'

**19–20 (V).** Then the proconsul ordered that Philip and his people be taken out of the sanctuary and be taken to the tribunal, telling the executioners, 'Strip Philip and his companions and discover the source of their magic!' So they stripped Philip first and then Bartholomew. They came also to Mariamne, dragged her out and said, 'Let us strip her naked, so that all may understand how she teams up with men, although she is a woman. For she in particular has been deceiving all the women.' The tyrant said to his priests (ill deserving of the name), 'Proclaim throughout the city that all should come, men and women alike, to see her disgrace, because she goes around with these mages, and no doubt they fornicate with her.' He commanded that Philip be suspended, that his ankles be pierced, that iron hooks be fetched, that they should be put through his heels, and that he should be hung upside down from a tree opposite the sanctuary. They stretched Bartholomew out opposite Philip and nailed his hands to the wall of the sanctuary gate.

**20.** Philip and Bartholomew laughed to see each other. It was as if they were subject to no torture. For their punishments were prizes and crowns. When they stripped Mariamne, at once the appearance of her body changed before them all, and to all it seemed that she was engulfed in a fiery cloud. They were wholly incapable of looking in her direction, and all fled from her.

**24 (V).** [John enters the city and arrives upon the scene.] And he said to the people of that city, 'Men of Ophiorhyme-Hierapolis, great is your ignorance. For you have erred down the road of error. The dragon [*drakōn*] has blown [*pneō*] into you with its breath [*pneō*] and blinded you in three ways, which is to say that it has blinded you in body, soul and spirit [*pneuma*], and you were stricken by the destroyer. Look at the whole of creation, on the earth, in the heavens and in the waters. See that the snake bears no similarity with any man, but its stock is one of corruption and destruction: it was destroyed by God, and this is the reason that it is twisting and crooked, and there is no life in it. There is only anger, fury, darkness, fire and smoke in its parts. Why then do you now punish these people? Because they have told you, "The snake is your enemy"?'

**26–8 (V)** John, Bartholomew and Mariamne tried to stop Philip [cursing the Ophianoi], saying, 'Our Teacher was thrashed and whipped, and made to drink gall and vinegar, yet he said, "Pardon them, for they know not what they do." And he also taught us this, saying, "Learn of me that I am gentle and humble in heart."' Philip said, 'Get away from me and do not try to mollify me, because I will not endure you, because they hung me upside down and pierced my ankles and feet with iron. And you, John, beloved of God, how much did you preach to them without being heeded? So let me do what I want. I will curse them and they will be utterly destroyed at a single stroke.' He began to curse them, calling upon the Lord and exclaiming in Hebrew, 'Father of our Lord Jesus Christ, sole, all-powerful God, before whom all have ever trembled, powerful and disinterested judge, whose name is in your power, Sabaoth Ael, you are blessed through the ages, the authorities of the heavenly powers tremble before you as do the censures of the living cherubim, which consist of fire, holy king of greatness, whose name reached the beasts of the desert, and they became tame and praised you with sensitive voice, you who watch over us and readily grant our prayers, you who knew us before we were created, overseer of all, now I beg you, let great Hades open up its mouth and let the great abyss swallow down these godless men, who refuse to receive the word of truth in this city. Yes, Sabaoth.'

**27.** And lo! all of a sudden the abyss was opened up and swallowed down the whole of that area containing the proconsul, the entirety of the sanctuary, the Echidna they worshipped and the priests of the Echidna, some seven thousand men, not counting women and children. Only the place in which the apostles were remained stable. The proconsul was swallowed into the abyss. Their voices came up, with wailing, from below, saying, 'Have pity on us, God of your glorious apostles, because now at last we see the judgements visited upon those that deny the crucified one. Lo! the cross enlightens us. Jesus Christ, manifest yourself, for we are all going down to Hades and being whipped, because we unjustly crucified your apostles.' A voice was heard, saying, 'I shall be propitious towards you with my shining cross.'

28. Stachys, his whole house, the proconsul's wife and another fifty women that put their trust in the Lord alongside her remained safe, as did another substantial number of men and women, and a hundred virgins who had not been thrown down because of their chastity, sealed as they were with the sign of Christ.

**32 (V).** [Jesus has now manifested himself at the scene.] The Saviour turned, put out his hand and traced a cross in the air that extended from the heavens above all the way down into the abyss. The abyss was filled with light, and the cross resembled a ladder with steps. The Saviour spoke into the abyss, saying, 'All of you, come back up by the cross, so that you may see the light of God again, because even the apostle has now had pity on you, by my grace.' And lo! the entirety of the multitude that had been carried down into the abyss came up again. But there remained below the proconsul and the Echidna they worshipped. When the crowds had come up they looked at Philip and saw him hanging upside down, and they lamented greatly about the lawlessness with which they had acted. They also saw Bartholomew and Mariamne, with their previous forms. And lo! the Lord ascended into heaven as Philip, Bartholomew, Mariamne, Stachys and all the faithful people watched. They glorified God silently, in fear and trembling. Then the whole crowd cried out, 'There is but one God, the one that sent the apostles for our salvation! There is but one God, the one that these people proclaim in truth! We now truly repent of our great error, because we are not yet worthy of eternal life. Now we believe, because we have seen great miracles, and because the Saviour led us up out of the abyss.' They all fell on their faces, abased themselves before Philip and exhorted him, ready as they were to escape from their error. They prayed to become worthy of Christ's presence.

**39 (V).** After saying this Philip gave up his spirit, as all the crowd looked upon him and wept. His life ended peacefully, and all cried out the 'Amen'.

**42 (V).** Forty days later the Saviour appeared in the form of Philip and said to Bartholomew and Mariamne, 'My beloved brethren, do you wish to rest in the peace of God? Paradise has been opened for me and I have entered into the glory of God. You too, go off now to your allotted places. For the seed destined for this city and planted in it will bear beautiful fruit.' They embraced their brothers, prayed for each of them and left the city of Ophiorhyme, Asian Hierapolis. Bartholomew went off to Lycaonia, whilst Mariamne travelled to Jordan. Stachys and his people stayed behind to maintain the church of Jesus Christ our Lord, whose is the power and the glory, now, forever and for ages upon ages, Amen.

These delightful adventures are preserved in two related texts, which (partially) survive in a number of different recensions: the *Acts of Philip* recounts the apostle's career and adventures as a whole; the *Martyrion of Philip* concentrates on the immediate circumstances of his death and martyrdom and helpfully makes good the lost ending of the *Acts of Philip*.

The city in and around which Philip's adventures take place is once referred to as Opheorhymos, which is explained (plausibly) to mean 'Road of

Snakes' (*Acts of Philip* 8.4; cf. 14.2) and several times as the first-declension equivalent, with a slightly different orthography, Ophiorhyme (*Acts of Philip* 14.2, *Martyrion* 2, 7, 24, 42). Its citizens are the Ophianoi 'Snake people' (*Acts of Philip* 8.15). The *Martyrion* consistently identifies it with the famous city of Hierapolis in Phrygia, the modern Pammukale, on occasion running the two names together as Ophiorhyme-Hierapolis. Hierapolis was indeed the site of Philip's tomb and cult, and there is every reason to suppose that the text was composed there within an Encratite-Christian community. This is indicated by the prominence given to Mariamne, who, in dressing as a man and denying her womanhood, anticipates the life of an Encratite nun (*Acts of Philip* 4.8, *Martyrion* 19). In context it is suggested is that Mariamne's female form constitutes a particular liability when confronting snakes, in the light of the snake of Eden's seduction of Eve (*Acts of Philip* 8.4).

The culminating battle (*Martyrion* 26–7) is against the presiding Echidna, 'Viper', also described as a *drakaina* (8.16–17) and as a *drakōn* in her own right (*Martyrion* 13, 24) and more particularly as 'the mother of snakes' (*Acts of Philip* 8.4, 8.17; cf. *Martyrion* 17). As such she strongly resembles the great Echidna of Hesiod's genealogy, who is there and subsequently presented as the ultimate progenitrix, together with Typhon, of most of the great anguiform monsters of the classical tradition (**1**; cf. also **2–3**). Just as Philip's Echidna is presented as presiding over all other *drakontes* and snakes, so too the two major *drakontes* encountered by Philip en route to the Ophiorhyme and the Echidna are shown in their turn to preside over a host of lesser (though still monstrous) snakes. The desert *drakōn* is attended by a host of snakes and a host of the offspring of snakes (*Acts of Philip* 9). The *drakōn* of the rocks addresses its fifty attendant snakes as 'children of Darkness and Bitterness', whilst they in turn declare that they are 'children of [its] race' (*Acts of Philip* 11.4–5). The configuration of a great *drakōn* presiding over a host of lesser snakes lurks behind Lucian's early parodic tale of the Chaldaean snake blaster (**130**) and is found also in the subsequent tale of Clement of Metz (**156**).

In contrast with her subordinate great *drakontes*, the Echidna is not clearly described. All we can say is that she lives in her gated (*Martyrion* 19) and presumably lavish and expansive sanctuary, where she licks the citizens' newborn babies as they are introduced to her (*Martyrion* 2), and which is the scene of the denouement of the action and Philip's martyrdom. The sanctuary also appears to contain an image of her (*Martyrion* 16). The notion that the Echidna needed to be given wine so that she could sleep is a curious one (*Martyrion* 17). The motif of giving a great unsleeping *drakōn* herbs or plant juices to send it to sleep is a familiar one from classical tradition (**M8.b.ii**), but it hardly seems relevant here: the Echidna does not guard anything, nor do her adoring worshippers attempt to steal anything from her.

The fight against the desert *drakōn* (*Acts of Philip* 9) deploys the classical themes of the symmetrical battle vigorously. The *drakōn* is itself a creature of fire, with a belly of embers and sparks. This is countered by Philip with lightning brought down from heaven, which blinds the desert *drakōn* and pulverises the eggs of its snakes; cf. *Acts of Philip* 6, where the *drakōn* of the rocks addresses Philip as a 'son of Thunder'. The deployment of lightning against *drakontes* is in itself an old classical motif (**M6.b.iv**). It can, however, be used more widely in hagiography, as when Thecla calls lightning down to kill the seals that are trying to eat her as she baptises herself (*Acts of Paul and Thecla* 34, late ii AD). And then there is the battle of the airs. The desert *drakōn* produces in its fieriness a great smoky mist that precedes it (**M6.a.ii, M7.a.ii**; cf. the cloud raised by the monster that Hermas encounters, **128**). Some attention is given to the darkness to which this mist gives rise, with a number of words devoted to it, notably a series built on the *gnoph-* root. No doubt the darkness of the satanic snake is contrasted with the light and illumination offered by Jesus (*Acts of Philip* 11.4, *Martyrion* 27, 32). This imagery of darkness is subsequently extended to identify the wicked proconsul with the Echidna and serpents he sponsors, with him being given the curious proper name Tyrannognophus (*Acts of Philip* 15.1). Philip and his team respond to the dark, smoky mist by sprinkling holy water into the air in the shape of the cross and thereby purifying it. Philip's prayer against the desert *drakōn*, with its reference to locking the enemy up in its own lair, makes an appeal to the imagery of the dragon of Revelation (**126**; cf. also **136–7**). The weaponry of fire resurfaces in other episodes. The *drakōn* of the rocks also breathes fire and indeed consists of fire (*Acts of Philip* 11.5). Philip deploys another beam of light, that of the monad that shines from his eyes, against the pair of *drakontes* that guard the gates of Ophiorhyme (*Acts of Philip* 13.2; cf. *Martyrion* 17). Also, liquid from the snake eggs 'inflames' Stachys's eyes (*Acts of Philip* 14.2). Philip eradicates it from his eyes with Mariamne's virgin saliva; as we learn from the Donatus tale (**146**), saintly saliva is caustic to snakes (*Acts of Philip* 14.7). And when the Ophianoi try to strip her, Mariamne protects herself by turning into a fiery cloud (*Martyrion* 20). The weaponry of air resurfaces too in the case of the pair of gate-guarding *drakontes*, for they blind strangers with their terrible breath (*Acts of Philip* 13.2). And then John tells the Ophianoi that they have all been metaphorically blinded by the breath of the *drakōn*-Echidna (*Martyrion* 24). These passages, alongside the tale of the blinding juice of the snake eggs, also offer an example of the symmetrical battle of vision, corresponding indirectly as they do with Philip's own blinding of the desert *drakōn* with his lightning bolt.

The *drakōn* of the rocks and its snakes (*Acts of Philip* 11.2–8) are similarly dark (*gnophōdēs*) and claim to be the children of Darkness (*Skotos*) and Blackness (*Melania*). They are identified with demons (in particular they recall the biblical Legion in their plurality: Mark 5.1–20, etc.) and as such are dealt with by the appropriate technique of exorcism. The familiar tropes of exorcism on display here include the invoking of a powerful name, the compulsion of the demon to show itself in its true form, admit its identity, confess its wrongs and quit the place (or person) it occupies, and its banishment to the wilderness. It was a commonplace of both classical and early Christian literature than demons and ghosts could be dark like Africans (cf. Lucian *Philopseudes* 16, 30–1, Pausanias 6.6.7–11, *PGM* VII.348–58, and the 'Egyptian' demon at **155**).

The narrative as it stands is confused about whether the demons' true shape is anguiform on the one hand or humanoid, dark and winged on the other. We seemingly have elements of three supposed true revelations awkwardly combined with one another: as snakes at 11.5; as winged humanoids at 11.7; and, in the case of the *drakōn* himself at any rate, as dark humanoid at 11.8. The second of these revelations at least shows itself to emerge from the over-elaboration and corruption of the notion that Philip transformed the demons from their former snake form into flying humanoids in order to enable them to carry out their work of building the church.

Some, but not all, of the confessions identify the snake demons with noteworthy wicked snakes of the Old Testament, the snake of Eden (we recall again Jesus's initial words of advice to Mariamne; cf. **122**) and, more particularly, the fifty snakes of the mages of Egypt devoured by the *drakōn* of the staff of Moses, a devouring they had evidently somehow contrived to survive (Exodus 4.3–4, 7.9–12, 7.15). These snakes boast beards: it is rare for any Christian text to acknowledge this familiar attribute of the classical *drakōn*.

The *drakōn* and its snakes appear to have been buried and confined in a cave (itself otherwise a suitable enough home for a *drakōn*) enclosed beneath a rock pile. It is almost as if they have already been the victims of an exorcism and so confined to such a wilderness home. We note that Philip was subsequently to confine the Echidna to the abyss. Perhaps we are to imagine that such a confinement was the direct consequence of their devouring by Moses's staff. But at any rate we sense here in a Christian source the ambiguity that sometimes lurks in classical ones: do *drakontes* live deep in the earth of their own accord, or are have they been confined there by a greater power (**M2.a.i, M2.a.iv**)? The serpents' paradoxical reluctance to leave their rocks when compelled to do so is perhaps forced upon them by the demands of traditional exorcism narrative. As Amsler et al. 1999 note in their commentary on this passage, the tumble of rocks, together with the seven springs they acquire in the course of the story, are evocative of the remarkable Travertine rock formations still to be seen outside Pammukale. The association in itself of a dragon with a spring, even with the creation of a spring, is of course old and classical (**73**; more generally, **M4.a**).

Is the cult of the Echidna and its snakes supposed to relate in any way to any actual pagan cult? It has been hypothesised that the Echidna is a distorted version of the actual great goddess of Hierapolis, Cybele, but, despite the best efforts of the hypothesis's advocates, there is no significant point of contact between the two beyond the fact that one presided over pagan Hierapolis in fact, the other in fiction. Insofar as any appeal is made to genuine pagan cult imagery, it is likely, rather, to be that of Asclepius and his daughter Hygieia. It is, after all, in precisely their territory, that of healing, that Philip and his team fight for the souls of the Ophianoi from their dispensary. The Echidna's evidently substantial sanctuary contains an idol in the form of a snake (*Martyrion* 16), whilst sanctuaries of Asclepius would have contained a great many snake images. The god's cult statues famously incorporated his snake avatar coiling around his staff, whilst his temples would also have been decorated with independent snake images presented to it as votives by the grateful healed. In carrying snakes on their shoulders (*Acts of Philip* 13.1), the citizens that guard Ophiorhyme seem to be adopting the traditional iconographic pose of Hygieia and her Roman counterpart, Salus, the pose also adopted by the prophet Alexander of Abonouteichos for his ritual appearances with his snake Glycon, the living embodiment of the 'New Asclepius' (Lucian *Alexander* 12–18, 26). The curious tale of Stachys's blinding becomes rather more intelligible and rather less arbitrary if one imagines that he is the priest of a healing god who manifests himself in snake form. The repeated assertion that Ophiorhyme has no healers, a want Philip and his team seek to correct, may then be read as a denial of the efficacy of pagan healing gods. To such an extent these documents might be seen as making an indirect attack on an actual pagan cult type. However, in assimilating the principal foe to the terrible Echidna of classical myth, the authors more positively help pagan readers identify with Philip in his campaign against her.

Almost certainly, the more direct attack is made on others. The people of Ophiorhyme are referred to as Ophianoi (*Acts of Philip* 8.15), which gives much away: it was an alternative name for the Gnostic community known more commonly as the Ophites, a name also signifying 'Snake Men', or as the Naassenes, a community whose beliefs were characterised by more traditional Christian writers—rightly or wrongly—as a variety of inverted Christianity. The knowledge (*gnōsis*) given by the all-important snake of Eden, identified with Leviathan, was a signally good thing (Clement of Alexandria *Stromateis* 7.17.108.2 [ca. 200–2 AD]; Origen *Contra Celsum* 6.28 [248 AD]). As Epiphanius tells us, they sanctified the bread of their Eucharist by laying it on an altar table and having a sacred snake coil over it; they then kissed the snake (Epiphanius *Panarion* [*Against the Heretics*] 2.57–8 [37], [374–7 AD]). The inverted baptism rite attributed to the people of Ophiorhyme, in which babies are kissed by the Echidna, looks very much at home alongside such a communion (*Martyrion* 2).

With their immunity to (or, rather, natural deterrence of) snakebite, the Ophianoi recall two miraculous peoples of classical legend, the Ophiogeneis (Snake-born) and the Psylli. Communities of the former supposedly lived in Phrygia, at Parium on the Hellespont and in Cyprus (Aelian *Nature of Animals* 12.39, Strabo C588, Pliny *Natural History* 28.30–1). The latter lived in the Libyan Syrtes (Varro *Antiquitates* 1.2.1, Aulus Gellius 9.12.12, Strabo C814–15, Celsus *On Medicine* 5.27, Lucan 9.890–937, Pliny *Natural History* 7.14, 8.93, 21.78, 28.30, Plutarch *Cato Minor* 56, Cassius Dio 51.14, Aelian *Nature of Animals* 1.57, 16.27, Stephanus of Byzantium s.v. *Psylloi*).Philip's great curse against the Ophianoi (*Martyrion* 26), with its multiple addresses to God under a diverse range of soubriquets and descriptions, and his invocation of the name Sabaoth would not be out of place amongst the curses and other invocations of the partly Jewish-influenced Greek Magical Papyri from Egypt, the bulk of which also date from around the fourth century AD (cf. e.g. *PGM* XII.14–95).

The shining ladder-cross by which Jesus brings the Ophianoi out of the abyss and up and away from the Echidna below recalls St Perpetua's ladder to heaven, the first step of which is constituted by the head of a *drakōn* (**129**). Bartholomew's near-fainting at the earthquake that accompanies the emergence of the snakes of the rocks reminds us of his reaction, all too well predicted by Jesus, to the release of Beliar from the abyss in the *Questions of Bartholomew* (**126**).

## 135 St Philip again

late vi AD

[Abdias] *Historia Apostolica* pp. 738–40 Fabricius

Latin

After the Saviour's ascension, the blessed Philip zealously preached the gospel to the peoples throughout Scythia for twenty years. When he was arrested by the peoples there and brought to the statue of Mars and compelled to make sacrifice, a huge dragon [*draco*] emerged from underneath the base on which the statue stood and bit the son of the priest who was looking after the sacrificial fire. It also bit two of the tribunes who were in charge of the province, the officials of which were holding the apostle in chains. Furthermore, all were brought to death's door by the breath of the dragon and began to be seriously ill. Seeing this, the apostle said to them, 'Listen to my advice, and you will recover your health; nay rather, even those who have died will all be resuscitated. And the snake too which was harmful to you will be put to flight in the name of the Lord.' The sick said to him, 'What are we to do?' The apostle replied to them, 'Cast down this Mars, and smash it up, and in the place in which it seems to stand fixed, establish a cross of my Lord Jesus Christ, and worship it.' Then those that were racked with pain began to cry out, 'Virtue will be restored in us, and we will cast down Mars.' When they had fallen silent the apostle said, 'I command you, dragon, in the name of the Lord Jesus Christ, come out from your place, and go and live in a deserted place, where men do not go, and where nothing is supplied of use for human well-being, so that you may harm no one in going there. Then that most fierce dragon came out and began to depart at speed, and was never seen anywhere again. But Philip revived the son of the priest who looked after the fire and the two tribunes who had been dead, and he restored to health the whole crowd that had been afflicted by diseases because of the dragon's breath. As a result of this it came about that all those who had been persecuting the Apostle Philip repented and worshipped him, considering him to be God.

There is little point of contact between this version of Philip's great dragon battle (which belongs chronologically with those reproduced in chapter 24) and those of the *Acts of Philip* and *Martyrion of Philip*, beyond the notion that the dragon's adversary should be tightly associated with a cult of the unbelievers.

The story has much in common with the *Gospel of Thomas* (**127**) and many of the other hagiographical narratives reproduced here, combining as it does the defeat of the dragon with the revivification of its most recent victims, these including a youth, the son of the priest (**M15.d.i**). It offers a striking example of the widespread motif of the dragon's pestilential breath (**M7.a.ii**). As in some of the other hagiographical tales, the dragon's production of the pestilential airs is directly linked with the persistence of pagan worship (cf. **136, 147, 156**).

This narrative makes the bond between a marauding dragon and a traditional pagan god more simply and explicitly than most of the saintly dragon-slaying stories do, but the choice of god, in pagan terms, is odd. Ares or Mars was prominent in myth but rather less so in cult, and, aside from the Dragon of Ares of Theban myth (**75–80**), he had little to do with dragons or snakes, in marked contrast to Asclepius. Perhaps he was chosen here for his divine province of making war, which could be projected, in short compass, as more directly antithetical to Christian aspirations than the gentle and healing Asclepius.

## FURTHER READING

Bovon 1988, Amsler et al. 1996, 1999, Rutherford 2007.

# 23
## St Silvester and the Dragon of Rome

The *Acts of Silvester* lies at the heart of a intriguing nexus of Christian texts that seek to build a series of good Christian dragon-fight stories onto the curiously mangled traditions of a once genuine classical snake cult. For Silvester see also **161** (com.).

### 136  St Silvester seals up the pestilential Dragon of Rome in its hole

late iv–ca. 500 AD

*Acts of Silvester* B (1), at Duchesne 1897:31–2 (ca. 500 AD)

**Acts of Silvester B (1):** There was a most monstrous dragon [*draco*] in the Tarpeian rock, on which the Capitol is located. Once a month mages, together with profane virgins, used to descend down 365 steps to this dragon, as if to Hell, with sacrifices and propitiatory offerings, titbits of which could be given to the dragon, large as it was. This dragon suddenly and unexpectedly came up and, although it did not come out of its hole, nonetheless it corrupted the air around about with its breath. As a result of this came the death of people and, in great measure, mourning for the death of children. St Silvester was having an argument with some pagans in defence of the truth, and it came to a point at which the pagans said to him, 'Silvester, go down to the dragon and in the name of your God make it desist from killing the human race even for just one year, so that we may believe that your Christ possesses the virtue of divinity.'

Figure 23  Maso di Banco (fl. 1336–46 AD): St. Silvester and the Dragon of Rome. Fresco, San Silvestro Chapel, Santa Croce, Florence, ca. 1337. © Mondadori Electa / The Bridgeman Art Library.

221

*Acts of Silvester* A (1), at Pohlkamp 1983:11 (late iv AD)

Latin

St Silvester said to them, 'My Christ, full of the virtue of divinity, will deign to demonstrate his virtue in this place. But in your lack of faith you will ever be looking for bogus objections to his divinity that can be of no benefit to your cause.'

Then Silvester called together the saints and the men of the Spirit and ordained a three-day fast for the whole church, together with an urgent prayer that Lord Jesus Christ should deign to take thought for the salvation of people in this place and to demonstrate the power of his name. And so, when the third day after the commencement of the fast had passed, the apostle St Peter appeared in a vision to Silvester and said, 'Take with you the presbyters Theodorus, Dionysius and Felicissimus and the deacons Honoratus and Romanus and at the very entrance, before you descend to the dragon with these men, offer sacrifice to God there. After this, take up a chain. When you have gone down you will find the lair in which the dragon lives. Before it there are bronze doors with rings. As soon as you have gone down, invoke the name of our Lord Jesus Christ, draw the doors shut and pull the chain through their rings. And when you have closed them, say, "So says Peter, apostle of Christ: Those doors open not save on the Day of Judgement." Bury the key to the chain where you want.' The pagans that were going down with St Silvester tried to frighten him. But he remained steadfast and went down undaunted. He carried out all the instructions given him by the apostle Peter. The whole city was liberated from the breath of the dragon from that day and thenceforth. But when one year had passed, and then a second, all the servants of the dragon, agreeing amongst themselves that it had been truly overcome and shut in, prostrated themselves before St Silvester, put their faith in Christ and were baptized.

**Acts of Silvester A (1):** And so, after several days had passed, all the priests of the temples are said to have made a suggestion to august Constantine along the following lines: 'Most holy emperor, ever august, your Roman people is continuously imperilled by the breath of a dragon [*draco*]. For sacred virgins in the temple of Vesta maintained the custom of descending to him every day of the calends and serving cakes of wheat to him. But from the point at which your piety received the Christian law, nothing has been taken in to it, and so, in its displeasure, it plagues the people every day with its breath. And so we beg you to command that the food that used to be given in tribute to its power be laid out for it, so that the city of Rome can give thanks to your piety for the health of all its citizens.'

The historical Silvester became pope in 314 AD, a year after the Edict of Milan, and enjoyed twenty-one years in office under Constantine, whom he predeceased by two years. Despite the momentous times in which he lived, little of a factual nature is known of him. But Christian fiction has been kind to him, making him, inter alia, the baptiser of Constantine and the recipient of the Donation by which the emperor was held to have made the sovereignty of the city of Rome, Italy and the western provinces over to the Church in perpetuity.

Given first here is a translation of the whole of the relevant episode from the *Acts of Silvester* B (1) text, dated ca. 500 AD (cf. the version supplied at Mombritius 1910:ii, 529). Given second is a translation of a portion of the same episode in the *Acts of Silvester* A (1) text of a century or so earlier (this brief excerpt was published by Pohlkamp in the course of his abortive preparation of a full edition of the A text). Both texts project the dragon as an object of pagan cult. The A text has the Vestal Virgins, no less, taking food down into its cave to it. The B text is less specific about the identity of the virgins and ascribes the lead role in its cult rather to an undefined group of 'mages', no doubt in a desire to emphasise the fraud and illegitimacy of the creature's worship. Whilst the A text does not specify the actual location of its dragon's cave, the B text locates it in the Tarpeian rock. This was some three hundred yards distant from Vesta's temple in the Forum. Cakes of grain and honey were regularly given to the sacred snakes, both real and imaginary, that lived in Greek and Roman shrines; cf. **124, 139**.

These narratives offer one of the most striking examples amongst Christian ones of the pestilential breath the dragon can produce (**M7.a.ii**). In the B text, as in other Christian narratives, the dragon's pestilential breath is aligned with the continuation (if not necessarily the continuing predominance) of pagan worship which the defeat of the dragon brings to an end, leading to and indeed symbolising, as it does, conversion (cf. **147, 156**). In the A text, more anomalously, the pestilential breath is produced rather by a dragon embittered by having been deprived of its cult after a signal act of mass conversion to Christianity.

Silvester's mechanism for defeating the dragon, locking it up with key and chain in an abyss, ostentatiously appropriates the imagery of Revelation, in which St Michael does the same thing to the Revelation dragon (**126**). The final result of Silvester's battle is that the dragon is confined deep inside the earth, albeit in its own hole: this is also the final fate of the dragons faced by Thomas (**127**) and Philip (**134**); cf. also **102**.

## 137 St Silvester seals up the pestilential Dragon of Rome in its hole: later accounts

vii AD

Aldhelm *De virginitate* (poetic version) lines 545–56 and *De virginitate* (prose version) pp. 257–8 Ehwald

Latin

**Poetic version:** Finally he overcame through virtue a scaly dragon [*draco*], drawing bonds tightly around it with iron chains. Before this it had breathed forth from its crypt with death-bringing flame and rightly terrorized groups of people in the Roman kingdom whilst they disdained to serve the one Christ, believing that the cult of the terrible snake should take precedence. But when he had confined the beast in a tight collar, reining in the deadly fires of the pestilential dragon [*draco*], there rose at once amongst the happy citizens a triumphant cry, 'The creature that used to rage against us had been confined to the depths!' For that reason the grace of baptism, shining from heaven, at once illumined the arches of Rome like the sun.

**Prose version:** Silvester undertook the priesthood of the pontifical seat at Rome and became famous throughout all the provinces of Europe and the verdant parishes of Italy, which the icy glades of the Alps surround with their precipitous, rocky crags, as the tales of his miracles were noised abroad. This is because, relying upon the pure chastity of his body, which was endowed with the self-denial of his continual abstinence, he is said to have descended down a hundred steps, deep inside its lair, to a death-bringing dragon [*draco*] that was lurking in the secret cave of a crypt in Rome and terrorising the unfortunate people in a savage fashion, corrupting the air with its venomous jaws and the pestilential blasts of its breath. The mistaken paganism of the heathens had had the custom of making the polluted offerings of a mad sacrifice to this same beast, which was of amazing size, in order to placate its crazed frenzy. He confined it in a collar from which it could not escape and inflicted perpetual punishment upon it for all time. He turned Rome, which had been cultivating a false idolatry, from the doom-laden path of animal sacrifice to the right path, with the truths and brilliant witness of the gospels.

Aldhelm was Abbot of Malmesbury and subsequently Bishop of Sherborne; he was the first Anglo-Saxon we know of to have achieved distinction in Latin letters. He produced his *On Virginity* in both a poetic and a prose version. As can be seen, his handling of parallel episodes in the two versions can vary significantly. Emphasis is given both to the dragon's production of pestilential air (**M7.a.ii**) and indeed to its breathing of fire (**M6.a.ii**). The technique of closing off the dragon's production of bad air given here, that of chaining it tightly at the throat, seems rather more satisfactory in itself than that given in the version of the *Acts of Silvester* B (1) reproduced at **136**, and also gratifyingly embraces another widespread motif of saintly dragon fights, that of attaching a lead to the beast's neck, as found in **M15.d.iii**. However, the cry attributed to the people in the poetic version seems to preserve a reminiscence of the *Acts'* version of the dragon's confinement.

## 138 The earlier Christian notion that the Vestals tended a dragon

ca. 207 AD–400 AD

Tertullian *Ad uxorem* 1.6.3 (ca. 207 AD).

Paulinus of Nola *Carmina* 32.143–6 (ca. 400 AD)

Latin

**Tertullian:** For at Rome the women that deal with that apparently inextinguishable fire and tend the omens of their own punishment and that dragon [*draco*] too are appointed on the basis of virginity.

**Paulinus:** I hear that those who are called the Virgins of Vesta carry meals for a dragon [*draco*] every five years. However, this dragon either does not exist or, if it does exist, is the Devil himself, that former enemy tempter of the human race. Yet they worship him, who now trembles weakly before the name of Christ and confesses all his deeds.

These texts, the second of which may postdate the *Acts of Silvester* A (1), are interestingly indicative of an earlier Christian tradition that the Vestals tended a dragon that flourished long before the existence of the historical Silvester and, inevitably, long before the tale of his defeat of the creature was developed. Tertullian makes light of a Christian woman's sacrifice in remaining celibate after widowhood, since even pagans, he notes, can manage it in the service of their own snake cults.

## 139 In the background: the pagan rites of Juno Sospita at Lanuvium

Hellenistic–iii AD

Propertius 4.8.2–14 (c. 16 BC, Latin)

Aelian *Nature of Animals* 11.16 (early iii BC, Greek)

Plutarch *Parallela minora* 14 (*Moralia* 309a–b; ca. 100 AD) = Pythocles of Samos *Italica*, *FHG* iv p. 488 F1 (Hellenistic)

Latin, Greek

**Propertius:** Lanuvium has long been protected by an ancient dragon [*draco*]. It is well worth the time to visit this curious place. For a sacred descent falls away sharply into a blind cavern. This is the route travelled by virgins, tributes for the ravenous serpent [*serpens*], when it demands its annual feed and sends its hissings twisting up from the depths of the earth. Journeys of this kind give rise to omens. The girls sent down for such rites grow pale as their gentle hands are nibbled at by the snake's mouth. It snatches up the titbits proffered by the virgins. Even the baskets shudder in the virgins' hands. If they have been chaste, they return to hug their parents, and the farmers cry, 'The year will be fertile.'

**Aelian:** In Lavinium [*recte* Lanuvium] a grove, large and densely wooded, is held sacred, and it has nearby a temple of Hera of the Argolid. In the grove there is a great, deep hole, and that is the lair of a dragon [*drakōn*]. On appointed days sacred virgins enter the grove with barley cakes in their hand and blindfolds over their eyes. A divine breath draws them directly to the lair of the dragon, and they advance slowly and gently and without tripping, just as if they were seeing with their eyes uncovered. If they are virgins, the dragon accepts their food as sacred and suitable for an animal dear to the god. But if they are not virgins, then their food is left untasted, because the dragon has foreknowledge of their corruption and divines it. Ants reduce the barley cake of the fallen girl to crumbs, so that they are easily transportable for them, and then carry them out of the grove, purifying the place. The locals learn what has been done. The girls that have entered the grove are examined, and the one that has brought shame upon her maidenhood is punished with the penalties laid down by law. This is how I would demonstrate the divinatory power of dragons.

**Plutarch/Pythocles:** When the Carthaginians and the Siceliots were arranging an alliance against the Romans [i.e. the commencement of the First Punic War, 264 BC], the general Metellus failed to sacrifice to Vesta alone of the gods. She sent a hostile wind [*pneuma*] against his ships. The seer Gaius Julius said that he could make the wind fall if he sacrificed his daughter. So constrained, Metellus brought his daughter forth, but Vesta took pity on her and substituted a heifer for the girl, taking her to Lanuvium and appointing her priestess to the dragon [*drakōn*] worshipped amongst the people there. So says Pythocles in the third book of his *Italica*.

The fascinating fertility rites described belong in fact to Juno Sospita and her shrine at Lanuvium. Juno is the Roman equivalent of Hera, and ancient authors commonly confuse Lanuvium and Lavinium. Pythocles' aetiology of the rite (strongly reminiscent of the myth of Iphigenia: Euripides *Iphigenia at Aulis* esp. 1540–1901, Apollodorus *Epitome* 3.21–2, etc.), indicates that Vesta also had an important though otherwise obscure role in the Lanuvium cult and offers a starting point for the Christian transfer of the dragon rite to the Vestal Virgins in Rome. The sacred virgins who feed the snake and who stand to suffer punishment if they have lost their virginity in any case bear more than a superficial resemblance to the Vestal priestesses. The rite is attested already prior to Propertius by some coins minted in 64 and 54 BC by L. Roscius Fabatus: the obverses of the coins display the head of Juno Sospita, whilst their reverses show a girl, just possibly a blindfolded one, feeding a rampant snake. She holds her dress out in front to make a hammock, and the cake or cakes, we may assume, rest in the fold.

What actually went on in this rite is hard to fathom. It seems to be suggested that the grove was never entered by anyone but the sacred virgins, and them only under blindfolds. The snake, in short, was never seen and so presumably did not exist. Whether it existed or not, it could not have eaten the barley cakes, whatever the species to which it belonged: no snake can eat anything other than eggs and live (or recently killed) prey. But it is hard to believe that every single girl that entered the grove was concluded to have lost her virginity.

We may note that the serpent of Lanuvium, fictional or otherwise, has, like all serpents, a distinctive breath, although the use to which it puts it is uniquely positive. For the drawing effect of a dragon's breath, cf. **98, 143–4**. In this regard, it is interesting that Vesta should be said to have stayed Metellus's ships with a *pneuma*, literally a 'breath'.

## 140 Refractions of Silvester (i): the Dragon of Rome is destroyed by a nameless monk and revealed to be a cruel mechanical contraption

v AD

*De promissionibus* 3.43, at *PL* 51, 835

Latin

In the city of Rome there was a certain cave in which there was a mechanical dragon [*draco*] of amazing size. It brandished a sword in its mouth, and its eyes consisted of red gemstones. Its appearance was fearful and terrible. Every year virgins, decked out with flowers, were dedicated to it, and given to it in sacrifice in that fashion. Unawares, they would carry offerings down to it. But when they reached that step of the staircase where the dragon hung, by the craft of the Devil, the impact of the sword would kill them and shed their innocent blood. The dragon was destroyed in the following fashion by a certain monk who was well known to the imperial courtier Stilicho on account of his good offices: The monk felt his way carefully down the staircase step by step with his hand and his staff, examining the steps carefully. He perceived that Devil's trap as soon as he touched it and so evaded it in his descent. He hacked the dragon up and dashed it into pieces. He also demonstrated that gods cannot be made by human hand.

This anonymous Latin text was written in Africa in the fifth century AD. Once the Christians had decided that the Dragon of Rome which they had long associated with the Vestals should be destroyed, more than one righteous candidate for the role of destroyer was found. In this wonderful version the chronological setting is the turn of the fourth and fifth centuries AD, this being the age of Stilicho. Silvester's role is taken instead by an anonymous monk. The fraudulence of the pagan rite is gratifyingly ramped up—the dragon is not even a real one—as is its cruelty: the virgins that process to the serpent are now to become actual blood sacrifices to it. But in some ways this tale cleaves closer than the Silvester ones to the details of the original Juno Sospita rite. Although it is not stated explicitly, it is a fundamental premise of this narrative that as the virgins progress down the steps towards their impaling they are unable to see, whether because they are blindfolded or simply because of the darkness in the cave. The sword of course takes the part of the dragon's projecting tongue (cf. the description of Marina's dragon, **149**).

## 141 Refractions of Silvester (ii): the Dragon of Rome is destroyed by Gildas

ix AD

*Vita i S. Gildae*, MGH Auctores antiquissimi 13.1, 95

Latin

Gildas heard that the Roman citizens were gravely ill because of the pestilential breath of a dragon [*draco*] that was lurking in a cave in some mountain. With its pestilential breath it had killed many of the Romans and the others who lived around about. Hearing this, the blessed Gildas came out of his lodging in utmost secrecy at daybreak and climbed the mountain with his staff in his hand. Making a prayer, he came to the mouth of a cave and, seeing the dragon, courageously invoked Christ by name and said: 'In the name of our Lord Jesus Christ I order to you to die at once, so that the people of the faithful should no longer be killed by you.' It immediately fell down dead upon the earth, and the people were delivered of its pestilence.

By the ninth century AD the tale of the defeat of the Dragon of Rome, in a somewhat reduced form but one retaining the key motif of its pestilential breath, had been transferred to the British saint Gildas, whose historical floruit was the earlier seventh century AD. An eleventh-century life of Gildas subsequently relocates the Dragon of Rome, more conservatively, back beneath the Tarpeian rock (*Vita ii S. Gildae* at *Catalogus* 1889–92:ii, 184).

## 142 Refractions of Silvester (iii): a noble soldier and the hole of the Dragon of Rome

xii AD

*Mirabilia urbis Romanae* 24

Latin

Near that house was the Palace of Catelina, where the church of St Antony was, next to which is the place which is called Hell, for the reason that in ancient times the place used to belch forth and bring great destruction on Rome. So that the city might be delivered, a certain noble soldier threw himself into it in his arms in accordance with an oracle of the gods, and the earth closed up. And so the city was delivered. That is where the temple of Vesta is, where a dragon [*draco*] is said to sleep below, as is told in the *Life of St Silvester*.

The story of the noble soldier hurling himself into a hole is a refraction of the ancient myth of the Lacus Curtius, which was appropriately adjacent to the temple of Vesta. Livy (7.6) tells how, in 359 BC, an unfillable hole opened up in the Roman Forum. Divination revealed that Rome would last forever so long as the principal strength of the Roman people was devoted to it. The brave youth Marcus Curtius concluded that Rome's principal strength lay in her arms and valour, so he put on his armour and rode into the hole on his horse. The *Mirabilia* author may be referring specifically to this story, but it seems more likely that he is referring to a tale of a subsequent Christian soldier calqued on it: the motif of the closing up of hell might encourage us to believe this, when we think of the earth closing over Thomas's Dragon (**131**) and Philip's Echidna (**134**; cf. **M3.a.iv**). This Christian soldier would then be a third refraction of Silvester.

### FURTHER READING

Silvester: Loenertz 1975, Pohlkamp 1983, Canella 2006.
Juno Sospita: Santinelli 1902, Douglas 1913, Pailler 1997.

# 24
## Saintly Tales Originating between the Fourth and Sixth Centuries AD

We progress now to a selection of saintly dragon-slaying tales originating in the fourth century BC (as do those of Philip and Silvester) and the following two centuries. The tales included here recycle a series of themes that will by now be all too familiar, but they combine them with an intriguing series of inventions, not least in respect of the dragons' *modus operandi* and of the slayers' techniques.

### 143   St Hilarion of Gaza slays a dragon in Dalmatia with a pyre

before 396 AD

Jerome *Life of St. Hilarion the Hermit* 39

Latin

St Hilarion also took himself to Epidaurus, a town in Dalmatia. He stayed for a few days on a nearby farm but could get no peace, for a dragon [*draco*] of huge proportions, of the variety locally known as *boas* from the fact that they are so large that they devour oxen [*boves*], was laying waste to the entire province, attacking not just the flocks and herds, but also the farmers and shepherds, which it sucked up with the power of its breath. He had a pyre prepared, prayed to Christ, summoned the creature, ordered it to mount the pile of wood and set fire to it. And so he burned the monstrous creature with all the people looking on.... This tale is told by Epidaurus and the entire local area still today. Mothers tell it to their children so that it will be handed down into posterity.

Figure 24 Jean Fouquet (ca. 1420–80 AD): St. Hilary of Poitiers confines the snakes of Gallinaria. Illustrated manuscript of *The Hours of Étienne Chevalier*, ca. 1445 AD. Musée Condé, Chantilly. Giraudon / The Bridgeman Art Library.

Jerome's *Life* is our sole (non-derivative) source of information for the historical St Hilarion, whose floruit was the mid-fourth century AD. This tale offers another clear example in the hagiographical tradition of the use of fire against a dragon (**M6.b**). Compare, in particular, the pseudo-Aristotelian tale in which a Thessalian witch summons a sacred snake into a ring of parching herbs (**100**); for the destruction of serpents by means of summoning them into great pyres more generally, see **C1, C9–10**. This tale also offers another example of a dragon's deployment of its terrible breath not to blow out its venom but to suck its victims in or down (cf. **98, C3, C12**; more positively, **139**). The siting of this tale in a city called Epidaurus, albeit the Dalmatian one, might have suggested to some ancient readers that the dragon in question was a manifestation of the great pagan anguiform god Asclepius.

## 144  A later account of the Hilarion tale

vii AD

Aldhelm *De virginitate* (prose version) at Ehwald 1919:266–7

Latin

Wherefore, distinguished by countless amazing miracles, he made himself the equal of the ancient patriarchs, inasmuch as he destroyed a terrible dragon [*draco*] with a scaly body near Epidaurus, a city in Dalmatia. They call this type of dragon a *boa*, because it is of such an enormous size that it slaughters oxen with the venomous teeth of its jaws and because it is in the habit of gulping them down into the gluttonous maw of its stomach. And they devour not just herds and flocks, but also farmers, ploughmen and swineherds, all drawn to them by the power of their breath. O powers above, avert such a monster from the earth! He destroyed it with the weapons of prayer in the following fashion: He had logs piled up high to form a pyre, set it ablaze it with lighted kindling and by the power of a terrifying command compelled the aforementioned basilisk, of marvelous size, to climb upon it as the people watched. He scorched its scaly flanks and curving spine in the roasting embers until they were rigid and burned them up savagely with fiery masses of brands, and so delivered the people from the pestilential blasts of the creature.

A more excited account of the same episode from Aldhelm, who makes his Dalmatian dragon a blower as well as a sucker, perhaps bearing in mind the Dragon of Rome, about which he also speaks (**137**). Aldhelm's parallel account of this episode in the poetic version of his *De virginitate* is rather more summary (lines 808–11, at Ehwald 1919:387).

## 145  Ammon the hermit and the dragons of the Egyptian desert

before 410 AD

Tyrannius Rufinus of Aquileia *Historia monachorum in Aegypto* 8, at *PL* 21, 420–2 (Ammonas)

Latin

I believe we should also mention what we heard about a holy man called Ammon. We saw the place in which he lived in the desert. So, after leaving the blessed Apollonius, we went forth into the southern part of the desert and in the sand we saw traces of the trail of a huge dragon [*draco*]. The trail was so big that it seemed as if some great beam of wood had been drawn through the sand. When we saw it, we were stricken with a great terror. But the brothers escorting us urged us to not to be afraid in any way, but rather to have faith and track the dragon down. 'For you will see,' they said, 'how powerful faith is, when you have seen it destroyed by us. We have killed by our own hands many dragons and snakes, including horned ones. For so it is written: "The Saviour gives to those that believe in him the power to trample underfoot snakes and scorpions and the entire strength of the enemy [cf. Luke 10.19 = **125**]."' But when they said this, we just became more and more afraid, because of our weakness and our lack of faith, and we begged them not to choose to track down the dragon [*draco*], but rather to let us continue on the proper path. However, one of them in his keenness quickly tracked the dragon down. When, after a short while, he had found its cave, he called us to go to him and see how the matter ended. But one of the brothers, who lived in that part of the desert, came up to us and stopped us from going after the dragon. He said that we would not be able to bear the sight of it, especially as we were not used to seeing anything of that sort. He said that he himself had often seen that creature of unbelievable size, and that it was fifteen cubits long. After prevailing upon us not to approach the place, he hurried off and drew aside the brother that was waiting for us as he stood ready to kill the beast. He urged him to come back with him and deterred him from his course after much begging, reluctant as he was to leave without destroying it. When he had returned to us, he refused to accept that we were cowardly and faithless.

We came to his cell, where he received us very hospitably and refreshed us. He explained to us that there had been in the place he lived a holy man by the name of Ammon, whose disciple he himself was. The Lord had brought about a great many miracles through him. Amongst other things, he told us the following stories about him.

He said that thieves had often come to him to steal his bread, on which alone he fed, together with anything they found him keeping to support his most austere of lifestyles. Although he had often endured this aggravation from them, one day he went out into the desert. He returned from it with two huge dragons [*dracones*] that he commanded to live with him, ordering them to stay at the mouth of his cell and guard its entrance. When the thieves arrived, as ever they did, they saw that there were guards on the threshold, and when they saw that they were dragons, they lost their strength and their minds, were struck dumb and collapsed at once. When the old man realised this, he came out and found them half dead. He came to them, set them on their feet again and told them off, with the words, 'You see now that you are rougher than the beasts, for by God's will they are obedient to me, but you neither fear God nor feel any compunction in disrupting the life of his servants.' Nonetheless, he invited them into his cell, set a table of food before them, and bade them eat. They were cut to the quick and turned away from all their monstrous thoughts. In a short time they became better than many that had begun to serve the Lord before them. For they were so proficient in their penitence that they themselves were soon bringing about the same signs and miracles.

Moreover, at another time, a monstrously huge dragon [*draco*] was ravaging the local area and killing many people. The occupants of the place came to the aforementioned father and asked him to eliminate the beast from the region. In hopes of moving the old man to pity, they also brought with them a shepherd's son. The mere sight of the dragon had terrified him, and he had lost his mind, whilst the mere breath of the beast had rendered him weak and swollen so that he had to be carried about. Then Ammon anointed him with oil and restored him to health. Urging himself on to kill the dragon the while, he refused to make any promise about it to the people, and gave the impression that he could not help them in any way. But at long last he arose and went off to the beast's lair, planted his knees on the ground and prayed to the Lord. Then the beast began to attack him at great speed, with the foulest blasts of breath, hissing and screeching. He feared none of these things, but turned to the dragon and said, 'May Christ the

Son of God kill you, he who killed the great sea monster [*cetus*: Isaiah 27.1 = **123**].' When the old man had said this, at once that most dreadful dragon burst in the middle with loud report, belching forth all its venom together with its life. When those that dwelled nearby gathered and were dumbfounded by the amazing deed, they could not bear the strength of its stench. So they heaped huge mounds of sand up over it, with Father Ammon still standing by, however, because they did not have the courage to approach the beast without him being there, even though it was dead.

Ammon was a historical figure of the late fourth century AD. After a hermit's life he was consecrated a bishop by Athanasius. There is much of interest here. The culminating dragon fight coordinates, as do several of the Christian (and post-Christian) narratives, the motifs of the revivification of a youth attacked by the dragon with the destruction of the dragon itself (**M15.d.i**). It is rare for a Christian saint to use a tangible healing agent in restoring people from the effects of dragons, as Ammon does here when he applies an ointment to the boy. Ammon kills the dragon by bursting it open, as do SS. Thomas (**131**) and Marina (**149**). In this narrative we have a hint of a rare variety of parallelism in weaponry: for the dragon has itself caused the youth to swell up first. Much attention is given to the pestilential stench of the dragon's breath (**M7.a.ii**) and then of its carcass (cf. **146**; **M7.a.vi**). The method adopted by the locals of dealing with the stench of the carcass, heaping sand over it, is unique within extant accounts of classical and early Christian dragon slayings, but it encourages us to believe that the notion of the massive, pestilential and all but intractable dragon carcass originated in the actual phenomenon of beached whales, in many cases of which this may have been the only practical method available for dealing with the stench.

The rather curious and frustrating preliminary episode at least serves to build up the terribleness of the dragons we will encounter in the stories of Ammon. It is interesting for the way in which it represents dragon slaying as little more than an exciting pastime for keen young Christians: a reflection, no doubt, of the extent to which the motif of dragon slaying had by this point already become hackneyed in the saintly literature. And once again the dragon lives in a cave (**M.3.a.ii**). In both these tales of dragon slaying, the actual and the aborted, the protagonists explicitly contextualise their work against biblical precedent. This episode is recycled, with a more predictable ending, in **154**.

The tale of the thieves shows that saintly dragon slayers, like their classical forebears, can also master and tame the creatures when they need to. We find a pair of dragons associated with a hermit cell also in the case of Caluppan (**150**), though the context is a very different one.

## 146 St Donatus slays the Dragon of Epirus by spitting into its mouth

440s AD

Sozomen *Ecclesiastical History* 7.26.1–4

Greek

At his time [that of the emperor Gratian, r. 375–83 AD] many bishops all round the known world achieved distinction, as did Donatus, the bishop of Euroea in Epirus. The natives of Epirus bear witness to the many miracles he performed, and the greatest were those in connection with his slaying of the dragon [*drakōn*] that had its lair beside the main road at Chamaegephyrae. It used to snatch sheep, goats, horses, oxen and humans. Donatus went against the beast without sword, spear or any other weapon. But when it noticed him and raised its head to attack him, he made the sign of the cross in the air before its face and spat at it. The beast received the saliva into its mouth and immediately collapsed. As it lay there dead it became apparent that it was at least as large as the snakes said to be associated with the Indians. And indeed, as I was told, the natives dragged it off to the nearby plain with eight yoke-pair of oxen and burned it, so that it would not befoul the air when it rotted and render it pestilential.

Once again we find symmetry in the fight between man and dragon: Donatus sanctifies the air with the sign of the cross as he goes into battle with it, whilst the dragon's carcass threatens to render the air foul as it rots. And there is more. At one level Donatus might be thought to be extinguishing the dragon's fire, and thereby its essence, by spitting into its mouth. But the classical tradition (of which Sozomen is keenly aware at this point, with his reference to the snakes of India) knew that human saliva was scalding to snakes and therefore acted upon them just as their own venom did on humans: Pliny *Natural History* 7.14–15, Lucan 6. 488–91: cf. **C8**. For the snakes of India see Pliny *Natural History* 37.158, Philostratus *Apollonius* 3.8. The Donatus tale is told in briefer compass at Isidore of Seville *Chronicle* 107 (*PL* 83, 1017–58 at 1051; *MGH Auctores Antiquissimi* xi.2, 391–489 at 470, c. 600 AD), where it is located within the thirteen years shared by the emperors Arcadius and Honorius, i.e. 393–408 AD. For Donatus's dragon see also **161** (com.).

## 147 St Victoria banishes the Dragon of Tribulanum in Italy to the wilderness (1)

ca. 500 AD

*The Passion of St Victoria* 5–7, pp. 158–9 Delehaye

Latin

**5.** . . . There prevailed in the town of Tribulanum a most evil dragon [*draco*], at the blast of which many men and cattle were dying. A great and unbearable grief was coming about, with the result that all were abandoning their town.

**6.** Now it so happened that Domicianus, who was master of the town, similarly came, out of pity, to the place of St Victoria's exile. He arrived and began to offer her fine loaves and wine. St Victoria said to him, 'I give thanks to our Lord Jesus Christ, who feeds me every day. But tell me why you have come in such a state of anxiety.' Domicianus responded and said, 'I have fled my town, and I have been staying near the town in my little cottage, because I could not escape the blasts of the dragon. I said in my heart that, if I stayed on the other side of the mountain, I would escape the harmful blasts of the dragon.' St Victoria said to him, 'If you were to abandon your idols and worship Christ, this dragon would flee at once from you, and you would be freed from oppression.' Domicianus said to her, 'No one is greater or more honoured than I am in the city of Tribulanum. If you expel the dragon from there, I will make all its citizens become Christians.' Then St Victoria said to him, 'After tomorrow I will come there at the cock's crow and in the name of our Lord Jesus Christ I will make it flee from your borders.' Then Domicianus went to the city of Tribulanum and told his citizens everything that St Victoria had said to him. On hearing this, all that had fled from the city came to await the arrival of St Victoria.

**7.** Now on that Friday after making her promise St Victoria fasted, and so too on the following Saturday, and as Sunday dawned she proceeded to pray. No sooner had she begun to pray and make petition than the angel of the Lord that had appeared to her came to accompany her and began to lead the way, saying to her, 'None of these people can see that I am with you. Be reassured therefore that although I do not show myself to them, I will not abandon you, and I will ensure that your commands to the dragon are fulfilled.' Comforted by the angel, St Victoria entered the city after the cock's crow. Domicianus ran to meet her with all the citizens, and the people followed as she entered. As she arrived at the dragon's cave, St Victoria shouted out in a clear voice and said, 'In the name of our Lord Jesus Christ, depart from this place, most villainous dragon, and give honour to the living and true God, and to Jesus Christ, his son, and go where neither men nor flocks live, and where there is nothing of interest to men, where neither the ploughman ploughs nor the voice of man is heard.' Then the dragon, with the speediest of courses, departed in flight, in such a fashion that you would think it was being thrashed with whips. But neither its smell nor any trace of it could be detected any more. Then they praised St Victoria, saying, 'She is a goddess.' But she entered the dragon's cave and, calling the people together, said, 'Hear me, and build here a place of prayer and give me virgin girls to help me.' Girls were found of nine years of age and above, whom their parents brought to her at their request, with the result that within a short time more than sixty were in conversation with her. She instructed them in hymns and psalms and canticles, working constantly with them ...

We come now to the first of our female Christian dragon fighters; she may be a wholly fictional creation. Perhaps in recognition of her femininity, she is not asked actually to kill her dragon, even in the hands-off fashion typical of her male Christian counterparts. Once again the dragon's pestilential breath is central to the tale (**M7.a.ii**). Here the relationship between the persistence of pagan belief and the corrupt atmosphere produced by the dragon is made explicit. Victoria is fortified in her battle against her dragon by the manifestation of an angel, much as Silvester had been fortified in his by the manifestation of St Peter (**136**). Like most of the Christian dragons, this one has its cave (**M3.a.ii**). For the saint's redeployment of the vacated cave as a place of worship after the dragon has been dealt with, cf. **156**.

## 148 St Victoria banishes the Dragon of Tribulanum to the wilderness (2): a later account

vii AD

Aldhelm *De virginitate* (prose version) at Ehwald 1919:308–9

Latin

And so the blessed Victoria, her name truly presaging the victory of Christ, was brought into territory of Tribula, so that, in exile there, she might be tortured by an abundance of hunger and a lack of food. It happened at that time that all the citizens who had lived in the city of Tribula were scorning the town, scattering in all directions, roaming this way and that, because they could not endure the venom and the blasts of a scaly dragon [*draco*]. Victoria freely promised these people that, if they would abandon their wretched little idols of gods, renounce the Lupercalia festivals of their temples and be converted to God, she would drive the venomous exhalations of the foaming basilisk far away and restore the city to a safe existence. For because of the venomous blasts of the terrible snake, the unfortunate people were being destroyed in multitudes, with huge loss of life; parents, with the natural order of things turned upside down, were having to witness the all-too-early funerals of their children and were bitterly overwhelmed by tearful lamentations for their bereavement. The mayor of the city made a promise on behalf of all the people that they would change their nature from one of promiscuous sex, lay open their hearts and believe in the girl's prophecies if the murderously cruel snake, which was bringing doom-laden pestilence upon the wretched citizens, could be driven farther off. Then the sainted virgin, supported by an angel, together with the crowds that were converging from the populous city on the spectacle in groups, was escorted to the dragon's cave as the chickens were beating their wings and the cockerel was crowing. Wavering in no way before the fearful actions she was undertaking, neither trembling nor pallid with fear, she addressed the beast as it lay hidden, with the words, 'In the name of Jesus Christ our Lord, go out from here, most villainous dragon, and give honour to God! Go to a place of the sort uninhabited by men!' The dragon obeyed the words and, fleeing with the swiftest of courses, departed. But she entered the lair of the beast and asked the people, now delivered from danger, to build a chapel for her in that same crypt and to entrust little girls to her care. They obeyed her command, and seventy little virgins were devoted to her service. They hymned in pleasant harmony and sweetly sang the harmonies of the psalms, adhering to the examples and advice given by Victoria.

A retelling of the same tale, in some respects more elaborate, with an emphasis upon the promiscuity and subsequent chastity of the townspeople appropriate to Aldhelm's broader subject. The Lupercalia, cited rather naughtily as the type rite of Roman paganism, was an anomalously wild and bizarre festival in which naked men ran amok whipping people (Plutarch *Caesar* 61). The tale of Victoria's dragon is treated in broadly similar fashion in the poetic version of Aldhelm's *De virginitate* (lines 2385–2415, at Ehwald 1919:450–1).

## 149   St Andrew slays the Dragon of Thessalonica

late vi AD

Gregory of Tours *Life of Andrew* 19

Latin

After this, a certain young man, who had long remained by the apostle Andrew's side, told his mother what had been done and summoned her to come and meet the saint. On arrival she fell at the apostle's feet and asked to hear the word of the Lord. This granted, she asked him, with much begging, to come to her farm, where there was a serpent [*serpens*] of amazing size which was laying waste to the whole area. As the apostle approached, it made a loud hiss and charged at him in rampant mode. It was fifty cubits long, and so all present were panic-stricken and threw themselves on the ground. Then the saint of God said to it, 'Killer, put away the head that you raised in the beginning to the destruction of the human race, submit to the servants of God and die.' At once the serpent let out a deep roar, coiled around a large oak which was nearby and, winding itself around it and vomiting out a stream of venom, died. But the sainted apostle then came to an estate on which a small boy whom the serpent had bitten lay dead. Seeing his parents weeping, he said, 'Our Lord, who wants you to be saved, sent me here, so that you might believe in him. But now, go off and see the killer of your son.' And they said, 'We do not grieve over the death of our son, if we see vengeance upon the enemy.' As they left, the apostle said to the proconsul's wife [a character not introduced in the narrative before this point], 'Go and rouse the boy.' Without hesitation she went to the body and said, 'In the name of my God, Jesus Christ, rouse yourself, boy, unharmed.' And at once he got up. His parents returned and, after seeing both the serpent dead and their son alive, they threw themselves down before the apostle and gave thanks to God.

The *Life of Andrew*, by Gregory, Bishop of Tours, is thought to reflect well an apocryphal life of the saint originating in the third century AD. While we cannot be fully sure that this dragon-slaying episode was to be found in the original version, its yoking of the motif of dragon slaying with that of the revivification of the youth who was its latest victim chimes well with Lucian's late second-century tale of the Chaldaean snake blaster (**130**) and with the early third-century tale of Thomas's dragon slaying (**131**; cf. **127, 132, 135, 145, 149, 154**). It also shares its farm context with Lucian's tale.

## 150  St Caluppan is accosted by snakes and dragons in his hermit cell in Cantal

581–94 AD

Gregory of Tours *Liber vitae patrum* 11.1, at *MGH Scriptores rerum Merovingicarum* i.2, 259–60

Latin

Caluppan noticed a valley not far from his monastery [of Méallet in Cantal] from the middle of which nature had raised a pinnacle of rock to the height of some fifty feet or more, completely separated from the mountains surrounding it. The centre of the valley was watered by a river that divided itself, gently lapping this pinnacle. So the sainted hermit entered into the cleft of this rock, which in former times had offered shelter to passing strangers, and, excavating the stone, established a home, which even now one can get to only by climbing up a very tricky ascent. Indeed that place was so hard to get up to that it was an effort even for wild beasts to reach it. In this place he somehow made a tiny chapel. When he prayed there, as he used to tell us with tears, snakes [*serpentes*] frequently used to fall down on his head and, wrapping themselves around his neck, inflict not the smallest terror upon him. But because the Devil was known to take the form of a cunning snake, he did not doubt that it was the Devil that was launching these attacks upon him. He used to stand absolutely still and would not move in response to any of the strikes of the snakes. But one day two snakes of immense size entered the chapel to confront him, initially holding back. One of these, the instigator of all temptation himself, as I think, was stronger than the other. It raised its breast and lifted its face up against the saint's as if it were about to whisper something to him. Caluppan was absolutely terrified and froze, just as if he were cast from bronze. He could not even move a limb, nor could he lift his hand in order to make the sign of the blessed cross against his opponent. When saint and snake had stood there in silence for a considerable time, it occurred to him pray to the lord in his spirit and to shout out to him with his heart, even if he could not move his lips. As he silently spoke, his limbs, which had been bound by the craft of the foe, gradually began to be loosened. Sensing that he now had his right hand free, he made the sign of the blessed cross before his own face, and then, turning to the snake, he drew the sign of the cross of Christ again, against it, saying: 'Are you not the one who cast forth the first-made man from his home in Paradise? Who bloodied the right hand of a brother with family-murder, who armed Pharaoh so that he could attack the people of God? Who ultimately incited the Hebrew people to attack the Lord, inflamed with envy? Depart from the servants of God, from whom you have often departed overcome and confounded. For you were cast forth in the form of Cain, tripped in the form of Esau, thrown to the ground in the form of Goliath and hanged in the form of the traitor Judas. And you were triumphed over and ground down, together with all your powers and empires, in that very cross of the Lord's virtue. Enemy of god, hide your head and abase yourself before the sign of the divine cross, because you have nothing to do with servants of God, whose inheritance is the kingdom of Christ.' As the saint said these and similar things, making the sign of the cross with each assertion, the dragon [*draco*] was confounded by the virtuous power of this sign and in response abased itself and sank to the earth. And while this was happening, that other dragon began to wind itself around the feet and shins of the saint to trap him. And when the saintly hermit saw this snake pouring itself around his feet he made a prayer and ordered it to go away, saying: 'Go back, Satan! You could do me no further harm, in the name of my Christ.' But the snake, after retreating as far as the threshold of the little chamber, emitted a loud noise through its lower part and filled the room up with such a stench that it could be believed to be nothing other than the Devil. But thenceforth neither snake nor dragon manifested itself before the Saint.

Here Gregory of Tours speaks of a saint closer to his own time and place. We find a number of familiar themes here: both of the two focal *dracones* are fully identified with the Devil, as is often the case (**M15.b.i**); and the saint protects himself from the serpent by making the sign of the cross (**M11.b.v**). For the monastic cell swarming with snakes, cf. **153**, and cf. also **145**, albeit the context is far different. But the glory of this text is its scatological treatment of the motif of the dragon's production of bad air (**M7.a**): it is difficult to believe that humour is not intended. For another scatologically diverting hagiographical monster, see the Onachus described at **161** (com.).

## 151   St Marcellus of Paris banishes a tomb-dwelling dragon

late vi AD

Venantius Fortunatus
*Vita S. Marcelli Pariensis episcopi* 10, at *MGH* Auctores antiquissimi iv.2, 53–4

Latin

Let us narrate too that glorious divine achievement of his that, for all it may be last in order, we place first in virtue. There was a certain matron of high family but low repute, who stained her shining stock with base sin. After the light was taken away and she brought the days of her fleeting life to an end, she was carried out to her tomb with an accompanying (though profitless) procession. What happened after she had been laid in this tomb, and after her funeral rites, I shudder to relate, because it gives rise to a double grief over the dead woman. Anyway, a most enormous serpent [*serpens*] began to visit in order to devour her body, and, to speak more plainly, the dragon [*draco*] itself became the burial place of the woman whose limbs the beast was devouring. The serpentine pallbearer appropriated her luckless obsequies in such a way that her corpse was not permitted to lie quiet. Although the ending of her life had permitted her to lie in one place, she was ever being transported around in punishment. What an accursed fate, truly to be dreaded! A woman who had not maintained her integrity towards her husband when in the world did not deserve to retain the integrity of her body in the tomb. For the snake, which had drawn the woman into sin when she lived, continued its cruelty against her corpse. Then the members of her family that remained in the city heard a loud noise, ran together and saw the huge beast coiling its way out of the tomb and gliding along with its vast bulk and its tail whipping. The people were utterly terrified by this and moved out of their homes. On learning this, the blessed Marcellus, knowing how to triumph over the foe, walked forth from the city, the people thronging around him. Then, leaving them at a distance, whilst remaining in their plain sight, he came to where it was his purpose to fight, with Christ as his guide. And when the snake returned to the tomb from the wood, coiling about to meet itself by turns, Marcellus uttered a prayer. The snake began to beg for forgiveness with its head inclined in supplication and its tail making blandishing gestures. Then the blessed Marcellus struck its head three times with his crosier, put his handkerchief on the serpent's neck, and dragged the object of his victory out before the eyes of the citizens. Thus before the gaze of this audience of the theatre of the spirit he fought alone against the dragon. Thence the people, reassured, ran up to the bishop, eager to see his captive enemy. With the priest leading a host of around three thousand, all followed him, giving thanks to the Lord and performing funeral obsequies for the foe [*sc.* in so far as the procession resembled that of a funeral]. Then the blessed Marcellus chided the snake and said, 'From this day forth either go and live in the desert, or plunge yourself into the sea.' With the beast immediately dispatched, no trace of it was ever found again. Lo, to think that the protection of the land depended upon a single priest, who overcame the foe with his insubstantial crosier more bravely than if ballista darts had been fired, for the wounded creature could have struck back at him if the divine principle had not vanquished it. O most saintly man, through whose light crosier the weight of virtue was shown, whose gentle fingers formed the serpent's chain! Thus the weapons of an individual prevailed over a public enemy, and a victory for all was celebrated over the prey taken by a single man. If one were to compare the deserving achievements of saintly men on the basis of their deeds, Gaul would hold Marcellus in admiration, just as Rome does Silvester. The only difference in their achievements is that the latter put a seal on his dragon, whereas the former drove his hither and thither. But who would have the strength to enumerate his miracles one by one in speech, or to bring forth in voice all the things he did without public knowledge, when the brilliant things he achieved before witnesses have already been recorded? For Marcellus, most saintly by virtue of these deeds, ever attentive, brilliant in conversation, outstanding in his achievements, glorious in his blessedness, rich in reward, destined to reign for eternity alongside the Lord, overcoming the uncleanness of the world, in his cleanliness passed over to Christ on the calends of November, in the reign of our Lord Jesus Christ, whose is the honour and the glory, the virtue and the power, throughout all ages of ages. Amen.

Despite Venantius Fortunatus's description of the dragon's arrival in the woman's tomb and its purpose in coming, the notion of a tomb-dwelling serpent seems to hark back to pagan beliefs, and one cannot help suspecting that it should be read at some level as an embodiment of the dead woman and therefore, in Christian terms, an expression of her wickedness: cf. **133**. We may compare *Beowulf*'s Firedrake, the dragon that takes up residence in the tomb of a wealthy man buried with his treasure and cherishes it as its own (**B2**). The motif of the saint tying a garment around the tamed dragon's neck to lead it along like a subservient dog harks back as far as Beliar (**126**) and was to become a popular one (**M15.d.iii**). The dispatching of the dragon to either the wilderness or the sea is, as we have seen, an exorcistic motif that identifies the dragon with a possessing demon (**M15.b.iii**), an identification that seems particularly appropriate in this case given that the dragon is also projected as the dead woman's former tempter. My translation does not agree in the interpretation of all details with the (partial) English translation (by Goldhammer) of this passage at le Goff 1980.

## 152 St Hilary of Poitiers confines the snakes of Gallinaria to a certain part of the island

late vi AD

Venantius Fortunatus *Vita S. Hilarii* [*Pictavensis*] 35–8, at *MGH* Auctores antiquissimi iv.2, 5

Latin

It would not be right for us to pass over this distinguished miracle. When he was in the region of the island of Gallinaria [off the Italian coast, near Andora], he learned from the locals that it was infested with unnumbered and enormous coiling snakes [*serpentes*]. Because of this, even though they could see the island nearby, they considered it remoter than Africa because of its inaccessibility. When he heard this, the man of God saw that victory was coming to him in a fight against the beasts. He disembarked onto the island invoking God's name and with the succour of the cross before him. Upon seeing him the snakes were turned to flight, because they were unable to tolerate the sight of him. Then he fixed his staff into the ground to serve as a boundary marker by which he designated, by the power of his virtue, the point up to which they were to be permitted to roam. They were no longer allowed to occupy the part he forbade. The island had a sea inlet. Since they ever feared to touch the forbidden part, it was easier for them to cross over the sea than to cross the place at which the saint had spoken: such was the immovable boundary fixed in place by his speech.

It is difficult to see exactly what point Venantius is trying to make in his discussion of the sea inlet: one wonders why, if the snakes could indeed swim over the sea, difficult as it no doubt was, they could not thereby bypass Hilary's boundary point. But at any rate, the ground is prepared for the subsequent famous tradition of Patrick's driving of snakes from the island of Ireland (**159**). For Hilary of Poitiers see also **161** (com.).

## 153   St Florentius of Valcastoria destroys a plague of snakes and disposes of the carcasses

593 AD

Gregory the Great
*Dialogues* 3.15.11–12

Latin

GREGORY: That man of God [Florentius] did another thing that should not be kept silent. When his fame had grown great far and wide, a certain deacon of a remote place was keen to come to him to ask him to pray for him. When he arrived at his little cell, he found the whole place all around full of unnumbered snakes. Absolutely terrified, he cried out and said, 'Servant of the Lord, make a prayer!' And then there was a wonderful peace. Florentius came out and directed his gaze and his hands to the sky, to ask God to remove the plague of snakes, as he knew he would. At his speech there was thunder in the sky, and this thunder [sc. a thunderbolt?] killed all those snakes that had occupied that same place. When Florentius, the man of God, saw the snakes killed, he said, 'See, Lord, you have killed them. Who is to remove them from here?' In immediate response to his speech there came as many birds as snakes had been killed. They each took one away and cast them forth afar, and rendered the area of that dwelling completely cleansed of snakes.

The historical Florentius had been abbot of Valcastoria some half a century before Gregory wrote. For the monastic cell swarming all around with snakes, cf. Caluppan's plight (**150**). For the direction of God's thunderbolts against snakes, cf. the tale of Philip and the desert dragon, **131**, and, more generally, **5–6**, **8–9**. Although there is no mention of the pestilential corruption of the air caused by snake carcasses (**M7.a.vi**), this consideration clearly underpins the tale's delightful final episode, with Florentius finding a novel solution to the age-old problem.

### FURTHER READING

Hilarion: Kelly 1975, Leclerc et al. 2007.
Ammon: Festugière 1961, 1964, 4.1.
Victoria: Mayr-Harting 1972 (for Aldhelm).
Andrew: Prieur 1989, Bremmer 2000.
Caluppan: Godding 2000.
Marcellus of Paris: Le Goff 1980:155–88.
Hilary of Poitiers: Brennan 1985 (for Venantius Fortunatus).
Florentius: Peterson 1984 (for Gregory).

# 25
## Saintly Tales of the Central Medieval Period

No attempt is made to give expansive coverage of the Christian dragon-slaying tradition beyond the sixth century AD, but the opportunity is taken here to supply a few interesting narratives recorded in the centuries prior to the emergence of the dragon and snake tales of SS. George and Patrick, to whom the final chapter is devoted. Once again, a mixture of familiar commonplaces and interesting invention will be found.

Figure 25 Jost Amman (1539–91 AD, attributed): St. Margaret of Antioch. Polyptych, Galleria e Museo Estense, Modena. The Bridgeman Art Library.

## 154  St Samson of Dol masters a series of dragons in southern Britain and northern France

vii–viii AD

*Vita i S. Samsonis, episcopi Dolensis* 1.50, 58–60

Latin

**1.50.** [The action takes place at Tricurius (Trigg, in Cornwall).] Then the count [Vediolanus] wisely had them all come to St Samson to have their baptisms confirmed. He came with them, praising God and saying, 'Behold the angel of God sent down from heaven. He has come to deliver us from our sin. But, Saint, we still have a great worry.' St Samson said, 'What is it?' The count replied, 'We have an outstanding region occupied by a venomous and most evil serpent [*serpens*]. This serpent lives in an impenetrable cave and ravages almost two whole districts, preventing anyone from living there.' On learning this St Samson, fearless, said, 'In the name of God let us go without hesitation. If you truly believe, you will see the great deeds of God with your own eyes in connection with this serpent.' So without hesitation and with common purpose they went off with St Samson. The young man who had recently been revived followed him, professing that he would join the clergy. And so St Samson proceeded at the head of the head of the army, and the recently revived boy served as his guide until, at dawn on the following day, they saw with their own eyes the terrible cave where the serpent lived. Then the boy said, 'Elect of God, do you see the cave across the river in which the serpent lives?' Trusting in the Lord, Samson ordered the army and his monks to remain there and then on his own, or rather in the company of God, crossed the river. His boy followed him and together they came to the mouth of the terrible cave. St Samson looked at the boy that followed him and said with a smile, 'Be brave, boy, and act like a man.' The boy said, 'Whom shall I fear, elect of God? God is with you.' Samson ordered him to stand a little way off and boldly entered the cave. When the serpent saw him, it shook violently and furiously strove to turn about to gnaw its tail. But he swiftly took the linen belt he was wearing and, with equal speed, put it on the serpent's neck. He then dragged the serpent along with him and threw it down from a great height, commanding it in the name of Jesus Christ to live no more. On seeing this, the boy quickly ran back to the count and the army and reported everything he had witnessed, blow by blow. On hearing, they immediately came to the saint in relief, to bestow apostolic honours upon him. He refused to receive any significant honour from them, but in order to glorify and publicise the miracle he ordered his monks to found a monastery near the cave. He himself lived a heavenly life in the cave for a while, applying himself to fasting and prayer.

**1.58.** [The scene has now moved to Brittany.] Then the king [Childebert], wishing to please St Samson in all things and bestowing apostolic honours upon him, promised to do right by the Judwal mentioned above and humbly said, 'Elect of God, we have a great worry. For we have an evil serpent destroying and laying waste to much of our land. We have heard that you have already been victorious in a case similar to this and so we would like you, if it would cause you no harm, to drive this one away from us.' St Samson said without hesitation, 'Give me someone who knows the path and believes in God and I will go and cast the dragon out by the power of God.' Then a believer who knew the path put himself forward to accompany him. He left his companions behind in the palace with the aforementioned Judwal and accomplished the journey just with two of his elect, and in the company of Christ. It came about that at last they came to the dreadful cave in which the serpent lived. Recognising this, St Samson said to his men, 'Stand firm and wait for me here, until I return to you.' Whilst they awaited him, he went out to the entrance of the dreadful cave, with God as his companion, naturally. There he performed an overnight vigil, fasting and praying, and at last he called the serpent to him in the name of Jesus Christ. When the serpent came, quivering, St Samson took his cloak and put it on the serpent's neck. Dragging it with him, and singing the customary psalm we have already mentioned [*sc.* Psalm 135], he commanded it to go beyond a river called the Sigona [the Seine] and ordered it to remain beneath a certain rock.

**1.59.** And so he went back with his companions and returned to the palace. His companions reported to the king and all their own people everything they had seen in connection with the serpent. Then all were seized by a great, constraining fear, with the result that no one dared to oppose him any more even in the smallest matter. St Samson wished to return to Brittany with Judwal, and the king readily consented. With the king's assistance he ordered the construction of a magnificent monastery in the place from which he had ejected the serpent. At the king's behest he detailed brothers to undertake the work there....

**1.60.** One day when he was in his home in France [*sc.* in his monastery at St-Samson-sur-Risle] he heard a dreadful report of a serpent that was doing no less harm that the earlier ones. Stricken in conscience, he journeyed to it and, dragging that one along too, threw it into the sea, commanding it to die in the name of Jesus, lest it do any more harm.

The narratives of Samson's three dragon battles are highly repetitive between themselves and deploy many familiar motifs: the dragon's cave home (twice) (**M3.a.ii**), the summoning of the dragon from its cave whilst companions wait at a distance (cf. **145**), the yoking of the rampant dragon's neck with an item of the saint's clothing (three times) (**M15.d.iii**), the associated conversion of the locals (**M15.a.iii**), the sealing of the dragon beneath the earth (**M3.a.iv**) and the construction of a monastery in the cave vacated by the dragon (**M15.d.v**). Comparison of the Trigg and Samson-sur-Risle episodes with the intervening Brittany one suggests that the author saw little difference between the killing of a dragon and the sealing of it beneath the earth.

Prior to the action described in 1.50, the boy guide that leads Samson to the dragon's cave had been dead for two hours; the saint restored him to life (1.49). He had not been killed by the dragon, but even so, we sense that the combination motif—the revivification of a boy victim plus the slaying of a dragon—familiar from many other Christian narratives (**M15.d.i**) lurks in the archaeology of this narrative.

In the ninth-century AD *Vita ii S. Samsonis*, Samson acquires a similarly repetitive series of dragon fights, now no fewer than four (*Vita ii S. Samsonis*, *Acta Bollandiana* 6, 98–100, 109–11, 128–30, 144–5). The first of these is curiously derivative of the first episode in Rufinus's account of dragons associated with the Egyptian hermit Ammon (**145**): again we have a travelling band including both faithful and pagan, one of the faithful of whom is now actually given the name Ammon; and again a dragon trail is found resembling that of a log dragged over the ground. However, the anomalous ending of Rufinus's episode, in which the dragon fight is aborted, is avoided, and Samson does indeed proceed to kill it. The other three episodes proceed *pari passu* with those of the earlier *Vita i* quoted here, albeit with a certain amount of kaleidoscoping of motifs and with a new emphasis on the general fieriness and smokiness of the dragons.

## 155 St Narcissus of Gerundum redeems the soul of Afra from a demon by tricking him into taking that of a local dragon instead

ca. 770 AD

*Conversio et passio ii S. Afrae,* MGH Scriptores rerum Merovingicarum iii, 60, §7

Latin

[The action takes place in Augusta (Augsburg, Germany) during the Persecution of Diocletian (303–11 AD). Bishop Narcissus of Gerundum (Girona, Spain) has redeemed the soul of the courtesan Afra from a demon who manifests himself in the form of an Egyptian, 'blacker than a crow, naked, his body covered with the scars of elephantiasis,' by promising to render another soul to him in her place on the following day.]

At daybreak the demon came and said, 'Remember, bishop, the oath that you uttered before God, and give me a soul, whose body I can kill, and keep the soul with me.' Replying to the demon, St Narcissus the bishop said, 'You too swear in the name of my God, that you will kill at once the one I give into your power, and affirm this for me: "If I do not kill the one, may God command me to go into the abyss."' The demon said to him, 'By God himself, who overcame us together with our master, so may he not order me to go into the abyss, because I will immediately kill the one you give into my power.' And Bishop Narcissus said to him: 'Go to the spring of the Julian Alps, from which no one can drink the water, not man, not beast of burden, not any wild animal, because a dragon [*draco*] lives there, and all who approach the spring are killed by its breath. Go and kill this dragon and take its soul into your power.' Then the demon shouted out and said, 'O that lying bishop! And what is more, he has bound me with an oath to kill my friend, and if I do not kill him I will be forced to go into the abyss.' Then the demon consented and killed the dragon, and the spring was liberated for the use of all, right up until the present day.

This tale is particularly interesting for its alignment of the demon and the dragon as friends and professional colleagues; we have seen elsewhere the tendency to assimilate dragons to demons, an assimilation that accommodates their banishment by exorcistic techniques (**M15.b.iii**). Some familiar themes recur: the dragon guards a water source (**M4.a.i**), and its breath is pestilential (**M7.a.ii**).

## 156 St Clement of Metz destroys a plague of pestilential snakes infesting that city's amphitheatre and banishes the dragon that presides over them

782–6 AD

Paul the Deacon (Paulus Diaconus, Paulus Warnefridus), *Gesta episcoporum Mettensium* at *PL* xcv, 711–13

Latin

When the blessed Clement had arrived at the city of Metz, he made his home, as they say, in the vaults of the amphitheatre which was sited outside the city. He also built a chapel to the Lord in this place and set up an altar in it in the name of the blessed apostle Peter, his master. So the venerable priest preached industriously to the peoples of the city, and the pity of God helped him in this. He liberated the greatest multitude of them from the unclean cults of idols and from the blindness of sin and brought them to the splendour of the true faith, and he achieved distinction as the first man to show the way to justice and truth in these parts. Now those who know this region tell that up until this present day no serpent [*serpens*] can abide the amphitheatre in which he originally made his home upon arrival, and that all venomous beasts shun the place from which the tokens of true salvation once shone forth. For the older sources tell us of a miracle, performed by this most holy bishop and apostle, so great that it is not right that it should be kept quiet, a miracle the tradition of which has been handed down most truthfully from age to age by previous devotees of our holy faith, older yet. At the point in time that the venerable priest came to the aforementioned city, the greatest calamity was destroying the people of the district, for the above-mentioned amphitheatre was filled with such a great multitude of serpents that not only did no one dare to come to this same place, but no one even dared to come near it. But their venomous breaths had given rise to exceptionally cruel deaths, not just of men, but also of horses, oxen, sheep and other animals. Now as the most blessed Clement was approaching the walls of the city itself, this same pestilence spread itself out in such a way that there was no means of going to the city and returning safely from it. For if anyone wished to exit the gates, even under compulsion of the greatest necessity, or indeed to go near them, he would immediately perish in the most wretched way, stricken by the power of the venom. Nor is it surprising if the snake, gliding over its vessels of choice, laid low the bodies of those from whose minds righteousness had as yet least dismissed through the water of the holy baptism...[lacuna]. So after the admirable worshipper of the Holy Trinity began to give his mind over fully to performing the duty of preaching laid upon him, the countless multitude of the sick soon flocked eagerly to where he was when they heard that he was preaching that the true God was the source of succour, and they learned from the mouth of the excellent shepherd how they had deservedly been infected by the serpents' venom. When he saw their manifest wretchedness, he made no delay in applying the most healthful medicine. So he pledged that they would have God's mercy all the more quickly if they did not refuse to abandon the detestable worship of idols. And so not only the sick but also the few who remained well promised on the basis of the healthful advice to renounce all effigies once they were delivered, so long as they were not cheated of their promised benefits by the bishop of God on high. When the man filled with God heard undertakings of this sort, which he had craved for so long, he prepared to submit himself to all dangers on their behalf and gave immediate thanks to the Creator of all. Then with a few brothers gathered around him he made the sacred oblation that the Lord Christ commanded the devotedly faithful to perform in his memory. But once he had fortified himself and his men with the offering, he did not fear to enter the contest with the ancient enemy. Putting his trust in the Lord of Heaven and Earth, he courageously entered the vaults of the amphitheatre to fight the ancient serpent, that is, the Devil. When they heard the sound of his feet approaching, the serpents at once began to come forth from the vaults in their competitive eagerness to devour the man of God. But he made the sign of the cross and rushed to join battle with them. Since they did not have the strength to resist his virtue any further, they immediately laid down their swelling necks. But the man of God, as antiquity relates, immediately took off the scarf he wore on his most holy neck and tied up the largest of the serpents, with all the people watching, and by his own hands led it in bonds to the river Salia [Seille], the stream of which was nearby. There he released the snake and said, 'In the name of the most holy and indivisible Trinity, which I recognise as the true God from the teaching of my most blessed master Peter, the chief of the apostles, I command that you should do no harm to man or beast and that you should at once cross this river together with the whole of your venomous entourage and go into those parts where mankind cannot live.' Scarcely had the sacred priest finished his words when lo! the most monstrous serpent began swiftly to depart with all the others, just as the excellent priest had commanded. And from that day the place has been shown to be so cleansed of the uncleanness of serpents that hardly ever is even the tiniest worm found there, as was noted above.

These events are set in the later first century AD, when St Peter supposedly sent Clement on his mission to Metz. Meagre traces of the amphitheatre in question, now engulfed by the modern city, may still be seen in le Sablon district.

Many commonplaces of the hagiographgical dragon-slaying tradition are to be found here: the destruction of a dragon (and its attendant snakes) is co-ordinated with the elimination of pagan worship (**M15.a.iii**), which is strongly identified with the blight of the snakes' pestilential breath (**M7.a.ii**); the snakes are identified directly with the Devil (**M15.b.i**); the saint fortifies himself with the sign of the cross before going into battle (**M11.b.v**); he is confronted with a host of snakes over which a greater single one presides (**M2.a.ii**); he ties an item of his clothing around the neck of the rampant dragon like a dog's lead (**M15.d.iii**); and rather than being killed, the dragon is exorcistically banished to the wilderness (**M15.b.iii**). For the rendering of earth poisonous to snakes, cf. **100** [with com.], **152**, **159**.

Clement's dragon enjoyed a vigorous afterlife in Metz's local traditions, and from the twelfth century AD its effigy participated in the city's rogation processions. In more recent centuries its effigy has returned to the streets for carnivals. The dragon's name is given in a number of related forms, of which Graoully is now standard; it is first attested in 1546 AD in the form Growelin.

## 157 Baby Jesus tames a group of dragons

viii–ix AD

*Gospel of Ps.-Matthew* 18, p. 81 Tischendorf

Latin

When they had come to a cave and wished to rest in it, the blessed Mary dismounted her mule and sat with the boy Jesus in her lap. Joseph had three boys with him and Mary a girl, all making the same journey. And lo! suddenly a great number of dragons [*dracones*] came out of the cave. Upon seeing them, the children cried out in the extremity of their terror. Jesus climbed down from his mother's lap and stood on his feet before the dragons. They worshipped him and withdrew from them. And then the utterance of the prophet David was fulfilled; he said, 'Dragons of the earth, praise the Lord, dragons and all from the abyss.' Little baby Jesus, walking about in front of them, commanded them to harm no one. But Mary and Joseph were terribly afraid that the little baby might be harmed by the dragons. Jesus said to them, 'Do not be concerned for me on the ground that I am a little baby. For I always have been and I continue to be perfect. All the beasts of the wilderness become tame before me.'

The *Gospel of Ps.-Matthew* is another of the non-canonical gospels. It was seemingly compiled in the eighth or ninth century AD, and was in part derivative of the *Gospel of Thomas* tradition. Indeed it provides its own version of the *Gospel of Thomas* tale given above (**127**) at §41 (p. 103 Tischendorf). The tale given here seems to be have been inspired by the same episode.

## 158 St Marina (Margaret) of Pisidian Antioch is swallowed by the Devil in the form of a dragon but bursts forth from its stomach

ix AD

*Martyrium of St Marina* pp. 24–7 Usener

Greek

[Olybrius, the governor of the East, falls in love with the Christian virgin Marina (Margaret) of (Pisidian) Antioch and declares that he will marry her if she gives up her faith. Upon her refusal, he has her thrown into prison and tortured. She prays to God to let her see her great opponent, the Devil.]

After she had finished her prayer there was in that place [25] a great earthquake, and the prison was shaken. And suddenly there emerged from the corner a great and most terrifying dragon [drakōn], with a skin of all colours. Its crest and beard were like gold. Its teeth flashed with lightning, and its eyes were like pearls. A flame of fire and a great deal of smoke issued from its nostrils. Its tongue was like a sword. Snakes coiled around its neck. The corners of its eyes were like silver. It stood in the middle of the gaol roaring and hissing. It ran around Marina in a circle with its sword-tongue unsheathed, and its hissing made a terrible stench in the gaol. The holy virgin was in great fear. Her limbs gave way, her vision became blurred and she forgot the prayer she had been making. But the Lord acted in accordance with it and showed her the enemy and adversary of all men. Now she knelt and began to pray and say, 'Unseen God, by your face the sea and the abyss are dried up. You are the one that sets boundaries to Hades. You are the one that frees the bonds of the earth, [26] so that it may not shake. You are the one that diminishes the power of the good-hating dragon [drakōn]. You are the one that binds Hades and liberates those shut within it. Now look at me and have pity on me. Do not stand by and see me harmed by an evil demon. Let your wish come to pass, Lord, so that I may conquer this creature's flame, the nature of which I did not know.' As she was saying this the dragon, greatly angered, hissed at her. The holy servant of God made a cross on her forehead and over her whole body and prayed with tears and said, 'Lord, chase this wicked wolf and mad dog and its stench away from me. And let the sweetness and goodness of your Holy Spirit [*literally* 'breath', *pneuma*] come to me.' And when she had said this the dragon raged against her and overwhelmed her. It raised its neck over the square stone [sc. to which prisoners would have been bound]. Its head was hanging down. Its legs reached the ground, running out from that part of its neck upon which the snakes grew, and the mouth of the dragon gaped open. The dragon drew the holy girl to itself, placed its mouth [27] on her neck, sent its tongue down under her feet and in this way hoisted her up like a lifting machine and gobbled her down into its belly. With her hands making the sign of the holy Christ, Christ went before her and ruptured the dragon's guts. And so the dragon fell from the square stone, made a loud noise, split in half and died. The holy girl came out of its belly unharmed. Turning back, she said to it, 'Truly you found what you were looking for.' The dragon remained where it was, fallen on the floor. And suddenly from the other corner of the prison a great demon fell upon the knees of the holy Marina...

[Marina eventually disposes of the demon by pulling out half his beard, knocking his right eye out with it, and then striking him on the forehead with a hammer.]

The *Martyrdom* is the earliest extant account of the fictional St Marina, whose adventures became enormously popular in the central medieval period in both the Latin and Greek churches. Whereas later accounts place Marina in the reign of Diocletian (284–305 AD), this one, which claims to have been written by one Theotimus, the fellow-prisoner who recovered her remains, gives no clear indication of at what point in the imperial period it imagines her to have lived. The narrative is rare amongst Christian ones for making its dragon a multiform: it has additional snake heads coiling around its neck (we think of Hydras and Gorgons) and, even more surprisingly, legs emerging from the same point on its neck. It seems to be visualised as part Gorgon, part *kētos*. Also relatively rare amongst Christian narratives is the explicit reference to the crest and beard the dragon sports (however, cf. **134**). For both the dragon's sword-tongue and its gem-like eyes, cf. **140**. The technique by which the dragon hoists Marina up into its mouth using its tongue is finely described. Particular emphasis is again given both to this dragon's fieriness (in eye and nose) and to the smoky stench it emits (**M6.a**). In the case of the latter the theme of the symmetrical battle is celebrated, with the dragon's evil breath being challenged by the breath of the Holy Spirit. For the arrival of a dragon preceded by an earthquake as it emerges from the earth, cf., again, **134**. As often, the saint defends herself against the dragon (and twice here) by making the sign of the cross (**M11.b.v**). For Marina see also **161** (com.).

## FURTHER READING

Samson: Flobert 1997, Rauer 2000:90–116, 150–9.
Clement of Metz: Chazan 2000, Michaux 2000, Goetz 2000, Wagner 2000.
*Gospel of Pseudo-Matthew*: Elliot 2005:84–99.
Marina: Larson 2002.

# 26
## St Patrick and St George

The tradition of saintly dragon-slaying narratives reviewed in the previous five chapters culminates in the much-loved tales attaching to SS. Patrick and George. So far as the preserved literary record is concerned, these two saints acquire their serpents only in the twelfth century AD, although there are indications that Patrick at any rate may have been associated with his snakes long before this. Nonetheless, the stories attaching to both saints lie conservatively within the tradition of saintly dragon-slaying tales that first took shape a millennium earlier.

Figure 26 Raphael (1483–1520 AD): St. George battles the dragon, ca. 1503–5. Musée du Louvre. Giraudon / The Bridgeman Art Library.

## 159 St Patrick casts the snakes of Ireland into the sea from Croagh Patrick

731–1267 AD

Bede *Ecclesiatical History of the English People* 1.1 (731 AD)

Gerald of Wales *On the Topography of Ireland* 1.28, at Brewer et al. 1861–91: v, 62 (1187 AD)

Jocelin of Furness *Life of St Patrick, Acta Sanctorum*, March ii, p. 574, §148 (ca. 1200–10 AD)

Jacobus de Voragine (Jacques de Varazzo) *Golden Legend* 50 (1263–7 AD)

Latin

**Bede:** One cannot see reptiles in Ireland, and no snake has the capacity to live there. For snakes have often been taken there from Britain, only for them to perish as soon as they come into contact with the smell of its air as the boat comes close to land. Indeed, almost everything that comes from the island is effective against venom. I have seen people that have been bitten by a snake. Then leaves of books originating in Ireland have been scraped and the scrapings put in water and given them to drink. By such a method all the power of the loitering venom has been nullified and the entire swelling of the distended body reduced and assuaged.

**Gerald of Wales:** But some people suppose, in a rather popular myth, that St Patrick and other saints of the land purged the island of harmful creatures.

**Jocelin of Furness:** The most outstanding pastor raised his staff with the hand of the Lord Jesus, and by raising it in a threatening fashion he assembled in one place all the venomous creatures from every part of Ireland, with the help of an angel, and then he compelled them all to flee onto the highest promontory (which at that point was called Croagh, but is now called Croagh Patrick [in County Mayo]). And there he cast down the whole pestilential host from the sheer precipice of the mountain. At his command they slid from the edge and were swallowed up by the ocean.

**Jacobus de Voragine:** And he brought it about that no venomous animal could live in the whole of the land of the Scots [i.e. Ireland].

These brief texts describe between them the establishment of the famous myth of St Patrick's expulsion of snakes from Ireland. As early as 731 AD Bede knew that the country of Ireland was repulsive to snakes. Although he says nothing of how the land came to be this way, it is difficult to imagine that he did not ascribe it to the action of a saint, especially in view of the well-established tradition of serpent expulsion in hagiography (see especially **153**). Whether the saint in question would have been Patrick is less clear. By 1187 AD Gerald of Wales was to imply that Patrick had the chief credit for dismissing the snakes but was not the only one with a claim. In Jocelin of Furness's *Life of St Patrick*, ca. 1200–10 AD, we finally find an explicit narrative of Patrick's feat. If Jacobus de Voragine (for whom see **161**) then referred only glancingly to the feat in his *Golden Legend* of 1263–7 AD, he nonetheless by doing so guaranteed it widespread fame across Europe.

The notion that a land's, usually an island's, earth should be hostile to snakes and curative of their bites (a phenomenon now known to folklorists as 'Irish earth') was already well established in the ancient world. Pliny associates it with Ebusus (Ibiza), Galata and Sicily (*Natural History* 3.78. 5.27, 37.54; cf. Pomponius Mela 2.7), Aelian with Crete and Astypalaea (*Nature of Animals* 5.2, 5.8) and others with Lemnos in particular (Dioscorides 5.113, Galen *De simplicium medicamentorum temperamentis ac facultatibus* xii.169 Kühn, Philostratus *Heroicus* 6.2).

We may note that Old Irish tradition had its own dragon fights, although the influence of hagiography upon these cannot be completely ruled out. See, for example, the originally seventh- or eighth-century AD saga of Fergus mac Léti's killing of the *muirdris* (C5).

## 160  St George slays the Dragon of Lasia: the earliest extant account of his deed

xii AD

*Miracula Sancti Georgii, Codex Romanus Angelicus* 46, §12

Greek

*Miracle of George the great martyr in connection with the dragon* [drakōn]. *Lord, bless it!* Turning, amongst miracles, to that of George, the great martyr and miracle worker, let us give glory to God, who exalted him and displayed the nature of his grace through the all-glorious martyr George. Has anyone through the ages ever yet heard of or seen a miracle of the sort performed by the all-blessed George?

In these times there was a city named Lasia, and it was ruled by a king named Selbius. He was a wicked idolater, lawless, impious and without pity or compassion for the believers in Christ. The Lord gave his people requital for their deeds. Near the city there was a lake with plentiful water. In that water was born a wicked dragon, and every day it would come out and eat them. Often the king would assemble all his armies and go out and do battle against the beast, but it would churn the waters up into turmoil so that they could not even get anywhere near the place. Since it was eating them, they were wickedly oppressed.

The people of the city came together and cried out to the king, 'See, king, our city is a fine and beautiful one to live in, but we are being destroyed in wicked fashion.'

The king said, 'A lot is to be given to each of you, and you must all register a name on it. I have an only daughter, a young girl, and I will put her name on my lot, just as you will name your own children on yours. And by this means let us not be wiped out of our own city.'

The speech pleased all, and they all began to provide their own children, day by day, until the king's lot came up. The king clothed his daughter in purple and linen and decked her out in gold, precious stones and pearls. Embracing her longingly, he kissed her and, lamenting tearfully over her as if she were already dead, said, 'Off you go, my sweetest, only child, light of my eyes. Upon whom, my sweetest child, shall I look hereafter to take even the tiniest cheer? When shall I arrange your marriage? When shall I see your bridal chamber? When shall I light the wedding torches for you? When shall I sing the wedding song for you? When shall I see the fruit of your belly? Alas, my sweetest child, go off to the place where you must die alone and without me.'

Then the king said to the people, 'Take gold, silver and my kingdom, and let my daughter off.' But no one would concede this to him because of the decree that the king himself had issued. So the king gnashed his teeth bitterly and sent the girl to the lake. The whole of the city, the great and the small alike, flocked together to watch her.

God, who loves mankind and knows pity, and who does not want sinners to die but rather to turn to him and live, wanted to bring about a sign by means of George, the all-glorious great martyr. This was the age of St George. He had the rank of count. It happened that his army had been lost, and he was travelling back to his fatherland, the land of Cappadocia. By God's design the saint arrived in that place and took his horse into the lake so that it could drink. He saw the girl sitting there, wetting her knees with tears, glancing about this way and that and wailing.

St George said to her, 'Lady, why are you sitting crying in this place?'

The girl said to him, 'I see, my lord, that you are handsome and brave, and I feel pity for your handsomeness and your youth. Why have you come here to die in a dreadful way? Get back on your horse and escape quickly!'

The saint said to her, 'Lady, who are you and who are the people standing yonder and watching you with great lamentation?'

The girl said, 'It is a long story, and I cannot tell it to you. But escape before you are killed in a dreadful fashion!'

The saint said to her, 'Tell me the truth, lady. For, by Lord God, I will die alongside you, because I surely will not leave you in the lurch.'

Then the girl groaned bitterly and said, 'My lord, our city was a fine and beautiful one to live in, but then a wicked dragon was born in the lake water. Every day it would come out of the water and eat the people of the city. I am the king's only daughter. My father issued a decree and everyone gave up their children for the dragon to eat. And then the decree rebounded upon my father, and he sent me off for the beast to eat. See now, I have told you everything. Get away from here in haste!'

Hearing this, the saint said to the girl, 'Fear not henceforth, but take courage!' He asked her, 'What is the religion of your father and his people?'

The girl said, 'They worship Heracles, Scamander, Apollo and the great goddess Artemis.'

The saint said to the girl, 'But you must believe in my God. Fear not henceforth, but take courage.' The blessed one raised his voice to God and said, 'O God, you who are enthroned over the cherubim and seraphim and who watch over the abyss, the one enduring, true God. You know that the hearts of men are foolish. You showed the dreadful signs to your servant Moses. Show your pity through me too, and engineer with me a sign for the good. Make the terrible beast fall at my feet, so that people will know that you are always with me.'

Then there came a voice from heaven, which said, 'Your prayer has been heard by the ears of the Lord. Do what you wish.'

At once the girl cried out, 'Alas, my lord, get away, because the terrible beast is coming.'

The saint ran to meet the dragon and made the sign of the cross with the words, 'Lord my God, make the beast a call to faith for the faithless people.' When he had said this, by the help of the same God and the prayer of the saint the dragon fell at his feet.

The saint said to the girl, 'Take off your belt and my horse's bridle and bring them to me here.' The girl took her belt off and gave the items to the saint. By God's design he tied them onto the dragon and handed it over to the girl with the words, 'Let us take it to the city.' Taking the dragon, they went to the city. When the people saw the unexpected miracle they took fright and were on the point of fleeing for fear of the dragon, but St George shouted to them, 'Do not be afraid, but stay, see the glory of God and believe in our Lord Jesus Christ, the true God, and I will kill the dragon.'

The king and the entire city cried out, 'We believe in the Father, the Son and the Holy Ghost, and in the consubstantial and indivisible Trinity.' Upon hearing this, the saint unsheathed his sword, killed the dragon and handed the girl over to her father. Most of the people gathered round and kissed the saint's feet, glorifying God. St George summoned the archbishop of Alexandria, and baptised the king, his nobles and the whole people, some 240,000, over a period of fifteen days. There was great joy in that place. Then the city of Lasia raised up a most sacred temple in the name of St George. As the temple was being built, the saint stood in a certain place and prayed, and a sacred spring burst forth. Then they believed in the Lord. St George authored many miracles and signs through the grace he had been given.

St George supposedly lived in the third century AD and his wider legend goes back to the sixth century AD, but his association with the dragon is not attested until this twelfth-century AD Greek version of the *Miracula Sancti Georgii*. Its telling of the story is frankly somewhat awkward, and one must sometimes rely upon a familiarity with the classical and Christian traditions that underlie it to make sense of its flow (for instance, with the king's telegraphic enunciation of the sortition).

The tale exhibits many familiar motifs: the dragon is associated with a water source (**M4.a.i**); the saint fortifies himself for battle with the sign of the cross (**M11.b.v**); the saint uses an item of clothing—albeit in this case the girl's, rather than his own—to make a lead for the rampant dragon (**M15.d.iii**); the slaying of the dragon is achieved by faith and in turn is associated with a mass conversion (**M15.a.ii–iii**); and a sacred spring is made to gush forth after the defeat of the dragon (**M4.a.iv**).

It is rare for a saint to kill a dragon in such a hands-on, physical way, but George is, after all, a knight. Furthermore, the killing with a sword of a dragon that churns up the depths is appropriate in the light of Septuagint Isaiah 27.1 ('On that day God will bring his holy, great and strong sword against the dragon [*drakōn*] as it flees, against the twisting dragon-snake [*drakōn ophis*], and he will slay the dragon') and of Job 41.23 ('He makes the abyss boil like a bronze cauldron. He controls the sea as if it were a little bottle of oil'); cf. **123, A9**.

It has been a popular contention that the legend of St George's dragon slaying was in origin derivative of the classical myth of Perseus, Andromeda and the sea monster (Hartland 1894–6:iii, 38–47, Fontenrose 1959:515–20, Hansen 2002:119–30). It must be admitted that, amidst the hackneyed motifs of the hagiographical dragon-slaying tradition, some distinctively classical motifs stand out. However, amongst all potential models, the classical motifs link the narrative much more compellingly to the myth of Hesione than they do to that of Andromeda:

- young victims are chosen by lot to be put out for the dragon to eat: cf. Hesione (**104, 106**);
- the king tries everything to spare his own daughter, but his indignant people will hear nothing of it: cf. Hesione (**103, 105–6**);
- the princess (who in subsequent tradition will acquire the name Sabra) is set out for the dragon to come and devour: cf. Hesione (**103–7**) and Andromeda (**108–17**);
- the dragon emerges from the water to devour the victim set out for it: cf. Hesione (**103–7**) and Andromeda (**108–16**);
- the hero finds the girl victim awaiting her fate with the dragon as he happens to pass by: cf. Hesione (**103–6**) and Andromeda (**108–16**); and
- after slaying the dragon, the hero fails to marry the princess he has delivered: cf. Hesione (**103–4**).

A corollary to the Perseus theory is the contention that Lasia, the site of the action, was supposed to be somewhere close to Joppa, which, as we have seen, in a minor tradition in classical terms, claimed to be the home of the Andromeda story (**117–18**). There is only the weakest of bases for this, namely the observation that some of St George's other adventures centre on the area of modern Israel and Lebanon, with Lydda, near Joppa, being the site of his martyrdom (one might do rather better to build upon the role of the bishop of Alexandria in the story at hand). The name Lasia itself seems to have no historical basis. Some have read it as a speaking name, 'Rough Place', though such a reading defies the text's explicit assertions that, dragon aside, it was a fine and beautiful place in which to live.

But the indications of the narrative itself, meagre as they are, are rather that the action takes place close to Troy, site of the action of the Heracles and Hesione myth:

- The list of pagan gods worshipped by the Lasians begins with Heracles himself, probably a self-conscious tribute to principal classical source. The second named, Scamander, can only be the famous river of Troy of that name. Apollo is next: Apollo Smintheus had a major cult on the Trojan plain and indeed initiated the action of the *Iliad*, while Apollo Thymbraeus, in myth at any rate, also had his cult on the Trojan plain and sent *drakontes* out of the sea to attack the children of Laocoon there (**92–6**). The 'great goddess Artemis' is admittedly harder to tie specifically to Troy.
- George comes across the princess as he is returning home to Cappadocia, in central Asia Minor. Although his starting point is unspecified, a return route from anywhere to the west or to south might well have brought him through Troy on the Asia Minor seaboard.

### 161   St George slays his dragon: the canonical and most influential account

1263–7 AD

Jacobus de Voragine
*Golden Legend* 58

Latin

George, a military tribune from Cappadocia, arrived by some chance at a city called Silena in the province of Libya. Near this city was a lake swamp like a sea in which a pestilential dragon [*draco*] used to lurk. Many times had the people taken up arms against it, only for it to turn them to flight. It would approach the walls of the city and kill everyone with its breath. Of necessity, accordingly, the citizens used to give it two sheep every day to placate its anger. Otherwise it would attack the city walls and infect the air, from which many would die. When, in due course, they had almost run out of sheep, and since, in particular, they could not find a supply of them, they took counsel and gave the serpent a single sheep with a human being in addition. So everyone's sons and daughters were being given to the serpent by lot, and no one was excluded from the lot. When almost all the sons and daughters had been eaten, by some chance the king's only daughter was selected by lot and destined for the dragon.

Then the king, in his grief, said, 'Take gold and silver and half my kingdom and spare my daughter from dying in such a way.'

The people responded to him in anger, 'It was you, king, that made this ruling, and all our children are now dead—and you want to save your daughter? Unless you do with your daughter what you have ordained for the others, we will burn you and your household.'

Observing this, the king began to weep for his daughter, and said, 'Alas me, my sweetest daughter, what am I to do about you? Or what am I to say? When now will I see your wedding?' He turned to the people and said, 'I beg you to allow me a postponement of eight days in which to grieve for my daughter.'

The people conceded this, but at the end of the eight days they returned and said in anger, 'Why are you destroying the people for the sake of your daughter? See, we are all dying because of the dragon's breath.'

Then the king, realising that he could not spare his daughter, dressed her in royal robes, embraced her tearfully and said, 'Alas me, my sweetest daughter, I used to believe that you would suckle sons at your royal bosom, and now you are off to be eaten by a dragon. Alas me, my sweetest daughter, I used to hope that I would invite princes to your wedding, decorate the palace with pearls, listen to the music of drums and pipes, and now you are off to be eaten by a dragon.' He kissed her warmly and sent her off with the words, 'Would that I had died before I lost you in this way, my daughter!'

Then she fell at her father's feet and sought his blessing. Her father tearfully blessed her, and she went off to the lake. By chance the blessed George was passing that way. When he saw her weeping he asked her what was the matter.

She said, 'Good young sir, get on your horse quickly and flee, lest you be killed alongside me.'

George replied to her, 'Do not be afraid, daughter, but tell me what you are waiting for here whilst all the people watch.'

She said, 'As I observe, good young sir, you have a great heart, but do you want to be killed alongside me? Flee quickly.'

George replied, 'I will not depart from here until you tell me what the matter is.'

So when she had explained the whole story to him, George said, 'Do not be afraid, daughter, because I will help you in the name of Christ.'

She said, 'But, good soldier, hurry to save yourself. Do not be killed alongside me! It is enough that I alone should die, for you could not deliver me and would perish alongside me.'

As they were saying this, lo! the dragon arrived and raised its head from the lake. Then the girl, shaking with fear, said, 'Flee, good lord, flee quickly.'

Then George got on his horse and, protecting himself with the sign of the cross, attacked the dragon boldly as it came against him. Bravely hurling his spear and entrusting himself to God, he dealt it a severe wound and dropped it to the ground. He said to the girl, 'Throw your belt around the serpent's neck, daughter. There is no need to hesitate.'

When she had done this, it followed her like the tamest dog. When, accordingly, she began to lead it to the city, the crowds began to flee over hills and mountains upon seeing it, saying, 'Woe for us, because now we shall all die!'

Then the blessed George signalled to them and said, 'Do not be afraid, for the Lord sent me to you for this, that I should liberate you from the punishments inflicted by the dragon. Only believe in Christ. If every one of you is baptized, I will kill this serpent.'

Then the king and all the crowds were baptized, and so the blessed George drew his sword and killed the serpent. He ordered it to be carried out of the city. Then four yoke-pair of oxen took it out into a great field. On that day twenty thousand people were baptized, not counting women and children. The king built a church of amazing size in honour of the blessed Mary and the blessed George. A lively spring gushes forth from its altar, the drinking of which cures all the sick. The king offered unlimited money to the blessed George, but he refused to accept it and asked that it be given to the poor. Then George gave the king brief instruction on four points, namely that he should care for God's churches, hold his priests in honour, heed the divine offices carefully and always remember the poor. He kissed the king and left.

However, in some books one reads that George protected himself with the sign of the cross and attacked and killed the serpent already as it was making its way towards the girl to eat her.

Jacobus de Voragine (Jacopo da Varazze) hailed from Varazze, near Genoa. He was a Dominican monk who went on, in 1292 AD, to become archbishop of Genoa. The instant popularity and canonisation of his compilation *Legenda Sanctorum* (*Readings of the Saints*) led to its being rechristened *Legenda Aurea* (*Golden Readings*, or *Golden Legend*). It became the fundamental handbook for the lives of the saints in the later medieval period, quickly and repeatedly translated into all the vernaculars of Western Europe. In particular, its narratives came to underpin the non-biblical religious art of the period, to which it remains an indispensable key for latter-day scholars of the same.

This narrative is broadly similar in shape and compass to that of the *Miracula Sancti Georgii*, but it is reproduced in addition to it here in the light of its subsequent influence. The scene of the action has now been transposed to the city of Silena in Libya. It also adds some further typical themes, namely the pestilential nature of the dragon's breath (**M7.a.ii**) and its carcass (**M7.a.vi**); for the deployment of oxen to drag the problematic carcass off, cf. **146**.

For other dragons and dragon fights in the *Golden Legend*, see: §§12 (St Silvester's dragon, which kills three hundred people a day with its breath, and the mouth of which Silvester binds shut with thread and wax, sealing it with the sign of the cross; cf. **136–7**), 17 (St Hilary confines the snakes on Gallinaria; cf. **152**), 49 (the manifestation of a dragon eager to devour him deters a monk wavering in his faith from quitting his monastery), 50 (St Patrick banishes snakes from Ireland: see **159**), 65 (St Philip banishes the Scythian dragon, in an account loosely resembling that of Pseudo-Abdias; his opponents in Hierapolis are no longer the Ophianoi but the snakeless Ebionites, heretics who hold that Christ was a phantom; cf. **135–6**), 86 (lustful dragons fly through the air and drip their sperm into wells and rivers, giving rise to plague; they are averted by the fumes from piles of burning animal bones, typically around the time of John the Baptist's feast day; cf. **M7.b.iv**); 90 (St Paul's viper, here transposed from Malta to Mytilene; cf. **125**), 93 (the dragon of St Margaret/Marina; cf. **158**), 98 (St Christina is surrounded by a number of venomous snakes, but they merely lick her; when a magician attempts to impel the creatures to bite her, they instead turn upon him and kill him; Christina restores him to life and banishes the snakes to the desert; cf. **M15.d.i**), 99 (the disciples of St James the Greater split a fire-breathing dragon in two by making the sign of the cross), 105 (St Martha bridles the dragon Tarasconus; it dwells in the river Rhone, is half fish and was born of Leviathan and the Onachus, the latter of which can shoot its dung like darts at its pursuers over the distance of an acre; the locals then kill it; in a separate but immediately following story, Martha restores a dead boy to life—cf. **M15.d.i**), 115 (St Donatus's dragon, which has here been polluting a spring and attacks the saint as he rides past on his ass; cf. **146**), 129 (a tangle of ten-foot-long snakes in the tomb of St Concordian is scattered upon the conversion of St Mamertinus; cf. **132–3, 151**), 140 (St Matthew casts sleep upon a pair of sulphurous-fire-breathing dragons sent by the Ethiopian sorcerers Zaroes and Arphaxat before banishing them), 143 (a snake slips inside a peasant's mouth as he sleeps and causes him stomach ache; he incubates in the church dedicated to SS. Cosmas and Damian, whereupon the snake slips out again by the same route); 145 (the archangel Michael and the Revelation Dragon; cf. **126**), 166 (St Martin averts a water snake).

## 162  Digenis Akritis destroys a shape-shifting three-headed dragon

ca. 1300 AD

*Digenis Akritis*
(Grottaferrata version)
6.42–80

(modern) Greek

At noon I turned to sleep. The noble girl sprinkled me with rose water whilst the nightingales and other birds sang. The girl felt thirsty and went off to the spring. As she was pleasantly dipping her feet, a dragon [*drakōn*] transformed itself into a handsome boy and accosted her with the intention of leading her into sin. But she recognised it for what it was and said, 'Dragon, give up your plan. I am not deceived. The man that loves me has been keeping vigil and has only just gone to sleep.' (To herself she said, 'This is a dragon. I have never yet seen such a sight.') 'If he wakes and discovers you, he will punish you.' But the dragon leaped up shamelessly and tried to rape her. The girl screamed at once and called to me, 'Wake up, my lord, and save your dearest girl!' The sound of her voice went right to my heart and I quickly sat up and saw the troublemaker, for I had advisedly slept in a place directly opposite the spring. No sooner had I drawn my sword than I found myself at the spring, for my feet carried me as swiftly as wings. As I got there it turned itself into a huge, terrifying vision, fearful for men: it had three massive heads, all shooting forth flame. From each of its heads it sent forth a lightning-like flame. It made the sound of thunder as it moved, with the result that the earth and all the trees seemed to shake. It inflated its body whilst drawing its heads together, but it drew in its hinder part and sharpened its tail. Alternately coiling and uncoiling, it launched its whole body against me. But I set what I saw at nought. I raised my sword up high, with all my strength, and brought it down upon the heads of the most terrible beast and took them all off at once. It fell to the ground and unravelled itself, twitching its tail up and down in its death throes. I wiped off my sword and put it back into my scabbard. I called my boys over from where they were some distance away and ordered them to remove the dragon immediately.

The earliest extant manuscript of the this curious but popular Byzantine epic, the *Grottaferrata*, derives from ca. 1300 BC, though the world it reflects is largely that of the ninth and tenth centuries AD, which is likely, therefore, to have been the age of its principal composition. The protagonist, Digenis Akritis, is a morally ambiguous Byzantine frontiersman who has here carried off the daughter of a general, Doukas. The vigorous narrative lacks the restraint of contemporary hagiographical accounts of dragon fights, such as that of St George, but exhibits some common themes with them: the dragon is associated with a spring (**M4.a**); it is strongly assimilated to a demon and as such can manifest itself in humanoid form (**M15.b.iii**); and its carcass presents a threat of pestilence (we infer) and so must be removed, a task which requires many hands (**M7.a.vi**).

Themes peculiar to modern Greek folklore peep through even in this early telling. As Jeffreys observes in her notes to these lines, the use of the term *drakōn* tends towards modern Greek *drakos*, signifying something more of an ogre than a reptile. And above all it is noon that is the 'dangerous hour', the hour at which demons and other unwelcome supernatural phenomena are wont to manifest themselves: see Blum and Blum 1970.

## FURTHER READING

Patrick: Krappe 1941a, 1947, Bieler 1949, Kenney 1968.
George: Aufhauser 1911:52–69, Fontenrose 1959:515–21, Fischer 1975–, Castellana 2000, Hansen 2002:119–30, Didi-Huberman et al. 1994.
Digenis Akritis: Jeffreys 1998.

# Appendix A
## World-foundational Dragon-Slaying Tales from the Ancient Near East and India

### A1. THE SUMERIAN DRAGON FIGHT: NINURTA AGAINST AZAG (SUMERIAN; LATE THIRD MILLENNIUM BC)

The Sumerian epic *Lugal-e* tells of the battle between Ninurta, the storm god, and Azag. Ninurta's battle mace Sharur, personified as a lion-headed bird, comes to him with news that a rival, Azag, a child of Heaven and Earth, fostered by wild beasts, has arisen in the highlands, that the plants have chosen him as their king and that he plans to employ his army of stones to take over Ninurta's kingdom. Ninurta rouses himself against Azag and his minions in an onslaught in which he rains down fire and coals and scorches the rebels. Although Azag initially prevails in the battle, Sharur escapes and appeals to Ninurta's father, Enlil, who settles Azag's firestorm (or dust storm) with a rainstorm, whereupon Ninurta and Sharur regroup for a second, successful attack upon Azag. Ninurta carves up Azag's corpse and proclaims that his name should no longer be uttered. The nature of Azag remains obscure. At heart, and especially in the final scene of the second battle, he appears to be a hardwood tree, an appropriate king for mountain plants and stones. Evidently, however, this is not a shape in which he can do battle. In the course of the initial battle he is assimilated to a serpent (176), and we are told elsewhere that he is venomous (230). Intriguingly, when he deploys the sky as a weapon, it too is assimilated to a snake (170). Azag appears to be the latest in a series

Figure A-1 Marduk battles Tiamat. Neo-Assyrian cylinder seal (impression), ca. 900–750 BC. British Museum. Redrawn by Eriko Ogden.

of serpentine opponents of Ninurta. In counselling the god, Sharur reminds him of his former victories, including at least two over other serpents, one of which is described as seven-headed (129, 133). Also, the introductory paean to Ninurta praises him for reaping the necks of the insubordinate like grain (6) and compares him to the right forepaw that a lion puts out against a snake (11). Curiously, Ninurta himself is also described metaphorically as a serpent (3) and as venom spitting (106–7); his mace, Sharur, is also venomous (254). The use of fire by both sides in a serpent battle resembles that found in classical narratives (**M6**).

**Source:** *Lugal*-e, esp. 1–337.

**Text:** van Dijk 1983.

**Translation:** Jacobsen 1987:233–72; van Dijk 1983 (French).

## A2. THE EGYPTIAN DRAGON FIGHT: RA AGAINST APOPHIS (EGYPTIAN; CA. 2000 BC)

The ca. 310 BC Hieratic-Egyptian Bremner-Rhind papyrus in the British Museum preserves a tale thought to have been composed ca. 2000 BC. This tells, somewhat obscurely, of the nightly victory of the sun god, Ra, over the serpent Apophis, the embodiment of darkness and night. Apophis is thirty cubits long, his head three cubits broad. He lives in a cave in the mountains of the west, and as Ra's sun barque approaches them on its daily course, Apophis attacks it. The battle rages all night, with the god deploying spear, arrows, sword, flame and magical spells against the serpent and eventually prevailing over him in the east. Ra hacks Apophis up with a knife and binds the parts beneath the earth, whereupon his barque rises again from that quarter.

**Source:** *P. Bremner-Rhind* xxvi–xxviii.

**Text:** Budge 1910, plates i–xix.

**Translation:** *ANET*³ 6–7 (J.A. Wilson).

## A3. THE BABYLONIAN DRAGON FIGHT: MARDUK AGAINST TIAMAT (AKKADIAN; EARLY SECOND MILLENNIUM BC)

The fourth tablet of the Middle Babylonian Akkadian *Enūma eliš* or *Epic of Creation* narrates the battle between Marduk and Tiamat, the female, serpentine, multi-headed embodiment of the sea and of chaos, who is supported by a host of monstrous associates which includes yet more snake-shaped creatures. Grasping a herb with which to counter her poison, he goes into battle against Tiamat herself. He launches an evil wind against her, which she swallows and which distends her belly. He then shoots an arrow at her inflated belly and pops it, splitting her down the middle and slitting her heart. Marduk constructs heaven and earth from her body.

**Source:** *Enūma eliš* tablet iv.

**Text:** Lambert and Parker 1966.

**Translations:** Dalley 2000:228–77, superseding *ANET*³ 60–72 (E.A. Speiser).

## A4. THE INDIAN DRAGON FIGHT: INDRA AGAINST VRITRA (SANSKRIT; CA. 1500–1000 BC)

The Sanskrit *Rigveda*, thought to have been composed between 1500 and 1000 BC, tells of the storm god Indra's defeat of Vritra. Vritra, the firstborn of the serpents, encompasses and dams up the world's waters. The poem explicitly acknowledges that his name means 'blockage'. Indra dashes him into pieces with a thunderbolt made for him by Tvastar, so that his body comes to resemble a series of logged branches lying on the earth. By killing the serpent, Indra releases the waters he has controlled, which then rise to cover and conceal his body. Vritra would appear to have been a pure serpent in form, although in the description of the great battle he is twice described as having shoulders.

**Source:** *Rigveda* 1.32; cf. also 1.52, 1.80, 2.11–12, 3.32, 4.18, 5.32, 6.17, 8.96, 10.113.

**Text:** van Nooten and Holland 1994.

**Translations:** Arya and Joshi 2001; West 2007:256–7 (1.32 only); Brereton and Jamison forthcoming.

## A5. THE CANAANITE-UGARITIC DRAGON FIGHT: BAAL-SAPON AGAINST YAM AND LITAN (UGARITIC; CA. XIV BC)

The story of Baal-Sapon's fight against Yam is preserved in a fragmentary series of fourteenth-century BC Ugaritic cuneiform tablets written by a scribe named Ilimilku. El grants rule to Yam(m)(u), the Principle of the Sea, but Baal-Sapon, the storm god, whom Yam seeks to enslave, challenges him. Baal-Sapon defeats Yam with two throwing clubs (i.e. thunderbolts) named 'Expeller' and 'Chaser' and made for him by the smith god Kothar. These fly from his hands like eagles. The first is thrown without effect, but the second strikes Yam on the head and brings him down, though it does not kill him. The defeat of Yam is associated with the slaying of a seven-headed serpent, Ltn, construable as 'Litan' or 'Lotan' and evidently corresponding to the biblical Leviathan, but the fragmentary nature of the tablets leaves it uncertain whether Yam and Litan are one and the same or are associates. Baal-Sapon then rules from a palace of silver, gold and lapis lazuli built for him by Kothar atop Mount Sapuna above Ugarit. Baal-Sapon initially refuses to have windows built in the palace because of his continuing fear of Yam, but eventually he permits a single one, and it is through this that he sends forth thunder.

**Sources:** *KTU* 1.1–2 (= *CTA* 1–2), *KTU* 1.3 (= *CTA* 3) iii 35–52, *KTU* 1.5 (= *CTA* 5) i2•–3.

**Text:** Smith 1994.

**Translations:** Coogan 1978, Gibson 1978, superseding *ANET*³ 129–42 (H.L. Ginsberg); Caquot et al. 1974 (French).

## A6. THE HURRIAN-HITTITE DRAGON FIGHT: TESHUB AGAINST HEDAMMU (HITTITE; CA. 1250 BC, REFLECTING HURRIAN MATERIAL UP TO TWO MILLENNIA OLDER)

The civilisation of the Hurrians flourished from the later third millennium until ca. 1330 BC. In a fragmentary Hittite dragon-slaying myth derived from them, the storm god Teshub (Teššub) defeats the voracious sea serpent Hedammu, son of the underworld god Kumarbi and Sertapsuruhi, daughter of the sea god. Teshub prevails upon his sister, Sauska (the equivalent of the Hittite Inara), to help him overcome Hedammu by seducing him and luring him out of the safety of the sea onto the land. So she goes to the bathhouse, washes herself and anoints herself with perfumed oil, whereupon, it is said, in a lovely image, that 'love ran after her like puppies'. She summons Hedammu from the deep with the help of a pair of musical instruments. As he raises his head from the sea he sees her naked form and determines to gobble her down, but she now gives him a love potion and then beer (or perhaps a love potion that consists of beer). The beer initially sends him to sleep, but when he wakes he becomes aroused and makes love to Sauska. The story's finale is missing: perhaps Teshub goes on to attack Hedammu while he is distracted in lovemaking, or perhaps he simply has the serpent at a disadvantage once they are on dry land.

**Source:** *CTH* 348, esp. F11.1–3, F12.1–2, F14, F16.1–3.

**Text:** Siegelova 1971:38–71.

**Translation:** Hoffner 1998:51–5; Siegelova 1971:38–71, esp. 44–5, 54–61, *TUAT* 3.856–8 (German).

## A7. THE HITTITE DRAGON FIGHT: TARHUNNA AGAINST ILLUYANKA (HITTITE; CA. 1250 BC)

The Hittite priest Kella's aetiology of the *purulli* festival is the tale of the storm god Tarhunna's (Tarhunta's) fight against the serpent Illuyanka(s) in Kiskilussa. 'Illuyanka' simply means 'serpent' and indeed may be a common rather than a proper noun. The aetiology is given in two variants, in both of which Illuyanka initially defeats Tarhunna. In the first variant Tarhunna relies upon the help of the goddess Inara and the mortal Hupasiya. Inara prepares an elaborate feast, with copious quantities of wine and beer. Then she in turn asks for help from a mortal, Hupasiya, in the town of Ziggaratta. Hupasiya tells her he will do whatever she wants if she will let him sleep with her, to which she agrees. Returning to the task at hand, Inara conceals Hupasiya in ambush. She puts on fine clothes and calls Illuyanka forth from his hole with an invitation to her feast. He duly comes, along with his offspring. They eat and drink everything, become drunk, and have no wish to go back down their hole again (probably because of their drunken insensibility, but just possibly because they have eaten themselves too fat to get into it). Hupasiya now emerges from concealment and ties Illuyanka up, whereupon Tarhunna arrives to kill the serpent.

In the second variant, which has interesting implications for duties towards in-laws in the Hittite world, Illuyanka initially defeats Tarhunna and in victory removes his heart and eyes. The blighted Tarhunna then marries a poor mortal woman, with whom he sires a son who goes on to marry the daughter of Illuyanka. Tarhunna instructs his son to demand his eyes and heart from his new bride, and seemingly also her father, as bride price, and these are duly ceded. Tarhunna, now made whole again, goes to the sea to attack the serpent and indeed his own son, who now fights alongside his father-in-law. As Tarhunna is on the point of defeating Illuyanka, his son pleads to be destroyed together with him, and Tarhunna does as he bids, killing them both.

Source: *CTH* 321.

Text: Beckman 1982:12–18.

Translations: Beckman 1982:18–20, Hoffner 1998:11–14, superseding *ANET*³ 125–6 (A. Götze).

## A8. THE IRANIAN DRAGON FIGHT: ATAR AND THRAĒTAONA AGAINST AŽI DAHĀKA (AVESTAN AND MIDDLE PERSIAN; CA. X–V BC)

The Zoroastrian sacred texts of the *Avesta* (ca. 1000–400 BC) feature two battles against Aži Dahāka, the first part of whose name is a cognate of the Greek word *ophis* ('snake'). As to the first battle, the world's good and evil principles, Angra Mainya and Spenta Mainyu respectively, are in competition for kingly splendour (*farr*), and they fight for it by means of missiles and by means of proxy champions. The evil principle creates the three-headed dragon Aži Dahāka as his champion, whilst the good principle creates Atar, the principle of fire, as his. Aži Dahāka first threatens to rush upon Atar and extinguish him, whereupon Atar threatens to send a stream of flame up through Aži Dahāka's bottom and out of his mouths ('I will enter thy hinder part, I will blaze up in thy jaws, so that thou mayest never more rush upon the earth'; *Avesta, Yašts* 19.50). Intimidated, Aži Dahāka withdraws.

The *Avesta* contains several overlapping references to Aži Dahāka's second battle, in which he is defeated by the hero Thraētaona, although we never find the fight itself narrated. These references tell us that, in addition to three mouths, Aži Dahāka also has three heads, six eyes and a thousand skills. Aži Dahāka offers sacrifices of thousands of animals either to Ardvi Sura Anahita or to the Waters and to Vayu (Storm Wind), the divider of the waters, in hopes of emptying the earth of men, but the deities prefer Thraētaona's equal sacrifices as he prays to rid the world of Aži Dahāka and to liberate his two beautiful wives, Savanghavach and Erenavach, from him. Middle Persian tradition, in the form of the *Dēnkard* and the *Bundahish*, offers further details of the defeat of Aži Dahāka, now known as Dahāg or Zohak (etc.), by Thraētaona, now known as Fredun (etc.), though it remains unclear how many of these are ancient. Amongst these details Thraētaona fights Aži Dahāka as a mere nine-year-old; when he strikes him, he releases a horde of harmful creatures from his body; and he eventually binds him down alive beneath Mt Demavend.

Source (Atar against Aži Dahāka): *Avesta, Yašts* 19.46–50.

Sources (Thraētaona against Aži Dahāka): *Avesta, Yašts* 5.28–35 (the principal account), 9.13–15, 14.40, 15.18–25, 9.7–8, *Avesta, Vidēvdat/Vendidād* 1.17, *Dēnkard* 7.1.26, *Bundahish* 29.8–9.

Texts: *Avesta*—Geldner 1886–96; *Dēnkard*—Sanjana 1874–1928; *Bundahish*—Justi 1868.

Translation: *Avesta*—Darmesteter and Mills 1880–87; *Dēnkard*—Sanjana 1874–28; *Bundahish*—Justi 1868.

## A9. THE JEWISH DRAGON FIGHT: GOD AGAINST LEVIATHAN AND RAHAB (HEBREW; CA. X–IV BC)

In a series of confusing allusive references in the Old Testament we meet the massive, serpentine sea monsters Leviathan and Rahab and their minions.

Leviathan's name, as we have seen, is a derivative or cousin of the Canaanite 'Litan'/'Lotan' (**A5**). Both Leviathan and Rahab preside over a chaotic ocean to which God brings peace, order and containment when he smites the creature into pieces. Almost certainly they are to be fully identified with each other. Job 41 speaks of a sea monster, which may or may not be Leviathan, that sends forth fire and smoke from its mouth and nostrils ('by his neesings a light doth shine', 41.18, in the words of the King James Bible) and churns up the sea like a boiling pot. The Septuagint's reflexes of these references are laid out at **123** (where the numeration for Job 41 differs slightly).

**Sources (Rahab):** Psalms 89.9–10 (x–vi BC), Isaiah 51.9–10 (vi BC [this part of the book]), Job 9.13, Job 26.5–14 (probably iv BC).

**Sources (Leviathan):** Psalms 74.13–14, 104.26 (x–vi BC), Isaiah 27.1 (late viii BC [this part of the book]), Job 3.8, 41.1–34 (probably iv BC); cf. also Job 7.12.

**Text:** Kittel et al. 1997.

**Translation:** *NEB*.

# Appendix B
## Germanic Dragon Fights of the Eighth to Thirteenth Centuries AD

### B1. SIGEMUND AGAINST A DRAGON: BEOWULF (ANGLO-SAXON; VIII–X AD)

The Anglo-Saxon epic *Beowulf* incorporates the following brief report of Sigemund's killing of a treasure-guarding dragon by transfixing it with his sword and pinning it to the wall of its own cave:

> Great fame sprang up for Sigemund after the day of his death. For the doughty warrior had laid low the worm [*wyrm*], the guardian of the hoard. Under the grey stone the prince's son attempted an audacious deed. He did not have Fitela with him. Nonetheless, it fell to him that his sword transfixed the portentous worm, so that the noble iron stood in the wall. The dragon [*draca*] died in the killing. By valour the dread warrior enabled himself to acquire the treasure hoard, as he wished. Wael's son [cf. 'Volsung'] loaded up his seagoing boat and bore the adornments in the bosom of his ship. The hot worm melted. (*Beowulf* 884–97 §13; trans. Ogden)

Figure B-1 Sigurd transfixes Fafnir. Wooden portal from Hylestad Church, Setesdal, Norway, Universitetets Oldsamksamling, University of Oslo, Norway. Ancient Art and Architecture Collection Ltd. / The Bridgeman Art Library.

This is an early version of a tale that was to morph into the more familiar account of the killing by Sigemund's son Sigurd (or Siegfried) of Fafnir. The term *draca* is derivative of the Latin *draco*. How much did the *Beowulf* poet know of the Latin dragon-slaying tradition?

Source: *Beowulf* 884–97, §13.

Text: Klaeber 1950.

Translations: e.g. Wright 1957, Porter 1991.

### B2. BEOWULF AGAINST THE FIREDRAKE: *BEOWULF* (ANGLO-SAXON; VIII–X AD)

The *Beowulf* poet casts his hero Beowulf in the mould of Sigemund, sending him in his turn similarly to defeat a fifty-foot-long, coiling, fire-breathing dragon (*fyrdraca*, *līgdraca*) which also has the ability to fly. A wealthy pagan, the last of his race, has been buried in an elaborate giant-built barrow on a headland. Inside is a secret stone vault of pillars and arches that contains the entire wealth of the lost people. A dragon has come to occupy the tomb and to cherish the treasure as its own. A runaway serf happens upon it and steals a jewelled cup whilst the dragon sleeps. Unable to track down the missing vessel or the thief when it wakes the following day, the dragon awaits nightfall and then exacts a terrible revenge on the local Geats, spewing fire and burning their dwellings, including Beowulf's own great hall, to the ground. Elderly though he now is, Beowulf prepares to fight the dragon by having an iron (as opposed to wooden) shield made for himself and sets out with a party of twelve other men, including the serf, who escorts them to the barrow. As they arrive they find flames issuing from the tomb's arches. Beowulf challenges the dragon to come forth, which it immediately does. At first Beowulf can do nothing to wound the dragon with his ancestral sword, Naegling, and the creature surrounds him with a burning ring of fire. Of his companions, only Wiglaf is brave enough to dive though the smoke and join in the fight. Beowulf brings Naegling down on the dragon's head, but it shatters without effect. The dragon then tears a chunk out of Beowulf's neck with its fangs, but Wiglaf is able to drive his own golden sword into its body, whereupon Beowulf slits its belly open with his dagger, killing it. However, the dragon's venom has entered his body, and he is doomed to die. Wiglaf retrieves some of the dragon's treasure from the barrow to show Beowulf before he breathes his last. He then heaves the dragon's carcass over the cliff into the sea before burying Beowulf in a magnificent tumulus.

Source: *Beowulf* 2200–3182 §§31–43

Text: Klaeber 1950.

Translations: e.g. Wright 1957, Porter 1991.

### B3. SIEGFRIED AGAINST THE DRAGON: *NIBELUNGENLIED* (MIDDLE HIGH GERMAN; CA. 1200 AD)

The Middle High German *Nibelungenlied*, which originated in Austria, makes only two brief and retrospective refererences to Siegfried's slaying of the dragon in passing. Siegfried had slain the dragon and bathed in his blood, and this had turned his skin hard like horn, so that no weapon could penetrate it (cf. the folktale type ATU 650C, 'The Youth who Bathed himself in the Blood of a Dragon'). However, as he was bathing, a leaf from a linden tree had fallen on his back between his shoulder blades, leaving just this one spot still vulnerable. The main narrative tells how the wicked Hagen tricks Siegfried's wife Krimhild into revealing the spot to him, so that he can treacherously slay him.

**Source:** *Nibelungenlied* §§100, 899–904.

**Text:** Reichert 2005.

**Translation:** Hatto 1965.

## B4. SIGURD AGAINST FAFNIR: *VOLSUNGASAGA* (OLD NORSE; CA. 1200–70 AD)

The greedy Fafnir kills his father Hreidmar and deprives his brother Regin of his share of the gold which they had all forcibly extorted from the Æsir gods, Odin, Loki and Hoenir, in compensation for their killing of a third brother, Otr, the man-otter. He takes it off into the wilderness of Gnita-Heath and is there transformed into a great serpent that then lies upon the gold in his cave, forever guarding it. The smith Regin persuades his foster-son, Sigurd, to go off to the heath and kill Fafnir, misleadingly telling him that it is no bigger than a water snake. He reforges Sigurd's broken sword, Gram, rendering it so strong and sharp that it will slice through an anvil for him. Following Regin's advice, Sigurd digs a pit in the track along which Fafnir comes down from his cave to the nearby river to drink, blowing venom before him as he goes. Sigurd sits in this and thrusts his sword up into Fafnir's heart as he crawls overhead. The dying Fafnir prophesies to Sigurd and tries to discourage him from taking his hoard of gold, warning him that it brings death to all that possess it: it has already been the death of its original owner—the dwarf-pike Andvari, from whom the Æsir gods had taken it—of Hreidmar and now of Fafnir himself. Regin joins Sigurd and drinks some of Fafnir's blood in the knowledge that it will bestow the gift of prophecy upon him. He asks Sigurd to roast Fafnir's heart for him, and as he does so Sigurd tests its juices by dipping his finger in them and licking it. In this way he too acquires the gift of prophecy, and specifically the ability to understand the prophetic language of birds. Immediately the nuthatches tell him in song that Regin is planning to betray him, and so Sigurd strikes the smith's head off with Gram. Riding to Fafnir's lair, he finds its massive iron doors open and proceeds to take the hoard, in defiance of the dragon's warning.

**Source:** *Volsungasaga* §§13–20.

**Text:** Olsen 1906–8, Jónsson 1954b, Thorsson 1985.

**Translation:** Byock 1990.

## B5. SIGURD AGAINST FAFNIR: SNORRI STURLUSON *PROSE EDDA* (OLD NORSE; CA. 1220 AD)

The ca. 1220 AD *Prose Edda* of Snorri Sturluson implies that Fafnir's transformation into a serpent is aided by his wearing of Hreidmar's Helm of Dread (cf. **B7**). The killing of Fafnir is described in much the same terms as in the

*Volsungasaga* (**B4**), with some minor variations. After Sigurd has killed Fafnir, Regin reveals that the dragon was his brother and then asks Sigurd to roast the heart as an act of settlement between them. Again Regin drinks Fafnir's blood but falls asleep immediately after doing so, which explains why he is not able to use his own newfound gift of prophecy to foresee his murder by Sigurd. Sigurd scalds his thumb accidentally on the heart and sucks it in response.

**Source:** Snorri Sturluson *Prose Edda*, *Skáldskaparmál* §§46–7 ('Otter's Ransom' and 'Fafnir, Regin and Sigurd').

**Text:** Jónsson 1931, Faulkes 1998.

**Translation:** Byock and Poole 2005.

## B6. SIGURD AGAINST REGIN: *THIDREKSSAGA* (OLD NORSE; CA. 1230–50 AD)

*Thidrekssaga* is an Old Norse saga based on lost German material. For this narrative the two key figures are Regin and his brother Mimir, but in this case it is Regin that becomes the dragon, with Mimir taking on the role of the smith. Regin has become a dragon as a result of his devotion to sorcery, but it is not clear whether this is by his own design. Sigurd is a clumsy and unruly apprentice to Mimir, and the smith decides to unburden himself of the young man by the ruse of sending him into the forest to make charcoal. There he is to meet Regin, the 'fire-dragon' (*linnormr*), whom Mimir has already asked to destroy the apprentice. Regin attacks Sigurd as he is burning his logs for the charcoal. Sigurd grabs the largest burning beam from the fire and strikes the dragon on the head with it, killing him. He then chops the carcass's head off with an axe (it is noteworthy that Regin is again decapitated, even though he has exchanged roles in this narrative; cf. **B4**). Sigurd stews the dragon up to make a meal for himself, scalds his fingers in the soup and sucks them, thereby acquiring the prophetic language of birds. He learns from them straightaway that Mimir is plotting to kill him and so returns to him and kills him first. He fortifies himself for the task by smearing either the dragon's sweat or its blood (the manuscript reading is insecure) over himself to give himself an impenetrable horny skin. However, he is unable to reach a small patch in the centre of his back (cf. **B3**).

**Source:** *Thidrekssaga* §§163–7.

**Text:** Bertelsen 1905–11 and Jónsson 1954a.

**Translation:** Haymes 1988.

## B7. SIGURD AGAINST FAFNIR: *POETIC EDDA* (OLD NORSE; CA. 1270 AD)

The *Poetic Edda* hews closely to the *Prose Edda*'s account (**B5**). From its *Reginsmal* we learn that Regin is himself a dwarf, whereas from its *Fafnismal* we learn that both Regin and Fafnir are giants. It may again be suggested that the Helm of Dread is responsible for transforming Fafnir into a dragon.

**Source:** *Poetic Edda*, *Reginsmal* and *Fafnismal*; cf. also *Gripisspa*.

**Text:** Dronke 1969–2010.

**Translations:** Larrington 1996:143–65, Dronke 1969–2010.

## B8. TRISTAN AGAINST THE DRAGON OF WEXFORD: GOTTFRIED VON STRASSBURG, *TRISTAN* (MIDDLE HIGH GERMAN; 1210 AD)

In Gottfried von Strassburg's *Tristan* a terrible fiery dragon is burning up the country and the people around Wexford. The king of Ireland offers the hand of his daughter Isolde to the hero that slays it. In the course of an extended battle the dragon eats half of his horse, but Tristan eventually tracks it down, kills it and cuts out its tongue, closing its mouth again after doing so. He stumbles away from the immediate scene only to be overcome by a mixture of exhaustion, the dragon's heat and the noxious fumes exuded by the tongue he has with him. Whilst he is out of action, the king's craven steward comes across the dragon's body, chops its head off and runs back to the king with it, claiming to have slain it and demanding the reward of Isolde's hand. In due course, however, there is a showdown at court in which the steward produces the head as evidence for his story, which is then refuted when Tristan produces the tongue. Thus Tristan wins Isolde. The reason for including this engaging tale here in Appendix B as opposed to Appendix C is, it must be conceded, slender, since Gottfried's *Tristan* is derived from French and ultimately Celtic forebears.

**Source:** *Tristan* books 13–14, esp. 13 lines 8963–9092.
**Text:** Krohn 1980.
**Translation:** Hatto 1960.

## B9. THOR AGAINST THE MIDGARD SERPENT: SNORRI STURLUSON, *PROSE EDDA* (OLD NORSE; CA. 1220 AD)

Snorri Sturluson tells that the Midgard ('mid-yard' or 'middle-earth') Serpent is the son of Loki. Odin casts it into the ocean that surrounds all the lands, where it grows to an enormous size and coils around the lands, biting its tail. Utgarda-Loki (Loki of the 'out-yard' or 'outer regions') disguises the serpent as a housecat and tricks Thor into attempting, in a trial of strength, to lift it off the ground. Thor can do no more than raise one of the cat's paws. Upon discovering the trick, the angry Thor goes out onto the ocean to fish for the serpent with the giant Hymir. He baits his hook with an ox head, which the serpent takes and then pulls on strongly. Thor braces himself so hard against the bottom of the boat that his feet smash through it, and he must brace himself against the ocean floor. Thor and the serpent, the latter spitting venom, lock eyes as they wrestle with the line. Thor finally pulls the serpent on board and raises his hammer to kill it, but the giant takes fright and cuts the line with the bait knife, causing the serpent to sink down to the bottom of the sea. However, Thor hurls his hammer after it and even so strikes its head off, before punching the giant behind the ear and knocking him into the sea. Snorri Sturluson intervenes in his own narrative at this point to deny that the serpent was killed and to assert that instead it lives on and still lies in the sea that surrounds the lands. At Ragnarok (the 'Twilight of the Gods') this still-living Midgard Serpent will writhe in fury and attack the land, spewing venom again into air and sea. Thor will again fight and kill the serpent, but he will also die himself from the venom it spits upon him.

**Source:** Snorri Sturluson *Prose Edda*, *Gylfaginning* §§34, 46–48, 51, 53.

**Text:** Jónsson 1931, Faulkes 1998.

**Translation:** Byock and Poole 2005.

### B10. THOR AGAINST THE MIDGARD SERPENT: *POETIC EDDA* (OLD NORSE; CA. 1270 AD)

The tale of Thor's fishing expedition for the Midgard Serpent is told in shorter compass in the *Poetic Edda*. The details of the killing, which are slightly compromised by a lacuna, resemble those of the *Prose Edda* (**B9**), save that there is no role in the denouement for the giant Hymir. After hauling the serpent onto the boat, Thor succeeds in striking its head with the hammer before letting the carcass sink back into the deep.

**Source:** *Poetic Edda*, *Hymiskvitha* §§17–26.

**Text:** Dronke 1969–2010.

**Translations:** Larrington 1996:143–65, Dronke 1969–2010.

### B11. THIDREK AND FASOLD AGAINST A FLYING DRAGON: *THIDREKSSAGA* (OLD NORSE; CA. 1230–50 AD)

*Thidrekssaga* further offers the wonderful tale of Thidrek and Fasold's rescue of Sistram from a flying dragon. (Thidrek is better known as Dietrich of Bern, i.e. Verona, a distant refraction of Theodoric.) Thidrek and Fasold espy a dragon flying low, skimming the ground with its iron-like claws. A half-swallowed fellow knight, spitting blood but still very much alive, protrudes from its mouth. It is the weight of the knight, swallowed weapons and all, that prevents the dragon from getting properly airborne, despite its size and strength. Sistram, for it is he, calls upon the pair to help him, sheepishly explaining that the dragon picked him up as he slept. Thidrek and Fasold strike at the creature with their swords but cannot penetrate its skin. Sistram hands them his own sword from the dragon's mouth, telling them that it will be more effective; he also asks them to be careful not to wound his own legs as they strike the creature, jammed well down its throat as they are. Thidrek and Fasold duly hack at the dragon as Sistram bids until they succeed in killing it.

**Source:** *Thidrekssaga* §105.

**Text:** Bertelsen 1905–11 and Jónsson 1954a.

**Translation:** Haymes 1988.

### B12. RAGNARR LODBROK AGAINST A PAIR OF MASSIVE VIPERS: SAXO GRAMMATICUS, *GESTA DANORUM* (LATIN; EARLY XIII AD)

The historical but heavily mythologised Ragnarr Lodbrok, king of the Danes, is pitted against a pair of serpents in Saxo Grammaticus's *Gesta Danorum*. Since this is a Latin text, the narrative is supplied in full translation:

> He redirected his love towards Thora, daughter of King Herodd, and wished to marry her. He repudiated Ladgerda. He mistrusted her loyalty, for he re-

membered that she once set beasts of the greatest ferocity upon him to destroy him. Meanwhile Herodd, king of the Swedes, was by chance hunting in the woods when his companions found two snakes. He took them back to his daughter to rear. She immediately obeyed her father's command and steeled herself to rear these viper specimens with her maiden hands. Indeed, she took care that their appetite should be satisfied by an entire ox carcass every day, unaware as she was that she was nurturing with her private food supplies a public disaster. When they were grown, they began to burn up the local area with their most pestilential breath. The king, repenting of his idle project, proclaimed that whoever eliminated the pest could marry his daughter. A great many young men were drawn there, attracted as much by lust as by the opportunity to display valour. But their labours were hazardous and in vain. Ragnarr learned what was happening from travellers between the two courts. He asked his nurse for a woollen cloak and some quite shaggy thigh protectors with which to deflect bites inflicted by the snakes. He had the idea of protecting himself by wearing clothing stuffed with hair, which would remain flexible and allow him to move freely. When his ship reached Sweden, a frost was falling. He purposefully threw his body into water, wetted his clothing and then exposed it to the cold to harden it and render it more impenetrable. Dressed in this fashion, he bade farewell to his companions, urged them to maintain their loyalty to Fridleif and made off on his own to the palace. When he saw it, he tied his sword to his flank and strapped his spear to his right hand. As he proceeded, a serpent [*serpens*] of unusual size slid up to confront him. Then a second, equal in size to the first, crawled up in the trail of the first. They strove both to batter him with their coils and to spew their vomit and venom all over him continuously. In the meantime the courtiers made for safe hiding places and watched the battle from a distance, just like frightened little girls. The king himself was equally terrified and took refuge in a small room with a few others. But Ragnarr, relying on the hardness of his frozen clothing, combated the venomous attacks not just with his weapons but also with what he was wearing. Fighting alone, he withstood the gaping pair in tireless battle as they showered forth their venom over him with a continuous blast of breath. He deflected the bites with his shield and the venom with his clothes. Eventually he launched his spear from his hand and drove it into the bodies of the beasts as they attacked him with all vigour. He penetrated both of their breasts with it and brought the fight to a happy conclusion. The king [Herodd] was intrigued by his clothing and studied it, when he noticed how hairy and bristly it was. He laughed out loud at the shagginess of his lower clothes in particular, and above all at the unkempt appearance of his breeches, and gave him the joking name of Lodbrok [Hairy Breeches]. When Ragnarr had recovered from his toils, the king invited him to a banquet with his friends. Ragnarr said that he first had to go back and see the witnesses he had left. He set out and brought them back smartly dressed in anticipation of the banquet. At long last, when the meal was done, he was given the appointed prize of victory [i.e. Thora]. With her he sired Radbard and Dunwat, who had splendid qualities. Nature gave them some additional brothers, Siward, Bjorn, Agnar and Iwar. (Saxo Grammaticus *Gesta Danorum* 9.252–3; trans. Ogden)

Alas, serpentkind eventually has its revenge upon Ragnarr. After the usurping king Harald attempts, in Ragnarr's absence, to introduce Christianity to

Denmark, Ragnarr returns, ousts him and restores the old religion. God then punishes him by allowing him to be captured by the Irish, who execute him by throwing him into a pit of snakes (9.262). For folkloric parallels to this narrative, Germanic and other, see Krappe 1941b, Davidson and Fisher 1998:ii, 152–3.

**Source:** Saxo Grammaticus *Gesta Danorum* 9.252–3, 262.

**Text:** Olrik and Raeder 1931.

**Translation:** Davidson and Fisher 1998:i.

# Appendix C
## *A Selection of Dragon- and Serpent-Slaying Tales of Folkloric Interest*

Figure C-1 The Wonderful Legend of the Lambton Worm. Cover, anonymous pamphlet, 1875 AD. After Simpson 1980:72.

## C1. KING JANAMEJAYA AND THE SERPENT SACRIFICE (SANSKRIT; CA. 300 BC AND 300 AD)

The *Adi Parvan* of the *Mahabharata* tells how the Naga-raja (cobra king) Takshaka disguises himself as a worm and hides himself in an apple King Parikshit of Hastinapura is eating. As Parikshit finds the worm, Takshaka reverts to his true Naga-raja form, bites him, destroys him with fire and burns down his house. Parikshit's son Janamejaya determines to avenge his father upon the entire Naga race. He learns from his Brahmins of a rite that will compel Takshaka to throw himself into a fire: the *Sarpa-sattra* or 'serpent sacrifice'. The Brahmins don black robes, mark off a sacrificial area, utter their mantras, perform their rites and kindle a fire. All the serpents of the world are drawn to it and compelled to hurl themselves into the flames. The serpents come in all colours; some are a mile long, and some are the size of elephants. Millions are destroyed by the rite in this way. Takshaka himself is on the point of being drawn into the flames when the youth Astika, who has won Janamejaya's admiration, intervenes and, asking for the favour that Janamejaya has granted him, bids him bring an end to the sacrifice.

Source: *Adi Parvan* of the *Mahabharata* §§49–58.

Text: Sukthankar et al. 1933–66.

Translation: van Buitenen 1977.

## C2. THE BUDDHA OVERCOMES CANDA, THE NAGA-RAJA OF URUVELA, WITH HIS OWN FIERY NATURE (PALI; I AD)

The Pali Buddhist text of the first century AD, the *Mahavagga*, tells of the night the Buddha spends in a monastery at Uruvela near Benares (Varanasi), where he encounters a fiery Naga-raja (cobra king). Upon arrival he asks the head of the monastery if he may sleep in the room where the sacred fire is kept. The monk grants the Buddha permission but repeatedly tries to dissuade him because the room is occupied by Canda, 'a savage Naga-raja of great magical power, a dreadfully venomous serpent'. But the Buddha remains true to his purpose and goes to sit in the room, cross-legged and alert. The Naga, enraged, attacks him with a cloud of smoke, whereupon the Buddha uses his own miraculous power to send forth a cloud of smoke in return. The Naga, angrier still, now sends forth flames, and the Buddha too, in response, converts his own body into fire and sends forth flames of his own. The Buddha thus overcomes the Naga and casts its body into his alms bowl. He then shows the Naga's remains to the head monk: 'His fire has been conquered by my fire.'

Source: *Mahavagga* 1.15.1–5.

Text: Moonesinghe and Hewavitarne 1958.

Translation: Davids and Oldenberg 1881:118–20.

## C3. ALEXANDER THE GREAT SLAYS A DRAGON NEAR PRASIAKE IN INDIA (SYRIAC; VII AD)

The Syriac version of the *Alexander Romance* consists of a translation, thought to have been made in the seventh century AD, of a Greek version of the

*Romance* closely related to the oldest surviving Greek recension ('alpha'), yet exhibiting enough differences from it to be regarded as a unique representative of a separate recension ('delta'). It tells how Alexander comes to a people adjacent to Indian Prasiake who tell him that his way across the mountain ahead will be blocked by a great god in the form of a dragon that lives in a temple beside a river upon it. It is capable of sucking up an elephant with its breath and often takes human victims. To keep the dragon placated, a local man devoted to the service of the god takes it two oxen a day. These he deposits, their legs tied, on the opposite bank of the river; he then retreats to the top of the mountain. In due course the dragon emerges from the temple and devours the oxen. On hearing this, Alexander concludes to himself that the creature is not a god, but a wicked demon. Alexander takes a stand on the mountaintop to watch the creature feed. He sees that it resembles a cloud because of the fog of smoke emanating from its mouth, and he observes it sucking the oxen into its mouth from afar. Alexander then commands that on the following day it be given only small oxen, so that it will be all the more hungry on the following one. Hungry already on the second day after its inadequate meal, it crosses the river a second time, wandering around in search of more food, and on finding nothing threatens to come up the mountainside to where Alexander and his army are positioned, but they drive it back with a shout. On the third day Alexander orders that two huge oxen be prepared for the dragon. Their flesh is to be removed and their hides filled with gypsum, pitch, lead and sulphur. The dragon crosses the river and inhales the two oxen at once, falling to the ground, its mouth agape, as the gypsum enters its belly and uprooting trees with its thrashing tail. Alexander then orders brass balls to be heated with a smith's bellows and thrown into the creature's mouth. After receiving five balls, the beast shuts its mouth and dies. Alexander leads his army on.

**Source:** *Syriac Alexander Romance* 3.7.
**Text and Translation:** Budge 1889.

## C4. ARDESHIR SLAYS THE WORM OF HAFTVAD (MIDDLE PERSIAN; CA. 706 AD, CA. 1000 AD)

Ferdowsi's *Shahnameh* of ca. 1000 AD contains a number of dragon-slaying tales, of which the most compelling is that of the Worm of Haftvad. According to this, Haftvad is originally a poor man of Kajaran. One day his daughter finds a small worm in a windfall apple. Recognising it as a luck-bringing creature, she keeps it in her spindle case, where she feeds it with apple. At once she is able to spin twice as much as usual, and soon the family becomes rich as a result of the luck conferred by the worm. Eventually Haftvad is able to use his vast wealth to make himself the tyrannical ruler of his region. He builds himself a castle from which he conquers a vast empire, good luck ever attending his army. All this time the worm has been growing. After it outgrew its spindle case, Haftvad made a chest for it. As the family moves into the castle, he builds a large stone cistern for it there. Five years on again, it has grown to the size of an elephant. Its diet too has moved on, from apple, then to rice and now to milk and honey. King Ardeshir grows concerned by this burgeoning empire and determines to put Haftvad down, but his initial military movements against him end in failure. Then two friendly brothers explain to Ardeshir that the worm is in fact a manifestation of Ahriman and that he will need trickery to defeat it, so he devises a ruse. Ardeshir approaches the castle with lavish gifts and claims to be a rich merchant of Khorasan who has made his money by virtue of his devotion to the worm, to which he has now come to pay his respects. He is admitted, gets the worm's attendants drunk on wine, and pours molten lead down its throat, splitting its bowels open; the cistern and the whole town surrounding the castle reverberate to the noise of the explosion. His talisman now gone, Haftvad's forces desert to Ardeshir, and the tyrant is soon captured and executed. The later part of this story (from the point at which Ardeshir clashes with Haftvad), is already attested in the surviving abridgement of the *Book of the Deeds of Ardeshir* (*Kārnāmag ī Araxšer ī Pābagān*, sometimes known as the *Ardeshir Romance*), which, in the form in which we have it, was probably composed fairly soon after 706 AD. Among its minor points of variation, Ardeshir pours brass, rather than lead, down the worm's throat.

**Source:** *Shahnameh* C.1381–91; *Deeds of Ardeshir* §§7–9 Grenet.

**Text:** Khaleghi-Motlagh 1988– (*Shahnameh*); Grenet 2003 (*Deeds of Ardeshir*).

**Translation:** Davis 2006:544–53, Warner and Warner 1912:vi, 232–45 (*Shahnameh*); Grenet 2003 (*Deeds of Ardeshir*, French).

## C5. FERGUS MAC LÉTI SLAYS A *MUIRDRIS* (OLD IRISH; XI AD, REFLECTING A VII–VIII AD FOREBEAR)

An Old Irish legal text preserves the following story. Fergus mac Léti, the king of Ulster, falls asleep on the coast, whereupon some leprechauns (appearing here for the first time in Irish tradition) attempt to carry him into the sea. But as his feet touch the water, he wakes and grabs hold of three of them. He agrees to release them in return for the granting of a wish, and he asks for the power to swim (indefinitely) underwater. This they grant him, with the proviso that he should not go under his own Loch Rudraige (Dundrum Bay). He is given herbs to put in his ears as he swims. The day comes when Fergus defies the leprechauns' proviso and swims under Loch Rudraige. In its waters he encounters a dreadful monster, a *muirdris*, which inflates and contracts itself like a smith's bellows. His terror at the sight of it leaves his mouth permanently wrenched around to the back of his head, and he flees back to the land. His charioteer bids him sleep to recover from his ordeal, but while Fergus does so, he goes to consult the wise men of Ulster, who are assembled at Emain Macha: what were they to do, since it was improper for them to have a disfigured king? But they agree that they want no other king but Fergus, and so they determine that he himself should never be permitted to discover his own disfigurement. To this end, all base and half-witted people are to be banished from the king's house, and he is only to have his face washed while lying on his back, so that he may not see his reflection in the water. In this way they are able to maintain the secret for seven years. But one day, as Fergus is having his face washed by his bondswoman Dorn, he becomes irritated with her for washing him too slowly and whips her. Stung by resentment, she taunts him with the truth of his disfigurement, whereupon he cuts her in half with his sword. He then returns to the loch, and its waters seethe for a day and a night as he does battle with the *muirdris*. At last he emerges carrying the creature's head, but then immediately drops down dead. The waters of the loch remain red with blood for a month.

Source: *Echtra Fergusa mac Léti* 4–8.
Text and Translation: Binchy 1952:41–4.

## C6. ESFANDYAR RIDES A SPIKED CHARIOT INTO THE MOUTH OF A DRAGON ON THE ROAD TO TURÁN (MIDDLE PERSIAN; CA. 1000 AD)

Ferdowsi's *Shahnameh* also relates how, amongst other perils on the road to Turán, Esfandyar encounters a dragon with a body resembling a flint mountain. It breathes forth fire and has bright, bloody eyes and sharp claws, and it sucks up fish out of the deep. Esfandyar has his carpenters build him a boxed-in chariot studded with projecting sword blades in which he rides to meet it. As they approach the dragon, his horses try to escape, but as it sucks them down, they draw the chariot in after them, which becomes lodged in the dragon's gullet. The beast's blood begins to gush forth, and it grows weak. Esfandyar rises from his box and hacks his way out with his sword upwards through the dragon's brain, but he is then overcome by the fumes of its venom. He is revived by his retinue with rosewater. All give thanks to Allah.

Source: *Shahnameh* V.1591–4.
Text: Khaleghi-Motlagh 1988–.
Translation: Warner and Warner 1912:5.125–8 (omitted from Davis 2006).

## C7. THE SONS OF KRAKUS SLAY THE DRAGON OF KRAKÓW (LATIN; 1190–1208 AD)

Wincenty Kadłubek's *Chronicle or Origin of the Kings and Princes of Poland* records the tale of how the elder Krakus prevailed upon his two sons to kill the Dragon of Kraków, 'Smok Wawelski'. The Latin text is given in a full formal translation:

> So Poland had been raised to greatness by the brilliant successes of Krakus. He was resolved that his offspring were the worthiest to succeed, and so they would have done had not one of his two sons been compromised by the crime of fratricide against the other. For there was in the recesses of a certain crag a monster of enormous savagery, which some men hold to be called a 'whole-swallower' [*holophagus*]. Every week, in accordance with the reckoning of days, a specific number of oxen were owed to its voracity. If the locals did not offer these to it as sacrificial victims, the monster would take revenge upon them by seizing an equivalent number of people. Krakus could not endure this blight, and since he was a merciful son more to his fatherland than he was a father to his own sons, he summoned his sons in secret, described his proposal and laid out his plan.... 'It is only right that you should take up arms to kill the monster, and fitting that you should be in the forefront of the battle against the monster, not spared from it, since

you are each half of my life, and the succession of this kingdom is owed to you.'...So the sons laid out, instead of the oxen, oxhides filled with burning sulphur in the accustomed place. When the whole-swallower gulped these down in its great greed, it was choked by the flames smoking inside it. But then the younger brother ambushed and killed the elder, regarding him not as a partner in victory and kingdom, but as a competitor for these. He wept for his death with crocodile tears and lied that he had been killed by the monster. Even so, he was embraced and congratulated as victor by his father. For often grief over death is overcome by the joy of victory. In this way the younger Krakus succeeded to his father's rule, a wicked heir! But the stain of his fratricide was to endure longer than the distinction of his rule. For his deception was uncovered shortly afterwards and he was condemned to exile in perpetuity in punishment for his crime....Anyway, a splendid city was soon founded on the whole-swallower's crag, called Kraków [Craccovia] after Krakus [Craccus], so that he should live forever in memory. The funeral obsequies were finally brought to an end by the completion of the city. Some people called it Kraków [Cracovia] because of the crowing [*crocitatio*] of the crows that had swarmed together over the body of the monster. The council, the leading men and the entire common people were so bound by their love for the dead prince that they chose his only child, his little virgin daughter, to succeed his father. Her name was Wanda....(Trans. Ogden)

**Source:** Wincenty Kadłubek *Chronica seu originale regum et principum Poloniae.*

**Text:** *Monumenta Poloniae historica* (Bielowski 1864–93) ii 256–7.

## C8. A NAMELESS SAINT SLAYS A DRAGON WITH A CIRCLE OF SPITTLE (LATIN; EARLIER XIV AD)

The French Dominican Jean Gobi (Johannes Gobii Junior) tells the following tale in his *Ladder to Heaven*:

It is told in the *History in Three Parts* that a most wicked dragon [*draco*] was devouring people and could not be repelled by the power of arms or by the power of men. Upon hearing of this, a certain saint said, 'My dear men, the power of a dragon is no greater than that of a demon, but the power of a demon is repelled by fasting and prayer. So let us mortify our flesh and our bodies by fasting, so that God may take pity on us.' When he had done this for ten days, he called all the people together and said, 'So that you may all learn how powerful fasting is, I want you all to spit into my bowl.' He took the spittle and made a circle around the dragon. It was unable to escape from the circle and died. Then the saint began to declare in loud voice, 'Just as the power of the corporeal fast killed this dragon, so the power of the spiritual fast repels all a demon's power and temptation.' (Trans. Ogden)

**Source:** Jean Gobi *Scala coeli* no. 13.
**Text:** Polo de Beaulieu 1991.

## C9. A SORCERER DESTROYS A PLAGUE OF SNAKES BY CHARMING THEM INTO A PYRE (AUSTRIAN GERMAN; TRADITIONAL, RECORDED 1859)

Zingerle records the following folk tale from Steeg, in the Tyrol. In Birchetsgump, near Steeg, the snakes proliferate in such numbers that the locals can barely mow or make hay. One day a foreign sorcerer comes and promises a remedy, provided that there is no white snake among the creatures. He is reassured that no such snake has ever been seen. So he goes onto the mountain, kindles a great fire and begins to read from a book of spells. As the first snake shoots into the fire, a high-pitched whistling is heard far off. Thereupon the sorcerer grows pale, says that he is done for and shouts to the people to get away. The snakes rush into the fire, but the last one is a white one with a little crown on its head, and it pierces the sorcerer through before it too falls into the fire.

**Source-text:** Zingerle 1859: 181–2 no. 302.

## C10. FRIDELO DESTROYS A PLAGUE OF SNAKES BY CHARMING THEM INTO A CIRCULAR PYRE (AUSTRIAN GERMAN; TRADITIONAL, RECORDED 1913)

Pehr records the following tale from Friedlach, in the Tyrol; it is reminiscent of C9 and also, in part, of the famous tale of the Pied Piper of Hamelin. Poisonous worms come to proliferate in the inhospitable lowlands around Friedlach, in Glantal. They then move up the hills, enter people's homes and eat the food out of their bowls from under their noses. Nothing is of any use against them: not, prayer, not fire, not poison. A stranger arrives from neighbouring Italy, one Fridelo. He undertakes to destroy all the snakes, provided that there is not a white one among them, for in that case he would be done for. Since no one recalls seeing such a snake, Fridelo sets to work. He has brushwood arranged in a wide circle around an old oak tree on a hill and then bids farewell to the townspeople, making them promise to establish an everlasting expiation for his soul should the terrible snake queen show herself after all and destroy him. He then takes up his position in the tree, has the brushwood kindled and begins to play a lovely tune on a small flute. Snakes by the hundreds dart this way and that out of rubble, houses and stables, from holes, furrows and ravines. As if drawn by an invisible force, they slither into the blazing fire, wanting in vain to leap over the embers. They all meet their death in the flames. The locals watch from the adjacent hills and, through the smoke and steam generated by the snakes' carcasses, see that Fridelo seems satisfied with his work. They give expression to their joy with a loud shout. But all of a sudden a ringing cry heralds the approach of the white snake. It is larger and stronger than all the others and winds itself in terrible coils. The snake queen leaps at Fridelo across the barrier of embers and kills him, along with herself, in the flames. The region is now liberated from the snake plague. The community make good their vow, and on the hill where Fridelo did his work they build the church of the modern parish of Friedlach, the name of which is (supposedly) derived from 'Fridelo's-oak' (originally Vridelosaich), whilst Count Wilhelm von Glanegg establishes the 'snake mass', which is recited annually until 1862 in the castle chapel.

**Source-text:** Pehr 1913:37 no. 18.

## C11. ASSIPATTLE SLAYS THE STOOR WORM BY SAILING INTO ITS MOUTH AND DIGGING BURNING PEAT INTO ITS LIVER (ORKNEY ENGLISH; TRADITIONAL, RECORDED 1891)

The Stoor Worm is a monstrous sea serpent that girds the earth with its length. One day it comes to attack Assipattle's homeland, the location of which is unstated, though the context suggests Scandinavia. The king is advised by his sage that he must placate the worm by feeding it seven virgins a week, and these are duly bound hand and foot and laid out for it on a rock by the shore. In due course the people, ever being deprived of their daughters, grow restive, and the king is advised that he must persuade the monster to depart once and for all by offering it the supreme sacrifice of his own daughter, the Princess Gem-de-Lovely, the most beautiful girl in the land. Asking his people for a few days' grace, the king makes proclamation throughout his land for a champion to take on the Worm, with the hand of Gem-de-Lovely, the succession to the throne and Snikkersnapper, the great sword inherited from Odin, for prizes. Assipattle, the idle but boastful son of a farmer, volunteers but is scorned by the king's messenger. So he steals his father's horse Teetgong, who has the ability to run like the wind when his rider gives him the secret sign by blowing through the windpipe of a goose. He rides to the coast, where he steals some burning peat from an old woman's fire, which she has in a bucket, and a small boat from the shore. He sails into the Worm's gaping mouth as it yawns and the waters are carried into it (it is in the habit of yawning seven times before snatching up the seven most available morsels with its forked tongue). He is carried down the serpent's gullet as if down a tunnel for miles on end and eventually is able to beach his boat by its liver. He cuts a hole in the liver and stuffs the burning peat into it. Returning to his boat, he sails back towards its mouth, is ejected as the serpent retches in pain and is carried all the way back to land. The Worm, now ablaze, shoots out its tongue in agony and briefly grips one of the moon's horns with it. As the tongue then falls back onto the earth it makes a great rift in the land into which the sea rushes, creating the Oresund Strait and the Baltic Sea. As the worm continues to writhe, it launches its head into the sky, only for it to crash down again, with its dislodged teeth forming Orkney, the Shetlands and the Faroe Islands. The bulk of its body becomes Iceland, with its liver still blazing within to create that land's volcanoes. Assipattle is duly rewarded with girl, kingdom and sword.

**Source-texts:** Dennison 1891:130–1, Marwick 1974:139–44, Simpson 1980:137–41.

## C12. HECTOR GUNN SLAYS THE WORM OF CNOC-NA-CNOIMH WITH PEAT AND PITCH (SCOTTISH ENGLISH; TRADITIONAL, RECORDED 1961)

A huge worm takes up residence in a hole in the side of a hill in Glen Cassley, Sutherland. Its principal threat lies in the venomous breath it emits, which hangs in a pall that extends for miles over the local countryside and brings death to all living things, leaving the valley desolate. Sometimes it coils around the top of its hill to survey the desolation it has caused with satisfaction, and so the hill acquires the name of Cnoc-na-Cnoimh (Worm's Hill). The king of Scotland, William the Lion (the historical king reigned 1165–1214 AD), offers reward to any knight that slays the dragon, but none is brave enough to come forward. However, a rough farmer from the Kyle of Sutherland, one Hector Gunn, does offer to try to dispatch the creature. On approach he finds that the worm is out its hole, snoozing and sunning itself on its hilltop. He rides near in an attempt to strike off its head with his broadsword but is driven back by its fumes and almost faints from them. Once he recovers, he tries another tack. He thrusts the end of his seven-ell spear through a great divot of peat, dips it in boiling pitch and rides off to attack the beast. This time it is awake and attempts to suck him into its maw with its venomous breath. As he tenders the peat and pitch, the serpent draws in their pungent fumes and begins to suffocate. In its agony it squeezes its coils tight around its hilltop. Hector is able thus to draw closer and actually thrust the burning peat down the worm's throat, finally killing it. The spiral indentations it created in the hill with its constrictions are still to be seen. King William rewards Hector with land and money.

**Source-text:** Robertson 1961:131–2.

## C13. BARON LINTON SLAYS THE WORM OF WORMISTONE WITH PEAT AND PITCH (ENGLISH; TRADITIONAL, RECORDED 1879)

William Henderson recorded the tale of the slaying of the Worm of Wormistone in the following form. A voracious worm has a lair, the 'Worm's Hole', in the hill of Linton. With its venomous breath it sucks flocks and herds into its maw. Sometimes it comes out and coils around another neighbouring hill, subsequently known as Wormistone or Wormington Hill. Rich rewards are offered to anyone who will destroy the worm, and finally the brave laird of Lariston comes forward. He first attacks it with conventional weapons but achieves nothing. He then returns to fight with a divot of peat dipped in scalding pitch fixed to the end of his lance. The aromatic fumes of the burning peat at once suffocate the monster and preserve the hero from the effects of its venomous breath. In its death throes the worm contracts its coils around Wormistone Hill, with the result that it is scarred with spiral indentations. The laird is rewarded with lands in the region.

**Source-text:** Henderson 1879:295–6. (I have not been able to confirm whether this tale was already included in the rare first edition of this volume published in 1866.)

## C14. SIR JOHN LAMBTON SLAYS THE LAMBTON WORM IN SPIKED ARMOUR AND WITH THE HELP OF A FAST-FLOWING RIVER (ENGLISH; TRADITIONAL, RECORDED, IN THIS VERSION, CA. 1875)

The young Sir John Lambton, heir to the Lord of Lambton, sacrilegiously fishes on a Sunday and catches an ugly little worm on his rod. He throws it down a well in disgust. There the worm grows, eventually to enormous size. It comes to coil itself three times around a local hill, subsequently to be known as Worm Hill, and then begins to lay waste to the local area, seizing lambs and sucking the cows' milk. Numerous knights challenge it in vain, losing life or limb. Whenever the worm is cut asunder, the pieces immediately rejoin themselves together. After seven years of the worm's marauding, Sir John, now a pious Christian, returns from the crusades to the scene of devastation and determines to go up against the dragon himself. Taking advice from a sibyl first, he learns that he is himself the cause of the blight and is told that he must face the worm in a suit of armour studded with spear blades; furthermore, he must vow that, should he be successful in slaying the creature, he will also kill the first living creature he meets afterwards, else no Lord of Lambton will die in his bed for nine generations. Sir John joins battle with the worm on a rock in the middle of a river. It coils around him and attempts to constrict him, impaling itself on his spikes, and thereby weakens itself so much that Sir John is able to hack it in two. The swift-flowing current carries one of its halves away so that it cannot reunite with its other half, and the creature consequently dies. Sir John's overjoyed father, the Lord of Lambton, rushes to congratulate him. Sir John cannot bear to kill him, and he breaks his vow. The second living creature he encounters is his favourite dog, which he kills with a heavy heart, forlornly hoping to fulfil his vow in this way. And so the curse falls upon the following nine generations of the family.

**Source-text:** Simpson 1980:124–7 (reproducing anonymous pamphlet of ca. 1875).

## 15. THE BLACKSMITH OF DALRY SLAYS THE WHITE SNAKE OF MOTE HILL IN ARMOUR WITH RETRACTABLE SPIKES (SCOTTISH ENGLISH; TRADITIONAL, RECORDED 1885)

Andrew Lang recorded the following tale from Dalry in Kirkcudbright. A huge, snow-white snake with an impenetrable skin terrorises Dalry. Its body is as thick as three bags of meal, and it coils itself three times around a large barrow adjacently to a river. It destroys the people and the cattle and even goes to the local churchyard and with its claws digs up the recently dead in order to devour them. The Lord of Galloway offers a reward to any of his knights that can deal with the blight. The first to come forward is swallowed up by the serpent, horse and all, in a single mouthful. A second knight comes forward, but bad omens deter his attempts to join to battle with the snake: first he is thrown by his horse; then he experiences a nosebleed as he gets into the saddle. Meanwhile a Dalry smith has been making his own preparations to face the snake: he has constructed a suit of armour with retractable spikes. No sooner has he made it than his young, beautiful wife dies and is buried in the churchyard. The night after the funeral a small child alerts the smith to the fact that the snake is scraping at her grave. He leaps to his feet, dons his armour, spikes retracted, and rushes to the churchyard. When he arrives, the snake pounces upon him at once and swallows him whole. Once inside the monster, the smith springs out his spikes. The spikes, well tempered as they are, allow the smith, with considerable effort, to tear his way through the snake's skin from the inside, leaving it dead. As the smith emerges victorious from the snake's carcass, the second knight arrives upon the scene and, in frustration at losing his own opportunity for glory, attacks the smith, who defeats him too. The river runs red for three days with the serpent's blood.

**Source-text:** Lang 1885:258.

# List of Editions Used

The following records the (for the most part critical) editions of the Greek and Latin texts upon which the foregoing translations have been principally based. Alternative readings have occasionally been adopted.

[Abdias] *Historia Apostolica*
   Fabricius 1719

Achilles Tatius
   Garnaud 1991

*Acts of St Marina*
   Usener 1886:15–46

Acts
   Aland et al. 1968

Acts of John
   Lipsius and Bonnet 1891–1903

Acts of Philip, Martyrion of Philip
   Amsler et al. 1999

Acts of Silvester A (1)
   Text reproduced at Pohlkamp 1983:11

Acts of Silvester B (1)
   Text reproduced at Duchesne 1897:31–2

Acts of Thomas
   Lipsius and Bonnet 1891–1903

Aelian
   Hercher 1864–6

Aeschylus *Phorcides*
   *TrGF* iii

Aldhelm *De virginitate* (prose and verse)
   Ehwald 1919

Alexander of Myndus
   *FGrH* 25

*Alexander Romance* (A text)
   Kroll 1926

Antoninus *Liberalis*
   Cazzaniga 1962

Apollodorus *Bibliotheca*
> Wagner et al. 1894–1902

Apollonius of Rhodes *Argonautica*
> Fraenkel 1961

Apuleius *Metamorphoses*
> Helm 1912

Aristonicus of Tarentum
> *FHG* iv, 337

Aristophanes
> Wilson 2007

[Aristotle] *Mirabilium auscultationes*
> Bekker 1831

Athenaeus
> Olson 2006–12

Athenagoras *Legatio*
> Diels and Krantz 1951–2, 1B13

Bacchylides
> Maehler 2003

Bede *Ecclesiastical History*
> Colgrave and Mynors 1969

Clement of Alexandria *Protrepticus*
> Früchtel et al. 1960–70

Conon
> *FGrH* 26

*Conversio et passio ii S. Afrae*
> *MGH Scriptores rerum Merovingicarum* 3, 41–64

Critias
> *TrGF* ii

Damascius *De principiis*
> Ruelle 1899

Demetrius of Magnesia
> *see* Diogenes Laertius

*De Promissionibus*
> *PL* 51, 733–856

*Digenis Akritis* (Grottaferrata version)
> Jeffreys 1998

Dio Chrysostom
> von Arnim 1893–6

Diodorus
> Fischer and Vogel 1888–1906

Diogenes Laertius
> Long 1964

Dionysius Periegetes
> Brodersen 1994

Dionysius of Samos
> *FGrH* 15

Dionysius Scytobrachion
> *FGrH* 32

Ephorus
> *FGrH* 70

[Eratosthenes] *Catasterismi*
> Wagner et al. 1894–1902

Euphorion
> Lightfoot 2009

Euripides
> *Fragments*: *TrGF* v
> *Bacchae, Medea*: Diggle 1981–94

Eustathius *Commentary on Dionysius Periegetes*
> GGM

*First Vatican Mythographer*
> Zorzetti and Berlioz 2003

Fulgentius
> Helm 1898

Gerald of Wales *On the Topography of Ireland*
> Brewer et al. 1861–91: v, 3–204 (Dimock)

Gospel of Ps.-Matthew
> Tischendorf 1876

Gospel of Thomas
> Tischendorf 1876

Gregory the Great *Dialogues*
> de Vogüé and Antin 1979

Gregory of Tours
> *Liber vitae patrum*: MGH Scriptores Rerum Merovingicarum 1.2
> *Life of St Andrew*: 1989:564–651

Hellanicus
> Fowler 2000

Heraclides of Pontus
> Wehrli 1944–78, 7

Heraclitus
> Wagner et al. 1894–1902

Herodorus of Heraclea
> Fowler 2000

Herodotus
> Legrand 1932–68

Hesiod
> *Shield*: Solmsen et al. 1990
> *Theogony*: West 1966

**Hesychius**
    Latte 1953–66
**Hippobotus**
    *see* Diogenes Laertius
**Homer**
    *Iliad*: West 1998–2000
    *Odyssey*: von der Mühll 1962
***Homeric Hymns***
    West 2003a
**Hyginus**
    *De astronomia*: Viré 1992
    *Fabulae*: Marshall 1993
**Isidore of Seville**
    Barney 2005
**Jacobus de Voragine *Golden Legend***
    Graesse 1850
**Jerome *Life of Hilarion the Hermit***
    Bastiaensen 1975
**Jocelin of Furness *Life of St Patrick***
    *Acta Sanctorum*, March ii, 540–80
**John Malalas**
    Dindorf 1831
**Josephus**
    Niese 1887–95
**Lucan**
    Housman 1926
**Lucian**
    Macleod 1972–87
**Luke**
    Aland et al. 1968
**Lycophron *Alexandra***
    Mascialino 1964
**Lycus**
    *FGrH* 570
**Manilius**
    Goold 1985
**Nonnus *Dionysiaca***
    Favant et al. 1976–2006
**Menander Rhetor**
    Russell and Wilson 1981
***Mirabilia urbis Romanae***
    Valentini and Zuchetti 1946
***Miracula Sancti Georgii, Codex Romanus Angelicus* 46**
    Aufhauser 1911:52–69

Origen *Contra Celsum*
  Borret 1967–9
*Orphic Argonautica*
  Vian 1987
Ovid *Metamorphoses*
  Bosselaar and van Proosdij 1951
Palaephatus
  Wagner et al. 1894–1902
Panyassis
  West 2003b
*Passion of SS. Perpetua and Felicitas*
  Musurillo 1972:106–31
*Passion of St Victoria*
  Delehaye et al. 1883
Paul the Deacon *Gesta episcoporum Mettensium*
  PL 95, 709–22
Paulinus of Nola *Carmina*
  de Hartel 1999
Pausanias of Antioch
  *FHG* iv, 467–71
Pausanias Periegetes
  Spiro 1903
Petronius
  Müller 1995
Pherecydes of Athens
  Fowler 2000:272–364
Pherecydes of Syrus
  Schibli 1990
Philochorus
  *FGrH* 323
Philostrati
  *Imagines*: Benndorf and Schenkl 1893
  *Life of Apollonius*: Jones 2005–6
Photius *Bibiliotheca*
  Henry 1959–77
Pindar *Nemeans, Olympians, Pythians*
  Snell and Maehler 1984–9
Pisander of Camirus
  West 2003b
Plautus *Amphitruo*
  Christenson 2000
Pliny *Natural History*
  Beaujeu et al. 1950–2003

Plutarch
>    *Failure of Oracles*: Sieveking 1929
>    *Parallela minora*: Nächstadt 1935

Pomponius Mela
>    Silberman 1988

Procles of Carthage
>    *FHG* iv, pp. 483–4

Propertius
>    Heyworth 2007

Ps.-: for pseudonymous texts *see under* relevant name

Pythocles of Samos
>    *FHG* iv, pp. 488–9

*Questions of Bartholomew*
>    Bonwetsch 1897

Quintus Smyrnaeus
>    Pompella 2002

Revelation
>    Aland et al. 1968

Scholia to Aristophanes *Peace*
>    Holwerda 1982

Scholia to Homer *Iliad*
>    Erbse 1971–88

Scholia to Lycophron (incl. Tzetzes)
>    Scheer 1958

Scholia to Nicander
>    Geymonat 1974

Scholia to Plato
>    Greene 1938

[Scylax] *Perplus*
>    GGM

Seneca
>    *Hercules Furens*: Billerbeck 1999
>    *Medea*: Chaumartin 1996–

Septuagint
>    Rahlfs 1935

Servius
>    Thilo and Hagen 1878–1902

Shepherd of Hermas
>    Whittaker 1967

Silius Italicus
>    Delz 1987

Sophocles *Trachiniae*
>    Easterling 1982

**Sozomen** *Ecclesiastical History*
  Bidez and Hansen 1960
**Statius** *Thebaid*
  Lesueur 1990–4
**Strabo**
  Meinecke 1877
**Tertullian**
  Reifferscheid et al. 1890–1957
**Theocritus**
  Gow 1950
**Timaeus**
  *FGrH* 566
**Tyrannius Rufinus** *Historia monachorum in Aegypto*
  *PL* 21, 391–462
**Tzetzes**
  *See* Scholia to Lycophron
**Valerius Flaccus**
  Liberman 1997
**Valerius Maximus**
  Briscoe 1998
**Venantius Fortunatus** *Vita S. Marcelli Pariensis Episcopi, Vita S. Hilarii [Pictavensis]*
  *MGH Auctores antiquissimi* 4.2
**Virgil** *Aeneid*
  Mynors 1972
***Vita i S. Gildae***
  *MGH Auctores antiquissimi* 13, 91–106
***Vita S. Samsonis, episcopi Dolensis***
  Flobert 1997
**Xenophon**
  Marchant 1900–20

# References

Acta Sanctorum. 1643–. Multiple vols. Antwerp.
Ahbel-Rappe, S. 2010. *Damascius' Problems and Solutions Concerning First Principles.* New York.
Aland, K., M. Black, C.M. Martini, B.M. Metzger and A. Wikgren. 1968. *The Greek New Testament.* 2nd ed. Stuttgart.
Alexiades, M.A. 1982. Οἱ Ἑλληνικὲς Παραλλαγὲς γιὰ τὸν Δρακοντοκτόνο Ἥρωα (Aarne-Thompson 300, 301A καὶ 301B). Παραμυθολογικὴ Μελέτη. Ph.D. diss., University of Ioannina. [English-language summary at 133–6.]
Amandry, P. 1948. 'Πύρπνοος Χίμαιρα' *Revue archéologique*, 1–11.
Amandry, P. 1952. 'Herakles et l'hydra de Lerne' *Bulletin de la Faculté des lettres de Strasbourg* 30, 293–322.
Amandry, P., and D. Amyx. 1982. 'Héraclès et l'Hydre de Lerne dans la céramique corinthienne' *Antike Kunst* 25, 102–16.
Amat, J. 1996. *Passion de Perpétue et Félicité suivi des Actes:* Introduction, texte critique, traduction commentaire et index. Paris.
Amsler, F., F. Bovon and B. Bouvier. 1996. *Actes de l'apôtre Philippe.* Turnhout.
Amsler, F., F. Bovon and B. Bouvier. 1999. *Acta Philippi.* 2 vols. [Vol. 1: Textus; Vol. 2: Commentarius.] Corpus Christianorum, Series Apocryphorum 11–12. Turnhout.
Andreae, B. 1989. *Laokoon und die Gründung Roms.* Mainz am Rhein.
Andreae, B., and B. Conticello. 1987. *Skylla und Charybdis: zur Skylla-Gruppe von Sperlonga.* Abhandlungen der Mainzer Akademie 14. Mainz am Rhein.
Arya, R.P., and K.L. Joshi, eds. 2001. *Rgveda Samhita: Sanskrit Text, English Translation, Notes and Index of Verses.* 4 vols. Delhi.
Aufhauser, J.B. 1911. *Das Drachenwunder des heiligen Georg in der griechischen und lateinischen Überlieferung.* Byzantinisches Archiv 5. Leipzig.
*Aufstieg und Niedergang der römischen Welt.* 1972–. Multiple volumes and parts. Berlin.
Ballabriga, A. 1990. 'Le dernier adversaire de Zeus: le mythe de Typhon dans l'épopée grecque archaïque' *Revue de l'histoire des religions* 207, 3–30.
Balty, J.-C. 1997. 'Kassiepeia' *LIMC* viii.1, 666–70.
Barney, S.A. 2005. *The Etymologies of Isidore of Seville.* Cambridge.
Basset, E.L. 1955. 'Regulus and the serpent in the *Punica*' *Classical Philology* 50, 1–20.
Bastiaensen, A.A.R., ed. 1975. *Vita di Martino—Vita di Ilarione—In memoria di Paola.* Milan.
Batto, B.F. 1992. *Slaying the Dragon: Mythmaking in the Biblical Tradition.* Louisville, KY.
Beaude, P.-M. 2000. 'Les dragons dans la Bible' in J.-M. Privat, ed., *Dans la gueule du dragon: Histoire—ethnologie—literature.* Sarreguemines. 135–43.
Beaujeu, J., et al. 1950–2003. *Pline l'ancien: Histoire naturelle.* 37 vols. Paris.
Beckman, G. 1982. 'The Anatolian myth of Illuyanka' *Journal of the Ancient Near Eastern Society* 14, 11–25.
Bekker, I. 1831. *Aristotelis opera.* Vol. 2. Berlin.
Belson, J.D. 1980. 'The Medusa Rondanini' *American Journal of Archaeology* 84, 373–78.

Benndorf, O., and K. Schenkl 1893. *Philostrati maioris imagines*. Leipzig.
Bernabé, A., and A.I. Jiménez San Cristóbal 2008. *Instructions for the Netherworld: the Orphic Gold Tablets*. Leiden. Trans. of *Instrucciones para el más allá: aas aaminillas Órfi cas de oro*. Madrid, 2002.
Bernand, A. 1970. *Le delta égyptien d'après les textes grecs*. 4 vols. Cairo.
Bertelsen, H., ed. 1905–11. *Thidriks Saga af Bern*. 2 vols. Copenhagen.
Besig, H. 1937. *Gorgo und Gorgoneion in der archaischen griechischen Kunst*. Berlin.
Bidez, J., and G.C. Hansen, eds. 1960. *Sozomenus: Kirchengeschichte*. Die griechischen Schriftsteller 50. Berlin.
Bieler, L. 1949. *The Life and Legend of St Patrick: Problems of Modern Scholarship*. Dublin.
Bielowski, A., ed. 1864–93. *Monumenta Poloniae historica*. 6 vols. Lvov.
Billerbeck, M. 1999. *Seneca: Hercules Furens*. Leiden.
Binchy, D.A. 1952. 'The saga of Fergus mac Léti' *Ériu* 16, 33–48.
Blaise, F. 1992. 'L' épisode de Typhée dans la Théogonie d' Hésiode' *Revue des études grecques* 105, 349–70.
Blinkenberg, C. 1924. 'Gorgone et lionne' *Revue archéologique* 19, 267–77.
Blum, R., and E. Blum. 1970. *The Dangerous Hour: the Lore and Culture of Crisis and Mystery in Ancient Greece*. London.
Boardman, J. 1987. 'Very like a whale—classical sea monsters' in A.E. Farkas, ed., *Monsters and Demons in the Ancient and Medieval Worlds*. Mainz. 73–84.
Boardman, J. 1990a. 'I. A. Herakles Dodekathlos' *LIMC* v.1, 5–16.
Boardman, J. 1990b. 'VII. B. Herakles fights a snake' *LIMC* v.1, 119–20.
Boardman, J. 1992. 'Lamia' *LIMC* vi.1, 189.
Boardman, J. 1997. 'Ketos' *LIMC* viii.1, 731–36; 8. 2, 496–501.
Bodson, L. 1981. 'Les grecs et leurs serpents: premiers résultats de l'étude taxonomique des sources anciennes' *AC* 50, 57–78 with plates i–iv.
Bömer, F. 1969–86. *P. Ovidius Naso Metamorphosen: Kommentar*. 7 vols. Heidelberg.
Bond, G.W., ed. 1963. *Euripides: Hypsipyle*. Oxford.
Bonnechere, P. 2003. *Trophonios de Lébadée: cultes et myths d'une cité béotienne au miroir de la mentalilté antique*. Leiden.
Bonwetsch, G.N. 1897. 'Die apokryphen Fragen des Bartholomäus' *Nachrichten von der königlichen Gesellschaft der Wissenschaften, Philol.-hist. Kl*. 9–29.
Boosen, M. 1986. *Etruskische Meermischwesen: Untersuchungen zu Typologie unde Bedeutung*. Rome.
Bornkamm, G. 1933. *Mythos und Legende in den apokryphen Thomas-Akten: Beiträge zur Geschichte der Gnosis und zur Vorgeschichte des Manichäismus*. Göttingen.
Borret, M. 1967–9. *Origène. Contre Celse*. 4 vols. Paris.
Bosselaar, D.E., and B.A van Proosdij. 1951. *P. Ovidii Nasonis Metamorphoseon Libri i–xv*. Leiden.
Boulotis, C. 1997. 'Hypsipyle i' *LIMC* viii.1, 645–60. [NB: This article is out of sequence within *LIMC*.]
Bovon, F. 1988. 'Les Actes de Philippe' *ANRW* ii.25.6, 4431–527.
Bovon, F. 2008. *Das Evangelium nach Lukas*. Vol. 2. 2nd ed. Neukirchen-Vluyn.
Braswell, B.K. 1988. *A Commentary on the Fourth Pythian Ode of Pindar*. Berlin.
Brazda, M.K. 1977. *Zur Bedeutung des Apfels in der Antiken Kultur*. Bonn.
Bremmer, J.N., ed. 1996. *The Apocryphal Acts of John*. Kampen.
Bremmer, J.N., ed. 2000. *The Apocryphal Acts of Andrew*. Leuven.
Bremmer, J.N., ed. 2001. *The Apocryphal Acts of Thomas*. Leuven.
Bremmer, J.N., ed. 2012. *Perpetua's Passions: Multidisciplinary Approaches to the* Passio Perpetuae et Felicitatis. Oxford.
Brendel, O. 1932. 'Die Schlangenwürgende Herakliskos' *Jahrbuch des deutschen archäologischen Instituts* 47, 191–238.
Brennan, B. 1985. 'The career of Venantius Fortunatus' *Traditio* 41, 49–78.
Brereton, J., and S.W. Jamison, eds. Forthcoming. *The Rig Veda: Translation and Explanatory Notes*. Oxford.

Brewer, J.S, J.F. Dimock and G.F. Warner, eds. 1861–91. *Giraldus Cambrensis: Works*. 8 vols. London.
Briscoe, J. 1998. *Valerii Maximi* Facta et dicta memorabilia. 2 vols. Leipzig.
Brodersen, K. 1994. *Dionysios von Alexandria: das Lied von der Welt*. Hildesheim.
Brommer, F. 1942. 'Herakles und die Hesperiden auf Vasenbildern' *Jahrbuch des deutschen archäologischen Instituts* 57, 105–23.
Brommer, F. 1955. 'Die Königstochter und das Ungeheuer' *Marburger Winckelmann Programm 1955*. Marburg. 3–15.
Budge, E.A.W. 1889. *The History of Alexander the Great, Being the Syriac Version of the Pseudo-Callisthenes*. Cambridge.
Budge, E.A.W. 1910. *Facsimiles of Egyptian Hieratic Papyri in the British Museum*. London.
Buitron-Oliver, D. 1992. *The Odyssey and Ancient Art*. Exhibition catalogue. Annandale-on-Hudson.
Burck, E. 1976. 'Die Befreiung der Andromeda bei Ovid und der Hesione bei Valerius Flaccus' *Wiener Studien* 10, 221–38.
Burkert, W. 1979. *Structure and History in Greek Mythology and Ritual*. Berkeley.
Burkert, W. 1983. 'Oriental myth and literature in the *Iliad*' in R. Hägg, ed., *The Greek Renaissance of the Eighth Century BC: Tradition and Innovation: Proceedings of the Second International Symposium at the Swedish Institute in Athens, 1–5 June 1981*. Stockholm. 51–6.
Burkert, W. 1992. *The Orientalizing Revolution*. Cambridge, MA.
Byock, J.L., trans. 1990. *The Saga of the Volsungs*. Berkeley.
Byock, J.L., and R. Poole, trans. 2005. *Snorri Sturluson: The Prose Edda*. London.
Canella, T. 2006. *Gli Actus Silvestri*. Spoleto.
Caquot, A., M. Sznycer and A. Herdner. 1974. *Textes ougaritiques i: mythes et légendes*. Paris.
Cassuto, U. 1961. *A Commentary on the Book of Genesis*. Jerusalem.
Castellana, M. 2000. 'Le regard du dragon dans la légende de saint Georges' in J.-M. Privat, ed., *Dans la gueule du dragon: Histoire—ethnologie—literature*. Sarreguemines. 159–72.
*Catalogus codicum hagiographicorum latinorum antiquiorum seaculo xvi qui asservantur in Bibliotheca Nationali Parisiensi*. 1889–93. 4 vols. Brussels.
Caterall, J.L. 1937. 'Perseus' *RE* 19.1, 978–92.
Cazzaniga, I. 1962. *Antoninus Liberalis: Metamorphoseon synagogue*. Milan.
Chaumartin, F.-R. 1996–. *Senèque: Tragédies*. Budé. 3 vols. Paris.
Chazan, M. 2000. 'Le dragon dans la légende de le saint Clément, premier évêque de Metz' in J.-M. Privat, ed., *Dans la gueule du dragon: histoire—ethnologie—literature*. Sarreguemines. 17–35.
Christenson, D.M. 2000. *Plautus: Amphitruo*. Cambridge.
Clauss, J., and S.I. Johnston, eds. *Medea*. Princeton.
Cockle, W.E.H. 1987. *Euripides: Hypsipyle. Based on a Re-examination of the Papyri*. Rome.
Colgrave, B., and R.A.B. Mynors. 1969. *Bede's Ecclesiastical History of the English People*. Oxford Medieval Texts. Oxford.
Collard, C., M.J. Cropp and K.H. Lee. 1995. *Euripides: Selected Fragmentary Plays*. Vol. 1. Warminster.
Collard, C., M.J. Cropp and J. Gibert. 2004. *Euripides: Selected Fragmentary Plays*. Vol. 2. Warminster.
Collins, N.L. 2000. *The Library at Alexandria and the Bible in Greek*. Leiden.
Coogan, M.D. 1978. *Stories from Ancient Canaan*. Philadelphia.
Cook, A.B. 1914–40. *Zeus: a Study in Ancient Religion*. 3 vols. Cambridge.
*Corpus Scriptorum Ecclesiasticorum Latinorum*. 1865–. Vienna.
Croon, J.H. 1955. 'The mask of the underworld demon—some remarks on the Perseus-Gorgon story' *Journal of Hellenic Studies* 75, 9–16.

Dalley, S., trans. 2000. *Myths from Mesopotamia*. Oxford World's Classics. Rev. ed. Oxford.

Daremberg, C., and E. Saglio, eds. 1877–1919. *Dictionnaire des antiquités grecques et romaines*. 5 vols. Paris.

Darmesteter, J., and L.H. Mills. 1880–7. *The Zend-Avesta*. 3 vols. The Sacred Books of the East, Vols 4, 23, 31. Oxford.

Davids, T.W., and H. Oldenberg, trans. 1881. *Vinaya Texts*. Part I, Sacred Books of the East, Vol. 13. Oxford.

Davidson, H.E., and P. Fisher. 1998. *Saxo Grammaticus: the History of the Danes, Books I–IX*. 2 vols. Rochester, NY.

Davies, M. 1988. *Epicorum Graecorum fragmenta*. Göttingen.

Davis, D., trans. 2006. *Albolqasem Ferdowsi: Shahnameh, the Persian Book of Kings*. New York.

Day, J. 1977. *God's Conflict with the Dragon and the Sea: Echoes of a Canaanite Myth in the Old Testament*. University of Cambridge Oriental Publications 5. Cambridge.

de Hartel, W., ed. 1999. *Paulinus of Nolanus: Carmina*. CSEL 30. Vienna.

Delehaye, H., et al., eds. 1883. 'Passio S. Victoriae' in *Analecta Bollandiana* 2, 157–60.

Delz, J. 1987. *Sili Italici* Punica. Stuttgart.

Dennison, W.T. 1891. 'Orkney Folklore: Sea Myths 3' *Scottish Antiquary* 5, 130–3.

Detienne, M., and J.-P. Vernant. 1978. *Cunning Intelligence in Greek Culture and Society*. Chicago. Trans. of *Les ruses d'intellegence: la Métis des grecs*. Paris, 1974.

de Vogüé, A., and P. Antin. 1979. *Grégoire le Grand: Dialogues, tome ii (livres i–iii)*. Paris.

Didi-Huberman, G., R. Garbetta and M. Morgaine 1994. *Saint Georges et le dragon: versions d'une légende*. Paris.

Diels, H., and W. Krantz, eds. 1951–2. *Die Fragmente der Vorsokratiker*. 3 vols. 6th ed. Berlin.

Diggle, J. 1981–94. *Euripides*. 3 vols. Oxford.

Dillon, J.E.M. 1990. The Greek Hero Perseus: Myths of Maturation. D.Phil. diss., Oxford University.

Dindorf, L. 1831. *Ioannis Malalae chronographia*. Bonn.

Dörig, J., and O. Gigon. 1961. *Der Kampf der Götter und Titanen*. Göttingen.

Douglas, E.M. 1913. 'Iuno Sospita of Lanuvium' *Journal of Roman Studies* 3, 60–72.

Drexler, W. 1886–90. 'Hesione' *ML* 1.2, 2591–94.

Dronke, U., ed. and trans. 1969–2010. *The Poetic Edda*. 3 vols. Oxford.

Duchesne, L. 1897. 'S. Maria Antiqua: notes sur la topographie de Rome au moyen-âge, viii' *Mélanges d'archéologie et d'histoire* 17, 13–37.

Dunand, F. 1969. 'Les representations de l'Agathodémon; à propos de quelques bas-reliefs du Musée d'Alexandrie' *Bulletin de l'Institut français d'archéologie orientale* 67, 9–48.

Dunand, F. 1981. 'Agathodaimon' *LIMC* i.1, 277–82. Zurich.

Dunbabin, T.J. 1951–3. 'Bellerophon, Herakles and Chimaera' in *Studies Presented to David Moore Robinson on his Seventieth Birthday*. 2 vols. St Louis. ii, 1164–84.

Easterling, P.E. 1982. *Sophocles: Trachiniae*. Cambridge.

Ebner, M., H. Gzella, H.-G. Nesselrath and E. Ribbat. 2001. *Lukian: die Lügenfreunde. Scripta antiquitatis posterioris ad ethicam religionemque pertinentia* 3. Darmstadt.

Edelstein, E.J., and L. Edelstein. 1945. *Asclepius: a Collection and Interpretation of the Testimonies*. 2 vols. Baltimore.

Ehrman, B.D. 2003. *The Apostolic Fathers* Vol. 2. LCL. Cambridge, MA.

Ehwald, R., ed. 1919. 'Aldhelm *De Virginitate*' in *Monumenta Germaniae historica*. Auctores antiquissimi 15. Berlin. 226–323 and 350–471.

Eitrem, S. 1921. 'Kerberos' *RE* 11.1, 271–84.

Elliot, J.K. 2005. *The Apocryphal New Testament*. 2nd ed. Oxford.

Erbse, H. 1971–88. *Scholia Graeca in Homeri Iliadem*. 7 vols. Berlin.

Evans, J.D. 1985. 'Semiotics and traditional lore: the medieval dragon tradition' *Journal of Folklore Research* 22, 85–112.

Fabricius, J.A., ed. 1719. *Codex apocryphus Novi Testamenti*. 2 vols. 2nd ed. Hamburg.
Fallon, F.T., and R. Cameron. 1988. 'The Gospel of Thomas: a Forschungsbericht and analysis' *ANRW* ii.25.6, 4195–251.
Farber, W. 1983. 'Lamaštu' *Reallexikon der Assyriologie* 6, 439–46.
Faulkes, A. 1998. *Edda by Snorri Sturluson: Skáldskaparmál*. 2 vols. London.
Favant, M.-C., et al. 1976–2006. *Nonnos de Panopolis: les dionysiaques*. 18 vols. Paris.
Feldman, T.P. [= T.P. Howe] 1965. 'Gorgo and the origin of fear' *Arion* 4, 484–94.
Fernández Marcos, N. 2000. *The Septuagint in Context: Introduction to the Greek Versions of the Bible*. Leiden.
Festugière, A.J. 1961. *Historia monachorum in Aegypto*. Brussels.
Festugière, A.J. 1964. *Les moines d'orient*. Paris.
Fischer, H. 1975–. 'Georg, Hl.' in K. Ranke et al., eds, *Enzyklopädie des Märchens: Handwörterbuch zur historischen und vergleichenden Erzählforschung*. 13+ vols. Berlin. v, 1030–9.
Fischer, K.T., and F. Vogel. 1888–1906. *Diodori bibliotheca historica*. 5 vols. 3rd ed. Leipzig.
Flobert, P., ed. 1997. *La vie ancienne de Saint Samson de Dol*. Paris.
Floren, J. 1977. *Studien zur Typologie des Gorgoneion*. Münster.
Foerster, W. 1935. 'Δράκων' in C. Kittel and G. Friedrich, eds, *Theologisches Wörterbuch zum Neuen Testament* ii, 284–86.
Foerster, W., J. Grether and J. Fichtner. 1957. 'ὄφις' in C. Kittel and G. Friedrich, eds, *Theologisches Wörterbuch zum Neuen Testament* v, 566–82.
Fontenrose, J. 1959. *Python: a Study of the Delphic Myth and its Origins*. Berkeley.
Fontenrose, J. 1968. 'The hero as athlete' *California Studies in Classical Antiquity* 1, 73–104.
Fontenrose, J. 1983. 'The building of the city walls: Troy and Asgard' *Journal of American Folklore* 96, 53–63.
Fowler, R.L. 2000. *Early Greek Mythography*. Vol. 1. Oxford.
Fraenkel, H. 1961. *Apollonii Rhodii* Argonautica. Oxford.
Fraser, P.M. 1972. *Ptolemaic Alexandria*. 3 vols. Oxford.
Frazer, Sir James G. 1921. *Apollodorus: The Library*. LCL. 2 vols. Cambridge, MA.
Früchtel, L., O. Stählin and U. Treu, 1960–70. *Clemens Alexandrinus*. Vols 2–3 (Vol. 2: 3rd ed.; Vol. 3: 2nd ed.). Berlin.
Furtwängler, A. 1886–90. 'Die Gorgonen in der Kunst' *ML* 1.2, 1701–27.
Ganschinietz/Ganszyniec, R. 1918. 'Agathodaimon' *RE Supplementband* 3, 37–59.
Ganschinietz/Ganszyniec, R. 1919. *De Agatho-daemone*. Warsaw.
Gantz, T. 1993. *Early Greek Myth: a Guide to Literary and Artistic Sources*. Baltimore.
Garnaud, J.-P. 1991. *Achille Tatius: le roman de Leucippé et Clitophon*. Paris.
Gathercole, S. 2012. *The Composition of the Gospel of Thomas: Original Language and Influences*. Cambridge.
Geisau, H. 1963. 'Python' *RE* 24.1, 606–10.
Geldner, K.-F. 1886–96. *Avesta: the Sacred Books of the Parsis*. Stuttgart.
Geymonat, M. 1974. *Scholia in Nicandri Alexipharmaca*. Milan.
Gibson, L. 1978. *Canaanite Myths and Legends*. Edinburgh.
Glotz, G. 1877–1919a. 'Gorgones' *DA* 2, 1615–29.
Glotz, G. 1877–1919b. 'Perseus' in C. Daremberg and E. Saglio, eds, *Dictionnaire des antiquités grecques et romaines*. Paris. 4, 398–406.
Godding, R. 2000. 'De Perpétue à Caluppan: les premières apparitions du dragon dans l'hagiographie' in J.-M. Privat, ed., *Dans la gueule du dragon: Histoire—ethnologie—literature*. Sarreguemines. 145–57.
Goetz, O. 2000. 'Le théâtre du monstre' in J.-M. Privat, ed., *Dans la gueule du dragon: Histoire—ethnologie—literature*. Sarreguemines. 53–78.
Goldman, B. 1961. 'The Asiatic ancestry of the Greek Gorgon' *Berytus* 14, 1–22 and plates i–ix.
Gooding, D.W. 1963. 'Aristeas and Septuagint Origins: a Review of Recent Articles' *Vetus Testamentum* 13, 357–79.

Goodman, M., J. Barton and J. Muddiman, eds. 2012. *The Apocrypha*. Oxford.
Goold, G.P. 1985. *M. Manilii Astronomica*. Stuttgart.
Gourmelen, L. 2004. *Kékrops, le roi-serpent: imaginaire athénien, représentations de l'humain et de l'animalité en Grèce ancienne*. Paris.
Gow, A.S.F. 1950. *Theocritus*. 2 vols. Cambridge.
Grabow, E. 1998. *Schlangenbilder in der griechischen schwartzfiguren Vasenkunst*. Münster.
Graesse, J.G.T., ed. 1850. *Jacobus de Voragine, Legenda aurea*. Leipzig.
Green, J.B. 1997. *The Gospel of Luke*. Grand Rapids, MI.
Greene, W.C. 1938. *Scholia Platonica*. Haverford, PA.
Grenet, F. 2003. *Le geste d'Ardashir fils de Pâbag: Kārnāmag ī Araxšer ī Pābagān*. Die.
Halm-Tisserant, M. 1986. 'Le gorgoneion, emblème d'Athena: introduction du motif sur le bouclier et l'égide' *Revue archéologique*, 245–78.
Hamilton, Sir William, and J.H.W. Tischbein. 1791–5. *Collection of Engravings from Ancient Vases*. 4 vols. Naples.
Hampe, R. 1935–6. 'Korfugiebel und frühe Perseusbilder' *Mitteilungen des deutschen archäologischen Instituts: athenische Abteilungen* 60–61, 269–99 and plates 93–100.
Hansen, W.F. 2002. *Ariadne's Thread: a Guide to International Tales Found in Classical Literature*. Ithaca.
Hansen, W.F. 2004. *Classical Mythology: a Guide to the Mythical World of the Greeks and Romans*. New York.
Hardie, P. 1986. *Virgil's* Aeneid: *Cosmos and Imperium*. Oxford.
Harrison, J. 1912. *Themis*. Cambridge.
Hartland, E.S. 1894–6. *The Legend of Perseus: a Study of Tradition in Story, Custom and Belief*. 3 vols. London.
Hartwig, P. 1893. 'Die Heraufholung des Kerberos auf rotfiguren Schalen' *Jahrbuch des deutschen archäologischen Instituts* 8, 157–73.
Hatto, A.T., trans. 1960. *Gottfried von Strasburg: Tristan*. London.
Hatto, A.T., trans., 1965. *The Niebelungenlied*. London.
Haymes, E.R., trans. 1988. *The Saga of Thidrek of Bern*. London.
Heffernan, T.J. 2012. *The Passion of Perpetua and Felicity*. New York.
Helm, R. 1898. *Fabii Planciadis Fulgentii v.c. opera*. Leipzig.
Helm, R. 1912. *Apuleii Platonici Madaurensis opera quae supersunt*. Vol. 1, *Metamorphoseon libri xi*. Leipzig.
Henderson, W. 1879. *Notes on the Folklore on the Northern Counties of England and the Border*. Publications of the Folklore Society 2. 2nd ed. London.
Henry, R. 1959–77. *Photius: Bibliothèque*. 8 vols. Paris.
Hercher, R. 1864–6. *Claudii Aeliani de natura animalium libri xvi, varia historia, epistolae, fragmenta*. 2 vols. Leipzig.
Hetzner, U. 1963. *Andromeda und Tarpeia*. Meisenheim am Glan.
Heydemann, H. 1886. *Jason in Kolchis*. Halle.
Heyworth, S.J. 2007. *Sexti Properti elegos*. Oxford.
Hillard, T.W. 1998. 'The *Agathos Daimon* abandons Alexandria: the Potter's Oracle and possible Roman allusions' in T.W. Hillard et al., eds, *Ancient History in a Modern University*, Vol. 1, *The Ancient Near East, Greece and Rome*. Grand Rapids, MI. 160–72.
Hillard, T.W. 2010. 'The god abandons Antony: Egyptian street theatre in 30 BC' in N. Kanawati, hon., A. Woods, A. McFarlane and S. Binder, eds, *Egyptian Culture and Society: Studies in Honour of Naguib Kanawati*. 2 vols. Cairo. 1, 201–17.
Himmelmann, N. 1991. 'Laokoon' *Antike Kunst* 34, 97–115.
Hine, H.M. 2000. *Seneca: Medea*. Warminster.
Höckmann, U. 1991. 'Zeus besiegt Typhon' *AA* [no serial no.], 11–23.
Hoffner, H.A. 1998. *Hittite Myths*. 2nd ed. Atlanta.
Holland, R. 1900. 'Mythographische Beiträge: 1. Der Typhoeuskampf' *Philologus* 59, 344–54.
Holwerda, D. 1982. *Scholia in Vespas, Pace, Aves et Lysistratam*. Groningen.

Housman, A.E. 1926. *Lucani Belli civilis libri x*. Oxford.
Howe, T.P. [= T.P. Feldman]. 1952. An Interpretation of the Perseus-Gorgon Myth in Greek Literature and Monuments through the Classical Period. Ph.D. diss., Columbia University.
Howe, T.P. 1953. 'Illustrations to Aeschylus' tetralogy on the Perseus theme' *American Journal of Archaeology* 57, 269–75.
Howe, T.P. 1954. 'The origin and function of the Gorgon-head' *American Journal of Archaeology* 58, 209–21.
Hughes, S.L., and J.A. Fernandez Bernades. 1981. 'Las Gorgonas: guardianas de lo sagrado' *Argos* 5, 53–73.
Isler-Kerényi, C. 2000. 'Immagini di Medea' in B. Gentili and F. Perusino, eds, *Medea nella letteratura e nell' arte*. Venice. 117–38.
Jacobsen, T. 1987. *The Harps that Once...: Sumerian Poetry in Translation*. New Haven.
Jacoby, F., et al., eds. 1923–. *Die Fragmente der griechischen Historiker*. Multiple volumes and parts. Berlin and Leiden.
Jacquemin, A. 1986. 'Chimaira' *LIMC* iii.1, 249–59.
Jacques, J.-M. 2002. *Nicandre: Œuvres*. Vol. 2. Paris.
Jacques, J.-M. 2007. *Nicandre. Œuvres*. Vol. 3. Paris.
Jakobsson, O. 1925. *Daimon och Agathos Daimon*. Lund.
Jameson, M.H. 1990. 'Perseus, the hero of Mykenai' in R. Hägg and G.C. Nordquist, eds, *Celebrations of Death and Divinity in the Bronze Age Argolid: Proceedings of the Sixth International Symposium at the Swedish Institute in Athens, 11–13 June, 1988*. Acta Instituti Atheniensis Regni Sueciae 40. Stockholm. 312–23.
Jameson, M.H., D.R. Jordan and R.D Kotansky. 1993. *A Lex Sacra from Selinous*. GRBS Monographs 11. Durham, NC.
Jeffreys, E., ed. and trans. 1998. *Digenis Akritis: the Grottaferrata and Escorial Versions*. Cambridge.
Jentel, M.-O. 1997. 'Skylla I' *LIMC* viii.1, 1137–45.
Jessen, O. 1914. 'Iason' *RE* 9.1, 75–71.
Johnson, L.T. 1992. *The Acts of the Apostles*. Collegeville, MN.
Johnston, S.I. 1999. *Restless Dead: Encounters between the Living and the Dead in Ancient Greece*. Berkeley.
Jones, C.P. 2005–6. *Philostratus: The Life of Apollonius of Tyana*. 3 vols. LCL. Cambridge, MA.
Jónsson, F., ed. 1931. *Edda Snorra Sturlusonar*. Copenhagen.
Jónsson, G., ed. 1954a. *Thithreks Saga af Bern*. 2 vols. Reykjavík.
Jónsson, G. 1954b. *Fornaldar sögur Northurlanda*. 4 vols. Akureyri.
Jouanno, C. 2002. *Naissance et métamorphoses du Roman d'Alexandre: domaine grec*. Paris.
Junod, E., and J.-D. Kaestli. 1988. 'Le dossier des Actes de Jean: état de question et perspectives nouvelles' *ANRW* ii.25.6, 4293–362.
Justi, F. 1868. *Der Bundehesh*. Leipzig.
Kaestli, J.-D. 1988. 'Où en est l'étude de l'"Évangile de Barthélemy"?' *Rev. Bib.* 95, 5–33.
Kahil, L. 1966. 'Apollon et Python' in K. Michalowski, hon., M.L. Bernhard, ed., *Mélanges offerts à Kazimierz Michalowski*. Warsaw. 483–90.
Kahil, L. 1994. 'Python' *LIMC* vii.1, 609–10.
Karagiorga, T.G. 1970. Γοργείη κεφαλή. Athens.
Kassel, R., and C. Austin. 1983–. *Poetae Comici Graeci*. 8 vols. Berlin.
Kelly, J.N.D. 1975. *Jerome: his Life, Writings and Controversies*. London.
Kenney, J.F. 1968. *The Sources for the Early History of Ireland: Ecclesiastical: an Introduction and Guide*. Shannon.
Kern, O. 1922. *Orphicorum fragmenta*. Berlin.
Kirk, G.S., J.E. Raven and M. Schofield. 1983. *The Presocratic Philosophers: a Critical History with a Selection of Texts*. 2nd ed. Cambridge.
Kittel, R., K. Elliger and W. Rudolph, eds. 1997. *Biblia Hebraica Stuttgartensia*. Stuttgart.

Khaleghi-Motlagh, D., ed. 1988–. *Abu al-Qasim Firdawsi: Shahnameh (The Book of Kings)*. 8+ vols. New York.

Klaeber, F. 1950. *Beowulf*. 3rd ed. Lexington.

Kleinknecht, H. 1944. 'Laokoon' *Hermes* 79, 66–111.

Klijn, A.F.J. 1962. *The Acts of Thomas: Introduction, Text, Commentary*. Leiden.

Klimek-Winter, R. 1993. *Andromedatragöden*. Stuttgart.

Knox, B. 1950. 'The serpent and the flame' *AJP* 71, 379–400; reprinted in S. Commager, *Virgil: a Collection of Critical Essays*. Englewood Cliffs, 1966. 124–42.

Koch, M. 2004. *Drachenkampf und Sonnenfrau: zur Funktion des Mythischen in der Johannesapokalypse am Beispeil von Apk 12*. Tübingen.

Kokkorou-Alewras, G. 1990a. 'IV. C. Herakles and the Lernaean Hydra (Labour II)' *LIMC* v.1, 34–43.

Kokkorou-Alewras, G. 1990b. 'IV. N. Herakles and the Hesperides (Labour XII)' *LIMC* v.1, 100–11.

Krappe, A.H. 1933. 'La légende de Persée' *Neuphilologische Mitteilungen* 34, 225–323.

Krappe, A.H. 1941a. 'Irish earth' *Folk-Lore* 52, 229–36.

Krappe, A.H. 1941b. 'Sur un épisode de la saga de Ragnar Lodbrók' *Acta Philologica Scandinavica* 15, 326–38.

Krappe, A.H. 1947. 'St Patrick and the snakes' *Traditio* 5, 323–30.

Krauskopf, I. 1986. 'Chimaira (in Etruria)' *LIMC* iii.1, 259–69.

Krauskopf, I. 1988. 'Gorgones (in Etruria)' *LIMC* iv.1, 330–45.

Krauskopf, I. 1994. 'Septem' *LIMC* vii.1, 730–48.

Krauskopf, I., and S.-C. Dahlinger. 1988. 'Gorgo, Gorgones' *LIMC* iv.1, 285–330.

Krohn, R. 1980. *Gottfried von Strassburg*. 3 vols. Stuttgart.

Kroll, J. 1932. *Gott und Hölle: der Mythos vom Descensuskampfe*. Leipzig.

Kroll, W., ed. 1926. *Historia Alexandri Magni (Pseudo-Callisthenes)*. Vol. 1, *Recensio vetusta*. Berlin.

Kuhnert, E. 1897–1909. 'Perseus' *ML* 3.2, 1986–2060.

Küster, E. 1913. *Die Schlange in der griechischen Kunst und Religion*. RVV 13.2. Giessen.

Lalleman, P.J. 1998. *The Acts of John: a Two-Stage Initiation into Johannine Gnosticism*. Leuven.

Lalonde, G. 2006. Horos Dios: *an Athenian Shrine and Cult*. Leiden.

Lambert, W.G., and S.B. Parker. 1966. *Enuma Eliš: the Babylonian Epic of Creation: the Cuneiform Text*. Oxford.

Lambrinudakis, W., and O. Palagia. 1984. 'Apollon' *LIMC* ii.1, 183–327.

Lane Fox, R. 2008. *Travelling Heroes*. London.

Lang, A. 1885. 'A Galloway nursery tale' *Academy* [*and Literature*] 702 (17 October), 257–58.

Langlotz, E. 1951. *Perseus*. Heidelberg.

Langlotz, E. 1960. *Der triumphierende Perseus*. Cologne.

Laroche, E. 1971. *Catalogue des textes hittites*. Paris.

Larrington, C., trans. 1996. *The Poetic Edda*. Oxford World's Classics. Oxford.

Larson, W.R. 2002. 'The role of patronage and audience in the cults of Sts Margaret and Marina of Antioch' in S.J.E. Riches and S. Salih, eds, *Gender and Holiness: Men, Women and Saints in Late Medieval Europe*. London. 23–33.

Latte, K. 1953–66. *Hesychii Alexandrini lexicon*. 2 vols. Copenhagen.

Leclerc, P., E.M. Morales and A. de Vogüé. 2007. *Jérôme: trois vies des moines (Paul, Malchus, Hilarion)*. Paris.

Le Goff, J. 1980. *Time, Work and Culture in the Middle Ages*. Chicago. Trans. of *Pour un autre Moyen Âge*. Paris, 1977.

Legrand, P.-E. 1932–68. *Hérodote: Histoires*. 9 vols. Paris.

Lesky, A. 1931. 'Medeia' *RE* 15, 29–65.

Lesky, A. 1967. 'Herakles und das Ketos' *Anzeiger der österreichischen Akademie der Wissenschaften, phil.-hist. Klasse* 104, 1–6.

Lesueur, R. 1990–4. *Stace: Thébaïde*. 3 vols. Budé. Paris.
*Lexicon Iconographicum Mythologiae Classicae*. 1981–99. 9 vols in 18 parts. Zurich and Munich.
Liberman, G. 1997. *Valerius Flaccus: Argonautiques*. 2 vols. Paris.
LiDonnici, L.R. 1995. *The Epidaurian Miracle Inscriptions: Text, Translation and Commentary*. Atlanta.
Lightfoot, J.L. 2009. *Hellenistic Collection: Philitas, Alexander of Aetolia, Hermesianax, Euphorion, Parthenius*. Cambridge, MA.
Lipsett, B.D. 2011. *Desiring Conversion: Hermas, Thecla, Aseneth*. Oxford.
Lipsius, R.A., and M. Bonnet, eds. 1891–1903. *Acta Apostolorum Apocrypha*. 2 vols. Leipzig.
Lochin, C. 1994. 'Pegasos' *LIMC* vii.1, 214–30.
Loenertz, R.J. 1975. 'Actus Silvestri, genèse d'une légende' *Revue d'histoire ecclésiastique* 70, 426–39.
Long, H.S. 1964. *Diogenis Laertii vitae philosophorum*. 2 vols. Oxford.
Macleod, M.D. 1972–87. *Luciani opera*. 4 vols. Oxford.
McPhee, I. 1990. 'Hesperides' *LIMC* v.1, 394–406.
McPhee, I. 1992. 'Ladon I' *LIMC* vi.1, 176–80.
Maehler, H. 2003. *Bacchylides: Carmina cum fragmentis*. Leipzig.
Marchant, E.C. 1900–20. *Xenophontis opera omnia*. 5 vols. Oxford.
Marinatos, S. 1927–8. Γοργόνες καὶ Γοργόνεια' Ἐφημερὶς Ἀρχαιολογική, 7–41.
Marshall, I.H. 1978. *The Gospel of Luke*. Exeter.
Marshall, P.K. 1993. *Hygini Fabulae*. Leipzig.
Marwick, E. 1974. *The Folklore of Orkney and Shetland*. London.
Mascialino, L. 1964. *Lycophronis Alexandra*. Leipzig.
Matthews, V.J. 1974. *Panyassis of Halikarnassos: Text and Commentary*. Leiden.
Mayr-Harting, H. *The Coming of Christianity to Anglo-Saxon England*. London.
Meinecke, A. 1877. *Strabonis Geographica*. 3 vols. Leipzig.
Melfi, M. 2007–. *I santuari di Asclepio in Grecia*. 1+ vols. Rome.
Merkelbach, R. 1959. 'Drache' *RAC* iv, 226–50.
Michaux, L. 2000. 'Le Graouilly, entre histoire et l'imaginaire' in J.-M. Privat, ed., *Dans la gueule du dragon: Histoire—ethnologie—literature*. Sarreguemines. 37–52.
Migne, J.P., ed. 1857–1904. *Patrologiae cursus completus: series Graeca*. Paris.
Migne, J.P., ed. 1884–1904. *Patrologiae cursus completus: series Latina*. Paris.
Miller, S.G., ed. 1990. *Nemea: a Guide to the Site and Museum*. Berkeley.
Milne, M. 1956. Review of Brommer 1955. *American Journal of Archaeology* 60, 300–2.
Mitropoulou, E. 1977. *Deities and Heroes in the Form of Snakes*. 2nd ed. Athens.
Mombritius, B., ed. 1910. *Sanctuarium sive vitae sanctorum*. 2 vols. 2nd ed. Paris. (1st ed. Milan, 1477–8.)
*Monumenta Germaniae historica*. 1826–. Berlin.
Moonesinghe, S.N.K., and W.D. Hewavitarne, eds. 1958. *Mahāwagga Pāli of Vinaya Pitaka*. 2 vols. Colombo, Sri Lanka.
Morris, P., and D. Sawyer, eds. 1992. *A Walk in the Garden: Biblical, Iconographical and Literary Images of Eden*. Journal for the Study of the Old Testament Supplement Series 136. Sheffield.
Müller, C.F.W., ed. 1855–82. *Geographi Graeci minores*. 3 vols. Paris.
Müller, C.F.W., ed. 1878–85. *Fragmenta historicorum Graecorum*. 5 vols. Paris.
Müller, K. 1995. *Petronii Arbitri Satyricon reliquiae*. Stuttgart.
Musurillo, H. 1972. *Acts of the Christian Martyrs*. Oxford.
Mynors, R.A.B. 1972. *P. Vergili Maronis opera*. Oxford.
Nächstadt, W. 1935. *Plutarchi Moralia*. Vol. 2, pt 2. Leipzig.
Napier, A.D. 1986. *Masks, Transformation and Paradox*. Berkeley.
Neils, J. 1990. 'Iason' *LIMC* v.1, 629–38.
*New English Bible*. 1961. Cambridge.
Niese, B. 1887–95. *Flavii Iosephi opera*. 6 vols. Berlin.

Nilsson, M.P. 1967–74. *Geschichte der griechischen Religion*. 2 vols. 3rd ed. Munich.
Oakley, J.H. 1997. 'Hesione' *LIMC* viii.1, 623–9.
Ogden, D. 2001. *Greek and Roman Necromancy*. Princeton.
Ogden, D. 2007. *In Search of the Sorcerer's Apprentice: the Traditional Tales of Lucian's Lover of Lies*. Swansea.
Ogden, D. 2008. *Perseus*. London.
Ogden, D. 2009. *Magic, Witchcraft and Ghosts in the Greek and Roman Worlds: a Sourcebook*. 2nd ed. New York.
Ogden, D. 2010. 'Dimensions of death in the Greek and Roman worlds' in P. Gemeinhardt and A. Zgoll, eds, *Weltkonstruktionen: Religiöse Weltdeutung zwischen Chaos und Kosmos vom Alten Orient biz zum Islam*. Orientalische Religionen in der Antike 5. Tübingen, 2010. 103–31.
Ogden, D. 2011. *Alexander the Great: Myth, Genesis and Sexuality*. Exeter.
Ogden, D. 2013. *Drakōn: Dragon Myth and Serpent Cult in the Greek and Roman Worlds*. Oxford.
Olrik, J., and H. Raeder, eds. 1931. *Gesta Danorum*. 2 vols. Copenhagen.
Olsen, M. 1906–8. *Völsunga saga ok Ragnars saga loðbrókar*. 2 vols. Copenhagen.
Olson, S.D. 2006–12. *Athenaeus: the Learned Banqueters*. 8 vols. LCL. Cambridge, MA.
Pache, C.O. 2004. *Baby and Child Heroes in Ancient Greece*. Urbana and Chicago.
Pailler, J.-M. 1997. 'La vierge et le serpent: de la trivalence à l'ambiguïté' *Mélanges de l'École française de Rome: Antiquité* 109, 513–75.
Paoletti, O. 1988. 'Gorgones Romanae' *LIMC* iv.1, 345–62.
Paribeni, E. 1988. 'Harmonia' *LIMC* iv.1, 412–14.
Parsons, P., and H. Lloyd-Jones. 1983. *Supplementum Hellenisticum*. Berlin.
Pauly, W.A., G. Wissowa and W. Kroll, eds. 1894–. *Realencyclopädie der klassischen Altertumswissenschaft*. Multiple volumes and parts. Munich.
Pehr, F. 1913. *Kärntner Sagen*. Klagenfurt.
Penglase, C. 1994. *Greek Myths and Mesopotamia: Parallels and Influence in the Homeric Hymns and Hesiod*. London.
Pervo, R.I. 2009. *Acts: a Commentary*. Minneapolis.
Pesch, R. 2003. *Die Apostelgeschichte (Apg 13–28)*. 2nd ed. Neukirchen-Vluyn.
Peter, H. 1906–14. *Historicorum Romanorum reliquiae*. 2 vols. 2nd ed. Leipzig.
Peterson, E. 1954. 'Die Begegnung mit dem Ungeheuer: Hermas, Visio IV' *Vigiliae Christianae* 8, 52–71.
Peterson, J.M. 1984. *The Dialogues of Gregory the Great in their Late Antique Cultural Background*. Toronto.
Petsalis-Diomidis, A. 2010. *Truly Beyond Wonders: Aelius Aristides and the Cult of Asklepios*. Oxford.
Phillips, K.M., Jr. 1968. 'Perseus and Andromeda' *American Journal of Archaeology* 72, 1–23, with plates 1–20.
Phinney, E., Jr. 1971. 'Perseus' battle with the Gorgons' *Transactions of the American Philological Association* 102, 445–63.
Pietersma, A., and B.C. Wright. 2007. *A New English Translation of the Septuagint*. New York.
Pietrzykowski, M. 1978. 'Sarapis-Agathos Daimon' in M.J. Vermaseren, hon., *Hommages à M.J. Vermaseren*. Études préliminaires aux religions orientales dans l'empire romaine 68. 3 vols. Leiden. iii, 959–66.
Pohlkamp, W. 1983. 'Tradition und Topographie: Papst Silvester I. (314–335) und der Drache vom Forum Romanum' *Römisch Quartalschrift für christliche Altertumskunde und Kirchengeschichte* 78, 1–100.
Polo de Beaulieu, M.-A. 1991. *La scala coeli de Jean Gobi*. Paris.
Pompella, G. 2002. *Quinti Smyrnaei Posthomerica*. Hildesheim.
Porter, J., trans. 1991. *Beowulf: Text and Translation*. Hockwold-cum-Wilton.
Porzig, W. 1930. 'Illujankas und Typhon' *Kleinasiatische Forschungen* 1, 379–86.

Pottier, E. 1877–1919. 'Draco (Δράκων)' in C. Daremberg and E. Saglio, eds, *Dictionnaire des antiquités grecques et romaines*. Paris. ii.1, 403–14.

Preisendanz, K., and A. Henrichs. 1973–4. *Papyri Graecae Magicae: die griechischen Zauberpapyri*. 2 vols. 2nd ed. Stuttgart.

Preller, L., and C. Robert. 1887–1926. *Griechische Mythologie*. 3 vols, multiple parts. 4th ed. Berlin. [Vol. 2 (in three parts) = C. Robert *Die griechische Heldensage*. Berlin, 1920–26.]

Prieur, J.-M., ed. 1989. *Acta Andreae*. Corpus Christianorum, Series Apocryphorum 6. 2 vols. Turnhout.

Pritchard, J.B., ed. 1969. *Ancient Near Eastern Texts Relating to the Old Testament*. 3rd ed. Princeton.

Privat, J.-M., ed. 2000. *Dans la gueule du dragon: Histoire—ethnologie—literature*. Sarreguemines.

Pülhorn, W. 1984. 'Archemoros' *LIMC* ii.1, 472–75.

Quaegebeur, J. 1975. *Le dieu égyptien Shaï dans la religion et l'onomastique*. Orientalia Lovaniensia Analecta 2. Leuven.

Quasten, J. 1949–60. *Patrology*. 3 vols. Utrecht. [N.B.: The inferior fourth volume that subsequently appeared under the name of Quasten is by other hands.]

Quispel, G. 1957. 'The Gospel of Thomas and the New Testament' *Vigiliae Christianae* 11, 189–207.

Radermacher, L. 1905. 'Lucian, *Philopseudes* Cap. 11 und 24' *Rheinisches Museum* n.F. 60, 315–17.

Rahlfs, A. 1935. *Septuaginta*. 2 vols. Stuttgart.

Rajak, T. 2011. *Translation and Survival: the Greek Bible of the Ancient Jewish Diaspora*. Oxford.

Rathmann, W. 1938. 'Perseus (4) Sternbild' *RE* 19.1, 992–96.

Rauer, C. 2000. *Beowulf and the Dragon*. Cambridge.

*Reallexikon für Antike und Christentum*. 1941–. Stuttgart.

Reichert, H. 2005. *Das Nibelungenlied*. Berlin.

Reifferscheid, A., et al. 1890–1957. *Quinti Septimi Tertulliani opera*. 4 vols. Vienna.

Resnick, I.M., and K.F. Kitchell, Jr. 2007. '"The sweepings of Lamia": transformations of the myths of Lilith and Lamia' in A. Cuffel and B. Britt, eds, *Religion, Gender, and Culture in the Pre-modern World*. Basingstoke. 77–104.

Riccioni, G. 1960. 'Origini e sviluppo del gorgoneion e del mito della Gorgone—Medusa nell' arte greca' *Rivista dell'Istituto Nazionale di Archeologia e Storia dell'Arte* 9, 127–206.

Riethmüller, J.W. 2005. *Asklepios: Heiligtümer und Kulte*. 2 vols. Heidelberg.

Robert, C. 1920–6. *Die griechische Heldensage*. 3 vols. 4th ed. Berlin [ = Preller and Robert 1887–1926, Vol. 2.].

Robertson, N. 1980. 'Heracles' "Catabasis"' *Hermes* 108, 274–99.

Robertson, R.M. 1961. *Selected Highland Folktales*. Edinburgh.

Roccos, L.J. 1994. 'Perseus' *LIMC* vii.1, 332–48.

Roes, R.A. 1934. 'The representation of the Chimaera' *Journal of Hellenic Studies* 54, 21–25.

Roes, R.A. 1953. 'The origin of the Chimaera' in *Studies Presented to David Moore Robinson on his Seventieth Birthday*. 2 vols. St Louis. 2, 1155–63.

Rohde, E. 1925. *Psyche*. London. [Translated from the 8th German ed.]

Röhrich, L. 1981. 'Drache, Drachenkampf, Drachentöter' in K. Ranke et al., eds, *Enzyklopädie des Märchens: Handwörterbuch zur historischen und vergleichenden Erzählforschung*. 13+ vols. Berlin. 3, 787–820.

Roscher, W.H., ed. 1884–1937a. *Ausführliches Lexikon der griechischen und römischen Mythologie*. 7 vols. Leipzig.

Roscher, W.H. 1884–1937b. 'Andromeda' *ML* i.1, 345–47.

Roscher, W.H. 1884–1937c. 'Gorgones' *ML* i.2, 1695–701.

Rossi, M.I. 1984. 'The *Passion* of St Perpetua: everywoman of late antiquity' in R.C. Smith and J. Lounibos, eds, *Pagan and Christian Anxiety: a Response to E.R. Dodds*. Lanham. 53–86.

Ruelle, C.É. 1899. *Damascii successoris dubitationes et solutiones*. 2 vols. Paris.

Russell, D.A., and N.G. Wilson. 1981. *Menander Rhetor*. Oxford.

Rutherford, I. 2007. 'Trouble in Snake-town: interpreting an oracle from Hierapolis-Pammukale' in S. Swain, S. Harrison and J. Elsner, eds, *Severan Culture*. Cambridge. 449–57.

Sancassano, M. 1997. *Il serpente e le sui immagini: il motivo del serpente nel poesia greca dall'Iliade all'Orestea*. Bibliotheca di Athenaeum 36. Como.

Sanjana, P.B., ed. 1874–1928. *The Dinkard*. 19 vols. Bombay.

Santinelli, I. 1902. 'Alcune questioni attinei ai riti delle Vergini Vestali' *Rivista di filologia e d'istruzione classica* 30, 244–69.

Schauenberg, K. 1960. *Perseus in der Kunst des Altertums*. Bonn.

Schauenberg, K. 1981. 'Andromeda I' *LIMC* i.1, 774–90.

Scheer, E. 1958. *Lycophronis* Alexandra. Vol. 2. Berlin.

Schefold, K., and F. Jung. 1988. *Die Urkönige: Perseus, Bellerophon, Herakles und Theseus in der klassischen und hellenistischen Kunst*. Munich.

Scherling, K. 1924. 'Ladon' *RE* 12.1, 385–95.

Schibli, H.S. 1990. *Pherekydes of Syros*. Oxford.

Schmidt, H. 1907. *Jona: eine Untersuchung zur vergleichenden Religionsgeschichte*. Forschungen zur Religion und Literatur des Alten und Neuen Testaments 9. Göttingen.

Schmidt, J. 1884–1937. 'Typhoeus, Typhon' *ML* v, 1426–54.

Schmidt, J. 1913. 'Skylla I' *RE* 2. Reihe 3.a, 647–55.

Schmidt, M. 1992. 'Medeia' *LIMC* vi.1, 386–98.

Schmitt, M.L. 1966. 'Bellerophon and the Chimaera in archaic Greek art' *American Journal of Archaeology* 70, 341–47 with plates 80–1.

Schwartz, J., ed. 1951. *Lucien de Samosate*. Philopseudès et De morte Peregrini, avec introduction et commentaire. Textes d'Études. Publ. Fac. Lettres Univ. Strasbourg 12. Paris.

Scobie, A., 1983. *Apuleius and Folklore: toward a History of ML3045, AaTh567, 449A*. London.

Séchan, L. 1927. 'La légende de Médée' *Revue des études grecques* 40, 234–310.

Servais-Soyez, B. 1981. 'En relisant l'iconographie de Cadmos' *Antiquité classique* 50, 733–43.

Sfameni Gasparro, G. 1997. 'Daimôn and Tuchê in the Hellenistic religious experience' in P. Bilde et al., eds, *Conventional Values of the Hellenistic Greeks*. Studies in Hellenistic Civilisations 7. Aarhus. 67–109.

Shepard, K. 1940. *The Fish-Tailed Monster in Greek and Roman Art*. New York.

Siegelova, J. 1971. *Appu-Märchen und Hedammu-Mythos*. Wiesbaden.

Sieveking, W. 1929. *Plutarchi Moralia*. Vol. 3. Leipzig.

Silberman, A. 1988. *Pomponius Mela: De chorographia*. Paris.

Simon, E. 1954. 'Die Typen der Medeadarstellungen in der antiken Kunst' *Gymnasium* 61, 203–27.

Simon, E. 1979. 'Archemoros' *Archäologischer Anzeiger*, 31–45.

Simon, E. 1984. 'Laokoon und die Geschichte der antiken Kunst' *Archäologischer Anzeiger*, 643–72.

Simon, E. 1992. 'Laokoon' *LIMC* vi.1, 196–201.

Simpson, J. 1980. *British Dragons*. London.

Sineux, P. 2007. *Amphiaraos, guerrier, devin et guérisseur*. Paris.

Smallwood, V. 1990. 'M. Herakles and Kerberos (Labour XI)' *LIMC* v.1, 85–100.

Smith, M.S. 1994. *The Ugaritic Baal Cycle*. Vetus Testamentum Supplement 55. Leiden.

Snell, B., R. Kannicht and S. Radt. 1971–2004. *Tragicorum Graecorum Fragmenta*. 5 vols. Göttingen.

Snell, B., and H. Maehler. 1984–9. *Pindari carmina*. 2 vols. Leipzig.

Solmsen, F., R. Merkelbach and M.L. West. 1990. *Hesiodi Theogonia, Opera et Dies, Scutum, Fragmenta*. 3rd ed. Oxford.
Sourvinou-Inwood, C. 1987. 'Myth as history: the previous owners of the Delphic oracle' in J. Bremmer, ed., *Interpretations of Greek Mythology*. London. 215–41.
Spaltenstein, F. 1986. *Commentaire des Punica de Silius Italicus*. 2 vols. Paris.
Sparkes, B. 1968. 'Black Perseus' *Antike Kunst* 11, 3–16.
Spiro, F. 1903. *Pausaniae Graeciae descriptio*. 3 vols. Leipzig.
Stoneman, R., ed. and trans. 2007. *Il romanzo di Alessandro*. Vol. 1. Milan.
Stoneman, R. 2008. *Alexander the Great: a Life in Legend*. Yale.
Stordalen, T. 2000. *Echoes of Eden: Genesis 2–3 and the Symbolism of the Eden Garden in Biblical Hebrew Literature*. Leuven.
Stothers, R.B., 2004. 'Ancient scientific basis of the "Great Serpent" from historical evidence' *Isis* 95, 220–38.
Sukthankar, V.S., et al. 1933–66. *The Mahābhārata: for the First Time Critically Edited*. 19 vols. Poona.
Tarn, W.W. 1928. 'The hellenistic ruler-cult and the daemon' *Journal of Hellenic Studies* 48, 206–19.
Taylor, L.R. 1930. 'Alexander and the serpent of Alexandria' *Classical Philology* 25, 375–78.
Teipel, J. 1922. *Typhoei Fabula qualis usque ad Pindari et Aeschyli Aetatem fuerit*. Münster.
*Texte aus der Umwelt des Alten Testaments*. 1982–. Gütersloh.
Thilo, S., and H. Hagen. 1878–1902. *Commentarii in Vergilii carmina Servii Grammatici*. 3 vols. Leipzig.
Thorsson, Ö. 1985. *Völsunga saga; og, Ragnars saga loðbrókar*. Reykjavik.
Tischendorf, C. 1876. *Evangelia apocrypha*. 2nd ed. Leipzig.
Tiverios, M.A. 1990. 'Kadmos' *LIMC* v.1, 863–82.
Touchefeu-Meynier, O., and I. Krauskopf. 1997. 'Typhon' *LIMC* viii, 147–52.
Turk, G. 1884–1937. 'Python' *ML* iii.2, 3400–12.
Uro, R. 2003. *Thomas: Seeking the Historical Context of the Gospel of Thomas*. London.
Ustinova, Y. 2005. 'Snake-limbed and tendril-limbed goddesses in the art and mythology of the Mediterranean and the Black Sea' in D.B. Braund, ed., *Scythians and Greeks: Cultural Interactions in Scythia, Athens and the Early Roman Empire (Sixth Century BC–First Century AD)*. Exeter. 64–79.
Uther, H.-J. 2004. *The Types of International Folktales: a Classification and Bibliography*. 3 vols. FFC. 284–6. Helsinki.
Valantasis, R. 1997. *The Gospel of Thomas*. London.
Valentini, R., and G. Zuchetti, eds. 1946. *Codice topografico della Città di Roma*. Rome.
van Buitenen, J.A.B., trans. 1977. *The Mahābhārata*. Vol. 1. Chicago.
van Dijk, J. 1983. *LUGAL UD ME-LAM-BI NIR-GAL*. Leiden.
van Nooten, B.A., and G.B. Holland. 1994. *Rig Veda: a Metrically Restored Text with Introduction and Notes*. Cambridge, MA.
Venit, M.-S. 1989. 'Herakles and the Hydra in the first half of the sixth century BC' *Hesperia* 58, 99–113, with plate 26.
Vermeule, E. 1971. 'Kadmos and the Dragon' in G.M.A Hanfmann, hon., D.G. Mitten et al., eds, *Studies Presented to George M.A. Hanfmann*. Mainz. 177–88.
Vermeule, E. 1977. 'Heracles brings a tribute' in F. Brommer, hon., U. Höckmann and A. Krug, eds, *Festschrift für Frank Brommer*. Mainz. 295–301.
Vernant, J.-P., and Ducroux, F. 1988. 'Features of the mask in ancient Greece' in J.P. Vernant and P. Vidal-Naquet, *Myth and Tragedy in Ancient Greece*. New York. 189–206.
Vian, F. 1951. *Répertoire des gigantomachies figurées dans l'art grec et romain*. Paris.
Vian, F. 1952a. *La guerre des Géants: le mythe avant l'époque hellénistique*. Paris.
Vian, F. 1952b. 'La guerre des Géants devant les penseurs de l'antiquité' *Revue des études grecques* 65, 1–39.
Vian, F. 1960. 'Le mythe de Typhée et le problème de ses origines orientales' in O. Eissfeldt et al., eds, *Eléments orientaux dans la religion grecque ancienne*. Paris. 17–37.

Vian, F. 1963. *Les origines de Thèbes*. Paris.
Vian, F. 1987. *Les Argonautiques orphiques*. Paris.
Vian, F., and M.B. Moore. 1988. 'Gigantes' *LIMC* iv.1, 191–270.
Viré, G. 1992. *Hygini de astronomia*. Stuttgart.
Visser, C.E. 1938. *Götter und Kulte im ptolemäischen Alexandrien*. Amsterdam.
Vojatzi, M. 1982. *Frühe Argonautenbilder*. Würzburg.
von Arnim, J. 1893–6. *Dionis Prusaensis quem vocant Chrysostomum quae exstant omnia*. 2 vols. 2nd ed. Berlin.
von der Mühll, P. 1962. *Homeri Odyssea*. Basel.
von Steuben, H. 1968. *Frühe Sagendarstellung in Korinth und Athen*. Berlin.
Wagner, P.-E. 2000. 'Le Graouilly: chronique d'une foklorisation' in J.-M. Privat, ed., *Dans la gueule du dragon: Histoire—ethnologie—literature*. Sarreguemines. 79–98.
Wagner, R., et al. 1894–1902. *Mythographi Graeci*. 3 vols. Leipzig.
Walcot, P. 1966. *Hesiod and the Near East*. Cardiff.
Warner, A.G., and E. Warner, trans. 1912. *The Sháhnáma of Firdausí*. 9 vols. London.
Waser, O. 1894. *Skylla und Charybdis in der Literatur und Kunst der Griechen und Römer*. Zurich.
Watkins, C. 1995. *How to Kill a Dragon: Aspects of Indo-European Poetics*. Oxford.
Wehrli, F. 1944–78. *Die Schule des Aristoteles*. 10 vols. Basel.
Weicker, G. 1912. 'Hesione' *RE* 8, 1240–42.
Wernicke, K. 1894. 'Andromeda' *RE* 1, 2154–59.
West, D.R. 1995. *Some Cults of the Greek Goddesses and Female Daemons of Oriental Origin*. Alter Orient und Altes Testament 233. Neukirchen-Vlyun.
West, M.L. 1966. *Hesiod: Theogony*. Oxford.
West, M.L. 1983. *The Orphic Poems*. Oxford.
West, M.L. 1997. *East Face of Helicon*. Oxford.
West, M.L. 1998–2000. *Homeri Ilias*. 2 vols. Stuttgart.
West, M.L. 2003a. *Homeric Hymns, Homeric Apocrypha, Lives of Homer*. Cambridge, MA.
West, M.L. 2003b. *Greek Epic Fragments*. Cambridge, MA. [Panyassis.]
West, M.L. 2007. *Indo-European Poetry and Myth*. Oxford.
Whittaker, M., ed. 1967. *Die apostolischen Väter*. Vol. 1, *Der Hirt des Hermas*. 2nd ed. Berlin.
Wickkiser, B.L. 2008. *Asklepios, Medicine and the Politics of Healing in Fifth-Century Greece*. Baltimore.
Wilk, S.R. 2000. *Medusa: Solving the Mystery of the Gorgon*. New York.
Will, E. 1947. 'La décollation de Méduse' *Revue archéologique* 27 (6th ser.), 60–76.
Wilson, J.C. 1995. *Five Problems in the Interpretation of the* Shepherd of Hermas: *Authorship, Genre, Canonicity, Apocalyptic, and the Absence of the Name 'Jesus Christ.'* Lewiston.
Wilson, N.G. 2007. *Aristophanis Fabulae*. Oxford.
Wilson, R.McL. 1960. *Studies in the Gospel of Thomas*. London.
Woodford, S. 1983. 'The iconography of the infant Heracles strangling snakes' in F. Lissarague and F. Thélamon, eds, *Image et céramique grecque: Actes du colloque de Rouen, 25–26 novembre 1982*. Rouen. 121–9.
Woodford, S. 1988. 'A. Herakles and the snakes' *LIMC* iv.1, 827–32.
Woodward, J. 1937. *Perseus: a Study in Greek Art and Legend*. Cambridge.
Worms, F. 1953. 'Der Typhoeus-Kampf in Hesiods Theogonie' *Hermes* 81, 29–44.
Wright, D. 1957. *Beowulf*. London.
Yalouris/Gialouris, N. 1953. 'πτερόεντα πέδιλα' *Bulletin de correspondance hellénique* 77, 3–17, 293–321.
Ziegler, K. 1912. 'Gorgo (1)' *RE* 7, 1630–55.
Zingerle, I.V. 1859. *Sagen aus Tirol*. Innsbruck.
Zinserling-Paul, V. 1979. 'Zum Bild der Medeia in der antiken Kunst' *Klio* 61, 407–63.
Zorzetti, N., and J. Berlioz. 2003. *Premier mythographe du Vatican*. Paris.

# Index of Greek and Latin sources

Note: This index directs to the numerical series of source passages.

[Abdias]
  *Historia Apostolica* pp. 738–40
    Fabricius: **135**
Achilles Tatius
  *Leucippe and Clitophon*
    3.6.3–3.7.9: **115**
*Acts of John*
  71–86: **132**
*Acts of Philip*
  8.4 (G), 8.7 (G), 8.15 (G),
    8.16–17 (V), 9 (V), 11.2–8 (A),
    13.1–4 (A), 14.1–3 (A), 14.7–9
    (A), 15.1 (A), *Martyrion of
    Philip* 2 (A), 7 (V), 12–17 (V),
    19–20 (V), 24 (V), 26–8 (V),
    32 (V), 39 (V), 42 (V): **134**
*Acts of Silvester*
  (A) 1, (B) 1: **136**
*Acts of Thomas*
  30–33: **131**
Aelian
  *Nature of Animals* 11.16: **139**
Aeschylus
  *Phorcides* F262 i *TrGF*: **57**
Aldhelm
  *De virginitate* (poetic version)
    545–56: **137**
  *De virginitate* (prose version)
    257–8 Ehwald: **137**
  *De virginitate* (prose version)
    266–7 Ehwald: **144**
  *De virginitate* (prose version)
    308–9 Ehwald: **148**
Alexander of Myndus
  *FGrH* 25 F5: **25**
  F 1.6 Wellmann (not in *FGrH*): **64**
*Alexander Romance*
  1.32.5–13: **101**
Antoninus Liberalis
  *Metamorphoses* 8: **73**

Apollodorus
  *Bibliotheca* 1.6.1–3: **5**
  *Bibliotheca* 2.3.2: **48**
  *Bibliotheca* 2.4.3: **108**
  *Bibliotheca* 2.4.8: **22**
  *Bibliotheca* 2.5.2: **23**
  *Bibliotheca* 2.5.9: **104**
  *Bibliotheca* 2.5.11: **28**
  *Bibliotheca* 2.5.12: **35**
  *Bibliotheca* 3.4.1, 3.5.4: **75**
Apollonius of Rhodes
  *Argonautica* 1.494–5, 503–6: **10**
  *Argonautica* 3.1176–90: **88**
  *Argonautica* 4.123–66: **87**
  *Argonautica* 4.1396–1407: **30**
Aristophanes
  *Frogs* 465–77: **37**
  *Thesmophoriazusae*
    1009–1135: **110**
Aristonicus of Tarentum
  *FHG* 4, 337 F2 **25**
[Aristotle]
  *Mirabilium auscultationes*
    845b: **100**
Athenaeus
  221b–e: **64**
Athenagoras
  *Legatio* 18: **11**

Bacchylides
  *Epinicians* 9.10–14: **82**
  F9 Maehler: **93**
Bede
  *Ecclesiatical History of the English
    People* 1.1: **159**
Bible: *see* New Testament,
    Septuagint

Clement of Alexandria
  *Protrepticus* 2.16 p.14 P: **12**

Conon
  FGrH 26 F1: **118**
Conversio et passio ii, S. Afrae
  MGH, SRM 3, 60, §7: **155**
Critias
  Pirithous TrGF 43 F1 lines
    10–14: **42**

Damascius
  De principiis 123.2, 1, 318 Ruelle
    = DK 1.B.12: **11**
Demetrius of Magnesia
  fragment: **133**
De promissionibus
  3.43: **140**
Digenis Akritis
  Grottaferrata version, 6.42–80: **162**
Dio Chrysostom
  Orations 5.1, 5–16, 18–21,
    24–7: **72**
Diodorus
  3.52, 54, 55: **61**
  3.70.3–6: **53**
  4.25.1, 4.26.1: **38**
  4.26.2–4: **34**
  4.36 and 38: **26**
  20.41.2–6: **69**
Diogenes Laertius
  5.89–90: **133**
Dionysius Periegetes
  788–92: **41**
Dionysius of Samos
  FGrH 15 F2: **121**
Dionysius Scytobrachion
  FGrH 32 F7: **61**
Duris of Samos
  FGrH 76 F17: **68**

Ephorus
  FGrH 70 F31b: **18**
[Eratosthenes]
  Catasterismi 1.4: **29**
  Catasterismi 15, 17: **109**
  Catasterismi 22: **57**
Euphorion
  F41 Lightfoot: **41**
  F71 Lightfoot: **42**
  F95 Lightfoot: **93**
Euripides
  Andromeda FF114–15, 117–18,
    122, 124–5, 127 TrGF: **110**
  Andromeda FF115a, 120, 129,
    129a, 136, 145, 146 TrGF: **109**
  Andromeda Testimonium iii.a (a):
    **109**
  Bacchae 1330–9, 1355–60: **77**
  Heracles 610–19: **42**
  Heracles 1274–5: **24**
  Hypsipyle FF754a, 757 TrGF: **81**
  Ion 987–97: **53**
  Iphigenia in Tauris 1234–57: **15**
  Medea 480–2: **86**
  Phoenissae 638–48, 657–75,
    818–21, 931–41, 1006–12,
    1060–66: **76**
  F472m TrGF: **69**
  F930 TrGF: **77**
Eustathius
  Commentary on Dionysius
    Periegetes 788–92: **41**

First Vatican Mythographer 1.57: **47**
Fulgentius
  Mitologiae 1.21: **66**

Gerald of Wales
  On the Topography of Ireland
    1.28: **159**
Gobi, Jean
  Scala coeli 13: **C8**
Gospel of Ps.-Matthew
  18, p. 81 Tischendorf: **157**
Gospel of Thomas
  16.1–2 (A): **127**
Gregory the Great
  Dialogues 3.15.11–12: **153**
Gregory of Tours
  Liber vitae patrum 11.1, MGH
    SRM 1.2, 259–60: **150**
  Life of Andrew 19: **149**

Hecataeus
  FGrH 1 F27: **45**
Hellanicus of Lesbos
  F51 Fowler: **75**
  F103 Fowler: **24**
Hellanicus of Tarsus
  Fragment: **11**
Heraclides of Pontus
  F16 Wehrli: **133**
Heraclitus
  De incredibilibus 1, 9, 13: **62**
  De Incredibilibus 15: **52**
  De incredibilibus 18: **27**
  De incredibilibus 33: **46**
  De incredibilibus 34: **69**
Herodorus of Heraclea
  F14 Fowler: **33**
  F23 Fowler: **24**
  F31 Fowler: **41**

Herodotus
    4.8–10: **3**
Hesiod
    *Theogony* 270–336: **1**
    *Theogony* 767–74: **36**
    *Theogony* 820–80: **6**
[Hesiod]
    *Shield* 216–37: **55**
Hesychius
    s.v. *eleutheron hydōr*: **42**
    s.vv. *Lamia, lamiai*: **70**
Hieronymus of Rhodes
    Fragment: **11**
Hippobotus
    fragment: **133**
Homer
    *Iliad* 6.152–95, 16.328–9: **49**
    *Iliad* 20.144–8: **103**
    *Odyssey* 12.73–126, 234–9: **119**
*Homeric Hymn* (3) *to Apollo*
    300–9, 349–73: **14**
Hyginus
    *Astronomia* 2.6: **29**
    *Astronomia* 2.14: **45**
    *Fabulae* 74: **81**
    *Fabulae* 140: **13**
    *Fabulae* 151: **2**

Isidore of Seville
    *Etymologies* 8.11.102: **70**

Jacobus de Voragine
    *Golden Legend* 50: **159**
    *Golden Legend* 58: **161**
Jerome
    *Life of St Hilarion the Hermit* 39: **143**
Jocelin of Furness
    *Life of St Patrick, Acta Sanctorum*,
        March ii, p. 574, §148: **159**
John Malalas
    *Chronographia* pp. 35–9 Dindorf:
        **65**
    *Chronographia* pp. 37–8 Dindorf: **9**
Josephus
    *Jewish War* 3.420: **117**

Kadłubek, Wincenty
    *Chronica seu originale regum et
        principum Poloniae, MPH* 2,
        256–7: **C7**

Livy
    summarised: **97**
Lucan
    9.619–99: **59**

Lucian
    *Dialogues of the Dead* 4: **44**
    *Dialogues in the Sea* 14: **116**
    *Hall* 22: **116**
    *Lover of Lies* 11–13: **130**
    *Lover of Lies* 22–4: **102**
Lycophron
    *Alexandra* 31–6, 470–8: **105**
    *Alexandra* 834–46: **112**
    *Alexandra* 951–5: **105**
Lycus
    *FGrH* 570 F3: **91**

Manilius
    *Astronomica* 5.538–618: **114**
*Martyrium of St Marina*
    pp. 24–7 Usener: **158**
Menander Rhetor
    *Peri epideiktikon* 3.17, 441–2
        Spengel: **17**
*Mirabilia urbis Romanae*
    24: **142**
*Miracula Sancti Georgii*
    Codex Romanus Angelicus 46,
        §12: **160**

New Testament
    Acts 28.3–6: **125**
    Luke 10.19: **125**
    Revelation 12–13, 20.1–3: **126**
Nicander
    paraphrase: **73**
Nonnus
    *Dionysiaca* 1.140–64, 184–202,
        213–18, 234–53, 258–76,
        294–309, 362–82, 387–403,
        409–47, 463–471, 478–94, 507–20,
        2.1–10, 20–52, 68–72, 237–58,
        273–90, 314–17, 339–52, 364–90,
        436–74, 508–39, 553–63, 606–24,
        663–79: **8**
    *Dionysiaca* 4.348–463: **79**

Origen
    *Contra Celsum* 6.42 and 6.43: **10**
*Orphic Argonautica*
    887–1021: **90**
Ovid
    *Metamorphoses* 3.28–98: **78**
    *Metamorphoses* 4.617–20: **58**
    *Metamorphoses* 4.633–62: **32**
    *Metamorphoses* 4.663–739: **113**
    *Metamorphoses* 4.772–803: **58**
    *Metamorphoses* 7.406–19: **41**
    *Metamorphoses* 14.8–74: **120**

Palaephatus
  3: **80**
  31: **60**
  37: **107**
  38: **27**
Panyassis
  *Heraclea* F3 Davies/F8
    West: **24**
  *Heraclea* F10 Davies/F15
    West: **29**
  *Passion of SS. Perpetua and Felicitas*
    4.3–9: **129**
  *Passion of St Victoria*
    5–7, pp. 158–9 Delehaye: **147**
Paul the Deacon
  *Gesta episcoporum Mettensium, PL*
    95, 711–13: **156**
Paulinus of Nola
  *Carmina* 32.143–6: **138**
Pausanias of Antioch
  *FHG* iv pp.467–8, F3: **9**
Pausanias Periegetes
  2.15.2–3: **84**
  2.21.5–7: **63**
  2.37: **24**
  3.25.4–6: **45**
  4.35.9: **117**
  9.26.7–8: **99**
Petronius
  *Satyricon* 89: **94**
Pherecydes of Athens
  F11 Fowler: **54**
  F16c Fowler: **31**
  F22a Fowler: **75**
  F69a Fowler: **22**
Pherecydes of Syros
  FF78 and 79 Schibli: **10**
Philochorus
  *FGrH* 328 F18b: **46**
Philostrati
  *Imagines* 1.18: **77**
  *Imagines* 1.29: **111**
  *Life of Apollonius* 4.25: **74**
Photius
  *Bibliotheca* cod. 186: **118**
  *Bibliotheca* cod. 190: **25**
Pindar
  *Nemeans* 1.33–59: **19**
  *Olympians* 13.60–6 and
    84–90: **50**
  *Pythians* 1.15–28: **7**
  *Pythians* 4.242–50: **85**
  *Pythians* 12.6–26: **56**
Pisander of Camirus
  *Heraclea* F3 Davies/F2 West: **24**

Plautus
  *Amphitruo* 1091–1124: **21**
Pliny
  *Natural History* 2.236: **52**
  *Natural History* 5.69, 5.128,
    6.182, 9.11: **117**
Plutarch
  *Failure of Oracles, Moralia* 414b
    and 417f–418c: **16**
  *Parallela Minora* 14, *Moralia*
    309a–b: **139**
Pomponius Mela
  1.11: **117**
  1.92: **41**
Procles of Carthage
  *FHG* 4, 483–4 F1: **63**
Propertius
  4.8.2–14: **139**
Ptolemy son of Hephaestion
  resume: **25**
Pythocles of Samos
  *FHG* 4, 488 F1: **139**

*Questions of Bartholomew*
  4.7–17, 18–28, 46, 60: **126**
Quintus Smyrnaeus
  *Posthomerica* 12.444–97: **95**

Rufinus of Aquileia
  *Historia monachorum in Aegypto* 8,
    *PL* 21, 420–2: **145**

Saxo Grammaticus
  *Gesta Danorum* 9.169–70: **B12**
Scholia to
  Apollonius *Argonautica* 2.353: **41**
  Aristophanes *Peace* 758: **68**
  Homer *Iliad* 2.793: **11**
  Homer *Iliad* 5.395–7: **39**
  Homer *Iliad* 6.76: **96**
  Homer *Iliad* 6.181: **52**
  Homer *Iliad* 8.479: **10**
  Homer *Iliad* 20.147: **103**
  Lycophron *Alexandra* 45: 121
  Lycophron *Alexandra* 1191: **10**;
    see also Tzetzes
  Nicander *Alexipharmaca* 13b: **41**
  Plato *Phaedo* 89c: **24**
[Scylax]
  *Periplus* 104: **117**
Seneca
  *Hercules Furens* 49–64: **42**
  *Hercules Furens* 524–32: **31**
  *Hercules Furens* 782–829: **40**
  *Medea* 684–709: **4**

Septuagint
  Bel and the Dragon (Septuagint; Theodotion version) 23–7: **124**
  Genesis (Septuagint) 3.1–20: **122**
  Isaiah (Septuagint) 27.1: **123**
  Job (Septuagint) 3.8, 9.13, 26.12–13, 40.25: **123**
  Psalms (Septuagint) 73.13–14, 103.25–6: **123**
Servius
  on Virgil *Aeneid* 2.201: **93**
  on Virgil *Aeneid* 6.287: **27**
*Shepherd of Hermas*
  vision 4: **128**
Silius Italicus
  *Punica* 6.140–293: **98**
Sozomen
  *Ecclesiastical History* 7.26.1–4: **146**
Statius
  *Thebaid* 1.562–669: **71**
  *Thebaid* 4.716–22, 739–45, 775–96, 5.505–587: **83**
Strabo
  C43: **117**
  C665: **52**
  C750–1: **9**

Tertullian
  *Ad uxorem* 1.6.3: **138**
Theocritus
  24.10–33, 56–9, 82–100: **20**

Timaeus
  *FGrH* 566 F53: **91**
Tzetzes
  *Commentary on Lycophron Alexandra* 17: **51, 67**
  *Commentary on Lycophron Alexandra* 615: **91**

Valerius Flaccus
  *Argonautica* 2.451–578: **106**
  *Argonautica* 8.54–121: **89**
Valerius Maximus
  1.8 ext. 19: **97**
Venantius Fortunatus
  *Vita S. Hilarii* [*Pictavensis*] 35–8, *MGH* AA 4.2, 5: **152**
  *Vita S. Marcelli Pariensis Episcopi* 10, *MGH* AA 4.2, 53–4: **151**
Virgil
  *Aeneid* 2.199–231: **92**
  *Aeneid* 4.480–6: **31**
  *Aeneid* 5.86–96: **133**
  *Aeneid* 6.417–25: **43**
*Vita i S. Gildae*
  *MGH* AA 13.1, 95: **141**
*Vita i S. Samsonis, episcopi Dolensis*
  1.50, 58–60: **154**

Xenophon
  *Anabasis* 6.2.2: **41**

# *General Index*

Note: This index directs to page numbers.

abyss xix, xxiii, 3, 16, 71, 131, 189, 192–3, 203–4, 214–15, 218–19, 223, 242, 244–5, 250–1; *see also* Hades, Hell, Tartarus, underworld
Acheron (underworld, Thesprotia) 64–5, 73, 100
  (Heraclea Pontica) 69
aconite 65, 68–9, 73–4, 131
Adam 18, 192, 208
Adrastus 100, 120–1, 123–4; *see also* Seven against Thebes
Aeacus 65, 70
Aeetes 1, 125–6, 128–30, 132
Aegis 22, 80–1
  *aegis* 27, 31, 80–1, 83–4, 87, 115, 117
Aeneas 71, 135, 152, 159, 183, 206
Afra, St 242
Agathos Daimon 9, 137, 149–50, 152
Aidoneus 73
Aigipan 21–2; *see also* Pan
airs xx–xxi, 3, 7, 87, 89, 95, 114, 142–3, 202, 209, 215–17, 220–1, 223–4, 232, 236, 238, 248, 252, 267; *see also* breath, winds
Ajax the Less 137
Alcmene 46–9, 60
Alcyoneus of Delphi 105, 147, 154
Alcyoneus (Giant) 20
Alexander of Abonouteichos 218
Alexander the Great 17, 62, 149–50, 272–3
Alexandria 9, 35, 149–50, 206, 250, 252
allegory xxiii, 61–2, 73–4, 94–6
altars 32, 112, 115, 121–2, 124, 132, 135, 138, 177, 206, 213, 219, 242, 253
Amazons 17, 77–8, 91, 105

Amisodarus 76–7
Ammon (god) 104, 158, 160, 163, 170–1
Ammon, St 229–31, 238
Amphiaraus 9, 120
Amphitrite 183–4
Amphitryon 14, 46–7, 49, 69–70, 88
Amymone 51–3, 116
Anchises 206
Andrew, St 234, 238
Andromeda 2, 26, 78, 93, 103, 154, 160–78, 183, 251
Anglo-Saxon 224, 263–4; *see also Beowulf*
anguipedes xvii, xix, 13, 15, 17, 19–23, 33, 36, 41, 97, 102, 104–5, 107, 113, 146, 152; *see also* Cecrops, Delphyne, Echidna, *empousai*, Hecate, Giants, Lamia, Typhon
Anigrus 59
Antioch (on the Orontes) 34–5, 150
Antioch (Pisidian) 154, 190, 239, 244–5
Aphrodite 23, 28, 32, 62, 110, 138, 178, 183
Apollo 18, 20, 22–3, 28, 39–44, 53, 62, 83, 97, 100–2, 110, 112, 122, 128, 130, 139, 154–6, 158–9, 250, 252
  A. Thymbraeus 101–2, 134–40, 252
Apollonius of Tyana 106–7
Apophis 258
apples 1, 14, 16, 57–62, 128, 272–3
Archemorus *see* Opheltes
Ardeshir 273–4
Ares 32, 128, 183
  Dragon of, 1–2, 33, 42, 62, 109–18, 123, 126, 128–9, 135, 145, 150
  Mars 113, 207, 219–20

309

Drusiana 204–5
Duris Cup 126

earth (often personified) xix,
    xxiii, 2, 14, 16, 18, 20–34, 36–7,
    39–41, 43, 52, 57–62, 64, 66,
    68, 70, 72–4, 79–81, 87–9, 92,
    96, 100, 110–12, 114–17,
    121–2, 124, 128–31, 138, 142–5,
    151–2, 156, 171, 174, 180,
    187–9, 191–3, 204, 209–10,
    214, 218–19, 223, 224, 226–7,
    229, 235, 241, 243–6, 248, 255,
    257–9, 261, 267, 278
Ebionites 254
Echidna 13–18, 20, 23, 25, 36, 38,
    56, 58, 65–6, 69, 76, 152, 204,
    207–19, 227; *see also* vipers
Echion 110
Echo 165–8
Eden, Snake of, 187–8, 190, 199,
    204, 216–17, 219
Edessa 204
eggs 36–8, 209, 211, 216–17, 225
Egypt, Egyptians 20, 23, 32, 35, 80,
    93, 158, 160, 164, 171, 209,
    217–19, 229, 241–2, 258; *see
    also* Alexandria
El 259
elephants 118, 151–2, 177, 272–3
Eleusis 64
*empousai* 106–7
Enceladus 20–1, 36
Encheleans 110
Encratites 203–16
*Enūma eliš* 258, 296
Enyo (Graea) 14, 83–4
Epidaurus (Argolid) 9, 229
Epidaurus (Dalmatia) 190, 228–9
Ericthonius 9, 136
Eros 22, 27, 33, 60, 164, 168–9
Esfandyar 154, 275
Ethiopia, Ethiopians 60, 88, 90,
    188, 210, 254
    Kētos of, 2, 5, 93, 147, 154, 160–78
Etna 2, 21, 23, 25, 69, 79
Eucrates 982, 150–1, 204
Euryale 14, 85–6, 90, 94–5
Eurybatus 105, 147, 154
Eurynome 36
Eurystheus 1, 51–2, 55, 58, 60,
    62–4, 66, 68–72, 84, 125, 153
Eve 187–8, 203, 208, 216
exorcism xxiii, 3, 194, 217–18, 237,
    242, 244

eyes xx–xxi, 3, 5, 7, 14–15, 20, 22–3,
    28, 31–2, 41, 47–8, 59–60, 67–70,
    83–4, 86, 88–93, 98–9, 101,
    103, 113–15, 121–3, 127–32,
    135, 138–9, 143–5, 151, 165,
    157–9, 170, 174, 180, 183, 188–9,
    192, 204, 209, 211–13, 217,
    225–6, 236, 240, 245–6, 249,
    260–1, 267, 275; *see also* sleep

Fafnir 57, 111, 140, 263–6
faith xxiii, 191, 196, 198, 212–13,
    215, 222, 226, 229–30, 241–4,
    250–1, 254
families *see* broods, genealogies
*farr* 261
farting xxi, 3, 235–6
Fasold 268
Fergus mac Léti 274–5
fire, fieriness *passim*, esp. xx–xxi,
    20–35, 47–8, 51, 53–6, 69–71,
    76–81, 103–5, 113–15, 120–3,
    129–30, 135–8, 142–5, 147–8,
    157–60, 183–4, 189–94,
    196–202, 208–19, 223–4,
    228–9, 231–2, 234–5, 237–8,
    240–1, 252–9, 261, 263–4,
    266–70, 272–9
Firedrake 237, 264
fleece, golden 1, 16, 59, 125–33
floods xx, 30, 35, 78, 103, 155–6,
    159, 163, 172, 177, 209
Florentius, St, 238
folklore, folktales 7, 9, 22, 58–9,
    148, 155, 163, 190, 248, 255,
    265, 270–80
Fortunatus 204–5
foundation of world, cities, cults,
    festivals xxii, 1, 7, 29, 35, 38,
    68–9, 102, 105, 110, 114,
    149–50, 157–8, 177, 203,
    257–62, 277
Four-lined snake 10
Fridelo 148, 277
Friedlach 277
fumigation xxi, 7, 47–8, 202

Gallinaria 228, 237, 254
Games, Nemean 119–20, 124
    Pythian 40, 43
Gem-de-Lovely 278
genealogies xx, 5, 13–18, 37, 57, 65,
    76, 84, 216
George, St, 3, 5, 76, 154, 162, 239,
    247, 249–55

Geryon 14–16, 18, 183
ghosts 64–5, 68–9, 73, 83, 98, 100, 106–7, 152, 201, 206, 212, 217, 250
Giants 15, 16–23, 26–31, 33, 35–8, 80, 88, 115–17, 143, 145, 267–8
gigantomachy 36, 38, 136–7
Gildas, St, 226–7
Glauce 18
Glaucetes 165, 168
Glaucus (father of Bellerophon) 76, 78, 133
Glaucus (lover of Scylla) 168, 181–3
Glycon 60, 218
Gnostics 194, 203, 205, 219
goats 2, 14, 16, 27–9, 76–7, 79–81, 83, 200, 208, 212, 231; *see also* Aegis, Chimaera
Gobi, Jean 276
gold 1, 14, 17, 48, 52–3, 57–62, 64, 84–6, 90, 96, 106, 111, 113, 123, 125–33, 143, 171, 176, 198, 206, 245, 249, 252, 259, 264–5; *see also* metal, treasure
*gorgoneia* 82, 86–7; *see also* Gorgons
Gorgons 2, 4, 14–16, 18, 64–6, 78, 80–98, 105, 115, 142, 151–2, 162–3, 166, 168, 171–3, 175–6, 183, 245
Gorgon-Aegis 80–1; *see also* Euryale, *gorgoneia*, Medusa, Stheno
Gottfried von Strassburg 163, 267
Graeae 14–15, 18, 83–6, 89–90, 98, 170
Gram 265
Greek Magical Papyri 94, 219
groves xx, 41, 70, 88, 113–14, 120–3, 126–9, 131–2, 142–5, 157, 159, 224–5; *see also* trees
guardians, serpents as xx, 1, 14, 16, 21, 57–62, 65–7, 71, 89, 110–12, 114–15, 117, 120, 123, 125–32, 136–7, 143, 149, 206, 211, 213, 216–18, 230, 242, 263, 265; *see also* water-sources, springs, treasure
Gunn, Hector 278–9
Gyges 152

Hades 14, 20, 24, 63–73, 83–5, 106, 151, 164–5, 174, 193, 214–15, 245; *see also* abyss, Hell, Tartarus, underworld

Haemus 21, 23
Hagen 265
halcyons 172
Harmonia 2, 27, 33, 36, 109–13, 137
*harpē* (sickle-sword) xxii, 1, 8, 21, 23, 83–4, 86, 88, 93, 171, 173–6
Harryhausen 129
heads, multiple xix, 1–2, 5, 14–16, 20, 22–5, 29–34, 37, 51–2, 55–6, 58, 63–4, 66–7, 69, 72–4, 76, 85–6, 104, 115, 132, 146, 152, 180–1, 183, 188, 190–1, 244–5, 255, 261; *see also* Cerberus, Hecate, Hydra, Ladon, Scylla, Typhon
healing, dragon gods of, 9, 218, 220
Hecate 20, 107, 127, 131–3, 146, 150–2, 181–4, 204
Hedammu 22, 33, 259–60
Helenus 137, 139
Hell 192, 221, 227; *see also* abyss, Tartarus, underworld
Hephaestus 20, 24–5, 39, 85–6, 183
Hera 14, 20, 22–3, 28, 30, 34, 37–41, 45–9, 52, 58, 60, 98–9, 120, 224–5; *see also* Juno Sospita
Heraclea Pontica 68–70, 73
Heracles 1–2, 14–18, 20–2, 33, 36–7, 40, 45–74, 77, 84, 91, 104–5, 120, 125, 128, 143, 147, 153–61, 170, 173, 179, 183–4, 250, 252
Heraclides of Pontus 205
herbs *see* drugs
Hermas 196–9, 209
Hermes 20–2, 33, 64, 83–4, 86, 88, 91, 169
Hermione 70
heroes (heroised dead) 8–9, 205
Hesione 2, 103, 137, 147, 153–63, 168, 251–2
Hesperides 1, 14, 16, 57–62, 71, 89, 128; see also Ladon
Hierapolis 16, 208, 212, 314–16, 218, 254; *see also* Ophiorhyme
*hieros ophis* 147–8
Hilarion, St, of Gaza 190, 228–9, 238
Hilary, St, of Poitiers 228, 237–8, 254
Hippomedon 121–3
Hittites 22, 25, 33, 35, 259–61

Holy Spirit xxi, 3, 7, 245–6
honey-cakes *see* cakes
horses, immortal 154
Hreidmar 265
Hupasiya 22, 33, 260
Hurrians 22, 33, 35, 259–60
Hydra 1, 14–16, 18, 47, 50–6, 58–60, 73, 79, 88, 111, 116, 122–3, 125, 129, 145, 159, 181, 245
Hygieia 10, 137, 218
Hymir 267–8
Hypsipyle 119–23

Illuyanka 22, 25, 33, 260–1
Illyria, Illyrians 32, 110, 116
immortality xix, 14, 20, 35, 51, 53, 58–9, 62, 95, 154, 180
Inara 22, 260–1
incantations xxi, 8, 18, 128–9, 148, 181–3, 199–202; *see also* prayers
incubation 10, 255
India, Indians 7, 80, 111, 151, 168, 174, 177, 202–3, 232, 259, 272–3
Indo-European 7
Indra 259
Iobates 76–8, 84
Iolaus 1, 14, 50–5
Iphicles 46–9, 55
Iran, Iranians *see* Persia
Ireland, Irish earth 238, 248, 254, 267, 270, 274–5

Jacob (brother of Jesus) 194, 201
Jacob's ladder 199
Janamejaya 272
Jason 1, 18, 71, 125–33, 147
Jesus Christ xxii, 3, 190–4, 199, 201, 203, 205, 208–10, 213–15, 217–24, 226, 228, 230, 232–37, 240–1, 243–5, 248–50, 253–4
John, St, 196, 204–6, 214, 217
Joppa 165, 177–8, 251
Judaism 177, 190, 219, 261–2
Juno Sospita 224–7

Kadłubek, Wincenty 275–6
Kasios, Mt, 21–2, 35
Kētōn xxiii, 160–1
*kētos*, defined xvii, 5
  Kētos, as personal or proper name, 160, 178
  *Kētos* of Ethiopia 162–78
  *Kētos* of Troy 153–61; *see also* Laocoon, Scylla

*kibisis* 83–5
Kirkcudbright 155, 280
Kiskilussa 25, 260
Kothar 259
Kraków 275–6
Krakus 275–6
Krimhild 265

Lacus Curtius 227
Ladon 1, 14–16, 18, 57–62, 71, 128, 143, 145, 160; *see also* Hesperides
Laestrygonians 98
Lamashtu 97, 108
Lambton Worm 271, 279–80
Lamia, *lamiai* 2, 15, 84, 93, 97–108, 128, 136, 142, 147, 152, 154, 163
landscapes xxii, 22–3, 43, 79, 278–9
Langia 121, 123
Lanuvium 224–5
Laocoon 5, 15, 46, 102, 134–40, 155, 252
Laomedon 136–7, 154–60, 163
Lasia 249–52
Lemnos, Lemnian earth 137, 248
leopards 26, 30, 33, 103, 191, 208, 210, 212
leprechauns 274
Lerna 1, 14, 16, 50–1, 55, 59, 122, 143, 145, 158–9
Lernus 55
Leto 28, 39–41
Leviathan 22, 188–9, 195, 219, 254, 259, 261–2
Libya 2, 49, 58, 62, 80, 86–93, 98–9, 103–5, 117, 142, 144, 164, 175, 219, 252, 254; *see also* Gorgons, Lamia, Psylli
licking 10, 139–40, 212, 216, 254, 265; *see also* sucking
Linton, Baron 279
Linus 103
lions 2, 14–16, 18, 23, 26–7, 29–34, 36–7, 52, 67, 75–81, 97, 103, 113–14, 142, 156–7, 191, 257–8
Loki 265, 267,
luck, good 9, 273; *see also* Agathos Daimon
*Lugal-e* 22, 257,
Lycia 2, 16, 75–80, 84, 106, 125

Mahavagga 272
Malta 190, 194, 254

Mamertinus, St, 254
marauding xx, 1, 4, 40, 42–3, 51, 76–7, 80, 139, 153, 220, 280
Marcellus, St, 205, 236–8
Marduk 257–8,
Mariamne 201, 208–18
Marina (Margaret), St, 3, 154, 190, 226, 231, 244–6, 254
Mars *see* Ares
Marsi 18
Martha, St, 254
Martin, St, 255
Maryandini 68
Massylians 60
Matthew, St, 254
measure, Pythian 43
Medea 1, 3, 13, 18, 22, 49, 61, 68, 71, 87, 125–33, 147–8
Medusa 2, 4, 14–16, 18, 22, 33, 35, 51, 58, 61, 64, 76, 78, 80, 82–96, 98, 126, 145, 160, 162, 170, 172, 175–6, 184; see also *gorgoneia*, Gorgons
Melampus 140
memorialisation xx, xxii, 23, 32, 40, 42–3, 86, 120
Menestratus 147, 154
Menippus (Lucian) 71–2
Menippus (Philostratus) 106–7
Menoeceus 111–12
Messina, Strait of, 181, 183
metal (bronze, iron) xix–xx, 1–2, 14, 20, 24, 31–2, 46, 66–9, 78, 84–8, 101, 109, 111, 113–17, 126, 130–2, 144, 147, 172, 174, 189, 191, 199, 210, 214, 222–3, 235, 251, 263–5, 268; *see also* gold, treasure
meteorology 95–6
Metz 201, 216, 242, 244, 246
Michael, St, 191–3, 223, 255
Midas 194, 199–201, 205
Midgard Serpent 267–8
Mimir 266
Mistresses of Animals 98
Mnesilochus 165–8
*muirdris* 248, 274–5
Mycenae, Myceneans 55, 70, 78
Myrina 91
mysteries 35, 28, 64, 66, 93

Naasenes 194 ,219
Naegling 264
Nagas, Naga-rajas 272
naiads xxii, 2–3, 121, 123, 145

names (for dragons) 60, 160
Narcissus, St, of Gerundum 242
Nemea, Dragon of, 46, 117, 119–24, 145, 158, 160
  Nemean Lion 14–15, 18, 52, 67
  Nemean Games 119–20
nereids 162–3, 172, 175–6, 181–2
Nessus 53–4
*Nibelungenlied* 264–5
Nicanora 212–13
Nile 149
Ninurta 22, 257–8
Norse 7, 22, 140, 155, 162, 265–8
nymphs xxii, 2, 14, 59, 83–4, 121–3, 138, 143, 160, 168; *see also* naiads, nereids

Odin 155, 265, 267, 278
Odysseus 65, 83, 179–84
Oeta, Mt, 53
Olympias 150
*omphalos* 102
Onachus 236, 254
Opheltes-Archemorus 119–24
Ophianoi 207–8, 214, 216–19, 254
Ophiogeneis 150, 219
Ophion(eus) 19, 35–8, 51
Ophiorhyme (Opheorhymos) 15, 208–9, 211–12, 214–19; *see also* Hierapolis
Ophiuchus 18, 26, 32–3, 72–3
Ophioussa 148
*ophis*: see *hieros ophis*
Ophites 219
Ophonion 36
oracles 20, 39–43, 54, 61, 69, 73–4, 93, 104–5, 110–12, 115, 119, 154–5, 160, 169, 227
Orkney 155, 278
Orontes 34–5, 94, 150
Orpheus 36, 66, 130–3
Orthus 14–15, 18, 63
Osiris 35
Otr 265

pairs of dragons or snakes xix–xx, 15, 33, 38, 40, 45–9, 54, 85, 102, 120, 134–40, 155, 217, 231, 254, 268–70
Pallas (Giant) 20, 22
Pallene 20
Pan 2, 21–2, 27, 33, 37
Parium 219
Parnassus, Mt, 39–41, 43, 61, 101, 105, 122

Patrick, St, 5, 238, 239, 247–8, 254, 256
Paul, St, 190, 194, 254
Pegasus 2, 14–16, 18, 75–8, 84, 87, 91, 95–6
Pemphredo 14, 83–4
Perpetua, St, 197, 199, 206, 219
Persephone 38, 64–7, 70, 73, 83
Perseus 2, 14, 22, 34–5, 55, 58, 61, 78, 80, 82–96, 126, 147, 154, 160, 162–78, 183, 251
Persia, Persians 17, 34–5, 42, 69, 93, 154, 189, 261, 273–5
*pharmaka* see drugs
Phidias 136
Philip, St 3, 5, 16, 32, 152, 198, 201, 204, 207–20, 223, 227, 228, 238, 254
Philoctetes 54, 137
Phineus 163, 177–8
Phlegra 20, 80, 88
Phoenicians 78, 80, 106, 111, 113, 117–18, 177–8
Phoenodamas 156–7, 163
Phorcides *see* Graeae
Phorcys (Phorcus) 14, 18, 83, 85, 88–90, 92, 94, 156–7, 183
Phrygia 73, 80, 138, 158–9, 216, 219; *see also* Hierapolis, Ophiorhyme
Picus-Zeus 93
Pirithous 64–6, 69, 73
Pluto (daughter of Cronus) 26, 34
*Poetic Edda* 22, 266, 268
poisons 7, 18, 22, 40, 53, 54, 59, 65, 68–9, 72–4, 87, 89, 129–30, 148, 158, 244, 258, 277; *see also* aconite, venom
Poland 275
Polybotes 20–1, 36
Polydectes 58, 83–6, 89, 126, 162
Pompeii 169
poppies 60
Porceus 137
Poseidon (Neptune) 14, 16, 18, 20, 39, 72, 76–7, 87, 93, 98, 135–7, 154–6, 158–9, 163, 173, 180, 183–4
Prasiake 272–3
prayers 3, 8, 35, 101–2, 131, 143, 152, 158, 168–9, 180–2, 201, 204–5, 208–9, 214–15, 217, 222, 226, 228–30, 232–3, 235–6, 238, 240–1, 244–5, 250, 261, 276–7; *see also* incantations

Priam 155, 159
Proetus 76
prophecy, prophets 32, 41, 43, 47, 62, 110–12, 114–15, 125, 128, 131, 139–40, 145, 156, 163, 170, 176, 205, 218, 233, 244, 265, 266; *see also* Cassandra, Helenus, Melampus, oracles, Tiresias
propitiation 9, 221
*Prose Edda* 155, 265–8
Psamathe 103
Psylli 49, 201, 219
Ptolemy II Philadelphus 187
Pytho *see* Delphi
Python 18, 39–44, 60, 62, 100, 102, 122–3, 160

Ra 258
Ragnarr Lodbrok 268–70
Rahab 188–9, 195, 261–2
Rat snakes 10
rationalisation xxiii, 15, 42–3, 52, 55–6, 62–3, 72–3, 79, 89–95, 99, 117–18, 140, 150, 160, 165, 174, 178, 183–4
Regin 265–6
Regulus 2, 141–5
Revelation Dragon 190–8, 198–9, 217, 223, 255; *see also* Beliar
Rhea 36
Rhegium 182
*Rigveda* 259
rivers xxii, 2–3, 14, 25–6, 31, 34–5, 43, 47, 51, 53, 59, 68–9, 72–3, 76, 90, 94, 100, 104–5, 114, 116, 121–2, 127, 129–30, 132, 139, 141–5, 150, 157–60, 191, 210, 235, 240–1, 243, 252, 254, 265, 273, 279–80; *see also* Achelous, Bagrada, Drakōn (rivers), Nile, Orontes, Sagaris, water-sources
rocks, stones xx, xxii–xxiii, 2, 14, 20, 23, 25–6, 28–31, 34, 47, 51–3, 58, 61, 64–6, 82–3, 86–92, 99, 105, 109–13, 116–17, 122–4, 133, 136, 138–9, 142, 155, 158–9, 163, 168–80, 182–4, 199, 201, 209–10, 216–19, 221, 223, 226–7, 235, 241, 245, 249, 257, 263–4, 273, 278, 280
Rome, Romans 2, 3, 9, 18, 71, 89, 92, 159, 173, 177, 183, 204, 218, 234

Dragon of R. 3, 193, 221–7, 229, 237; *see also* Bagrada Dragon
Roscius Fabatus 225
Rostam 17
rotting 3, 7, 40–1, 59, 232

Sabazius 19, 38
Sabra 251
Sagaris 72–3
saliva xx–xxi, 7, 201, 212, 217, 231–2, 276
Salus 218
Samosata 202, 204
Samson, St, of Dol 240–1, 246
Sarpa-sattra 272
Sauska 33, 260
Saxo Grammaticus 268–70
Scamander 139, 250, 252
Scaurus 177
Scipio Africanus 206
Scylla 5, 15–16, 24, 139, 152–3, 157, 179–84
Scythes 17
Scythia, Scythians 13, 16–18, 53, 68, 159, 165–8, 219, 254
sea-monsters, sea-serpents *see kētos*
Seriphos 83–5, 89–90, 176
*serpens* (the term) 4
Seth 23, 35
Seven against Thebes 112, 119–24; *see also* Adrastus, Hippomedon, Capaneus
*Shahnameh* 17, 154, 273–5
shields (their blazons, their strap-decorations) 47, 66–7, 82, 84–5, 87–8, 91, 113–16, 120, 133, 135–7, 143, 174–5, 264, 269
ships, sea-monsters as, xxiii, 178
sibyls 71, 152, 280
Sicily 2, 20–1, 23, 25, 32, 69, 157, 183, 248; *see also* Etna
sickle *see harpē*
Sigemund (Siegmund) 263–4
Sigurd (Siegfried) 140, 263–6
Silena 252, 254
silence xxi, 8, 132, 215, 235
Silvester, St, 3, 5, 193, 221–8, 233, 237, 254
sinews 21–2, 28–9, 33–4
siring by dragon 62, 150
Sistram 268
slaver 5, 68–9, 85, 143–4
sleep, unsleeping dragons, sleep-casting xxi, 1, 7–8, 16, 18, 34, 59–61, 67, 71, 83–4, 86–9, 98, 126–33, 147–8, 163, 175, 205, 213, 216, 2227, 254–5, 260, 264, 266, 274; *see also* eyes
Sleipnir 155
smell 104, 142, 233
*see also* airs, breath, farting, rotting, winds
Smok Wawelski 275
snakes *passim*; Sacred Snake see *hieros ophis*; *see also* vipers
Solymi 77–8
sound xxi, 8, 23, 27–31, 67, 85, 148, 152, 255; *see also* incantations, prayers, silence
source *see* water-source
Sparta, Spartans 69, 90, 140, 168, 206
Spartoi, of Thebes, 109–18
of Colchis 127–9
spears (javelins) xxii, 2, 31–2, 76, 78, 80–1, 91–3, 113–14, 116, 120, 122, 128, 135, 137, 142–5, 199, 231, 253, 258, 269, 279–80
Sphinx, sphinxes 14–16, 18, 103
springs xxii, 1–3, 14, 16, 25–6, 29–30, 34, 40–1, 51–3, 70, 78, 95, 100, 105, 109–17, 119–24, 128, 132, 142, 150, 158, 177, 183, 210, 218, 242, 250–1, 253–5, 260; *see also* Amymone, Castalia, Cynadra, Dirce, Langia, Sybaris, rivers, Telphusa, water-sources
Stachys 211–18
Steeg 277
Stheno 85–6, 90, 94–5
Sthenoboea *see* Anteia
Stilicho 226
stones *see* rocks
Stoor Worm 155, 278
Sturluson, Snorri 155, 265–8
Styx 65, 71, 142, 145
sucking xxi, 143–4, 180, 203–4, 228–9, 266, 273, 275, 279; *see also* licking
sulphur xx, 47–8, 202, 254, 273, 276
Sumeria, Sumerians 22, 257–8
Svadilfari 155
sweat 266
swords xix, xxii, 3, 14, 46, 64, 84–5, 91–2, 95–6, 101, 116, 132, 151–2, 154, 57, 171, 174–6, 188, 191–2, 199, 213, 226, 231, 245–6, 250–1, 253, 255, 258, 263–5, 268–9, 274–5, 278–9; *see also harpē*

Sybaris 99, 102, 105, 136, 147, 154, 163
symmetry of battle xx–xxii, 7–8, 23, 34, 54, 202, 216–17, 232, 246
Syrtes 49, 99, 103–5, 219

Taenarum 64, 67, 69–70, 72–3
Tamineh 17
Tarasconus 254
Tarhunna 22, 25, 33, 260
Tartarus 20, 22–5, 36, 66, 132, 145, 151, 189, 192, 193, 203; *see also* abyss, Hell, underworld
teeth xix, 1–2, 5, 15, 30, 47, 68, 83–5, 101, 109–18, 121, 126, 129, 138, 156, 158, 160, 172–3, 180–1, 183, 189, 213, 229, 245, 249, 278; *see also* Graeae, Spartoi
Tempe 42
Tenedos 135, 137–9
Tenos 147–8
Teshub 22, 33, 259–60
Thalestris 17
Thebes 1, 52, 55, 109–19, 121, 123, 128, 145, 150; *see also* Cadmus, Ares (Dragon of), Seven against Thebes
Thegri 198
Themis 43, 61
Theseus 64, 66–8, 70, 73
Thespiae, Dragon of, 105, 136, 147, 154, 163
Thessalonica 234
Thessaly, Thessalians 22, 87, 147–8, 200, 229
Thidrek 266, 268
Thomas, St, 152, 196, 201–4, 206, 223, 227, 231, 235
Thor 23, 267–8
Thrace, Thracians 21, 23, 90, 158
Thraētaona 261
thunderbolts xx–xxi, 2–3, 7–8, 14, 20–35, 48, 54, 69, 121, 123, 129, 138, 151, 158–9, 192, 194, 209–10, 216–17, 238, 245, 255, 259
Tiamat 257–8
Tiresias 47, 111–12
Tiryns 14, 69–70
Titans 20–1, 23–4, 30, 35, 88, 127, 181
Tityus 43
tombs xix, 112, 122, 124, 131–2, 139, 158, 199–201, 204–6, 216, 236–7, 254, 264
tongues xix, 3, 18, 23, 26, 47, 85, 88, 100, 113, 118, 121–2, 129, 135, 138, 143–5, 163, 198, 211–12, 226, 245–6, 267, 278
Trachis 47, 53–4
treasure xx, 1, 57, 59, 61, 237, 263–4; *see also* gold, guardians, metal
trees xx, 1, 16, 20, 26, 28, 30–3, 39, 52–3, 57, 59–61, 93–4, 114, 121, 126, 128, 130–3, 139, 143–5, 150–1, 174, 180, 187–8, 214, 255, 257, 265, 273, 277; *see also* groves
Tribulanum 3, 232–3
Trigg 240–1
tripod 40–1, 102
Tripodisci 102
Tristan 163, 267
Triton (sea god) 156, 168, 175–6
Troezen 64, 69
Troilus 140
Trophonius 9
tsunami *see* floods
Typhon 2, 14–38, 40–1, 54, 58, 60, 66, 72, 76, 80, 109, 115–16, 138–9, 152, 160, 173, 193, 216
Tyrannognophus 212, 217
Tyrol 148, 277

Ugarit 259
underworld xix–xx, 16, 37, 63–74, 83, 107, 114, 127, 145, 150, 152, 158, 200, 202, 204, 260; *see also* abyss, caves, Cerberus, earth, Hell, Tartarus
Uranus 20–1
Uruvela 272

venom xx–xxi, 5, 7,18, 26–7, 29, 31–3, 47, 49, 51–5, 59, 72, 87–9, 100, 104, 113–16, 121–3, 130, 135, 142, 144–5, 148–9, 173, 199, 201, 203–5, 208, 210, 212, 223, 229, 231–4, 240, 242–3, 248, 254, 257–8, 264–5, 267, 269, 272, 275, 278–9; *see also* poisons
Vesta, Vestal Virgins 3, 222–7
Victoria, St, 3, 232–4, 238
vipers 3, 7, 13–14, 17, 20, 26, 28–30, 33, 53, 56, 66, 68–9, 80, 88, 110, 115, 117, 147, 190, 194, 199–202, 208, 216, 254, 268–70; *see also* Echidna
virgins 2–3, 80, 85, 88, 117, 153, 157–8, 167, 172–3, 176, 192, 198–9, 201–2, 215, 217, 221,

222, 224–6, 233–4, 244–5, 276, 278; *see also* Medea, Hesperides, Hygieia, Lanuvium, Vestal Virgins
volcanoes xxii–xxiii, 2, 79, 278; *see also* Etna
*Volsungasaga* 265–6
vomit 5, 23, 29, 68–9, 143, 180, 234, 269
Vritra 259

water-sources xx, xxii, 34, 41, 51, 105, 110, 120, 123, 142, 145, 159, 242, 251; *see* rivers, springs
wealth, dragon gods of 9
whales 170, 177, 180, 231
White Snake of Mote Hill 155, 280
Wiglaf 264
winds xx–xxi, 7, 20, 24, 26, 28, 30–1, 39, 47, 103, 116, 132, 143, 158, 168, 170–1, 208, 210, 225, 258, 261, 278; *see also* airs, breath

wings 1, 20, 22, 29, 37, 85, 87–9, 91, 132, 168, 170–2, 174–5, 191–3
witches 1, 22, 61, 87, 126–7, 147–8, 181, 229; *see also* Circe, Medea, Thessalians
wolves 30, 101, 245
wombs 23, 41, 101–2, 116; *see also* broods
Wormistone 279

Yam 259

Zaroes and Arphaxat 254
Zeus (Jupiter) 2, 14, 19–40, 46–8, 53–4, 58–61, 67, 76, 80, 84, 86–8, 91, 93, 98–9, 106, 109–12, 115–16, 121, 123–4, 131–2, 145, 147, 149, 151, 154–5, 159, 163, 165–7, 171, 173, 176
Z. Meilichios 9

*Dragons, Serpents,
and Slayers in the Classical
and Early Christian Worlds*